Financial Accounting for Executives

By

KENNETH R. FERRIS

JAMES S. WALLACE

The Peter F. Drucker and Masatoshi Ito
Graduate School of Management

Claremont Graduate University

Cambridge
BUSINESS PUBLISHERS

FINANCIAL ACCOUNTING FOR EXECUTIVES, First Edition, by Kenneth Ferris and James Wallace

ISBN 0-9787279-5-9

Bookstores & Faculty: to order this book, contact the company via email customerservice@cambridgepub.com or call 800-619-6473.

Retail Customers & Students: to order this book, please visit the book's website and order directly online.

For permission to use material from this text, contact the company via email permissions@cambridgepub.com.

Printed in the United States of America.
10 9 8 7 6 5 4 3 2 1

ABOUT THE AUTHORS

KENNETH R. FERRIS   Kenneth R. Ferris is a Professor at The Peter F. Drucker and Masatoshi Ito Graduate School of Management at The Claremont Graduate University. He received a B.B.A. and an M.B.A. from George Washington University and an M.A. and a Ph.D. from The Ohio State University. He previously served on the faculties of Northwestern University, Southern Methodist University, and Thunderbird School of Global Management, and has taught at numerous academic institutions in Australia, Hong Kong, Japan, and New Zealand. Professor Ferris is the author or co-author of eleven books, over fifty academic and professional publications and over eighty case studies. He previously served as a director of several NYSE-listed companies and is active in executive education programs around the world.

JAMES S. WALLACE   James S. Wallace is an Associate Professor at The Peter F. Drucker and Masatoshi Ito Graduate School of Management at The Claremont Graduate University. He received his Bachelors of Arts from the University of California, Santa Barbara, his MBA from the University of California, Davis, and his PhD from the University of Washington. Professor Wallace also holds a CPA certification from the state of California. He previously served on the faculty of the University of California, Irvine and has served as a visiting professor at the University of California, San Diego. Professor Wallace's work has appeared in leading academic journals including the Journal of Accounting and Economics, the Journal of Corporate Finance, and Information Systems Research, along with leading applied journals such as the Journal of Applied Corporate Finance, the Journal of Accountancy, Issues in Accounting Education and Accounting Horizons. Prior to his career in academics, Professor Wallace worked in public accounting and in industry with a Fortune 500 Company. He has done consulting work with numerous companies in multiple industries.

STATEMENT OF PURPOSE

If you have prior business experience, either working for a company or managing your own business, then you have personal experience that an understanding of financial statements is essential to do just about any job successfully. Although business decisions often involve a careful analysis of non-financial factors, they almost always involve a significant consideration of accounting information. Initiating a multi-million dollar marketing campaign, restructuring a subsidiary, deciding on the sales price of a new product, or assessing whether to acquire another company and at what price—these are just some of the business decisions that require a basic understanding of accounting and financial statements. This textbook is written to facilitate that understanding and to facilitate the reader's personal goal of gaining a more complete understanding of financial statements and their use in business decisions.

KEY FEATURES

Analytically-oriented. A defining feature of this textbook is that it was explicitly written for an EMBA, MBA, and an advanced undergraduate student market. This marketplace tends to be characterized as more analytically and decision-focused. Unlike undergraduate textbooks in accounting which use the classic debit and credit paradigm to explain key concepts, this textbook uses a more intuitive spreadsheet approach to explain the fundamentals of accounting, specifically to demonstrate how accounting data is processed and how financial statements are constructed. Not only is this approach more user-friendly (i.e., most managers routinely use spreadsheets in their daily professional lives), but it is also far less labor and time-intensive than the classic debit/credit paradigm.

Real-world based. Accounting information is an integral part of business decision-making at just about every level in a business. Consequently, the discussion of important accounting and finance concepts is grounded in the context of actual corporate decisions (e.g. What is this business worth? Should I invest in or lend to this company?). To this end, the text contains over 60 illustrations from actual corporate financial reports and disclosures, highlighting the role and impact of accounting information generally, and financial statements specifically, in financial decision-making.

International in context. There is an increasing overlap between generally accepted accounting practice (GAAP) in the U.S. and around the world. This text emphasizes the commonality of U.S. and international GAAP, but also identifies where major divergences arise. We make few references to specific FASB or IASB standards but rather explain the general approaches adopted worldwide. Understanding how stock options are accounted for, for example, is far more valuable to a manager, shareholder or an investment professional than knowing the title and specific content of FAS No. 123R. A unifying theme throughout the book is how measures of firm performance are affected by the application of U.S. and global accounting principles.

Decision-focused. A key skill set for all investment professionals, lenders, managers, and shareholders is the ability to use accounting information for decision-making purposes. In this book, we focus on two key decisions and link the discussion of all topics to these key decisions:

1. Should I extend credit to this company?
2. Should I invest in this company, and if so, at what price?

Thus, the analysis of financial statements is a key organizational theme that pervades each chapter.

Valuation theme. Related to the two key decisions, a central theme of this textbook is how knowledge of financial accounting can aid the user in determining the value of a firm. The first four chapters lay the groundwork for assessing firm value by introducing the basic financial statements and tools for their analysis. The next seven chapters provide additional structure for this analysis, with each chapter including a section that discusses how the chapter's content should be analyzed and how that analysis will impact firm value. Finally, chapter 12 introduces various methodologies to assess the value of a company.

Tied to academic research in finance and accounting. Increasingly, students of accounting and finance are interested in exploring such empirical questions as "How do the capital markets respond to accounting policy changes?" and "Which EPS measure—Basic EPS or Diluted EPS—is used by the capital market to value a company's stock?" Where appropriate, we have made reference to the extant research in accounting and finance to address some of these empirically-based questions within the text itself, while also enabling the interested reader to further her/his knowledge of these questions by accessing the original research effort.

ORGANIZATION

The text is twelve chapters in length, with the chapters organized around the following decision-focused thematic structure:

  I. The Foundations of Accounting and Financial Statement Analysis (Chapters 1-4)

 II. Operating Resources and Decisions (Chapters 5-6)

III. Investing Resources and Decisions (Chapters 7-8)

IV. Financing Decisions (Chapters 9-11)

 V. Equity Valuation (Chapter 12)

SUPPLEMENTAL MATERIALS

An Instructor's Manual is available with this text. The Instructor's Manual provides suggestions for classroom use and suggested solutions for the end-of-chapter exercises and problems. Check figures for selected exercises and problems are provided at the following website <u>http://www.cambridgepub.com/ farferris/</u>. Exercises and problems for which check figures are available are identified with a check mark preceding the exercise or problem number.

The development of this textbook and the accompanying instructor's manual has benefited from the assistance of Ms. Torrey Mann. Our special thanks to her for her help. We also appreciate the extensive review comments provided by Professor Mark DeFond. Finally, Professor Graeme Rankine made a significant academic contribution to the development of this book; and, our thanks are extended to him for his involvement.

Kenneth R. Ferris
James S. Wallace

TABLE OF CONTENTS

Chapter **Three**

Measuring Performance: Cash Flow and Net Income   **3.1**

Chapter **Four**

Using Financial Statements for Investing and Credit Decisions   4.1

Part II   Operating Resources and Decisions

Chapter **Five**

Operating Cycle, Revenue Recognition and Receivable Valuation   5.1

Chapter **Six**

Operating Expenses, Inventory Valuation, and Accounts Payable   **6.1**

Part III   Investing Resources and Decisions

Chapter **Seven**

Long-Lived Fixed Assets, Intangible Assets, and Natural Resources   7.1

Chapter **Eight**

Other Corporate Entities, Joint Ventures, and Mergers and Acquisitions 8.1

Part IV   Financing Decisions

Chapter **Nine**

Debt Financing: Bonds, Notes, and Leases   9.1

Chapter **Ten**

Commitments and Contingent Liabilities, Deferred Tax Liabilities, and Retirement Obligations **10.1**

Chapter **Eleven**

Equity Financing and Shareholders' Equity **11.1**

Part V **Equity Valuation**

Chapter **Twelve**
Using Accounting Information in Equity Valuation 12.1

Chapter One

Economic Environment of Accounting Information

TAKEAWAYS

When you complete this chapter you should be able to:

1. Identify the basic financial statements—the income statement, the balance sheet, the statement of cash flow, and the statement of shareholders' equity.

2. Explain how companies acquire capital from investors who purchase the debt and equity securities issued by such firms to obtain an expected return commensurate with the risk the investors assume.

3. Describe the role of accounting standards in facilitating a properly functioning capital market.

4. Explain the conflicts of interest that can arise between executives, debtholders, and shareholders of a corporation and the costs associated with the divergent incentives that can arise when ownership and management of a company are separated.

Where are we?

In this chapter, the financial statements of Amazon.com are used to illustrate the accounting information that companies provide to debtholders and shareholders. The chapter discusses how the demand for capital by companies that have insufficient funds to meet their investment needs and the supply of capital come together in a capital market to set equilibrium prices for stocks and bonds. The chapter also discusses how the credibility of accounting information is enhanced when a reputable external auditor provides an opinion about the accounting information. Finally, the chapter investigates the use of accounting data in internal decision-making by management and its use in contracts between shareholders and managers and between shareholders and debtholders to attenuate the conflicts of interest that can arise between the various constituencies of a company.

Where are we going?

In the next chapter we illustrate how accounting events are analyzed, quantified, summarized, and ultimately disclosed in a company's basic financial statements. Concepts such as assets, liabilities, revenues, expenses, and cash flow are defined and used in an example that demonstrates the preparation of basic financial statements. The chapter also introduces the use of financial statements for purposes of evaluating a company's financial performance. Finally, several recent accounting scandals are used to illustrate how some managers enhance their company's reported financial performance through the selection and use of alternative accounting methods.

Amazon.com, Inc. was one of the first, and became perhaps the best known, internet-based reseller of retail goods. The company was one of the high-flying internet stocks that became a favorite of equity investors during the stock market bubble period of the late 1990s. Like many dot.com companies that lacked a history of proven earnings, investors began to question Amazon's business model following the U.S. stock market decline of 2001–2002. Investors also began questioning the way the stock market valued companies during this period of so-called "irrational exuberance." As a consequence, there eventually occurred a shift back to firm valuations based on such business fundamentals as strong operating earnings and a solid balance sheet.

Amazon.com was founded by Jeff Bezos in 1995 under the name Cadabra.com as an online bookstore to compete with traditional "brick-and-mortar" bookstores and mail-order catalogs. Bezos renamed the company "Amazon" after the world's largest river and took the company public in 1997. Like the South American river, Amazon.com was huge in scale, offering many times the selection of products of even its largest competitors. Amazon has since greatly expanded its product offerings to include DVDs, music CDs, computer software, video games, electronics, clothing, furniture, food, toys and much more.

Bezos believed in the long-term prospects for his company, although he did not expect the business to produce a profit for many years. As history has since demonstrated, Bezos' business strategy proved successful. Unlike many internet companies, Amazon grew at a steady pace and focused on such business fundamentals as revenue growth, cash flows, and attaining profitability. The bursting of the dot.com bubble in the early 2000s forced many e-companies out of business. Amazon, however, persevered and eventually reported its first profit in the fourth quarter of 2002. Amazon.com has continued to report profits every year since then, earning net income of $35 million in 2003, $588 million in 2004, $359 million in 2005, and $190 million in 2006. Despite its recent financial success, however, Amazon's cumulative profit remains negative, largely as a consequence of its early history of operating losses. Today, Amazon.com trades on the NASDAQ stock exchange under the symbol AMZN and is a member of the prestigious Standard and Poor's 500 Index, an index of the shares of the 500 largest companies traded on U.S. stock exchanges.

In this chapter, we examine the financial statements of Amazon, as well as consider the generally accepted accounting principles that have been established to ensure a level of comparability among the many public companies, like Amazon, that produce financial statements for use by investors, lenders, and shareholders.

EXECUTIVE OUTLINE

Economic Environment of Accounting Information

Financial Accounting and Its Relevance	Generally Accepted Accounting Principles	Financial Accounting in Investment Decisions	The Changing Economic Landscape
■ Financial Accounting: What is it? ■ Qualitative Attributes of Accounting Information ■ Amazon's Accounting Methods and the Role of the Independent Auditor	■ Role of the U.S. Securities and Exchange Commission ■ The FASB and Standard Setting	■ Demand for and Supply of Capital ■ Relation Between Risk and Return	■ The Sarbanes-Oxley Act ■ Principles-Based GAAP

FINANCIAL ACCOUNTING AND ITS RELEVANCE

Most individuals are familiar with the game of baseball and its many rules. Most know, for instance, that according to the rules of the game, the team with the most runs scored at the completion of play is considered to be the winner. Of course the rules do much more than decide the measure by which we are able to determine which team won and which team lost; they also provide a framework within which to play the game and settle disagreements along the way. Imagine the chaos that might ensue if there were no mutually-accepted rules of the game? How would it be determined, for instance, if a base-runner was out or was safe, if a pitch was a ball or a strike, and so on? Without an accepted set of rules governing the game, it would be impossible to play the sport and insure a consistent set of outcomes.

Keeping score with an accepted set of rules applies to more activities than just baseball; it also applies to running a business like Amazon.com. In fact, the similarities between baseball and financial accounting are probably closer than you might imagine. Understanding the "rules of the game" also helps us do more than simply declare the winner of a game or calculate the annual profit of a business; it enables us to keep track of various measures which can be used to determine the quality of a team's play or the quality of a business' operations. Our knowledge of the rules and how teams or businesses have performed in the past—for example, team batting averages, pitching records, and fielding percentages for baseball teams and assorted financial ratios such as the return on assets, return on equity or return on sales for a business—can, in turn, help us to predict how teams and businesses will perform in the future. This knowledge, as you will see in subsequent chapters, is invaluable when attempting to assess the value of a sports franchise or a business enterprise.

Simply reading a rule book, however, may not be sufficient to obtain a complete understanding as to how a game is played and scored. It is also critical to understand the limitations regarding how the rules are applied, along with what is not covered by the rules. This caveat especially applies to financial accounting. Imagine the difficulty that would occur if each baseball team got to decide the distance from home plate to first base in its home stadium? Or imagine the confusion if, with the bases loaded, a team could choose which direction to run toward home plate, scoring either from first base or from third base? Unfortunately, as we will see in the following chapters of this textbook, financial accounting permits considerable flexibility in determining the applicability of its "rules" to individual business enterprises. As a consequence, the rules governing financial accounting will be seen to involve considerable managerial judgment. In baseball, for example, while general guidelines exist as to whether a pitch should be called a ball or a strike, it is up to an umpire's judgment to make the exact call. In a similar fashion, while general accounting guidelines exist as to what is considered revenue for a business, financial accounting often requires that corporate managers exercise judgment in assessing just how much revenue a business earned in a given fiscal period. In addition to the obvious analytical challenges that can result from this flexibility in the application of the rules of the game, business analysis is also often hampered by a lack of certain key information. Many of the factors that are critical to a business' operating success, to include the quality of its workforce and a well-recognized brand name, are not measured and reported under current financial accounting rules.

A theme that will be repeated throughout this textbook is that accounting information is useful not only for keeping score of a business' past operating performance and financial health but also for predicting its future performance and financial well-being, and ultimately, for helping to assess firm value. However, to be a good scorekeeper and a good analyst, one needs to know not only the rules of the game, but also how to interpret the data resulting from the application of the rules, the limitations of the rules, and when to make adjustments to the information to aid in its use for decision-making purposes.

Financial Accounting: What is it?

Financial accounting concerns the preparation and use of the accounting information provided in a company's publicly-available financial statements. Users of financial accounting information include, among others, a company's management, the shareholders who own the company through the shares they purchase, debtholders from whom the company borrows money, investment professionals who provide financial advice about the company, and governmental agencies like the U.S. Securities and Exchange Commission which regulates the dissemination of accounting information to the investing public. Unlike the external focus of financial accounting, managerial accounting focuses on the production of accounting information internal to a firm for deciding such operational questions as how much inventory to produce, what price to charge customers, and for measuring and rewarding the performance of a firm's managers and employees. Managerial accounting information is rarely provided to anyone other than a firm's board of directors, managers, and employees to avoid revealing proprietary information that might adversely affect a firm's competitive position. The focus of this textbook is on financial accounting, and how financial advisors, investors, lenders, managers, and shareholders use this information for decision-making purposes.

Before getting into the details of how financial statements are prepared and analyzed, it is useful to see the end result of the financial accounting process—the financial statements themselves. For the moment, don't worry about the numerous details that you will see since these details will be explored in later chapters. Company financial reports include many items besides the basic financial statements, such as explanatory footnotes, a chairman's statement, and a management discussion and analysis of recent events and company performance. For simplicity, these latter items have been omitted and will be considered in subsequent chapters.

To begin, it is useful to obtain a "big picture" view of a company by reading the introductory information about a company's business and its business strategy—that is, management's view of where the company is going based on the resources it has available (human, physical, and financial). Reading the financial statements will help you determine whether a company has the necessary financial resources, or can acquire them, to get where they want to be.

Consider, for example, the business strategy of Amazon.com:

> Amazon.com seeks to be the world's most customer-centric company, where customers can find and discover anything they might want to buy online at a great price.

No small thinking here! If Amazon's customer friendliness can attract the millions of customers that the company has the capacity to handle, and each customer buys something from Amazon, Amazon's future sales could be substantial.

Investment professionals who track the performance of companies like Amazon formalize sales and sales growth projections by gathering data regarding consumer demand, product shipments, product prices and sales discounts. These projections are integral to the analytical reports developed by investment professionals concerning a company's current financial health, and hence, its fair market value. Your review of Amazon's financial statements is likely to be enhanced by obtaining and reviewing a copy of a reputable analyst's report from any one of a variety of financial websites such as Yahoo.com or MSN.com or from a financial services company like **Merrill Lynch** or **Salomon Smith Barney**. As to the claims that the company is "customer-centric" and that "customers can find and discover anything they might want to buy," you can verify these assertions yourself by logging on to Amazon's website (www.Amazon.com) if you haven't done so already.

The basic financial statements for **Amazon.com**, Inc.—the balance sheet, the income statement, and the statement of cash flow—are provided in Exhibits 1.1, 1.2, and 1.3. (A fourth financial statement, the statement of shareholders' equity, will be discussed later in this chapter.) The **balance sheet** in Exhibit 1.1 shows, for example, what resources the company currently has and who provided the financing to acquire the various resources—debtholders

> Access to corporate financial statements has increased greatly in recent years thanks to the World Wide Web. Companies such as Amazon often provide financial statements on their corporate website.

or shareholders. Specifically, Amazon's balance sheet reveals the amount and type of assets owned, the obligations outstanding, and the shareholders' investment in the company. In essence, two investment constituencies provided the necessary financing for Amazon's assets—the shareholders who own the company as a consequence of their share purchases and debtholders who have loaned money and other assets to the company.

Amazon's balance sheet is based on the basic **accounting equation** which asserts that a business' assets must always equal the sum of its liabilities and its shareholders' equity. By the end of 2005, Amazon's balance sheet reveals that it had acquired nearly $3.7 billion in assets while the company's debt

> The basic accounting equation, Assets = Liabilities + Shareholders' equity, provides the foundation not for only the balance sheet, but more importantly for the entire methodology underpinning the recording of all accounting transactions. Each transaction that is recorded must be done so such that the equation remains in balance. For this reason, the term "double-entry" accounting is often used to describe this method of recording transactions.

stood at $3.45 billion ($1.929 billion plus $1.521 billion) and its shareholders' equity totaled just $246 million. Notice that although the shareholders contributed over $2.2 billion to the business since its inception in 1997, only $246 million in shareholders' equity remains. To identify the cause of this decline in shareholders' equity, we will need to explore Amazon's income statement, which we consider shortly.

The presence of various accounts on Amazon's balance sheet such as **accounts receivable**, the amount that Amazon expects to receive from its customers for prior online purchases, and **accounts payable**, the amount that Amazon expects to pay to its suppliers for prior credit purchases of inventory,

> An alternative to the accrual basis of accounting is the **cash basis of accounting**. Under the cash basis, the financial effects of a business event are recorded in the financial statements when the cash effect of the transaction occurs. Thus, a company records revenue from a sales transaction *only* after cash has been collected from the customer; similarly, expenses are recorded *only* when they are paid.

indicates that this financial statement was prepared using the **accrual basis of accounting**. This approach requires Amazon to record the financial effects of a business transaction *without* regard to the timing of the cash effects of the event. Thus, Amazon records the revenue from each sales transaction when it occurs regardless of whether the customer has paid for the ordered goods or not. Similarly, Amazon records the cost of doing business when such costs are incurred regardless of whether those costs have been paid or not. The balance sheets and income statements of most businesses are prepared using the accrual basis of accounting as this approach is widely recognized as being superior to all other approaches for measuring the financial performance and health of a company.

accrual basis recognizes revenues + costs when they occur not when $ changes hands

EXHIBIT 1.1	Consolidated Balance Sheet		

Amazon.com
Consolidated Balance Sheet

		December 31	
($ millions)		**2005**	**2004**
Assets			
Current assets			
Cash and cash equivalents		$1,013	$1,303
Marketable securities		987	476
Inventories		566	480
Accounts receivable and other current assets.		363	280
Total current assets		2,929	2,539
Fixed assets, net		348	246
Other assets		419	463
Total assets.		$3,696	$3,248
Liabilities and stockholders' equity (deficit)			
Current liabilities			
Accounts payable.		$1,366	$1,142
Other current liabilities		563	478
Total current liabilities.		1,929	1,620
Long-term debt and other		1,521	1,855
Stockholders' equity (deficit)			
Common stock, 5,000 authorized shares, issued and outstanding shares—			
416 and 410 shares		4	4
Additional paid-in-capital		2,263	2,123
Accumulated other comprehensive income.		6	32
Accumulated deficit		(2,027)	(2,386)
Total stockholders' equity (deficit)		246	(227)
Total liabilities and stockholders' equity (deficit)		$3,696	$3,248

An important tenant underlying the accrual basis of accounting is the going concern assumption; that is, the notion that the basic financial statements are prepared assuming that a business will continue operating in the future unless there is substantial evidence to the contrary. If a business is expected to continue operating in the future, investors will focus on revenues and net income from the income statement in order to forecast a firm's future operating performance. If, on the other hand, a business is expected to cease operations, investors are likely to focus their attention more closely on shareholders' equity on the balance sheet to determine what an investor might receive if, and when, the company is liquidated. Academic research consistent with the going-concern assumption indicates that in setting share prices, investors place relatively more weight on shareholders' equity on the balance sheet when a business is facing financial distress but on net income on the income statement when a business is financially healthy.[1]

Amazon's income statement in Exhibit 1.2 reports how much merchandise the company sold and how much profit, if any, it made from those sales. Amazon's consolidated statement of income reveals

---

[1] See M. Barth, W. Beaver and W. Landsman, "Relative Valuation Roles of Equity Book Value and Net Income as a Function of Financial Health," *Journal of Accounting and Economics* (February 1998).

that the company's sales grew to nearly $8.5 billion by 2005. The 'bottom line' of the income statement indicates that Amazon earned a profit in each of the three years covered by the income statements (2003 to 2005). In contrast, Amazon racked up losses of just over $3 billion in the years prior to 2003. A review of Amazon's historical financial statements (not presented here) reveals that from 1996 until 2002, Amazon failed to earn a profit in any of the six years since it became a public company! This history of operating losses explains why the shareholders' investment on the balance sheet was nearly wiped out.

Exhibit 1.2 presents Amazon's consolidated income statement. But just what was "consolidated" and what remains "unconsolidated"? Under the accounting standards of most countries, when one company obtains a majority of the voting shares of another company, the financial results of the two companies are combined and reported on a "consolidated" basis. Thus, in the case of Amazon, the consolidated income statement includes the complete financial results of Amazon's majority-owned subsidiaries but only summary results of its subsidiaries in which its ownership interest is less than a majority.

You are probably wondering how a company like Amazon can sustain six years of operating losses and still remain in business! The answer to this question resides in Amazon's statement of cash flow to which we now turn.

| EXHIBIT 1.2 | Consolidated Income Statement |

Amazon.Com Inc.
Consolidated Statement Of Operations

($ millions)	Year Ended December 31,		
	2005	2004	2003
Net sales.	$8,490	$6,921	$5,264
Cost of sales.	6,451	5,319	4,007
Gross profit.	2,039	1,602	1,257
Operating expenses	1,607	1,162	987
Income from operations	432	440	270
Interest income.	44	28	22
Interest expense.	(92)	(107)	(130)
Other income (expense), net	44	(6)	(123)
Total non-operating expense.	(4)	(85)	(231)
Income before income taxes	428	355	39
Provision for income taxes.	95	(233)	4
Income before change in accounting principle	333	588	35
Cumulative effect of change in accounting principle.	26	—	—
Net income.	$ 359	$ 588	$ 35

Exhibit 1.3 presents Amazon's statement of cash flow. The **statement of cash flow** tells us how much cash Amazon.com generated from its core business operations or received from its shareholders and debt-holders, and how much it spent to buy software and equipment. Investors are usually very interested in the statement of cash flow because it provides insight into a business beyond that provided by a balance sheet, which reflects a firm's current financial health, or an income statement, which depicts a firm's recent operating performance. Amazon's statement of cash flow shows, for instance, that its operating activities generated $733 million in cash in 2005 despite reporting net income of only $359 million. Although Amazon's total cash and cash equivalents decreased by $290 million in 2005, the company's cash holdings on

the balance sheet were still in excess of $1.0 billion! Thus, Amazon has substantial cash on hand despite reporting many years of operating losses on the income statement and despite maintaining an accumulated shareholder deficit on the balance sheet. These seemingly conflicting financial results are possible because of Amazon's use of the accrual basis of accounting in the preparation of its income statement and its balance sheet.

There exists substantial empirical evidence that investors who buy and sell shares use information about the past, especially financial statement information, to help make predictions about a company's future. Financial analysts, individual investors, bankers, and many other interested parties spend considerable time and resources predicting a company's future earnings and cash flows to help assess what a company's share price should currently be worth. We will have more to say about how to value a company's shares in Chapter 12; however, let it suffice for the moment that the value of a share of stock today is thought to be a function of a company's *future* earnings.

EXHIBIT 1.3	Consolidated Statement of Cash Flow

Amazon.Com Inc.
Consolidated Statement Of Cash Flow

	Year Ended December 31,		
($ millions)	2005	2004	2003
Cash and cash equivalents, beginning of period.	$1,303	$1,102	$ 738
Operating activities			
Net income.	359	588	35
Adjustments to reconcile net income to cash provided by operating activities:			
Depreciation.	121	76	76
Stock-based compensation.	87	58	88
Other operating expenses (income).	7	(8)	3
Gains on sales of marketable securities, net.	(1)	(1)	(10)
Non-cash interest expense and other	33	(251)	144
Cumulative effect of change in accounting principle.	(26)	—	—
Changes in operating assets and liabilities:			
Inventories	(104)	(169)	(77)
Accounts receivable, net and other current assets	(84)	(2)	2
Accounts payable and other current liabilities.	341	275	132
Net cash provided by operating activities	733	566	393
Investing activities			
Purchase of fixed assets	(204)	(89)	(46)
Acquisitions, net of cash acquired.	(24)	(71)	
Sales and maturities of marketable securities and other investments.	836	1,427	813
Purchase of marketable securities.	(1,386)	(1,584)	(536)
Proceeds from sales of subsidiary.	—	—	5
Net cash (used in) provided by investing activities	(778)	(317)	236
Financing activities			
Proceeds from exercises of stock options and other.	66	60	163
Proceeds from long-term debt and other.	11	—	—
Repayment of long-term debt and capital lease obligations	(270)	(157)	(495)
Net cash used in financing activities	(193)	(97)	(332)
Foreign-currency effects on cash and cash equivalents	(52)	49	67
Net increase (decrease) in cash and cash equivalents	(290)	201	364
Cash and cash equivalents, end of period.	$1,013	$1,303	$1,102

You might think that Amazon.com, which only recently began to earn an operating profit and with liabilities nearly as large as its assets, would have a share price that was close to zero. Yet Exhibit 1.4 shows that Amazon's share price soared by nearly 5,000 percent since its initial public offering while the much broader Standard and Poor's 500 Index was relatively stable over the same period. Amazon's share price at its initial public offering was $1, but by mid 2007, its share price was over $72 per share giving the company a market value of nearly $30 billion. This illustrates an important distinction between a company's financial statements and its share price—the former is largely concerned with the past while the latter is concerned with the future. Financial statements are a description of the historical financial performance of a company, whereas share prices reflect investor *expectations* regarding a firm's future financial health and performance. The fact that Amazon's market value is nearly $30 billion versus a balance sheet value of just $246 million for shareholders' equity suggests that the stock market is optimistic that Amazon's future is going to be much brighter than its past.

EXHIBIT 1.4	**Stock Price of Amazon.com versus Standard and Poor's 500 Index**

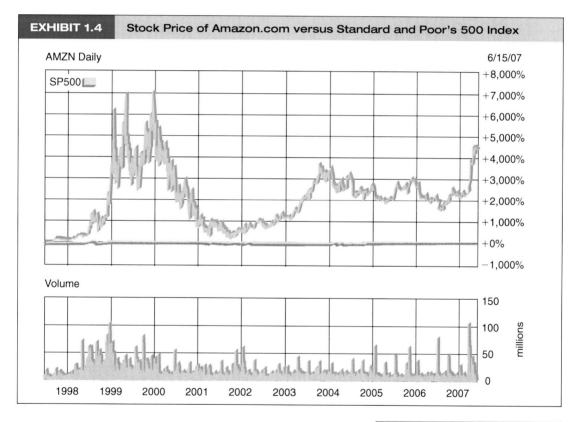

To summarize then, companies like Amazon.com who obtain capital from such external sources as debtholders and shareholders are expected to periodically provide these interested stakeholders with financial accounting information. This information includes an income statement, a balance sheet, and a statement of cash flow. A fourth statement—the statement of shareholders' equity—is also typically provided. The relation between these four financial statements is illustrated in Exhibit 1.5.

Publicly listed companies in the United States are required to file a quarterly financial report (Form 10-Q) and an annual set of financial statements (Form 10-K) with the U.S. Securities and Exchange Commission. This information is also mailed or e-mailed to shareholders and debtholders.

EXHIBIT 1.5	Relation Among the Basic Financial Statements

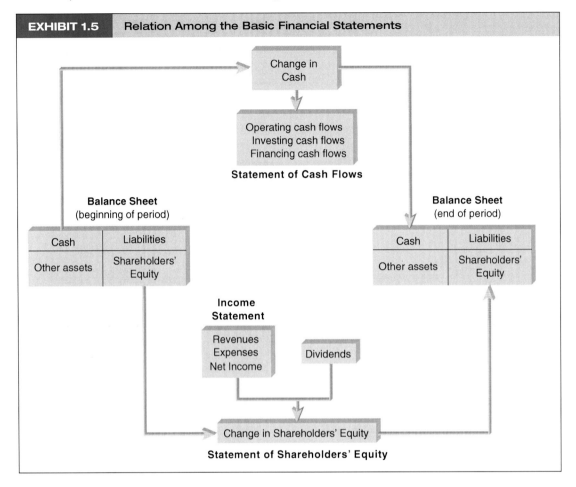

Exhibit 1.5 illustrates a number of important points about the basic financial statements. First, a balance sheet is a description of a business' assets, liabilities, and shareholders' equity as of a particular point in time, usually the end of the fiscal year or the end of a quarter. The balance sheet is represented by the basic accounting equation: Total assets equal Total liabilities plus Shareholders' equity. Second, the income statement describes a firm's performance over the fiscal period; it is represented by the equation: Revenues minus Expenses equals Net income. Third, the net income earned by a business may be either distributed to shareholders as a dividend or retained in the business to provide financing for future operations. The statement of shareholders' equity captures this decision—it reveals how the shareholders' investment in a business grew by the amount of any net income retained in the business or declined as a consequence of any dividend distributions to shareholders or any operating losses sustained by a business. This statement also reveals whether the shareholders' investment in a business increased by any new share sales or declined by any share repurchases. Fourth, the statement of cash flow reports the cash flow from operations, the cash flow from investing, and the cash flow from financing for a firm. The net cash flow for a fiscal period equals the change in the cash account on the balance sheet from the beginning of the period to the end of the period. Finally, note that the financial statements

are not independent, but rather they are interrelated. (The interrelationship of the basic financial statements is referred to in accounting jargon as "articulation;" that is, the basic financial statements are said to articulate with one another.) As you will see in subsequent chapters, there is unique, but interrelated information in each of the basic financial statements that is of interest to lenders, managers, shareholders, and investment professionals.

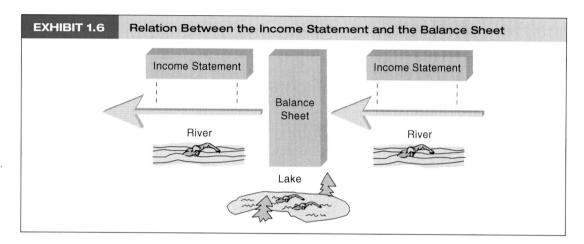

| **EXHIBIT 1.6** | **Relation Between the Income Statement and the Balance Sheet** |

Exhibit 1.6 illustrates another example of the interrelationship of the basic financial statements, in this case between the income statement and the balance sheet, using an analogy of a river and a lake. An income statement, like a river, measures performance over a period of time—a flow concept. On the income statement, performance is measured in terms of earnings in dollars, and with a river, performance is measured in terms of the flow of water in cubic feet or meters. Balance sheets and lakes, in contrast, measure levels— a stock concept. Balance sheets measure the level of net assets

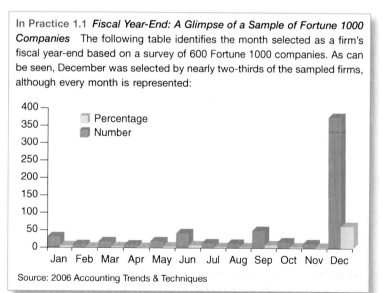

In Practice 1.1 *Fiscal Year-End: A Glimpse of a Sample of Fortune 1000 Companies* The following table identifies the month selected as a firm's fiscal year-end based on a survey of 600 Fortune 1000 companies. As can be seen, December was selected by nearly two-thirds of the sampled firms, although every month is represented:

Source: 2006 Accounting Trends & Techniques

and lakes measure the level of water, both at a point in time. Just as a lake's level of water rises and falls because of the inflow and outflow of water from a river, the level of net assets on the balance sheet rises and falls as a consequence of the operating earnings or losses generated by a business and reported on its income statement. A similar analogy could be used between the cash balance on the balance sheet and the statement of cash flow. The cash account on the balance sheet reports the level of cash currently available to a business, whereas the statement of cash flow reports the inflows and outflows of cash that occurred over the fiscal period. To repeat, the balance sheet discloses the available "stocks" of various assets, while the income statement and the statement of cash flow reveal the various "flows" of those assets.

Why Accounting Information is Important

If you have prior business experience, either working for a company or managing your own business, then you have personal experience that a working knowledge of accounting is essential to do just about any job successfully. Although business decisions may involve a careful analysis of non-financial factors, they almost always involve a significant consideration of accounting information. Initiating a multi-million dollar marketing campaign, restructuring a subsidiary, acquiring another company, deciding on the sales price for a product—these are just some of the business decisions that require at least a basic knowledge of accounting. That's why, for instance, Anne Mulcahy, Chief Executive Officer of **Xerox Corporation** had to learn about accounting and finance when she took over at Xerox in 2001. As *Fortune* magazine explained,

> She knew she had to get to the bottom of Xerox's problems quickly. She cast about for someone, anyone, who could teach her Balance Sheet 101. The guy she found, Joe Mancini Jr., director of corporate financial analysis . . . became her tour guide in deciphering the company's $30 billion balance sheet. He taught her about debt structure, inventory trends, and the impact of taxes and currency moves so that she could understand what would generate cash and how each of her decisions would affect the balance sheet. (*Fortune*, June 9, 2003).

Executives, such as Anne Mulcahy, are getting up to speed on accounting issues because the post-Enron corporate environment in the United States puts these individuals at risk for civil and criminal law suits.[2] Under the **Sarbanes-Oxley Act**, passed into law by the United States Congress in 2002, the Chief Executive Officer (CEO) and Chief Financial Officer (CFO) of each company (foreign or domestic) with public debt or equity sold in the United States must certify in writing that the information contained in the company's publicly-disseminated financial statements presents, in all material respects, the company's financial condition and results of operations. The Sarbanes-Oxley Act provides for both financial penalties (up to $5 million) and incarceration (up to 20 years) for executives who falsely certify their company's financial data.

Qualitative Attributes of Accounting Information

It is generally agreed that accounting information is valuable to analysts, creditors, investors, managers, and shareholders because it contributes to the making of important economic decisions. For instance, managers use accounting information to decide the price that they must charge for their company's products; bank credit analysts use accounting information to decide whether to extend a loan to a business; and, investors use accounting information to decide whether to invest in the shares of a company and at what price. Thus, accounting information is said to have **decision usefulness**.

There are two specific attributes which make accounting information decision useful—relevance and reliability. **Relevance** refers to the capacity of accounting information to impact a decision. Relevant

---

[2] *The Wall Street Journal* (July 22, 2003) reported that 70 percent of the executives who took a test of basic accounting principles shortly after the passage of the Sarbanes-Oxley Act failed to earn a passing score. A survey of executives taken two years following the passage of the legislation indicates that executive understanding of accounting and finance issues has substantially improved since the legislation's enactment (*CFO Magazine*, May 2005).

information is timely and possesses feedback value, predictive value, or both. Timeliness alone does not make accounting information relevant, but a lack of timeliness can render accounting information irrelevant. By preparing periodic financial statements it is possible for companies to provide analysts, managers, and investors with timely information. Feedback value pertains to decisions and actions already taken. Accounting information allows financial statement users to measure those actions and evaluate their success. Predictive value, on the other hand, suggests that accounting information helps financial statement users form predictions about future outcomes. Investment professionals and shareholders use the historical financial statements to help predict a firm's future operating performance, and hence, its market value.

Because too much information can overwhelm financial statement users (i.e., the problem of information overload), the criteria of materiality is used worldwide to help guide just how much accounting information should be disclosed in the financial statements. Information that

> Materiality is a disclosure criterion used by companies to decide what, and how much, information to provide in their financial statements. Although the definition of materiality varies from firm to firm, and often between external auditors, a common threshold for the income statement is five percent of revenues. Hence, any income statement item that equals or exceeds five percent of revenues presumably merits disclosure on a firm's income statement as such items are numerically large enough to potentially influence an investor's assessment of firm performance.

is immaterial is unlikely to be relevant to a decision-maker. Finally, reliability refers to the fact that accounting information is, or should be, free from error or bias; that is, accounting information should be both objective and verifiable. Unfortunately, the attributes of relevance and reliability are often in conflict with one another, forcing trade-offs between the two. A major role of the independent auditor, to which we now turn, is to review a company's publicly-available accounting information to insure that it is largely error free.

Amazon's Accounting Methods and the Role of the Independent Auditor

By now, one question that you have probably considered about Amazon's financial statements is: Could Amazon have computed its accounting results in more than one way? The answer is yes. Nearly every country around the world maintains a set of generally accepted accounting principles—or GAAP—that provides guidance to companies regarding the preferred way to measure and report their performance. The confusing aspect about GAAP, however, is its flexibility. For example, consider the depreciation on a building. Instead of having just one approach to calculate depreciation on a building, the GAAP of most countries allows for multiple methods, all of which are considered "generally accepted." As you will see in Chapter 7, just which depreciation method is selected can have a dramatic effect on a firm's reported performance.

Consider, for instance, the $566 million reported by Amazon.com for inventory on its 2005 balance sheet in Exhibit 1.1. Was this the amount that Amazon paid for the inventory? Or, was it what the inventory could be sold for at the end of the year? Or, was it what the same inventory would cost to replace if it were purchased at the end of 2005? Companies provide details about their accounting methods and how the various accounts are measured in the footnotes to their financial statements. For example, the footnotes to Amazon's 2005 financial statements report that:

> Inventories, consisting of products available for sale, are accounted for using the FIFO method, and are valued at the lower of cost or market value. This valuation requires us to make judgments (emphasis

added), based on currently available information, about the likely method of disposition, such as through sales to individual customers, returns to product vendors, or liquidations, and expected recoverable values of each disposition category. Based on this evaluation, we adjust the carrying amount of our inventories to lower of cost or market value.

There are several points to observe here. First, Amazon's financial statements are prepared by the company itself, raising the concern that the company might be tempted to boost its inventory value to make it appear that Amazon has more assets than it really does. Second, Amazon's top management and financial staff "make judgments" in deciding what inventory values to report. But since the financial statements provided by Amazon's management are potentially affected by these judgments, an investor might skeptically discount the reported information and reduce their estimate of what the company is presumably worth. This issue is known as the **lemons problem.**[3]

One solution to the lemons problem is for a credible, independent party to provide a "warranty" as to the quality of the product offered. For example, in the used car market, an auto dealer might promise to take a vehicle back if the buyer experiences any problems. In the "accounting market," independent audit firms such as **Deloitte & Touche, Ernst & Young, KPMG,** and **PricewaterhouseCoopers** provide assurance of the reliability of the financial statements of the companies they audit in an **audit report** that accompanies the financial statements. Audit firms work hard to provide this assurance because errors in detecting defective financial statements can result in the loss of an audit firm's valuable reputation, and ultimately, as illustrated by the demise of **Arthur Andersen** in 2002, the collapse of an entire audit firm. Audit firms may also bear civil and criminal penalties from lawsuits brought by shareholders, debtholders and/or governmental agencies like the U.S. Securities and Exchange Commission (SEC) if their work is found to be negligent.

In Practice 1.2 *Financial Statement Rounding: A Glimpse of a Sample of Fortune 1000 Companies*   The following table identifies the degree of rounding in financial statements in a survey of 600 Fortune 1000 companies. Nearly all of the sampled firms rounded their reported numbers, with rounding to the nearest thousand dollars the most commonly used choice:

Source: 2006 Accounting Trends & Techniques

The independent auditors' report by Ernst & Young for Amazon's financial statements is provided in Exhibit 1.7. The first paragraph of the report indicates that the scope of Ernst & Young's audit includes Amazon's balance sheet, income statement, statement of shareholders' equity, statement of cash flow

---

[3] G.A. Ackerlof, "The Market for Lemons: Quality Uncertainty and the Market Mechanism," *The Quarterly Journal of Economics,* (1970). In markets where buyers are uncertain about the quality of goods offered for sale, markets may break down because buyers reduce the price that they are willing to pay, causing sellers with high quality products to withdraw from the market. The downward price spiral continues as products of continually decreasing quality become the only products available for sale, and eventually, market breakdowns can occur.

EXHIBIT 1.7	Independent Auditors' Report

REPORT OF ERNST & YOUNG LLP
INDEPENDENT REGISTERED PUBLIC ACCOUNTING FIRM

The Board of Directors and Stockholders Amazon.com, Inc.

We have audited the accompanying consolidated balance sheets of Amazon.com, Inc. as of December 31, 2005 and 2004, and the related consolidated statements of operations, stockholders' equity (deficit), and cash flows for each of the three years in the period ended December 31, 2005. Our audits also included the financial statement schedule listed in the Index as Item 15(a)(2). These financial statements and schedule are the responsibility of the Company's management. Our responsibility is to express an opinion on these financial statements and schedule based on our audits.

We conducted our audits in accordance with the standards of the Public Company Accounting Oversight Board (United States). Those standards require that we plan and perform the audit to obtain reasonable assurance about whether the financial statements are free of material misstatement. An audit includes examining, on a test basis, evidence supporting the amounts and disclosures in the financial statements. An audit also includes assessing the accounting principles used and significant estimates made by management, as well as evaluating the overall financial statement presentation. We believe that our audits provide a reasonable basis for our opinion.

In our opinion, the financial statements referred to above present fairly, in all material respects, the consolidated financial position of Amazon.com, Inc. at December 31, 2005 and 2004, and the consolidated results of its operations and its cash flows for each of the three years in the period ended December 31, 2005, in conformity with U.S. generally accepted accounting principles. Also, in our opinion, the related financial statement schedule, when considered in relation to the basic financial statements taken as a whole, presents fairly in all material respects the information set forth therein.

As discussed in Note 1 to the consolidated financial statements, the Company adopted Statement of Financial Accounting Standards No. 123 (revised 2004), Share-Based Payments, effective January 1, 2005.

We also have audited, in accordance with the standards of the Public Company Accounting Oversight Board (United States), the effectiveness of Amazon.com, Inc.'s internal control over financial reporting as of December 31, 2005, based on criteria established in Internal Control-Integrated Framework issued by the Committee of Sponsoring Organizations of the Treadway Commission and our report dated February 16, 2006 expressed an unqualified opinion thereon.

/S/ ERNST & YOUNG LLP
Seattle, Washington
February 16, 2006

and other financial items. This paragraph also highlights the fact that the auditor's responsibility is only to provide an opinion, whereas the responsibility for the preparation of the statements themselves lies with Amazon's management. The second paragraph discloses that the audit firm's procedures used in the review of Amazon's financial data were in accordance with **generally accepted auditing standards** as prescribed by the Public Company Accounting Oversight Board, but that accepted auditing procedures do not consider every business transaction and instead rely only on a set of sampled transactions to form an opinion. An audit of a company like Amazon would be prohibitively expensive if every single business transaction was examined to reach an opinion.

The third paragraph provides Ernst & Young's opinion that Amazon has prepared its financial statements in accordance with generally accepted accounting principles and that there are no important (material) errors in representing the firm's accounting information. The fourth paragraph reports that Amazon changed its accounting methods to comply with a new generally accepted accounting standard for the expensing of employee stock options. In effect, this paragraph highlights significant changes in accounting methods that could potentially affect a user's interpretation of the accounting information provided. The final paragraph indicates that, in addition to its audit of the financial statements, Ernst & Young performed an audit of the effectiveness of Amazon's internal controls over its financial reporting.

Amazon's audit opinion refers to **generally accepted accounting principles**, or GAAP. But what principles are generally accepted, who accepted them, how did they get accepted, and why were they accepted?

GENERALLY ACCEPTED ACCOUNTING PRINCIPLES

Generally accepted accounting principles arose to mutually benefit the capital market participants who use financial statements to evaluate a security's **expected return** and **risk**. The standardized conditions provided by the use of GAAP give market participants confidence that the investment decisions they make using accounting information will be the best possible decisions. In the United States, the ultimate power to set accounting standards rests with the U.S. Congress, which established the **Securities and Exchange Commission (SEC)** by giving it the power to regulate securities markets and establish and enforce the accounting standards used by companies issuing those securities. The oversight role of the SEC is depicted in Exhibit 1.8. The stock market crash of 1929 and the Great Depression of the early 1930s brought turbulent times to the U.S. financial markets. The scandalous behavior of corporate executives in the downfall of some companies and the sight of ordinary citizens who had lost all of their savings were all that the U.S. Congress needed to step in and establish the SEC.

> The expected **return** on an investment refers to the expected income to be earned on the investment, whereas the **riskiness** of an investment refers to the uncertainty associated with the expected return. In general, risk and expected return are positively correlated; that is, investments with higher risk generally earn a higher rate of a return.

Similar events occurred again 70 years later. Calls for action in the aftermath of the **Enron, WorldCom** and **Global Crossing** debacles resulted in the passage of the **Sarbanes-Oxley Act in 2002**, bringing greater regulation of the accounting profession by a new organization called the **Public Company Accounting Oversight Board (PCAOB)**, which became responsible for overhauling auditing standards, inspecting accounting firms and disciplining wayward auditors. The PCAOB supplanted a system of self-regulation in which accountants at the **American Institute of Certified Public Accountants (AICPA)** oversaw their peers.

Although the SEC has the final authority over the form and content of financial statements, it has delegated the responsibility for establishing U.S. GAAP to a private sector organization called the **Financial Accounting Standards Board (FASB)**. The FASB's position under the oversight of the SEC is depicted in Exhibit 1.8. The FASB was established in 1973 after the Accounting Principles Board (APB), the predecessor to the FASB, was discontinued. The APB was abandoned after losing public confidence and support for its role in setting accounting standards. The FASB is administered by the **Financial Accounting Foundation (FAF)**, whose trustees are drawn from several different groups including the American Accounting Association, the American Institute of Certified Public Accountants, the Association for Investment Management and Research, the Financial Executives Institute, and the Securities Industry Association.

The FASB has seven full-time members who must relinquish all ties to their former employers and accept no other paid employment during their five-year terms. The FASB issues exposure drafts of its accounting standards for comment at public hearings where interested parties have the opportunity to express their opinion about the proposed rules. The passage of a proposed accounting rule, called a **Financial Accounting Standard (FAS)**, requires the support of five of the seven members. The FASB issued its first standard in 1973, but as of the time of the printing of this textbook, it had issued 158 FASs.

EXHIBIT 1.8	Economic Environment of Accounting Information

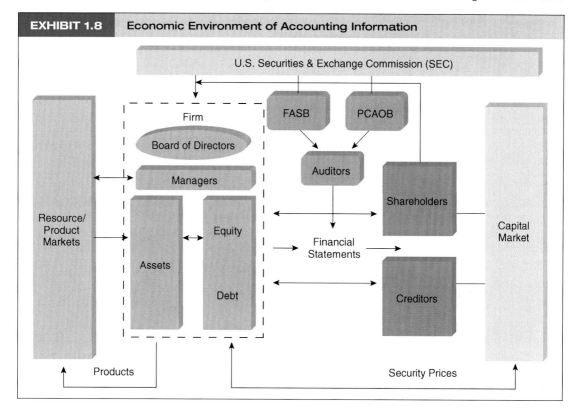

An example of a financial accounting standard is FAS 2, *Accounting for Research and Development Costs*, issued in 1974, requiring that "All research and development costs . . . be charged to expense when incurred." Financial statement users may disagree with the required accounting treatment of research and development (R&D) costs under FAS 2, but the knowledge that all companies are required to use the same method is likely to be valuable to analysts and investors when reviewing the financial statements of companies that incur significant R&D costs.

To the layperson, the notion that accounting standards generate heated debates is almost laughable. But in the late 1990's, the FASB issued an exposure draft that required companies to charge the cost of executive stock options against corporate net earnings. Many technology companies feared that the decline in their reported income after implementation of this proposed accounting standard would cause their company's share price to materially decline. The debate over stock option accounting even reached the floor of the U.S. Congress. Senator Joseph Lieberman of Connecticut proposed a law prohibiting the SEC from requiring that executive stock options be expensed. The FASB, under intense political pressure, ultimately backed down with the issuance of FAS 123. The final standard gave firms a choice of deducting the cost of stock options against net income or disclosing in their footnotes what a firm's net income would have been if the options had been charged against its income.

Stock option accounting resurfaced as a controversial topic in the aftermath of the Enron, WorldCom, and Global Crossing scandals as critics attributed the collapse of these companies, at least in part, to the incentive that option-holding executives have to drive share prices higher by inflating reported corporate earnings. Numerous companies began to voluntarily charge the cost of employee stock options against earnings while other companies (such as Microsoft) abandoned stock options in favor of other compensation arrangements. As of 2006, FAS 123 has been revised to FAS 123R such that it is now mandatory to charge the expense of employee stock options against corporate earnings. (We will have more to say about employee stock options in Chapter 11.)

GLOBAL PERSPECTIVE

Accounting standards have traditionally been established on a country-by-country basis. Unfortunately, this situation made the comparability and transparency of financial information across national borders difficult at best. To overcome the diversity in transnational GAAP, the **International Accounting Standards Board** was established in 1973 to "harmonize" global accounting practice. Many countries (Bulgaria, Estonia, Jamaica, New Zealand, Russia, Tanzania, and the Ukraine) have replaced their national GAAP with the **International Financial Reporting Standards (IFRS)** issued by the IASB. Beginning in 2005, the European Union (EU) required that all publicly-held companies in EU-member states and EU-applicant states use IFRS in their consolidated financial statements. Foreign companies that raise capital in the U.S., however, must issue financial statements prepared using U.S. GAAP, or if prepared using some other form of GAAP (such as IFRS or national GAAP), present a reconciliation of their net income and shareholders' equity under U.S. GAAP and the foreign GAAP.

As a concluding observation, it is helpful to understand that, in most countries, GAAP are used only to prepare the financial statements distributed to such external parties as financial analysts, shareholders, and debtholders. It is rare that GAAP are used to prepare a company's income tax statements because income tax regulations are customarily set by elected legislators or governmental agencies, not accounting professionals. The internal financial statements used by managers to run a company may also differ from those statements issued to shareholders and debtholders. In short, it is not unusual for a company to maintain three (or more) sets of financial data—for managers, for the taxation authorities, and for analysts, shareholders, and debtholders. The focus of this textbook is on those financial statements prepared using GAAP for such external constituencies as financial advisors, lenders, investors, and shareholders.

ROLE OF FINANCIAL ACCOUNTING IN INVESTMENT DECISIONS

In very simplified terms, the lifetime profile of an individual consists of 12 to 16 years of education, 35 years of employment, 15 to 20 years of retirement, and finally death. During the first few years of employment, individuals spend most of their earnings acquiring assets like a car, a house, and taking the occasional vacation. After the basics are acquired, most individuals begin to consider the possibility that they will need substantial funds to maintain a lifestyle in retirement that they will have grown accustomed to in their working life. That means developing a retirement plan. The basic retirement plan consists of decisions about how long to work, the amount of funds to set aside over the employment period, and how to allocate those funds across different types of investments.

Individuals typically invest some of their retirement funds in the shares of companies or in a portfolio of companies to diversify their holdings. The old adage *Don't put all your eggs in one basket!* is good advice since a diversified portfolio reduces risk. Over the last decade, more and more individuals have begun simplifying the process of diversifying their equity investments by buying shares in mutual funds. By investing in a spectrum of companies, the value of mutual fund shares is not unduly influenced by the share price performance of a single company but instead by the broad movement of stock prices in general. Stock market indices such as the Dow Jones Industrial Average (DJIA) and the Standard and Poor's 500 Index (S&P 500) are examples of indexes of a large portfolio of stocks that mutual funds often try to mimic.

Individuals also typically put a sizeable portion of their retirement funds in tax-deferred company-sponsored pension plans. Some individuals dislike risk so they put more of their funds in government debt securities that provide interest payments and repayment of principal. Securities issued by the United States government, and the governments of most developed countries, are considered to be risk-free because of the very low probability that these entities will fail to pay the interest and principal on their debt securities.

The portfolio decisions of millions of individuals and businesses in allocating funds across different investment opportunities can be thought of as the supply of capital. At the same time, there are companies that have opportunities to invest in assets that far exceed their ability to generate the needed investment funds. These unfunded investment opportunities of millions of businesses can be thought of as the demand for capital. The capital market, on the other hand, can be thought of as the market place in which funds are traded between the suppliers of capital and those firms in search of capital. The financial statements provided by the multitude of firms seeking capital are used by the various suppliers of capital to evaluate the investment alternatives. Equilibrium prices for equity and debt securities result when millions of buyers and sellers agree to exchange capital on mutually acceptable terms.

Individual companies raise funds—that is, obtain capital—by issuing shares to shareholders and/or by borrowing from creditors such as financial institutions and bond investors. For shareholders, the return on their investment is derived from dividend payments and any appreciation (or depreciation) experienced from changes in a company's share price. In general, the return (r) for an equity security over a given period, such as a month or a year, is a function of its price at the end of the period (P_t), any dividends received during the period (D_t) and its price at the beginning of the period (P_{t-1}). That is,

> Companies "go public"—that is, sell ownership shares in the public capital market—as a means to gain access to capital to grow, to provide the original investors with "liquidity" (the ability to sell their ownership interests), and to have shares to be used to facilitate future mergers and acquisitions.

$$r_t = (P_t + D_t - P_{t-1})/P_{t-1}$$

For lenders, a return is generated by the interest payments paid by borrowers and the full and timely repayment of their initial capital investment.

In Practice 1.3 provides data on the average annual return for various types of securities sold in the United States over the 76 year period of 1926 to 2002. The In Practice also shows the standard deviation of the annual returns, a measure of the variation around the average return, which is often used as an indication of the riskiness of a given investment. According to the data, large company shares earned an average return of 12.7 percent per year compared to a return of 5.7 percent for long-term government

---

In Practice 1.3 *Average Annual Rate of Return by Type of Security: 1926–2002*

Security Classification	Average Return	Standard Deviation
Large company stocks....................	12.7%	20.2%
Small company stocks....................	17.3	33.2
Long-term corporate bonds...............	6.1	8.6
Long-term government bonds.............	5.7	9.4
Intermediate-term government bonds........	5.5	5.7
U.S. Treasury bills.......................	3.9	3.2
Inflation...............................	3.1	4.4

Source: Ibbotson, Stocks, Bonds, Bills and Inflation

bonds but the standard deviation of the returns for large company stocks was much higher, 20.2 percent versus 9.4 percent. Small company shares have done even better than large company shares, having earned an average annual return of 17.3 percent, but the standard deviation of 33.2 percent is also considerably higher. The high standard deviation for small company shares means that the actual return in any year will vary considerably more than for large company shares. In short, when small company share prices fall (rise), they tend to fall (rise) farther than large company share prices; and thus, small company shares are considered to be a riskier investment than large company shares.

The data in In Practice 1.3 indicate that investments in shares have provided higher average annual returns than investments in government bonds. If the standard deviation of the return is a reasonable measure of risk, the data indicate that shares have higher risk than government bonds, supporting the intuitive notion that higher returns come at the price of bearing higher risk. Investors in common shares can lose all of their investment whereas an investment in government bonds is considered to be risk-free (which means, an investor will receive all interest payments when due and will receive a full return of invested capital). The data also provide support for the notion that shareholders of large firms bear more risk than corporate bondholders since the standard deviation of corporate bonds is only 8.6 percent versus 20.2 percent for stocks. Yet, shareholders are compensated for this additional risk by earning higher returns, 12.7 percent versus 6.1 percent for bondholders.

What is the role of accounting information in the capital markets? For investors who follow an active investment strategy, one very important role for financial statement information is to provide better assessments of the expected return and risk of individual securities so that the investor can make the best possible investment decisions. This is called the **information role** of financial statements. For passive investors who follow a buy-and-hold strategy, accounting information may have only limited value since these investors implicitly operate under the premise that security prices reflect all information that is publicly available. Passive investors (such as, individuals who invest in index funds) believe that it is not possible to earn excess returns above the general market return because the capital markets are efficient. A market in which security prices correctly reflect all publicly available information (for example, the information contained in financial statements) is referred to as an **efficient market.**

Debtholders, on the other hand, use accounting information to assess financial risk—that is, the risk that a firm may not pay its debt service charges and principal payments on a timely basis. When debtholders determine that financial risk is high, they will demand commensurately higher returns (by charging higher interest rates) to compensate them for the additional risk assumed by lending to such a firm.

CHANGING ECONOMIC LANDSCAPE

Enron, WorldCom and Global Crossing are now household names synonymous with the most egregious corporate wrongdoing in the United States in the last 70 years. These financial scandals brought about significant changes in U.S. corporate regulation. To demonstrate that it was responsive to the public's demand for action, numerous corporate executives and employees from Arthur Andersen, auditor for all three failed companies, were questioned on the floor of the U.S. Congress. In response to their findings, the U.S. Congress quickly enacted the Sarbanes-Oxley Act, establishing the Public Company Accounting Oversight Board to regulate the accounting profession.

Some observers believe, however, that the enacted changes didn't go to the root cause of the financial scandals, the seeds of which were sown in regulation changes made 30 years ago. They cite changes made in the 1970s to increase competition in audit markets by permitting accountants to advertise and solicit clients and to changes in the law which permitted auditors to be sued more easily for financial statement errors as causes of the 'race to the bottom.'[4] With decreasing fees from competition and increased legal costs, accounting firms introduced changes in auditing methodologies to reduce audit costs and lobbied for more precise standards to better defend themselves in lawsuits. Accounting firms also diversified into corporate consulting to reduce their dependence on auditing fees, the less profitable side of the business, and, by rewarding partners on the basis of client retention and new client acquisition, encouraged a compliant attitude to financial reporting disagreements. Observers also cite regulatory changes that abolished fixed brokerage commissions as another root-cause of the scandals. With the profitability of the securities business reduced, the research side of the securities industry focused more on pleasing clients that brought in underwriting and investment-banking business by releasing favorable earnings forecasts and assessments. Thus, analysts lost their objectivity and failed to perform hard-nosed fundamental analysis that previously provided value to investors.[5]

Over the years, generally accepted accounting standards have become increasingly complicated, often requiring detailed manuals to interpret the rules and guide companies in their implementation. For example, FAS 2 occupied only 19 pages when it was issued in 1974, while FAS 133, a complicated standard on derivatives issued in 1998, is 213 pages in length. The Sarbanes-Oxley Act mandated, among other things, an investigation of the possibility of using "principles" rather than increasingly detailed "rules" as a basis for U.S. accounting standards. Whether principles become the guiding influence in setting future accounting standards remains to be seen.

ETHICS PERSPECTIVE

There is an intense debate within the U.S. accounting standard-setting community as to whether accounting principles should be rules-based, as is the case with U.S. GAAP, or principles-based, as is the standard with international GAAP. The fundamental difference between these approaches is that principles-based accounting provides a conceptual basis for accountants to follow instead of a list of detailed rules. The landmark Sarbanes-Oxley legislation called for the U.S. Security and Exchange Commission to study the adoption of principles-based standards for U.S. GAAP. The subsequent SEC staff report recommended that U.S. GAAP move toward a principles-based approach. In April 2003, the auditing firm of PricewaterhouseCoopers placed a full-page advertisement in the *Wall Street Journal*. Joining the debate over whether GAAP should be more principles versus rules-based, the audit firm wrote: "Rules-based systems encourage creativity (and not the good kind) in financial reporting. They allow some to stretch the limits of what is permissible under the law, even though it may not be ethically or morally acceptable. A principles-based system requires companies to report, and auditors to audit, the substance or business purpose of transactions, not merely whether they can qualify as acceptable under incredibly complex or overly technical rules." The accounting firm advertisement further stated: "A rules-based system allows managers to ignore the substance and, instead ask, 'Where in the rules does it say I can't do this?'"

SEVEN ACCOUNTING MYTHS

It is rare that someone starting an introductory course in financial accounting begins the experience with a blank mental slate. Rather, most individuals bring with them a set of expectations. Almost everyone has had experience with some aspect of accounting, from balancing a checkbook or filling out a credit card

---

[4] P.M. Healy and K.G. Palepu, "How the Quest for Efficiency Corroded the Market," *Harvard Business Review* (July 2003).
[5] ibid.

application, to reading a set of financial statements. Through these experiences, and from discussions with others, a certain accounting mystery develops along with the formation of certain myths and misconceptions. It is the goal of this textbook to take you on a journey through the world of financial accounting, and along the way, attempt to solve many of the mysteries and debunk many of the myths and misconceptions.

The first two myths about accounting relate to the underlying rules that govern how accounting numbers are calculated and reported. This set of rules is known as **generally accepted accounting principles**, or GAAP. Perhaps the most widely held myth that we explore is the belief that:

1. Generally-accepted accounting principles are a set of rigid rules that, if followed correctly, will lead to a unique, "correct" representation of the financial performance and health of a firm.

Closely related to myth number one is the belief that:

2. GAAP is created from a comprehensive analytical process, which is free from political influence.

The following four myths relate to the basic financial statements which are the output of the accounting process:

3. The basic financial statements, consisting of a balance sheet, an income statement, a statement of shareholders' equity, and a statement of cash flow, reflect a complete, accurate, and timely portrayal of the financial performance and well-being of a firm.

4. All of a firm's identifiable assets and liabilities appear on the balance sheet, and the difference between a firm's assets and its liabilities represents the value of the firm.

5. Each of the financial statements is independent, with each reflecting a different aspect of a firm's performance and financial health.

6. Cash flow is ultimately what matters to a firm and its investors; therefore, it is not really necessary to worry about the definition of earnings used in the preparation of the income statement. Rather, one need only consider the sources and uses of cash as reflected on a firm's statement of cash flow.

Lastly, and what we feel is perhaps the biggest myth of all is:

7. A knowledge of accounting is only necessary for someone who wants to be an accountant.

Some of the terminology from the above list of myths may be unfamiliar to you at this point. One thing that is certainly not a myth is that a major challenge associated with learning accounting is to simply understand all of the jargon. Perhaps we should have added an additional myth: Accounting is hard! While this is certainly a subjective assessment that each student will make, we believe that the approach followed in this textbook will go a long way to turning this challenge into a myth as well.

While most individuals reading this book do not plan to pursue a career in accounting, we believe that it is critical for anyone planning a career in management to understand the fundamentals of accounting, for it is the language of business. To use an analogy from sports, you don't have to be a great baseball player to enjoy the game of baseball. Stated alternatively, it is not critical to be trained as an accountant but you must understand how the game is played and scored.

Accounting, as noted above, has its own language. Two of the words that seem to strike fear into new accounting students are "debit" and "credit." Debits and credits represent a mechanism for accountants to record business transactions, in other words to keep score of the game. For those executives planning to continue their accounting studies to a more advanced level, we have included details on using debits and credits in the appendixes to many of the chapters. Sometimes, however, it is difficult to see the forest through all of the trees. Therefore, we utilize a spreadsheet approach to recording transactions within the chapters to explain the accounting process in a more straightforward, intuitive manner.

EXECUTIVE SUMMARY

In this chapter we considered the basic financial statements of Amazon.com, an online retailer of products. We examined how the financial statements can be used by debtholders and shareholders to predict the expected return and risk of individual securities. We also considered the role of the FASB, the IASB, and the SEC in setting accounting standards and the role of auditors in monitoring compliance with those standards.

As a validation of your understanding of the content of this chapter, you should now be able to:

- Identify the basic financial statements—the income statement, the balance sheet, the statement of shareholders' equity, and the statement of cash flow.
- Understand that companies acquire capital from investors who purchase the debt and equity securities issued by such firms to obtain an expected return commensurate with the risk the investors assume.
- Understand the role of accounting standards in facilitating a properly functioning capital market.
- Understand the conflicts of interest that may arise between the executives, shareholders, and debtholders of a corporation, and the costs associated with the divergent incentives which may arise when the ownership and management of a company are separated (see appendix).

In Chapter 2, we consider how the basic financial statements are developed from accounting events.

KEY CONCEPTS AND TERMS

Accounting equation, 1.5
Accounts receivable, 1.5
Accrual basis of accounting, 1.5
Agency costs, 1.24
American Institute of Certified
  Public Accountants, 1.16
Audit report, 1.14
Balance sheet, 1.5
Capital market, 1.19
Cash basis of accounting, 1.5
Consolidated income
  statement, 1.7
Contracting role of accounting, 1.24
Corporate charter, 1.23
Corporate governance, 1.24
Corporation, 1.23
Debt covenant, 1.25
Decision usefulness, 1.12
Demand for capital, 1.19
Efficient market, 1.20

Expected return, 1.16
Feedback value, 1.13
Financial accounting, 1.4
Financial Accounting
  Foundation, 1.16
Financial Accounting Standard, 1.16
Financial Accounting Standards
  Board, 1.16
Footnotes, 1.13
Generally accepted accounting
  principles, 1.22
Going concern assumption, 1.6
Generally accepted auditing
  standards, 1.15
Income statement, 1.6
Information overload, 1.13
Information role of accounting, 1.20
International Accounting Standards
  Board, 1.18

International Financial Reporting
  Standards, 1.18
Lemons problem, 1.14
Limited liability, 1.24
Managerial accounting, 1.4
Materiality, 1.13
Predictive value, 1.13
Public Company Accounting
  Oversight Board, 1.16
Relevance, 1.12
Reliability, 1.13
Risk, 1.16
Sarbanes-Oxley Act, 1.12
Securities and Exchange
  Commission, 1.16
Statement of cash flow, 1.7
Statement of shareholders'
  equity, 1.10
Supply of capital, 1.19

APPENDIX 1A: Agency Costs and the Separation of Management and Capital Providers

Today, businesses are often organized as **corporations** owned by shareholders under the laws of the state or province in which a company is incorporated. State incorporation laws require a company to have a **corporate charter**—a set of by-laws governing the rights and responsibilities of the board of directors to a firm's shareholders and covering such topics as annual meetings, the election of directors, the type and quantity of shares to be sold, and shareholder voting rights. Shareholders usually delegate the task of running a business on their behalf to a board of directors who are elected by shareholders at the annual shareholders' meeting. The board of directors, on the other hand, has oversight responsibility for the company but the day-to-day management of the firm is directed by the chief executive officer (CEO) who appoints the senior management team including the president, the chief operating officer (COO) and the chief financial officer (CFO). With the assistance of top management, the board of directors recommends a firm's independent auditors to shareholders who vote on audit firm appointment (and reappointment) at the annual meeting. These arrangements are collectively referred to as a company's **corporate governance**, a topic much debated since the collapse of **Enron**, **WorldCom**, **Global Crossing**, and a host of other trouble-ridden firms.

A noteworthy characteristic of the corporate form of organization is the principle of **limited liability**, a feature that limits the liability of a business' shareholders for the debts incurred by the business. Thus, if a corporation's assets are insufficient to pay off a business' liabilities when they mature, the lenders are unable to satisfy their claims against the company by attempting to gain control of the personal assets of the company's shareholders.

BUSINESS PERSPECTIVE

The corporate form of business is one of the two primary organizational forms of companies. The other form is a partnership, also known as a sole proprietorship when there is only one partner. There are several key differences between these alternative organizational forms, the principal ones being limited liability, tax status, and ease of ownership transferability. The primary advantage of the corporate form of business is the limited liability provision in which shareholders are only liable for the debts of a business to the extent of their investment in the business. Partners in a partnership, in contrast, face joint and severable liability wherein each partner is liable for not only their own acts, but also for the acts of the other partners. In addition, a partner's liability is not limited to just his/her partnership investment, but liability extends to their personal assets as well. The limited liability attribute of corporations is essential to their ability to raise large amounts of capital because shareholders can invest in a corporation without risking their entire personal wealth. This attribute also facilitates the transferability of ownership interests in a corporation relative to a partnership.

Corporations are not without negatives, however, and the principal one is tax status. Corporations face a corporate income tax on their earnings, which may lead to a situation of "double taxation" when any previously taxed corporate income is taxed again to the shareholders when they receive a dividend distribution. Partnerships are not taxed separately; instead, the partnership income is taxed only once at the individual-partner level. In addition to these two primary organizational forms, several hybrid forms exist that have attributes of both corporations and partnerships. These hybrid forms include limited partnerships, limited liability partnerships, sub-chapter S corporations, and limited liability corporations.

The development of the concept of limited liability was significant because it enabled the ownership of a firm to be separated from the day-to-day management of the firm; and, consequently, permitted the segmentation of risk bearing by shareholders from the operational control of a business by its team of managers. Unfortunately, the separation of the ownership of a business from the management of a business often leads to a conflict of interest between the preferences of shareholders for greater wealth and the preferences of managers for increased leisure and on-the-job "perks" such as a company-financed jet. The separation of ownership and the provision of debt financing can also potentially create a conflict of interest between shareholders with preferences for higher-valued shares and debtholders with preferences for timely debt servicing and loan repayment. The costs associated with these divergent self-interests are referred to as **agency costs.**

Since conflicts of interest are likely to arise among the various constituencies that comprise a corporation (i.e., shareholders, managers, and creditors), the agency costs associated with these conflicts must be born by the company's shareholders by virtue of their ownership of the firm. Consequently, it is normally in the shareholders' interest to engage in various "monitoring" and "contracting" activities to help control or reduce these conflicts. For example, financial statement information is often used in employment contracts between managers and shareholders to measure, monitor, and control managerial behavior. This is referred to as the **contracting role** of accounting information.

Conflicts between Managers and Shareholders

Since shareholders must bear the agency costs associated with the conflicting self-interests that result from the separation of management and ownership of a corporation, they are incentivized to develop contracts with corporate management that direct or control managerial behavior. For example, the shareholders of a business often develop and institute incentive contracts with a business' executives that tie an executive's compensation to the company's share price, via stock options or a restricted stock plan, or to the company's accounting earnings which have been shown to be correlated with a company's share price. Thus, incentive contracts work to align the financial interests of managers with those of a company's shareholders, thereby encouraging the managers to simultaneously work to maximize their own wealth as well as that of the shareholders. Amazon.com, for example, reported that the company granted bonus opportunities to various executive officers payable upon the achievement of *certain performance goals*. Undoubtedly, some of the performance goals were measured in terms of such accounting numbers as sales, cash flow or profits. By linking executive compensation to measurable accounting variables, management is more likely to take appropriate actions to see that the performance goals are met or exceeded, thereby increasing the wealth of the shareholders, and that of their own.

Conflicts between Debtholders and Shareholders

Agency costs can also arise from conflicts between debtholders and shareholders. An extreme example of such behavior would occur in the case of a firm whose shareholders borrow a large amount of money from debtholders only to pay the borrowed funds out as a dividend. In effect, the shareholders redistribute the borrowed wealth from the debtholders to themselves, potentially leaving the debtholders with a worthless corporate shell and no resources to repay the loan. By virtue of their ownership of the firm, shareholders bear the agency costs of this conflict via higher interest rates because debtholders can anticipate these potentially unconstrained actions by shareholders. A solution to this conflict is for shareholders to agree to be bound by a legally enforceable loan contract containing provisions that restrict the shareholders' behavior. These contract provisions are called **debt covenants,** and may, for example, restrict the amount of dividends that may be paid.

> When a company borrows funds, the terms of the loan agreement are formalized in a legal contract. Typically, these loan contracts contain provisions, called **covenants**, which restrict the actions of the borrower. For example, a common debt covenant limits the amount of dividends that can be paid to shareholders. Covenants are used by lenders to reduce financial risk and increase the likelihood that borrowers pay their interest and principal repayments in a timely manner.

To illustrate, the following disclosure relates to the long-term debt that appears on Amazon's balance sheet:

The indenture governing the 4.75% Convertible Subordinated Notes contains certain affirmative covenants for us, including making principal and interest payments when due, maintaining our corporate existence and properties, and paying taxes and other claims in a timely manner. We were in compliance with these covenants through December 31, 2005.

Another example of a corporate action creating agency costs is the issuance of new debt with repayment priority over existing debt. In this situation, there is a redistribution of wealth from the initial debtholders to the shareholders. A solution to this conflict is for the shareholders to agree to a legally enforceable contract that limits the firm's ability to issue new debt with priority over the old debt. For example, Amazon's borrowing agreements have covenants that restrict the company's ability to borrow by requiring that the ratio of aggregate indebtedness divided by pre-tax operating earnings be less than 6 to 1. Under the terms of this covenant, Amazon is required to periodically provide debtholders with audited financial statements from which measures of aggregate indebtedness and pre-tax operating earnings can be taken and used to evaluate the firm's compliance with the covenant. How does this help Amazon? By agreeing to the restrictions imposed by the covenant, Amazon.com is able to obtain a loan that it might not otherwise gain access to.

DISCUSSION QUESTIONS

Q1.1   **Financial Statement Data Users.** Financial statement data is utilized by a variety of user-groups to include a company's board of directors, bondholders, corporate employees and executives, customers, investment advisors, labor unions, loan officers and credit analysts, shareholders and suppliers. For each user-group, discuss how financial statement data might be used in their decision-making process.

Q1.2   **Accounting Standards.** Discuss why accounting standards (generally-accepted accounting principles) are important to investors and to a properly functioning, efficient capital market. How do accounting standards help capital markets be (or become) "efficient"?

Q1.3   **Corporate Governance.** Discuss what "corporate governance" is and why it is important to shareholders.

Q1.4   **Risk, Return, and Accounting Information.**   Discuss the relationship between investment risk and the expected rate of return on an investment. Explain why accounting information is useful in evaluating the risk/return trade-off inherent in all investments.

Q1.5   **Global GAAP.**   Discuss the major impediments to the acceptance of a global set of generally accepted accounting principles. Prepare a list of those key impediments. Of the items on your list, which do you think will be the most difficult to overcome? Why? Why is having a global set of GAAP desirable?

Q1.6   **Asymmetric U.S. GAAP.**   Under U.S. GAAP, long-lived assets such as real estate are carried on the balance sheet at the original purchase price of the asset. In the event that the value of a real estate asset becomes "impaired"—that is, the current value of the real estate falls below its original purchase price and is unlikely to recover the lost value in the foreseeable future—the asset's book value is written down to the lower current value and a loss is recorded on the firm's income statement. Under no circumstances, however, can a firm write-up the value of its real estate assets in the event that current value exceeds original purchase price. Discuss whether U.S. GAAP should be changed to allow a symmetric treatment of asset value increases and decreases? What are the implications of this asymmetry in the accounting treatment of assets (like real estate) for current U.S. financial statement users?

Q1.7   **Human Assets.**   The balance sheet allegedly reports all of the assets of a business. But one of the most important assets of any business is its employees, and this asset is omitted from the balance sheet of every company in every country in the world. Thus, it can be concluded that the balance sheet of any company understates the true value of its assets. Discuss what types of companies and which industries are most likely to be impacted by this situation. Prepare a list of the companies that you feel are most adversely affected by this accounting practice. Why did you select these companies?

Q1.8   **Key Performance Indicators: Amazon.com.**   Based upon your reading of the chapter, specifically a review of the financial statements of **Amazon.com**, identify five key indicators of performance (KPIs) for Amazon.com. Explain why you selected the five KPIs. Identify five KPIs that are not present in Amazon's financial statements but that you believe are important to consider when making a decision about whether to invest in Amazon.com.

Q1.9   **Audit Reports.**   Review **Amazon.com**'s audit report in Exhibit 1.7 and discuss what the report tells you about Amazon's financial statements. Is there anything in the audit report that causes you concern? Why or why not? According to the independent auditors, who has ultimate responsibility for the preparation of and fairness of the company's financial statements?

Q1.10   **Accounting Assumptions and Concepts.**   Discuss the following accounting assumptions and concepts:
- Accrual basis of accounting
- Cash basis of accounting
- Going-concern assumption
- Materiality concept
- Information role of accounting
- Contracting role of accounting

Why are the assumptions and concepts important?

Q1.11 **The Basic Financial Statements.** Describe or define the four basic financial statements:
- Income statement
- Balance sheet
- Statement of shareholders' equity
- Statement of cash flow

Discuss how the four statements are interconnected.

Q1.12 **Debt Covenants.** American Airlines has outstanding lines of credit and various loan agreements with a number of financial institutions. Under the terms of these debt contracts, American is required to (a) maintain a minimum balance of $1.25 billion of unrestricted cash and short-term investments, (b) maintain a ratio of operating cash flow to interest expense of at least 1.3 to 1.0, and (c) restrict any dividend payments to American shareholders to not more than 25 percent of net income. Discuss why American's lenders would impose these financial and operating restrictions on the airline. Discuss why American would agree to the restrictions.

Q1.13 **Debt Covenants.** Titanium Metals Corporation (TIMET) is one of the world's leading producers of titanium products, a key component used in the manufacture of commercial and military aircraft. In TIMET's 2005 annual report, the company disclosed the following:

> Under the terms of the company's U.S. asset-based revolving credit agreement, borrowings are limited to the lesser of $105 million or a formula-determined borrowing-base . . . . Borrowings are collateralized by substantially all of the company's U.S. assets.

> The U.S. credit agreement prohibits . . . the payment of dividends on the company's common stock . . . , limits additional indebtedness, requires compliance with certain financial covenants including a minimum net worth covenant and a fixed charge ratio covenant . . . .

Discuss why TIMET's U.S. lenders would impose such restrictions on the company. Discuss why TIMET would agree to such restrictions?

Q1.14 **Separation of Ownership and Management (appendix).** Describe a conflict that may arise between the shareholders of a company and the managers of the company. Discuss what the shareholders might do to overcome that conflict and explain why you feel that your solution to the conflict would be effective.

Q1.15 **Conflicts between Shareholders and Debtholders (appendix).** Describe a conflict that may arise between the shareholders of a company and the debtholders of the company. Discuss what the debtholders might do to resolve that conflict and explain why you feel that your solution to the conflict would be effective.

Q1.16 **The Going Concern Assumption.** Ernst & Young, LLP is the independent public accountant for AMR Corporation, the parent company of American Airlines and American Eagle. In 2002, Ernst & Young gave AMR a "clean opinion," indicating that its financial statements were fairly presented. In the 2002 auditors' report for AMR, however, Ernst & Young notes:

> The accompanying financial statements have been prepared assuming the Company will continue as a going concern . . . the Company's recent history of significant losses, negative cash flow from operations, uncertainty regarding the Company's ability to reduce its operating costs to offset the declines in its revenues, the potential failure of the company to satisfy the liquidity requirements in certain of its credit agreements, raise substantial doubt about the Company's ability to continue as a going concern.

Discuss why Ernst & Young would issue a "clean opinion" on the financial statements of AMR Corporation given its many doubts about the firm's ability to "continue as a going concern."

Q1.17 **Is the Sarbanes-Oxley Act Effective?** In 2006, BusinessWeek magazine (April 17, 2006) carried an opinion piece which questioned the effectiveness of the Sarbanes-Oxley Act of 2002. According to the author, Professor D. Moore, "key business failures that cost investors and employees tens of billions of dollars are all but sure to happen again. The calamitous scandals of Enron and many other companies were possible only because of breaches in a bulwark of our free market system—auditor independence." Professor Moore states that the Sarbanes-Oxley Act will be ineffective in preventing future corporate scandals because the act fails to address the real underlying problem, namely the lack of auditor objectivity. Do you agree with Professor Moore? If so, why? If not, why not?

Q1.18 **Should the Sarbanes-Oxley Act be revised?** In late 2006, **BusinessWeek** magazine (December 18, 2006) carried a report on the aftermath of the passage of the Sarbanes-Oxley Act. According to the piece, "the intentions were good, but in the two years since its passing, the Sarbanes-Oxley Act has collapsed into a glob of regulatory confusion costing U.S. businesses billions of dollars a year in compliance costs." The article further noted that "(T)he act never got the vetting it deserved because of the race to approve it after the **Enron** and **WorldCom** meltdowns. . ." Nevertheless, one direct consequence of the Act was that a record number of U.S.-listed firms—1,300 companies, or over 8 percent of the total—restated their earnings in 2005. Discuss whether the criticisms of the Act noted in the *BusinessWeek* article are justified given the large number of firms that found it necessary to restate their reported earnings following the passage of the Act.

Q1.19 **(Ethics Perspective) Rules-based versus Principles-based Accounting.** Do you believe that rules-based accounting leads to unethical managerial behavior? If so, why? Do you think that rules-based GAAP allows businesses to design their financial reporting so as to stay within the letter of the accounting standards even if they clearly violate the spirit of the standards?

⊘ **indicates that check figures are available on the book's Website.**

EXERCISES

E1.20 **Account Identification.** Presented below is a list of financial statement accounts. Using the letter A for assets, L for liabilities, SE for shareholders' equity, R for revenue, E for expenses, and NA for not applicable, identify (a) whether the listed accounts appear on the balance sheet (B/S) or income statement (I/S), and if so, (b) the nature of the account (A, L, SE, R, E, or NA).

1. Accounts receivable	9. Depreciation expense
2. Common stock	10. Accounts payable
3. Sales	11. Cash flow from operating activities
4. Land	12. Cash
5. Retained earnings	13. Cost-of-goods sold
6. Notes payable	14. Equipment
7. Dividends paid	15. Selling expense
8. Inventory	16. Interest income

E1.21 **Account Identification.** Presented below is a list of financial statement accounts. Using the letter A for assets, L for liabilities, SE for shareholders' equity, R for revenue, E for expenses, and NA for not applicable, identify (a) whether the listed accounts appear on the balance sheet (B/S) or the income statement (I/S), and if so, (b) the nature of the account (A, L, SE, R, E, or NA).

1. Cash flow for investing activities	9. Amortization expense
2. Prepaid rent	10. Common stock
3. Cost-of-goods sold	11. Accounts receivable
4. Long-term investments	12. Dividends paid
5. Accounts payable	13. Service revenue
6. Retained earnings	14. Inventory
7. Income tax expense	15. Wages payable
8. Cash	16. Property and land

E1.22 **The Balance Sheet Equation.** The Arcadia Company reported the following financial results during its first two years of operations:

Year End	Assets	=	Liabilities	+	Shareholders' Equity
Year 1 ...	$80,000	=	$60,000	+	$20,000
Year 2 ...	70,000	=	40,000	+	30,000

Assuming that no dividends were declared and that no additional capital was invested in Year 2, determine Arcadia's net income (or loss) for Year 2.

⊘ E1.23 **The Balance Sheet Equation.** The Claremont Company reported the following financial results during its first two years of operations.

Year End	Assets	=	Liabilities	+	Shareholders' Equity
Year 1 ...	$110,000	=	$60,000	+	$50,000
Year 2 ...	125,000	=	80,000	+	45,000

Assuming that no dividends were declared and that no additional capital was invested in Year 2, determine the net income (loss) for the Claremont Company in Year 2.

⊘ E1.24 **Key Relations: Revenues, Expenses, Dividends, and Retained Earnings.** Compute the missing amounts (in millions) in the following table. (The balance in retained earnings at year-end 2006 was $2.2.) Comment on the firm's performance over the three year period after calculating the level of expenses as a percentage of total revenues and net income as a percentage of total revenues. What advice would you give to this company in regards to its dividend policy?

	2004	2005	2006
Retained earnings (beginning)	$1.2	$ 2.0	?
Revenues	8.8	11.8	11.8
Expenses	7.4	?	11.0
Dividends	?	.6	.6

E1.25 **Key Relations: Revenues, Expenses, Dividends, and Retained Earnings.** Compute the missing amounts in the following table. (At the end of 2006, retained earnings had a balance of negative $2,086.) Comment on the company's performance over the three year period after calculating the relationship of expenses as a percentage of revenues and net income as a percentage of revenues. Do you agree with the company's dividend policy? Why?

	2004	2005	2006
Retained earnings (beginning)	$(1,746.5)	$(1,830.5)	$(2,653.0)
Revenues	4,840.5	5,327.0	?
Expenses	?	5,628.0	5,425.0
Dividends	-0-	?	17.5

E1.26 **Financial Statement Results.** In its 2005 annual report to shareholders, The General Electric Company reported the following financial results:

- Revenues increased from $134.5 billion in 2004 to $149.7 billion in 2005.
- Net income decreased from $16.8 billion in 2004 to $16.4 billion in 2005.
- Total assets decreased from $750.0 billion in 2004 to $673.5 billion in 2005.
- Shareholders' equity decreased from $110.8 billion in 2004 to $109.4 billion in 2005.

- For 2005, the cash flow from operating activities was $37.6 billion, the cash flow from investing activities was negative $35.1 billion, and the cash flow from financing activities was negative $6.2 million.

Discuss the possible explanations for the financial results of the General Electric Company from 2004 to 2005.

E1.27 **Financial Statement Results.** In its 2005 annual report to shareholders, The Johnson and Johnson Company, a consumer-products company, reported the following financial results:

- Revenues increased from $47.7 billion in 2004 to $50.5 billion in 2005.
- Net income increased from $8.5 billion in 2004 to $10.4 billion in 2005.
- Total assets increased from $53.3 billion in 2004 to $58.1 billion in 2005.
- Shareholders' equity increased from $31.8 billion in 2004 to $37.9 billion in 2005.
- For 2005, the cash flow from operating activities amounted to $11.9 billion, the cash flow from investing activities amounted to negative $0.3 billion, and the cash flow from financing activities amounted to negative $4.5 billion.

Discuss the possible explanations for the financial results of The Johnson and Johnson Company from 2004 to 2005.

E1.28 **Financial Statement Results: Global.** In its 2005 annual report to shareholders, the Ericsson Company of Sweden reported the following financial results (all values are in Swedish Krona):

- Sales increased from 117,738 million in 2004 to 131,972 million in 2005.
- Net income increased from negative 10,844 million in 2004 to 19,024 million in 2005.
- Total assets increased from 182,372 million in 2004 to 183,040 million in 2005.
- Shareholders' equity increased from 60,481 million in 2004 to 77,299 million in 2005.
- Cash and cash equivalents increased from 73,207 million in 2004 to 76,554 million in 2005.
- For 2005, the cash flow from operating activities was 22,479 million, the cash flow from investing activities was negative 4,788 million, and the cash flow from financing activities was negative 14,344 million.

Discuss the possible explanations for the financial results of Ericsson from 2004 to 2005.

E1.29 **Calculating Security Returns.** Presented below are the beginning-of-year common share price (P_{t-1}), the end-of-year common share price (P_t), and the annual dividend (D_t) for three competitors—The Johnson and Johnson Company, The Procter & Gamble Company, and Novartis AG:

	P_{t-1}	P_t	D_t
Johnson & Johnson.....................	$65.50	$60.25	$1.32
Procter & Gamble......................	55.75	58.50	1.24
Novartis AG	48.50	52.50	0.90

Calculate the annual return for each of the three companies. Which security provided the highest return over the one year period?

◐ E1.30 **Calculating Security Returns.** Presented below are the beginning-of-year common share price (P_{t-1}), the end-of-year common share price (P_t), and the annual dividend (D_t) for three competitors—General Electric Company, Phillips Electronics NV, and Siemens AG.

	P_{t-1}	P_t	D_t
General Electric Co.	$32.01	$34.50	$0.86
Phillips Electronics NV	72.52	72.90	1.28
Siemens AG	27.20	25.36	0.52

Calculate the annual return for each of the three individual securities. Which security provided the greatest return over the one year period? What other information would you need to assess the return/risk tradeoff on each of these individual securities?

PROBLEMS

⊘ P1.31 **Key Financial Statement Relations: Balance Sheet, Income Statement, and Statement of Cash Flow.** Compute the missing amounts in the following financial statements. You may assume that accounts receivable relate only to credit sales and that accounts payable relate only to credit purchases of inventory. There were no sales of property and equipment during 2006 and any purchases of property and equipment were made using cash:

Balance Sheet at	December 31, 2005	December 31, 2006
Current assets		
Cash	$?	$ 25,000
Marketable securities	3,000	5,000
Accounts receivable	12,000	37,000
Merchandise inventory	52,000	23,000
Prepaid advertising	15,000	18,000
Total current assets	92,000	108,000
Property, plant and equipment (cost)	175,000	?
Accumulated depreciation	(35,000)	(63,000)
Land	15,000	?
Intangible assets	?	7,000
Total assets	$258,000	$342,000
Current liabilities		
Accounts payable	$ 12,000	$ 23,000
Wages payable	?	18,000
Interest payable	6,000	5,000
Dividends payable	3,000	?
Taxes payable	17,000	12,000
Total current liabilities	43,000	60,000
Long-term debt	?	86,000
Shareholders' equity		
Common stock	150,000	172,000
Retained earnings	23,000	32,000
Treasury stock	(10,000)	?
Total liabilities and shareholders' equity	$258,000	$342,000

Income Statement for Year Ending	December 31, 2006
Sales revenue.	$?
Cost of sales.	123,000
Gross profit.	162,000
Expenses:	
Wages.	15,000
Advertising	18,000
Depreciation	?
Amortization	4,000
Total expenses	65,000
Operating profit	97,000
Interest	?
Income (loss) before taxes	88,000
Tax expense	35,000
Net income.	$ 53,000

Statement of Cash Flow for Year Ended	December 31, 2006
Cash flow from operating activities	
Cash collections from customers.	$ 260,000
Cash payments for:	
Inventory.	(83,000)
Wages.	(2,000)
Taxes	(40,000)
Interest	(10,000)
Advertising	?
Net cash provided by operations	104,000
Cash flow from investing activities	
(Purchases) sale of property, plant and equipment	(111,000)
(Purchase) sale of marketable securities	?
(Purchase) sale of land	11,000
Net cash provided by investing activities.	(102,000)
Cash flow from financing activities	
Issuance (repayment) of long-term debt	34,000
Payment of dividend	(45,000)
Issuance (repurchase) of common stock	?
(Purchase) sale of treasury stock	2,000
Net cash provided by financing activities.	13,000
Change in cash.	$?

P1.32 **Key Financial Statement Relations: Balance Sheet, Income Statement, and Statement of Cash Flow.** Compute the missing amounts in the following financial statements. You may assume that accounts receivable relate only to credit sales and that accounts payable relate only to credit purchases of inventory. There were no sales of property and equipment during 2006 and any purchases of property and equipment were made using cash:

Balance Sheet at	December 31, 2005	December 31, 2006
Current assets		
Cash.	$ 18,000	$?
Marketable securities	2,000	5,000
Accounts receivable.	8,000	10,000
Merchandise inventory.	41,000	58,000
Prepaid advertising.	13,000	16,000
Total current assets	82,000	104,000
Property, plant and equipment (cost)	?	201,000
Accumulated depreciation	(41,000)	(52,000)
Land.	12,000	19,000
Intangible assets	12,000	?
Total assets.	$227,000	$282,000
Current liabilities		
Accounts payable.	$ 18,000	$?
Wages payable.	15,000	18,000
Interest payable	?	6,000
Dividends payable	2,000	4,000
Taxes payable.	5,000	1,000
Total current liabilities.	48,000	50,000
Long-term debt	46,000	?
Shareholders' equity		
Common stock.	121,000	160,000
Retained earnings	22,000	32,000
Treasury stock	?	(12,000)
Total liabilities and shareholders' equity.	$227,000	$282,000

Income Statement for Year Ending	December 31, 2006
Sales revenue.	$140,000
Cost of sales.	87,000
Gross profit.	53,000
Expenses	
Wages.	?
Advertising	5,000
Depreciation.	?
Amortization	2,000
Total expenses	24,000
Operating profit	29,000
Interest	3,000
Income (loss) before taxes	26,000
Tax expense	?
Net Income.	$ 18,000

Statement of Cash Flow for Year Ended	December 31, 2006
Cash flow from operating activities	
Cash collections from customers.	$?
Cash payments for:	
Inventory.	(101,000)
Wages.	(3,000)
Taxes	(12,000)
Interest	(5,000)
Advertising	(8,000)
Net cash provided by operations	9,000
Cash flow from investing activities	
(Purchases) sale of property, plant and	(39,000)
equipment.	
(Purchase) sale of marketable securities	(3,000)
(Purchase) sale of land	?
Net cash provided by investing activities.	(49,000)
Cash flow from financing activities	
Issuance (repayment) of long-term debt	6,000
Payment of dividend	(6,000)
Issuance (repurchase) of common stock	39,000
(Purchase) sale of treasury stock	(2,000)
Net cash provided by financing activities.	37,000
Net cash flow	(3,000)
Change in Cash	$ (3,000)

P1.33   Key Financial Statement Relations: Balance Sheet, Income Statement, and Statement of Cash Flow. Compute the missing amounts in the following financial statements. You may assume that accounts receivable relate only to credit sales and that accounts payable relate only to credit purchases. There were no sales of property and equipment during 2006 and any purchases of property and equipment were made using cash.

Balance Sheet	December 31, 2005	December 31, 2006
Current assets		
Cash.	$?	$ 34,000
Marketable securities.	6,000	5,000
Accounts receivable.	12,000	?
Merchandise inventory.	72,000	61,000
Prepaid advertising	13,000	12,000
Total current assets	132,000	118,000
Property, plant and equipment (cost).	201,000	?
Accumulated depreciation.	?	(101,000)
Land	16,000	14,000
Intangible assets	13,000	10,000
Total assets.	$273,000	$286,000

continued

continued from previous page

Balance Sheet	December 31, 2005	December 31, 2006
Current liabilities		
Accounts payable	$ 25,000	$ 37,000
Wages payable	6,000	14,000
Interest payable	8,000	14,000
Dividends payable	3,000	2,000
Taxes payable	?	8,000
Total current liabilities	47,000	75,000
Long-term debt	87,000	32,000
Shareholders' equity		
Common stock	121,000	?
Retained earnings	28,000	40,000
Treasury stock	?	(15,000)
Total liabilities and shareholders' equity	$273,000	$286,000

Income Statement for Year Ending	December 31, 2006
Sales revenue	$245,000
Cost of sales	?
Gross profit	78,000
Expenses:	
Wages	?
Advertising	15,000
Depreciation	12,000
Amortization	?
Total expenses	50,000
Operating profit	28,000
Interest	7,000
Income (Loss) before taxes	21,000
Tax expense	6,000
Net income	$ 15,000

Statement of Cash Flow for Year Ended	December 31, 2006
Cash flow from operating activities	
Cash collections from customers	$251,000
Cash payments for:	
Inventory	(144,000)
Wages	(12,000)
Taxes	(3,000)
Interest	(1,000)
Advertising	?
Net cash provided by operations	$ 77,000

continued

continued from previous page

Statement of Cash Flow for Year Ended	December 31, 2006
Cash flow from investing activities	
(Purchase) sale of property, plant and equipment . . .	$ (44,000)
(Purchase) sale of marketable securities	1,000
(Purchase) sale of land	?
Net cash provided by investing activities.	(41,000)
Cash flow from financing activities	
Issuance (repayment) of long-term debt	?
Payment of dividend	(4,000)
Issuance (repurchase) of common stock	33,000
(Purchase) sale of treasury stock	(5,000)
Net cash provided by financing activities.	(31,000)
Net cash flow	5,000
Change in cash (on balance sheet)	$ 5,000

CORPORATE ANALYSIS

CA1.34 The Procter and Gamble Company.   The 2005 annual report of **The Procter and Gamble Company** (**P & G**) is available at www.pg.com/annualreports/2005/pdf/pg2005annualreport.pdf. After reviewing P & G's annual report, respond to the following questions:

a. Prepare a list of some of the products produced by P & G. In what industry does P & G operate? Who are some of P & G's key competitors? (To identify the key competitors for P & G, you will need to access the Internet (e.g., http://finance.yahoo.com) or obtain a copy of a recent research report for P & G.)

b. How much net income did P & G earn in 2003, 2004, and 2005? How much operating revenue did P & G report in 2003, 2004, and 2005? Are the trends in operating revenue and net income consistent and positive (i.e., increasing)?

c. How much cash flow from operations was generated by P & G in 2003, 2004, and 2005? Is the trend in the cash flow from operations consistent with the trend in operating revenue and net income? Calculate the ratio of the cash flow from operations divided by net income for 2003, 2004, and 2005. (Note: The ratio of cash flow from operations divided by net income is called the "operating funds ratio.") What does this ratio tell you?

d. Calculate the ratio of total liabilities divided by total assets for 2004 and 2005. What does this ratio tell you? Is P & G principally debt-financed or principally equity-financed? Is the form of P & G's financing changing over time?

e. Consider the audit report for P & G. Who are P & G's auditors? What does P & G's audit report say about the firm's financial statements? Is there anything in P & G's audit report that causes you any concern? If so, what?

CA1.35 **Internet-based Analysis.** Consider a publicly-held company whose products you are familiar with. Some examples might include:

Company	Product	Corporate Website
• Johnson & Johnson Company	• Band-Aids	• www.jnj.com
• Microsoft Corporation	• Windows XP software	• www.microsoft.com
• Nokia Corporation	• Cellular phones	• www.nokia.com
• Intel Corporation	• Pentium processors	• www.intel.com
• Kimberly-Clark Corporation	• Kleenex	• www.kimberly-clark.com

Access the company's public website and search for its most recent annual report. (Some companies will provide access to their financial data through an "investor relations" link, while others will provide a direct link to their "annual reports.") After locating your company's most recent annual report, open the file and review its contents. After reviewing the annual report, for your selected company, prepare answers to the following questions:

1. Prepare a list of the company's products.
2. Identify which accounting firm audited the company's financial data. Briefly describe the contents of the audit report.
3. How much net income did the company earn in each of the past two years?
4. How much cash flow from operations did the company generate in each of the last two years?
5. Explain why the amount of net income and the cash flow from operations differed?
6. Comment on the company's performance and financial health over the last two years. Is the company's performance and financial health improving or declining? Why?

Chapter Two

From Accounting Events to Financial Statements

TAKEAWAYS

When you complete this chapter you should be able to:

1. Explain the accounting meaning behind the terms asset, liability, shareholders' equity, revenue, expense, and matching.

2. Prepare financial statements from accounting events.

3. Apply selected financial ratios to evaluate a company's financial performance.

4. Apply the balance sheet equation to understand the managerial motives for selecting between alternative accounting methods.

Where have we been?	Where are we?	Where are we going?
Chapter 1 examined why individuals use accounting information when making financial decisions and how this information can be made more valuable through the development and use of accounting standards. It also examined the demand for and the supply of capital and how accounting information can help make capital markets efficient. Finally, the chapter appendix examined the conflicts of interest that can arise between capital providers and business managers and how accounting information can be used to attenuate those conflicts.	In this chapter, we examine the balance sheet equation and how financial statements are derived from a set of accounting events that affect a business. We also investigate how to use financial statements to evaluate a firm's performance and to understand the managerial motives for selecting between alternative accounting methods.	Chapter 3 examines the various components of the income statement and how cash flow statements can be derived from an income statement and a set of balance sheets. The chapter also examines the alternative ways that investment professionals define and measure earnings and cash flows when they evaluate the financial performance of a business.

CRAZY EDDIE   Symbol: CRZY

Crazy Eddie was a discount consumer electronics store chain based in New York. The business was started in 1971 by Eddie Antar and his cousin, Sam, and soon became well known for its loud radio and television commercials which featured a frenetic spokesperson who promoted the chain's "insa-a-a-a-ane prices." Eventually, the chain grew to 43 stores and generated over $300 million in revenues. In 1984, Eddie and Sam took the company public (symbol: CRZY) at an IPO price of $8 per share; by early 1986, the shares were selling for more than $75 per share.

Almost from the start of business, Eddie and Sam engaged in various forms of financial fraud. Court records indicate that they routinely skimmed an estimated $4 million per year from the business, which they deposited in offshore bank accounts. In the early 1980s, Eddie hired his nephew, Sammy, who had earned a degree in accounting, to assist with the fraud. With the help of Sammy who had become the CFO, Eddie and Sam inflated same-store sales by an estimated $15 to $20 million per year, and likewise falsified store inventories to justify the inflated revenue figures. Court records indicate that Sammy coerced store employees, using threats of termination, to falsify sales invoices so that the company's independent auditors would not suspect the presence of fraud.

By mid-1986, the magnitude of the fraud became almost impossible to cover up, and the stock market began to become suspicious. By October 1986, the share price had fallen to $17.50 per share, and shortly thereafter, Eddie resigned as the company's chief executive officer. Just prior to his resignation, Eddie cashed out of his Crazy Eddie stock, sending some $50 million to his off-shore accounts in Israel.

In June 1989, Crazy Eddie filed for Chapter 11 bankruptcy protection. Shortly thereafter, the U.S. Securities and Exchange Commission charged Eddie Antar with securities fraud and illegal insider trading. In January 1990, a U.S. Federal district judge ordered Antar to repatriate the more than $50 million from stock sales that he had illegally transferred to Israel. Instead, Eddie fled the U.S. using a fake passport; but, in June of 1992, he was arrested in Tel Aviv and extradicted to the U.S. In 1996, Eddie Antar was sentenced to 8 years in prison for stock fraud and racketeering and was ordered to pay more than $150 million in fines.

In 2004, the Crazy Eddie trademark was acquired by the Trident Growth Fund, which placed the trademark and internet domain name "crazyeddie.com" on eBay for sale. The auction ended without the reserve price of $800,000 being met; the highest bid was just $30,100.

In this chapter, we examine the balance sheet equation and how financial statements can be derived from a set of accounting events, real or fraudulent.

EXECUTIVE OUTLINE

From Accounting Events to Financial Statements

The Balance Sheet Equation	Preparing Financial Statements from Accounting Events	Evaluating Business Performance and Making Financial Decisions	Managerial Discretion and Accounting Methods
■ Accounting Equation ■ Defining some Accounting Terms ■ Accounting Equation Spreadsheet	■ Preparing Basic Financial Statements ■ Articulation of Financial Statements ■ Accounting Policy Decisions at Russian River Valley Winery	■ Evaluating Firm Profitability ■ Return on Equity Analysis ■ Evaluating Financial Risk	■ Operating Revenues at B.J.'s Wholesale Club ■ Operating Expenses at America Online

BALANCE SHEET EQUATION

Graduation from a university is an exciting time in life. Graduates usually say farewell to old friends and look to life's next set of challenges. This phase of life is likely to bring added responsibilities including a job and possibly a family. It may even involve the decision to buy a house. But before you do, you will probably need to take out a loan, typically called a mortgage. A mortgage is a loan from a financial institution secured by the home itself, and possibly other assets. In the event that you fail to make the agreed upon interest and principal payments on your mortgage, the financial institution may exercise its contractual right to foreclose on your house—that is, to seize the property and sell it to recover the value of the outstanding loan.

Before lending any money, a financial institution will usually request certain information to assess whether an individual or a business represents a good credit risk. Exhibit 2.1 presents one of the forms that will need to be completed in order to have a loan application considered. If you have never completed one of these forms, now is a good time to try it out.

Let's focus on the left side of the form—your assets. The caption "cash or market value" indicates that the numbers that you are requested to insert should be your assets' current value. The top part of the form asks for the balance of your cash and checking/savings accounts, with the names and addresses of the institutions where you keep these accounts so that the lender can verify the reported amounts. The section below cash and checking/savings accounts asks for the value of all your stocks and bonds. To fill in this information, you will need to know the number of stocks and bonds that you own of each company and the current price for each security. If the stocks and bonds are traded on an exchange such as the New York Stock Exchange, the London Stock Exchange, or the Tokyo Stock Exchange, you can simply access a financial internet site to find the current price for each of the securities. Next, you will have to get the cash surrender value of any life insurance policies. If you have a life insurance policy, your insurance agent can provide that information.

The section below life insurance asks for the market value of any real estate owned, such as a rental house or a vacation home. Where do you get the market value for your real estate properties? It is harder to get this type of information because real estate does not have an actively traded market like the London, New York, or Tokyo Stock Exchanges. You will have to hire an appraiser who will estimate the value of your house by considering comparable properties—that is, houses with the same number of bedrooms, bathrooms, and in the same neighborhood. But determining the market value for your real estate holdings is considerably more subjective than coming up with a value for your stock or bond portfolio. If you hired three different appraisers, you would probably get three different estimates. After you have included any remaining assets that you own, such as a car or a business, you can then total them all up and put a number in the box for "total assets a."

Now turn to the far right column where you are asked to insert amounts for the unpaid balances on all of your outstanding loans, including credit cards, student loans, and real estate or automobile loans. For each of these loans you must also disclose the names and addresses of the people you owe money to so that the lender can verify your reported amounts. The sum of all of these items can be put in the box labeled "total liabilities b."

Finally, the form asks you to come up with your "net worth," described as "a minus b." Your net worth is simply the difference between your total assets and total liabilities. This is an important relationship so let's write it out:

$$A - L = NW$$

EXHIBIT 2.1	A Typical Loan Application

VI. ASSETS AND LIABILITIES

This statement and any applicable supporting schedules may be completed jointly by both married and unmarried Co-borrowers if their assets and liabilities are sufficiently joined so that the Statement can be meaningfully and fairly presented on a combined basis; otherwise separate Statements and Schedules are required. If the Co-Borrower section was completed about a spouse, this Statement and supporting schedules must be completed about that spouse also.

Completed ☐ Jointly ☐ Not Jointly

ASSETS	Cash or Market	Liabilities and Pledged Assets. List the creditor's name, address and account number for all outstanding debts, including automobile loans, revolving charge accounts, real estate loans, alimony, child support, stock pledges, etc. Use continuation sheet, if necessary. Indicate by (*) those liabilities which will be satisfied upon sale of real estate owned or upon refinancing of the subject property.		
Description	Value			
Cash deposit toward purchase held by:	$			
		LIABILITIES	**Monthly Payt. & Mos. Left to Pay**	**Unpaid Balance**
		Name and address of Company	$ Payt./Mos.	$
List checking and savings accounts below				
Name and address of Bank, S&L, or Credit Union				
		Acct. no.		
		Name and address of Company	$ Payt./Mos.	$
Acct. no.	$			
Name and address of Bank, S&L, or Credit Union				
		Acct. no.		
		Name and address of Company	$ Payt./Mos.	$
Acct. no.	$			
Name and address of Bank, S&L, or Credit Union				
		Acct. no.		
		Name and address of Company	$ Payt./Mos.	$
Acct. no.	$			
Name and address of Bank, S&L, or Credit Union				
		Acct. no.		
		Name and address of Company	$ Payt./Mos.	$
Acct. no.	$			
Stocks & Bonds (Company name/ number & description)	$			
		Acct. no.		
		Name and address of Company	$ Payt./Mos.	$
Life insurance net cash value				
Face amount: $	$			
Subtotal Liquid Assets	$			
Real estate owned (enter market value from schedule of real estate owned)	$	Acct. no.		
Vested interest in retirement fund	$	Name and address of Company	$ Payt./Mos.	$
Net worth of business(es) owned (attach financial statement)	$			
Automobiles owned (make and year)	$			
		Acct. no.		
		Alimony/Child Support/Separate Maintenance Payments Owed to:		
Other Assets (itemize)	$		$	
		Job Related Expense (child care, union dues, etc.)	$	
		Total Monthly Payments	$	
Total Assets a.	$	**Net Worth (a-b)** $	**Total Liabilities b.**	$

This expression says that your personal net worth (NW) is equal to the amount left over from your assets (A) after paying off all of your liabilities (L). Notice that this expression implicitly suggests that your creditors have first claim on your assets and you get what remains. Since the lenders have first claim, they are in a less risky position. As we observed in Chapter 1, there is a positive relationship between the amount of assumed risk and the expected return on an investment; that is, greater (less) assumed risk implies a higher (lower) expected return.

If we add L to both sides of our expression, we can rearrange the relationship as follows:

$$A = L + NW$$

This new expression is called the **balance sheet equation**. It shows that the total assets on the left side must exactly equal the sum of the claims on those assets on the right side. There are two types of claims—the lenders who have first claim on your assets—and you—the person who gets what is left over. It should now be clear why the balance sheet equation always balances –NW is just a balancing or plug figure!

> In some countries, the balance sheet equation is formatted as:
>
> $$A - L = NW$$
>
> This format emphasizes the measurement of net worth. Regardless of which format is adopted, the information contained in a balance sheet is exactly the same.

Now if we think about a company instead of an individual, shareholders are those individuals or entities which purchase ownership shares in the business. In the case of a business, the term NW is usually replaced by the term SE, for shareholders' equity. Therefore, the balance sheet equation that we will use to refer to a business instead of an individual is:

$$A = L + SE$$

In a nutshell, the right side of the balance sheet equation tells us that a business obtains cash and/or other assets (A) from shareholders by issuing shares (SE) and from lenders by promising to pay interest on any debt and repay any borrowed funds (L). As you will see in subsequent chapters, some companies borrow sparingly and thus are financed principally by shareholders. Other companies borrow extensively, and we will refer to these companies as being **leveraged**. The relative mix of funding from shareholders versus lenders is an important **financing decision** that can have a dramatic effect on a firm's financial performance.

The left side of the balance sheet equation shows how a business invests its resources in various assets (A)—this is known as the **investment decision**. Who makes the investment decision? Technically, the shareholders have the right to make such decisions but they usually delegate these decisions to a management team. Not surprising, shareholders are preoccupied with maintaining and growing their wealth; thus, they expect the management team to make investment decisions that increase SE over time.

Defining some Accounting Terms

We have used the terms "asset," "liability" and "shareholders' equity" without precisely defining these terms. From the loan application above, it is clear that assets include cash, stocks, bonds, and real estate, among other things. For now, we will define an **asset** as an economic resource that is expected to generate future benefits for a business. As we will see, assets may comprise a variety of economic resources to include those mentioned above, as well as inventory, property and equipment, and various intangible assets such as copyrights and patents, among others.

From the loan application above, liabilities include car loans, credit card debt, student loans, and mortgages. But as you will soon see, a business' liabilities may include many types of obligations. For now, we define a liability simply as an obligation to make future cash payments. This definition implies that if a business is obliged to make cash payments in the future, then the obligation qualifies as a liability. In subsequent chapters, we will see that some liabilities that satisfy this definition need not be (and often are not) reported on the balance sheet. We will refer to these unreported obligations as off-balance-sheet debt. (Subsequent chapters will reveal that many of a firm's economic assets also fail to appear of the balance sheet!) Finally, we define shareholders' equity as the residual value of a business—that is, the value of any assets remaining after all liabilities have been satisfied. Shortly, we will see that shareholders' equity has two key components—the value of the shareholders' direct investment in a business, called contributed capital or common stock (CS), and the amount of any profits retained in the business to support future operations, called retained earnings (RE). Incorporating these two components of SE into the balance sheet equation yields the following:

$$A = L + (CS + RE)$$

Preparing Financial Statements from Accounting Events

Recording Transactions

You may feel that there is little reason why you should be subjected to the rigors of learning how to record transactions since you probably have little, if any, desire to become an accountant. In fact, most managers are apt to hire an accountant to execute these activities. But having some knowledge of the recording process can be invaluable, and this can be illustrated by way of an analogy.

It is doubtful that the readers of this book will go on to a career in auto repair. Many readers, in fact, may never even look under the hood of a car. Each of you, however, likely drive a car; and, many of you likely have experienced mechanical problems at one time or another. It would certainly be helpful to the mechanic who will ultimately be responsible for repairing your car if you have the ability to provide detailed information regarding what is wrong. It could also prove financially beneficial if you have some understanding of what the mechanic plans to charge you for. You certainly do not want to be completely at their mercy. The same applies for business transactions. While you may not be responsible for the actual recording of a transaction, as a manager you may be responsible for the reported financial statements. If so, wouldn't you want to be able to intelligently discuss with your accountant what needs to be done and to also understand what should be done? A basic understanding of the recording process can give you this necessary competence.

We follow two approaches in this textbook for the recording of transactions. The approach we illustrate in this chapter utilizes a horizontal spreadsheet built upon the basic accounting equation of Assets equaling Liabilities and Shareholders' equity. This spreadsheet approach is appreciated by many readers for its simplicity; however, this is not the method used by accounting professionals. Many of you will find the spreadsheet approach more intuitive, and you will be heartened to know that this approach yields the exact same result as that used by accounting professionals.

The second approach, shown in the appendix to this chapter, represents how transactions are actually recorded. The recording is most often done by accounting software rather than by hand. This approach involves first recording transactions as journal entries, utilizing a double-entry system of debits and credits. These terms probably sound quite foreign, and rightly so. Unlike much in the natural sciences that is determined by nature, the accounting process of recording transactions is completely designed by man and is therefore somewhat arbitrary. The important thing, however, is that it works. And, not only does it work, but it also has a built-in error detection mechanism. While many of the readers may struggle to understand the accounting process, most come to see this system as somewhat of an art form, poetic in its elegance.

To demonstrate how financial statements are prepared from accounting events, an illustration involving the hypothetical Russian River Valley Winery is presented. Our approach for organizing the firm's accounting data is a simple spreadsheet based on the balance sheet equation, $A = L + SE$, as follows:

Russian River Valley Winery Spreadsheet							
Assets				=	Liabilities	+	Shareholders' Equity
Cash	Buildings	Land	Intangible Assets		Bank Loan Payable		Common Stock / Retained Earnings

Because the balance sheet equation must always balance, we know that the value of the winery's assets on the left side of the spreadsheet will always equal the value of the winery's liabilities plus its shareholders' equity on the right side of the spreadsheet.

THE RUSSIAN RIVER VALLEY WINERY

Matt and Kate Miller established the Russian River Valley Winery near Healdsburg, California. They owned a small parcel of farmland on which the winery would be operated. Kate further agreed to use her inheritance from her grandparents to construct buildings suitable for the new business.

Since Matt and Kate lacked sufficient land to grow their own grapes, they decided that the winery would purchase grapes from local growers. The wines would be aged in oak barrels, then bottled, corked, and held for a minimum of six months before sale.

Recognizing that the winery would need additional financial resources, Kate and Matt approached an old friend, Bob Buck, who worked as a loan officer at the Hap e-Loan Corporation. Via e-mail, Bob indicated that the business plan for the winery looked promising but that Hap e-Loan would need to review a comprehensive set of forecasted financial statements before the Miller's $4.8 million loan request would be considered. The loan agreement proposed a fixed interest rate of 6 percent per year on the outstanding loan balance and called for the borrowed amount to be repaid over 10 years in equal annual installments payable at the end of the year.

Establishing the Business   On the basis of discussions with the company's legal advisors, Kate and Matt determined that the following events would likely occur during the start-up phase of the business:

1. Matt would receive four million shares of common stock, valued at $1 per share, in the Russian River Valley Winery, Inc., in exchange for contributing his land to the business. This transaction would increase the business' land (A) account by $4 million and increase the common stock (SE) account by $4 million.

One of the most important skills a manager can develop is the ability to prepare forward-looking financial forecasts. These forecasts are often prepared as pro-forma financial statements. The terms pro-forma and forecasted can be used interchangeably. Capital providers such as banks usually require such statements for new businesses in order to help determine whether the business represents a prudent investment.

Russian River Valley Winery Spreadsheet						
	Assets			=	Liabilities	+ Shareholder' Equity
Cash	Buildings	Land	Intangible Assets		Loan Payable	Common Stock
1		4,000				4,000

2. Kate would receive two million shares of common stock in the winery for the buildings that she would finance with her inheritance. This would increase the winery's buildings (A) account by $2 million and increase the common stock (SE) account by $2 million.

Russian River Valley Winery Spreadsheet						
	Assets			=	Liabilities	+ Shareholder' Equity
Cash	Buildings	Land	Intangible Assets		Loan Payable	Common Stock
2	2,000					2,000

3. When the $4.8 million bank loan was approved and the cash disbursed to the Russian River Valley Winery, the cash (A) account would increase by $4.8 million and the bank loan payable (L) account would increase by $4.8 million.

Russian River Valley Winery Spreadsheet						
	Assets			=	Liabilities	+ Shareholder' Equity
Cash	Buildings	Land	Intangible Assets		Loan Payable	Common Stock
3	4,800				4,800	

4. Cash fees expected to be paid for incorporation costs during the start-up phase were estimated at $100,000. This would decrease cash (A) by $100,000 and increase intangible assets (start-up costs) by the same amount. (Recall that an asset is presumed to generate future benefits for a business. Thus, the cost of opening a business can reasonably be expected to provide such benefits since they are necessary to enable the enterprise to begin operations; consequently, such costs are often considered to be an asset on the balance sheet of many new businesses.)

> Most recorded assets such as cash or buildings have an actual physical presence and are sometimes referred to as tangible assets. In addition, certain recorded assets lack a physical presence, but still provide future benefits to the organization. These intangible assets include such items as patents and start-up costs.

Russian River Valley Winery Spreadsheet						
	Assets			=	Liabilities	+ Shareholder' Equity
Cash	Buildings	Land	Intangible Assets		Loan Payable	Common Stock
4	−100			100		

Following the pre-opening events identified by Kate and Matt, the Russian River Valley's balance sheet at the start of business would appear as follows:

Russian River Valley Winery Spreadsheet

	Assets				=	Liabilities	+	Shareholder' Equity
	Cash	Buildings	Land	Intangible Assets		Loan Payable		Common Stock
1			4,000					4,000
2		2,000						2,000
3	4,800					4,800		
4	−100			100				
Totals	4,700	2,000	4,000	4,100		4,800		6,000
			10,800		=	4,800	+	6,000

Russian River Valley Winery, Inc.
Pre-Opening Balance Sheet

($ thousands)

Assets		Liabilities & Shareholders' Equity	
Cash.	$ 4,700	Liabilities	
Buildings.	2,000	Bank loan payable	$ 4,800
Land	4,000	Shareholders' equity	
Intangible assets	100	Common stock.	6,000
Total assets	$10,800	Liabilities & shareholders' equity	$10,800

The winery's total assets of $10.8 million equal the sum of the winery's liabilities plus shareholders' equity of $10.8 million.

Projected Business Events

To comply with the bank's request for **forecasted financial statements**—that is, financial statements prepared on an "as if" basis using assumptions about what might happen in the future—Matt and Kate compiled a list of the important events that would likely occur during the first year of operations. These events appear below as accounting events Number 1 through 14. Matt and Kate's analysis of how each of the events would affect the winery's balance sheet equation appears as bullet items. Observe that the analysis of each event leads to the identification of (at least) two financial effects on the balance sheet equation; and, that the financial effects of each transaction are recorded in the appropriate columns of the winery's spreadsheet. Further, notice in the Russian River Valley spreadsheet that after each event is analyzed, the balance sheet equation remains in balance, with total assets equal to the sum of total liabilities and shareholders' equity. To help understand how the balance sheet equation is affected by the various events, each asset account is labeled with an A, each liability account with an L, and each shareholders' equity account as SE. Finally, notice that the account balances from the winery's pre-opening balance sheet have been entered into the spreadsheet in the row labeled "beginning balance."

1. The winery would purchase $380,000 of inventory (grapes, corks, bottles, labels). All purchases would initially be on credit and would subsequently require payment within 30 days of the initial purchase transaction. It was estimated that the unpaid balance of this credit purchase would be $20,000 at the end of the year.

Russian River Valley Winery Spreadsheet

		Assets							=	Liabilities			+	Shareholders' Equity	
	Cash	Accounts Receivable	Inven- tory	Equip- ment	Build- ings	Accum. Deprec.	Land	Intangible Assets		Accounts Payable	Taxes Payable	Loan Payable		Common Stock	Retained Earnings
Beg. Bal.	4,700	0	0	0	2,000	0	4,000	100		0	0	4,800		6,000	0
1(a)			380							380					
1(b)	−360									−360					

- In 1(a) the winery purchases inventory, but does not immediately pay for the inventory. Thus, inventory (A) increases by $380,000 and accounts payable (L)—that is, amounts owed by the winery to its suppliers—increases by $380,000.
- In 1(b) the winery pays $360,000 ($380,000 less $20,000) to its suppliers; thus, cash (A) decreases by $360,000 and accounts payable (L) decreases by $360,000.

2. The winery would spend $1.5 million in cash to acquire equipment to be used in crushing, separating and fermenting the grape juice.

> Kate and Matt's analysis of Russian River Valley's credit purchase of inventory reflects the accrual basis of accounting discussed in Chapter 1. Their analysis also reflects the Entity Principle of accounting, which stipulates that the financial affairs of a business must be maintained separate and distinct from the affairs of the owners of the business.

		Assets							=	Liabilities			+	Shareholders' Equity	
	Cash	Accounts Receivable	Inven- tory	Equip- ment	Build- ings	Accum. Deprec.	Land	Intangible Assets		Accounts Payable	Taxes Payable	Loan Payable		Common Stock	Retained Earnings
Beg. Bal.	4,340	0	380	0	2,000	0	4,000	100		20	0	4,800		6,000	0
2	−1,500			1,500											

- The winery increases the equipment (A) account by $1.5 million and decreases cash (A) by $1.5 million.

3. The winery would spend $2 million in cash to purchase oak aging barrels. The barrels would be considered a long-term investment in equipment because the barrels typically last five or more years.

		Assets							=	Liabilities			+	Shareholders' Equity	
	Cash	Accounts Receivable	Inven- tory	Equip- ment	Build- ings	Accum. Deprec.	Land	Intangible Assets		Accounts Payable	Taxes Payable	Loan Payable		Common Stock	Retained Earnings
Beg. Bal.	2,840	0	380	1,500	2,000	0	4,000	100		20	0	4,800		6,000	0
3	−2,000			2,000											

- Cash (A) is reduced by $2 million and equipment (A) is increased by $2 million.

4. The Russian River Valley Winery would sell two types of wine—bulk wine and bottled wine. It was estimated that bulk wine sales would total 100,000 gallons at $15 per gallon. Sales of bottled wine were estimated to be 50,000

> Matt and Kate's analysis and recording of accounting events 2 and 3 reflects the historical cost principle of accounting, which stipules that all assets should initially be recorded at their acquisition or historical cost.

bottles at $8 per bottle. About 20 percent of the sales would be immediately paid for in cash, with 80 percent of the sales on credit with payment expected in 30 days after the sale transaction. Of that latter amount, $800,000 was expected to be uncollected at year-end.

		Assets							=	Liabilities			+	Shareholders' Equity	
	Cash	Accounts Receivable	Inven- tory	Equip- ment	Build- ings	Accum. Deprec.	Land	Intangible Assets		Accounts Payable	Taxes Payable	Loan Payable		Common Stock	Retained Earnings
Adj. Bal.	840	0	380	3,500	2,000	0	4,000	100		20	0	4,800		6,000	0
4(a)	380	1,520													1,900
4(b)	720	−720													

- In 4(a), total sales are projected to be $1.9 million (100,000 gallons @ $15 plus 50,000 bottles @ $8). Of this total amount, the winery expects to collect $380,000 in cash (20 percent of $1.9 million) and will be owed the balance of $1.52 million by its customers. Thus, cash (A) is increased by $380,000, accounts receivable (A) is increased by $1.52 million, and shareholders' equity (specifically, revenue, a component of retained earnings) is increased by $1.9 million. Accounts receivable represent amounts owed to the winery by its customers.

  The relation between revenues and expenses, components of the income statement, and retained earnings, a component of the shareholders' equity por-

> Revenues (R) are increases in shareholders' equity that result from providing goods and services to customers. Revenue is reported on the income statement when it has been earned—that is, when a company has provided substantially all of the goods or services it has promised to provide—and when the collectibility of the cash from the customer is reasonably assured. This important concept is known as the revenue recognition principle. Recognizing revenue is a wealth-increasing event for a business and its shareholders, and this is reflected by an increase in shareholders' equity.

tion of the balance sheet, is illustrated below. As you will recall from exhibits 1.5 and 1.6 from chapter 1, the income statement articulates with the balance sheet through the retained earnings account. Revenues, which increase net income, also increase retained earnings, whereas expenses, which decrease net income, also decrease retained earnings. We further illustrate this articulation of the financial statements later in this chapter.

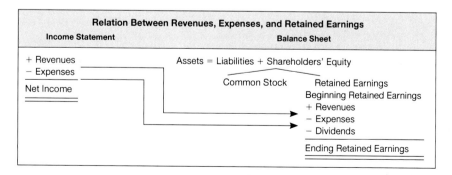

Relation Between Revenues, Expenses, and Retained Earnings

- In 4(b), customers are expected to owe the winery $800,000 at year-end; hence, they must have paid $720,000 in cash during the year. Thus, cash (A) is increased by $720,000 and accounts receivable (A) is decreased by $720,000.

5. Payroll expenses for employees were estimated to require cash payments of $100,000 during the year. Selling and administrative expenses of $300,000 were also expected to be paid.

	Assets								=	Liabilities			+	Shareholders' Equity	
	Cash	Accounts Receivable	Inven- tory	Equip- ment	Build- ings	Accum. Deprec.	Land	Intangible Assets		Accounts Payable	Taxes Payable	Loan Payable		Common Stock	Retained Earnings
Adj. Bal.	1,940	800	380	3,500	2,000	0	4,000	100		20	0	4,800		6,000	1,900
5(a)	−100														−100
5(b)	−300														−300

- In 5(a), the winery pays $100,000 in cash for employee wage expense; thus, cash (A) decreases by $100,000 and shareholders' equity (specifically, expenses, a component of retained earnings) decreases by $100,000.

- In 5(b), the winery reduces cash (A) by $300,000 for the payment of selling and administrative expenses. Since these services are consumed in the process of generating revenues from wine sales, the cost of these used-up resources are matched with revenues, thus reducing retained earnings (SE) by $300,000.

6. The loan agreement requires payment of principal and interest at the end of the year.

> Expenses (E) represent the using up of goods and services associated with the production of revenues by a business. Since expenses reduce assets, expenses are a wealth-reducing event. The cost of the goods and services consumed in generating revenues are said to be matched with the revenues they generate; as a consequence, a business is able to compare its accomplishments (revenue) with its effort (expenses). This important concept is known as the matching principle of accounting.

	Assets								=	Liabilities			+	Shareholders' Equity	
	Cash	Accounts Receivable	Inven- tory	Equip- ment	Build- ings	Accum. Deprec.	Land	Intangible Assets		Accounts Payable	Taxes Payable	Loan Payable		Common Stock	Retained Earnings
Adj. Bal.	1,540	800	380	3,500	2,000	0	4,000	100		20	0	4,800		6,000	1,500
6(a)	−480											−480			
6(b)	−288														−288

- In 6(a), cash (A) is reduced by $480,000, the first of 10 annual loan repayments ($4.8 million divided by 10), and the loan payable (L) account is reduced by the same amount.
- In 6(b), cash (A) is reduced by $288,000 (6 percent of $4.8 million) for the first year's interest payment. Interest is the cost of borrowing funds from a financial institution and is a financing expense of the business. Hence, retained earnings (SE) are also reduced by $288,000 as this business expense must be matched with the enterprise's revenues.

7. The winery's policy was to order only as much inventory as would be needed for the current year's sales. Thus, it was estimated that the ending inventory would be zero.

		Assets							=	Liabilities			+	Shareholders' Equity	
	Cash	Accounts Receivable	Inven- tory	Equip- ment	Build- ings	Accum. Deprec.	Land	Intangible Assets		Accounts Payable	Taxes Payable	Loan Payable		Common Stock	Retained Earnings
Adj. Bal.	772	800	380	3,500	2,000	0	4,000	100		20	0	4,320		6,000	1,212
7			-380												-380

- The entire available inventory is assumed to have been used up in the production and sale of wine. Thus, inventory (A) decreases by $380,000, as does retained earnings (SE). The cost of inventory sold is an expense to be matched with revenues. Notice that inventory is first classified as an asset since it is assumed to provide future benefit to the enterprise in the form of future cash inflows. When the inventory is sold, and therefore used up, the asset is removed from the balance sheet and an expense, called cost of goods sold, is recognized as a reduction in shareholders' equity. This is an example of the matching principle in which the cost of goods sold is matched with the revenues from the sale of the goods, all recognized in the same accounting period.

8. Depreciation for the year was determined as follows: $175,000 for equipment, based on an expected useful life of 20 years, and $50,000 for buildings, based on an expected useful life of 40 years.

		Assets							=	Liabilities			+	Shareholders' Equity	
	Cash	Accounts Receivable	Inven- tory	Equip- ment	Build- ings	Accum. Deprec.	Land	Intangible Assets		Accounts Payable	Taxes Payable	Loan Payable		Common Stock	Retained Earnings
Adj. Bal.	772	800	0	3,500	2,000	0	4,000	100		20	0	4,320		6,000	832
8(a)						-175									-175
8(b)						-50									-50

- Depreciation refers to the systematic expensing of an asset as a consequence of the passage of time. Accountants often estimate the amount of depreciation to be taken on an asset by estimating the expected useful life of the asset and then allocating its cost equally across all years of the asset's expected useful life, a method called straight-line depreciation. In 8(a), the expected life of the equipment is 20 years so depreciation expense (E) is $175,000 ($3.5 million divided by 20 years). Hence, retained earnings (SE) are decreased by $175,000. Of course, the asset must also be decreased, but by convention, the equipment account is not decreased directly. Another account—called accumulated depreciation—is decreased, and thus, reflects the negative $175,000. The accumulated depreciation account is then subtracted from the equipment account. We show an increase in accumulated depreciation as a negative number under the assets section of the spreadsheet. This is because accumulated depreciation is actually a contra-asset, where by convention it maintains a balance of the opposite sign as a regular asset. We will have much more to say about both depreciation expense and accumulated depreciation in chapter 7. Another important point to note is that the purpose of depreciation is not to reduce the asset's book value in an attempt to equate its book value with its market value. Rather, the purpose of depreciation is to allocate the cost

> Balance sheet accounts which are subtracted from other accounts (such as accumulated depreciation) are known as contra-accounts (CA). The difference between the cost of an asset (e.g. equipment) and its accumulated depreciation is called the book value of the asset.

of the asset over time in an attempt to match the asset's cost with the revenue generated by the asset in each future period, an application of the matching principle.

- In 8(b), the depreciation expense associated with using the building for a year is estimated to be $50,000 ($2 million divided by 40 years); hence, retained earnings (SE) are decreased by $50,000. As in 8(a), accumulated depreciation (CA) is decreased by $50,000 and deducted from the building account.

9. Kate and Matt decide that the start-up costs of the business should be expensed over two years.

		Assets							=	Liabilities			+	Shareholders' Equity	
	Cash	Accounts Receivable	Inven-tory	Equip-ment	Build-ings	Accum. Deprec.	Land	Intangible Assets		Accounts Payable	Taxes Payable	Loan Payable		Common Stock	Retained Earnings
Adj. Bal.	772	800	0	3,500	2,000	−225	4,000	100		20	0	4,320		6,000	607
9								−50							−50

- The write off of the start-up costs, called amortization, is an expense of the business. Thus, the intangible asset account (A) is reduced by $50,000 ($100,000 divided by 2 years), as is retained earnings (SE). If Matt and Kate had estimated a five-year expected life for the start-up costs instead of just two years, the amortization expense would be only $20,000 per year ($100,000 divided by five years). Estimating the expected useful life of equipment, buildings, and such intangible assets as start-up costs is an important managerial activity. An incorrect estimate of an asset's expected useful life can have a dramatic positive (or negative) effect on a firm's reported performance. As you will see, many accounting numbers, like amortization expense, are just estimates, and as such, can be quite imprecise.

10. Matt and Kate issue 200,000 additional shares to an outside investor for $2 per share to finance future expansion plans.

		Assets							=	Liabilities			+	Shareholders' Equity	
	Cash	Accounts Receivable	Inven-tory	Equip-ment	Build-ings	Accum. Deprec.	Land	Intangible Assets		Accounts Payable	Taxes Payable	Loan Payable		Common Stock	Retained Earnings
Adj. Bal.	772	800	0	3,500	2,000	−225	4,000	50		20	0	4,320		6,000	557
10	400													400	

- The issuance of additional common shares increases common stock (SE) by $400,000 and increases cash (A) by the same amount. As a consequence of selling shares to the outside investor, Matt and Kate must now share control of the business and its profits with the investor who has become a co-owner of the winery. Kate and Matt must have forecasted that they would need the extra cash badly enough to relinquish some control of the business. If you look at the cash column you can see why—there is a large quantity of cash outflows.

11. Matt and Kate intend to buy grapes from the most respected local growers; and thus, they expect that their wines will be well received by their customers. As a consequence, Matt and Kate believe that their ownership shares in the business will be worth considerably more by the end of the year and that this should be reflected in the projected financial statements.

		Assets							=	Liabilities			+	Shareholders' Equity	
	Cash	Accounts Receivable	Inven-tory	Equip-ment	Build-ings	Accum. Deprec.	Land	Intangible Assets		Accounts Payable	Taxes Payable	Loan Payable		Common Stock	Retained Earnings
Adj. Bal. 11	1,172	800	0	3,500	2,000	−225	4,000	50		20	0	4,320		6,400	557

- The winery records no transaction for this information. Even though a good company reputation and widely-recognized brand name are valuable assets to a business, they are not recorded in the financial statements.

> Brand names are not reported in the balance sheet unless purchased from other entities; in some countries (such as France), however, estimating the value of a brand name and placing that asset on the balance sheet is permitted.

12. Federal income taxes were estimated to be $240,000 with 60 percent being paid by year-end.

		Assets							=	Liabilities			+	Shareholders' Equity	
	Cash	Accounts Receivable	Inven-tory	Equip-ment	Build-ings	Accum. Deprec.	Land	Intangible Assets		Accounts Payable	Taxes Payable	Loan Payable		Common Stock	Retained Earnings
Adj. Bal.	1,172	800	0	3,500	2,000	−225	4,000	50		20	0	4,320		6,400	557
12	−144										96				−240

- Income taxes are a cost of doing business, and consequently, this expense must be matched with the winery's revenue; hence, retained earnings (SE) are reduced by $240,000. Since the winery expects to pay $144,000 (60 percent of $240,000), cash (A) is reduced by $144,000 and the remaining amount of $96,000 is still owed; thus, taxes payable (L) increase by $96,000.

13. On the last day of the year, Kate and Matt expect to acquire $60,000 of new grape inventory in anticipation of the following year's production. The purchase would be on credit, with payment terms of 30 days.

> In competitive business environments, it is often necessary to permit customers to buy goods and services on credit, allowing them to pay for the purchased goods over 30, 60, or even 90 days without incurring any interest charges. Extending credit to customers, however, carries a hidden cost to a business, called an opportunity cost. This opportunity cost is equal to a business' cost of borrowing over the time period during which the purchase price remains unpaid. We will have more to say about opportunity costs in Chapter 5. You may also want to read the appendix at the end of this book for insights about the time value of money.

		Assets							=	Liabilities			+	Shareholders' Equity	
	Cash	Accounts Receivable	Inven-tory	Equip-ment	Build-ings	Accum. Deprec.	Land	Intangible Assets		Accounts Payable	Taxes Payable	Loan Payable		Common Stock	Retained Earnings
Adj. Bal.	1,028	800	0	3,500	2,000	−225	4,000	50		60	96	4,320		6,400	317
13			60							60					

- Inventory (A) increases by $60,000 and, since this purchase is not immediately paid for, accounts payable (L) increases by an equivalent amount.
14. Matt and Kate expect to declare and pay cash dividends of $260,000.

Russian River Valley Winery Spreadsheet

	Cash	Accounts Receivable	Inven- tory	Equip- ment	Build- ings	Accum. Deprec.	Land	Intangible Assets	=	Accounts Payable	Taxes Payable	Loan Payable	+	Common Stock	Retained Earnings
				Assets					=		**Liabilities**		+	**Shareholders' Equity**	
Beg. Bal.	4,700	0	0		2,000	0	4,000	100		0	0	4,800		6,000	0
1(a)			380							380					
1(b)	−360									−360					
2	−1,500			1,500											
3	−2,000			2,000											
4(a)	380	1,520													1,900
4(b)	720	−720													
5(a)	−100														−100
5(b)	−300														−300
6(a)	−480											−480			
6(b)	−288														−288
7			−380												−380
8(a)						−175									−175
8(b)						−50									−50
9								−50							−50
10	400													400	
11															
12	−144										96				−240
13			60							60					
14	−260														−260
End Bal.	768	800	60	3,500	2,000	−225	4,000	50		80	96	4,320		6,400	57
				$10,953					=		$4,496		+	$6,457	

- The dividend that Matt and Kate expect to pay is a distribution of the winery's earned profit; hence, it reduces cash (A) by $260,000 and retained earnings (SE) by $260,000. A dividend is considered to be a distribution of a business' earnings to its owners and not a cost of doing business; consequently, dividends are not considered in the calculation of net income on the income statement, although they are reflected in the calculation of retained earnings on the statement of shareholders' equity.

Preparing the Financial Statements

Since all of the projected financial events for the first year of operations for the winery have been analyzed and the financial effects entered into the spreadsheet, it is now possible to complete the spreadsheet by summing up the various values in each of the columns. These final balances are entered in the row labeled "ending balance." The completed spreadsheet for the Russian River Valley Winery thus becomes the basis for preparing the company's basic financial statements. The ending balance row of the spreadsheet, for example, provides the necessary inputs (the ending account balances) for the winery's balance sheet as of the end of the first year of operations, and this statement is presented in Exhibit 2.2.

EXHIBIT 2.2	An Illustrative Balance Sheet

Russian River Valley Winery, Inc.
Balance Sheet

($ thousands)	Pre-Opening	End of Year 1		Pre-Opening	End of Year 1
Assets			**Liabilities and shareholders' equity**		
Current assets			Current liabilities		
Cash.	$ 4,700	$ 768	Accounts payable.	$ 0	$ 80
Accounts receivable.	0	800	Taxes payable.	0	96
Inventory.	0	60	Loan payable-current.	0	480
Total current assets	4,700	1,628	Total current liabilities.	0	656
Noncurrent assets			Noncurrent liabilities		
Property, plant & equipment			Loan payable-noncurrent . . .	4,800	3,840
Equipment	0	3,500	Total liabilities	4,800	4,496
Buildings.	2,000	2,000	Shareholders' equity		
Land	4,000	4,000	Common stock ($1 par)	6,000	6,400
	6,000	9,500	Retained earnings	0	57
Accumulated depreciation	0	(225)	Total shareholders' equity . .	6,000	6,457
Property, plant & equipment (net). .	6,000	9,275	**Total liabilities &**		
Intangible assets	100	50	**shareholders' equity. . . . . .**	$10,800	$10,953
Total noncurrent assets	6,100	9,325			
Total assets	$10,800	$10,953			

    Exhibit 2.2 reveals that the winery's total assets are projected to grow from $10.8 million at the beginning of the year to $10.953 million by year-end. By comparing the various account balances at the beginning of the year with those at the end of the year, it is possible to identify just which accounts increased and which ones decreased. One of the objectives in reviewing a company's balance sheet is not only to understand what assets and liabilities a company has, but also whether and which of these accounts is increasing or decreasing.

    Russian River Valley's balance sheets in Exhibit 2.2 also provide information beyond just a listing of the company's assets, liabilities, shareholders' equity, and whether their balances changed over the fiscal period.

In Practice 2.1 **Balance Sheet Title: A Glimpse of a Sample of Fortune 1000 Companies** The following table identifies the title used on the balance sheet by a sample of 600 Fortune 1000 companies. The title preferred by over 96 percent of the surveyed firms is "balance sheet:"

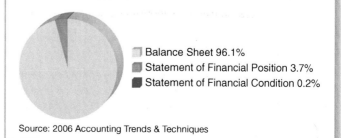

Balance Sheet 96.1%
Statement of Financial Position 3.7%
Statement of Financial Condition 0.2%

Source: 2006 Accounting Trends & Techniques

The balance sheet provides information, for example, about when a business' non-cash assets are likely to be converted into cash and when they are expected to be consumed as part of the business' regular operations, as well as information about when its liabilities are likely to require payment. This information is evident from the classification of the assets and liabilities into the categories of "current" and "noncurrent." **Current assets** are those assets that are expected to be converted into cash or used to support operations during the next 12 months, while **noncurrent assets** are those assets expected to be available to support the continuing operations of a business for many years in the future. **Current liabilities** are those liabilities that are expected to require payment within the next 12 months, whereas **noncurrent liabilities** are obligations that are not expected to require payment for more than one year. The phrase "long-term" is often used instead of "noncurrent."

Notice in Exhibit 2.2 that since the second annual principal payment of $480,000 on the winery's outstanding bank loan is due within 12 months of the date when the balance sheet is prepared, this amount is reclassified from the noncurrent liabilities section of the balance sheet to the current liabilities section of the winery's balance sheet. This reclassification is important because it will enable Kate and Matt to fully understand just how much cash will be needed to satisfy the various claims against the business in the coming year.

Can other information be obtained from the Russian River Valley Winery spreadsheet? Recall that the retained earnings column of the spreadsheet contained all of the revenue and expenses of the business. Thus, an income statement can be readily prepared from data contained in the retained earnings column of the spreadsheet. The income statement for the first year of operations for the winery is presented in Exhibit 2.3.

EXHIBIT 2.3	An Illustrative Income Statement

Russian River Valley Winery, Inc. Income Statement	
($ thousands)	Year 1
Revenues.	$1,900
Cost of goods sold.	380
Gross profit	1,520
Operating expenses	
Wages and salaries	100
Selling & administrative	300
Depreciation.	225
Amortization.	50
Total operating expenses	675
Operating income.	845
Interest expense.	288
Income before income taxes	557
Income taxes	240
Net income	$ 317

Like the balance sheet, the Russian River Valley income statement provides a number of useful pieces of information. For instance, the income statement highlights several key measures of firm performance: revenues, gross profit, operating income, and net income. **Revenues** measure the inflow of cash and other assets (such as, accounts receivable) from a firm's primary business activity. **Gross profit**, on the other hand, measures the amount of cash and assets remaining after deducting the cost of sales, or what is often called the cost of goods sold. **Operating income** refers to a firm's net income before deducting such items as interest expense and income taxes; and, **net income** is the firm's bottom-line performance—the business' net income after all expenses are deducted, both operating and non-operating, recurring and non-recurring.

Observe that the top section of the income statement, through operating income, reflects the results of the company's primary business activities—that is, the winery's core business of producing and selling wine, which is often referred to as its **recurring operations**. The section below operating income reflects the financing activities of the business and any non-recurring operations. The winery doesn't expect to have any non-recurring activities for the year but it does expect to have costs associated with financing its business, namely interest expense on the outstanding bank loan. The winery's net income of $317,000 is the "bottom line" profit available to shareholders. The management of a business must decide whether to reinvest these earnings in the business or to distribute them to shareholders as a dividend, and this decision is reflected in the statement of shareholders' equity.

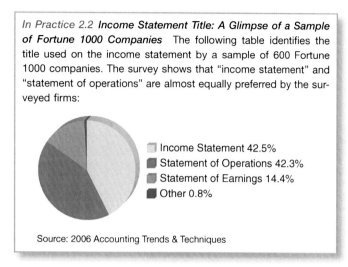

In Practice 2.2 Income Statement Title: A Glimpse of a Sample of Fortune 1000 Companies The following table identifies the title used on the income statement by a sample of 600 Fortune 1000 companies. The survey shows that "income statement" and "statement of operations" are almost equally preferred by the surveyed firms:

- Income Statement 42.5%
- Statement of Operations 42.3%
- Statement of Earnings 14.4%
- Other 0.8%

Source: 2006 Accounting Trends & Techniques

The statement of shareholders' equity reveals how the shareholders' direct investment in a business increased (decreased) due to the company's sale (repurchase) of its own common stock and how the retained earnings of a business were increased by net income and decreased by any net losses or dividends paid to shareholders. A statement of shareholders' equity for the Russian River Valley Winery is presented in Exhibit 2.4. Like the income statement, the information needed to prepare a statement of shareholders' equity is available from the sharcholders' equity columns of the winery's spreadsheet. Exhibit 2.4 shows that the winery expects to begin the year with a zero balance in retained earnings but is expected to end the year with a balance of $57,000, and that the winery expects to begin the year with $6 million in common stock but is expected to end the year with a balance of $6.4 million. Notice how these figures reconcile with the data reported for retained earnings and common stock on the winery's balance sheet in Exhibit 2.2. In accounting jargon, we say that the data from the statement of shareholders' equity "articulate" with the data from the winery's balance sheet.

EXHIBIT 2.4	An Illustrative Statement of Shareholders' Equity		
Russian River Valley Winery, Inc.			
Statement of Shareholders' Equity			
($ thousands)	Common Stock	Retained Earnings	Total
Balance at beginning of year 1.	$6,000	$ 0	$6,000
Net income.		317	317
Dividends paid		(260)	(260)
Sale of common stock	400		400
Balance at end of year 1	$6,400	$ 57	$6,457

In addition to generating profits, a business must make sure that its profits translate into cash so that cash is available to pay the business' expenses and obligations as they come due. The information about a company's available cash flow can be obtained from its statement of cash flow, which can be prepared from the cash inflows and outflows reported in the cash column of the completed spreadsheet. Exhibit 2.5 presents a statement of cash flow for the Russian River Valley Winery. Notice that all of the cash inflows and outflows from the cash column of the spreadsheet are included in this statement.

EXHIBIT 2.5	An Illustrative Statement of Cash Flow

Russian River Valley Winery, Inc. Statement of Cash Flow	
($ thousands)	Year 1
Operating activities	
Cash receipts	
Cash sales	$ 380
Cash collections on account	720
Total cash receipts	1,100
Cash disbursements	
Cash payments for inventory.	360
Cash payments for interest	288
Cash payments for wages & salaries.	100
Cash payments for selling & administrative.	300
Cash payments for taxes.	144
Total cash disbursements.	1,192
Cash flow from operations	(92)
Investing activities	
Purchases of property, plant & equipment	(3,500)
Cash flow from investing.	(3,500)
Financing activities	
Sale of common stock.	400
Repayment of loan.	(480)
Payment of common stock dividends	(260)
Cash flow from financing.	(340)
Net cash flow	(3,932)
Cash balance, beginning of year	4,700
Cash Balance, End of year.	768
Change in cash.	$(3,932)

The statement of cash flow classifies a business' cash flow into the three activity categories of operating, investing, and financing, which correspond to the main activities of any business. The **operating activities** section provides information about the day-to-day cash inflow and outflow from core business operations. The **investing activities** section contains information about the purchase and sale of long-term assets by the firm. This section provides insights about a company's investment strategy. Finally, the **financing activities** section provides information regarding how a business was financed during the period, for example whether the company raised cash from issuing debt or equity or used cash to repay debt or buy back its shares. This section provides insight about a firm's financing strategy. Notice that the cash dividend paid to shareholders is included in the financing section, yet the cash paid for interest on the bank loan is listed in the operating section. Under the accounting rules of most countries, interest expense is an operating cash outflow, whereas dividends are a financing cash outflow. Finally, notice that the "bottom-line" of the statement of cash flow—the net cash flow for the period—equals the change in the cash account from a company's balance sheet. In the case of the Russian River Valley Winery, the change in cash as reported in Exhibit 2.2 is negative $3,932 ($768 − $4,700 = −$3,932). In essence, a statement of cash flow provides the detailed information to explain how and why the cash account on the balance sheet changed from the beginning of the fiscal period to the end. We will have more to say about the statement of cash flow in Chapter 3.

Articulation of the Financial Statements

It should be apparent at this point that the basic financial statements of the Russian River Valley Winery are highly interconnected and are not independent from one another. In accounting parlance, we refer to this interconnectedness as **articulation**. Using the schematic from Exhibit 1-5 in Chapter 1, the articulation of the Russian River Valley Winery's basic financial statements can be illustrated as follows:

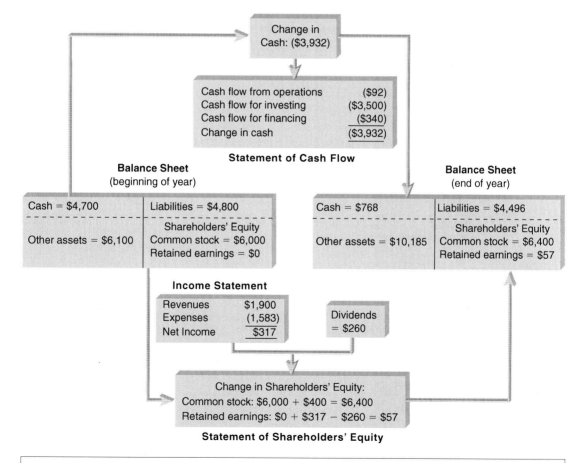

The divergent treatment of interest, the cost of debt financing, and dividends, the cost of equity financing, in the statement of cash flow is attributable to the fact that a statement of cash flow is prepared from the perspective of shareholders, reporting the residual cash flows from operations accruing to the owners after all expenses have been paid but *before* any cash distributions for dividends have been made.

Notice that:

- The change in the cash account ($-$3,962) on the balance sheet from the beginning of the year to the end of the year equals the sum of the cash flow from operations ($-$92), the cash flow from investing ($-$3,500), and the cash flow from financing ($-$340) on the statement of cash flow.
- The change in retained earnings ($57) on the balance sheet equals the sum of the beginning balance ($0) in retained earnings plus net income ($317) from the income statement less any dividends ($-$260) paid to shareholders.
- The change in shareholders' equity ($457) on the balance sheet equals the change in retained earnings ($57) plus the change in common stock ($400) as reported on the statement of shareholders' equity.

Although the basic financial statements articulate with one another, they present different types of information about a business. The income statement, for example, describes a firm's operating performance for the current fiscal period, whereas the balance sheet describes the firm's financial condition as of the beginning or end of the fiscal period. The statement of shareholders' equity, on the other hand, describes how the shareholders' investment changed over the period, and the statement of cash flow explains why (and how) one very important business asset—cash—increased or decreased over the fiscal period. Like the income statement, the statement of cash flow also describes the firm's operating performance for the current period. The difference between these statements, however, relates to the definition of "firm operating performance." The income statement defines firm performance in terms of accrual net earnings whereas the statement of cash flow defines performance in terms of operating cash flow. Thus, although interconnected, the financial statements each depict a different aspect of a business' financial information. It is also important to note that the balance sheet is *at a period in time,* sometimes referred to as a snapshot. In contrast, the other statements are reported *for a period of time*, such as a year.

Accounting Policy Decisions at Russian River Valley Winery

While identifying the expected future events for the winery, Matt and Kate implicitly made a number of accounting policy decisions that affected the forecasted financial statements of the winery, and thus, its likelihood of getting the bank loan. For example, by assuming that all of the $800,000 of outstanding accounts receivable at year-end was reasonably assured of collection, the winery's net income is potentially overstated. For most businesses, the existence of unpaid accounts receivable will usually mean that some future losses can be anticipated for uncollectible accounts. By not estimating what these losses might be, and by not matching those potential losses with the related operating revenue, Kate and Matt may have allowed the winery's projected performance for the first year of operations to be overstated.

Further, depreciation on the equipment and buildings was estimated by Matt and Kate based on expected useful lives of 20 and 40 years, respectively. If Kate and Matt over-estimate the length of the useful lives of these assets, the annual depreciation expense on the income statement will be understated and projected net income overstated. Finally, the expected life chosen to amortize the start-up costs was estimated to be two years. If Kate and Matt underestimate this expected life, the amortization expense will be overstated and the winery's net income understated.

These policy choices illustrate a little appreciated fact about accounting: Financial statements require managers to make many estimates and assumptions which may prove incorrect, and consequently, cause the financial statements to incorrectly characterize a company's performance. Because of the many estimates and assumptions inherent in preparing financial statements, it is wise to remember that accounting data, and hence, the financial statements themselves, are not precise descriptions of a business' financial performance.

To illustrate this point, consider the following statement from the General Motors Corporation annual report to shareholders:

> The consolidated financial statements of GM are prepared in conformity with generally accepted accounting principles, which require the use of estimates, judgments and assumptions . . . . Management believes that the accounting estimates employed are appropriate and resulting balances are reasonable; however, actual results could differ from the original estimates, requiring adjustments to these balances in future periods.

EVALUATING BUSINESS PERFORMANCE AND MAKING FINANCIAL DECISIONS

Producing financial statements about a business is important, particularly if those statements are useful in decision-making. Matt and Kate would certainly be interested in using the financial statement information in Exhibits 2.2, 2.3, 2.4, and 2.5 to decide whether they should proceed with their proposed winery. Similarly, Bob Buck of Hap e-Loan Corporation will find the data in the forecasted financial statements invaluable in helping to decide whether lending money to Russian River Valley is a prudent idea. While a business' owners are primarily interested in the profitability of the business, a financial institution is primarily interested in assessing the financial risk that it will be exposed to when lending to a business. But how can the financial statements help us learn about business profitability and the risks inherent in lending to a business? Stated alternatively, how can financial statements help us make investment and lending decisions?

Evaluating Firm Profitability

To evaluate the profitability of a business, it is often useful to consider various performance indicators from the financial statements. To illustrate, let's consider the most basic measure of firm performance—whether a business made a profit. The income statement in Exhibit 2.3 shows that net income for the Russian River Valley Winery is indeed expected to be positive—net income is projected to be $317,000 for its first year of operations. That's good news! But just looking at the absolute level of profits ignores how much investment it took to generate those profits. In

> Financial Ratios are frequently used to evaluate firm performance. They permit valid comparisons of performance over time or between competitors. By dividing one accounting measure (such as, net income) by a second accounting measure (such as, net sales), the resulting ratio is standardized, thereby enabling an "apples-to-apples" comparison of firm performance.

GLOBAL PERSPECTIVE

The preparation of financial statements around the world proceeds in exactly the same fashion. Not surprisingly, however, some differences in the actual format of the financial statements and in the labels used to describe various financial statement accounts do arise. For example, in North America, the labels "revenue" and "sales" are used to describe the value of the goods sold by a company as reported on its income statement. In the United Kingdom, however, the label "turnover" is used instead to represent the sales of a business. These labeling differences are superficial and in no way alter the content or purpose of the basic financial statements. In essence, worldwide, an income statement is an income statement; and, a balance sheet is a balance sheet!

addition, it is hard to compare the performance of firms of different sizes or of a company over time by just comparing the level of their profits. For example, one would certainly expect a firm such as **General Electric**, with over $670 billion dollars in reported assets, to have a higher level of profit than a small winery. With far greater levels of sales and investments, it is only natural for General Electric to show a higher level of profit. Consequently, the use of financial ratios provides one approach to make useful comparisons of performance between firms of differing size and for a given firm over various time periods.

One profitability measure that considers relative firm size is the **return on sales** ratio (ROS), or net income divided by sales revenue:[1]

Ratio	Financial Variables	Computation	Result
Return on sales (ROS)	$\dfrac{\text{Net income}}{\text{Sales revenue}}$	$\dfrac{\$317}{\$1,900}$	16.7%

The ROS ratio, which is also referred to as the **profit margin ratio**, for the Russian River Valley Winery is forecasted to be 16.7 percent, which indicates that for every dollar of sales revenue, the winery is expected to generate nearly 17 cents of bottom-line profit. You don't have to know much about wineries to recognize that a 16.7 percent return on sales is quite high. But to be certain, it would be wise to compare the Russian River Valley Winery's ROS against the ROS for other small wineries or against the average ROS for the wine industry. By making such inter-firm and industry comparisons, it is possible to more clearly benchmark the winery's performance and to determine how successfully the business is expected to perform.

Another measure of profitability that considers relative firm size is the **return on assets** (ROA) ratio, or net income plus after-tax interest expense divided by total assets:

Ratio	Financial Variables	Computation	Result
Return on assets (ROA)	$\dfrac{[\text{Net income} + \text{Interest expense} \times (1 - \text{Tax rate})]}{\text{Total assets}}$	$\dfrac{\$317 + \$288 \times (1 - (\$240/\$557))}{\$10,953}$	4.4%

The return on assets ratio represents the amount of earnings available to a business' capital providers, to include both its lenders and its shareholders. Since lenders obtain their return in the form of interest payments, and since this expense is subtracted in the calculation of net income, it is necessary to add the interest expense back to net income to produce a measure of the total return available to a firm's capital providers. Interest expense, however, is tax deductible by the business, and therefore, effectively reduces a firm's total income tax expense. The positive impact of interest expense on a firm's income tax expense is referred to as a "tax shield." In order to correctly account for the **tax shield**, the amount of interest added back to net income should be reduced by the amount of the tax shield which is already reflected in a firm's income tax provision, and hence, in its net income. The income tax rate used in this calculation is the company's **effective tax rate**, or a firm's tax expense divided by its income before income taxes. Note

---

[1] Some investment professionals calculate the ROS ratio on an "unlevered" basis as follows:

$$\text{Unlevered ROS} = \frac{\text{Net income} + \text{Interest} \,(1 - \text{Tax rate})}{\text{Net sales}}$$

Unlevering the ROS ratio–that is, adding the interest expense paid by a company net of the tax benefit of the interest expense back to net income–creates a measure of net income as if the company were all equity financed. This alternative measure of ROS allows the analyst to focus on the efficacy of management's operating decisions independent of management's financing decisions. We will have more to say about unlevered ROS in Chapter 4.

that no such adjustment is needed for dividends paid to shareholders since dividends are not tax deductible and are not subtracted in the calculation of net income, and consequently, do not need to be added back.

Russian River Valley's expected ROA, also referred to as the return on investment, is 4.4 percent, indicating that it takes about $1 of assets to generate about four and a half cents of net income. Is that good? One benchmark—the six percent interest rate (but only 3.4 percent after considering the interest tax shield) to be charged by Hap e-Loan Corporation on the proposed bank loan—suggests that the winery's expected ROA is quite low. While the winery will earn slightly more than its 3.4 percent after-tax cost of borrowed funds, this is not a very large margin.[2] The low projected ROA for Russian River Valley may indicate several things—that the wine business is highly competitive, producing only marginal returns, or alternatively, that the winery's business model needs more work to enable the business to be more profitable.

From a shareholder perspective, the size of a business' profit relative to the shareholders' investment in the business is an important measure of profitability, and this can be evaluated by the return on shareholders' equity (ROE) ratio, or net income divided by shareholders' equity.[3] This ratio indicates how much profit was generated given the shareholders' investment in a business:

Ratio	Financial Variables	Computation	Result
Return on equity (ROE)	$\dfrac{\text{Net income}}{\text{Shareholders' equity}}$	$\dfrac{\$317}{\$6,457}$	4.9%

The Russian River Valley Winery's expected ROE is 4.9 percent, which indicates that for every dollar of shareholders' equity invested in the winery, the business is expected to generate less than five cents of profit for its shareholders. This is a little higher than the after-tax 3.4 percent interest rate to be charged by Hap e-Loan Corporation on the bank loan, yet Matt and Kate bear much more risk than the lender. (Recall that assuming higher risk should result in higher returns.) We can tentatively conclude that this expected return is high enough to justify the investment that Kate and Matt will have to make. But, the two entrepreneurs will certainly want to focus on ways of improving the profitability of the business and its ROE.

Return on Equity Analysis

Investment professionals have devised an ingenious way of analyzing the profitability of a business by breaking the return on shareholders' equity (ROE) ratio into three component financial ratios—the return on sales, asset turnover, and financial leverage:

----

[2] Russian River Valley's after-tax cost of borrowed funds is calculated as follows:

$$\text{After-tax cost of borrowing} = \text{Before-tax cost of borrowing} \times (1 - \text{Tax rate})$$

In the case of Russian River Valley, the effective tax rate is 43 percent ($240/$557); hence, the after-tax cost of borrowing is:

$$3.4\% = 6.0\% \times (1 - .43)$$

[3] Many investment professionals define the return on shareholders' equity (ROE) ratio as:

$$\text{ROE} = \frac{\text{Net income} - \text{Preferred stock dividends}}{\text{Common shareholders' equity}}$$

This ratio definition reflects the widely-held view that preferred stock is a quasi-form of debt, and hence, the cost of preferred stock (preferred stock dividends) should be subtracted from net income just as the cost of debt financing (interest expense) is subtracted from net income. Common shareholders' equity is then defined as total shareholders' equity less preferred stock equity. Since many firms do not issue preferred shares, the ROE ratio collapses to just net income divided by shareholders' equity. In addition, some ratios, like ROE, include a metric in the numerator that is measured over time (such as net income) and a metric in the denominator that is measured at a point in time (such as shareholders' equity). Because of this mismatch of the time dimension of a ratio's components, some analysts use averages, rather than ending balances, for the denominator of these ratios.

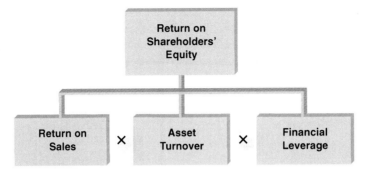

This paradigm reveals that there are four ways to improve a company's ROE, and hence, a firm's profitability: 1) improve a business' return on sales; 2) improve a business' asset turnover; 3) improve a business' use of financial leverage; or, 4) some combination of items 1, 2, and 3. Asset turnover is a measure of how effectively a business' assets are being used by the management team to generate sales revenue. This ratio is calculated as sales revenue divided by total assets. This metric is an important indicator of firm performance since the principal objective of any business is to generate income, and that is only possible after the business first generates operating revenue. Financial leverage, on the other hand, refers to the relative mix of debt versus equity financing

Financial leverage refers to the use of debt to finance a business' assets and/or its operations. The cost of debt financing is defined as the rate of interest specified in a debt contract. If a firm is able to earn a return on its borrowed assets greater than its after-tax cost of borrowing, the excess return accrues to the firm's shareholders. And, as a consequence, a company's ROE will exceed its ROA—for example, 4.9 percent versus 3.4 percent for The Russian River Valley Winery. Thus, when we observe that a firm's ROE exceeds its ROA, we can conclude that the firm has been able to successfully utilize financial leverage.

used by a business and is calculated as total assets divided by shareholders' equity. Since the after-tax interest rate on the winery's debt is only 3.4 percent, financing some of the Russian River Valley's assets with debt takes advantage of this cheaper source of financing.[4] We can apply ROE analysis to the winery's forecasted financial data as follows:

Return On Equity	=	Return On Sales	×	Asset Turnover	×	Financial Leverage
$\dfrac{\text{Net income}}{\text{Shareholders' equity}}$	=	$\dfrac{\text{Net income}}{\text{Sales revenue}}$	×	$\dfrac{\text{Sales revenue}}{\text{Total assets}}$	×	$\dfrac{\text{Total assets}}{\text{Shareholders' equity}}$
$\dfrac{\$317}{\$6,457}$	=	$\dfrac{\$317}{\$1,900}$	×	$\dfrac{\$1,900}{\$10,953}$	×	$\dfrac{\$10,953}{\$6,457}$
4.9%	=	16.7%	×	0.173	×	1.70

The ROE analysis for the Russian River Valley Winery reveals why the winery's expected return on equity (4.9 percent) is low. Although the winery's expected ROS is a healthy 16.7 percent, Russian River Valley's expected asset turnover is only 0.173, which indicates that each dollar invested in the business' assets is expected to generate less than 18 cents in sales. Further, the winery has a financial leverage ratio of 1.70, indicating that the winery's assets are forecasted to be about 1.7 times the amount of shareholders'

---

[4] For all businesses, the cost of debt financing is cheaper than the cost of equity financing. Recall that since buying shares in a business is riskier than lending to a business, the returns expected by shareholders should be higher than the returns expected by lenders–lenders have first claim on the assets of a business and shareholders get what is left over.

equity invested in the business. Put another way, the Russian River Valley Winery assets are financed with relatively more equity ($6,457) than debt ($4,496). Since the winery is able to earn a slightly higher return on its borrowed funds than the after-tax cost that the business will be charged for the use of these funds, the winery's expected ROE is enhanced by its use of financial leverage.

To enable us to benchmark the expected performance of the winery, Exhibit 2.6 presents an ROE analysis for ten wine companies over a recent five year period. The data confirms the assessment that Russian River Valley has a low expected return on equity and asset turnover but a relatively high expected return on sales, as compared to the average of the other ten wineries. Observe, for instance, that while the expected ROS for Russian River Valley is 16.7 percent, it averages only about 6.3 percent for the ten wineries; and, while Russian River Valley's expected asset turnover is only 0.173, it averages 0.59 for the ten wineries, or more than three times higher than the turnover forecasted by the winery. This kind of information can be very useful to Kate and Matt in that it highlights the various financial strengths and weaknesses of their proposed business, and thus, highlights those areas in which Matt and Kate should try to improve their business plan. We will have more to say about ROE analysis in Chapter 4.

EXHIBIT 2.6	ROE Analysis: Median Values for 10 Firms in the Wine Industry					
Return On Equity	=	**Return On Sales**	×	**Asset Turnover**	×	**Financial Leverage**
7.97%	=	6.28%	×	0.59	×	2.15

Source: *Compustat*

Evaluating Financial Risk

The concern that the Russian River Valley Winery may have insufficient cash to pay its annual interest payments and repay the principal on its proposed bank loan on a timely basis are the types of financial risk that financial institutions must consider when lending to a business. Two financial ratios that assess this form of risk include the long-term debt-to-equity ratio and the interest coverage ratio:

Ratio	Financial Variables	Computation	Result
Long-term debt-to-equity	$\dfrac{\text{Long-term debt}}{\text{Shareholders' equity}}$	$\dfrac{\$4,320}{\$6,457}$	0.67
Interest coverage	$\dfrac{\text{Operating income}}{\text{Interest expense}}$	$\dfrac{\$845}{\$288}$	2.93

The long-term debt-to-equity ratio reveals the relative investment of long-term lenders versus that of the shareholders in the Russian River Valley Winery. A high debt-to-equity ratio, for example, indicates a financing strategy heavily dependent on borrowed versus shareholder-invested funds. The interest coverage ratio, on the other hand, reveals the extent to which current operating earnings "cover" current debt service charges (interest expense). A high interest coverage ratio, also referred to as the times-interest-earned ratio, indicates that a business has strong operating earnings (or low interest charges), and thus, has the capacity to take on additional debt and additional debt service costs, as well as to easily service its existing debt.

The Russian River Valley Winery's expected long-term debt-to-equity ratio is 0.67, indicating that its long-term debt of $4,320 ($3,840 + $480) is about two-thirds the amount of its shareholders' equity of $6,457. The winery's expected interest coverage ratio is 2.93, suggesting that the winery's operating income is projected to be almost three times the expected interest expense for the period. Both ratios indicate that there is a fair amount of cushion for the business' lenders. Overall, with a reasonable debt-to-equity ratio and interest coverage ratio, the winery should have a good chance of getting the proposed $4.8 million loan because it appears to have a good chance of paying both the annual interest charge and principal repayments in a timely manner.

MANAGERIAL DISCRETION AND ACCOUNTING METHODS

The balance sheet equation used for analyzing the various accounting events of a business can be helpful in understanding the accounting method choices that a company makes and how those choices affect a business' financial statements. To illustrate, we use the balance sheet equation to examine how B.J.'s Wholesale Club accounted for the membership fees it charges its customers and how America Online accounted for the cost of computer diskettes it used to attract new internet customers.

Operating Revenues at B.J.'s Wholesale Club

B.J.'s Wholesale Club Inc. is a wholesale membership club in the United States. Customers pay an annual fee of $45 for the right to shop at any of B.J.'s outlets which offers its customers lower prices on goods which it buys in very large quantities. B.J.'s accounts for the $45 membership fee as operating revenue when it is received. To illustrate the financial effects associated with this practice, assume that a customer paid the $45 fee on July 1, half way through B.J.'s fiscal year which ends on December 31. B.J.'s would report the event by increasing cash (A) by $45 and increasing operating revenue and retained earnings (SE) by $45 (see Panel A, Exhibit 2.7).

EXHIBIT 2.7	B.J.'s: Accounting for Membership Fees		
Panel A	Cash	Liabilities	Retained Earnings
July 1	$45.00		$45.00
Ending Balance	$45.00		$45.00
Panel B	Cash	Liabilities	Retained Earnings
July 1	$45.00	$45.00	
December 31		−$22.50	$22.50
Ending Balance	$45.00	$22.50	$22.50

B.J.'s accounting for membership fees, however, came under criticism from the U.S. Securities and Exchange Commission which required that the company abandon the practice and instead recognize the fee ratably over the 12-month membership period.[5] Under the new accounting policy, on July 1, B.J.'s would show an increase in cash of $45 and an increase in a liability account (called "unearned revenue") of $45 to recognize B.J.'s obligation to provide member services to its customer for the coming year (see Panel B). By December 31, B.J.'s has satisfied six months (or one-half) of its obligation and thus, would

---

[5] Some investment professionals refer to B.J.'s original accounting treatment of its membership fees as front-end loading of revenues. Under this practice, the cash flows from the sale of a membership are immediately recognized as revenue even though some portion of the revenue may relate to services to be delivered in a future period.

recognize $22.50 of operating revenues and a reduction in the liability for future services of $22.50. At the end of the year, B.J.'s has a remaining liability of $22.50 for services it has agreed to provide for the next six months.

Let's compare B.J.'s former accounting policy with its new policy by contrasting the account balances in Panels A and B in Exhibit 2.7. The former policy increases earnings by $22.50 for the year, reduces liabilities by $22.50, and increases shareholders' equity by $22.50. Thus, under the old policy, the performance of the company appears superior. Yet, the cash flows under both accounting policies are identical.

An astute observer might notice that with no new customers next year, the old accounting policy will result in zero earnings in year two. This observation highlights a fundamental difference between accrual accounting and cash accounting. Accrual accounting, with its adherence to revenue recognition and expense matching, creates timing differences between earnings recognition and cash flows. Over the two year period, there will be no difference in cumulative net income; but, under B.J.'s new accounting policy, earnings will be $22.50 in the second year. Thus, the new policy shifts some revenues and earnings from the current year to the following year but does not change the total revenues or earnings over the two year period. But suppose there are more customers in each succeeding year—then earnings will be higher under the old accounting policy than under the new accounting policy—and B.J.'s management team will appear to be doing a better job.

Operating Expenses at America Online

America Online (AOL) was a pioneer internet service provider which blanketed the United States with computer diskettes to entice customers to sign up for the company's service. For accounting purposes, AOL accounted for the cost of the diskettes as an asset on the balance sheet, called "deferred marketing costs," and expensed the resulting asset over a two-year period.[6] To see the effect of this accounting policy on AOL's balance sheet, assume that it costs $2 to produce and distribute each AOL diskette and that a diskette is shipped on January 1. (AOL's fiscal year ends on December 31.) On January 1, AOL reduces cash (A) by $2 and increases intangible assets (A) by the same amount. On December 31, AOL expenses $1 by reducing intangible assets by $1 and reducing retained earnings (SE) by $1. These events are illustrated in Panel A of Exhibit 2.8.

EXHIBIT 2.8	AOL: Accounting for Advertising Costs		
Panel A			
	Cash	**Intangible Asset**	**Retained Earnings**
June 30.	−$2.00	$2.00	
December 31		−$1.00	−$1.00
Ending Balance	−$2.00	$1.00	−$1.00
Panel B			
	Cash	**Intangible Asset**	**Retained Earnings**
June 30.	−$2.00		−$2.00
Ending Balance	−$2.00		−$2.00

---

[6] Some investment professionals refer to AOL's treatment of deferred marketing costs as **rear-end loading of expenses**. Under this practice, the cash outflows for advertising and marketing are capitalized to the balance sheet as an asset even though some (or all) of the expenditure should be currently recognized on the income statement as an expense.

After repeated criticism from Wall Street analysts regarding this policy, AOL switched to immediately expensing the cost of the diskettes. Under immediate expensing, AOL would reduce cash (A) by $2 for the cost of a diskette and reduce retained earnings (SE) by the same amount. The event would be recorded as shown in Panel B of Exhibit 2.8.

Contrasting the account balances from Panels A and B of Exhibit 2.8 reveals the effect of AOL's decision to change its accounting policy. Immediately expensing the cost of the diskettes reduces assets on the balance sheet by $1 at December 31 and reduces earnings for the year by $1. Yet, there is no cash flow effect associated with the change since cash is initially reduced by $2 under both methods. Over a two year period, there is no difference in AOL's performance under the two policies; however, under the old policy, net income is higher in year one.

In both examples—B.J.'s and AOL—the selection of a firm's accounting policies can materially impact reported firm performance, in many instances making the operating performance look better than it really was. A theme throughout each of the following chapters is that informed financial statement users must look beyond the reported numbers and also consider the accounting policy choices made by a company's management. Evaluating a company's profits without knowledge of how that number is derived is like reporting the temperature on a given day without understanding what temperature scale was used—Centigrade or Fahrenheit (32 degrees Fahrenheit is quite cold while 32 degrees Centigrade is quite pleasant). As we will see from actual corporate examples, some managers will make judicious accounting policy choices in an attempt to manage the level of reported firm performance, and consequently, to influence the perceived value of a firm.

ETHICS PERSPECTIVE

B.J.'s Wholesale Club Inc. and America Online represent two examples of how managers can use their discretion to manage the reported earnings of a firm. Much of this discretion is within the flexible guidelines that are part of the institutional setting of accounting; however, sometimes managers cross the line of acceptable accounting practice and engage in fraudulent reporting. Very often the line between the two is quite grey, where it is difficult to separate aggressive financial reporting from fraudulent financial reporting. In either case, it can be argued that the intent of some corporate managers is to deceive the investing public by misrepresenting a firm's financial performance.

In the post-Enron environment, and with the enactment of the Sarbanes-Oxley Act, many firms are proactively portraying themselves as being "ethical." Ethical behavior is, for example, part of the Corporate Social Responsibility movement. This behavior includes many dimensions, including the ethical treatment of employees and the environment, as well as ethical financial reporting. Academic research has found a positive correlation between a firm's reputation and its financial performance. Do you feel that strong ethics makes good business sense? Why do you think that there is a positive correlation between ethical behavior and successful corporate financial performance?

REVIEW PROBLEM

The Arcadia Company was founded by Thomas Smith and began operations in July 2006 as a neighborhood hardware store, selling branded lawn and garden supplies, household products, and small tools. The following transactions occurred during the second half of 2006:

1. Smith established The Arcadia Company by contributing $250,000 of his personal funds and receiving all of the company's capital stock in return for his equity investment.

2. The company purchased a small shop in a strip mall for $150,000 cash.
3. Needing working capital to purchase inventory, the company borrowed $120,000 cash from a local bank, using the recently purchased store as collateral for the loan. Interest on the loan was set at six percent per year, payable every six months. The loan could be repaid at any time, but full loan repayment was required within three years.
4. Smith used the entire loan amount of $120,000 to purchase inventory. In addition, he purchased $30,000 of inventory on credit. By the end of 2006, all but $6,000 of the credit purchase had been repaid.
5. Smith decided to use a simple rule-of-thumb for pricing his inventory for sale—all goods would be marked-up 100 percent above their cost. By year-end, Smith noted that he had sold inventory with a cost basis of $80,000. All sales were for cash or on a debit/credit card.
6. Smith decided to depreciate his shop on a straight-line basis, using an expected useful life of 20 years.
7. During the latter half of 2006, Smith withdrew $20,000 in cash from the business as his salary. Since The Arcadia Company had been set-up as a sole proprietorship, there would be no income taxes to pay at the business level.

Required

1. Prepare a spreadsheet for The Arcadia Company using the balance sheet equation, reflecting the financial effects of the above transactions.
2. Prepare an income statement, balance sheet, and statement of cash flow for The Arcadia Company at the end of the first year of operations.
3. Compute for the Arcadia Company the following ratios; (1) Return on Sales, (2) Return on Assets, (3) Return on Equity.
4. Show that Return on Equity is equal to the multiplicative combination of Return on Sales, Asset Turnover, and Financial Leverage

Solution

The Arcadia Company
Spreadsheet

	Assets				=	Liabilities		+	Shareholders' Equity	
	Cash	Inventory	Building	Accum. Deprec		Accts Payable	Loan Payable		Capital Stock	Retained Earnings
1	250,000								250,000	
2	−150,000		+150,000							
3a	+120,000						+120,000			
3b	−3,600									−3,600 (E)*
4a	−120,000	+120,000								
4b		+30,000				+30,000				
4c	−24,000					−24,000				
5a	+160,000									+160,000 (R)**
5b		−80,000								−80,000 (E)
6				−3,750						−3,750 (E)***
7	−20,000									−20,000 (E)
	212,400	70,000	150,000	−3,750		6,000	120,000		250,000	52,650

* ($120,000 × .06)/2 = $3,600
** $80,000 × 2 = $160,000
*** ($150,000/20)/2 = $3,750

The Arcadia Company
Income Statement

Revenues	$160,000
Less: Cost of goods sold.	80,000
Depreciation expense	3,750
Wage expense	20,000
Interest expense.	3,600
Net income.	$ 52,650

The Arcadia Company
Balance Sheet

Assets		Liabilities	
Cash	$212,400	Accounts payable.	$ 6,000
Inventory.	70,000	Loan payable	120,000
Total current assets	282,400	Total liabilities	126,000
Building	150,000	**Shareholders' equity**	
Less Accum. Deprec.	(3,750)	Capital stock	250,000
	146,250	Retained earnings	52,650
		Total	302,650
Total assets	$428,650	Total liabilities & shareholders' equity.	$428,650

The Arcadia Company
Statement of Cash Flow

Operating Activities	
Cash sales	$ 160,000
Payments for inventory	(144,000)
Cash wages	(20,000)
Interest payment	(3,600)
Cash flow from operations.	(7,600)
Investing Activities	
Purchase of building	(150,000)
Cash flow from investing	(150,000)
Financing Activities	
Sale of capital stock	250,000
Bank loan	120,000
Cash flow from financing	370,000
Cash, beginning	-0-
Cash, end	212,400
Change in cash.	$212,400

3. ROS = 52,650 / 160,000 = 32.9%
   ROA = (52,650 + 3600) / 428,650 = 13.1%
   ROE = 52,650 / 302,650 = 17.4%
4. ROE = 52,650/160,000 × 160,000/428,650 × 428,650/302,650
      =   0.329   ×   0.373   ×   1.42   = 17.4%

EXECUTIVE SUMMARY

In this chapter we examined the balance sheet equation and how financial statements are derived from a set of accounting events that affect a business. We also considered some of the estimates and assumptions inherent in the financial statement preparation process, observing that since estimates and assumptions can be incorrect, financial statements should never be considered to be a precise representation of a company's financial performance. Finally, we investigated how to use financial statement data to evaluate a business' operating performance and its financial risk.

As a validation of your understanding of the content of this chapter, you should now be able to:

- Explain the accounting meaning behind the terms asset, liability, shareholders' equity, revenue, expense, and matching.
- Prepare financial statements from accounting events.
- Use selected financial ratios to evaluate a company's financial performance.
- Use the balance sheet equation to understand the managerial motives for selecting between alternative accounting methods.

In the next chapter, we examine the various components of the income statement and also learn how to prepare a statement of cash flow from just an income statement and a set of balance sheets.

KEY CONCEPTS AND TERMS

APPENDIX 2A: Technical Language of Accounting– The Debit and Credit Paradigm

The spreadsheet approach used in Chapter 2 to analyze the effects of various accounting events on the balance sheet equation is intuitive and closely resembles how modern electronic accounting systems process accounting information. Yet financial professionals often use the technical accounting language of "debit" and "credit" when referring to accounting transactions. To help you understand this technical language, we revisit the accounting events of the Russian River Valley Winery and process them using the debit/credit mechanism and double-entry bookkeeping. But first a little history!

Luca Pacioli, an Italian monk, is credited with being the first to describe double-entry bookkeeping in his book, ***Summa de Arithmetica, Geometria, Proportioni et Proportionalita,*** published in Latin in 1494. Some claim that Luca didn't really invent double-entry bookkeeping; he just took the time to observe what Italian merchants were doing and then documented his observations. Instead of using pluses and minuses, Luca invented the T-account having two sides. The left side was referred to as the debit side—often represented as Dr—and the right side he called the credit side—or Cr for short. The T-account Luca invented looked like this:

T-Account

Debit	Credit
(Dr)	(Cr)

Of course, Luca had to decide which side would be a positive and which would be negative. So, he concluded that an increase in assets would be a debit (the left side) and a decrease in assets would be a credit (the right side). Similarly, an increase in a liability must be a credit and a decrease in a liability a debit. And, since shareholders' equity is on the same side of the balance sheet equation as the liabilities, an increase (decrease) in shareholders' equity would be a credit (debit). The reasons why Luca selected this particular convention have been lost with time. Be careful to note that the words debit and credit are not synonymous with increase and decrease. Instead, they merely identify the left or right side of the T-account. The following diagram summarizes the debit/credit convention described by Luca:

Asset		=	Liability		+	Shareholders' Equity	
Debit	Credit		Debit	Credit		Debit	Credit
(+)	(−)		(−)	(+)		(−)	(+)

The Accounting Cycle

The process of analyzing and recording accounting data for a business is often referred to as the **accounting cycle**. The cycle begins when an accounting event involving a business occurs. The event is analyzed and a determination made as to which of the business' accounts are affected. This analysis is then entered into the firm's accounting system by means of a **journal entry**, which will be illustrated shortly. Immediately after the data is entered into the firm's accounting system, it is transferred, or **posted**, to the appropriate T-accounts. The preparation of journal entries and posting of data to the T-accounts are daily activities at a business.

At the end of each fiscal period, prior to the preparation of any financial statements, a number of data verification checks are undertaken. First, **adjusting entries** are prepared to update various accounts for any new or previously unreported financial information and to correct any observed data errors. Second, a **trial balance** is prepared to insure that the amount of recorded debits equals the amount of recorded credits. Finally, the financial statements are prepared, typically in the following sequence: income statement, statement of shareholders' equity, balance sheet, and statement of cash flow. The preparation sequence reflects the fact that the basic financial statements are interdependent—that is, they articulate with one another.

Prior to the preparation of the statement of shareholders' equity, **closing entries** are prepared. Closing entries transfer the results of a business' operating activities—that is, its revenues, expenses, and dividends—to retained earnings on the statement of shareholders' equity (and hence, the balance sheet). The accounts appearing on the income statement, along with the dividend account, are referred to as temporary accounts because they are closed, or zeroed out, at the end of each accounting period. Each of these accounts will therefore start the next accounting period with a zero balance. This makes intuitive sense since we wish to measure performance over a period of time and thus need to start each period with a blank slate. The accounts appearing on the balance sheet, in contrast, are referred to as permanent accounts because they are not closed out at the end of each accounting period. In fact, the temporary accounts are closed to a permanent account, retained earnings. Again, this makes intuitive sense since it is the purpose of the balance sheet to report a business' financial condition at a point in time, rather than for a period of time. Considered a different way, the various accounts such as cash or accounts payable that exist at the end of the period should still exist at the start of the next period unless all cash is paid out and all accounts payable are paid in full. After the closing entries are executed, the remaining financial statements—the statement of shareholders' equity, the balance sheet, and the statement of cash flow—can be prepared.

To summarize, the various steps in the accounting cycle are:

1. Record the daily accounting events using journal entries.
2. Post the journal entry data to the appropriate T-accounts.
3. At the end of the fiscal period, record any needed adjusting entries.
4. Prepare a trial balance.
5. Record the closing entries for the revenue, expense, and dividend accounts.
6. Prepare the financial statements.

The Accounting System

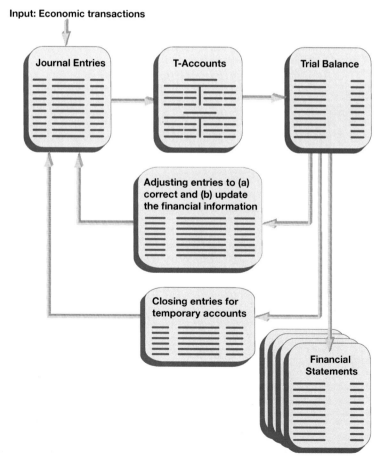

There are three arrows originating from the Trial Balance. Each of these loops represents a different version of the trial balance—(a) pre-adjustment, (b) post-adjustment, and (c) post-closing trial balances. It is the final post-closing trial balance that is used to create the company's financial statements.

To illustrate the accounting cycle, we return to the pre-opening balance sheet for the Russian River Valley Winery presented in Exhibit 2A.1.

EXHIBIT 2A.1	
Russian River Valley Winery, Inc. **Balance Sheet**	
($ thousands)	**Pre-Opening**
Assets	
Cash	$ 4,700
Buildings	2,000
Land	4,000
Intangible assets	100
Total assets	$10,800
Liabilities and equity	
Loan payable	$ 4,800
Shareholders' equity	
Common stock	6,000
Liabilities and shareholders' equity	$10,800

Step 1—*Record the accounting events using journal entries.*

The 14 events for the Russian River Valley Winery are recorded below using journal entries and the debit/credit paradigm. The convention is to record the debit portion of a journal entry on top and then to record the credit part of the entry below. Care must be exercised that the total of the debit portion of each entry exactly equals the credit portion.

Event	Accounts	Debit	Credit
1(a)	Inventory . . . . Accounts Payable	380	380
1(b)	Accounts Payable . . . . Cash	360	360
2	Equipment . . . . Cash	1,500	1,500
3	Equipment . . . . Cash	2,000	2,000
4(a)	Cash . . . . Accounts Receivable . . . . Sales Revenue	380 1,520	1,900
4(b)	Cash . . . . Accounts Receivable	720	720
5(a)	Wage Expense . . . . Cash	100	100

continued

continued from previous page

Event	Accounts	Debit	Credit
5(b)	Selling & Administrative Expense.	300	
	Cash.		300
6(a)	Loan Payable	480	
	Cash.		480
6(b)	Interest Expense.	288	
	Cash.		288
7	Cost of Goods Sold	380	
	Inventory.		380
8(a)	Depreciation Expense—Equipment	175	
	Accumulated Depreciation.		175
8(b)	Depreciation Expense—Buildings	50	
	Accumulated Depreciation.		50
9	Amortization Expense	50	
	Intangible asset		50
10	Cash.	400	
	Common Stock		400
11	(No event is recorded.)		
12	Income Tax Expense	240	
	Income Taxes Payable		96
	Cash.		144
13	Inventory.	60	
	Accounts Payable		60
14	Retained Earnings (dividend declared).	260	
	Cash.		260

Step 2—Post the journal entry data to the appropriate T-accounts.

If you examine the T-accounts below, you will see that each of the debits and credits from the journal entries above have been entered into the appropriate T-accounts. Notice that the ending balance for each of the T-accounts exactly corresponds to the ending balances obtained using the spreadsheet approach followed in the chapter.

	Cash		
Bal	4,700		
4(a)	380	360	1(b)
4(b)	720	1,500	2
		2,000	3
		100	5(a)
		300	5(b)
		480	6(a)
		288	6(b)
10	400	144	12
		260	14
Bal	768		

	Accounts Payable		
		0	Bal
		380	1(a)
1(b)	360		
		60	13
		80	Bal

	Common Stock		
		6,000	Bal
		400	10
		6,400	Bal

	Retained Earnings		
		0	Bal
14	260		
Bal	260	317	17
		57	Bal

	Income Summary		
		1,900	15
16	1,583		
17	317		
		0	Bal

continued

Accounts Receivable			
Bal	0		
4(a)	1,520		
		720	4(b)
Bal	800		

Income Taxes Payable			
		0	Bal
		96	12
		96	Bal

Sales Revenue			
		1,900	4(a)
15	1,900		
		0	Bal

Inventory			
Bal	0		
1(a)	380		
		380	7
13	60		
Bal	60		

Loan Payable			
		4,800	Bal
6(a)	480		
		4,320	Bal

Cost of Goods Sold			
7	380		
		380	16
Bal	0		

Equipment			
Bal	0		
2	1,500		
3	2,000		
Bal	3,500		

Wage Expense			
5(a)	100		
		100	16
Bal	0		

Buildings			
Bal	2,000		

Depreciation Expense			
8(a)	175		
8(b)	50		
Bal	225		
		225	16
Bal	0		

Accumulated Depreciation			
		0	Bal
		175	8(a)
		50	8(b)
		225	Bal

Selling & Admin Expense			
5(b)	300		
		300	16
Bal	0		

Land			
Bal	4,000		

Interest Expense			
6(b)	288		
		288	16
Bal	0		

Intangible Assets			
Bal	100	50	9
Bal	50		

Amortization Expense			
9	50		
		50	16
Bal	0		

Income Tax Expense			
12	240		
		240	16
Bal	0		

Step 3—At the end of the fiscal period, make any needed adjusting entries.

Accounting events such as the recording of depreciation expense (8(a)) and amortization expense (8(b)) are considered to be adjusting entries. They are often recorded at the end of each fiscal period when a company's accounting staff reviews the business' financial data for completeness. Other examples of adjusting entries include correcting any amounts that were previously incorrectly recorded and estimating and recording the estimated losses associated with any uncollected accounts receivable.

Step 4—Prepare a trial balance.

The trial balance is a listing of the account balances from the company's various T-accounts. Russian River Valley's trial balance is presented in Exhibit 2A.2. Notice in the winery's trial balance that the total debit balance ($13,021) for the winery's T-accounts equals the total credit balance ($13,021). If the balances were not equal, it would indicate that an error had been made in recording some piece of accounting information.

EXHIBIT 2A.2		
Russian River Valley Winery, Inc. **Trial Balance**		
Account	**Debit**	**Credit**
Cash.	$ 768	
Accounts receivable.	800	
Inventory.	60	
Equipment	3,500	
Buildings.	2,000	
Accumulated depreciation		$ 225
Land	4,000	
Intangible assets	50	
Accounts payable.		80
Taxes payable.		96
Loan payable		4,320
Common stock.		6,400
Retained earnings	260	
Sales revenue.		1,900
Cost of goods sold.	380	
Wages expense	100	
Depreciation expense.	225	
Selling & administrative expense	300	
Interest expense.	288	
Amortization expense.	50	
Tax expense	240	
Totals	$13,021	$13,021

Step 5—Record closing entries for the temporary accounts.

Closing entries (events 15, 16, and 17) transfer the ending balances from the revenue and expense T-accounts to an income summary account, and then ultimately to the retained earnings account on the statement of shareholders' equity, and thus, the balance sheet. Closing entries also serve another function—they set the revenue and expense T-accounts equal to zero at the end of each fiscal period (see the closing balances for the T-accounts from Step 2). By doing so, the revenue and expense T-accounts only contain information from the current period, thus facilitating comparisons of net income from one fiscal period to the next.

Event	Account	Debit	Credit
15	Sales revenue.	1,900	
	Income summary		1,900
16	Income summary	1,583	
	Cost of goods sold		380
	Wage expense.		100
	Depreciation expense		225
	Selling & administrative expense.		300
	Interest expense		288
	Amortization expense		50
	Tax expense.		240
17	Income summary	317	
	Retained earnings		317

Step 6—Prepare the financial statements.

The financial statements prepared from data organized using the debit/credit paradigm will be identical to those derived using the spreadsheet approach, as presented in Exhibits 2.2 through 2.5, and consequently, are not reproduced here.

Summary

The use of journal entries and T-accounts to record accounting information is still integral to those businesses in which financial data is hand-collected. Increasingly, however, accounting data is processed electronically; and, consequently, the technical language of accounting is changing to reflect this reality.

DISCUSSION QUESTIONS

Q2.1   **Accounting Terminology.**   Describe or define the following terms:

- Asset
- Liability
- Shareholders' equity
- Revenue
- Expense

Discuss how the five terms relate to one another.

Q2.2   **Historical versus Forecasted Financial Statements.**   Discuss the difference between historical and forecasted (or pro forma) financial statements. How are these different sets of financial statements used by managers and shareholders for decision-making purposes?

Q2.3   **Accounting Principles.**   Consider the following accounting principles:

- Entity principle
- Revenue recognition principle
- Matching principle

Define these accounting principles. Discuss how these principles relate to one another.

Q2.4   **Balance Sheet Classifications.**   Most balance sheets are defined as "classified balance sheets" in that both the assets and liabilities are dichotomized into the categories of current and non-current. (Note: In those industries in which the business operating cycle is longer than one year (such as the wine industry, the real estate industry, the financial services industry), classified balance sheets are not required under U.S. GAAP.) Discuss how the balance sheet classifications of current versus non-current convey important information about a firm's financial condition to managers and shareholders.

Q2.5 **Key Performance Indicators: The Income Statement.** Describe or define the following key performance indicators (KPIs) from the income statement:

- Operating revenue
- Gross profit
- Operating income
- Net income

Discuss how each of these measures depicts a firm's performance.

Q2.6 **Key Performance Indicators: The Statement of Cash Flow.** Describe or define the following key performance indicators (KPIs) from the statement of cash flow:

- Cash flow from operating activities
- Cash flow from investing activities
- Cash flow from financing activities

Discuss how each of these measures conveys important information about firm performance to managers and shareholders.

Q2.7 **Return on Shareholders' Equity.** The return on shareholders' equity ratio can be decomposed into three separate financial ratios—the return on sales, total asset turnover, and financial leverage. Define each of the ratios assuming the firm is all equity financed and discuss what actions a manager might take to increase a firm's return on shareholders' equity.

Q2.8 **Evaluating Financial Risk.** Investment professionals use a variety of financial ratios to evaluate a company's financial risk. Two popular financial risk ratios include:

- Total debt-to-total assets ratio
- Interest coverage ratio

Define each ratio and discuss what actions a manager might take to reduce a firm's financial riskiness.

Q2.9 **Managing Operating Revenues.** Some corporate executives have reportedly attempted to manage their firm's operating revenues through such actions as "front-end loading" or "rear-end loading" of operating revenues. Explain the concepts of front-end loading and rear-end loading of operating revenues. Discuss why some managers might undertake these actions. Discuss how you might be able to identify that a manager is managing a firm's operating revenues.

Q2.10 **Net Income, Cash Flow from Operations, and Dividend Policy.** The Arizona Corporation reported positive net income but negative cash flow from operations. Further, despite the negative cash flow from operations, the company continued to pay its regular dividend on its common shares. Discuss why it is possible for a company to report positive net income when the cash flow from operations is negative. Do you agree with the firm's strategy of maintaining its regular dividend? Why or why not?

Q2.11 **Debt Covenants.** Bristol-Myers Squibb (BMS) Company reports that it maintains a $2 billion, five-year revolving line of credit with a syndicate of lenders. The company disclosed in its annual report that:

> The availability of the line of credit is subject to the Company's ability . . . . to meet certain conditions, including a financial covenant in which net debt-to-capital cannot exceed 50 percent.

Discuss why BMS would agree to the above financial covenant. Discuss why the syndicate of lenders would impose such a constraint on BMS. How would you calculate the "net debt-to-capital" ratio? What does the ratio reveal about a company?

Q2.12 **Managing Operating Expenses.** Some corporate executives have reportedly attempted to manage their firm's operating expenses through such actions as "front-end loading" or "rear-end loading" of their operating expenses. Explain the concepts of front-end loading and rear-end loading of operating expenses. Discuss why some managers might undertake these actions. Discuss how you might be able to identify that a manager is managing a firm's operating expenses.

Q2.13 **Net Loss, Cash Flow from Operations, and Dividend Policy.** The Phoenix Corporation reported a net loss but a positive cash flow from operations. Further, despite the net loss, the company continued to pay its regular dividend. Discuss why it is possible for a company to report a net loss while also reporting a positive cash flow from operations. Do you agree with the company's decision to continue the payment of its regular dividend? Why or why not?

Q2.14 **(Ethical Perspective) Corporate Social Responsibility and Ethics.** In the post-Enron environment, and with the enactment of the Sarbanes-Oxley legislation, many firms are proactively portraying themselves as being "ethical." Ethical behavior is, for example, part of the Corporate Social Responsibility movement. This behavior includes many dimensions, from the ethical treatment of employees and the environment, to ethical financial reporting. Academic research has found a positive correlation between a firm's reputation and its financial performance. Do you feel that strong ethics makes good business sense? Why do you think that there is a positive correlation between ethical behavior and successful corporate financial performance?

⊘ **indicates that check figures are available on the book's Website.**

EXERCISES

E2.15 **The Balance Sheet Equation.** Fernandez & Co. experienced the following six events during the current year:

1. The sale of common stock to investors for $5 million cash.
2. The sale of a new bond issue to investors for $10 million cash.
3. The purchase of $500,000 of inventory for cash.
4. The purchase of $700,000 of equipment using bank financing.
5. The payment of $100,000 cash for income taxes associated with last year's operations.
6. The CFO determined that net income for the most recent month was $2 million.

Using the balance sheet equation as illustrated in this chapter, describe how each of the above six events would affect the balance sheet of Fernandez & Co.

E2.16 **The Balance Sheet Equation.** R.J. Miller & Company experienced the following six events during the current year:

1. Sold common stock to investors for $10 million cash.
2. Borrowed $20 million cash from a bank.
3. Purchased $1 million of inventory for cash.
4. Purchased $1.5 million of new machinery by signing a note payable.
5. Paid $2 million of cash dividends to shareholders.
6. Net income for the year totaled $4.5 million.

Using the balance sheet equation as illustrated in this chapter, describe how each of the above six events would affect the balance sheet of R. J. Miller & Company.

E2.17 **Account Classification.** Presented below is a list of income statement and balance sheet accounts:

a. Interest expense	j. Depreciation expense
b. Land	k. Equipment
c. Cost of goods sold	l. Loan payable
d. Intangible assets	m. Wages and salaries expense
e. Income tax expense	n. Buildings
f. Inventory	o. Retained earnings
g. Revenues	p. Selling and administrative expense
h. Accounts payable	q. Amortization expense
i. Accounts receivable	r. Cash

For each account, indicate whether it would appear on the balance sheet (B/S) or the income statement (I/S). For those accounts appearing on the balance sheet, indicate whether the account is an asset (A), liability

(L), or shareholders' equity (SE) account. For those accounts appearing on the income statement, indicate whether the account is a revenue (R) account or an expense (E) account.

E2.18   **Account Classification.**   Presented below is a list of income statement and balance sheet accounts:

a. Deferred income
b. Patent
c. Accumulated depreciation
d. Interest payable
e. Gain on sale of land
f. Prepaid insurance
g. Dividend income
h. Currently-maturing portion of long-term debt
i. Allowance for uncollectible accounts

j. Dividend payable
k. Supplies inventory
l. Insurance expense
m. Interest income
n. Goodwill
o. Other receivables
p. Mortgage payable
q. Preferred stock
r. Office supplies expense

For each account, indicate whether it would appear on the balance sheet (B/S) or the income statement (I/S). For those accounts appearing on the balance sheet, indicate whether the account is an asset (A), liability (L), or shareholders' equity (SE) account. For those accounts appearing on the income statement, indicate whether the account is a revenue (R), expense (E), gain (g), or loss (l) account.

E2.19   **Asset or Expense.**   The Rankine Corporation reported net income of $10 million in 2006, and it appears that net income for 2007 will be the same. During 2007, the company made the following expenditures:

1. $250,000 was spent to resurface the company parking lot. The resurfacing has to be done about every five years.
2. $500,000 was spent to upgrade the company's air filtration system in the plating department. The system worked satisfactorily, but the U.S. Department of Labor recently promulgated new rules (effective three years from today) that would have required the changes the company made voluntarily.
3. $900,000 was paid to a consultant for the design of a new manufacturing facility. The new plant was the dream of the prior CEO but had been shelved because the current CEO was uncertain about the firm's future.
4. $600,000 was spent on the development of a new inventory control system. The system was designed to allow salespeople in the field to electronically enter orders into the system so that they could be shipped the next day. The system appeared to be on track, but another $200,000 would have to be spent before it could be demonstrated that it would function as planned.
5.   The company's Arizona plant was shut down for three months because of the slow economy. The company struggled to find ways to keep its employees busy so they could retain as many as possible. Some employees agreed to accept half pay while the company found maintenance work and training for the other employees. At the end of three months, about 85 percent of the workforce was still on the payroll when the company resumed normal production. The maintenance work done by the employees during this time cost about $1 million; the training cost the company another $800,000.

Indicate whether the above expenditures should be considered as an asset or as an expense. Be prepared to justify your answer.

E2.20   **The Statement of Cash Flow.**   The following cash flow information was taken from The Johnson and Johnson Company (J&J) 2005 annual report. Compute the missing values in the table (amounts are in millions). Based on this data, how does J&J finance its on-going operations and asset purchases?

	2005	2004	2003
Cash, beginning balance	$ 9,013	$?	$3,171
Cash flow from operating activities	11,877	?	10,595
Cash flow from investing activities.	(279)	(2,347)	?
Cash flow from financing activities.	?	(5,148)	(3,863)
Cash, ending balance.	$16,055	$?	$5,377

E2.21 **The Statement of Cash Flow.** The following cash flow information was taken from **The General Electric Company (GE)** 2005 annual report. Compute the missing values in the table (amounts are in millions). Based on this data, describe GE's cash flow performance for the three year period.

	2005	2004	2003
Cash, beginning balance	$?	$12,664	$?
Cash flow from operating activities	37,641	36,484	29,229
Cash flow from investing activities.	?	(38,414)	(21,843)
Cash flow from financing activities.	(6,119)	?	(3,632)
Cash, ending balance.	$11,801	$15,328	$?

E2.22 **Preparing the Basic Financial Statements.** Andrew James began his business by obtaining an equity investment of $12,000 cash from his family and by borrowing an additional $10,000 in cash from a local bank. He used some of this cash to purchase equipment costing $16,000. During the year, he leased the equipment to Ana Amphlett for $6,000 in cash. By year-end, his expenses had amounted to $5,000, which he paid in cash. Since it had been a good year, Andrew decided to pay his equity investors a cash dividend of $1,600.

Using the balance sheet equation as illustrated in this chapter, analyze the above economic events. Prepare an income statement, a statement of shareholders' equity, a balance sheet, and a statement of cash flow for the year. Do you agree with Andrew's decision to pay his investors a $1,600 cash dividend? Explain.

E2.23 **Preparing the Basic Financial Statements.** Marilyn Miller opened a floral shop using $5,000 of her own cash savings and with $15,000 in cash borrowed from her parents. She signed a lease on a small store for one year, agreeing to pay $350 per month in rent. During the first year of operations, Marilyn purchased fresh flowers from a local nursery for $2,500, paid $1,200 for utilities, and generated floral sales totaling $12,000. (Assume all transactions were cash transactions.) Marilyn was hoping to be able to repay her parents one-half of the borrowed money at the end of the first year of operations.

Prepare an income statement, balance sheet, and statement of cash flow for the floral shop. Can Marilyn achieve her goal of repaying one-half of the $15,000 loan at the end of the first year of operations?

E2.24 **Preparing Cash Flow Data.** Andrew James began the second year of his business with a cash balance of $20,000. Using the following information, which all occurred during Year 2, prepare a statement of cash flow for Andrew. Evaluate Andrew's cash management practices in Year 2.

1. Borrowed $25,000 in cash from a bank.
2. Generated operating revenues of $35,000, collecting $30,000 of that amount in cash.
3. Incurred operating expenses of $28,000, of which $18,000 was paid in cash.
4. Purchased new equipment costing $15,000 with a down payment of $5,000 cash and signing a note for $10,000.
5. Paid shareholders a cash dividend in an amount that would enable James to establish an ending cash balance of $30,000.

E2.25 **Preparing Cash Flow Data.** Marilyn Miller began the second year of her floral business with $12,000 in cash in her bank account. Using the information below, all of which occurred during Year 2, prepare a statement of cash flow for Marilyn. Evaluate her cash management strategy during Year 2.

1. Sold an equity interest in the business for $13,000 cash.
2. Generated revenue from floral sales of $20,000, collecting all but $5,000.
3. Incurred operating expenses totaling $9,000, of which $2,000 remained unpaid at the end of Year 2.
4. Purchased new store equipment for $5,000, with a down payment of $2,500 cash and signing a note payable for $2,500.
5. Paid shareholders a cash dividend of $2,800.

PROBLEMS

⊘ P2.26 **Accounting Event Analysis and Financial Statement Preparation.** Smith & Co. experienced the following six events in its first year of operations:

1. Shareholders contributed $60,000 cash.
2. Purchased land for $40,000 cash.
3. Borrowed $18,000 in cash from a bank.
4. Provided services for $16,000, which will be paid to Smith & Co. next year.
5. Paid $11,000 cash for miscellaneous operating expenses.
6. Paid a $1,000 cash dividend to shareholders.

Required

Using the balance sheet equation as illustrated in this chapter, identify how each of the above six events affected the various accounts involved. Prepare an income statement, a statement of shareholders' equity, a balance sheet, and a statement of cash flow for the first year of operations.

P2.27 **Accounting Event Analysis and Financial Statement Preparation.** Wilmot Real Estate Company experienced the following events during its first year of operations:

1. Received $50,000 in cash from investors as an equity investment.
2. Borrowed $40,000 in cash from a bank.
3. Purchased two parcels of land, each costing $15,000, for a total of $30,000 cash. The land was purchased for resale purposes.
4. Paid $10,000 cash to rent office equipment for the year.
5. Provided real estate appraisal services valued at $25,000, receiving $20,000 in cash and an account receivable for an additional $5,000.
6. Paid miscellaneous expenses totaling $11,000 in cash.
7. Sold one parcel of land, costing $15,000, for $22,000 cash.
8. Paid a $5,000 cash dividend to shareholders.

Required

Using the balance sheet equation as illustrated in this chapter, identify how each of the above events affect the balance sheet equation of $A = L + SE$. Prepare an income statement, a statement of shareholders' equity, a balance sheet, and a statement of cash flow for the first year of operations.

P2.28 **Accounting Event Analysis and the Income Statement.** The following events occurred for The Thomas Magnum Corporation during 2006:

1. Sales of products totaled $219,000, of which $15,000 remained uncollected at year-end.
2. The cost of goods sold during the year was $56,000.
3. A cash disbursement of $50,000 was made on July 1, 2006, to pay for a 12-month office equipment lease that expires on June 30, 2007.
4. Depreciation expense for the year on the company's warehouse amounted to $7,500.
5. Employee wages for the year totaled $40,000, of which $2,000 was unpaid at year-end.
6. Selling, general, and administrative expenses amounted to $10,000 for the year and were paid in full.
7. A cash payment of $25,000 was made to reduce the balance of accounts payable.
8. Interest expense on long-term debt was $18,000 for the year, of which $4,500 was unpaid at year-end.
9. The company paid income taxes on its pre-tax income at a rate of 40 percent.

Required

1. Using the balance sheet equation as illustrated in this chapter, analyze the effect of the above events.
2. Prepare an income statement for 2006 for the company.

⊘ P2.29 **Accounting Event Analysis and the Balance Sheet.** Presented below are the balance sheet accounts of the Mayfair Company as of December 1, 2006. The accounts are listed in random order.

Machinery & equipment (net)	$15,000	Cash	$10,000
Accounts payable.	10,000	Notes payable	9,500
Note receivable	2,000	Accounts receivable.	15,000
Inventory.	3,000	Goodwill	8,000
Bank loan	10,500	Additional paid-in-capital	76,000
Building (net).	30,000	Land	40,000
Capital stock ($1 par value)	5,000	Retained earnings	12,000

During the month of December 2006, the following events occurred:

1. Purchased inventory on credit that cost $3,000.
2. Issued capital stock at par value in exchange for machinery and equipment valued at $12,000.
3. The building was appraised at a value of $45,000 by a certified real estate appraiser.
4. The note receivable of $2,000 was collected.
5. $8,000 cash was paid on the outstanding accounts payable.
6. Purchased land valued at $25,000, paying $3,000 in cash and signing a five year note for the remaining amount.

Required
1. Prepare the balance sheet as of December 1, 2006, for the Mayfair Company
2. Prepare a spreadsheet using the balance sheet equation as illustrated in this chapter for the December events.
3. Prepare the balance sheet as of December 31, 2006, for the Mayfair Company.

P2.30 **Preparing a Balance Sheet.** The following financial information is known about **Pfizer, Inc.** as of December 31, 2005 (all amounts in millions):
a. The balance of cash and cash equivalents was $2,247.
b. Short-term investments have a fair market value of $19,979.
c. Gross accounts receivable total $9,948, which includes $183 that is not expected to be collected.
d. Inventory has a cost basis of $6,900 but a replacement cost of $6,709.
e. Prepaid expenses total $3,196.
f. Property, plant and equipment have a cost basis of $29,587, a current fair value of $42,500, and accumulated depreciation taken to date of $10,000.
g. Intangible assets have a cost basis of $76,582 and accumulated amortization of $20,500.
h. Accounts payable total $2,226; accrued expenses payable total $14,633; and, short-term borrowings total $11,589.
i. Long-term debt totals $6,347, and post-retirement benefit obligations total $17,143.
j. Shareholders' equity totals $65,627, composed of retained earnings of $37,608, other comprehensive income of $479, treasury stock of negative $39,767, and contributed capital of $67,307.

Required
Prepare a balance sheet for Pfizer, Inc. as of December 31, 2005. Evaluate Pfizer's financial risk at year-end 2005.

P2.31 **Analysis of Financial Statement Data.** The following data was taken from the financial statements of The Amphlett Corporation, which is all equity financed.

	2005	2006
Net sales.	$145,860	$161,585
Net income.	24,765	28,340
Total assets.	171,225	192,440
Shareholders' equity	101,975	121,165

Required
1. Calculate the following ratios for 2005 and 2006:

    a.   Return on equity
    b.   Return on assets
    c.   Return on sales
    d.   Total assets-to-shareholders' equity (financial leverage)
    e.   Total asset turnover
2.   Comment on the financial performance of The Amphlett Corporation based on your ratio calculations.

P2.32   **Analysis of Financial Statement Data.**   The following data was taken from the financial statements of The Mann Corporation, which is all equity financed.

	2005	2006
Net sales.	$1,300,000	$2,320,000
Net income.	100,000	220,000
Total assets.	558,659	894,309
Shareholders' equity	303,030	371,622

Required
1.   Calculate the following ratios for 2005 and 2006:
    a.   Return on equity
    b.   Return on assets
    c.   Return on sales
    d.   Total assets-to-shareholders' equity (financial leverage)
    e.   Total asset turnover
2.   Comment on the financial performance of The Mann Corporation based on your ratio calculations.

P2.33   **Analyzing Financial Statement Information.**   The Thunderbird Corporation has applied to the Biltmore National Bank for a $100,000 loan to purchase new equipment for its manufacturing operations. As part of the loan application, the chief financial officer of Thunderbird submitted the following financial statement information:

	2006	2005
Balance sheet		
Current assets	$ 49,000	$ 42,000
Non-current assets	175,000	150,500
Total assets	224,000	192,500
Current liabilities	24,500	21,000
Non-current liabilities.	91,000	73,500
Shareholders' equity	108,500	98,000
Income statement		
Operating revenues	122,500	112,000
Operating expenses.	(80,500)	(91,000)
Net income.	42,000	21,000
Statement of cash flow		
Cash flow from operating activities	52,500	31,500
Cash flow from investing activities	(49,000)	(42,000)
Cash flow from financing activities	24,500	17,500
Change in cash	$ 28,000	$ 7,000

Required
Analyze the financial statement information of The Thunderbird Corporation and indicate whether you believe that the firm's loan application should be approved. And, if so, why?

P2.34 **Analyzing Financial Statement Information.** The San Gabriel Company has applied for a $75,000 loan at the La Verne National Bank to purchase new equipment and machinery for its manufacturing operations. As part of the loan application, San Gabriel's chief financial officer submitted the following financial statement information:

	2006	2005
Balance sheet		
Current assets	$ 45,000	$ 40,000
Non-current assets	90,000	75,000
Total assets	135,000	115,000
Current liabilities	35,000	20,000
Non-current liabilities.	45,000	35,000
Shareholders' equity	55,000	60,000
Income statement		
Operating revenues	460,000	445,000
Operating expenses.	(390,000)	(360,000)
Net income.	70,000	85,000
Statement of cash flows		
Cash flow from operating activities	60,000	75,000
Cash flow from investing activities	(40,000)	(25,000)
Cash flow from financing activities	(25,000)	(40,000)
Change in Cash	$ (5,000)	$ 10,000

Required

Analyze the financial statement information of The San Gabriel Company and indicate whether you believe that the firm's loan request should be approved. And, if so, why?

◉ P2.35 **The Operating Cycle and Financial Statements.** Presented below is the year-end 2005 balance sheet for The Little Corporation.

The Little Corporation
Balance Sheet
December 31, 2005

Assets			Liabilities & Shareholders' Equity	
Current			**Current liabilities**	
Cash.		$ 510,000	Accounts payable	$ 650,000
Accounts receivable (net). . . .		564,000	Wages payable	173,000
Inventory		720,000	Interest payable	56,000
Prepaid rent		222,000	Total current liabilities	879,000
Total current assets		$2,016,000	**Non-current liabilities**	
Non-current			Bank loan.	450,000
Long-term investments		496,500	Bonds payable.	1,950,000
Equipment	$1,440,000		Total liabilities	3,279,000
Less Accum depreciation . . .	(288,000)			
		1,152,000	**Shareholders' equity**	
Machinery	2,850,000		Common stock (no par value) . . .	1,200,000
Less Accum depreciation . . .	(712,500)		Retained earnings	1,548,000
		2,137,500	Total shareholders' equity	2,748,000
Intangible assets (net)		225,000	**Total liabilities &**	
Total assets.		$6,027,000	**shareholders' equity.**	$6,027,000

During 2006, the company entered into the following events:

1. Sales to customers totaled $2 million, of which $1.6 million were on credit and the remainder was cash sales. The cost of goods sold totaled $800,000.
2. Purchased $700,000 of inventory on credit.
3. Paid $620,000 cash to employees as wages. (This amount includes the wages payable at December 31, 2005.)
4. Collected $1.75 million cash from customers as payment on outstanding accounts receivable.
5. Paid $1.2 million cash to suppliers on outstanding accounts payable.
6. Sold machinery for $120,000 cash. The machinery had cost $370,000 and at the time of sale it had a net book value of $160,000.
7. Paid miscellaneous expenses totaling $98,000 cash.
8. Sold common stock (no par value) for $450,000 cash.
9. Invested $200,000 of excess cash in short-term marketable securities.
10. Declared and paid a cash dividend of $100,000.

As part of the year-end audit, the internal audit staff identified the following additional information:

1. $180,000 of prepaid rent was consumed during the year.
2. The equipment had a remaining useful life of ten years and the machinery of 20 years. The company uses straight-line depreciation.
3. The intangible assets had a remaining useful life of ten years.
4. Interest on the bank loan and bonds payable was ten percent. During the year, interest payments totaling $260,000 had been paid in cash.

Required
1. Using the balance sheet equation as illustrated in this chapter, the events affecting the Little Corporation during 2006.
2. Prepare the income statement for 2006.
3. Prepare the statement of shareholders' equity, balance sheet, and statement of cash flow for 2006.

P2.36 **Preparing Financial Statements from Accounting Events** On June 30, 2005, Cynthia Hayes and Cathy Swales, doing business as Cayman Islands Divers Ltd., purchased the operating assets of Sister Islands Divers Ltd. for $200,000 cash. The newly incorporated Cayman Islands Divers (hereafter CID Ltd.) would maintain a small administrative office in George Town, the capital of the Cayman Islands, while diving operations would be conducted from each of the three islands comprising the Cayman Islands. The company had been initially capitalized in the amount of $240,000 cash, for which Cynthia and Cathy each received 120,000 common shares (par value = $1.00). Of this initial amount, $200,000 in cash had been paid to the owners of Sister Islands Divers for the following assets (see Exhibit 1):

$ 19,000	Retail inventory
10,800	Rental equipment inventory
6,000	(3) Air compressors
4,200	Cash register, personal computer, display cabinets, fax/copy machine
60,000	(2) 40 foot dive boats
60,000	(1) 55 foot dive boat
40,000	Intangibles: business goodwill ($25,000), 5-year covenant-not-to-compete ($15,000)
$200,000	

In addition, CID Ltd. assumed the lease on a small retail shop located in the Holiday Inn Hotel on Seven-Mile Beach on Grand Cayman Island.

Business Transactions

June. After depositing their $240,000 in cash in the Cayman National Bank in George Town, Cynthia and Cathy paid Trevor Neckles, an attorney, $5,000 cash to incorporate CID Ltd.. According to company documents, CID Ltd. officially incorporated on June 20, 2005.

July. During July the following events occurred. Unless otherwise noted, all transactions were in cash.

1. For each of the 31 days of July, CID Ltd. provided services to an average of 53 divers, with revenues of $75 per diver.
2. Equipment rentals averaged $560 per day.
3. Salaries paid to the boat crews, office personnel, and dive instructors for the month totaled $4,500.
4. Gasoline and repairs to the three boats totaled $1,860.
5. Instructional fees received from student-divers totaled $4,000.
6. Retail equipment sales totaled $21,700; the mark-up on the sold equipment was 100 percent above cost.
7. The lease payment of $350 on the George Town office was paid, as was the Holiday Inn lease of $750. These payments included all utilities.
8. A severe storm arose unexpectedly on July 31, and scuba tanks valued at $300 were lost overboard in water too deep to mount a recovery operation.
9. On July 31, several boat-loads of divers from a neighboring scuba shop had been taken out for night diving after the shop's own boat had broken down. CID Ltd. expected to receive $800 for the services in early August.
10. Received $1,200 in cash as advance deposits for diving services to be provided in August.
11. Since July had been a relatively successful month, Cynthia and Cathy decided to pay themselves a salary of $10,000 cash each.

Required

1. Prepare a balance sheet for CID Ltd. at the end of the day on June 30, 2005.
2. Using the balance sheet equation as illustrated in this chapter, analyze the effect of the July events.
3. Prepare a balance sheet as of July 31, 2005, an income statement and a statement of cash flow for the month of July.

EXHIBIT 1	Cayman Islands Divers Ltd.

Beginning Asset Inventory

A. Rental equipment inventory

Estimated Value	Items	Estimated Remaining Useful Life
$ 3,000	40 buoyancy control devices	2 years
4,800	40 regulator set-ups (including gauges)	4 years
2,250	90 aluminum diving tanks (80 cubic foot capacity)	10 years
750	Weights, weight-belts, fins, masks, snorkels, exposure suits, boots	1 year
$10,800		

B. Equipment inventory

Estimated Value	Items	Estimated Remaining Useful Life
$ 6,000	(3) air compressors	5 years
4,200	Cash register, personal computer, fax/copy machine, display cabinets	3 years
60,000	(2) 40 foot dive boats (12-15 diver capacity)	6 years
60,000	(1) 55 foot dive boat (20-24 diver capacity)	6 years

P2.37   **Preparing Financial Statements from Accounting Events**   Photovoltaics, Inc. is an Arizona-based manufacturer and distributor of photovoltaic solar energy units. The company was founded in 2005 by Arthur
Manelas and Harry Linn. Manelas, formerly a research scientist with NASA, had been operating a small
photovoltaic manufacturing company in Massachusetts when Linn, a marketing consultant to industry and
himself an owner of a solar energy company in Oregon, proposed the joint venture.

Convinced that excellent market opportunities for the solar arrays existed, Linn began preparing a
prospectus that could be used to help raise capital to significantly expand Manelas's current operations. The
two founders had located a manufacturing facility in Tucson, Arizona, that would cost approximately $8
million to acquire and equip with updated production equipment. Based on his prior experience, Linn knew
that prospective venture capital investors would expect to see the following:

- A balance sheet identifying the company's assets and equities as they would appear at the start of
  operations.
- A pro forma income statement for the first year of operations.
- A pro forma balance sheet as it would appear at the end of the first year of operations.
- A pro forma statement of cash flow for the first year of operations.

In anticipation of preparing these reports, Linn collected the following information and arrived at the following projections for the first year of operations:

Data related to pre-opening events

1. Ten million shares of common stock (par value $1) were authorized for sale by the company's charter
   of incorporation. Manelas received 500,000 shares in exchange for the rights to the photovoltaic patent,
   and Linn received an equal number of shares after contributing $500,000 in personal funds to the firm.
2. Incorporation and attorney's fees (start-up costs) amounted to $27,000 and would be paid in cash.
3. Sales of common stock to venture capitalists would total 2.5 million shares. A selling price
   of $3.25 per share was set, and transaction costs of 1.5 percent of the stock proceeds were
   projected.
4. The $8 million purchase price of the manufacturing facility was to be allocated as follows: building
   − $4.5 million; land − $750,000; and, equipment − $2.75 million. In addition, raw materials and
   partially completed solar units would be purchased on credit from Manelas's original manufacturing
   company at a cost of $1.3 million. A note, secured by the inventory itself and accruing interest at a
   rate of 10 percent per year on the unpaid balance, would be issued to Manelas.

Projected events

5. Revenues from the sale of solar arrays for the first year were projected to be $480,000, with 20
   percent of this amount estimated to be uncollected at year-end. The company had decided to follow
   a particularly rigid credit granting policy until operations were well established; hence, no provision
   for bad debts would be established because no uncollectible accounts were anticipated.
6. Cash purchases of inventory were estimated at $70,000; the cost of inventory sold was projected to
   be $215,000.
7. Insurance on the building, equipment, and inventory was expected to cost $2,700 per year.
8. Employee wages were estimated at $72,000; selling and administrative costs were projected at 2
   percent of gross sales.
9. The useful life of the acquired assets were estimated as follows:

Building	20 years
Equipment	10 years

Linn decided to write the patent off over its remaining legal life of 17 years and to write off the start-
up costs over five years.

10. Salaries to Linn and Manelas were set at $20,000 each for the first year.
11. Interest payments, but no principal repayments, would be made on the ten percent notes issued to Manelas during the first year of operations.
12. Income taxes were estimated at 22 percent of pre-tax net income.
13. A cash dividend of $100,000 would be paid at the end of the first year to the equity investors.

Required

1. Using the balance sheet equation as illustrated in this chapter, prepare the following financial statements:
   a. Opening balance sheet as of the start of operations.
   b. Income statement for the first year.
   c. Balance sheet at the end of the first year.
   d. Statement of cash flow for the first year.
2. As a prospective investor in the company, what factors would you look for in the financial statements to help you decide whether to invest in the venture? Do you agree with the decision to pay a $100,000 cash dividend at the end of the first year of operations? Why?

P2.38 **Preparing Financial Statements from Accounting Events.** In January 2005, Susan and Clark Shipley, co-owners of Island Foods, Inc. began discussing the possibility of expanding their restaurant business from a single location in Glendale, Arizona to two additional locations—one in Scottsdale and a second in Phoenix. Although the Glendale restaurant had only been open for about two years, it had attracted a loyal customer base from neighborhood businesses and schools. Despite the success of the Glendale restaurant in its first two years of operations, the Shipley's would still need to borrow money to finance the two new restaurants. Susan and Clark knew that they would be expected to present a set of recent financial statements as part of any loan proposal. So, the co-owners spent an afternoon compiling data regarding the key transactions of the two preceding years.

Background

In early 2003, Clark and Susan Shipley moved from the damp, gray environs of Seattle, Washington to the dry, sunny climate of Phoenix, Arizona. After some reflection on their life in Seattle, as well as an analysis of the local business environment in the Phoenix area, they concluded that they would like to own and manage a restaurant. Glendale was Arizona's third largest city, but it was not noted for a plethora of eating establishments, and those that did exist were principally Italian, Mexican, or fast food. The Shipley's concluded that their restaurant would feature Japanese rice bowls and operate under the name "Island Teriyaki".

With that decision made, Clark and Susan began the long and difficult process of setting up their restaurant. In March 2003, they formed Island Foods, Inc. by contributing $10,000 in cash in exchange for all of the company's 1,000 shares of stock. Clark convinced his parents to loan the new venture $120,000 in cash, with principal payable at the rate of $12,000 per year over ten years and interest payable at a rate of 7.5 percent on the outstanding balance as of the beginning of the year. The loan agreement was signed on March 31, 2003, and provided that both principal and interest would be paid only once a year on March 31.

During March, the Shipley's searched for a suitable location for the restaurant. Clark negotiated a lease for approximately 2,000 square feet of retail space at a rate of $1,400 per month. The lease agreement ran for five years, with an option to renew for five more years. The landlord agreed to give the Shipley's three months of free rent on the front-end of the lease in order to help the new business survive the critical start-up period.

Also during the month of March, Clark arranged to buy a commercial refrigerator, range, and grill for $26,000 in cash, to be delivered and installed on March 31. Discussions with the seller indicated that the kitchen equipment should last for five years. Clark and Susan also purchased a computer system, with restaurant-specific software already installed, at a cost of $12,000 cash. While the system could last indefinitely, Susan suggested that it be depreciated over six years. Other purchases included food preparation equipment at a cost of $1,200 cash and various restaurant furniture and fixtures at a cost of $2,700 in cash; the equipment, furniture and fixtures were expected to have a useful life of three years.

To enable the restaurant to be fully operational on April 1, the landlord allowed the Shipley's carpenter, electrician, painters, and plumbers to begin renovations to the leased store on March 30 and 31. Working round-the-clock, the workmen completed all necessary improvements and renovations to the leased space at a cost of $68,000 in cash. On March 31, the purchased kitchen equipment was delivered and "Island Teriyaki" opened for business as planned on April 1, 2003.

First Two Years of Operations

Although Susan and Clark had prepared a timely U.S. income tax return in April of 2004 (for 2003 income taxes), they had not bothered to prepare a full set of financial statements using the accrual method of accounting. Since Clark had "backed-up" the hard drive on their computer system on a weekly basis, he had a CD containing all of the 2003 transactions and one of 2004 transactions. Working from the CD, Clark generated the necessary accounting information regarding the first two years of operations; he assembled the cash flow information in columnar form (see below) and relevant accrual information by each income statement account:

cash in columns

	2003	2004
• **Revenues**	$212,000	$327,000
In general, all restaurant sales were cash transactions; however, the Shipley's had developed a personal relationship with the general manager of one of Glendale's local businesses. As a courtesy to him, they had agreed to cater the company's New Year's Eve party each year and to bill the company directly. The billings totaled $3,000 in 2003 and $5,000 in 2004, and were paid by the company within 15 days of the following month.		*includes $3000 from 2003*
• **Expenses**		
o **Food costs**	$60,000	$105,000
Susan usually sat down once a week to write checks for any recent bills. Consequently, by year-end, only one week of food costs remained unpaid, totaling $9,000 in 2003 and $12,000 in 2004.		*$9000 pays for food exp of 2003*
o **Supply costs** *cash costs of $96, $12 unpaid = $108 total*	$4,800	$6,200
Since payment on delivery was required for these miscellaneous restaurant supplies (such as ice, napkins, etc.), Susan usually paid this bill directly out of petty cash.		
o **Utility charges**	$8,000	$12,000
At year-end one month's payment for electricity, telephone, and water remained due.		
o **Employee wages**	$44,000	$76,000
Because Clark did much of the cooking himself while Susan worked on food and sauce preparation, the Shipley's were able to keep their labor costs fairly low. They also made a conscious decision to hire local high school and college students. At year-end, Clark determined that one week of wages, amounting to $1,100 in 2003 and $1,400 in 2004, were due to the employees.		
o **Licenses**	$900	–
Clark paid the one-time Glendale "new business license" fee at 9am on April 1, 2003, to enable the business to immediately begin operations.		

continued

continued from previous page

	2003	2004
o **Insurance**	$18,000	–

o **Insurance**
On April 1, 2003, the Shipley's purchased a three-year "all risks" insurance policy for $18,000 cash. The policy was very comprehensive, covering loss due to theft, fire, or storm damage, as well as such business-related risks as lawsuits arising from customer injury while on the restaurant premises.

o **Income taxes**   –   –
For purposes of preparing the accrual financial statements, Clark and Susan decided to assume that income taxes would be paid on April 15 at a rate of 15 percent.

o **Owner compensation** $25,000 $40,000
A review of the stored data revealed that the Shipley's had withdrawn $25,000 in cash for personal use in 2003 and $40,000 in 2004. For purposes of the loan proposal, Susan decided to treat these withdrawals as dividends.

Required

1. Prepare a balance sheet for Island Foods, Inc. as of March 31, 2003.
2. Prepare a balance sheet, income statement, and statement of cash flow as of December 31, 2003.
3. Prepare a balance sheet, income statement, and statement of cash flow as of December 31, 2004.
4. Calculate the following financial ratios for the restaurant for 2003 and 2004.

Probability	Solvency
• Return on sales	• Financial leverage
• Return on assets	• Total debt-to-equity
• Return on equity	• Interest coverage ratio
Liquidity	Asset management
• Quick ratio	• Total asset turnover

Would you extend a loan to the Shipley's in the amount of $200,000 in order to open two new restaurants?

P2.39   **(Appendix) Recording Transactions using the Debit/Credit Paradigm.**   Miller & Co. experienced the following six events in its first year of operations:

1. Shareholders contributed $60,000 cash.
2. Purchased land for $40,000 cash.
3. Borrowed $18,000 in cash from a bank.
4. Provided services for $16,000, which will be paid to Miller & Co. next year.
5. Paid $11,000 cash for miscellaneous operating expenses.
6. Paid a $1,000 cash dividend to shareholders.

Required
Prepare journal entries using the debit/credit paradigm to record the above transactions.

P2.40   **(Appendix) Recording Transactions using the Debit/Credit Paradigm.**   RJM Real Estate Company experienced the following events during its first year of operations:

1. Received $50,000 in cash from investors as an equity investment.
2. Borrowed $40,000 in cash from a bank.

3. Purchased two parcels of land, each costing $15,000, for a total of $30,000 cash. The land was purchased for resale purposes.
4. Paid $10,000 cash to rent office equipment for the year.
5. Provided real estate appraisal services valued at $25,000, receiving $20,000 in cash and an account receivable for an additional $5,000.
6. Paid miscellaneous expenses totaling $11,000 in cash.
7. Sold one parcel of land, costing $15,000, for $22,000 cash.
8. Paid a $5,000 cash dividend to shareholders.

Required

Prepare journal entries using the debit/credit paradigm to record the above transactions.

P2.41 **(Appendix) Recording Transactions using the Debit/Credit Paradigm.** The following events occurred for The KMF Corporation during 2006:

1. Sales of products totaled $219,000, of which $15,000 remained uncollected at year-end.
2. The cost of goods sold during the year was $56,000.
3. A cash disbursement of $50,000 was made on July 1, 2006, to pay for a 12-month office equipment lease that expires on June 30, 2007.
4. Depreciation expense for the year on the company's warehouse amounted to $7,500.
5. Employee wages for the year totaled $40,000, of which $2,000 was unpaid at year-end.
6. Selling, general, and administrative expenses amounted to $10,000 for the year and were paid in full.
7. A cash payment of $25,000 was made to reduce the balance of accounts payable.
8. Interest expense on long-term debt was $18,000 for the year, of which $4,500 was unpaid at year-end.
9. The company paid income taxes of $25,000 on its earnings.

Required

Prepare journal entries using the debit/credit paradigm to record the above transactions.

CORPORATE ANALYSIS

CA2.42 **The Procter and Gamble Company.** The 2005 annual report of The Procter and Gamble Company (P & G) is available at www.pg.com/annualreports/2005/pdf/pg2005annualreport.pdf. After reviewing P & G's annual report, respond to the following questions:

a. P & G's net income increased each year from 2003 through 2005. Looking at the company's income statement, explain why P & G's net income increased if every one of its operating expenses also increased over the same period. (To answer this question, divide each of P & G's operating expenses by operating revenues and consider the trend over the three year period.)
b. P & G's total assets increased by approximately $4.5 billion from 2004 to 2005. Which assets principally accounted for this growth? Is this growth a problem? If so, why? If not, why not?
c. Consider the change in P & G's total debt and total shareholders' equity from 2004 to 2005. Did P & G finance the $4.5 billion growth in its assets principally with debt or principally with equity? Do you agree with this strategic financing decision? Why or why not?
d. Consider P & G's statement of cash flow. What were the four major cash outflows for the company in 2005? How did P & G finance these cash outflows?
e. Compare P & G's dividend payments to its net income in 2004 and 2005. (Note: The ratio of dividends paid divided by net income is called the dividend payout ratio.) What percentage of net income does P & G pay to its shareholders? How does this payout percentage compare to P & G's competitors (such as Johnson and Johnson, Kimberly-Clark Corporation)? Do you agree with this dividend payment policy? What message does this policy convey to investors about the company's future growth potential?

CA2.43 **Internet-based Analysis.** Consider a publicly-held company whose products you are familiar with. Some examples might include:

Company	Product	Corporate Website
• **Johnson & Johnson Company**	• Band-Aids	• www.jnj.com
• **Microsoft Corporation**	• Windows XP software	• www.microsoft.com
• **Nokia Corporation**	• Cellular phones	• www.nokia.com
• **Intel Corporation**	• Pentium processors	• www.intel.com
• **Kimberly-Clark Corporation**	• Kleenex	• www.kimberly-clark.com

Access the company's public website and search for its most recent annual report. (Note: Some companies will provide access to their financial data through an "investor relations" link, while others will provide a direct link to their "annual reports.") After locating your company's most recent annual report, open the file and review its contents. After reviewing the annual report for your selected company, prepare answers to the following questions:

1. Calculate the cost of goods sold, operating expenses, and net income as a percentage of net sales for the last two years. What is the trend in each of these percentages? Explain what might be driving the trend.
2. Calculate the company's total liabilities as a percentage of total assets for the last two years. Did this percentage increase or decrease? Is the company principally debt-financed or equity-financed?
3. Determine if the company paid dividends to its shareholders. (Hint: Look at the statement of shareholders' equity or the statement of cash flow.) If the company paid dividends, calculate the ratio of dividends paid divided by net income. (Note: This ratio is known as the dividend payout ratio.) What percentage of its net income did the company pay to its shareholders in each of the last two years?
4. Review the company's statement of cash flow. Identify the major sources of financing used by the company in each of the last two years?
5. Review the company's "Summary of Significant Accounting Policies." Identify how the company recognizes revenue. Identify if the company uses any estimates in the preparation of its financial statement, and if so, prepare a list of the estimates used in its financial report.

Chapter Three

Measuring Performance: Cash Flow and Net Income

TAKEAWAYS

When you complete this chapter you should be able to:

1. Interpret a statement of cash flow to explain a company's financing and investing strategies.
2. Prepare a statement of cash flow using the indirect method.
3. Interpret the components of net income to evaluate a company's sustainable earnings.
4. Explain the difference between EBITDA, free cash flow, and discretionary cash flow.

Where have we been?	Where are we?	Where are we going?
Chapter 2 illustrated how accounting events are analyzed, quantified, summarized, and ultimately, reported in a company's financial statements. The chapter also examined how the financial information of a business can be analyzed and used to make investment and credit decisions. Finally, the notion that, in some instances, management can make strategic accounting policy choices to enhance reported firm performance was introduced and illustrated with two corporate examples.	In this chapter, we explore the content and preparation of the statement of cash flow. The chapter demonstrates how cash flow statements can be prepared using only balance sheet and income statement information and how cash flow statements can be analyzed to understand a company's sources and uses of cash. The chapter then turns its attention to the income statement and explores the components of net income to help in identification of a company's sustainable earnings. Financial theory posits that the value of a share of stock is a function of a company's recurring, sustainable earnings. Finally, alternative definitions of cash flow as used by investment professionals—EBITDA, free cash flow, and discretionary cash flow—are defined and explored.	In Chapter 4, additional financial statement analysis tools to evaluate a company's financial performance are introduced and their use illustrated. Specifically, financial statement analysis techniques to assess a firm's profitability, asset management, and financial risk are explored. These techniques are then used to illustrate how lenders evaluate the risk associated with extending debt financing to Outback Steakhouse, a casual dining restaurant company. Finally, the preparation of pro forma financial statements are discussed and illustrated.

BRISTOL-MYERS SQUIBB COMPANY   Symbol: BMY

The **Bristol-Myers Squibb Company** was formed in 1989 with the merger of pharmaceutical companies Bristol-Myers Company and the Squibb Corporation. The company is best known for its prescription pharmaceutical drugs such as TAXOL for use in chemotherapy treatment; however, it also manufactures over-the-counter drugs and health-care products, and sells nutritional products through its subsidiary Mead Johnson. The company has been rumored to be an acquisition target for one of the larger European pharmaceutical companies, such as **Glaxosmithkline plc, Novartis AG**, or **Sanofi-Aventis SA**.

Lance Armstrong, seven-time winner of the Tour de France and a cancer survivor, acts as the company's spokesperson, perhaps to deflect attention away from recent adverse publicity resulting from an accounting scandal. In 2002, Bristol-Myers Squibb agreed to pay $150 million to the U.S. Department of Justice and the U.S. Securities and Exchange Commission in settlement of a lawsuit alleging improper recording of $2.5 billion in revenue between 1999 and 2001. According to the government allegation, the company engaged in "channel stuffing" in order to report higher product sales on its income statement, presumably to meet Wall Street earnings' expectations. Channel stuffing refers to the practice of shipping unordered goods to retailers, usually with a guarantee to allow the retailers to return any unsold merchandise.

Bristol-Myers Squibb apparently felt it was important to report strong results on its income statement even if it meant violating the "rules of the game." There was, however, one telltale sign that something was wrong with the company's reported results: While the company was reporting inflated sales and earnings on the unordered product it shipped to its customers, its operating cash flow failed to reflect the apparent increase in sales. Where would this information appear in a company's financial statements?

In addition to the income statement that included the inflated sales, Bristol-Myers Squibb was also required to disclose its statement of cash flow to its shareholders. This statement includes a reconciliation of a firm's reported net income and its corresponding cash flow from operations. In 2001, the year prior to the alleged channel stuffing, Bristol-Myers reported net earnings in excess of $2 billion and cash flow from operations in excess of $5 billion. The company had in prior years consistently reported cash flow from operations that equaled or exceeded its reported net income. This changed in 2002, however, when the company reported net income in excess of $2 billion, but cash flow from operations of less than $1 billion.

In this chapter, we examine how firm performance is measured. Both the income statement and the statement of cash flow contain important indicators of a company's operating performance. Public companies like Bristol-Myers Squibb are required to include both financial statements in their filings with the U.S. Securities and Exchange Commission and in their annual report to shareholders. To be fully informed, financial statement users must understand the information that each statement conveys about a company's operating performance.

EXECUTIVE OUTLINE

Measuring Performance: Cash Flow and Net Income

Analyzing and Computing Cash Flow Information	Identifying and Understanding Sustainable Earnings
■ Statement of Cash Flow	■ Special Items and Extraordinary Items
■ Presenting Cash Flow Information	■ Discontinued Operations
■ Computing Cash Flow under the Indirect Method	■ Earnings per Share
■ Cash Flow Ratios	■ Pro Forma Earnings
■ Alternative Measures of Cash Flow	

ANALYZING AND COMPUTING CASH FLOW INFORMATION

In the minds of most investment professionals, lenders, and managers, the two most important measures of a firm's financial health and performance are its operating cash flow and its net income. In this chapter, we explore these two measures in greater detail, examining their similarities and differences, and how they are interrelated. We will see that the accrual accounting process imbeds estimates of future cash flow into current net income, and as a consequence, that current period net income is often a very good predictor of future operating cash flow.

We begin this chapter by considering the various ways that cash flow data can be presented. We then consider how cash flow information can be extracted from balance sheets and income statements. Finally, we consider the important concept of sustainable earnings and the various alternative measures of cash flow used by investment professionals.

Statement of Cash Flow

The statement of cash flow summarizes a firm's inflows and outflows of cash by segmenting a firm's total cash flow into three activity categories:

- Cash flow from operating activities
- Cash flow from investing activities
- Cash flow from financing activities

These three categories represent the three key activities undertaken by all businesses—providing a good or service (operating activities), obtaining the assets necessary to provide a good or service (investing activities), and financing both the basic operations of a business and the investment in assets required to produce a product or provide a service (financing activities). The three basic activities can be illustrated with a simple example of a pizza delivery business. Before the business can start delivering pizzas, it must first obtain the necessary funds to buy a delivery van. Taking out a loan at a bank is an example of a financing activity. The borrowed cash can then be used to buy the van, representing an investing activity. Having purchased the van, the business can then begin using it to make deliveries and collecting cash from customers, an operating activity.

Analyzing and understanding the contents of the statement of cash flow provides financial statement users with critical insights about a company's operating, investing, and financing strategies. Exhibit 3.1, for example, provides an illustration of a typical statement of cash flow. This exhibit reveals that the cash flow from operations represents the aggregate of the cash received from the sale of goods and services less the cash spent on operating expenses. The cash flow from investing, on the other hand, is the aggregate of the cash received from the sale of investments, property and equipment, and intangible assets less the cash spent to acquire these various types of assets. Finally, the cash flow from financing represents the aggregate of the cash received from the sale of debt and equity securities less the cash paid to retire debt, repurchase equity securities, or pay dividends to shareholders.

The statement of cash flow can be presented in two alternative formats—the direct and indirect method—to which we now turn.

EXHIBIT 3.1	An Illustrative Statement of Cash Flow

Operating Activities
  Cash received from the sale of goods and services
  − Cash spent on operating expenses
  ⎱ Operating Strategy

  Cash Flow from Operations (CFFO)

Investing Activities
  Cash received from the sale of investments, property and
  equipment, or intangible assets
  − Cash invested in investments, property and equipment, or
  intangible assets
  ⎱ Investing Strategy

  Cash Flow from Investing (CFFI)

Financing Activities
  Cash received from the sale of debt or equity securities
  − Cash paid to retire debt or equity securities and to
  pay dividends
  ⎱ Financing Strategy

  Cash Flow from Financing (CFFF)

Presenting Cash Flow Information

There are two formats available under GAAP to present the statement of cash flow—the direct method format and the indirect method format. These approaches differ only in how the cash flow from operations is constructed. The cash flow from investing and the cash flow from financing are identical under the two formats.

Since the vast majority of publicly-held companies (about 99 percent) utilize the indirect method format, we will principally focus on this format. Appendix B to this chapter illustrates how to construct a direct method statement of cash flow. Under the direct method statement of cash flow, cash flow from operations is computed directly from the company's cash transactions.

Under the indirect method a company computes its cash flow from operations by making various adjustments to convert its accrual-based net income to its cash-based cash flow from operations. In other words, cash flow from operations is computed indirectly by starting with accrual net income and then making adjustments to determine cash flow from operations. Exhibit 3.2 presents an indirect method statement of cash flow for **Sun Microsystems.**

Exhibit 3.2 reveals that Sun's cash flow from operations begins with the company's 2005 net loss of $107 million and then reports the various adjustments needed to convert its net loss under the accrual basis of accounting to its cash flow from operations of $369 million under the cash basis of accounting. Sun's statement of cash flow reveals that the principal positive adjustments to its net loss from operations were depreciation and amortization expense ($671 million), the change in accounts payable ($105 million), and the change in accounts receivable ($111 million). These accrual accounting adjustments illustrate how it is possible for a company like Sun Microsystems to report negative net income while also reporting a positive cash flow from operations—net income includes, among other things, such non-cash expenses as depreciation and amortization expense.

Sun's statement of cash flow also reveals the company's investing and financing strategies. In 2005, for example, the company used its available cash flow to acquire property, plant and equipment ($257 million), spare parts and other assets ($90 million), and for various acquisitions ($95 million). Financing for these

EXHIBIT 3.2	Illustration of the Indirect Method for Statement of Cash Flow

Sun Microsystems, Inc.
Consolidated Statements of Cash Flows

Fiscal Years Ended June 30 (in millions)	2005	2004 (Restated)	2003 (Restated)
Cash flows from operating activities			
Net loss	$ (107)	$ (388)	$(3,384)
Adjustments to reconcile net loss to net cash provided by operating activities			
Depreciation and amortization	671	730	918
Amortization of other intangible assets and unearned equity compensation	96	83	110
Impairment of goodwill and other intangible assets	—	49	2,125
Tax benefits from employee stock plans	25	4	9
Deferred taxes	(315)	620	654
Loss on investments, net	9	64	84
Purchased in-process research and development	—	70	4
Changes in operating assets and liabilities			
Accounts receivable, net	111	61	387
Inventories	32	(44)	181
Prepaid and other assets	(19)	(288)	(231)
Accounts payable	105	158	(133)
Other liabilities	(239)	1,107	313
Net cash provided by operating activities	369	2,226	1,037
Cash flows from investing activities			
Purchases of marketable debt securities	(7,154)	(8,469)	(6,958)
Proceeds from sales of marketable debt securities	6,181	5,795	6,476
Proceeds from maturities of marketable debt securities	941	854	578
Purchases of equity investments	(1)	(19)	(21)
Proceeds from sales of equity investments	50	49	17
Acquisition of property, plant and equipment, net	(257)	(249)	(373)
Acquisition of spare parts and other assets	(90)	(71)	(217)
Payments for acquisitions, net of cash acquired	(95)	(201)	(30)
Net cash used in investing activities	(425)	(2,311)	(528)
Cash flows from financing activities			
Acquisition of common stock	—	—	(499)
Proceeds from issuance of common stock, net	218	239	182
Principal payments on borrowings and other obligations	(252)	(28)	(201)
Net cash provided by (used in) financing activities	(34)	211	(518)
Net increase (decrease) in cash and cash equivalents	(90)	126	(9)
Cash and cash equivalents, beginning of year	2,141	2,015	2,024
Cash and cash equivalents, end of year	$2,051	$2,141	$2,015
Supplemental disclosures of cash flow information			
Interest paid (net of interest received from swap agreements of $62, $72 and $70 in fiscal 2005, 2004 and 2003, respectively)	$ 27	$ 26	$ 36
Income taxes paid (received) (net of refunds of $34, $143 and $351 in fiscal 2005, 2004 and 2003, respectively)	$ 371	$ 70	$ (91)
Supplemental schedule of noncash investing activities			
Stock and options issued in connection with acquisitions	$ 1	$ 125	$ 193

capital investments came from the issuance of new common stock ($218 million), net of payments on corporate borrowings ($252 million), and from the company's operating cash flow. Notice that the sum of Sun's operating cash flow ($369 million) plus its financing cash flow (−$34 million) was insufficient to cover its capital investment of $425 million in 2005, forcing the company to draw down on its existing cash.

Computing Cash Flow under the Indirect Method

Although a statement of cash flow is a required corporate disclosure for public companies in their annual report to shareholders and their annual 10-K filing with the U.S. Securities and Exchange Commission, it is not a required disclosure for unaudited financial data (such as, quarterly financial data). Thus, an important skill for investors, investment professionals, and managers is the ability to estimate a company's cash flow using only those statements that are routinely available, namely income statements and balance sheets. (This skill is also important in the construction of pro forma financial statements, which are discussed in Chapters 4 and 12.) In this section, we illustrate how to prepare an indirect method statement of cash flow using only two balance sheets and an income statement.

To begin, it is important to understand exactly what we are accomplishing with the statement of cash flow. This statement details a firm's cash flow activity during a given fiscal period. It reveals how the cash balance on the balance sheet increased or decreased from the beginning of the period to the end of the period (the change in cash). The principle events that cause a firm's cash balance to change include the sale of goods, the purchase of inventory, the payment of operating expenses, the payment of dividends, the purchase or sale of property and equipment, and the sale or repurchase of stock, among other things. In short, all of the financial events that result in a change in a company's cash account are reported in some form on the firm's income statement or balance sheet. And, as a consequence, a statement of cash flow can be prepared using only a company's income statement and the changes in its balance sheet accounts. This can be seen by reference to the balance sheet equation:

$$\text{Assets (A)} = \text{Liabilities (L)} + \text{Shareholders' Equity (SE)} \tag{1}$$

Separating a firm's assets into its cash assets (CA) and its non-cash assets (NCA):

$$\text{CA} + \text{NCA} = \text{L} + \text{SE} \tag{2}$$

And, rewriting the balance sheet equation in changes form yields:

$$\Delta\text{CA} + \Delta\text{NCA} = \Delta\text{L} + \Delta\text{SE} \tag{3}$$

Finally, rearranging the components of the balance sheet equation shows that the change in cash can be computed from the change in all of the other balance sheet accounts:

$$\Delta\text{CA} = \Delta\text{L} - \Delta\text{NCA} + \Delta\text{SE} \tag{4}$$

Five Steps to Cash Flow. Since you are already familiar with the financial affairs of the Russian River Valley Winery from Chapter 2, we will use this data for purposes of illustrating an approach for generating cash flow data from balance sheets and income statements. The process involves five steps, resulting in the preparation of an indirect method statement of cash flow. The approach begins by focusing initially only on the balance sheet and then proceeds to integrate a business' income statement through a series of systematic adjustments to a preliminary statement of cash flow derived solely from balance sheet data. Exhibit 3.3 presents the beginning of year (column 1) and end of year (column 2) balance sheets for the Russian River Valley Winery.

Step One. Using just the beginning and ending balance sheets (see Columns 1 and 2 in Exhibit 3.3), calculate the change in each balance sheet account by subtracting the beginning balance sheet amount from the ending amount. The results of this step for Russian River Valley are presented in Column 3 of Exhibit 3.3. To simplify this step, the change in the property, plant, and equipment accounts are calculated as an aggregate amount after deducting any accumulated depreciation (on a net of accumulated depreciation basis).

To verify the accuracy of the Step One calculations, simply compare the sum of the changes in the asset accounts ($153) to the sum of the changes in the liability and shareholders' equity accounts ($153). These totals must be equal. If the totals are not equal, it indicates the presence of a subtraction error that must be identified and corrected before progressing to Step Two.

EXHIBIT 3.3	Preparing a Statement of Cash Flow: The Indirect Method			
	Russian River Valley Winery, Inc.			
	Balance Sheet			
	(1)	(2)	(3)	(4)
	Beginning	End of	Change	Cash Flow
($ thousands)	Of Year 1	Year 1	For Year	Classification
Current assets				
Cash.	$ 4,700	$ 768	$(3,932)	Net cash flow
Accounts receivable.	0	800	800	Operating
Inventory.	0	60	60	Operating
Total current assets	4,700	1,628		
Non-current assets				
Equipment	0	3,500		
Buildings.	2,000	2,000		
Land	4,000	4,000		
	6,000	9,500		
Accumulated depreciation	0	(225)		
Property, plant & equipment, net	6,000	9,275	3,275	Investing/Operating
Intangible assets, net	100	50	(50)	Investing/Operating
Total assets.	$10,800	$10,953	$ 153	
Current liabilities				
Accounts payable.	$0	$80	$ 80	Operating
Taxes payable.	0	96	96	Operating
Notes payable, current.	0	480	480	Financing
Total current liabilities.	0	956		
Notes payable, non-current	4,800	3,840	(960)	Financing
Shareholders' equity				
Common stock, $1 par.	6,000	6,400	400	Financing
Retained earnings	0	57	57	Financing/Operating
Shareholders' equity	6,000	6,457		
Liabilities & shareholders' equity	$10,800	$10,953	$ 153	

An important figure identified during Step One is the final result of the statement of cash flow, namely the change in the cash account. The bolded area in Exhibit 3.3 reveals that the cash account of the Russian River Valley Winery declined by $3,932 from the beginning of the year to the end of the year. Hence, all of the various cash inflows and outflows for the winery must aggregate to this figure.

Step Two. Step Two involves identifying the appropriate cash-flow activity category—operating, investing, or financing—for each balance sheet account, and this is illustrated in Column 4 of Exhibit 3.3. Although measuring the change in the balance sheet accounts in Step 1 is straight-forward, there can be some confusion over the correct activity classification for some of the balance sheet accounts in Step 2. Accounts receivable, inventory, accounts payable and taxes payable are all easily identified as operating activity items because they are associated with the day-to-day operations of a business. Notes payable (current and non-current) and common stock, on the other hand, are clearly financing activity items because they are associated with raising capital to finance a business. Net property, plant and equipment (P,P&E), however, can be both an investing activity item and an operating activity item. Purchases and sales of P,P&E are associated with the capital investment needed to run a business, and thus, are an investing activity item; but, the depreciation expense associated with P,P&E is an operating activity item since the depreciation of P,P&E is deducted as an operating expense in the calculation of accrual net income. Similarly, intangible assets can be both an investing activity item and an operating activity item because the acquisition or sale of intangibles is an investing activity item, whereas the amortization of intangibles is an operating expense deducted in the calculation of accrual net income, and hence, an operating activity item. Finally, retained earnings can be both an operating activity item and a financing activity item because retained earnings is increased by net income, an operating activity item, but decreased by the payment of dividends, a financing activity item.

> **In Practice 3.1** *Balance Sheet Caption: A Glimpse of a Sample of Fortune 1000 Companies* The following table identifies the caption used by a sample of 600 Fortune 1000 companies on their balance sheets to describe the cash account. The overwhelming majority of firms utilize the caption "cash and cash equivalents."
>
> | Balance Sheet Captions | Number | Percentage |
> |---|---|---|
> | Cash . . . . | 22 | 3.7 |
> | Cash and cash equivalents* . . . . | 528 | 88.0 |
> | Cash and equivalents . . . . | 34 | 5.6 |
> | Cash combined with marketable | | |
> | securities . . . . | 13 | 2.2 |
> | Other. . . . . | 3 | 0.5 |
> | Total . . . . | 600 | 100.0 |
>
> Source: 2006 Accounting Trends & Techniques
>
> * As this textbook went to press in 2007, the FASB took steps to eliminate the term "cash equivalents" from corporate financial statements. Items currently classified as cash equivalents, such as certificates of deposit and money market accounts, will now be classified as "short-term investments."

As a general rule, the following cash flow activity classifications apply, although exceptions will exist:

Balance Sheet Account	Cash Flow Activity Category
Current assets	Operating
Non-current assets.	Investing/Operating
Current liabilities.	Operating
Non-current liabilities	Financing
Capital stock	Financing
Retained earnings	Operating/Financing

Examples of exceptions to the above general activity classifications include the following:

- Marketable securities, a current asset, are an investing activity item.
- Current maturities of long-term debt, a current liability, are a financing activity item.
- Employee pension obligations, a noncurrent liability, are an operating activity item.

Step Three. Having completed Steps One and Two, you are now ready to build a **preliminary statement of cash flow** using the calculated increases or decreases in the various balance sheet accounts from Step One and the identified activity classifications from Step Two. The preliminary statement of cash flow for the Russian River Valley Winery, using the values from Column 3 of Exhibit 3.3 and the cash flow activity categories from Column 4, is presented in Exhibit 3.4.

EXHIBIT 3.4	An Illustration of a Preliminary Statement of Cash Flow: The Indirect Method

Russian River Valley Winery Inc. Preliminary Statement of Cash Flow	
($ thousands)	Year 1
Operating activities	
Retained earnings	$ 57
Accounts receivable.	(800)
Inventory	(60)
Accounts payable	80
Taxes payable	96
CFFO	(627)
Investing activities	
Property, plant & equipment (net)	(3,275)
Intangible assets (net)	50
CFFI	(3,225)
Financing activities	
Notes payable, current.	480
Notes payable, non-current.	(960)
Common stock	400
CFFF.	(80)
Change in cash (from balance sheet).	$(3,932)

Since a statement of cash flow measures the inflows and outflows of cash for a business, it is important to note that the sign of the asset account changes calculated in Step One must be reversed for purposes of preparing the preliminary statement of cash flow in Exhibit 3.4. This can be seen in equation (4) above in which the change in non-cash assets has a negative sign. For instance, Exhibit 3.3 shows that the change in accounts receivable was an increase of $800, whereas the change in intangible assets was a decrease of $50. When preparing the indirect method cash flow statement, an $800 increase in accounts receivables represents a subtraction from net income (a cash outflow), and a decline in intangible assets of $50 represents an addition to net income (a cash inflow), to arrive at the cash flow from operations. To illustrate why an increase in accounts receivable must be subtracted from net income to arrive at operating cash flow, consider how sales are initially recorded. Recall that under the indirect method, cash flow from operations begins with accrual net income. Therefore we will need to make adjustments to accrual net income in order to find the cash that has been received or used. Assume that a $2,000 sale of inventory is paid for with $1,200 in cash and the remaining $800 recorded as an increase in accounts receivable. In this example, net income increases by $2,000 but cash is only increased by $1,200. Therefore, net income must be reduced by the $800 increase in accounts receivable to yield the correct cash flow from operations. Similar logic explains why it is necessary to add back the decrease in intangible assets to net income to arrive at the correct cash flow from operations. Intangible assets were reduced by amortizing the cost of the asset by $50. This $50 expense reduced net income; however, no cash outflow was involved. Therefore, it is necessary to add $50 back to net income to yield the correct change in operating cash flow. Hence, when preparing the preliminary statement of cash flow in Step Three, it is important to remember to reverse the sign of the change values for the asset accounts. This is unnecessary for the liability and shareholders' equity accounts as can be seen from equation (4) above.

Exhibit 3.4 presents the preliminary statement of cash flow for the Russian River Valley Winery. This preliminary statement suggests that the firm's cash flow from operating activities (CFFO) for the period was negative $627, the cash flow from investing activities (CFFI) was negative $3,225, and the cash flow from financing activities (CFFF) negative $80. As required, the cash inflows and outflows aggregate to the change in the cash account from the balance sheet of a decrease of $3,932.

Step Four. To this point we have used the balance sheet exclusively to provide the needed inputs to our statement of cash flow. For most businesses, however, cash flow will be generated by the firm's on-going operations and not just by various events affecting the balance sheet accounts. Hence, it is now appropriate to introduce the operations-related data found on the winery's income statement (see Exhibit 3.5).

EXHIBIT 3.5	Income Statement	
Russian River Valley Winery, Inc. **Income Statement**		
($ thousands)		**Year 1**
Revenue		$1,900
Cost of goods sold.		380
Gross profit.		1,520
Operating expenses		
Wages & salaries		100
Selling, general & administrative		300
Depreciation		225
Amortization		50
Total operating expenses		675
Operating income.		845
Interest expense.		288
Income before income taxes		557
Income tax expense.		240
Net income.		$ 317

In this step, we will accomplish two important actions involving our preliminary statement of cash flow in Exhibit 3.4. First, we will replace the change in retained earnings from the balance sheet with net income from the income statement. In the event that the change in retained earnings does not equal net income, we will assume that any difference represents cash dividends paid to shareholders. For the Russian River Valley Winery, net income is $317 and the change in retained earnings is $57. Thus, it is necessary to gross up the change in retained earnings by $260 to equal the current net income ($57 + $260 = $317) under the operating activities section; and, to keep the statement of cash flow in balance with the decrease in cash of $3,932, insert the cash outflow for dividends ($260) under the financing activities section.

Second, we will adjust Russian River Valley's net income for any **non-cash expenses** such as the depreciation of plant and equipment and the amortization of intangibles that were deducted in the process of calculating the firm's accrual net income. These non-cash expenses must be added back to net income in the Operating Activities section to correctly measure the firm's operating cash flow. However, to keep the preliminary statement of cash flow in balance with the check figure of a decrease in cash of $3,932, it is also necessary to subtract equivalent amounts in the investing activities section.

To summarize, the adjustments to the Russian River Valley Winery preliminary statement of cash flow in Exhibit 3.4 are as follows:

> Depreciation expense and amortization expense are called **non-cash expenses** because these expenses do not involve any current period cash outflow. Depreciation expense, for example, represents the allocation of the purchase price of plant and equipment over the many periods that these assets produce revenues for a business. The matching principle requires that the cost of plant and equipment be matched with the revenues produced by these assets, and this is accomplished on the income statement by the inclusion of the periodic depreciation expense.

1. Net income of $317 replaces the change in retained earnings of $57 in the Operating Activities section. This action added $260 to the CFFO. To keep the statement of cash flow in balance with the check figure of negative $3,932 (the decrease in cash), it is necessary to subtract $260 elsewhere on the statement. Since retained earnings is calculated as follows:

   > Retained earnings (beginning)
   > + Net income for the period
   > − Dividends paid
   >
   > Retained earnings (ending)

   the outflow of $260 is reflected as a cash dividend paid to shareholders under the Financing Activities section.

2. Depreciation expense of $225, a non-cash deduction from net income, is added back to net income to avoid understating the cash flow from operations. However, to keep the statement of cash flow in balance with the change in cash of negative $3,932, a similar amount must be subtracted from property and equipment under the Investing Activities section.

3. Amortization expense of $50, another non-cash deduction from net income, is added back to net income to avoid understating the cash flow from operations. To insure that the statement is in balance with the check figure of negative $3,932, an equivalent amount is subtracted from intangible assets under the Investing Activities section.[1]

In Practice 3.2 *Method of Reporting the Cash Flow from Operations: A Glimpse of a Sample of Fortune 1000 Companies* The following table identifies the method of reporting the cash flow from operations as used by a sample of 600 Fortune 1000 companies. Over 98 percent of all companies surveyed used the indirect method:

Method of Reporting	Number	Percentage
Indirect method	592	98.7
Direct method.	8	1.3
Total	600	100.0

Source: 2006 Accounting Trends & Techniques

---

[1] Another example of a non-cash/non-operating item that will need to be removed from net income when calculating the CFFO is any "income (loss) from equity investments." We will have more to say about this adjustment and the accounting for equity investments in Chapter 8.

The results of these adjustments are displayed in Exhibit 3.6, which presents the final statement of cash flow for the Russian River Valley Winery. Note that the winery's statement of cash flow remains in balance with the change in the cash account of negative $3,932 after the three adjustments. This result is possible because whatever amount was added to (or subtracted from) net income under the CFFO, an equal amount was subtracted from (or added to) CFFI or CFFF.

Step Five. To provide the most useful cash flow data, a final step is required: Make any appropriate adjustments to the CFFO to calculate the recurring or sustainable CFFO. As noted above, the CFFO should include only the cash flow from operating activities. Consequently, to calculate the CFFO of a business, it is necessary to review a company's income statement to identify and remove the financial effects of any non-operating and/or non-recurring transactions. (An exception is interest expense, which many investment professionals view as a financing activity item; regardless, interest payments are required to be included in the CFFO under U.S. GAAP.)

To illustrate this point, assume that the Russian River Valley Winery sold property and equipment during the year at a loss of $25 and that the loss was included in its net income. This event is an investing activity and therefore properly belongs under CFFI. To correctly calculate the winery's CFFO, it is necessary to remove this loss from net income in the Operating Activity section and to add it to property and equipment under the Investing Activities section. These actions allow us to correctly measure the company's CFFO, as well as to correctly assess its cash flow for property and equipment. We will have more to say about this type of operating cash flow adjustment in subsequent chapters.

Exhibit 3.6 presents the final indirect method statement of cash flow for Russian River Valley and includes not only the adjustments from Step Four, but also, if needed, any adjustments to remove any

EXHIBIT 3.6	Statement of Cash Flow: Indirect Method

Russian River Valley Winery, Inc. Statement of Cash Flow	
($ thousands)	**Year 1**
Operating activities	
Net income.	$ 317
Depreciation	225
Amortization	50
(Increase) in accounts receivable	(800)
(Increase) decrease in inventory.	(60)
Increase (decrease) in accounts payable.	80
Increase (decrease) in taxes payable	96
Cash flow from operations	(92)
Investing activities	
Purchase of property, plant & equipment.	(3,500)
Cash flow from investing.	(3,500)
Financing activities	
Sale of common stock	400
Payment of notes payable (current)	(480)
Payment of cash dividends	(260)
Cash flow from financing.	(340)
Net cash flow	(3,932)
Change in cash (on balance sheet).	$(3,932)

non-operating or non-recurring gains and losses from the CFFO (Step 5). Russian River Valley's cash flow statement in Exhibit 3.6 using the indirect method reveals that the cash flow from operating activities is negative $92, the cash flow from investing activities is negative $3,500, and the cash flow from financing activities is negative $340. The resulting net cash flow of negative $3,932 exactly equals the decrease in cash on the balance sheet of $3,932, as required. (Appendix B to this chapter illustrates the construction of the statement of cash flow for Russian River Valley Winery on a direct method basis.)

The following illustration summarizes the five step process to preparing an indirect method statement of cash flow:

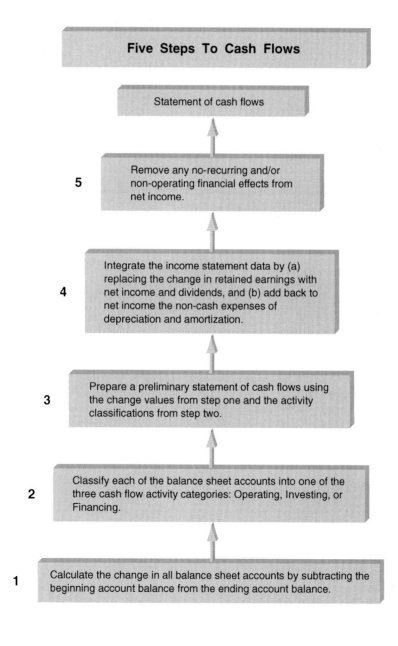

Five Steps To Cash Flows

Statement of cash flows

5   Remove any no-recurring and/or non-operating financial effects from net income.

4   Integrate the income statement data by (a) replacing the change in retained earnings with net income and dividends, and (b) add back to net income the non-cash expenses of depreciation and amortization.

3   Prepare a preliminary statement of cash flows using the change values from step one and the activity classifications from step two.

2   Classify each of the balance sheet accounts into one of the three cash flow activity categories: Operating, Investing, or Financing.

1   Calculate the change in all balance sheet accounts by subtracting the beginning account balance from the ending account balance.

Cash Flow Ratios

Investment professionals frequently use components of the statement of cash flow to form financial ratios that help highlight certain aspects of a firm's operating performance that might otherwise be obscured from financial statement users. For example, the operating funds ratio indicates the portion of a business' cash flow from operations provided by a firm's earnings and is calculated as follows:

$$\text{Operating Funds Ratio} = \frac{\text{Cash flow from operations}}{\text{Net income}}$$

This ratio frequently approximates one for most firms, although during a period of business expansion (contraction), the ratio may decrease (increase) to less (more) than one. The operating funds ratio is not meaningful for the Russian River Valley Winery since its cash flow from operations is negative.

Another cash flow-based ratio is the operating cash flow-to-current liabilities ratio, which is calculated as follows:

$$\text{Operating Cash Flow-To-Current Liabilities Ratio} = \frac{\text{Cash flow from operations}}{\text{Current liabilities}}$$

This ratio provides insights about a firm's liquidity, specifically the extent to which a company's current obligations can be satisfied by its operating cash flow. This ratio highlights the fact that business liquidity is available not only from a firm's existing liquid assets and its ability to borrow or refinance, but also from its on-going operations.

A final cash flow-based ratio is the cash conversion ratio, calculated as follows:

$$\text{Cash Conversion Ratio} = \frac{\text{Cash from sales}}{\text{Net sales}}$$

This ratio reveals the extent to which the sales reported on the income statement are converted into cash. Like the operating funds ratio, this ratio typically approximates one, although smaller (or larger) ratio values are possible depending upon the growth (or decline) in a firm's accounts receivable and its deferred or unearned revenue. Since this ratio features the cash collected from sales, it is most readily calculated when using the direct method format of the statement of cash flows. The cash conversion ratio for the Russian River Valley Winery is 0.58, indicating that the winery is projected to collect only $0.58 for each dollar of reported revenue during its first year of operations. (Can you verify the calculation of this ratio? Hint: Read Appendix B to this chapter.)

> **Cash from sales** is calculated as net sales plus/minus the change in accounts receivable plus/minus the change in unearned (or deferred) revenue.

Alternative Measures of Cash Flow

Although the statement of cash flow highlights the three cash flow measures of CFFO, CFFI, and CFFF, investment professionals often use other cash flow measures depending upon the purpose of their analysis. Three widely used alternative measures are EBITDA, free cash flow, and discretionary cash flow.

EBITDA, or earnings before interest, taxes, depreciation and amortization (and other non-cash charges, extraordinary items and non-recurring charges) is often used as an alternative measure of a firm's operating cash flow in those industries commonly referred to as capital intensive—that is, in those industries characterized by large capital investments in property, plant and equipment and/or intangible assets. The financial statements of firms in capital-intensive industries typically include large non-cash expenses for amortization and depreciation. As a consequence, the net income of companies in these industries may be substantially burdened by these charges, particularly as compared to companies in non-capital intensive industries.

To make more effective performance comparisons between companies from different industries and even within the same industry, some analysts rely on such metrics as EBITDA to level "the performance playing field." For example, to help analysts correctly evaluate the company's performance, **CSK Auto Corporation** reports both EBITDA and EBITDAR in its annual report. According to the company,

> While EBITDA is not intended to represent cash flow from operations as defined by GAAP, it is included herein because we believe it is a meaningful measure which provides additional information with respect to our ability to meet our future debt service, capital expenditure and working capital requirements. EBITDAR, on the other hand, represents EBITDA plus operating lease rental expense. Because the proportion of stores leased versus owned varies among industry competitors, we believe that EBITDAR permits a meaningful comparison of operating performance among industry competitors. We lease substantially all of our stores.

EBITDA is thought to provide an easily calculated alternative to operating cash flow as both measures begin with net income and both measures adjust for the non-cash operating expenses of depreciation and amortization.

Another cash flow measure, **free cash flow (FCF)**, is often used by analysts to evaluate a company's cash-flow strength. For instance, **Acxiom Corporation**, a company that integrates data, services and technology, reported that it generated free cash flow of $199.0 million in fiscal 2003, compared to operating cash flow of $253.8 million. The company noted that "free cash flow provides investors with a useful alternative measure of operating performance by allowing an assessment of the amount of cash available for general corporate and strategic purposes after funding operating activities and capital expenditures, capitalized software expenses and deferred costs." FCF is an important performance reference point for many investment professionals because it is less subject to the accounting trickery that often characterizes accrual net income. Free cash flow is calculated as follows:

$$FCF = CFFO - CapEx$$

In Practice 3.3 *Average Dollar Amount of the Adjustments to net income when computing the cash flow from operations using the indirect method format.* The largest adjustment to net income is the depreciation and amortization expense, which averaged 83 percent of net income.

Operating activities (in millions)	
Net income	$171.9
Depreciation and Amortization	142.7
Gain on sale of assets	(12.8)
Earnings from subsidiaries	(2.3)
Funds from operations—other	59.8
Increase in accounts receivable	(28.8)
Increase in inventory	(56.8)
Increase in accounts payable	18.4
Increase in taxes payable	2.2
Sources of funds—other	16.9
Cash flow from operations	$311.2

Source: Standard and Poor's Compustat, based on 6,316 firms reporting cash flow from operations in 2005.

where CapEx is the required reinvestment in the assets of a business necessary to enable the firm to maintain itself as a going concern. It should be clear that a firm with strong free cash flow will carry a higher firm value than one with weak (or no) free cash flow. Some investment professionals incorporate the construct of free cash flow into a ratio called the free cash flow yield to facilitate inter-firm comparisons of cash flow strength. A firm's free cash flow yield is defined as its free cash flow divided by its market capitalization. Businesses with high free cash flow yields are frequently seen as attractive additions to a portfolio of investment securities. We will have more to say about FCF in Chapter 12.[2]

While FCF addresses the issue of "How much cash is available for general corporate use?", the concept of discretionary cash flow addresses the question "How much internally-generated operating cash flow is available to permit a company's management to undertake a discretionary, value-creating action?" A business' discretionary cash flow (DisCF) is calculated as follows:

$$\text{DisCF} = \text{CFFO} - \text{Required debt payments} - \text{Dividend payments}$$

This expression reveals that DisCF is a company's internally-generated operating cash flow less any required payments to debtholders and any expected dividend payments to shareholders. Thus, DisCF is a measure of the excess internally-generated operating cash flow available to a business enterprise to undertake a discretionary project, for example investing in a new plant or acquiring a company. When DisCF is large, it indicates that a firm's internally-generated cash flow is strong relative to existing claims on those flows. When DisCF is small, it indicates that a firm will need additional external funding to facilitate a plant expansion, merger or acquisition, or debt retirement. Some analysts look to a business' discretionary cash flow as another indication of a business' cash flow health.

IDENTIFYING AND UNDERSTANDING SUSTAINABLE EARNINGS

Net income or net earnings is the "bottom line" measure of firm performance. It is a measure that depends on such accrual accounting procedures as the revenue recognition and expense matching policies selected by a firm's management. Generally-accepted accounting practice has historically emphasized the importance of accounting earnings because past accounting earnings have been found to be a good predictor of a firm's future operating cash flow. In Chapter 12, we will see that in earnings-based valuation models, the value of a company's share price largely depends on a firm's expected future earnings. Thus, an important role for historical accounting numbers is their use in forecasting a company's future earnings, and hence, a firm's market capitalization.

> Market capitalization refers to a firm's current fair market value, calculated as its market price per share times the number of shares outstanding. A business' market capitalization reflects the capital market's outlook regarding the company's future operating performance and differs from a firm's book value (i.e., the value of its shareholders' equity) which is based on past performance.

One of the determinants of the ability of historical earnings to predict future earnings is the extent to which earnings reoccur over time, or what is known as earnings persistence. Since the value of a share

---

[2] A company's capital expenditures, or CapEx, are frequently segmented into maintenance CapEx and incremental CapEx. Maintenance CapEx is the amount of capital investment required to leave a going-concern as well off at the end of a fiscal period as it was at the start of the fiscal period. Maintenance CapEx is frequently estimated by the amount of depreciation expense taken in a given period. Incremental CapEx, on the other hand, is any capital investment in excess of maintenance CapEx and is usually associated with an expansion in the productive capacity of a business.

of stock today is a function of a firm's ability to consistently generate earnings year in and year out, the sustainability or persistence of a company's operating earnings is closely linked to its value. Sustainable earnings are also sometimes referred to as **permanent earnings**, whereas non-sustainable earnings are often referred to as **transitory earnings**. In general, transitory earnings include such single-period items as extraordinary gains/losses, special items, restructuring charges, changes in accounting principle, and discontinued operations.

To assist investors in their assessment of a company's sustainable earnings, and hence in assessing a firm's **intrinsic value**, companies are required under GAAP to classify income statement accounts in a manner that aids the user in assessing a firm's sustainable earnings. Exhibit 3.7 illustrates the basic format of the income statement. Notice that the income statement is organized in such

> Intrinsic value refers to the underlying economic value of a business as a going-concern; that is, the value that a business could be sold for in an efficient market.

a way that items with greater persistence are reported higher in the income statement, whereas items considered more transitory are reported further down in the statement. Thus, accounts representing financial events that are both usual and frequent are reported first. Usual refers to whether an item is central to a firm's core operations, whereas **unusual items** display a high degree of abnormality and are unrelated, or only incidentally related, to the ordinary and typical activities of the enterprise.

EXHIBIT 3.7   **The Income Statement**

Savanna Company
Income Statement
For Year Ended December 31

Sales.		$500	Usual and frequent
Cost of goods sold.		200	Usual and frequent
Gross profit.		300	
Operating expenses	$200		Usual and frequent
Special items	50	250	Unusual or infrequent
Net operating income.		50	
Other income and expense			
Interest income.	25		Unusual
Interest expense.	(35)		Unusual
Gain on sale of equipment	15	5	Unusual
Net income from continuing operations before tax		55	
Income tax		20	
Net income from continuing operations.		35	
Gain (loss) on disposal of segment, net of tax.		10	Infrequent
Net income before extraordinary item		45	
Extraordinary gain (loss), net of tax		(15)	Unusual and infrequent
Net income.		$ 30	
Earning per share (100 shares outstanding)			
Net income from continuing operations		$ .35	
Disposal of business segment.		.10	
Extraordinary item		(.15)	
Total earnings per share		$ .30	

Frequent refers to how often an item is expected to occur, with infrequent items not reasonably expected to recur in the foreseeable future.[3] Usual and frequent items typically consist of such income statement accounts as sales, cost of goods sold, and other operating expenses. Just below these usual and frequent items are items that are either unusual or infrequent, but not both. Examples of these special items include such financial events as asset write-downs and restructuring charges. While these items are not expected to occur regularly, they are not considered unusual in nature. Income statement accounts such as interest expense, interest income, and gains on sales of equipment are often frequently recurring items; however, they are not considered part of a firm's central operations and therefore are considered unusual. Each of the above items is reported as part of continuing operations and is shown before any tax expense. GAAP, however, requires two single-period items, or one-time events, to be reported on an after-tax basis. These two items, discontinued operations and extraordinary items, are each shown net of any applicable income taxes. Reporting these items on a net-of-tax basis allows the income tax expense reported on the income statement to reflect only the income taxes associated with a firm's continuing operations, consequently enabling financial statement users to more readily predict a firm's future expected effective income tax rate.

Special Items and Extraordinary Items

There is no generally-accepted definition as to what constitutes a special item, therefore there is some variation in what firms will classify as "special." Special items often include gains or losses that are outside a firm's normal operations. For example, litigation settlements, impairment charges for long-lived assets, and the gains or losses associated with the sale of property, plant and equipment are typically classified as special items. The income statement for CSK Auto Corporation presented in Exhibit 3.8 reveals several special items, including a litigation settlement of $8.8 million in 2001, a write-off of unamortized management fee of $3.6 million in 1999, and $770,000 for the cost of a secondary share offering in 1999.

A controversial type of special item that some companies include in their income statement involves restructuring charges associated with changing a business' operations. Restructuring—also sometimes referred to as right-sizing or down-sizing—usually involves employee layoffs, closing facilities, and changing the company's financial structure by paying down debt with the issuance of new equity. For example, in Exhibit 3.8, CSK Auto Corporation reports "transition and integration expenses" in each year from 1999 to 2001 for the conversion of acquisition-related stores to the CSK format, store closing costs associated with the closure of CSK stores that overlapped with better situated acquired stores, and the operating losses of acquired automotive service centers that were closed.

In recent years, there has been increasing criticism of companies that report annual restructuring charges because it is believed that these write-offs have become a device for managing earnings. For example, Eastman Kodak Company has taken "one-time restructuring charges" every year for fourteen consecutive years, from 1992 to 2005. By taking recurring write-downs of property and equipment, management may attempt to convey the impression to investors, shareholders and investment professionals that the resulting restructuring charges are one-time events—that is, that they are transitory in nature and consequently should be ignored for purposes of valuing the firm. It should be observed, however, that these charges effectively reduce the regular depreciation expense on the income statement, and thus improve future operating income on an annual basis. Critics of this practice also note that restructuring charges are

---

[3] Accounting Principles Board, Opinion No. 30, "Reporting the Results of Operations," 1973. The Accounting Principles Board was the predecessor to the Financial Accounting Standards Board.

| EXHIBIT 3.8 | An Illustration of Extraordinary and Special Items | | |

CSK Auto Corporation
Consolidated Statements of Income

($ thousands)	2001	2000	1999
Net sales.	$1,452,109	$1,231,455	$1,004,385
Cost of sales.	769,043	636,239	531,073
Gross profit.	683,066	595,216	473,312
Other costs & expense			
Operating & administrative	568,873	471,340	391,528
Store closing costs	6,060	4,900	335
Legal settlement	8,800	—	—
Transition & integration expenses	23,818	30,187	3,075
Equity in loss of joint venture.	3,168	—	—
Goodwill amortization	4,799	1,941	—
Write-off of unamortized management fee	—	—	3,643
Secondary stock offering costs	—	—	770
Operating profit	67,548	86,848	73,961
Interest expense, net	62,355	41,300	30,730
Income before income taxes, extraordinary loss & cumulative effect of change in accounting principle.	5,193	45,548	43,231
Income tax expense.	193	17,436	15,746
Income before extraordinary loss & cumulative effect of change in accounting principle	5,000	28,112	27,485
Extraordinary loss, net of $4,236 of income taxes	—	—	(6,767)
Income before cumulative effect of change in accounting principle.	5,000	28,112	20,718
Cumulative effect of change in accounting principle, net of $468 of income taxes.	—	(741)	—
Net income.	$ 5,000	$ 27,371	$ 20,718

often taken in a 'bad year' in which operating earnings are unusually weak. Lumping restructuring charges in years characterized by poor operating results to enhance the probability of improved performance in future years has become known as **taking a bath**. Available evidence suggests that restructuring charges are often reversed in subsequent periods to enable a firm to beat analysts' earnings forecasts, to avoid reporting losses, or to avoid a decline in earnings from a prior year.[4]

Another one-time item is the additional income or charges that result from the implementation of a voluntary or mandatory **change in accounting principle**. Mandatory accounting changes occur when an accounting regulatory body, such as the FASB or IASB, changes the generally accepted accounting practice that is applicable to all audited companies. For example, in Exhibit 3.8, CSK Auto Corporation discloses that in 2000 it implemented a mandatory change in its method of accounting for store opening costs, from deferring these costs to immediately expensing the costs. This accounting policy change resulted in a reduction in CSK's net income of $741,000, net of income tax savings of $468,000.

---

[4] S.R. Moehrle, "Do Firms Use Restructuring Charge Reversals to Meet Earnings Targets?" *The Accounting Review* (April 2002).

A basic principle within U.S. GAAP is the **consistency principle**. Consistency requires that a firm use the same accounting measurement principles from one fiscal period to the next. This is not to be confused with uniformity, where all firms would need to report their financial results using a uniform set of principles and methods. Instead, consistency allows different firms to use different reporting methods; however, a firm is expected to report its performance on a consistent basis from one year to the next. The consistent use of accounting policies enables financial statement users to make valid, and hence useful, comparisons of performance across multiple time periods. Voluntary accounting policy changes can, and do occur, however, when the management of a company and its independent auditor decide that an alternative accounting method better reflects a firm's operations. Fortunately, voluntary changes in accounting methods don't happen very often—on average, less than two accounting policy changes per firm over a 20 year period. The capital market generally regards voluntary accounting policy changes suspiciously, often penalizing the share price of companies which make such changes. We will have more to say about voluntary accounting policy changes in Chapter 7.

As reflected in Exhibit 3.8, firms like CSK Auto Corporation were required in the past to separately show the cumulative financial effect of an accounting policy change, net of any income tax effect, as a separate line item on the income statement following the income from continuing operations. Under a new GAAP standard, the financial effect of a change in a company's accounting policies are now applied retrospectively to all prior periods to which the change can be estimated, with the financial effect of the change reported as an adjustment to retained earnings on the statement of shareholders' equity rather than on the income statement.

Extraordinary gains (losses) are gains (losses) that are both *unusual* and *infrequent* in nature. Extraordinary items are reported in the income statement *net* of any applicable income taxes and are reported after income from continuing operations—that is, the unusual and infrequent nature of these items is highlighted by prominently displaying them near the bottom of the income statement. Just what constitutes an extraordinary item, however, can be confusing. Consider, for example, a company whose uninsured building in California was destroyed in an earthquake. The firm would not be able to classify the loss as extraordinary because although the occurrence of earthquakes in California is infrequent, it would be not be considered unusual since it is part of the business risk of operating in California. Extraordinary items include such items as a gain or loss resulting from a natural disaster when such events are unusual and infrequent (such as a hurricane) or a gain or loss resulting from new government regulations, such as an asset expropriation by a foreign government (such as Venezuela's 2007 expropriation of international oil company assets). CSK Auto Corporation's income statement presented in Exhibit 3.8 includes an extraordinary item of $6.7 million, net of $4.2 million of income tax benefits, for losses incurred in connection with the retirement of some of the company's outstanding debt (see bolded area). This disclosure is consistent with the prior reporting requirement under U.S. GAAP, since revised, that gains and losses from early debt retirement be classified as an extraordinary item.[5]

Discontinued Operations

When a company discontinues a separately identifiable business unit, such as an existing division, to focus on other activities, it will generally incur costs to layoff employees, liquidate inventory, and shutter facilities. These costs and the profits (or losses) from operating the business unit until it can be disposed of are categorized as **discontinued operations** on the income statement. GAAP requires that companies

---

[5] FAS No. 145, issued in 2002, rescinded the requirement that gains (losses) on the early retirement of debt be classified as extraordinary under U.S. GAAP.

BUSINESS PERSPECTIVE: KOHL'S CORPORATION

Operating versus Non-Operating Earnings

The income statement for **Kohl's Corporation** is presented below. Kohl's consolidated income statement discloses such operating expenses as the cost of merchandise sold, depreciation and amortization on property and equipment, and selling and administrative expenses (see bolded areas). Kohl's separates the results of its core retailing business from the financing of its business by reporting interest expense as a non-operating item. It also separates the financial investing side of its business from its core business by reporting interest income on its investments and security holdings as a non-operating item. The underlying logic of this distinction is that Kohl's could relatively quickly change the way it finances its business and/or liquidate its investments—hence these items are considered to be transitory—but that exiting its core retailing business would require a longer period of time.

Kohl's Corporation
Consolidated Statements of Income

($ thousands, except per share data)	Fiscal Year Ended		
	January 28, 2006	January 29, 2005 (Restated)	January 31, 2004 (Restated)
Net sales.	$13,402,217	$11,700,619	$10,282,094
Cost of merchandise sold	8,639,278	7,586,992	6,887,033
Gross margin	4,762,939	4,113,627	3,395,061
Operating expenses			
Selling, general and administrative	2,963,472	2,582,996	2,157,030
Depreciation and amortization. . . .	338,916	288,173	239,558
Pre-opening expenses. . . .	44,370	49,131	47,029
Total operating expenses	3,346,758	2,920,300	2,443,617
Operating income. . . .	1,416,181	1,193,327	951,444
Other expense (income)			
Interest expense. . . .	72,086	64,761	76,371
Interest income	(1,695)	(2,309)	(3,440)
Income before income taxes	1,345,790	1,130,875	878,513
Provision for income taxes. . . .	503,830	427,474	332,050
Net income. . . .	$ 841,960	$ 703,401	$ 546,463
Net income per share			
Basic	$2.45	$2.06	$1.61
Diluted	$2.43	$2.04	$1.59

separate the results of their continuing operations from their discontinued operations to facilitate shareholder assessment of sustainable earnings. As shown in Exhibit 3.9, **Ford Motor Company**'s income from discontinued operations, after applicable income taxes, totaled $41 million in 2005. This amount is further partitioned into two components—operating income from discontinued operations and a loss on discontinued operations. Whereas the first component represents the net operating income for the period up to the time of the disposition of the discontinued operations, the second component represents the difference between the proceeds from the sale and the depreciated cost of the net assets disposed.

EXHIBIT 3.9	Illustration of Discontinued Operations

Ford Motor Company and Subsidiaries
Notes to the Financial Statements

Note 4. Discontinued Operations, Held-for-Sale Operations, Other Dispositions, and Acquisitions (continued)

Financial Services Sector

Discontinued Operations.   Consistent with our strategy to focus on our core business, we completed the disposition of the operations discussed below.

In 2004, we committed to a plan to sell Triad Financial Corporation, our operation in the United States that specialized in automobile retail installment sales contracts with borrowers who generally would not be expected to qualify, based on their credit worthiness, for traditional financing sources such as those provided by commercial banks or automobile manufacturers' affiliated finance companies. During 2005, we completed the sale of this business and recognized a pre-tax loss of approximately $16 million.

In 2004, we completed the sale of AMI Leasing and Fleet Management Services, our operation in the United States that offered full service car and truck leasing. During 2003, we recognized a pre-tax charge of $50 million, reflected in *Income/(loss) from discontinued operations* for the loss on sale. This amount represented the difference between the selling price of these assets, less costs to sell them, and their recorded book value.

In 2003, we completed the sale of Axus, our all-makes vehicle fleet leasing operations in Europe, New Zealand and Australia. In 2002, we recognized a pre-tax charge of $31 million, reflected in *Income/(loss) from discontinued operations* for the loss on sale. This amount represented the difference between the selling price of these assets, less costs to sell them, and their recorded book value.

The results of all discontinued Financial Services sector operations are as follows (in millions):

	2005	2004	2003
Revenues	$118	$493	$550
Operating income (loss) from discontinued operations	59	138	84
Gain (loss) on discontinued operations	(16)	—	(50)
(Provision for) benefit from income taxes.	(2)	(57)	(36)
Income (loss) from discontinued operations	$ 41	$ 81	$ (2)

Earnings per Share

Since investors own shares whose prices are customarily quoted in terms of a price per share, public companies are required to provide earnings numbers that are scaled by the number of shares held by its shareholders. For example, **basic earnings per share** (EPS) are net income divided by the actual number of common shares outstanding—that is, the number of shares held by a company's shareholders. **Diluted earnings per share**, on the other hand, is net income divided by the number of shares outstanding but adjusted for the possibility that some existing claims against the business might be converted into additional shares of common stock, thus increasing the number of shares outstanding. Claims against a firm that can be satisfied by the issuance of additional shares of common stock are called **dilutive claims** because the issuance of shares to satisfy these claims will lower, or dilute, basic EPS. Examples of **dilutive claims** include convertible bonds, employee stock options, and convertible preferred shares (which are discussed in Chapters 9 and 11, respectively).

Since Kohl's diluted EPS in 2005 was $2.43 versus a basic EPS of $2.45 (see Business Perspective: Kohl's Corporation), the company must have had some dilutive claims outstanding. Does the capital market consider the impact of these dilutive claims by relying more heavily on diluted EPS than on basic EPS when assessing a company's intrinsic value? Available evidence that diluted EPS explains more of the variation in share prices than basic EPS does suggest that investors do indeed focus more closely on diluted EPS in setting share prices.[6] However, available evidence also suggests that alternative EPS measures that better capture the potential dilutive effect of employee stock options explain more of the variation in share prices than does even diluted EPS.[7] This is consistent with the notion that investors make additional adjustments to diluted EPS when assessing the performance of firms that issue employee stock options.

Pro Forma Earnings

In recent years, companies have begun reporting a variety of alternative measures of earnings that *exclude* certain expenses or write-offs, jokingly referred to by investment professionals as EBBS or "earnings before bad stuff." One such measure is **pro forma earnings**. While there is no generally-accepted definition for the calculation of pro forma earnings, a commonly-used calculation is net income before discontinued operations, restructuring charges, extraordinary and special items, and the effect of any mandatory or voluntary accounting policy changes.

Under the requirements of the Sarbanes-Oxley Act passed in 2002, companies that include a non-GAAP financial measure such as pro forma earnings with their audited financial statements must also provide the most directly comparable GAAP numbers. These firms must also provide a reconciliation between the two sets of numbers. For example, **Eastman Kodak Company** reported a loss of $0.04 per share for the last quarter of 2004 using GAAP. Yet, on a pro forma basis, Kodak announced "operational earnings" of $0.78 per share, a swing of $0.82 per share from GAAP EPS. Kodak's pro forma earnings, a figure tracked by analysts who follow the company, excluded such costs as the company's restructuring charges.

The divergence between the generally higher pro forma earnings and GAAP earnings has increased over time. In Practice 3.4 presents, for example, GAAP EPS and pro forma EPS for the fourth quarter of 2004 for a selection of S&P 500 companies. Unfortunately, the capital market's reliance on pro forma earnings as a performance metric has also increased as suggested by evidence that share prices track pro forma earnings

In Practice 3.4 *GAAP EPS versus Pro Forma EPS**

Company	4th Quarter 2004		
	GAAP EPS	Pro Forma EPS	Percentage Difference
Eastman Kodak	$−0.04	$0.78	NM
Georgia Pacific	0.06	0.51	750
Rowan	0.02	0.15	650
Ford Motor	0.05	0.28	460
Clorox..................	0.72	3.69	413
Genzyme	−0.42	0.52	NM
Halliburton	−0.45	0.44	NM

*Source: *CFO Magazine* (May 2005). NM = not meaningful.

[6] R. Jennings, M.J. LeClere and R.B. Thompson, "Evidence on the Usefulness of Alternative Earnings per Share Measures," *Financial Analysts Journal* (November/December 1997).

[7] J.E. Core, W.R. Guay and S.P. Kothari, "The Economic Dilution of Employee Stock Options: Diluted EPS for Valuation and Financial Reporting," *The Accounting Review* (July 2002).

more closely than GAAP earnings.[8] To ensure that investors consider GAAP EPS, the U.S. Securities and Exchange Commission adopted Regulation G in 2003, which requires that firms put GAAP-based earnings first in their public earnings announcements, as well as to reconcile any non-GAAP earnings numbers (e.g., pro forma earnings) with their GAAP-based earnings. The intent of Regulation G is to insure transparency regarding the differences between GAAP earnings and any non-GAAP earnings reported by companies.

ETHICS PERSPECTIVE

One of the potential problems associated with the corporate form of business is the agency costs that can result from the separation of the ownership of a corporation from those that manage the corporation. One mechanism used to mitigate these potential agency costs are employment compensation contracts. The theory underlying this mechanism is that if a compensation contract is properly structured, goal congruence between the manager and the corporation's shareholders will result. Thus, properly-structured employment contracts provide performance incentives that result in larger amounts of compensation being paid when managers achieve better financial performance.

A potential unintended consequence of executive compensation contracts is that managers may also have an incentive to "cook the books" in order to report higher firm performance, and therefore, achieve higher personal compensation. In other words, rather than achieving goal congruence by working hard to sell more goods or to produce goods more efficiently, higher performance may be achieved through accounting trickery. Clearly, earnings management for purely personal gain can be argued to be an ethical breach of an executive's job.

REVIEW PROBLEM

The following balance sheet and income statement data were taken from the financial records of The Arcadia Company.

The Arcadia Company Balance Sheets					
	2006	**2005**		**2006**	**2005**
Assets			**Liabilities & Shareholders' Equity**		
Cash.	$ 30,000	$ 7,000	Accounts payable.	$ 63,000	$ 65,500
Marketable securities	60,000	67,500	Wages payable.	47,500	37,000
Inventory.	22,500	49,000	Total current liabilities.	110,500	102,500
Prepaid insurance.	4,500	6,000	Bank loan payable	85,000	83,000
Total current assets	117,000	129,500	Capital stock	75,000	75,000
Building (net).	190,000	187,500	Retained earnings	36,500	56,500
Totals	$307,000	$317,000	Totals	$307,000	$317,000

---

[8] M.T. Bradshaw and R.G. Sloan, "GAAP versus The Street: An Empirical Assessment of Two Alternative Definitions of Earnings," *Journal of Accounting Research* (March 2002).

The Arcadia Company Income Statement (2006)	
Revenues	$ 480,000
Less	
Cost of goods sold	320,000
Depreciation expense	28,500
Wage expense	93,000
Insurance expense	46,000
Interest expense	10,500
Net loss	$ (18,000)

Required

Prepare an indirect method statement of cash flow for The Arcadia Company for 2006 and calculate the following cash flow ratios for 2006: (a) operating funds ratio; (b) operating cash flow-to-current liabilities ratio; (c) cash conversion ratio.

Solution

The Arcadia Company Statement of Cash Flow	
(Indirect Method)	
Operating Activities	
Net loss	$(18,000)
Depreciation expense	28,500
Inventory	26,500
Prepaid insurance	1,500
Accounts payable	(2,500)
Wages payable	10,500
Cash flow from operations	46,500
Investing Activities	
Marketable securities	7,500
Building, net	(31,000)
Cash flow from investing	(23,500)
Financing Activities	
Bank loan	2,000
Dividends paid	(2,000)
Cash flow from investing	-0-
Net increase in cash	$ 23,000
Cash, beginning of year	7,000
Cash, end of year	30,000
Change in cash (from balance sheet)	$ 23,000

Operating funds ratio = $46,500/$(18,000) = Not meaningful
Operating cash flow-to-current liabilities ratio = $46,500/$110,500 = 0.42
Cash conversion ratio = $480,000/$480,000 = 1.00

EXECUTIVE SUMMARY

In this chapter, we examined the components of a company's net income in an effort to identify its sustainable earnings. Sustainable earnings are those operating and non-operating income flows that are expected to persist over many fiscal periods; they are the permanent earnings of a business. Sustainable earnings are important to managers and investors because they are a key determinant of firm value.

We also illustrated how a company's statement of cash flow can be prepared from its income statement and balance sheet. Finally, we examined the various alternative measures of cash flow that investors and investment professionals use to evaluate a firm's financial health: EBITDA, free cash flow, and discretionary cash flow.

As a validation of your understanding of the content of this chapter, you should now be able to:

- Use a statement of cash flow to explain a business' financing and investing strategies.
- Prepare a statement of cash flow using the indirect method.
- Explain the difference between EBITDA, free cash flow, and discretionary cash flow.
- Understand the components of net income to evaluate a company's sustainable earnings.

KEY CONCEPTS AND TERMS

Accruals, 3.27
Basic earnings per share, 3.22
Capital intensive, 3.15
Cash conversion ratio, 3.14
Cash flow for financing, 3.3
Cash flow for investing, 3.3
Cash flow from operations, 3.3
Change in accounting principle, 3.19
Consistency principle, 3.20
Diluted earnings per share, 3.22
Dilutive claims, 3.22
Direct method, 3.4

Discontinued operations, 3.20
Discretionary cash flow, 3.16
Earnings persistence, 3.16
EBITDA, 3.15
Extraordinary gain (loss), 3.20
Free cash flow, 3.15
Free cash flow yield, 3.16
Indirect method, 3.4
Intrinsic value, 3.17
Market capitalization, 3.16
Non-operating accruals, 3.30
Non-cash expenses, 3.11
Operating accruals, 3.27

Operating cash flow-to-current liabilities, 3.14
ratio, 3.14
Operating funds ratio, 3.14
Permanent earnings, 3.17
Pro forma earnings, 3.23
Restructuring charges, 3.18
Single period items, 3.17
Special items, 3.18
Taking a bath, 3.19
Transitory earnings, 3.17
Unusual items, 3.17

APPENDIX 3A: Accruals—Estimates of Expected Future Cash Flows

In this chapter, we illustrated how to prepare a statement of cash flow. Some investment professionals believe that a firm's operating cash flow is the best indicator of firm performance. The mantra goes something like this: Cash is fact, earnings are fiction. Part of this belief is due to the numerous estimates and accounting policy choices inherent in the calculation of net earnings under GAAP. With cash, in contrast, you either have it or you don't have it; there is no middle ground!

Accrual accounting was developed to address certain shortcomings of cash as a performance measure. Stated simply, cash is "lumpy." A measure of firm performance was needed that could smooth out this lumpiness and better measure period-by-period operating performance. Accrual earnings, with its foundation in revenue recognition and expense matching, do just that. A highly stylized example can provide an illustration:

> Just Magazines, Inc sells three-year magazine subscriptions. The company receives the entire $900 purchase price of a subscription at the start of the first year and magazines are then delivered for the following three-year period. The cost of producing and delivering the magazines is exactly one-half of the sales price, or $150 per year. This cost is paid for equally in each of the three years. Now assume that Just Magazines sells only one subscription. On a cash basis the company would show a healthy $750 profit ($900 − $150) in its first year. Unfortunately, the next two years would show losses of $150 each since there would be no cash coming in and only cash going out. So how representative of firm performance is the company's cash flow

in any one year? Imagine that you were an investor looking to buy Just Magazines' stock. What would you think after seeing the first year profits? If you had invested in the company, you would likely end up paying too much for the stock and being quite disappointed with year two and year three performance. As you can see, year one cash flow is a very poor predictor of the operating cash flow in year two or year three.

Now let's redo the example using accrual accounting. The first question is how much revenue should be recorded in the first year? Since Just magazines, Inc. earns revenue by producing and delivering magazines, the answer is $300.[9] The same can be said of years two and three. The next step is to match the expenses with the revenue that has been recognized. This amounts to $150 in each year. Thus, the firm reports net income of $150 each year, in essence smoothing out the lumpiness of the cash flows. Notice that in total, over the three year period, each method reports the exact same operating performance: $450. The difference is all in the timing. But which method provided a better period-by-period measure of performance? And, which measure provided a better prediction of future performance? At least in this example, earnings is the clear winner!

Research has shown that the capital market appears to pay more attention to earnings than operating cash flow since security returns are more highly correlated with earnings than cash flow.[10] Even if earnings were not considered a better measure of periodic firm performance, it is still important to understand how it is derived in order to compute cash flow. Recall that we start with net income in order to compute the cash flow from operations (CFFO) under the indirect format. It is nearly impossible to directly predict a firm's future operating cash flows that are needed for firm valuations. Instead, finance professionals first predict sales, cost of goods sold, inventory needs, etc.; and, they then adjust, much as we did in Chapter 3, to predict the firm's operating cash flow. We now turn our attention to accrual accounting and the income statement to illustrate how net earnings includes estimates of future cash flows.

In Chapter 3, we illustrated how to convert a business' accrual net income to its cash flow from operations using the indirect method format. That conversion process highlights an important aspect of net income—namely, the inclusion of **accruals**, or estimates of *next* period's cash inflows and outflows, in the current period's net income. The accrual basis of accounting utilized in the preparation of the income statement introduces accruals into the measurement of net income, but these accruals are then removed for purposes of preparing a statement of cash flow. An appreciation of accruals is important to fully understand how accounting conventions such as revenue recognition and the matching concept give rise to the all-important concept of net income. Further, a knowledge of accruals facilities an understanding of the behavior of earnings and cash flow over time, and how management might attempt to boost earnings through accruals management.

As discussed in Chapter 2, the accrual basis of accounting enables a business to measure and report its revenue and expenses independent of the cash inflows and outflows associated with its operations. Thus, for instance, a business' revenue is reported as the aggregate of its cash and credit sales transactions. Similarly, a business' expenses may include not only those expenses paid in the current period, but those expenses paid for in a prior period but charged against revenues in the current period, as well as those expenses matched with revenue in the current period but not yet paid for. In general, accruals fall into two categories—operating accruals and non-operating accruals. It is important to keep in mind that accruals simply create timing differences between the recognition of revenues and expenses and the receipt and payment of cash.

Operating Accruals

Operating accruals refer to financial events associated with such operating assets as accounts receivable and inventory and such operating liabilities as accounts payable and income taxes payable. For example, when converting the Russian River Valley's CFFO from the indirect method to the direct method (see Appendix B to Chapter 3), we observed that the company's revenues of $1,900 less the increase in its accounts receivable (ΔAR) of $800 was equal to the amount of cash the winery collected from its customers (i.e. $1,100). Recall also from Chapter 2 that the winery's sale of wine and its collections on accounts receivable were recorded as follows:

---

[9] You may be wondering what to do with the additional $600 in cash received in year one; the $600 is recorded as unearned revenue, a liability account, reflecting the firm's future obligation to deliver the magazine in years two and three.

[10] R. Bowen, G. Biddle, and J. Wallace, "Does EVA beat earnings? Evidence on association with stock returns and firm values," *Journal of Accounting and Economics* (December 1997).

	Assets			=	Liabilities	+	Shareholders' Equity
Event	Cash	Accounts Receivable	Inventory		Accounts Payable		Retained Earnings
Sale of wine	380	1,520					1,900
Cash collection.	720	−720					
	1,100	800					1,900

Stated alternatively,

$$\text{Revenues} = \text{Cash collections from customers} + \Delta AR$$
$$\$1,900 = \$1,100 + \$800$$

This relation highlights the fact that the current period's revenues are equal to the cash collected from sales in the current period plus any increase in the firm's accounts receivable, ΔAR. The change in accounts receivable is an operating accrual and represents management's estimate ($800) of the cash flows it *expects* to collect in the next period from sales transactions that occurred in the *current* period. Of course, if management doesn't really expect to collect all of this cash in the future, then currently reported revenue will be overstated and management is required under GAAP to provide an additional accrual to estimate any future bad debts from these current uncollected receivables. (We will have more to say about the bad debt estimate in Chapter 5.) Similarly, had accounts receivable decreased in the current period, the winery would need to subtract this amount from cash collections to compute revenues. This is because some of the net cash collected in the current period resulted from the collection of cash associated with previously recognized credit sales.

Accruals for revenues are not the only operating accruals included in a company's net income. The conversion process under the direct method also revealed that the Russian River Valley's cost of goods sold less its increase in inventory (ΔI) plus its increase in accounts payable (ΔAP) was equal to its cash payments for inventory. In Chapter 2, we recorded those credit purchases of inventory and payments on accounts for the winery as follows:

	Assets			=	Liabilities	+	Shareholders' Equity
Event	Cash	Accounts Receivable	Inventory		Accounts Payable		Retained Earnings
Purchase inventory on account			380		380		
Payment on account	−360				−360		
Purchase inventory on account			60		60		
Inventory sold.			−380				−380
	−360		60		80		−380

That is,

$$\text{Cost of goods sold} - \Delta I + \Delta AP = \text{Cash payments for inventory}$$
$$-\$380 - \$60 + \$80 = -\$360$$

Rearranging this expression so that cost of goods sold is equal to cash payments for inventory plus the change in inventory (ΔI) less the change in accounts payable (ΔAP) yields the following:

$$\text{Cost of goods sold} = \text{Cash payments for inventory} + \Delta I - \Delta AP$$
$$-\$380 = -\$360 + \$60 - \$80$$

This expression reveals that the current period's cost of goods sold excludes any unsold inventory purchased this period (ΔI) but includes any sold inventory purchased in the current period, as well as any sold inventory not paid for in the current period (ΔAP). Recall from Chapter 2 that the matching concept requires that the current period revenues be matched with the costs incurred to generate those revenues. Thus, the current period cost of good sold excludes the cost of inventory *expected* to be sold next period, as well as the cash that is *expected* to be paid next period for inventory purchases made in the current period. In short, the cost of goods sold includes two accruals, ΔI and ΔAP. Of course, if management doesn't really expect to sell this inventory in the future for at least the amount recorded for inventory, it will have effectively understated its cost of goods sold by including the inventory accrual (ΔI) that it doesn't expect to convert to cash. Management is required under GAAP to provide an additional accrual to estimate this possibility. We will have more to say about this lower-of-cost-or-market accrual for inventory in Chapter 6.

Another operating accrual included in net income is income taxes. The conversion process under the direct method revealed that Russian River Valley's income tax expense plus the increase in its taxes payable (ΔTP) was equal to its cash payment for income taxes. That is,

$$\text{Income tax expense} + \Delta\text{TP} = \text{Cash payments for income taxes}$$
$$-\$240 + \$96 \qquad = \qquad -\$144$$

Rearranging this expression so that the income tax expense is equal to the cash paid for income taxes less the change in taxes payable yields:

$$\text{Income tax expense} = \text{Cash paid for income taxes} - \Delta\text{TP}$$
$$-\$240 \qquad = \qquad -\$144 - \$96$$

Consider now a business whose only expenses are the cost of goods sold and income taxes. For this business, net income will be equal to revenues less cost of goods sold and income taxes, or:

$$\text{Net income} = \text{Revenue} - \text{Cost of goods sold} - \text{Income taxes}$$
$$= \$1,900 - \$380 - \$240$$
$$= \$1,280$$

Using the expressions above for revenue, cost of goods sold, and income taxes, the measurement of net income can be formulated as follows, where each of the changes are increases:

$$\text{Net income} - (\text{Cash collections from customers} + \Delta\text{AR}) - (\text{Cash payments for inventory} - \Delta\text{I} + \Delta\text{AP}) - (\text{Cash payments for income taxes} + \Delta\text{TP})$$

And, after rearranging terms:

$$\text{Net income} = (\text{Cash collections from customers} - \text{cash payments for inventory} - \text{cash payments for income taxes}) + \Delta\text{AR} + \Delta\text{I} - \Delta\text{AP} - \Delta\text{TP}$$
$$= \$1,100 - \$360 - \$144 + \$800 + \$60 - \$80 - \$96$$
$$= \$1,280$$

Since our hypothetical business is relatively simple (for example, there are only two expenses), the cash flow from operations (CFFO) is equal to cash collections from customers less cash payments for inventory and income taxes ($\$1,100 - \$360 - \$144 = \$596$). Hence, the expression for net income can be reformulated as follows:

$$\text{Net income} = \text{CFFO} + \Delta\text{AR} + \Delta\text{I} - \Delta\text{AP} - \Delta\text{TP}$$
$$= \$596 + \$800 + \$60 - \$80 - \$96$$
$$= \$1,280$$

This expression reveals that net income is equal to the cash flow from operations plus the accruals for credit sales (ΔAR), inventory (ΔI), accounts payable (ΔAP), and taxes payable (ΔTP). Since **operating accruals** are defined as the sum of the four accruals, ΔAR, ΔI, ΔAP, and ΔTP, net income becomes:

$$\text{Net income} = \text{CFFO} + \text{Operating accruals}$$
$$= \$596 + \$684$$
$$= \$1{,}280$$

Under the accrual basis of accounting, net income is said to "lead" the CFFO by including the expected net cash flows ($684) associated with the current period earnings that will be collected (less amounts paid) in the following period. On the other hand, the CFFO is said to "lag" net income because it waits until next period to include the net cash flow from the operating accruals when the cash is actually collected. As a performance measure, a company's accounting net income recognizes performance in the period in which it occurs, in this case earlier than does its CFFO, and that difference is what differentiates the accrual basis of accounting used to measure net income from the cash basis of accounting used to measure the cash flow from operations.

Non-Operating Accruals

In the illustration above, our hypothetical firm's net income was the difference between revenues, cost of goods sold, and income taxes; and net income included the four operating accruals ΔAR, ΔI, ΔAP, and ΔTP. But net income can also include non-operating accruals. Exhibit 3.6 in the Chapter 3, for example, reveals that the process of converting net income to the cash flow from operations also involves removing the accruals associated with such non-cash expenses as depreciation and amortization.

If we allow Dep to represent the firm's depreciation expense and Amort to represent the firm's amortization expense, the relationship between net income and the CFFO can be expressed as follows:

$$\text{Net income} - \Delta AR - \Delta I + \Delta AP + \text{Dep} + \text{Amort} + \Delta TP = \text{CFFO}$$
$$\$317 - \$800 - \$60 + \$80 + \$225 + \$50 + \$96 \qquad = \$(92)$$

And, this expression can be rearranged as,

$$\text{Net income} = \text{CFFO} + \Delta AR + \Delta I - \Delta AP - \Delta TP - \text{Dep} - \text{Amort}$$

If operating accruals are now represented by $\Delta AR + \Delta I - \Delta AP - \Delta TP$ and non-operating accruals by Dep + Amort, accrual net income can be expressed as follows:

$$\text{Net income} = \text{CFFO} + \text{operating accruals} - \text{non-operating accruals}$$

Thus, net income includes the cash flows from operation, as well as operating accruals and non-operating accruals. Businesses outlay cash to acquire long-lived assets such as factories, equipment and patents, which are used to produce various products. These long-lived assets generate cash flow over many future periods. Under the accrual basis of accounting, the entire cash outlay for these tangible and intangible assets is not charged against net income in the period of acquisition, but instead is allocated over the many periods that these assets are assumed to produce revenues. Thus, the non-operating accruals of depreciation and amortization are non-cash expenses and represent an allocation of the cost of an asset over the asset's *estimated* economic life. The amount of the asset's cost that is not charged against the current period net income is capitalized on the balance sheet as an asset to be matched against future revenues.

Managerial Discretion and Earnings Management

Because of the inclusion of various operating and non-operating accruals in accrual net income, the current period's net income embodies estimates of net cash flows *expected* in future periods. As a consequence of uncertain economic conditions such as the changing fortunes of a business's credit customers or inventory that becomes obsolete as a consequence of technological change, operating and non-operating accruals are often subject to forecasting error. Thus, a business may outlay more (less) net cash flow next period than was represented by, for example, its operating accruals in the current period, causing net income to be misstated. That does not necessarily mean that the company's management intentionally overestimated (underestimated) operating accruals to boost (reduce) net income. Management may have forecasted in good faith but adverse economic conditions may simply have affected the performance of the business.

To gain a more accurate picture of whether earnings misstatement is intentional or not, it is necessary to be able to measure a "normal" amount of variation in a business' accruals to capture an "abnormal" component that may be due to manipulation. For example, if management expected a decline in sales next period, management might recognize additional revenues by "stuffing the channel" at the end of the year, a practice whereby wholesalers agree to take delivery of a supplier's inventory, usually with a big discount as an inducement.[11] The abnormal increase in the operating accrual ΔAR might reveal the existence of the channel stuffing, and hence, the "management" of the business' revenue and net income. Another strategy might be to reduce the amount of a company's non-operating accruals by lengthening the depreciable life of a company's plant and equipment. Lengthening the depreciable life of an asset lowers the periodic depreciation expense, reducing the non-operating accrual, and increasing net income. We will have more to say about these non-operating discretionary accrual changes in Chapter 7.

Because the preparation of accounting information involves the use of estimates and assumptions involving operating and non-operating accruals, accounting information is subject to the risk of managerial manipulation. The motivation for such actions might involve the incentive contracts designed to motivate executives, risk of technical default on debt covenants, or the considerable external pressures from Wall Street professionals to meet previously identified performance targets (such as earnings estimates). Failure to meet Wall Street expectations can lead to significant share price declines, and thus, some managers have resorted to the manipulation of the operating and non-operating accruals in an effort to avoid this undesirable consequence.

APPENDIX 3B: Converting Indirect Method Cash Flows to Direct Method Cash Flows

Although it is quite straightforward to create a direct method statement of cash flow given access to a company's internal accounting records, such access is rarely available to anyone except a company's management team. The Russian River Valley cash flow statement that appears in Exhibit 2.5 in the previous chapter, for example, is simply a compilation of the cash inflows and outflows reported in the cash column from the Russian River Valley spreadsheet. All that is necessary is to pull the numbers directly off the spreadsheet and place them in the appropriate section of the cash flow statement. This is why, in fact, the direct method is referred to as "direct"—the cash flow from operations is taken directly from the company's accounting records rather than being indirectly computed from net income. Unfortunately, investors and lenders rarely have access to such proprietary internal data. Thus, it is necessary to be able to create direct method cash flow information using only such publicly-available data as the indirect method statement of cash flow.

The process of converting an indirect method statement of cash flow to the direct method requires two steps. First, replace net income (the first line-item under the Operating Activities section of the indirect method statement format) with the key line items appearing on a firm's income statement. For instance, Russian River Valley's income statement in Exhibit 3.5 contains the following key line items (in thousands):

Revenue	$1,900
Cost of goods sold	(380)
Operating expenses	(675)
Interest	(288)
Income taxes	(240)
Net income	$ 317

Thus, for the winery, we begin by replacing the net income of $317 under the Operating Activities section in Exhibit 3.6 with the five key income statement line items shown above, which aggregate to $317.

---

[11] **Bristol-Myers Squibb Co.** admitted to overstating its revenues by $2.5 billion between 1999 and 2001 through the practice of channel stuffing, (*The Wall Street Journal*, July 1, 2005).

The second step involves adjusting the key income statement line items identified in step one with the remaining line items from the Operating Activities section of the indirect method statement of cash flow. Using Russian River Valley's data in Exhibit 3.6, those adjustments would appear as follows:

Income Statement Line Items		Operating Activities Line Items	Direct Method Cash Flow	
Revenues	$1,900	Less $800 Accounts receivable	Cash collections from customers	$1,100
Cost of goods sold	(380)	Less $60 Inventory Add $80 Accounts payable	Cash paid for inventory	(360)
Operating expenses	(675)	Add $225 Depreciation Add $50 Amortization	Cash paid for operating expenses	(400)
Interest	(288)	(no adjustment required)	Cash paid for interest	(288)
Income taxes	(240)	Add $96 Taxes payable	Cash paid for income taxes	(144)
Net income	$ 317		Cash flow from operations	$ (92)

Exhibit 3A.1 presents the winery's direct method statement of cash flow after undertaking the above two steps. As expected, the direct method CFFO of negative $92 is exactly equivalent to the indirect method CFFO of negative $92 as reported in Exhibit 3.6. Note that the CFFI and CFFF are exactly the same in both Exhibit 3.6 and Exhibit 3A.1. The only difference between the two exhibits is the manner in which the CFFO is calculated. In Exhibit 3.6, the CFFO is calculated by beginning with net income and then adjusting for various non-cash expenses (e.g., depreciation and amortization), as well as adjusting for the changes in the various working capital accounts (e.g., accounts receivable, inventory, accounts payable, and taxes payable). In Exhibit 3A.1, net income is replaced with the key income statement line items and the non-cash expenses and working capital adjustments are disaggregated to the individual line items. But in each case, the CFFO total remains the same.

EXHIBIT 3A.1	Statement of Cash Flow: The Direct Method

Russian River Valley Winery, Inc. Statement of Cash Flow ($ thousands)	Year 1
Operating activities	
Cash from customer collections	$ 1,100
Cash paid for inventory	(360)
Cash paid for operating expenses.	(400)
Cash paid for interest.	(288)
Cash paid for income taxes.	(144)
Cash flow from operations	(92)
Investing Activities	
Purchase of property, plant & equipment	(3,500)
Cash flow from investing	(3,500)
Financing Activities	
Sale of common stock.	400
Payment of notes payable (current).	(480)
Payment of common stock dividends	(260)
Cash flow from financing.	(340)
Net cash flow	(3,932)
Change in cash (on balance sheet).	$(3,932)

DISCUSSION QUESTIONS

Q3.1   **Building Shareholder Value.**   Describe at least three ways that corporate managers can build shareholder value (increase their firm's share price). Rank-order the various managerial actions you identified according to their effectiveness in building shareholder value. Be prepared to justify your rank-ordering.

Q3.2   **Litigation, Reported Income and Share Price.**   In early 2006, Merck AG, a global pharmaceutical company, saw its share price decline dramatically after a jury in the United States found the company guilty of failing to warn consumers about safety issues surrounding one of the company's products, a pain-killer drug called *Vioxx.* Although Merck was found not guilty in one case involving a plaintiff who died while taking the drug, the company was found guilty in a second case, with the court awarding the survivors of the deceased plaintiff $4.5 million in compensatory damages. At the time of the trial, over 5,000 separate *Vioxx*-related lawsuits had been filed against Merck. Discuss how Merck should disclose the $4.5 million lawsuit award in its 2006 annual report. How should Merck disclose the 5,000 pending lawsuits in its 2005 financial statements <u>before</u> the court case was decided against the company? How should Merck report the pending *Vioxx*-related lawsuits in its 2006 annual report?

Q3.3   **Basic versus Diluted Earnings per Share.**   In 2005, Pfizer, Inc. reported that its basic earnings per share would be $1.11 per share while its diluted earnings per share would be $1.08 per share. Discuss the factors that might cause the number of shares used in the calculation of earnings per share to increase, and thus, cause diluted earnings per share (EPS) to be less than basic earnings per share. Which measure do you feel is most important to shareholders—basic EPS or diluted EPS? Why?

Q3.4   **Assessing the Quality of Reported Earnings using Cash Flow Data.**   Although much of the work of an equity analyst involves quantitative analysis, some analysts also engage in various qualitative analyses to help them assess the persistence of a firm's current earnings. Consider, for example, the case of Blockbuster Entertainment Corporation. In 1989, Lee J. Seidler, a senior analyst with Bear, Stearns & Co., issued a research report critical of Blockbuster's earnings. Mr. Seidler observed that although Blockbuster's 1988 net income was $15.5 million and its cash flow from operating activities $48.4 million, his review of the firm's cash flow data revealed that Blockbuster's purchases of new videocassette rental inventory had been classified as an "investing activity" rather than as an "operating activity" on the company's statement of cash flow. Presented below is selected financial statement information for Blockbuster:

(in millions)	1988	1987
Net income.	$15.5	$4.09
Cash flow from operations.	48.3	10.3
Purchases of videocassette rental inventory	(51.3)	(14.3)

Discuss how the statement of cash flow can be used to help evaluate the quality of a company's reported earnings. Describe how Blockbuster's cash flow data can be used to illustrate this. Do you agree with Blockbuster's decision to classify its videocassette inventory purchases as an "investing activity"? Why or why not? How does Blockbuster's cash flow classification of its video inventory purchases affect its cash flow from operations?

Q3.5   **Earnings Announcements and Share Prices.**   In April 2006, Alcoa, Inc., the world's largest aluminum company, reported its highest quarterly income in the company's history. Alcoa's earnings per share increased by more than 100 percent from $0.30 per share in 2004 to $0.69 per share in 2005. In response to the announcement, the company's share price rose over six percent, or an increase of $2.00 per share. On the same day, the Shaw Group, Inc., an engineering company, also reported an 100 percent increase in earnings per share, from $0.14 per share a year earlier to $0.31 per share in 2005. The Shaw Group's share price, however, fell $1.97 per share, or six percent. Discuss why the earnings announcement of Alcoa led to a share price increase and why the earnings announcement of the Shaw Group might have led to its share price decline.

Q3.6 **Managing Earnings.** Some members of the financial community allege that corporate managers "manage" their company's reported accounting results. Discuss the possible motivations behind this behavior. Can you envision a situation where a manager might manage a company's earnings downward? If so, why?

Q3.7 **Goodwill Impairment and Sustainable Earnings.** In 2002, the FASB adopted Statement of Financial Accounting Standard No. 142. Under SFAS No. 142, the amortization of goodwill is no longer required, and instead, goodwill is subject to an annual impairment test to verify that its value has not declined. If a decline in value is observed, the goodwill account is written down and an "impairment loss" is recorded on the income statement.

On February 27, 2006, **Vodafone**, a United Kingdom-based mobile telecommunications company, announced that it would write off $49 billion of goodwill associated with its $192 billion acquisition of Germany's Mannesmann AG. Vodafone's share price dropped three percent following the news announcement. At the time of the impairment announcement, the company's market capitalization was $140 billion while its book value was $202 billion.

Discuss how Vodafone will account for the goodwill write-down in its financial statements. How will the impairment charge affect the firm's book value? How will the impairment charge impact the firm's sustainable earnings? Why was the firm's market capitalization less than its book value?

Q3.8 **Special Charges.** On September 11, 2001, two American Airlines aircraft were hijacked and destroyed in terrorist attacks on The World Trade Center in New York City and the Pentagon in northern Virginia. As a consequence of these actions, **AMR Corporation**, the parent company of American Airlines, concluded that its fleet of aircraft had become impaired, and consequently, took a special charge of $718 million against 2001 net income and an additional $1,466 million charge against 2002 net income.

Discuss how these special charges will be reflected in AMR's financial statements? Given the unusual circumstances associated with these charges, could they be considered extraordinary? Why or why not? Will these charges be included in the company's sustainable earnings? Why or why not?

Q3.9 **New Accounting Standard.** Effective January 1, 2002, the FASB required the implementation of Statement of Financial Accounting Standard No. 142, "Goodwill and Other Intangible Assets" (SFAS No. 142). SFAS No. 142 requires that a company annually evaluate the value of its goodwill and indefinite-lived intangible assets for impairment. During 2002, **AMR Corporation**, the parent company of American Airlines and American Eagle, adopted SFAS No. 142 and conducted an impairment test of its existing goodwill. Based on this test, AMR Corporation concluded that its entire balance of $1.4 billion of goodwill had been impaired. Consequently, at year-end 2002, the company recorded a one-time, non-cash charge to write off all of its goodwill. The charge-off of AMR's goodwill was reported as a "cumulative effect of accounting change" in the amount of $988 million, net of the related income tax effect of $412 million, on its consolidated statement of earnings.

Discuss AMR's treatment of its goodwill impairment charge. Do you agree with the disclosure adopted by the company? Why or why not? How will the impairment affect the firm's future sustainable earnings?

Q3.10 **Market Capitalization, Book Value, and Intrinsic Value.** Discuss the concepts of book value, intrinsic value, and market capitalization. Using a financial website such as **Yahoo.Finance** or **MSN.Money**, identify the market capitalization and book value of **The Procter and Gamble Company**. Calculate the difference between these values. Why do these measures differ in value?

Q3.11 **Accounting Statement Restatements.** According to *CFO Magazine* (April, 2006), the number of companies that issued corrections to their financial statements hit a new high in 2005. A total of 1,195 U.S. public companies, or about 8.5 percent of the total, filed financial statement restatements in 2005. That amount was approximately twice the total restatements (613) filed in 2004. The major types of accounting restatements for the period 2003 to 2005 were identified as follows:

Number of Restatements	2003	2004	2005
Lease accounting	23	22	249
Stock option accounting	30	39	71
Hedge accounting	13	25	57

Discuss why the number of financial statement restatements increased so dramatically from 2004 to 2005. Discuss how and why the capital markets respond to financial statement restatements?

Q3.12 **(Ethics Perspective) Earnings Management to Prevent Technical Defaults.** Earnings management may be used to avoid a technical default of a covenant under a loan agreement. Loan covenants are written into loan agreements in order to protect a lender from various actions that a borrower might undertake. These covenants often require attainment of certain target financial ratios calculated using reported GAAP numbers. Failing to achieve these minimum target ratios, and hence falling into technical default, can be very costly to a firm. Earnings management to prevent a technical default will likely save a corporation and its shareholders from experiencing a large loss in market value, without necessarily providing any direct personal benefit to the company's managers. Is earnings management to avoid a loan covenant violation an ethical breach by management?

⊘ **indicates that check figures are available on the book's Website.**

EXERCISES

E3.13 **Classifying Accounting Events.** Presented below is a list of accounting events for the Longo Corporation. Classify each of the events as an Operating (O) activity event, an Investing (I) activity event, a Financing (F) activity event, or as none-of-the-above (N).
1. Sale of common stock for cash
2. Collection of cash on accounts receivable
3. Purchase of equipment for cash
4. Sale of inventory on credit
5. Borrowed cash from a bank
6. Payment of a cash dividend
7. Payment of utility expense using cash
8. Purchase of land using bank financing
9. Repurchase of previously issued stock using cash
10. Cash payment of interest on a bank loan

⊘ E3.14 **Classifying Accounting Transactions.** Presented below is a list of accounting transactions for the Davis Company. Classify each of the transactions as an Operating (O) activity transaction, an Investing (I) activity transaction, a Financing (F) activity transaction, or as none-of-the-above (N).

1. Purchase of machinery for cash
2. Cash payment on loan principal
3. Collection of cash on outstanding accounts receivable
4. Payment of a stock dividend
5. Sale of preferred stock for cash
6. Prepaid the office rent for six months
7. Cash payment of income tax expense
8. Sale of land held as an investment for cash
9. Declared (but did not pay) a cash dividend
10. Purchased treasury stock using cash

E3.15 **Classifying Accounting Transactions.** Presented below is a list of accounting transactions for The Mila Corporation. Classify each of the transactions as an Operating (O) activity transaction, an Investing (I) activity transaction, a Financing (F) activity transaction, or as none-of-the-above (N).

1. Purchased machinery using cash
2. Sold common stock for cash in an initial public offering
3. Converted a bond payable into common stock
4. Sold inventory for cash
5. Paid interest expense on a bank loan
6. Purchased a building using a cash down payment and by issuing a note payable for the remainder
7. Paid employee wages
8. Paid a cash dividend
9. Repurchased common stock for cash
10. Exchanged land for a new plant

E3.16 **Analyzing Cash Flow Data.** Presented below is cash flow information for two competitors—The Longo Corporation and The Davis Company (amounts in thousands):

| Company | Operating Profit | Cash Flow From | | |
		Operations	Investing	Financing
Longo Corporation......................	$(6,050)	$(1,320)	$ (693)	$ 415
Davis Company	(2,980)	(3,260)	1,502	1,809

Describe the cash management strategy of each company by identifying the key sources and uses of cash by each firm. Explain why the cash flow from operations of The Longo Corporation differs from the company's operating loss of $6,050. Calculate the change in the cash balance for The Davis Company.

E3.17 **Analyzing Cash Flow Data.** Presented below is cash flow information for two competitors—**Pfizer, Inc.** and **The Johnson and Johnson Company** (amounts in millions):

| Company | Operating Profit | Cash Flow From | | |
		Operations	Investing	Financing
Pfizer, Inc.	$ 8,085	$14,733	$(5,072)	$(9,222)
Johnson and Johnson	10,411	11,877	(279)	(4,521)

Describe the cash management strategy of each company by identifying the key sources and uses of cash by each firm. Calculate the change in the cash balance for each firm. Explain why the cash flow from operations for Pfizer, Inc. of $14,733 is greater than its operating profit of $8,085.

E3.18 **Income Statement Classification.** Net income for Global Enterprises, Inc. for the year just ended was $20 million. There is some debate, however, about the income statement classification of certain events that could be considered material. Global Enterprises manufacturers and distributes a line of automobile after-market products which are sold through Checker Auto Parts. The events that follow all occurred or were recognized during the year just ended:

1. A fire destroyed a warehouse in Ohio. The loss was $5 million, half of which was covered by insurance.
2. The company completed a contract that produced $2.5 million in profit. The company hopes to bid on similar contracts in the future but is unsure whether there will be future opportunities.

3. An order of batteries for a West Coast auto parts chain was found to be defective and was returned and scrapped. The loss on the order was $500,000. The company gave the customer a discount of $100,000 on future orders in hopes of maintaining the business relationship.

4. The company spent $2 million on the development of an internet website to be used to sell parts online. The website has an expected useful life of 24 months.

5. To ensure the availability of its merchandise, the company made an investment in several European auto parts suppliers. An opportunity arose to sell one of those investments at a substantial gain. The company received $8 million in cash, realized a $4 million gain, and invested the entire proceeds in a new supplier who was just beginning operations in Mexico.

6. A loan to a manufacturer of car radios was written off this year. It had been clear for some time that the $3 million note receivable was worthless, but the radio manufacturer was part of a complex of companies, some of whom were important customers to Global Enterprises. Global's CEO elected not to press the company for payment for fear of alienating the other companies in the group. But now Global Enterprises forced the hand of the radio producer, pushing it into bankruptcy.

Indicate how each event should be reported on the income statement of Global Enterprises, Inc. (i.e., as an special, extraordinary, or ordinary item) and whether it should be reflected in the current year's income statement, next year's income statement, or in a prior year's income statement (e.g., as a prior period adjustment).

E3.19 **Calculating Earnings per Share.** During 2006, Mayfair Enterprises had the following securities outstanding:

1. 250,000 shares of common stock with an average market price of $25 per share.
2. Convertible preferred stock, which had been sold at its par value of $100. The preferred stock is convertible into three shares of common stock and 3,000 preferred shares are currently outstanding.

During 2006, Mayfair Enterprises earned net income after income taxes of $3.2 million. Calculate the (a) basic earnings per share and (b) diluted earnings per share for Mayfair Enterprises for 2006.

⊘ E3.20 **Calculating Earnings per Share.** Little, Inc. reported earnings of $159,000 for 2006, and at the end of the year, had the following securities outstanding:

1. 60,000 shares of common stock. (The year-end share price was $25 per share.)
2. Employee stock options for the purchase of 8,000 common shares at an exercise price of $22 per share. (The options are fully vested.)

Calculate the (a) basic earnings per share and (b) diluted earnings per share for Little, Inc. for 2006.

E3.21 **Analyzing Cash Flow and Earnings Data.** Consider the financial statement data for Casual Clothing Inc. presented in Problem 3.28. Consider also the statement of cash flows that you prepared as part of Problem 3.28.

1. Calculate the following ratios for Casual Clothing Inc.
   a. Operating funds ratio
   b. Operating cash flow-to-current liabilities ratio
   c. Cash conversion ratio
2. Calculate the following alternative measures of cash flow:
   a. Earnings before interest, taxes, depreciation and amortization (EBITDA)
   b. Free cash flow
   c. Discretionary cash flow
3. What can you conclude about the cash flow health of Casual Clothing Inc. from your answers above?

E3.22   **Permanent versus Transitory Earnings.**   Entrust, Inc. is a global provider of security software; it operates in one business segment involving the design, production, and sale of software products for securing digital identities and information. Presented below are the consolidated statements of operations for the period 2002 to 2004 (all values in thousands). On January 1, 2002, the Entrust common shares traded at $10.40 per share; by year-end 2004, the shares traded at $3.80 per share. The company's cash flow from operations was $(27,411), $(20,908), and $9,606, for 2002, 2003, and 2004, respectively.

Calculate the permanent earnings of Entrust, Inc. for each of the three years. Compare the company's reported net income (loss) with its permanent earnings. Does Entrust's share price at year-end 2004 reflect the firm's apparent turn-around? Why or why not?

Entrust, Inc. Consolidated Statements of Operations			
Year Ended December 31 ($ thousands)	**2004**	**2003**	**2002**
Revenues			
Product	$29,295	$ 30,974	$ 44,734
Services and maintenance.	61,662	56,920	58,013
Total revenues	90,957	87,894	102,747
Cost of Revenues			
Product	4,149	5,341	5,281
Services and maintenance.	29,105	29,825	32,073
Amortization of purchased product rights	384	568	1,136
Total cost of revenues	33,638	35,734	38,490
Gross profit.	57,319	52,160	64,257
Operating expenses			
Sales and marketing	26,322	34,985	44,128
Research and development.	17,266	22,566	24,151
General and administrative	12,569	13,143	14,840
Impairment of purchased product rights	—	1,134	—
Restructuring charges and adjustments	—	13,623	(1,079)
Total operating expenses	56,157	85,451	82,040
Income (loss) from operations	1,162	(33,291)	(17,783)
Other income (expense)			
Interest income	1,281	1,680	3,346
Foreign exchange gain (loss)	429	(431)	(72)
Loss from equity investments	(1,111)	(603)	(602)
Realized loss on investments	—	—	(220)
Write-down of long-term strategic investments	—	(2,780)	(1,238)
Total other income (expense)	599	(2,134)	1,214
Income (loss) before income taxes and minority interest.	1,761	(35,425)	(16,569)
Minority interest in subsidiary.	4	—	—
Income (loss) before income taxes.	1,765	(35,425)	(16,569)
Provision for income taxes	687	441	1,350
Net income (loss)	$ 1,078	$(35,866)	$(17,919)

E3.23 **Converting Indirect Method Cash Flows to Direct Method Cash Flows (Appendix B).** The Miller Corporation disclosed the following statement of earnings in its 2005 annual report (amounts in thousands):

Earnings Statement	
	2005
Revenues	$1,430
Cost of goods sold.	(500)
Gross margin	930
Selling, general and administrative expenses	(200)
Operating income.	730
Unusual gain on sale of land	70
Net income.	$ 800

In addition, the company reported the following data regarding its operating cash flow in its year-end statement of cash flow (amounts in thousands):

Statement of Cash Flow	
(Indirect Method)	**2005**
Operating Activities	
Net income.	$800
Depreciation and amortization expense	260
Accounts receivable.	(150)
Inventory	(15)
Accounts payable	50
Gain on sale of land.	(70)
Cash flow from operating activities	$905

Using the above information for 2005, construct the Miller Company's cash flow from operating activities on a direct method basis.

E3.24 **Measuring Sustainable Earnings.** **Harnishfeger Corporation** was a mining machinery and equipment company based in Wisconsin. The company voluntarily changed its depreciation accounting policy from the accelerated method to the straight-line method. It disclosed the cumulative effect of this accounting policy change, equal to $11.005 million (net of applicable income taxes), in its financial statements. In addition, the company also voluntarily changed the estimated useful lives of certain of its U.S. plant and equipment. This estimate change increased its pretax reported profit by $3.2 million. The following are selected excerpts from the company's financial statements:

	(in thousands)
Income before income taxes, equity items, and cumulative effect of accounting method change.	$ 5,738
Provision for income taxes.	(2,425)
Income after taxes	3,313
Equity items	858
Cumulative effect of change in depreciation method	11,005
Net income.	$15,176

Calculate Harnishfeger's sustainable earnings. How would the capital market react to the company's decision to change its depreciation accounting policy and to change the estimated useful lives of its depreciable assets? Why?

PROBLEMS

P3.25 **Statement of Cash Flow.** Presented below are the financial statements for the Amphlett Corporation, as of year-end 2005 and 2006.

Amphlett Corporation Consolidated Balance Sheets		
As of Year-End ($ thousands)	**2005**	**2006**
Assets		
Current		
Cash.	$ 90,000	$ 15,000
Marketable securities.	—	200,000
Accounts receivable (net).	440,000	590,000
Inventory	615,000	600,000
Total current assets	1,145,000	1,405,000
Noncurrent		
Long-term investments	390,000	310,000
Property & equipment	1,100,000	1,800,000
Less: Accumulated depreciation	(500,000)	(500,000)
Property & equipment (net)	600,000	1,300,000
Intangibles (net)	105,000	95,000
Total noncurrent assets	1,095,000	1,705,000
Total assets.	$2,240,000	$3,110,000
Liabilities & Shareholders' Equity		
Accounts payable	$ 850,000	$ 900,000
Short-term bank debt	—	190,000
Total liabilities	850,000	1,090,000
Shareholders' equity		
Common stock, $10 par value.	675,000	775,000
Additional paid-in-capital.	300,000	380,000
Retained earnings	415,000	865,000
Total shareholders' equity	1,390,000	2,020,000
Total liabilities & shareholders' equity	$2,240,000	$3,110,000

Amphlett Corporation Consolidated Income Statement		
For Year Ended ($ thousands)	2005	2006
Revenues	$1,200,000	$1,430,000
Less: Cost of goods sold	420,000	500,000
Gross margin	780,000	930,000
Less: Selling, general & administrative expenses	120,000	150,000
Operating income.	660,000	780,000
Gain on sale of investments.	—	70,000
Net income before taxes	660,000	850,000
Less: Income taxes	11,000	50,000
Net income after taxes.	$ 649,000	$ 800,000

The footnotes to the Amphlett Corporation's financial statements revealed the following additional information:

1. Property and equipment costing $450 million was sold for its book value of $200 million.
2. Long-term investments were sold for $150 million, which included a gain of $70 million.

Required
Using the above financial data for the Amphlett Corporation, prepare the firm's statement of cash flow for 2006 using the indirect method.

⊘ P3.26 **Statement of Cash Flow.** Presented below are the consolidated financial statements of The Mann Corporation as of year-end 2005 and 2006.

The Mann Corporation Consolidated Balance Sheets		
As of Year-End ($ thousands)	2005	2006
Assets		
Current assets		
Cash.	$ 250,000	$ 400,000
Accounts receivable (net).	760,000	990,000
Inventory	400,000	710,000
Prepaid expenses	100,000	100,000
Total current assets	1,510,000	2,200,000
Investments in affiliate companies.	—	100,000
Property and equipment.	800,000	1,310,000
Less: Accumulated depreciation	(80,000)	(110,000)
Property & equipment (net).	720,000	1,200,000
Total assets.	$2,230,000	$3,500,000

continued

continued from previous page

The Mann Corporation Consolidated Balance Sheets		
As of Year-End ($ thousands)	**2005**	**2006**
Liabilities & Shareholders' Equity		
Current liabilities		
Accounts payable	$ 500,000	$ 570,000
Accrued expenses payable	220,000	200,000
Dividends payable	—	70,000
Total current liabilities.	720,000	840,000
Note payable—due in ten years.	—	500,000
Total liabilities	720,000	1,340,000
Shareholders' equity		
Common stock ($5 par value)	200,000	300,000
Additional paid-in-capital.	1,160,000	1,200,000
Retained earnings	150,000	660,000
Total shareholders' equity	1,510,000	2,160,000
Total liabilities & shareholders' equity	$2,230,000	$3,500,000

The Mann Corporation Consolidated Income Statement		
For Year Ended ($ thousands)	**2005**	**2006**
Sales.	$12,000,000	$16,800,000
Cost of goods sold.	10,400,000	14,000,000
Gross margin	1,600,000	2,800,000
Selling & administrative expenses	1,048,000	1,930,000
Depreciation expense.	20,000	30,000
Income tax expense.	152,000	240,000
Net Income.	$ 380,000	$ 600,000

Required

Using the above financial data, prepare the statement of cash flow for 2006 using the indirect method.

P3.27   **Statement of Cash Flow.**   Presented below are the condensed financial statements for the Grand Canyon Company for 2005 and 2006.

Grand Canyon Company Condensed Balance Sheet	2006	2005
Assets		
Cash and cash equivalents	$ 104	$ 147
Accounts receivables (net).	912	693
Inventories	1,750	1,670
Land.	81	66
Building and equipment (net).	2,928	2,572
Long-term investments	103	85
Other assets and goodwill (net)	220	146
Total assets.	$6,098	$5,379
Liabilities & Shareholders' Equity		
Accounts payables & accrued expenses.	$1,067	$ 790
Income tax payable	198	133
Notes payable	430	404
Deferred income tax	23	(24)
Long-term debt	948	1,011
Total liabilities	2,666	2,314
Shareholders' Equity		
Common stock	180	177
Retained earnings	3,252	2,888
Total Liabilities & Shareholders' Equity	$6,098	$5,379

Grand Canyon Company Condensed Income Statement	2006	2005
Sales.	$8,598	$7,738
Cost of goods sold*	(6,957)	(6,262)
Other operating expenses	(844)	(760)
Income tax expenses.	(232)	(209)
Total expenses	(8,033)	(7,231)
Net income.	$ 565	$ 507
* Depreciation expense (included in Cost-of-Goods Sold)	$370	$303

Required

Using the above financial data, prepare the firm's statement of cash flow for 2006 using the indirect method.

⊘ P3.28   **Statement of Cash Flow.**   Presented below are the consolidated financial statements of Casual Clothing, Inc.

Casual Clothing Inc. Consolidated Balance Sheet		
	2006	2005
Assets		
Current Assets		
Cash and cash equivalents	$ 8,794	$ 7,352
Merchandise inventory.	94,153	42,045
Accounts receivable (net).	25,700	17,800
Other current assets	35,103	25,393
Total current assets	163,750	92,590
Noncurrent Assets		
Buildings, furniture & equipment (net)	1,826,863	1,658,990
Land.	2,279,946	1,458,832
Construction-in-process	615,722	414,725
Intangibles (net)	9,780	6,700
Total assets.	$4,896,061	$3,631,837
Liabilities & Shareholders' Equity		
Current liabilities		
Notes payable	$ 779,904	$ 176,884
Current maturities of long-term debt.	250,000	350,000
Accounts payable	167,207	185,945
Accrued expenses & other liabilities	384,209	351,710
Income taxes payable	17,824	26,263
Total current liabilities.	1,599,144	1,090,802
Long-term liabilities		
Long-term debt	880,216	780,925
Total liabilities	2,479,360	1,871,727
Shareholders' Equity		
Common stock ($.05 par value).	146,961	146,961
Additional paid-in-capital.	1,294,967	1,294,967
Retained earnings	974,773	318,182
Total shareholders' equity	2,416,701	1,760,110
Total liabilities & shareholders' equity	$4,896,061	$3,631,837

Casual Clothing, Inc. Consolidated Statement of Earnings	
	2006
Net sales.	$13,673,460
Costs & expenses	
Costs of goods sold.	8,599,442
Operating expenses.	3,629,257
Interest expense (net).	62,876
	12,291,575
Earnings before income taxes	1,381,885
Income taxes	504,388
Net earnings.	$ 877,497

Note: In 2006, amortization expense for intangibles was $2,700 and depreciation expense for buildings, furniture & equipment was $123,000.

Required

Using the above financial data, prepare the statement of cash flow for 2006 for Casual Clothing, Inc. using the indirect method.

P3.29 **Statement of Cash Flow.** The following financial data were taken from the records of the Thomas Magnum Company.

Thomas Magnum Company Balance Sheet Data		
	2005	**2006**
Assets		
Cash.	$ 2,800	$ 12,000
Accounts receivable (net).	27,000	24,000
Inventory	19,600	9,000
Prepaid insurance	2,400	1,800
Total current assets	51,800	46,800
Building (net)	75,000	76,000
Total assets.	$126,800	$122,800
Liabilities & Shareholders' Equity		
Accounts payable	$ 26,200	$ 25,200
Wages payable	14,800	19,000
Total current liabilities.	41,000	44,200
Bonds payable.	34,000	34,000
Total liabilities	75,000	78,200
Capital stock	30,000	30,000
Retained earnings	21,800	14,600
Total shareholders' equity	51,800	44,600
Total liabilities & shareholders' equity	$126,800	$122,800

Thomas Magnum Company Income Statement: 2006	
Revenues	$192,000
Cost of goods sold.	128,000
Gross margin	64,000
Depreciation expense.	11,400
Insurance expense	18,400
Interest expense.	4,200
Wage expense	37,200
Net income (loss)	$ (7,200)

Required

Using the financial data for the Thomas Magnum Company, prepare the statement of cash flow using the indirect method.

P3.30 **Statement of Cash Flow.** The following financial data were taken from the Catalina Divers Supply Company for the year ended December 31, 2006.

Catalina Divers Supply Company Balance Sheet Data		
	2006	**2005**
Assets		
Cash.	$ 12,000	$ 10,800
Accounts receivable (net).	22,400	18,000
Inventory	30,000	31,200
Prepaid rent	2,400	3,600
Total current assets	66,800	63,600
Equipment (net)	116,000	104,000
Total Assets	$182,800	$167,600
Liabilities & Shareholders' equity		
Accounts payable	$ 22,400	$ 29,200
Wages payable	18,000	13,600
Interest payable	3,000	4,400
Deferred revenue	13,000	9,400
Total current liabilities.	56,400	56,600
Bank loan.	56,000	56,800
Total liabilities	112,400	113,400
Capital stock	20,000	20,000
Retained earnings	50,400	34,200
Total Shareholders' equity	70,400	54,200
Total Liabilities & Shareholders' equity	$182,800	$167,600

Catalina Divers Supply Company Income Statement For the Year Ended December 31, 2006	
Revenues	$218,200
Cost of goods sold	112,000
Gross margin	106,200
Wage expense	30,400
Rent expense	18,000
Interest expense.	5,800
Depreciation expense.	12,400
Loss on sale of equipment	8,400
Net income before income taxes	31,200
Income tax expense	8,800
Net income.	$ 22,400

Required

Using the above data, prepare the 2006 statement of cash flow for Catalina Divers Supply Company using the indirect method.

P3.31 **Analyzing and Interpreting Cash Flow Data: A Growing Enterprise.**   Presented below are cash flow data for **L.A. Gear Inc.** During this period of time, the manufacturer of athletic shoes and sportswear experienced a 1200 percent growth in net income.

L.A. Gear Inc. Statement of Cash Flow			
(in thousands)	Year 1	Year 2	Year 3
Cash flow from operations			
Net income.	$ 4,371	$22,030	$55,059
Depreciation	133	446	1,199
Noncash compensation to employees.	—	—	558
Increase in accounts receivable.	(12,410)	(34,378)	(51,223)
Increase in inventories	(1,990)	(50,743)	(72,960)
Increase in prepayments	(599)	(2,432)	(8,624)
Increase in accounts payable.	1,656	7,197	17,871
Increase (Decrease) in other current			
Liabilities.	(537)	11,193	10,587
Cash flow from operations.	(9,376)	(46,687)	(47,533)
Cash flow from investing			
Sale of marketable securities	5,661	—	—
Acquisition of property, plant & equip.	(874)	(2,546)	(6,168)
Acquisition of other noncurrent assets.	(241)	(406)	(246)
Cash flow from investing	4,546	(2,952)	(6,414)
Cash flow from financing			
Increase (Decrease) in short-term borrowing	4,566	50,104	(19,830)
Issue of common stock	—	495	69,925
Cash flow from financing	4,566	50,599	50,095
Change in cash.	$ (264)	$ 960	$ (3,852)

Required

1. Explain why the cash flow from operations is negative.
2. How did the company finance its operations during the three year period? Explain the logic of this strategy.
3. Depreciation expense as a percent of net income is only two to three percent during this period? What might explain this?

P3.32 **Analyzing and Interpreting Cash Flow Data: A Failing Enterprise.** **L.A. Gear,** a manufacturer of sports shoes and sportswear, began operations in the early 1980s. By late 1996, however, the company was in bankruptcy. Presented below are cash flow data for the company for the period 1995–1996.

L.A. Gear Inc. **Consolidated Statements of Cash Flow**		
($ thousands)	**1995**	**1996**
Operating activities		
Net loss	$(51,397)	$(61,689)
Adjustments to reconcile net loss to net cash provided by (used in) operating activities		
Depreciation and amortization	7,266	4,555
Minority interest in net loss of joint venture	(1,324)	(6,986)
Loss on sale or abandonment of property and equipment . .	417	77
Increase in reserve for unused barter credits.	4,568	—
Write-off of goodwill	1,012	8,324
Unrealized foreign exchange gain	(570)	—
(Increase) decrease, net of effects of acquisitions, in		
Accounts receivable, net	30,603	20,581
Inventories	6,100	18,095
Prepaid expenses & other current assets.	3,320	1,507
Other assets	1,624	(12)
Increase (decrease), net of effects of acquisitions, in		
Accounts payable & accrued liabilities.	(12,831)	16,166
Net cash provided by (used in) operating activities	(11,212)	618
Investing activities		
Capital expenditures	(3,256)	(710)
Net cash used in investing activities	(3,256)	(710)
Financing activities		
Costs related to issuance of Series B Shares	—	(661)
Net (repayments) borrowings under international credit facilities	622	(1,216)
Net cash (used in) provided by financing activities	622	(1,817)
Effect of exchange rate changes on cash & cash equivalents. . . .	92	252
Net (decrease) increase in cash & cash equivalents	(13,754)	(1,717)
Cash & cash equivalents at beginning of year	49,710	35,956
Cash & cash equivalents at end of year.	$ 35,956	$ 34,239

Required

Explain how L.A. Gear generated cash to sustain its operations during the period prior to its bankruptcy filing. What other financing options were available to the company?

P3.33   **Statement of Cash Flow: International.**   Presented below are recent financial statements for The Hoechst Group, a German conglomerate with operations in agriculture, chemicals, pharmaceuticals, and veterinary products:

The Hoechst Group Consolidated Balance Sheet (in millions of Deutsche Marks)		
	Year 2	Year 1
Intangible assets	15,077	15,200
Property, plant & equipment.	12,958	15,861
Investments	7,336	7,562
Non-current assets.	35,371	38,623
Inventories	5,507	6,739
Receivables & prepaid items	14,630	14,908
Liquid assets	391	635
Current assets	20,528	22,282
Total assets.	55,899	60,905
Equity of Hoechst AG stockholders.	16,599	16,012
Minority interests	2,580	3,097
Stockholders' equity	19,179	19,109
Provisions for pensions & similar obligations.	6,883	6,910
Other provisions.	8,751	9,476
Provisions.	15,634	16,386
Corporate debt.	12,509	16,165
Liabilities & deferred income	8,577	8,795
Total stockholders' equity & liabilities	55,899	60,905

The Hoechst Group Consolidated Statement of Profit & Loss (in millions of Deutsche Marks)		
	Year 2	Year 1
Net sales.	43,704	52,100
Cost of goods sold.	(25,533)	(31,533)
Gross profit.	18,171	20,567
Distribution & selling costs.	(8,940)	(10,206)
Research & development costs	(3,820)	(3,990)
General & administrative costs.	(2,680)	(2,808)
Other operating income	2,331	1,834
Other operating expense	(1,891)	(1,744)
Operating profit	3,171	3,653
Result on sale & transfer of business.	64	304
Investment income, net	1,062	309
Interest expense, net	(1,037)	(1,019)
Other financial expense, net.	(157)	(90)
Profit before taxes on income	3,103	3,157
Taxes on income	(944)	(1,383)
Income before minority interests	2,159	1,774
Minority interests	(264)	(431)
Net income.	1,895	1,343

The following additional information was contained in the company's footnotes:

1. Depreciation expense of 2,190 in Year 2 was included in the cost of goods sold.
2. Amortization of intangible assets totaled 1,000 in Year 2 and was included in "General and Administrative Costs".
3. A gain on the sale of investments of 300 in Year 2 was included in "Investment income, net".
4. There were no sales or repurchases of Hoechst capital stock during Year 2.

Required

Prepare a statement of cash flow for The Hoechst Group for Year 2 using the indirect method.

P3.34 **Statement of Cash Flow: International.** Presented below are recent financial statements for **Beige Holdings Ltd.**, headquartered in Johannesburg, South Africa. Beige specializes in the manufacturer and distribution of pharmaceuticals, cosmetics, and consumer products, principally in South Africa.

Beige Holdings Ltd. Consolidated Balance Sheet (in thousands of Rands)		
	Year 2	Year 1
Assets		
Fixed assets	29,351	6,179
Capital investments	21,642	41,830
Investments	72	—
Current assets	128,044	54,689
Inventories	50,189	17,594
Accounts receivable.	60,441	19,171
Loan to directors	502	—
Taxation prepaid	1,548	595
Cash resources	15,364	17,329
Total employment of capital & assets.	179,109	102,698
Equity & Liabilities		
Ordinary shares & premium	50,061	69,690
Retained earnings	12,492	9,127
Long-term liabilities	6,831	1,578
Long-term debt	42,075	6,960
Deferred taxation	1,059	223
Current liabilities.	66,591	14,850
Accounts payable	44,371	12,315
Current portion of long-term liabilities	3,258	953
Accrued expenses payable	1,500	—
Taxation payable	443	1,582
Bank overdraft	17,019	—
Total capital employed & liabilities	179,109	102,698

Beige Holdings Ltd. Consolidated Income Statements		
	Year 2	Year 1
Sales.	316,549	63,378
Cost of goods sold.	(257,550)	(41,736)
Gross profit.	58,999	21,642
Other operating costs.	(55,691)	(16,430)
Operating income.	3,308	5,212
Abnormal items	(1,158)	(801)
Net income after abnormal items.	2,150	4,411
Income from investments.	5,358	1,845
Net income from activities before finance charges	7,508	6,256
Finance charges	(4,553)	(1,294)
Net income before taxation	2,955	4,962
Taxation	(2,790)	(1,210)
Net income after taxation.	165	3,752
Extraordinary gain	3,200	5,375
Retained income for the year	3,365	9,127

The company's footnotes also revealed the following:

1. Depreciation expense for Year 2 totaled 5,870 and was included in cost of goods sold.
2. The extraordinary gain of 3,200 in Year 2 involved the sale of fixed assets having a cost basis of 1,800.

Required
Prepare a statement of cash flow for Year 2 using (a) the indirect method and (b) the direct method (see Appendix B).

CORPORATE ANALYSIS

CA3.35 **The Procter and Gamble Company.** The 2005 annual report of **The Procter and Gamble Company** (P & G) is available at www.pg.com/annualreports/2005/pdf/pg2005annualreport.pdf. After reviewing P & G's annual report, respond to the following questions:

a. P & G's 2005 statement of cash flow is presented using the indirect method format. Convert P & G's indirect method cash flow from operating activities to the direct method format (see Appendix B). After converting the indirect method to the direct method, calculate P & G's cash conversion ratio for 2005. What does the cash conversion ratio tell you about P & G's operating revenues? Is this good news or bad news? Why?

b. Calculate P & G's EBITDA, free cash flow, and discretionary cash flow for 2003, 2004, and 2005. What can you conclude about P & G's cash position from these measures?

c. Calculate P & G's sustainable earnings for 2003, 2004, and 2005. What can you conclude about the persistence of P & G's earnings?

CA3.36 **Internet-based Analysis.** Consider a publicly-held company whose products you are familiar with. Some examples might include:

Company	Product	Corporate Website
• **Johnson & Johnson Company**	• Band-Aids	• www.jnj.com
• **Microsoft Corporation**	• Windows XP software	• www.microsoft.com
• **Nokia Corporation**	• Cellular phones	• www.nokia.com
• **Intel Corporation**	• Pentium processors	• www.intel.com
• **Kimberly-Clark Corporation**	• Kleenex	• www.kimberly-clark.com

Access the company's public website and search for its most recent annual report. (Note: Some companies will provide access to their financial data through an "investor relations" link, while others will provide a direct link to their "annual reports.") After locating your company's most recent annual report, open the file and review its contents. After reviewing the annual report for your selected company, prepare answers to the following questions:

1. Identify the company's basic and diluted earnings per share (EPS) for the past two years. Is there a difference between these EPS numbers? If so, what dilutive claims are responsible for the decline in basic earnings per share?

2. Review the company's income statement. Are there any extraordinary or special items, restructuring charges, changes in accounting principles, or discontinued operations in either of the last two years? If so, calculate the company's sustainable earnings for each year.

3. Consider the company's statement of cash flow. What format—indirect or direct—is used to present the cash flow from operations? Convert the company's cash flow from operations from the indirect (direct) format to the direct (indirect) format (see Appendix B).

4. Calculate the company's EBITDA, free cash flow, and discretionary cash flow for each of the past two years. Comment on the company's cash flow health.

Chapter Four

Using Financial Statements for Investing and Credit Decisions

TAKEAWAYS

When you complete this chapter you should be able to:

1. Analyze financial statements to evaluate company profitability, asset management, and financial risk.

2. Construct pro forma financial statements to evaluate a company's ability to generate future earnings and cash flows.

3. Explain the return on equity model of financial analysis.

4. Describe the limitations of financial statement analysis.

Where have we been?	Where are we?	Where are we going?
In Chapter 3, a company's net income was shown to occasionally include such one-time items as restructuring charges, asset write-offs, extraordinary and unusual items, and discontinued operations that can obscure a company's sustainable earnings. The preparation of cash flow statements and the analysis of cash flow information were also investigated, as were the alternative measures of cash flow used by investment professionals, such as EBITDA, free cash flow, and discretionary cash flows.	In this chapter, financial statement analysis techniques are explained and then used to evaluate the profitability, asset management, and financial risk of **Outback Steakhouse**, a rapidly growing casual dining restaurant chain. Financial ratios are used to illustrate how lenders evaluate the risk associated with extending short-term trade credit or long-term capital asset financing to companies like Outback. Finally, since many business decisions, including investment and lending decisions, are based on a firm's ability to generate future earnings and cash flow, the construction of pro forma financial statements are discussed in an appendix to the chapter.	In Chapter 5, the important concept of revenue and how companies in various industries measure and report their revenue is examined. Since many businesses extend credit to their customers as a means to generate incremental sales, the related topics of managing and valuing accounts receivable are considered. The chapter also explores how companies estimate the potential losses they can expect to experience as a consequence of extending credit to their customers. Finally, the chapter investigates how some companies manage their reported performance through their revenue recognition and receivable valuation policies.

OUTBACK STEAKHOUSE   Symbol: OSI

Outback Steakhouse is a casual dining restaurant chain with over 900 locations in 23 countries throughout North and South America, Europe, Asia, and Australia. The company was founded in 1988 and is owned and operated by OSI Restaurant Partners, Inc. The company's shares trade on the New York Stock Exchange under the symbol OSI.

OSI operates restaurants under a number of well-recognized brand names, including Outback Steakhouse, Carrabba's Italian Grill, Fleming's Prime Steakhouse, Roy's, Lee Roy Selmon's, Bonefish Grill, and Cheeseburger in Paradise. OSI's principal brand is Outback Steakhouse which specializes in prime steaks, chicken and other offerings in a rustic Australian-inspired décor. Menu items are often named after locations in Australia, including "Ayers Rock Strip," "Alice Springs' Chicken," and "Rockhampton Ribeye." The "Bloomin' Onion," a one-pound fried onion sliced to "bloom" open, is a signature menu item. The company's strategy is to differentiate its restaurants by emphasizing high-quality food and service at moderate prices in a casual dining environment.

During 2005, Outback's restaurant growth was substantial, with over 130 new restaurant location openings, representing approximately 10 percent of its total worldwide restaurants. In 2006, the company expects similar growth with the addition of 125 new restaurants. By year-end 2006, the company expects to own and operate over 950 Outback Steakhouse locations worldwide.

In November 2006, OSI announced that it had agreed to be acquired by a private equity partnership composed of Bain Capital Partners, Catterton Partners, and a group composed of company management and executives. The agreed upon sale price was $40 per share, or about $3 billion. Wall Street professionals speculated that the reasons that the restaurant chain was a target for private equity investors was because the business produced a steady stream of operating cash flow, had little debt and significant quantities of real estate that could be used as collateral to lever up the company. Some investment professionals, however, questioned the integrity of the buyout deal since members of OSI's management team were part of the acquisition group. These professionals suggested that a conflict of interest existed such that instead of maximizing shareholder value, OSI's management team was now incentivized to try to buy the company from its shareholders at the lowest possible price. According to Morningstar Research Inc., the fair value of OSI's shares was over $48 at the time of the tender offer.

In this chapter, we examine various financial statement analysis techniques that can be used to evaluate the profitability, asset management effectiveness, and financial risk of a company like Outback Steakhouse. The results of a historical financial analysis can then be used to help assess the fair value of a company's share price. (The OSI Restaurant Partners sale was completed in June of 2007 for a per share price of $41.15, totaling approximately $3.5 billion.)

EXECUTIVE OUTLINE	**Using Financial Statements for Investing and Credit Decisions**	
Analyzing Financial Performance	**ROE Model Framework**	**Limitations of Financial Statement Analysis**
■ Fundamentals of Financial Statement Analysis ■ Common-Size Statements ■ Financial Ratios ■ Credit Risk Analysis ■ Benchmarking Companies	■ ROE Model Components ■ ROE Analysis of Outback Steakhouse ■ Estimating Sustainable Growth	■ Measurement Issues ■ Incomplete Data ■ Differing Accounting Methods ■ Biased Data ■ Lack of Timeliness

ANALYZING FINANCIAL PERFORMANCE

The financial statements of a company are an important source of information when making credit-granting and investment decisions. Credit-granting decisions involve a judgment about a firm's ability to make timely payments on existing or pending credit obligations. Investment decisions, on the other hand, involve determining an appropriate intrinsic value for a security based on a firm's ability to generate future payoffs (such as earnings and/or cash flow) whose value is greater than the resources used to generate those payoffs.

Since credit and investment decisions are often largely based on estimates of future revenues and expenses, a thorough evaluation of a company's past financial performance can be a useful guide to predicting its future financial performance. (A discussion of the development of forecasted financial statements is presented in Appendix 4B to this chapter.) In this section, the historical financial statements of Outback Steakhouse Inc. are analyzed to illustrate how assessments of a company's recent and past profitability, asset management, and financial risk can be developed. These assessments can then be used to help forecast Outback's future performance, and hence, the company's fair market or intrinsic value.

Outback Steakhouse Inc. is an international operator of casual dining restaurants. During 2005, Outback's store growth was substantial, with over 130 new restaurant openings. In 2006, the company expects similar growth with the addition of 125 new restaurants. You may wish to obtain additional information about the company at its corporate website at www.osirestaurantpartners.com.

Fundamentals of Financial Statement Analysis

The most basic technique of financial statement analysis is "ocular regression"—that is, examining a firm's financial statements to observe any trends in its account balances. This technique is also called trend analysis or longitudinal analysis. Outback's consolidated income statement in Exhibit 4.1 shows, for example, that the company grew rapidly over the period 2003 to 2005, with revenues increasing from nearly $2.7 billion in 2003 to over $3.6 billion in 2005 (see bolded areas in Exhibit 4.1), representing an annual growth rate of over 16 percent. Although revenues increased over the reported period, Outback reported a slight decrease in net income from $167.3 million in 2003 to $149.6 million in 2005.

Outback also disclosed a number of single-period items on its income statements—in each year for impaired assets and in 2004 and 2005 for weather-related losses. Without these one-time charges, income from operations would have increased approximately $1 million, from $264.2 million in 2003 ($258.9 plus $5.3) to over $265.2 million ($234.1 plus $31.1) in 2005, rather than showing a decline of nearly 10 percent ($258.9 million in 2003 to $234.1 million in 2005).

Outback's consolidated balance sheet in Exhibit 4.2 shows that the company's total assets grew from over $1.7 billion in 2004 to over $1.9 billion in 2005 (see bolded areas in Exhibit 4.2), with over half of the growth ($154 million) due to an increase in property, fixtures and equipment. The increase in property and equipment is consistent with the opening of over 130 new restaurants during this time period. Outback's balance sheet also reveals that property, fixtures and

In Chapter 2, an asset was defined as an economic resource that is expected to generate future benefits for a firm. When the expected value of the future benefits (e.g. cash flows) is revised downward, the value of the asset is said to be "impaired." Generally accepted accounting practice requires that when an asset becomes impaired, its carrying value on the balance sheet should be written down, with a parallel impairment loss reported on the income statement. We will have more to say about asset impairments and impairment losses in Chapter 7.

EXHIBIT 4.1	Outback Steakhouses Inc.: Consolidated Statement of Income		
$ thousands, except per share amounts, for period ended	**2005**	**2004**	**2003**
Revenues			
Restaurant sales.	$3,579,818	$3,183,297	$2,647,991
Other revenues	21,848	18,453	17,786
Total revenues.	3,601,666	3,201,750	2,665,777
Costs and expenses			
Cost of goods sold	1,307,899	1,193,262	983,362
Labor and other related	926,485	811,922	666,532
Other restaurant operating	779,187	660,878	534,703
Depreciation and amortization	127,198	104,310	84,876
General and administrative.	197,135	174,047	138,063
Hurricane property losses	3,101	3,024	
Provision for impaired assets and restaurant closings	26,995	2,394	5,319
Contribution for "Dine Out for America"	1,000	1,607	—
Income from operations of unconsolidated affiliates	(1,479)	(1,725)	(5,996)
	3,367,521	2,949,719	2,406,859
Income from operations	234,145	252,031	258,918
Other income (expense), net	(2,070)	(2,104)	(1,100)
Interest income.	2,087	1,349	1,479
Interest expense.	(6,848)	(3,629)	(1,810)
Income before provision for income taxes and elimination of minority partners' interest	227,314	247,647	257,487
Provision for income taxes.	76,418	82,175	87,700
Income before elimination of minority partners' interest	150,896	165,472	169,787
Elimination of minority interest.	1,295	9,415	2,532
Net income	$ 149,601	$ 156,057	$ 167,255
Basic Earnings Per Common Share			
Net income	$2.02	$2.11	$2.22
Basic weighted average number of common shares outstanding	76,541	77,549	78,393
Diluted Earnings Per Common Share			
Net income.	$1.95	$2.01	$2.13
Diluted weighted average number of common shares outstanding	76,541	77,549	78,393

equipment is the single largest asset account on the company's balance sheet, which is not surprising for a restaurant chain. Outback Steakhouse is a capital-intensive business—that is, a business requiring a large investment in such long-lived assets as property, plant and equipment.

Outback's balance sheet also reveals that the company is financed with relatively little debt— long-term debt plus the current portion of long-term debt totaled only $154 million in 2005 versus nearly

To evaluate a business' capital-intensity, some investment professionals calculate a capital intensity ratio as follows:

$$\text{Capital Intensity} = \frac{\text{Fixed assets} + \text{Intangible assets}}{\text{Total assets}}$$

A higher intensity ratio indicates higher levels of capital investment. Outback's capital intensity ratio for 2005 is 71 percent; can you calculate the capital intensity ratio for 2004?

EXHIBIT 4.2	Outback Steakhouse Inc: Consolidated Balance Sheet		
$ thousands, for period ended		**2005**	**2004**
Current Assets			
Cash and cash equivalents		$ 84,876	$ 87,977
Short term investments		1,828	1,425
Inventories		68,468	63,448
Deferred income tax assets		17,719	12,969
Other current assets		51,746	53,068
Total current assets		224,637	218,887
Property, fixtures and equipment, net		1,389,605	1,235,151
Investments in and advances to unconsolidated affiliates, net		21,397	16,254
Deferred income tax asset		33,073	6,660
Goodwill		111,318	107,719
Intangible assets		11,562	21,683
Other assets		142,114	71,438
Notes receivable collateral for franchisee guarantee		31,150	30,239
Total Assets		$1,964,856	$1,708,031
Current Liabilities			
Accounts payable		$ 98,020	$ 74,162
Sales taxes payable		17,761	26,735
Accrued expenses		130,583	97,124
Current portion of partner deposit and accrued buyout liability		15,175	13,561
Unearned revenue		110,448	100,895
Income taxes payable		695	87
Current portion of long-term debt		63,442	54,626
Total current liabilities		436,124	367,190
Partner deposit and accrued buyout liability		71,591	63,102
Deferred rent		55,206	44,075
Long-term debt		90,623	59,900
Guaranteed debt of franchisee		31,283	30,343
Other long-term liabilities		45,890	6,114
Total liabilities		730,717	570,724
Commitments and contingencies			
Interest of minority partners in consolidated partnerships		45,573	48,905
Stockholders' Equity			
Common stock, $0.01 par value, 200,000 shares authorized; 78,750 and 78,554 shares issued; and 74,854 and 73,767 outstanding as of December 31, 2005 and 2004, respectively		788	788
Additional paid-in capital		291,035	271,109
Retained earnings		1,104,423	1,025,447
Accumulated other comprehensive income (loss)		384	(2,118)
Unearned compensation related to outstanding restricted stock		(40,858)	—
		1,355,772	1,295,226
Less treasury stock, 3,896 shares and 4,983 shares at December 31, 2005 and 2004, respectively, at cost		(167,206)	(206,824)
Total stockholders' equity		1,188,566	1,088,402
Total liabilities and stockholders' equity		$1,964,856	$1,708,031

$1.2 billion of shareholders' equity. Consequently, it appears that while Outback's use of debt financing is increasing, the company's management has made a strategic decision to largely finance their new restaurant growth using internally-generated operating cash flow and equity financing.

Outback's consolidated statement of cash flow in Exhibit 4.3 reveals that the company generated a positive cash flow from operations in all three years from 2003 to 2005 (see bolded areas in Exhibit 4.3). Outback's cash flow from operations increased over 38 percent from $269 million in 2003 to $372 million in 2005. It should be apparent that the company's capital expenditures of $194.8 million, $254.9 million, and $327.9 million in 2003, 2004, and 2005, respectively, were financed principally using internally-generated funds—Outback's **discretionary cash flow** from operations over the three year period totaled $613 million versus its cash outflow for capital expenditures of $777.5 million.[1]

In summary, a trend analysis of Outback's financial statements suggests that the following trends characterized the business over the three year period of 2003 to 2005:

- Outback's operating revenues grew, while its profit declined, over the three year period.
- Outback's total assets increased due to substantial new restaurant growth.
- The company financed its new restaurant growth principally with internally-generated cash flow from existing restaurant operations.

Common-Size Financial Statements

A widely-used technique for analyzing a company's financial performance is the preparation of common-size financial statements. A **common-size income statement**, for example, shows all of the income statement items expressed as a percentage of net revenues for the year. **Net revenues** are gross revenues less any **sales discounts** and/or **sales returns**. The advantage of a common-size income statement is that it allows the financial statement user to readily compare the performance of firms of different size or to compare the performance of the same firm that grows or shrinks in size over time. As an example, one would expect that as Outback's sales revenue increase over time, its cost of goods sold would also increase. Unfortunately, it is difficult to ascertain the relative rate of change in the cost of goods sold (or any other operating expense) just by examining the dollar-value of the expense. Common-size income statements make the analysis much simpler by highlighting whether, in what direction, and in percentage terms, how much each operating expense changed relative to a company's operating revenue.

A common-size income statement for Outback Steakhouse is presented in Exhibit 4.4. This data shows that all of Outback's major expense categories remained relatively constant over the period 2003 through 2005. The largest

> In highly competitive industries it is often necessary to offer customers the opportunity to buy a company's products on credit. To minimize the opportunity cost (the time value of money) associated with extending credit to customers, some businesses offer their customers an incentive for quick payment of credit purchases. Quick payment incentives typically take the form of a price reduction called a **sales discount**. Sales discounts are subtracted from gross revenues, and thus, represent a contra-revenue account. Another contra-revenue account is the **sales returns** account, which represents the value of goods allowed to be returned by customers who are dissatisfied with a product. We will have more to say about sales discounts and sales returns in Chapter 5.

---

[1] Can you replicate the calculation of Outback's discretionary cash flows of $613 million over the three year period? Recall from Chapter 3 that:

$$\text{Discretionary cash flow} = \text{CFFO} - \text{Required debt repayments} - \text{Dividend payments}$$

EXHIBIT 4.3	Outback Steakhouse Inc.: Consolidated Statements of Cash Flow		
$ thousands, for period ended December 31	**2005**	**2004**	**2003**
Cash flows from operating activities			
Net income.	$149,601	$156,057	$167,255
Adjustments to reconcile net income to net cash provided by operating activities			
Depreciation and amortization.	127,198	104,310	84,876
Provision for impaired assets and restaurant closings and hurricane losses	30,096	5,418	5,319
Stock-based compensation.	6,756	—	—
Employee partner stock buyout expense.	6,718	7,495	4,791
Income tax benefit credited to equity.	16,514	14,527	13,189
Minority partners' interest in consolidated partnerships' income	1,295	9,415	2,532
Income from operations of unconsolidated affiliates	(1,479)	(1,725)	(5,996)
Change in deferred income taxes	(31,163)	(9,290)	(1,667)
Loss on disposal of property, fixtures and equipment.	3,605	4,102	3,705
Change in assets and liabilities, net of effects of acquisitions and FIN 46R consolidation			
Increase in inventories	(5,635)	(2,773)	(24,102)
Increase in other current assets.	(436)	(10,031)	(5,614)
(Increase) decrease in other assets	(10,301)	(20,440)	2,610
Increase in accounts payable, sales taxes payable and accrued expenses.	48,387	33,603	13,761
Increase in partner deposit and accrued buyout liability	9,003	7,956	2,534
Increase in deferred rent.	11,131	6,620	6,873
Increase in unearned revenue	9,553	16,637	13,441
Increase (decrease) in income taxes payable	608	(541)	(13,425)
Increase (decrease) in other long-term liabilities	776	925	(1,000)
Net cash provided by operating activities	372,227	322,265	269,082
Cash flows from investing activities			
Purchase of investment securities	(5,568)	(60,125)	(78,557)
Maturity and sales of investment securities.	5,165	79,524	78,309
Cash paid for acquisitions of businesses, net of cash acquired	(5,200)	(28,066)	(47,677)
Cash paid for designation rights	—	(42,500)	—
Capital expenditures	(327,862)	(254,871)	(194,754)
Proceeds from the sale of property, fixtures and equipment.	11,508	2,583	2,275
Proceeds from the sale of designation rights.	—	11,075	—
Increase in cash from adoption of FIN 46R	—	1,080	—
Payments from unconsolidated affiliates	131	1,361	13,518
Distributions to unconsolidated affiliates.	—	(121)	(1,830)
Investments in and advances to unconsolidated affiliates, net	(1,463)	(800)	(1,345)
Net cash used in investing activities	(323,289)	(290,860)	(230,061)
Cash flows from financing activities			
Proceeds from issuance of long-term debt	174,373	127,444	29,497
Proceeds from minority partners' contributions.	8,635	5,100	13,825
Distributions to minority partners.	(17,502)	(12,810)	(4,841)
Repayments of long-term debt.	(141,084)	(71,369)	(23,663)
Proceeds from sale-leaseback transactions	5,000	—	—
Dividends paid	(38,753)	(38,524)	(36,917)
Payments for purchase of Treasury Stock	(92,363)	(95,554)	(143,191)
Proceeds from re-issuance of Treasury Stock	49,655	39,393	41,583

continued

continued from previous page

EXHIBIT 4.3	Outback Steakhouse Inc.: Consolidated Statements of Cash Flow		
$ thousands, for period ended December 31	2005	2004	2003
Net cash used in financing activities	(52,039)	(46,320)	(123,707)
Net decrease in cash and cash equivalents.	(3,101)	(14,915)	(84,686)
Cash and cash equivalents at the beginning of the year	87,977	102,892	187,578
Cash and cash equivalents at the end of the year	$ 84,876	$ 87,977	$102,892
Supplemental disclosures of cash flow information			
Cash paid for interest.	$ 6,916	$ 3,683	$ 1,964
Cash paid for income taxes	88,516	79,117	81,944
Supplemental disclosures of non-cash items			
Purchase of employee partner's interests in cash			
flows of restaurants	$ 4,208	$ 1,833	$ 8,402
Litigation liability and insurance receivable	39,000	—	—
Debt assumed from acquisition	—	—	20,717
Assets received for note.	—	14,700	5,569
Debt assumed under FIN 46R	—	30,339	—
Issuance of restricted stock	44,202	—	—

percentage increases were in "Other restaurant operating" and in the "Provision for impaired assets and restaurant closings." As noted above, these expense categories contain several one-time items. Mostly as the result of these items, Outback's **return on sales**, defined as net income divided by net sales, declined from 6.3 percent in 2003 to approximately 4.2 percent in 2005 (see bolded area in Exhibit 4.4).

A common-size balance sheet for Outback Steakhouse is presented in Exhibit 4.5. A **common-size balance sheet** shows all of the balance sheet accounts expressed as a percentage of total assets. Exhibit 4.5 reveals that Outback's properties, fixtures and equipment account for over 70 percent of the company's total assets (see bolded area in Exhibit 4.5). Consistent with the trend analysis of Outback's financial statements, the common-size balance sheet highlights the fact that Outback has relatively little long-term debt on its balance sheet—long-term debt plus the current portion of long-term debt is just 7.8 percent of total assets while shareholders' equity is over 60 percent of total assets. This finding reinforces the prior observation that Outback is principally equity financed, with little dependency on debt financing.

Financial Ratios

Another technique for analyzing a company's financial performance is the calculation of **ratios** of relevant accounting variables—that is, dividing (or standardizing) one accounting measure by another economically relevant measure. A company may, for instance, report a numerically large net income, but the reason for the firm's success in generating a large net income may simply be a function of its size and not that the business is well run. To address this analytical issue, it is useful to compute such ratios as the return on assets (ROA), which provides an assessment of whether net income is large relative to a firm's size, as defined by its investment in assets. Financial ratios enable financial statement users to make valid comparisons of firm operating performance, over time for the same firm and between comparable companies.

EXHIBIT 4.4 Outback Steakhouses Inc.: Common-Size Statement of Income			
In percent, for period ended	**2005**	**2004**	**2003**
Revenues			
Restaurant sales.	99.39	99.42	99.33
Other revenues	0.61	0.58	0.67
Total revenues	100.00	100.00	100.00
Costs and expenses			
Cost of goods sold.	36.31	37.27	36.89
Labor and other related	25.72	25.36	25.00
Other restaurant operating	21.63	20.64	20.06
Depreciation and amortization.	3.53	3.26	3.18
General and administrative.	5.47	5.44	5.18
Hurricane property losses	0.09	0.09	
Provision for impaired assets and restaurant closings	0.75	0.07	0.20
Contribution for "Dine Out for America".	0.03	0.05	
Income from operations of unconsolidated affiliates	(0.04)	(0.05)	(0.22)
	93.50	92.13	90.29
Income from operations	6.50	7.87	9.71
Other income (expense), net	(0.06)	(0.07)	(0.04)
Interest income (expense), net	(0.13)	(0.07)	(0.01)
Income before provision for income taxes and elimination			
of minority partners' interest	6.31	7.73	9.66
Provision for income taxes.	2.12	2.57	3.29
Income before elimination of minority partners' interest	4.19	5.17	6.37
Elimination of minority interest.	0.04	0.29	0.09
Net income	4.15	4.87	6.27

When analyzing a firm's financial health, investment professionals, lenders, managers, and shareholders are usually interested in gaining insights about a firm's profitability, asset management, and financial risk. **Profitability** refers to how much income was generated by a business, particularly relative to the amount of total assets invested in the business or relative to the amount of assets specifically invested by a company's shareholders. **Asset management**, on the other hand, refers to how effectively the invested assets were used in the business by the company's management team. Finally, **financial risk** refers to a firm's ability to repay its borrowings in a timely manner and may be evaluated both in terms of a firm's short-term debt repayment capability and its long-term debt repayment capacity. **Liquidity** refers to the ability of a company to generate cash and is often considered a good indication of a company's ability to pay its outstanding *short-term* obligations. Short-term sources of liquidity include existing current assets, ongoing operations, and available lines-of-credit. **Solvency**, on the other hand, generally refers to the ability of a company to repay its outstanding *long-term* obligations. Liquidity and solvency are related concepts since a company must have sufficient liquidity to remain solvent. Firms that borrow extensively are said to be highly leveraged and carry greater financial risk; they are also said to be less solvent. **Leverage** refers to the use of borrowed funds to finance operations and/or asset purchases. Solvency and leverage are inversely related—that is, everything else being equal, a highly leveraged firm is less solvent than a firm which uses little or no debt to finance its business.

EXHIBIT 4.5	Outback Steakhouse Inc: Common-Size Balance Sheet	
In percent, for period ended	**2005**	**2004**
Current Assets		
Cash and cash equivalents	4.32	5.15
Short term investments	0.09	0.08
Inventories	3.48	3.71
Deferred income tax assets	0.90	0.76
Other current assets.	2.63	3.11
Total current assets	11.43	12.82
Property, fixtures and equipment, net	70.72	72.31
Investments in and advances to unconsolidated affiliates, net	1.09	0.95
Deferred income tax asset	1.68	0.39
Goodwill	5.67	6.31
Intangible assets	0.59	1.27
Other assets.	7.23	4.18
Notes receivable collateral for franchisee guarantee	1.59	1.77
Total Assets	100.00	100.00
Current Liabilities		
Accounts payable.	4.99	4.34
Sales taxes payable	0.90	1.57
Accrued expenses	6.65	5.69
Current portion of partner deposit and accrued buyout liability	0.77	0.79
Unearned revenue	5.62	5.91
Income taxes payable	0.04	0.01
Current portion of long-term debt	3.23	3.20
Total current liabilities.	22.20	21.50
Partner deposit and accrued buyout liability	3.64	3.69
Deferred rent	2.81	2.58
Long-term debt	4.61	3.51
Guaranteed debt of franchisee.	1.59	1.78
Other long-term liabilities	2.34	0.36
Total liabilities	37.19	33.41
Commitments and contingencies		
Interest of minority partners in consolidated partnerships.	2.32	2.86
Stockholders' equity		
Common stock, $0.01 par value, 200,000 shares authorized; 78,750		
and 78,554 shares issued; and 74,854 and 73,767 outstanding		
as of December 31, 2005 and 2004, respectively	0.04	0.05
Additional paid-in capital	14.81	15.87
Retained earnings	56.21	60.04
Accumulated other comprehensive income (loss)	0.02	(0.12)
Unearned compensation related to outstanding restricted stock	(2.08)	0.00
	69.00	75.83
Less treasury stock, 3,896 shares and 4,983 shares at December 31,		
2005 and 2004, respectively, at cost	(8.51)	(12.11)
Total stockholders' equity	60.49	63.72
Total liabilities and stockholders' equity.	100.00	100.00

Some of the financial ratios that are commonly calculated by investment professionals, lenders, and managers are presented and explained in Exhibit 4.6. The application and interpretation of these ratios can be illustrated using the financial data of Outback Steakhouse, to which we now turn.

EXHIBIT 4.6	Key Financial Ratios	
Ratio	**Definition**	**Explanation**
Profitability		
• Return on shareholders' equity (ROE)	$$\frac{\text{Net Income} - \text{Preferred Stock Dividends}}{\text{Shareholders' Equity}}$$	Rate of return generated by a business for its common shareholders.
• Return on assets (ROA)	$$\frac{\text{Net Income} + [\text{Interest Expense} (1 - \text{Tax Rate})]}{\text{Total Assets}}$$	Rate of return generated on a company's investment in assets from all sources.
• Return on sales (ROS)	$$\frac{\text{Net Income}}{\text{Net Sales}}$$	Percentage of net income remaining from a dollar of sales after subtracting all expenses.
• Gross profit margin ratio	$$\frac{(\text{Net Sales} - \text{Cost of goods sold})}{\text{Net Sales}}$$	Percentage of income generated from sales after deducting the cost of goods sold.
Asset Management		
• Receivable turnover	$$\frac{\text{Net Sales}}{\text{Accounts Receivable}}$$	Number of sales/collection cycles experienced by a firm.
• Receivable collection period	$$\frac{365}{(\text{Net Sales/Accounts Receivable})}$$	Number of days required, on average, to collect an outstanding account receivable.
• Inventory turnover	$$\frac{\text{Cost of goods sold}}{\text{Inventory}}$$	Number of production/sales cycles experienced by a firm.
• Inventory-on-hand period	$$\frac{365}{(\text{Cost of goods sold/Inventory})}$$	Number of days, on average, required to sell the inventory currently on hand.
• Asset turnover	$$\frac{\text{Net Sales}}{\text{Total Assets}}$$	Amount of sales generated from each dollar invested in assets.
Liquidity		
• Cash and marketable securities-to-total assets	$$\frac{(\text{Cash} + \text{Marketable Securities})}{\text{Total Assets}}$$	Percentage of total assets held as highly liquid assets.
• Quick ratio	$$\frac{(\text{Cash} + \text{Marketable Securities} + \text{Accounts Receivable})}{\text{Current Liabilities}}$$	Amount of liquid assets available to pay short-term liabilities.
• Current ratio	$$\frac{\text{Current Assets}}{\text{Current Liabilities}}$$	Amount of current assets available to service current liabilities.
• Accounts payable turnover	$$\frac{\text{Cost of goods sold}}{\text{Accounts Payable}}$$	Number of account payment cycles experienced by a firm.
• Days' payable period	$$\frac{365}{\text{Cost of goods sold/}\textit{Accounts Payable}}$$	Number of days, on average, required to pay an outstanding account payable.

continued

continued from previous page

EXHIBIT 4.6	Key Financial Ratios	
Ratio	Definition	Explanation
Solvency		
• Long-term debt-to-total assets	$$\frac{\text{(Long-term Debt + Current Portion of Long-Term Debt)}}{\text{Total Assets}}$$	Percentage of total assets provided by creditors.
• Long-term debt-to-shareholders' equity	$$\frac{\text{(Long-term Debt + Current Portion of Long-Term Debt)}}{\text{Shareholders' Equity}}$$	Relative investment of long-term creditors versus shareholders in a business.
• Interest coverage ratio	$$\frac{\text{Net Income Before Taxes + Interest Expense}}{\text{Interest Expense}}$$	Extent to which current operating income covers current debt service charges.

Financial ratios assessing the profitability, asset management, liquidity and solvency for Outback Steakhouse are shown in Exhibit 4.7. You may wish to replicate these calculations using Outback's financial statements in Exhibits 4.1, 4.2, 4.3, and the ratio definitions in Exhibit 4.6.

There is no generally-accepted definition for most of the financial ratios presented in Exhibit 4.6, and consequently, the ratios may be calculated in a variety of ways. For example, to calculate the return on assets ratio, some analysts use an average of the beginning and ending total assets as the denominator, while others use only the ending or beginning balance of total assets. This is done to match the numerator (i.e. net income), which is computed over a period of time, with the denominator (i.e. total assets), which is computed at a point in time. In general, unless there has been a large movement in the level of the denominator over the time period being analyzed, the definition used to define a ratio's calculation won't make much difference when ranking companies from best to worst, although it will affect the absolute value of a ratio. What is important is to define ratios consistently over time and between companies so that any performance comparisons are "apples to apples" and not "apples to oranges."

With respect to corporate profitability, Outback's cost of food used in prepared meals decreased slightly relative to sales over the two year period 2004 to 2005, enabling the company to register a small increase in its **gross profit margin ratio** from 62.5 percent of revenues in 2004 to 63.5 percent in 2005. However, Outback generated a **return on sales** (ROS) of only 4.2 percent in 2005, down slightly from 4.9 percent in 2004.[2] This means that for every dollar of sales in 2005, Outback earned just 4.2 cents after subtracting all expenses. An ROS of 4.2 percent may seem low, although it should be noted that the restaurant industry is extremely competitive, with new entrants and departures of failed businesses recorded every year. Outback's **return on assets (ROA)** of 7.8 percent in 2005 was also down from the company's 2004 ROA of 9.3 percent. The company's **return on equity** (ROE), down from its 2004 level of 14.3 percent, was still 12.6 percent in 2005, more than 5 percentage points over its ROA and 1.4 percentage points above its cost of equity. (See Appendix 4C for a discussion of how to calculate a company's cost of equity financing.)

---

[2] Many investment professionals use an alternative calculation of the return of sales (ROS) ratio, called the unlevered ROS ratio, calculated as follows:

$$\text{Unlevered ROS} = \frac{\text{Net income + Interest (1 − tax rate)}}{\text{Net sales}}$$

The unlevered ROS ratio enables the analyst to evaluate the effectiveness of a company's operating strategy independent of its financing strategy; that is, unlevering ROS restates a firm's net income as if the firm were all equity financed. A discussion of unlevering ratios is presented in Appendix 4A to this chapter.

EXHIBIT 4.7	Financial Ratios: Outback Steakhouse Inc.		
Fiscal Year Ending		**2005**	**2004**
Ratio			
Profitability			
Gross Profit Margin Ratio.		63.5%	62.5%
Return on Sales (ROS)		4.2%	4.9%
Return on Assets (ROA)		7.8%	9.3%
Return on Equity (ROE)		12.6%	14.3%
Asset Management			
Receivable turnover		NA	NA
Receivable collection period		NA	NA
Inventory turnover		19.1x	18.8x
Inventory-on-hand period.		19.1 days	19.4 days
Asset Turnover		1.8	1.9
Liquidity			
Cash & Marketable Securities-to-Total Assets.		0.04	0.05
Quick Ratio.		0.20	0.24
Current Ratio		0.52	0.60
Accounts Payable Turnover		13.3x	16.1x
Days' Payable Period.		27.4 days	22.7 days
Solvency			
Long-term Debt- to-Total Assets		7.8%	6.7%
Long-term Debt-to-Shareholders' Equity.		13.0%	10.5%
Interest Coverage Ratio		34.2x	69.2x

One measure of how well a company utilizes its borrowed funds involves a comparison of the company's ROE with its ROA. Since the ROA represents the return to all capital contributors while ROE is the return to just the company's shareholders, an ROE in excess of ROA indicates that a firm is earning more on its borrowed funds than its cost to borrow those funds. For example, if a firm borrows funds at an interest rate of five percent and subsequently earns eight percent from the use of those funds, the excess earnings accrue to the shareholders. Since Outback reported an ROE that was five percentage points greater than its ROA, the company can be described as being able to effectively utilize **financial leverage.** We will discuss financial leverage in greater detail shortly.

With respect to asset management, Outback's **inventory-on-hand** period—that is, the average number of days that a business' inventory remains on hand before being sold—indicates that Outback keeps very modest amounts of inventory on hand (i.e, 19.1 days in 2005), as would be expected for a restaurant chain whose differentiating strategy is to provide well-prepared, fresh food. The **receivable collection**

GLOBAL PERSPECTIVE

Financial statement analysis is executed, worldwide, in exactly the same fashion. Common-size financial statements and financial ratios, for example, are currency-neutral and can be effectively utilized anywhere in the world. Not all ratios are relevant, however, in all countries. For example, in lesser-developed countries which lack the infrastructure to support a credit system, ratios involving accounts receivables (such as receivable turnover and the receivable collection period) or accounts payable (such as accounts payable turnover and the day's payable period) are likely to be irrelevant for purposes of financial statement analysis.

period—that is, the average number of days that customers take to pay their bills—is not applicable to Outback because customers pay for their restaurant purchases in cash or with a debit/credit card. The company's **asset turnover** ratio indicates that, in 2005, every dollar invested in the business' assets generated $1.80 in sales, down slightly from $1.90 in 2004. Outback disclosed in its annual report that revenue growth in 2005 was disappointing due to several factors, including poor consumer confidence, the economic and emotional impact of the hurricane season, and unfavorable food costs and labor trends.

Analysts often combine the inventory-on-hand period with the receivable collection period to estimate the length of a company's **cash collection period**. This measure identifies the amount of time, on average, needed from the outlay of cash for inventory, through the sale of that inventory, until the ultimate collection of cash from the sale. In other words, the cash collection period represents the cash-to-cash cycle of a business. Since companies often acquire inventory on credit, without the necessity of paying interest on the credit purchase, an amount representing the average time taken to pay a company's accounts payable is often subtracted when estimating the cash collection period. The number of days needed to pay a firm's accounts payable is calculated as 365 / (Cost of goods sold /Accounts Payable) and is referred to as the **days' payable period**. Thus, a firm's cash collection period can be estimated as follows:

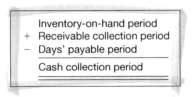

```
  Inventory-on-hand period
+ Receivable collection period
− Days' payable period
  ───────────────────────────
  Cash collection period
  ═══════════════════════════
```

In the case of Outback Steakhouse, the cash collection period for 2005 was minus 8.3 days (19.1 days + 0 days − 27.4 days). Since Outback's business is cash-intensive (all sales transactions are executed in cash), and its inventory turnover very rapid, the company is able to finance its business operating cycle using interest-free trade credit from its suppliers. This business attribute contributes significantly to Outback's profitability in the very competitive restaurant industry.

The financial ratios in Exhibit 4.7 also indicate that Outback is relatively illiquid—that is, it has limited liquid resources to pay its current obligations as they come due. Outback's **current ratio**—the ratio of current assets to current liabilities—is well below one in both years. Hence, if all of the company's current assets were converted to cash, there would not be sufficient cash to pay off Outback's current obligations. The **quick ratio**, which excludes Outback's potentially illiquid inventory, is 0.20 in 2005 and indicates that Outback's highly **liquid assets**, such as cash and marketable securities, are only 20 percent as large as the total of the obligations due within one year. Use of these ratios to analyze liquidity implicitly assumes that these assets can be converted into cash at a rate sufficient to match the timing of when the current obligations become due. Investment professionals often couple their analysis of the current and quick ratios with additional ratios such as the receivable collection period and the inventory-on-hand period,

> A company's liquid assets include cash, cash equivalents, marketable securities and accounts receivable, but exclude inventory and prepaid expenses which are often illiquid. Cash equivalents are very short-term (90 days or less) investments in highly liquid, risk-free certificates of deposits or government securities.

which indicate how quickly cash can be generated. While on the surface these ratios may appear to indicate a problem for Outback, the reality is that the company generates a great deal of operating cash flow, as evidenced by the $372 million cash flow from operations disclosed on the statement of cash flow. Because of the cash generating ability of the restaurant industry, it is not necessary for a company like Outback to maintain high liquid asset balances, as is often observed in some industries.

Credit Risk Analysis

Current shareholders, investment advisors, and top management are vitally interested in a company's profitability and asset management because these factors are closely linked to future increases and decreases in a company's share price. Lenders, on the other hand, are less interested in these factors because creditors generally don't share in the upside potential of a firm when its share price appreciates. Creditors are more concerned with downside risk—that is, getting paid the interest and principal they were promised. But what factors affect credit risk?

In general, the more indebtedness a firm has, the more likely it is that an unforeseen decline in sales and/or an increase in expenses will reduce a firm's capacity to meet its loan servicing commitments. The ratios of long-term debt, including the current portion of long-term debt, to total assets and to shareholders' equity are two ratios that measure the relative amount of a company's outstanding debt, and thus, its solvency. Similarly, the more operating income a company generates relative to the amount of its annual interest expense—the **interest coverage ratio**—the more likely it is that a company will be able to make timely interest payments from operating cash flow.

At the end of 2005, Outback's long-term debt was only 13 percent of its outstanding shareholders' equity. Further, Outback's interest coverage ratio—the ratio of operating income to interest expense—was a massive 34.2 times in 2005 and 69.2 times in 2004, respectively. On both counts, Outback's ability to take on additional debt with little risk to its lenders seems substantial. That puts the company in an excellent position to negotiate favorable credit terms such as a large loan with a low interest rate. With the company's strong operating cash flow of over $372 million in 2005, it should have little difficulty in paying interest charges or principal payments in a timely manner.

But how can you be sure that Outback has reported all of its outstanding debt on its balance sheet? Following the Enron Corporation scandal, it is likely that many more investors will carefully read the footnotes that accompany a company's financial statements, and in the case of Outback, such **due diligence** would be revealing. Outback's footnotes indicate that the company leases a number of its restaurant locations through operating leases. Under an **operating lease** agreement, the value of the leased asset and the related lease liability do **not** appear on the company's balance sheet. Outback's footnotes reveal that the company has minimum future lease payments under operating leases of nearly $580 million due over the next ten years. That means that Outback's debt ratios measured using only the debt listed on Outback's balance sheet *understate* the total level of corporate debt! Even if those **off-balance sheet liabilities** were considered, however, Outback appears to be an excellent credit risk.

> Because of complex accounting standards, some obligations (such as operating leases) do not appear on the face of the balance sheet, and thus, understate a firm's true debt position. These unreported liabilities are often referred to as **off-balance sheet liabilities** and are described in detail in Chapters 9 and 10.

Benchmarking: Comparisons with Similar Companies

Assessing the significance of financial ratios can be substantially enhanced by comparing a company's financial ratios with those of competing companies in the same industry or the same line of business. This process is called **benchmarking** or **cross-sectional analysis**. Outback Steakhouse is classified as being in North American Industry Classification System (NAICS) code 722110—The Eating and Drinking Places Industry. **Darden Restaurants Inc.** is another restaurant company in NAICS code 722110, and thus, is a competitor of Outback Steakhouse. Darden Restaurants, Inc. is the largest publicly-held casual dining restaurant company in the world.

> The North American Industry Classification System is a system for classifying companies into common industry groups.

In Practice 4.1 *Financial Ratio Benchmarks by Industry* The following table presents industry median benchmarks for a set of selected financial ratios:

Industry	ROE	ROA	ROS	A/R Turnover	Inventory Turnover	Current Ratio	Debt-to-Equity
Agriculture Crops	10.2	4.4	2.8	12.3	9.3	1.6	72.6
Oil Gas Extraction.	14.4	6.9	7.3	5.4	34.2	1.4	82.1
Food, Kindred Product	11.2	5.0	2.5	13.3	13.0	1.7	105.3
Apparel Related Products	10.9	5.1	2.5	9.6	7.8	2.4	74.8
Printing, Publishing	15.0	5.9	3.2	8.5	26.7	1.9	95.1
Rubber & Plastics	12.7	5.5	2.6	8.0	10.3	2.1	96.7
Fabricated Metal Products	14.6	6.7	3.3	8.0	11.1	2.2	85.3
Electrical Equipment	9.2	4.3	2.9	6.9	7.2	2.6	57.5
Trucking & Warehousing.	19.9	7.4	2.6	10.5	168.4	1.7	121.7
Transportation Services	21.9	8.1	2.0	9.8	43.3	1.5	138.3
Communication	8.3	1.8	1.9	8.9	36.7	1.4	95.2
Wholesale Trade	12.9	5.2	1.9	9.6	8.5	1.9	113.8
Eating Drinking Places	13.6	6.2	2.9	82.9	83.8	1.0	102.9
Miscellaneous Retail Stores	8.8	4.1	1.5	22.7	8.2	2.1	80.9
Real Estate	13.2	4.3	7.1	20.2	20.5	1.9	86.7
Personal Services.	10.7	5.6	2.9	11.5	38.2	1.7	97.3
Misc. Business Services.	17.6	7.0	3.0	7.6	37.0	1.7	93.9
Health Services	9.1	4.4	3.7	7.7	60.4	2.0	83.8
Educational Services	6.9	3.6	5.0	16.7	163.1	2.1	68.2

Source: Dunn & Bradstreet Industry Norms & Key Business Ratios 2005–2006

As of 2005, the company operated over 1,400 restaurants in the United States and Canada under the names Red Lobster, Olive Gardens, Bahama Breeze, Smokey Bone Barbeque & Grill, and Seasons 52.

Comparison ratios for Outback and Darden are reported in Exhibit 4.8. With regard to firm profitability, Darden reported a higher gross profit margin in 2005, 69.8 percent versus Outback's 63.5 percent, along with a return on sales over one percentage point higher than Outback's—5.5 percent versus 4.2 percent. This suggests that Darden does a better job than Outback controlling both its food costs and non-food costs. Darden's return on assets of 10.9 percent was higher than Outback's ROA of 7.8 percent. Darden also reported a significantly higher return on equity—22.8 percent versus 12.6 percent. As a consequence, it is difficult to avoid the conclusion that Darden is more profitable than Outback.

In terms of asset management, Darden holds significantly more inventory than Outback—57 days versus 19 days for Outback—which may reflect the different supply chain arrangements between the two companies or possibly the effect of different inventory valuation methods (a topic that will be considered in Chapter 6). Outback's asset turnover is higher at 1.8 versus just 0.54 for Darden. Darden is even less liquid than Outback. Darden's cash and marketable securities balance is only one percent of assets versus four percent for Outback. Neither company may see the need to maintain large cash balances on hand to take advantage of unforeseen opportunities because they may have standby financing arrangements with various financial institutions to extend credit should a cash need arise. On all three measures of solvency, Darden has a greater likelihood of being unable to meet its debt service obligations. For example, Darden's **long-term debt-to-equity** ratio is 51.1 percent versus just 13 percent for Outback. And, Darden's interest coverage ratio is also substantially lower than Outback's—10.5 versus 34.2—and a low interest coverage ratio indicates higher financial risk.

To summarize, although Outback is profitable, Darden has been able to generate higher levels of profitability by taking on greater risk through a more highly leveraged financing policy. Taking on higher financial risk is a strategic decision made by management regarding the benefits of higher growth versus the costs of additional credit risk. In the event of a declining economy, and a consequent downturn in casual dining restaurant sales, however, Darden may have greater difficulty weathering the downturn.

EXHIBIT 4.8	Financial Ratios: Outback Steakhouse versus Darden Restaurants				
		Outback		Darden	
Fiscal year ending		**2005**	**2004**	**2005**	**2004**
Profitability					
Gross profit margin ratio.		63.5%	62.5%	69.8%	69.5%
Return on sales (ROS)		4.2	4.9	5.5	4.5
Return on assets (ROA)		7.8	9.3	10.9	9.3
Return on equity (ROE).		12.6	14.3	22.8	19.3
Asset Management					
Receivable collection period		NA	NA	2.52	2.21
Inventory-on-hand period.		19.1	19.4	56.92	47.52
Asset turnover		1.8	1.9	0.54	0.55
Liquidity					
Cash & market securities-to-total assets		0.04	0.05	0.01	0.01
Quick ratio		0.20	0.24	0.08	0.10
Current ratio		0.52	0.60	0.39	0.51
Days' payable period		27.4	22.7	17.0	13.6
Solvency					
Long-term debt-to-total assets		7.8	6.7	22.1	23.5
Long-term debt-to-shareholders' equity		13.0	10.5	51.1	55.6
Interest coverage ratio		34.2	69.2	10.5	8.5

ROE MODEL FRAMEWORK

In Chapter 2, the return on equity (ROE) model was briefly introduced as a paradigm for analyzing the profitability of a business. This analytical framework provides an innovative structure for decomposing the return on shareholders' equity (ROE) into its three component ratios of return on sales (ROS), asset turnover (AT), and financial leverage (LEV):[3]

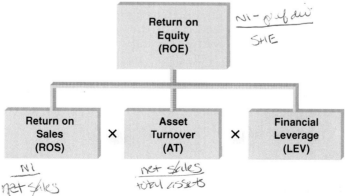

---

[3] Appendix 4A to this chapter presents a reformulation of the ROE Model using unlevered ratios.

The framework shows that a business can increase its return on equity by increasing one or more of the following factors:

- Return on sales (such as by increasing the price of products sold and/or by reducing operating expenses).
- Asset turnover (such as by using the key operating assets of accounts receivables, inventory and property and equipment more efficiently, for example by generating the same volume of sales with a smaller investment in these assets or generating greater sales volume with the same level of investment in these assets).
- Financial leverage (such as by financing the business with debt to leverage the use of high return assets with a lower after-tax cost of funds).

Data for computing an ROE analysis for Outback Steakhouse is presented in Exhibit 4.9. Outback's ROE has consistently been around 14 percent, although the trend in this ratio is in the wrong direction (see bolded area in Exhibit 4.9). Nevertheless, it is reasonable to conclude that, based on the 2005 ROE of 12.6 percent, Outback is a profitable company.

EXHIBIT 4.9	ROE Model Analysis: Outback Steakhouse Inc.				
($ thousands)	2005	2004	2003	2002	2001
Total revenues	$3,601,666	$3,201,750	$2,665,777	$2,362,106	$2,127,133
Net income.	149,601	156,057	167,255	156,364	133,377
Total assets.	1,964,856	1,708,031	1,474,787	1,389,575	1,237,748
Shareholders' equity	1,188,566	1,088,402	1,005,224	1,052,976	941,844
ROE analysis					
ROE (NI/Shareholders' equity)	12.6%	14.3%	16.6%	14.8%	14.1%
ROS (NI/Revenues).	4.2	4.9	6.3	6.6	6.3
AT (Revenues/Total assets).	1.83	1.87	1.81	1.70	1.72
LEV (Total assets/ SE).	1.65	1.57	1.46	1.32	1.32

But just what factors contributed to the decline in Outback's ROE from 16.6 percent in 2003 to 12.6 percent in 2005? The decline in Outback's ROE was entirely due to a decline in ROS from 6.3 percent in 2003 to 4.2 percent in 2005. Partially offsetting the decline in ROS was a very slight increase in asset turnover and a small increase in the use of financial leverage.

In summary, Outback's experienced a substantial decline in its ROE in recent years. Despite that decline, the company' share price remained relatively stable in the low $40s. Ignoring the very modest decline in ROS, the decline in Outback's ROE appears largely attributable to a failure on the part of Outback's management to effectively control costs while sales grew. In addition, while Outback is able to earn returns well above its cost of borrowing, management has been reluctant to utilize more than a minimum amount of leverage. The fact that Outback's return on assets of 7.8 percent in 2005 exceeded its after-tax cost of borrowing suggests that the firm is foregoing the opportunity to maximize shareholder value.

Estimating Sustainable Growth

Sales growth is one of the key factors of interest to all financial statement users, in part because of the high correlation between sales growth and growth in share price. Many investment professionals believe, for example, that the key driver of share price is the rate of growth in business revenue. In the case of Outback

Steakhouse, Exhibit 4.1 revealed that revenues grew from $2.7 billion in 2003 to over $3.6 billion in 2005, an annual growth rate of over 16 percent. But revenue growth comes at a cost, namely the related growth in a firm's investment in such operating assets as accounts receivable, inventory, and property, plant and equipment. And, an increase in a firm's investment in operating assets presents a secondary problem—the need to finance the required investment in new operating assets.

As previously discussed, firms may finance their asset purchases with debt, new equity, or with internally-generated funds. In general, financing new capital investments with the sale of equity is the least desirable financing option as equity is the most expensive form of financing. (See Appendix 4C for a discussion of how to estimate a firm's cost of equity.) Hence, financing a firm's growth in operating assets with debt and/or internally-generated funds are the options preferred by most managers.

Although sales growth is desirable, excessively rapid growth can strain the financial resources of a business, even to the point of destroying a business by inducing bankruptcy. To help managers avoid this situation, investment professionals have developed an approach to estimate a firm's maximum desired rate of growth, called the **sustainable growth rate** (SGR), which is calculated as follows:

Sustainable growth rate = Return on equity × Dividend retention rate

The **dividend retention rate** (DRR) is equal to the percentage of net income not paid to shareholders in the form of dividends, and consequently, which is retained in a business.[4] Thus, a business' SGR is the rate of return on shareholders' equity available to be reinvested in the business. Since a firm's ROE can be decomposed into its three component ratios of return on sales (ROS), asset turnover (AT), and financial leverage (LEV), we can identify the key drivers of a firm's SGR as follows:

SGR = ROS × AT × LEV × DRR

Thus, a firm can increase its SGR by increasing any of its key components—the return on sales, total asset turnover, financial leverage, or the dividend retention rate.

To illustrate the use of SGR, let's apply the concept to Outback Steakhouse. For the period 2003 through 2005, Outback's dividend retention rate was 78 percent, 75 percent, and 74 percent, respectively.[5] Exhibit 4.9 reports Outback's ROE for the same period. Multiplying Outback's ROE with its DDR yields the following sustainable growth rates:

	SGR	Actual Growth Rate in Sales
2003	12.95%	12.86%
2004	10.73%	20.11%
2005	9.32%	12.49%

---

[4] The dividend payout ratio (discussed in Chapter 11) is the percentage of net income paid out to shareholders in the form of dividends (Dividends paid/Net income). Thus, the dividend retention ratio can be calculated as 1 minus the dividend payout ratio. The dividend retention ratio is also sometimes referred to as the "plow-back percentage."

[5] Can you replicate the calculation of Outback Steakhouse's DRR? For 2003, Outback's DRR is calculated as follows:

$$DRR = [1 - (\text{Dividends paid/Net income})]$$
$$= (1 - 0.22) = 0.78$$

Beginning in 2004, Outback's actual rate of growth in sales of 20.11 percent exceeded its sustainable growth rate of 10.73 percent by almost ten percent, although the excess of the actual growth rate above the sustainable rate declined in 2005 to just slightly more than three percent. Nonetheless, these results suggest that Outback's growth strategy is on a collision course with its financing strategy. Consequently, it is clear that Outback's management needs to consider alternative options, for example, reducing the rate of new restaurant openings in 2006 and beyond or increasing the use of financial leverage to help finance the growth in new restaurants.

LIMITATIONS OF FINANCIAL STATEMENT ANALYSIS

It is important to understand not only what can be learned about a company by using the financial statement analysis techniques illustrated in this chapter, but also to understand that there are limitations to these techniques. One limitation is the ratios themselves. There is no GAAP that prescribes which ratios should be used in any given analysis, nor even how the ratios that are used should be calculated. As such, it is critical that a manager or an investment professional either compute the ratios directly or be sure to learn how any provided ratio has been computed. For example, it is entirely possible to obtain the same ratio, such as the return on assets, from two different data sources and have them calculated differently. Without knowing this, it is possible to make incorrect inferences when comparing the performance of different companies.

Just knowing how a ratio has been computed, however, does not insure the validity of the analysis. It is also quite possible that the numbers from which a ratio is calculated contain problems. Some of the potential problems that may exist with the underlying financial statement data include:

1. **Measurement concerns.** Arguably, the most relevant method of measurement for a company's assets and liabilities is their market value. After all, for valuation purposes you would expect to pay what something is currently worth, not what it was worth at some point in the past. Unfortunately, market values are often much more subjective than what accounting standard setters consider acceptable for use in the basic financial statements, and therefore, the more reliable historical cost concept pervades financial statement measurement. Thus, while the price paid for land in Manhattan, New York forty years ago may be a reliable number, it is not terribly relevant to today's valuation of a business operating in New York City.

2. **Incomplete data.** Although the historical cost concept does help insure that the reported financial statement numbers are reliable, the relevance of many of the reported assets and liabilities values on the balance sheet are lessened, and many are not even be reported at all. One accounting construct that impedes the relevance of financial statement data is that of conservatism. **Conservatism** dictates that, when in doubt, a company should report its accounts such that assets are understated, liabilities are overstated, the recognition of losses are accelerated, while the recognition of gains are delayed. Many important assets such as a company's trained workforce, management talent, internal processes, and brand go unreported on the balance sheet. In addition, money spent on public relations and advertising to enhance a company's brand image, or research and development expenditures to create future products, are expensed as incurred even though these expenditures arguably generate future benefits for a business. Conservatism dictates that these items not be capitalized as assets on the balance sheet because their future value is uncertain and because they cannot be reliably measured. In an apparent contradiction to conservatism, some liabilities are also excluded from the balance sheet. These so called off-balance sheet liabilities include some leases and certain contingencies.

3. **Differing accounting methods.** GAAP is not a one-size-fits-all set of rules. Instead, management is allowed significant flexibility in choosing the accounting methods that are used to report a firm's performance. Choices among alternative depreciation methods, alternative inventory cost flow assumptions, and alternative revenue recognition approaches are but a small sample of the policy choices that can dramatically alter reported income in any given year. This flexibility creates difficulties when comparing companies that use different accounting methods.

4. **Biased data.** GAAP allows not only the flexibility to choose different accounting methods, but also significant discretion in the various accrual estimates used in the preparation of the income statement and the balance sheet. A partial list of estimates that impact reported earnings include estimates for uncollectible accounts, warranty expense, and sales returns, along with estimates for such things as asset write-downs, pension expense, and asset lives. Because many employment contracts are written using reported accounting numbers, managers often have a perverse incentive to bias the estimates used in financial statements as a means to favorably influence the outcome of such contracts.

5. **Lack of timeliness.** The expression "old news is no news" was probably not written about accounting data, but it certainly applies to some extent. Security markets react nearly instantly to any news deemed valuation-relevant. Certainly company performance is valuation-relevant; however, the performance reported in a company's financial statements is not timely. The annual 10-K report containing a company's financial statements, for example, is often filed with the U.S. Securities and Exchange Commission over two months after a company's fiscal year-end. As a consequence, much of the information contained in the report is already known by the time the 10-K becomes public information. Further, the accounting reports are, by definition, backward looking reports,

ETHICS PERSPECTIVE

Financial analysts are one of the primary user-groups of the financial information considered in this chapter. There are two principal types of financial analysts – buy-side analysts and sell-side analysts. **Buy-side analysts** work primarily for investment management companies such as Fidelity Investments or The Vanguard Group. The job of these analysts is to provide unbiased research that helps the portfolio managers of these mutual fund companies select securities for inclusion in their mutual fund portfolios. A second type of analyst, the **sell-side analyst,** works primarily for large financial services/investment banking companies such as Merrill Lynch or Morgan Stanley. Unlike buy-side analysts who do their research for a company's internal use, sell-side analysts provide their research for sale and use by their company's customers.

It has been argued that sell-side analysts are sometimes put under unreasonable pressure to be less than completely objective in their recommendations. Several apparent lapses in ethical behavior by sell-side analysts have come to light in recent years, eventually leading to mandated changes prescribed in the Sarbanes-Oxley Act. The purpose of these changes was to eliminate many of the conflicts of interest that sell-side analysts were exposed to and included:

- A prohibition of the solicitation of investment banking business by sell-side analysts.
- The creation of separate organizational structures for sell-side analysts and investment bankers.
- Restrictions placed on the interactions between, and contact with, sell-side analysts and investment bankers.
- Imposition of policies designed to prevent investment bankers from influencing the content of analysts' research reports.
- Creation of analyst compensation packages in which a significant portion of a sell-side analyst's compensation is linked to the quality and accuracy of the analyst's research.

reporting on what has already occurred. Investment professionals, in contrast, want timely information that helps them predict what the future holds.

REVIEW PROBLEM

The following balance sheet and income statement data were taken from the financial records of The Arcadia Company:

The Arcadia Company Balance Sheets					
	2005	**2006**		**2005**	**2006**
Assets			**Liabilities & Shareholders' Equity**		
Cash	$ 30,000	$ 7,000	Accounts payable........	$ 63,000	$ 65,500
Accounts receivable.....	60,000	67,500	Wages payable..........	47,500	37,000
Inventory..............	22,500	49,000	Total current liabilities.....	110,500	102,500
Prepaid insurance.......	4,500	6,000	Bank loan payable	85,000	83,000
Total current assets	117,000	129,500	Capital stock	75,000	75,000
Building (net)...........	190,000	187,500	Retained earnings	36,500	56,500
Total	$307,000	$317,000	Total	$307,000	$317,000

The Arcadia Company Income Statements		
	2005	**2006**
Revenues	$430,000	$480,000
Less: Cost of goods sold	240,000	250,000
Gross margin	190,000	230,000
Less: Depreciation expense.......................	22,000	22,000
Wage expense	86,000	90,000
Insurance expense	16,000	16,000
Interest expense	6,800	6,600
Net income before taxes	59,200	95,400
Less: Tax expense (30%)	17,800	28,600
Net income.....................................	$ 41,400	$ 66,800

Required

1. Calculate the following ratios for The Arcadia Company for 2005 and 2006:

- Return on equity
- Return on sales
- Total asset turnover
- Financial leverage
- Receivable collection period
- Inventory-on-hand period
- Accounts payable period
- Total debt-to-total assets
- Long-term debt-to-equity
- Interest coverage
- Quick ratio
- Current ratio
- Gross profit margin

2. Comment on the trends in profitability, asset management, and financial risk for The Arcadia Company from 2005 to 2006.

Solution

1. Ratio Analysis

	2005	2006
Return on equity.	37.1%	50.8%
Return on sales	9.6	13.9
Total asset turnover	1.40	1.51
Financial leverage.	2.75	2.41
Receivable collection period	50.9 days	51.3 days
Inventory-on-hand period.	34.1 days	71.6 days
Accounts payable period	95.8 days	95.6 days
Total debt-to-total assets	63.7	58.5
Long-term debt-to-equity.	76.2	63.1
Interest coverage	9.7x	15.5x
Quick ratio	0.8x	0.7x
Current ratio	1.1x	1.3x
Gross profit margin.	44.2	47.9

2. The profitability of The Arcadia Company is up dramatically from 2005 to 2006, as revealed by the trend in the return on equity and return on sales ratios. The gross profit margin increase suggests that the company was able to realize some economies of scale over this same period. Overall, the company's asset management was up from 2005 to 2006, as revealed by the trend in the total asset turnover ratio, despite a small increase in the receivable collection period and a larger increase in the inventory-on-hand period. The cash collection cycle grew dramatically, however, from minus 10.8 days in 2005 to over 27 days in 2006 (a swing of over 37 days). The financial riskiness of the company improved from 2005 to 2006, as indicated by a decline in the use of financial leverage (see the financial leverage and the total debt-to-equity ratios). This improvement is also reflected in an improving interest coverage ratio and current ratio.

EXECUTIVE SUMMARY

In this chapter, we considered a variety of financial analysis techniques: ocular regression (or trend analysis), common-size financial statements, and financial ratios. These analytical techniques are used to gain an understanding of a company's historical financial performance. The performance areas of interest include profitability, asset management, and financial risk. As a validation of your understanding of the content of this chapter, you should now be able to:

- Analyze a company's financial statements to evaluate its profitability, asset management, and financial risk.
- Construct pro forma income statements, balance sheets, and statements of cash flow. (See Appendix 4B.)
- Explain the Return on Equity model of financial analysis.
- Understand the limitations of financial statement analysis.

KEY CONCEPTS AND TERMS

Annuity, 4.3

Asset management, 4.9

Asset turnover, 4.14

Benchmarking, 4.15

Beta, 4.27

Buy-side analyst, 4.21

Capital asset pricing model, 4.27

Capital intensive business, 4.4

Cash equivalents, 4.14

APPENDIX 4A: Unlevering Financial Ratios

In Chapter 4, the return on equity (ROE) model was introduced as an approach to organize the analysis of a company's financial performance and health. The ROE of a company was shown to be composed of three component ratios, as follows:

Return on Equity = Return on sales × Asset turnover × Financial leverage

Further, since the return on assets (ROA) ratio was revealed to be a function of the return on sales (ROS) ratio and asset turnover (AT), the ROE ratio could also be expressed as:

Return on equity = Return on assets × Financial leverage

Because ROA is a measure of the return generated by a business' total investment in assets, to include those assets contributed by shareholders as well as those assets loaned to the business by its creditors, many investment professionals "unlever" the ROA ratio by adding the current period interest expense paid to creditors back to the business' net income. Unlevering the ROA ratio grosses up net income for a business' cost of debt, yielding a measure of net income before any returns are distributed to either debtholders or shareholders. The resultant unlevered ROA is calculated as follows:

$$\text{Return on assets} = \frac{[\text{Net income} + \text{Interest } (1 - \text{Tax rate})]}{\text{Total assets}}$$

The interest expense added back to net income is multiplied by (1 − Tax rate), or one minus a firm's effective tax rate (Income tax expense/Net income before taxes). As a consequence, the amount of the interest expense added back to net income is reduced by the income tax savings associated with the tax deductibility of interest expense. These tax savings are referred to as the interest tax shield and must be removed to avoid double-counting their positive impact on net income (it is already reflected in the provision for income taxes used in the calculation of net income).

Some investment professionals believe that a similar unlevering adjustment should be made to the ROS ratio, as follows:

$$\text{Return on sales} = \frac{[\text{Net income} + \text{Interest } (1 - \text{Tax rate})]}{\text{Net sales}}$$

Unlevering ROS allows the financial analyst to focus on the effectiveness of a company's operating decisions, independent of the effectiveness of its financing decisions. Incorporating the unlevered ROS ratio into the calculation of ROA yields the following formulation:

$$\begin{array}{c}\text{Unlevered return} \\ \text{on assets}\end{array} = \begin{array}{c}\text{Unlevered return} \\ \text{on sales}\end{array} \times \begin{array}{c}\text{Total asset} \\ \text{turnover}\end{array}$$

$$\begin{aligned}\text{ROA} &= \frac{[\text{Net income} + \text{Interest} (1 - \text{Tax rate})]}{\text{Net sales}} \times \frac{\text{Net sales}}{\text{Total assets}} \\ &= \frac{[\text{Net income} + \text{Interest} (1 - \text{Tax rate})]}{\text{Total assets}}\end{aligned}$$

Unlevering ROS also facilitates a reformulation of the ROE Model, as follows:[6]

$$\text{ROE} = \begin{array}{c}\textbf{Unlevered} \\ \textbf{ROS}\end{array} \times \begin{array}{c}\textbf{Asset} \\ \textbf{turnover}\end{array} \times \begin{array}{c}\textbf{Financial} \\ \textbf{leverage}\end{array} \times \begin{array}{c}\textbf{Common equity share} \\ \textbf{of operating earnings}\end{array}$$

where the **common equity share of operating earnings (CSOE)** is defined as:

$$\text{CSOE} = \frac{\text{Net income}}{\text{Net income} + \text{Interest} (1 - \text{Tax rate})}$$

and represents the portion of a company's operating earnings allocable to the common shareholders. Incorporating CSOE into the ROE model yields the following:

$$\text{ROE} = \frac{\text{Net income} + \text{Interest} (1 - \text{Tax rate})}{\text{Net sales}} \times \frac{\text{Net sales}}{\text{Total assets}} \times \frac{\text{Total assets}}{\text{Shareholders' equity}} \times \frac{\text{Net income}}{\text{Net income} + \text{Interest} (1 - \text{Tax rate})}$$

When a company is all (or substantially) equity financed, the unlevered ROA and ROS ratios collapse to their familiar levered form, as does the ROE Model:

Return on equity = Return on sales × Total asset turnover × Financial leverage

APPENDIX 4B: Pro Forma Financial Statements

Lenders, managers, investment professionals, and shareholders are often interested in how a firm might perform in the future under various economic scenarios. For example, lenders might be interested in assessing whether Outback Steakhouse's business can generate sufficient cash in the future to make the principal payments on a proposed bank loan. But how can you forecast the future, and especially, how can you forecast a firm's ability to repay debt? The past is often an excellent guide to the future because many financial variables remain relatively constant from one year to the next and many financial variables maintain a relatively stable relationship with sales or total assets over time.

Forecasted financial statements are called **pro forma statements**—that is, financial statements prepared on an "as if" basis using assumptions about what might happen in the future. Excel™ spreadsheets are handy devices for preparing pro forma financial statements because it is possible to build a spreadsheet in such a manner as to easily change the underlying assumptions to see what will happen under alternative operating scenarios.

The process of preparing pro forma financial statements typically involves five steps:

1. Forecast sales, cost of goods sold, gross profit, and other operating expenses on the income statement, and the cash balance on the balance sheet.
2. Forecast accounts receivables, inventory, accounts payable, property and equipment, long-term debt, and short-term loans payable on the balance sheet.
3. Forecast depreciation expense and interest expense on the income statement.

---

[6] The development of the ROE Model using unlevered ratios is generally attributed to C. Stickney and T. Selling, "The Effects of Business Environment and Strategy on a Firm's Rate of Return on Assets," *Financial Analysts' Journal* (1989).

4. Forecast any remaining items on the income statement, expected dividend payments, and then, the statement of shareholders' equity and the balance sheet.
5. Prepare the pro forma statement of cash flow from the forecasted income statement and forecasted balance sheets using the indirect method format.

When developing pro forma data, it is often the case that a plug figure will be needed to balance the pro forma balance sheet. If a plug figure is needed to balance the asset side of the pro forma balance sheet, most investment professionals use the current asset account "marketable securities" as their plug figure. When a firm is producing excess cash flow from its operations, that excess will usually be invested in short-term marketable securities to enable the firm to earn a higher rate of return than would be possible if the excess funds were invested in a lower yielding cash account. Similarly, when additional cash is needed to support operations, the first source of that cash is likely to be the liquidation of any available short-term marketable securities. If, on the other hand, a plug figure is needed to balance the liability side of the pro forma balance sheet, most professionals use a short-term interest-bearing line-of-credit as the plug. A short-term line-of-credit is used as a plug figure because this form of financing is cheaper than financing with long-term debt, which of course, is cheaper than financing with equity, and therefore, likely to be the first choice of new financing by management.

The principle challenge to preparing pro forma statements is to determine how to forecast each of the income statement and balance sheet accounts. (It is unnecessary to forecast the pro forma statement of cash flow because the data for this statement can be indirectly derived from the pro forma income statements and balance sheets using the process described in Chapter 3.) The first account to be forecasted is revenue on the income statement, and this forecast is usually arrived at after a careful assessment of the expected external demand for a company's products. Most expenses on the income statement can be forecasted by reference to the common-size income statement percentages generated while developing the historical financial statement analysis of a company's past performance. Some expenses, however, must be forecasted by reference to items on the pro forma balance sheet. For example, depreciation expense is a function of a company's past and current investment in property, plant and equipment. Similarly, interest expense is a function of a company's past and current borrowings. And, income tax expense is a function of a firm's pre-tax net income and its expected effective tax rate. To forecast these expenses using historical common-size income statement percentages would mistakenly link the change in these expenses to the change in revenues.

On the balance sheet, many accounts are forecasted by reference to ratios which link the balance sheet account to a firm's operations. For example, here is a list of typical balance sheet accounts and the ratios that are commonly used to forecast them once a pro forma income statement has been prepared:

Balance Sheet Account	Ratio
Accounts receivable........	Receivable turnover
Inventory.................	Inventory turnover
Fixed assets..............	Fixed asset turnover
Total assets..............	Total asset turnover
Accounts payable.........	Accounts payable turnover

For many income statement and balance sheet accounts which are immaterial in amount, investment professionals often forecast the account balance as a constant on grounds of immateriality. And, in the case of some balance sheet accounts (such as the cumulative foreign currency translation adjustment), whose future value is not readily forecasted, the investment professional will often merely assume a constant future value. The key to well-constructed pro forma financial statements is to thoughtfully forecast the key income statement accounts (such as operating revenue and expenses) and the key balance sheet accounts (such as operating assets and liabilities).

It is important to recognize that forecasting income statements and balance sheets is not a hard-and-fast science. There are many different approaches used by investment professionals, and for this reason, forecasting is referred to as "an art and not a science." We will have more to say about developing and using pro forma financial statements in Chapter 12.

APPENDIX 4C: Calculating the Cost of Equity Financing

Shareholders buy shares in a company because they expect a return, either in the form of dividends or in the form of share price appreciation, or both. Since shareholders assume more risk than creditors, they are entitled to a higher rate of return. But how can the rate of return expected by shareholders be estimated? Stated alternatively, how can we calculate the expected cost of equity financing for a company?

A widely accepted approach to estimating the cost of equity financing – that is, the rate of return expected by shareholders – is through the **capital asset pricing model**, or CAPM.[7] The CAPM posits that there is a linear relationship between a company's systematic risk (β) and the expected return required by investors (r_e). The model states that if investors can earn the risk-free rate of return (r_f) by investing in government securities, then the expected return on a risky investment (such as common stock) should equal the risk-free rate of return plus an incremental return proportional to the company's risk. The incremental return associated with investing in equity securities versus risk-free securities is called the **equity risk premium**. The formula for the CAPM is given as follows:

$$r_e = r_f + \beta \times \textbf{(Equity risk premium)}$$

where

r_e = Cost of equity financing.

r_f = Risk-free rate of return, often proxied by the current yield to maturity of the U.S. ten-year treasury bond.

β = Measure of the systematic risk of a business, proxied by a firm's equity beta (available from any financial internet website).

The equity risk premium is estimated as follows:

$$\textbf{Equity risk premium} = r_m - r_f$$

where

r_m = Market rate of return for a diversified portfolio of equity securities, often proxied by the rate of return on the Standard & Poor's 500 Index.

The equity risk premium expected by investors on a diversified portfolio of equity securities is often assumed to be 7.5 percent, which is the average risk premium observed in the U.S. capital market over the 72 year period of 1926 to 1998.

To illustrate the use of the CAPM, assume that our goal is to estimate the cost of equity financing for Outback Steakhouse. Yahoo!Finance reports Outback's beta (β) to be 0.95, suggesting that if the U.S. stock market increases by $1, Outback's share price will increase by $0.95; that is, there is a 95 percent correlation between movements of the U.S. equity market and Outback's share price. Beta is a reflection of the **systematic risk** associated with a company's share price. Systematic risk is the risk that a company's share price will fall (rise) in some proportion to a fall (rise) in the overall stock market. **Non-systematic risk** is the risk that a company's share price will fall (rise) as a consequence of firm-specific and industry-specific information. Thus, Outback's share price will fall (rise) as a consequence of overall market movements (systematic risk) or as a consequence of new information about the company's performance or about the restaurant industry in general (non-systematic risk).

If the current yield on the U.S. ten-year Treasury bill is assumed to be 5 percent, and if we assume that the equity risk premium—that is, the incremental risk of investing in equity securities rather than in risk-free government bonds—is 7.5 percent, Outback's cost of equity can be estimated using the CAPM as follows:

$$r_e = 5.0\% + 0.95(7.5\%) = 11.265\%$$

---

[7] W.F. Sharpe, "Capital Asset Prices: A Theory of Market Equilibrium," *Journal of Finance*, 1964.

As a basis of comparison, if Outback had been a less well established company (more risky), investors would have expected a higher rate of return on their investment. Private equity investors, for example, who invest in non-public companies often expect a 20 to 40 percent return on their investments because these investments are less liquid than investments in publicly-traded companies like Outback Steakhouse—a reduced ability to sell shares (lower liquidity) implies higher risk for an investor. Similarly, venture capital investors who invest in high-risk new business ventures expect returns ranging from 40 to 100 percent, or more. As previously noted, the assumption of greater risk is typically associated with an expectation of higher returns.

In Chapter 4, our ratio analysis of Outback Steakhouse revealed that the company's return on equity (ROE) was a healthy 12.6 percent in 2005. Thus, Outback is able to earn a return on its equity that exceeds the cost of its equity funds ($12.6\% - 11.265\% = 1.335\%$), and as a consequence, Outback is able to build value for its shareholders.

DISCUSSION QUESTIONS

Q4.1 **Using Financial Ratios to Evaluate Firm Performance.** Financial statement analysis is a process whereby the basic financial statements are reviewed and evaluated to assess a firm's financial health and/or performance. Calculating financial ratios is an integral part of financial statement analysis. Discuss what a ratio is and why the use of ratios is helpful in assessing firm performance and financial condition.

Q4.2 **Using Financial Leverage Effectively.** Many corporations finance at least a part of their operations and asset purchases using debt, principally because the cost of debt financing is cheaper than equity financing. Moreover, some firms are able to use leverage more effectively than others - that is, the returns to shareholders as a result of financing with debt are higher for some firms than for other firms. Using the ROE model, discuss when the use of financial leverage is most effective and least effective. When should a firm stop using debt to finance its operations or asset purchases?

Q4.3 **Calculating the Return on Shareholders' Equity.** When calculating a firm's return on shareholders' equity (ROE), some investment professionals modify the ROE ratio by subtracting any dividends paid by the firm to its preferred stock shareholders as follows:

$$\text{Return on shareholders' equity} = \frac{(\text{Net income} - \text{Preferred stock dividends})}{(\text{Total shareholders' equity} - \text{Preferred stock equity})}$$

This modified ROE ratio is often referred to as the "return on common equity," or ROCE. Discuss why and when ROCE might be a superior assessment of a firm's return on equity.

Q4.4 **Unlevering the Return on Assets.** When calculating a firm's return on total assets (ROA) ratio, some investment professionals modify the ROA ratio by adding back the interest expense paid by a firm to its creditors, on a net-of-taxes basis, as follows:

$$\text{Return on assets} = \frac{[\text{Net income} + i(1 - \text{Tax rate})]}{\text{Total assets}}$$

where i is the actual interest expense paid by a firm and the tax rate is a firm's "effective tax rate" (income tax expense divided by pre-tax net income). Adjusting net income for the interest expense paid by a firm is called "unlevering net income" because the adjustment yields a measure of net income as if the firm were all equity financed (with no debt financing). Discuss when and why unlevering ROA might produce a more useful measure of the return on assets of a firm.

Q4.5 **Evaluating a Firm's Liquidity and Solvency.** The Manhattan Company has $265 million in assets, $90 million in current liabilities, $135 million in non-current liabilities, and $40 million in shareholders' equity. Of the company's $85 million in current assets, the company's cash and cash equivalents total $23 million, accounts receivable total $24.5 million, inventory totals $26.4 million, and other current assets total $11.1 million. Is the Manhattan Company solvent? Why or why not? Is the company liquid? Why or why not?

Q4.6   **Evaluating Capital Intensity.** Presented below are selected financial data (in millions) for 2005 for Bristol-Myers Squibb, Coca-Cola Enterprises, and the General Electric Company. Calculate the capital intensity ratio for each of the three firms and discuss the relative capital intensity of the firms.

	Fixed Assets	Intangible Assets	Total Assets
Bristol-Myers Squibb	$ 5,693	$ 6,744	$ 28,138
Coca-Cola Enterprises	6,560	15,394	25,357
General Electric Company	67,528	81,726	673,342

Q4.7   **Identifying the Unknown Companies.** Presented below are common-sized income statement data for three well-known companies representing three different industries (pharmaceutical, beverage, and diversified):

- **Bristol-Myers Squibb**
- **Coca-Cola enterprises**
- **General Electric Company**

Identify which of the three companies goes with each of the common-size data profiles. Discuss the rationale for your choice.

	Company 1	Company 2	Company 3
Common-size income statement			
Net sales.	100.0%	100.0%	100.0%
Cost of goods sold	30.9	44.3	59.8
Marketing, selling & admin.	22.6	13.0	32.6
Research & development	14.3	6.0	—
Other expenses	12.6	26.0	4.9
Net income	15.6%	10.7%	2.7%

Q4.8   **Evaluating the Return on Assets.** Presented below are selected financial data for two competitors. Discuss why the return on assets increased for Company A but decreased for Company B.

	Return on Assets		Return on Sales		Total Asset Turnover	
	Year 1	Year 2	Year 1	Year 2	Year 1	Year 2
Company A.	7.9%	10.7%	12.3%	15.6%	.637	.683
Company B	9.2	6.9	21.6	15.7	.427	.436

Q4.9   **Evaluating the Return on Assets.** Presented below are selected financial data for two competitors. Discuss why the return on assets increased for each firm.

	Return on Assets		Return on Sales		Total Asset Turnover	
	Year 1	Year 2	Year 1	Year 2	Year 1	Year 2
Company C	16.0%	17.9%	18.0%	20.6%	0.89	0.87
Company D	15.8	21.4	24.6	31.2	1.27	1.37

Q4.10 **Evaluating the Return on Equity.** Presented below are selected financial data for two competitors. Discuss why the return on equity decreased for each firm.

	Return on Equity		Return on Sales		Total Asset Turnover		Financial Leverage	
	Year 1	Year 2	Year 1	Year 2	Year 1	Year 2	Year 1	Year 2
Company X.	15.2%	15.0%	30.6%	27.3%	.073	.089	6.8	6.2
Company Y.	11.1%	9.1%	3.4%	2.8%	0.67	0.74	4.92	4.40

Q4.11 **(Ethics Perspective) Ethics and Financial Analysts.** Explain why a sell-side analyst might be less objective than a buy-side analyst in his/her research reports. If an analyst is working for **Merrill Lynch**, where should the analyst's loyalties lie—with Merrill Lynch, with the companies that the analyst reviews and evaluates, or with the clients who purchase the analyst's research?

⊘ **indicates that check figures are available on the book's Website.**

EXERCISES

E4.12 **Analyzing Financial Statement Data.** Presented below are summary financial data from the 2005 Bristol-Myers Squibb annual report. Using the ratio definitions from Exhibit 4.6, calculate the following ratios: return on equity, return on assets, return on sales, total asset turnover, and financial leverage. (Assume that the company is all equity financed.) Does the company appear to be a good investment? Why or why not?

(amounts in millions)	2004	2005
Balance sheet		
Total assets	$30,435	$28,138
Shareholders' equity	10,202	11,208
Income statement		
Net sales	$19,380	$19,207
Net income.	2,388	3,000

⊘ **E4.13** **Analyzing Financial Statement Data.** Presented below are summary financial data from the 2005 **Pfizer, Inc.** annual report. Using the ratio definitions from Exhibit 4.6, calculate the following ratios: return on equity, return on assets, return on sales, total asset turnover, and financial leverage. (Assume that the company is all equity financed.) Does the company appear to be a good investment? Why or why not?

(amounts in millions)	2004	2005
Balance sheet		
Total assets	$123,078	$117,565
Shareholders' equity	68,278	65,627
Income statement		
Net sales	$ 52,516	$ 51,298
Net income.	11,361	8,085

E4.14   **Analyzing the Return on Equity.**   Presented below are summary financial data from the 2005 Johnson and Johnson Company annual report. Using the ratio definitions from Exhibit 4.6, calculate the following ratios: return on equity, return on assets, return on sales, total asset turnover, and financial leverage. (Assume that the company is all equity financed.) Does the company appear to be a good investment? Why or why not?

(amounts in millions)	2004	2005
Balance sheet		
Total assets	$53,317	$58,025
Shareholders' equity	31,813	37,871
Income statement		
Net sales	$47,348	$50,514
Net income.	8,509	10,411

E4.15   **Analyzing the Return on Equity.**   Presented below are summary financial data from the 2005 General Electric Company annual report. Using the ratio definitions from Exhibit 4.6, calculate the following ratios: return on equity, return on assets, return on sales, total asset turnover, and financial leverage. (Assume that the company is all equity financed.) Does the company appear to be a good investment? Why or why not?

(amounts in millions)	2004	2005
Balance sheet		
Total assets	$750,507	$673,342
Shareholders' equity	110,821	109,354
Income statement		
Net sales	$ 55,005	$ 59,837
Net income.	16,819	16,353

E4.16   **Analyzing the Return on Equity.**   Presented below are summary financial data from the 2005 Coca-Cola Enterprises, Inc. annual report. Using the ratio definitions from Exhibit 4.6, calculate the following ratios: return on equity, return on assets, return on sales, total asset turnover, and financial leverage. (Assume that the company is all equity financed.) Does the company appear to be a good investment? Why or why not?

(amounts in millions)	2004	2005
Balance sheet		
Total assets	$26,461	$25,357
Shareholders' equity	5,378	5,643
Income statement		
Net sales	$18,158	$18,706
Net income.	596	514

E4.17   **Analyzing Financial Risk.**   Presented below are summary financial data from the 2005 Bristol-Myers Squibb annual report. Using the ratio definitions from Exhibit 4.6, calculate the following liquidity and solvency ratios: cash and marketable securities-to-total assets, quick ratio, current ratio, long-term debt-to-total assets, long-term debt-to-shareholders' equity, and the interest coverage ratio. Evaluate Bristol-Myers' liquidity and solvency.

(amounts in millions)	2004	2005
Balance sheet		
Cash and cash equivalents	$ 3,680	$ 3,050
Marketable securities.	3,794	2,749
Accounts receivable (net).	4,373	3,378
Total current assets	14,801	12,283
Total assets	30,435	28,138
Current liabilities	9,843	6,890
Current portion of long-term debt	1,883	231
Long-term debt	8,463	8,364
Shareholders' equity	10,202	11,208
Income statement		
Interest expense	$ 310	$ 349
Net income before taxes	4,418	4,516

E4.18   **Analyzing Financial Risk.**   Presented below are summary financial data from the 2005 **Pfizer, Inc.** annual report. Using the ratio definitions from Exhibit 4.6, calculate the following liquidity and solvency ratios: cash and marketable securities-to-total assets, quick ratio, current ratio, long-term debt-to-total assets, long-term debt-to-shareholders' equity, and the interest coverage ratio. Evaluate Pfizer's liquidity and solvency.

(amounts in millions)	2004	2005
Balance sheet		
Cash and cash equivalents	$ 1,808	$ 2,247
Marketable securities.	18,085	19,979
Accounts receivable (net).	9,367	9,765
Total current assets	39,088	41,896
Total assets	123,078	117,565
Current liabilities	26,458	28,448
Current portion of long-term debt	11,266	11,589
Long-term debt	7,279	6,347
Shareholders' equity	68,278	65,627
Income Statement		
Interest expense	$ 359	$ 488
Net income before taxes	14,007	11,534

E4.19   **Analyzing Financial Risk.**   Presented below are summary financial data from the 2005 **Johnson and Johnson Company** annual report. Using the ratio definitions from Exhibit 4.6, calculate the following liquidity and solvency ratios: cash and marketable securities-to-total assets, quick ratio, current ratio, long-term debt-to-total assets, long-term debt-to-shareholders' equity, and the interest coverage ratio. Evaluate Johnson and Johnson's liquidity and solvency.

(amounts in millions)	2004	2005
Balance sheet		
Cash and cash equivalents	$ 9,203	$16,055
Marketable securities.	3,681	83
Accounts receivable (net).	6,831	7,010
Total current assets	27,320	31,394
Total assets	53,317	58,025
Current liabilities	13,927	12,635
Current portion of long-term debt	280	668
Long-term debt	2,565	2,017
Shareholders' equity	31,813	37,871
Income statement		
Interest expense	$ 187	$ 54
Net income before taxes	12,838	13,656

⊘ **E4.20** **Analyzing Financial Risk.** Presented below are summary financial data from the 2005 **General Electric Company** annual report. Using the ratio definitions from Exhibit 4.6, calculate the following liquidity and solvency ratios: cash and marketable securities-to-total assets, quick ratio, current ratio, long-term debt-to-total assets, long-term debt-to-shareholders' equity, and the interest coverage ratio. Evaluate General Electric's liquidity and solvency.

(amounts in millions)	2004	2005
Balance sheet		
Cash and cash equivalents	$ 12,152	$ 9,011
Marketable securities.	56,923	53,144
Accounts receivable (net).	14,233	14,851
Total current assets	93,086	87,480
Total assets	750,507	673,342
Current liabilities	200,137	204,927
Current portion of long-term debt	157,195	158,156
Long-term debt	207,871	212,281
Shareholders' equity	110,821	109,354
Income statement		
Interest expense	$ 11,656	$ 15,187
Net income before taxes	19,771	22,129

E4.21 **Analyzing Financial Risk.** Presented below are summary financial data from the 2005 **Coca-Cola Enterprises, Inc.** annual report. Using the ratio definitions from Exhibit 4.6, calculate the following liquidity and solvency ratios: cash and marketable securities-to-total assets, quick ratio, current ratio, long-term debt-to-total assets, long-term debt-to-shareholders' equity, and the interest coverage ratio. Evaluate the company's liquidity and solvency.

(amounts in millions)	2004	2005
Balance sheet		
Cash and cash equivalents	$ 155	$ 107
Marketable securities.	–0–	–0–
Accounts receivable (net).	1,884	1,802
Total current assets	3,371	3,395
Total assets	26,461	25,357
Current liabilities	3,451	3,846
Current portion of long-term debt	607	944
Long-term debt	10,523	9,165
Shareholders' equity	5,378	5,643
Income statement		
Interest expense	$ 619	$ 633
Net income before taxes	818	790

E4.22 **Analyzing Asset Management Effectiveness.** Presented below are select financial data from the 2005 **Bristol-Myers Squibb** annual report. Using the ratio definitions from Exhibit 4.6, calculate the following ratios: accounts receivable turnover, receivable collection period, inventory turnover, and the inventory-on-hand period. Evaluate Bristol-Myers' receivable and inventory asset management effectiveness.

(amounts in millions)	2004	2005
Balance sheet		
Accounts receivable (net).	$ 4,373	$ 3,378
Inventory	1,830	2,060
Income statement		
Net sales	$19,380	$19,207
Cost of goods sold	5,989	5,928

E4.23 **Analyzing Asset Management Effectiveness.** Presented below are select financial data from the 2005 **Pfizer, Inc.** annual report. Using the ratio definitions from Exhibit 4.6, calculate the following ratios: accounts receivable turnover, receivable collection period, inventory turnover, and the inventory-on-hand period. Evaluate Pfizer's receivable and inventory asset management effectiveness.

(amounts in millions)	2004	2005
Balance sheet		
Accounts receivable (net).	$ 9,367	$ 9,765
Inventory	6,660	6,039
Income statement		
Net sales	$52,516	$51,298
Cost of goods sold	7,541	8,525

E4.24 **Analyzing Asset Management Effectiveness.** Presented below are select financial data from the 2005 **General Electric Company** annual report. Using the ratio definitions from Exhibit 4.6, calculate the following ratios: accounts receivable turnover, receivable collection period, inventory turnover, and the inventory-on-hand period. Evaluate General Electric's receivable and inventory asset management effectiveness.

(amounts in millions)	2004	2005
Balance sheet		
Accounts receivable (net)..	$14,233	$14,851
Inventory	9,778	10,474
Income statement		
Net sales	$84,705	$92,589
Cost of goods sold	61,759	66,814

⊘ **E4.25** **Analyzing Asset Management Effectiveness.** Presented below are select financial data from the 2005 Coca-Cola Enterprises, Inc. annual report. Using the ratio definitions from Exhibit 4.6, calculate the following ratios: accounts receivable turnover, receivable collection period, inventory turnover, and the inventory-on-hand period. Evaluate Coca-Cola Enterprise's receivable and inventory asset management effectiveness.

(amounts in millions)	2004	2005
Balance sheet		
Accounts receivable (net)..	$ 1,884	$ 1,802
Inventory	763	786
Income statement		
Net sales	$18,158	$18,706
Cost of goods sold	10,771	11,185

E4.26 **Debt Covenants and Financial Analysis.** During 2006, The Mann Corporation borrowed $500,000 from The Biltmore National Bank. The loan agreement included a debt covenant restricting the company's level of debt relative to shareholders' equity. The covenant specified that Mann's long-term debt-to-equity ratio could not exceed 1-to-1 at anytime during the loan period. The Mann Corporation's 2006 year-end balance sheet appeared as follows:

	2006
Total assets...	$2,001,600
Current liabilities..	$ 542,100
Long-term debt	625,500
Shareholders' equity	834,000
	$2,001,600

Calculate The Mann Corporation's long-term debt-to-equity ratio at year-end 2006. What is the company's maximum borrowing capability at year-end 2006 without violating the long-term debt-to-equity covenant of the existing loan agreement? What is the maximum dividend that the company can pay at year-end without violating the debt covenant? If the company pays a cash dividend of $100,000 at year-end 2006, what is the company's maximum borrowing capability without violating the debt covenant?

E4.27 **Estimating Sustainable Growth.** The following information is taken from **Procter and Gamble's** 2005 annual report:

(in millions)	2003	2004	2005
Income statement			
Net sales	$43,377	$51,407	$56,741
Net earnings.	5,186	6,481	7,257
Balance sheet			
Shareholders' equity	—	17,278	17,477
Statement of cash flow			
Dividends to shareholders	2,246	2,539	2,731

Calculate the company's actual and sustainable rate of growth in sales. How do the two growth rates compare? What advice would you give to P & G's management on the basis of these two rates of growth?

E4.28 **Estimating Sustainable Growth.** The following information is taken from the Fossil, Inc. 2005 annual report:

(in thousands)	2003	2004	2005
Income statement			
Net sales	$781,175	$959,960	$1,040,468
Net earnings.	68,335	90,569	78,059
Balance sheet			
Shareholders' equity	—	524,000	526,149
Statement of cash flow			
Dividends to shareholders	0	0	0

Calculate Fossil's actual and sustainable rate of growth in sales. How do the two rates of growth compare? What advice would you give to Fossil's management on the basis of these rates of growth?

E4.29 **Estimating Sustainable Growth.** The following information was taken from the 2005 annual report of **Microsoft Corporation**:

(in millions)	2003	2004	2005
Income statement			
Net sales	$32,187	$36,835	$39,788
Net earnings.		8,168	12,254
Balance sheet			
Shareholders' equity	—	74,825	48,115
Statement of cash flow			
Dividends to shareholders	0	1,729	36,968

Calculate Microsoft's actual and sustainable rate of growth in sales. How do the two rates of growth compare? What advice would you give to Microsoft's management on the basis of these two rates of growth? (Note: In 2005, Microsoft paid a special dividend to shareholders of $3.00 per share, amounting to $32.7 billion.)

PROBLEMS

P4.30 **Analyzing Financial Statements.** Presented below are selected financial data from the 2005 annual report of the **Bristol-Myers Squibb Company**:

(amounts in millions)	2004	2005
Balance sheet		
Cash and cash equivalents	$ 3,680	$ 3,050
Marketable securities.	3,794	2,749
Accounts receivable (net).	4,373	3,378
Inventory	1,830	2,060
Other current assets	1,124	1,046
Total current assets	14,801	12,283
Total assets	30,435	28,138
Current liabilities	9,843	6,890
Non-current liabilities.	10,390	10,040
Shareholders' equity	10,202	11,208
Income statement		
Net sales	19,380	19,207
Cost of goods sold	5,989	5,928
Interest expense	310	349
Net income.	$ 2,388	$ 3,000

Required

Using the ratio definitions from Exhibit 4.6, calculate the financial ratios for Bristol-Myers Squibb and determine whether the company is a good investment. Assume an effective tax rate of 30 percent.

P4.31 **Analyzing Financial Data: Trend Analysis.** Presented below is selected financial data for **The Gap, Inc.**, a large apparel company, for the five year period 1998 to 2002.

(in billions, except per share amounts)	1998	1999	2000	2001	2002
Net sales	$6.5	$9.1	$11.6	$13.7	$13.8
Cost of goods sold.	3.8	5.0	6.4	8.0	8.9
(as a percent of net sales)	58.0%	55.4%	54.7%	58.7%	64.3%
Operating expenses.	1.6	2.4	3.0	3.6	3.8
(as a percentage of net sales)	24.6%	26.4%	25.9%	26.2%	27.5%
Net income (loss)	0.5	0.8	1.1	0.9	(.008)
(as a percent of net sales)	7.7%	8.8%	9.5%	4.4%	(0.1)%
Cash dividend per share	0.09	0.09	0.09	0.09	0.09
Cash flow from operations.	0.8	1.3	1.4	1.2	1.3
Return on assets	17.9%	22.6%	24.6%	14.4%	(0.1)%
Return on equity.	33.0%	52.2%	59.2%	34.0%	(0.3)%

Required

1. Net sales more than doubled over the five year period, although net income did not. Why?
2. Comment on the company's use of financial leverage over the five year period.
3. Comment on the company's total asset turnover.
4. The company maintained its dividend of $0.09 per share over the five year period. Do you agree with this decision? Why?

P4.32 **Financial Statement Analysis using the ROE Model.** Presented below are the consolidated balance sheets and income statements for **Mann and Miller, Inc.**, a multinational consumer products company, for the period 2003 to 2005:

Mann & Miller, Inc. Consolidated Statement of Earnings			
(Dollars in Millions)	2005	2004	2003
Sales to customers.	$36,298	$32,317	$29,172
Cost of goods sold.	10,447	9,581	8,957
Gross profit.	25,851	22,736	20,215
Selling, marketing & administrative expense	12,216	11,260	10,495
Research expense	3,957	3,591	3,105
Purchased in-process research & development	189	105	66
Interest income.	(256)	(456)	(429)
Interest expense, net of portion capitalized.	160	153	204
Other (income) expense, net	294	185	(94)
	16,560	14,838	13,347
Earnings before provision for income taxes.	9,291	7,898	6,868
Provision for income taxes	2,694	2,230	1,915
Net earnings	$ 6,597	$ 5,668	$ 4,953
Basic net earnings per share	$2.20	$1.87	$1.65
Diluted net earnings per share	$2.16	$1.84	$1.61

Mann & Miller, Inc. Consolidated Balance Sheets			
(Dollars in Millions)	2005	2004	2003
Current assets			
Cash and cash equivalents	$ 2,894	$ 3,758	$ 4,278
Marketable securities.	4,581	4,214	2,479
Accounts receivable.	5,399	4,630	4,601
Inventories	3,303	2,992	2,905
Deferred income taxes	1,419	1,192	1,174
Prepaid expenses & other receivables.	1,670	1,687	1,254
Total current assets	$19,266	$18,473	$16,691

continued

continued from previous page

Mann & Miller, Inc. Consolidated Balance Sheets			
(Dollars in Millions)	2005	2004	2003
Marketable securities, non-current	$ 121	$ 969	$ 657
Property, plant & equipment, net	8,710	7,719	7,409
Intangible assets, net	9,246	9,077	7,535
Deferred income taxes	236	288	240
Other assets..	2,977	1,962	1,713
Total assets...	$40,556	$38,488	$34,245
Liabilities & Shareholders' Equity **Current liabilities**			
Loans & notes payable......................................	$ 2,117	$ 565	$ 1,489
Accounts payable...	3,621	2,838	2,122
Accrued liabilities payable	3,820	3,135	2,793
Accrued salaries, wages & commissions.....................	1,181	969	529
Income taxes payable	710	537	322
Total current liabilities	11,499	8,044	7,255
Long-term debt	2,022	2,217	3,163
Deferred income tax liability................................	643	493	255
Employee-related obligations................................	1,967	1,870	1,804
Other liabilities	1,778	1,631	1,373
Shareholders' equity			
Common stock—par value $1.00 per share (authorized 4,320,000,000 shares; issued 3,119,842,000 shares)	3,120	3,120	3,120
Note receivable from employee stock Ownership plan	(25)	(30)	(35)
Accumulated other comprehensive income......................	(843)	(530)	(461)
Retained earnings	26,571	23,066	18,113
Gross shareholders' equity..................................	28,824	25,626	20,737
Less: Common stock held in treasury, at Cost (151,547,000 and 72,627,000)...............................	(6,127)	(1,393)	(342)
Net shareholders' equity	22,697	24,233	20,395
Total liabilities & shareholders' equity	$40,556	$38,488	$34,245

Required

1. Calculate the following ratios for Mann & Miller, Inc (M & M):
   - *a.* Return on equity
   - *b.* Return on assets
   - *c.* Financial leverage
   - *d.* Return on sales
   - *e.* Total asset turnover
   - *f.* Receivable collection period
   - *g.* Inventory-on-hand period
   - *h.* Property, plant, and equipment turnover
   - *i.* Quick ratio
   - *j.* Long-term debt-to-shareholders' equity
   - *k.* Interest coverage ratio
   - *l.* Common-size income statements

2. In what areas is the company's performance improving? In what areas is the company's performance declining?
3. Assume that M & M's weighted-average cost of debt is approximately six percent. What is the company's after-tax cost of debt? Is the company using leverage effectively?

P4.33 **Financial Statement Analysis and Debt Covenants.** Wilmot Real Estate Co. had the following balance sheet at year-end 2005:

Wilmot Real Estate Co. Balance Sheet Year-end 2005			
Assets		**Liabilities and Shareholders' Equity**	
Current assets	$ 60,000	Current liabilities.	$ 45,000
Real estate investments.	250,000	Long-term liabilities	150,000
Other noncurrent assets.	25,000	Shareholders' equity	140,000
Total assets.	$335,000	Total liabilities & shareholders' equity	$335,000

In early 2006, the company took out a $200,000 two-year bank loan to finance new real estate investments. The loan specified that Wilmot must maintain a current ratio of at least 2-to-1 at all times during the loan period. Failure to satisfy this debt covenant would represent a "technical default" of the loan agreement, enabling the bank to demand immediate repayment of the outstanding loan balance and any accrued interest.
During 2006, Wilmot experienced the following events:

1. Generated $750,000 in revenues, of which $700,000 was collected by year-end 2006.
2. Incurred $650,000 in expenses, of which $575,000 was paid in cash.

Required

1. Prepare a balance sheet at year-end 2006 assuming that Wilmot invested the maximum allowable amount of the bank loan in new real estate investments in early 2006.
2. Evaluate Wilmot's compliance with the current ratio debt covenant assuming (a) the bank loan is included in current liabilities and (b) the bank loan is included in long-term liabilities.
3. Calculate the maximum dividend that Wilmot can distribute to its shareholders in 2006 assuming the bank loan is included in long-term liabilities.

P4.34 **(Appendix B) Pro Forma Income Statements.** Using the 2005 **Mann & Miller Inc.** (M&M) consolidated statement of earnings in Problem 4.32 as your base year, prepare pro forma income statements for M&M for 2006 and 2007 using an EXCEL spreadsheet. Relevant assumptions that you should use include:

*   Sales growth is twelve percent per year.
*   Gross profit margin is 70 percent.
*   Effective income tax rate is 29 percent.
*   All expenses, except interest expense, vary as a function of sales to customers.
*   Interest expense is eight percent of the beginning balance of long-term debt.

Required
Discuss the expected profitability of Mann & Miller in 2006 and 2007.

P4.35 **Financial Statement Analysis Using the ROE Model: International.** Presented below are the consolidated balance sheets and income statements for the **Kirin Brewery Company, Ltd.**, a multinational beverage company based in Japan for the period 2002–2004.

Kirin Brewery Company, Limited and Consolidated Subsidiaries For the years ended December 31			
Millions of Yen	**2004**	**2003**	**2002**
Sales	¥1,654,886	¥1,597,509	¥1,583,48
Less liquor taxes	430,957	431,749	445,935
Net sales	1,223,929	1,165,760	1,137,313
Cost of goods sold.............................	577,092	555,223	554,264
Gross profit	646,835	610,536	583,048
Selling, general and administrative expenses..............	537,444	508,981	493,259
Operating income	109,392	101,555	89,789
Non-operating income			
Interest income	750	835	1,147
Dividend income	3,341	2,919	2,614
Equity in earnings of affiliates	5,112	—	2,102
Rental income	1,621	—	—
Gain on transactions related to gift coupon	—	2,315	—
Return on funds in trust.......................	—	—	210
Other	3,209	4,109	4,143
Total	14,034	10,179	10,217
Non-operating expenses			
Interest expense	10,221	9,822	8,955
Loss on sale and disposal of finished goods..............	1,326	1,374	1,452
Equity in loss of affiliates	—	2,189	—
Other	5,315	3,671	5,154
Total	16,864	17,057	15,562
Ordinary income...............................	106,562	94,676	84,443
Special income			
Gain of sale of fixed assets	1,766	896	3,401
Reversal of allowance for doubtful accounts..............	331	503	—
Gain on sale of investment securities	319	77	420
Gain on release from the substitutional portion of the government's welfare pension insurance scheme	26,162	2,883	—
Gain on sale of shares of subsidiaries and affiliates	8,333	—	—
Reversal of allowance for furnace overhaul..............	—	—	700
Total	36,913	4,361	4,521
Special expenses			
Loss on disposal of fixed assets	5,743	3,747	6,715
Loss on sale of fixed assets.....................	251	1,757	379
Loss on impairment...........................	12,419	—	—
Loss on devaluation of investment securities	1,150	810	2,236
Loss on sale of investment securities	17	316	7
Business restructuring expense.....................	912	8,637	—
Loss on devaluation of fixed assets of foreign subsidiaries.........................	12,962	—	—
Expense of reserve for loss on repurchase of land	—	4,969	—
Loss on devaluation of land......................	—	650	—

continued

continued from previous page

Kirin Brewery Company, Limited and Consolidated Subsidiaries			
For the years ended December 31			
Millions of Yen	2004	2003	2002
Loss on devaluation of real estate in trust.................	—	—	3,352
Premium on employee's retirement benefits	—	—	1,755
Total	33,458	20,890	14,447
Income balance before income taxes minority interests	110,018	78,147	74,517
Income taxes—current....................................	39,738	41,236	37,092
Income taxes—deferred.................................	13,518	(2,094)	(878)
Minority interests	7,662	6,610	5,762
Net Income	¥ 49,099	¥ 32,392	¥ 32,540

Kirin Brewery Company, Limited and Consolidated Subsidiaries		
December 31		
Millions of Yen	2004	2003
Current Assets		
Cash...	¥ 183,501	¥ 133,108
Notes and accounts receivable, trade......................	292,708	283,661
Marketable securities......................	800	493
Inventories	83,296	88,831
Deferred tax assets	19,919	19,474
Other	45,111	45,072
Allowance for doubtful accounts......................	(4,489)	(5,312)
Total Current Assets......................................	620,848	565,327
Fixed Assets		
Property, plant and equipment (Net of accumulated depreciation and accumulated loss from impairment)		
Buildings and structures	190,537	185,404
Machinery, equipment and vehicles	165,881	182,997
Land...	154,474	165,980
Construction in progress	33,567	30,330
Other	41,819	45,276
Total	586,279	609,989
Intangible Assets		
Goodwill..	22,016	29,788
Consolidation differences	40,275	43,339
Other	72,652	76,135
Total	134,945	149,262

continued

continued from previous page

Kirin Brewery Company, Limited and Consolidated Subsidiaries December 31		
Millions of Yen	2004	2003
Investments and Other Assets		
Investment securities.	372,095	351,323
Long-term loans.	5,629	7,069
Life insurance investments	36,491	36,243
Deferred tax assets	17,970	39,487
Deferred tax asset due to land revaluation	—	1,929
Other	53,464	31,295
Allowance for doubtful accounts.	(3,935)	(4,060)
Total	481,716	463,288
Total Fixed Assets	1,202,941	1,222,540
Total Assets.	¥1,823,790	¥1,787,867

Kirin Brewery Company, Limited and Consolidated Subsidiaries December 31		
Millions of Yen	2004	2003
Liabilities, Minority Interests and Shareholders' Equity		
Current Liabilities		
Notes and accounts payable, trade.	¥ 111,418	¥ 109,264
Short-term loans payable and long-term debt with current maturities	24,882	16,896
Liquor taxes payable	117,066	117,119
Income taxes payable	13,523	19,532
Accrued expenses	78,656	60,312
Deposits received	51,176	58,172
Other	46,124	62,065
Total Current Liabilities.	442,847	443,363
Long-term Liabilities		
Bonds.	171,564	167,428
Long-term debt	67,119	93,617
Deferred tax liability due to land revaluation	3,197	—
Employees' pension and retirements benefits.	73,227	84,771
Retirement benefits for directors and corporate auditors	1,132	1,541
Reserve for repair and maintenance of vending machines	8,421	7,697
Reserve for loss on repurchase of land	5,157	4,969
Deposits received	73,374	72,282
Other	40,273	30,575
Total Long-term Liabilities	443,469	462,884
Total Liabilities	886,317	906,247
Minority Interests	78,857	77,737

continued

continued from previous page

Kirin Brewery Company, Limited and Consolidated Subsidiaries **December 31**		
Millions of Yen	**2004**	**2003**
Shareholders' Equity		
Common stock		
Authorized—1,732,026,000 shares		
Issued—984,508,387 shares.	102,045	102,045
Capital surplus.	70,984	70,868
Retained earnings	687,905	651,078
Land revaluation difference	(4,713)	(1,673)
Net unrealized holding gains on securities	52,463	29,875
Foreign currency translation adjustments	(35,614)	(34,128)
Treasury stock, at cost 18,577,240 and 18,416,607		
shares in 2004 and 2003, respectively	(14,456)	(14,183)
Total shareholders' equity.	858,615	803,882
Total Liabilities, Minority Interests and Shareholders' Equity	¥1,823,790	¥1,787,867

Required

1. Calculate the following ratios for Kirin Brewery:

   a. Return on equity
   b. Return on assets
   c. Return on sales
   d. Financial leverage
   e. Total debt-to-equity ratio
   f. Long-term debt-to-equity ratio
   g. Current ratio
   h. Quick ratio

   i. Interest coverage ratio
   j. Accounts payable turnover
   k. Accounts receivable turnover
   l. Inventory turnover
   m. Fixed asset turnover
   n. Total asset turnover
   o. Common-size income statements
   p. Common-size balance sheets

2. In what areas is the company's performance improving? In what areas is the company's performance declining? (Note: Kirin's weighted-average cost of debt in 2004 was 3.3 percent; what was the company's after-tax cost of debt?)

P4.36 **(Appendix 4B) Pro Forma Financial Statements.** The venture capital division of a major U.S. financial institution has elected to fund an investment in an oil and gas exploration and production company that will operate both onshore and offshore in Texas and Louisiana in the United States. The initial financing commitment from the bank was for $40 million.

The company's strategic plan called for an aggressive drilling program to be carried out during 2004. Hofstedt Oil & Gas estimated that it would drill 50 wells at an average cost of $800,000 per well and that 30 of those wells would yield aggregate crude oil reserves of approximately 10 million barrels. The remaining 20 wells were expected to be commercially unproductive. These forecasts were based on the expert opinion of geologists familiar with the properties and were confirmed by petroleum engineers employed directly by the bank.

The company's production plan called for a maximum exploitation effort to earn the highest financial return. Tom Hofstedt, president of the company, developed the following production scenario:

Year	Number of Barrels To Be Produced	Estimated Selling Price Per Barrel	Estimated Lifting Cost Per Barrel
2004	1,000,000	$30	$5
2005	1,500,000	30	5
2006	1,500,000	35	6
2007	2,500,000	40	7
2008	3,500,000	45	8

Hofstedt Oil & Gas was very concerned about the impact of this operation on its financial statements and on the company's share price. Consequently, any available accounting policy choices loomed as very important in the overall evaluation of the investment. As a result, Hofstedt sent a terse memo to the company's controller, the closing line of which stated, "Prepare pro forma statements showing the alternative accounting effects on cash flow, income before tax, and total assets if we elect to use the successful efforts method or the full cost method." Under the full cost method, the cost of all wells—successful and unsuccessful—are capitalized to the balance sheet and then depleted over the expected productive life of the successful wells. Under the successful efforts method, only the cost of the successful wells are capitalized (the cost of any unsuccessful wells are immediately expensed) to be depleted over their expected productive life. (See Chapter 7 for additional discussion of the full cost and successful efforts methods.)

Required
For purposes of pro forma statement preparation, assume that the $40 million loan agreement will be repaid as follows: (1) $10 million principal repayment per year to be paid on December 31 beginning on December 31, 2005; and (2) interest payments of 10 percent per year on the balance of the loan outstanding as of the beginning of the year. Ignore income taxes and all other operations. Based on your pro forma cash flows, income statements, and balance sheets for the period 2004 through 2008, what accounting method (successful efforts or full cost) recommendation would you make to Tom Hofstedt, and why?

P4.37 **(Appendix 4B) Pro Forma Financial Statements.** **Handy Dan, Inc.** operates warehouse-style stores, selling a variety of home building products and lawn and garden supplies. Presented below are Handy Dan's historical financial statements for Year 1 and Year 2:

Handy Dan, Inc. **Statement of Income** (amounts in millions)	Year 2
Sales.	$980
Cost of goods sold.	727
Gross profit.	253
Depreciation expense.	8
Other operating expenses	217
Operating income.	28
Interest expense.	21
Income before taxes.	7
Income tax expense.	2
Net income.	$ 5

Handy Dan, Inc.
Balance Sheets

(amounts in millions)	Year 1	Year 2	Equities	Year 1	Year 2
Assets			**Equities**		
Cash.	$ 10	$ 14	Accounts payable	$ 74	$104
Accounts receivable (net).	27	38	Short-term loans payable	10	29
Inventory	153	214	Long-term debt	207	289
Total current assets	190	266	Total liabilities.	291	422
Property & equipment (cost)	199	279	Contributed capital	50	62
Accumulated depreciation.	(9)	(17)	Retained earnings	39	44
	190	262	Total shareholders' equity	89	106
Total assets.	$380	$528	Total liabilities & shareholders' equity.	$380	$528

Handy Dan, Inc.
Statement of Retained Earnings

(amounts in millions)	Year 2
Retained earnings (Year 1)	$29
Add: Net income	5
Less: Dividends	0
Retained earnings (Year 2)	$44

Handy Dan, Inc.
Statement of Cash Flow

(amounts in millions)	Year 2
Operations	
Net income.	$ 5
Depreciation expense	8
Accounts receivable (net).	(11)
Inventory	(61)
Accounts payable	30
Cash flow from operations.	(29)
Investing activities	
Purchase of property & equipment	(80)
Cash flow from investing	(80)
Financing activities	
Short-term borrowing	19
Long-term borrowing.	82
Stock sales	12
Dividend payment	0
Cash flow from financing	113
Change in cash.	$ 4

Required

Using the following set of assumptions, prepare pro forma financial statements for Handy Dan, Inc. for Year 3:

- Sales are projected to grow by 40 percent.
- Cash is expected to increase at the same rate as sales.
- Assume the following ratios to forecast the identified accounts:

Account	Financial Ratio		
Accounts receivable..........	Receivable turnover	=	25.9x
Inventory...................	Inventory turnover	=	3.39x
Property & equipment	Fixed asset turnover	=	3.52x
Cost of goods sold...........	Gross profit margin percentage	=	25.9%
Operating expenses..........	Operating expenses ÷ sales	=	22.1%
Accounts payable............	Payable turnover	=	7.55x

- Depreciation expense is based on a 30 year expected life with no salvage value; any property and equipment acquired during the year is depreciated for only one-half year.
- Interest expense is based on a six percent short-term cost of debt and eight percent long-term cost of debt; only one-half year of interest is charged on loans taken out during the year.
- Effective income tax rate is 33.33 percent.
- The mix of short-term loans payable, long-term debt and contributed capital is set to satisfy an existing debt covenant that requires the company to maintain a current ratio of 2.0 (or greater) and a total debt-to-total assets ratio of 80 percent (or less).

Discuss the expected profitability and operating cash flow of Handy Dan in Year 3.

P4.38   **Benchmarking Firm Performance.**   Presented below are profitability ratios for three competitors for 2005: **Bristol-Myers Squibb (BMS)**, **Pfizer, Inc. (PFE)**, and the **Johnson and Johnson Company (J&J)**:

2005	BMS	PFE	J&J
Return on equity (ROE).........................	26.8%	12.3%	27.5%
Return on assets (ROA)	10.7%	6.9%	17.9%
Return on sales (ROS)	15.6%	15.7%	20.6%
Total asset turnover	.683	.436	0.87
Price-to-earnings multiple	16.1x	22.5x	17.5x

Required

Compare the relative profitability of the three firms. Which one appears most profitable? Which one would you prefer to add to a portfolio of securities? Why?

P4.39   **Evaluating Financial Performance.**   Presented below are selected financial statement data for three global energy firms for 2004:

(amounts in millions)	Chevron Texaco Corporation	Conoco Phillips Corporation	Marathon Oil Corporation
Balance sheet			
Total assets	$ 93,036	$ 91,756	$ 20,733
Short-term debt	816	632	16
Long-term debt	10,217	14,370	4,057
Total debt	47,806	49,033	12,622
Shareholders' equity	45,230	42,723	8,111
Income statement			
Revenues	$155,300	$135,076	$ 49,598
Net income.	13,328	8,129	1,261
Cash flow from operations	14,690	11,959	3,730
Ratios			
Receivable collection period	29.2 days	14.7 days	23.2 days
Inventory-on-hand period	10.4 days	13.7 days	18.2 days
Long-debt-to-total assets	11.0%	26.0%	24.0%
Return on assets	14.3%	8.8%	5.4%
Return on equity	29.5%	19.0%	15.5%

Required
1. Compare the three firms in terms of their size and their financing strategy.
2. Evaluate the performance of the three firms in 2004. Was performance linked to firm size?

P4.40 **Evaluating Financial Performance: Global.** Presented below are selected financial statement data for three global energy firms for 2004:

(amounts in millions of U.S. dollars)	Exxon Mobile Corp (US)	Statoil ASA (Norway)	Total SA (France)
Balance sheet			
Total assets	$191,304	$41,105	$58,388
Short-term debt	3,280	788	2,838
Long-term debt	5,013	5,243	7,239
Total debt	89,548	26,933	35,888
Shareholders' equity	101,756	14,172	22,500
Income statement			
Revenues	$298,035	$51,036	$90,798
Net income.	25,330	4,153	7,112
Cash flow from operations	40,551	6,468	10,678
Ratios			
Receivable collection period	31.0 days	37.8 days	41.7 days
Inventory-on-hand period	21.3 days	13.5 days	NA
Long-debt-to-total assets	11.0%	23.0%	24.0%
Return on assets	13.0%	10.0%	11.4%
Return on equity	24.9%	29.3%	30.7%

Required
1. Compare the three firms in terms of their size and their financing strategy.
2. Evaluate the performance of the three firms in 2004. Was performance linked to firm size?

P4.41   **(Appendix 4A) Calculating ROE using Unlevered Financial Ratios.**   Presented below are summary financial data from the 2006 annual report of The William Likert Company. Using the ratio definitions from Appendix A, calculate the following financial ratios: unlevered return on sales, total asset turnover, financial leverage, and common equity share of operating earnings. Evaluate the trend in the company's return on equity. Assume an effective income tax rate of 30 percent.

(amounts in thousands)	2005	2006
Balance sheet		
Total assets	$30,435	$28,138
Shareholders' equity	10,202	11,208
Income statement		
Net sales	28,000	26,000
Interest expense	310	349
Net income after taxes.	4,418	4,516

P4.42   **(Appendix 4A) Calculating ROE using Unlevered Financial Ratios.**   Presented below are summary financial data from the 2006 annual report of The Hazen Company. Using the ratio definitions from Appendix A, calculate the following financial ratios: unlevered return on sales, total asset turnover, financial leverage, and common equity share of operating earnings. Evaluate the trend in the company's return on equity. Assume an effective income tax rate of 30 percent.

(amounts in thousands)	2005	2006
Balance sheet		
Total assets	$123,078	$117,565
Shareholders' equity	68,278	65,627
Income Statement		
Net sales	130,000	140,000
Interest expense	3,590	4,800
Net income after taxes.	14,007	11,534

P4.43   **(Appendix 4C) Calculating the Cost of Equity.**   The following information is available for The Philippi Winery Company, Inc.

	2004	2005	2006
Beta	0.70	0.75	0.80
Risk-free rate of return	5.00	5.25	5.50
Equity risk-premium	7.00	7.30	7.50

Calculate the company's cost of equity capital for 2004, 2005, and 2006 using the Capital Asset Pricing Model discussed in Appendix 4C. Discuss the trend in the company's beta and its cost of equity.

CORPORATE ANALYSIS

CA4.44 **The Procter and Gamble Company.**   The 2005 annual report of **The Procter and Gamble Company** (P & G) is available at www.pg.com/annualreports/2005/pdf/pg2005annualreport.pdf. After reviewing P & G's annual report, respond to the following questions:

   a.   Prepare common-size income statements for the period 2003 through 2005. What major trends can you identify from this data?

    b. Prepare common-size balance sheets for 2004 and 2005. What major trends can you identify from this data?

    c. Calculate the following ratios for P & G for 2004 and 2005:

- Return on shareholders' equity
- Return on assets
- Return on sales
- Gross profit margin ratio
- Accounts receivable turnover
- Receivable collection period
- Inventory turnover

- Inventory-on-hand period
- Total asset turnover
- Quick ratio
- Current ratio
- Long-term debt-to-total assets
- Interest coverage ratio
- Financial leverage ratio

What major trends can you identify from this data?

    d. Develop an overall assessment of the financial performance of P & G for the period 2003 through 2005.

CA4.45 **Internet-based Analysis.** Consider a publicly-held company whose products you are familiar with. Some examples might include:

Company	Product	Corporate Website
• **Johnson & Johnson Company**	• Band-Aids	• www.jnj.com
• **Microsoft Corporation**	• Windows XP software	• www.microsoft.com
• **Nokia Corporation**	• Cellular phones	• www.nokia.com
• **Intel Corporation**	• Pentium processors	• www.intel.com
• **Kimberly-Clark Corporation**	• Kleenex	• www.kimberly-clark.com

Access the company's public website and search for its most recent annual report. (Note: Some companies will provide access to their financial data through an "investor relations" link, while others will provide a direct link to their "annual reports.") After locating your company's most recent annual report, open the file and review its contents. After reviewing the annual report for your selected company, prepare answers to the following questions:

1. Prepare common-size income statements and common-size balance sheets for the past two years. What significant trends can you identify from these common-size statements?

2. Calculate the following ratios for the past two years. (Note: Use the ratio definitions in Exhibit 4.6.)

Gross profit margin	Total asset turnover
Return on sales	Cash and marketable securities-to-total assets
Return on assets	Quick ratio
Return on equity	Current ratio
Receivable turnover	Long-term debt-to-total assets
Receivable collection period	Current ratio
Inventory turnover	Long-term debt-to-shareholders' equity
Inventory-on-hand period	Interest coverage ratio

What significant trends in the company's profitability, asset management, or financial risk can you identify from your calculations?

3. Identify several key competitors of your selected company. Go to Yahoo.Finance.com and benchmark your company against its key competitors on the following metrics:

Market capitalization	Return on assets
Return on sales	Return on equity

4. Review the company's long-term debt footnotes. Is the company subject to any debt covenants? If so, what are the covenants and is the company currently in compliance with the covenant(s).

Chapter Five

Operating Cycle, Revenue Recognition and Receivable Valuation

TAKEAWAYS

When you complete this chapter you should be able to:

1. Explain how retail, service and manufacturing companies recognize their operating revenue.
2. Describe how revenue is recognized under the completed contract and percentage of completion methods.
3. Explain how accounts receivables are valued and how the allowance for uncollectible accounts and bad debt expense are estimated.
4. Describe why the effective management of accounts receivable is important for a business.

Where have we been?	Where are we?	Where are we going?
Chapter 4 examined how to use financial statement data to evaluate a company's profitability, asset management, and financial risk. We saw that financial statement analysis may take many forms—trend analysis, common-size statement analysis, and ratio analysis. We also learned that financial statements should not be used in a vacuum without considering other sources of information. Finally, we discussed some of the limitations inherent in the use of accounting data for company financial analysis.	In this chapter, the important concept of operating revenue is investigated along with how companies in various industries measure and report their operating revenue. Since most businesses extend credit to their customers in an effort to generate incremental sales revenue, the related issue of measuring and reporting accounts receivable is considered. We will see that accounts receivable are valued at their net realizable value and will explore how companies estimate the potential losses that they experience as a consequence of extending credit to customers. We also consider how some companies manage their earnings through revenue recognition and receivable valuation policies.	In Chapter 6, we examine how, and at what cost, companies acquire the various resources needed to manufacture products or provide services to their customers. We will see that the cost of a company's inventory on hand and the cost of inventory sold depends on the inventory valuation method selected by management and that this choice is often influenced by income tax and income reporting considerations. Some of the inventory valuation methods that are explored include FIFO (First-in, First-out), LIFO (Last-in, First-out), and the Weighted-average cost method.

MICROSOFT CORPORATION   Symbol: MSFT

Microsoft Corporation is the world's largest personal computer software developer. The company also provides internet search services through its subsidiary MSN.com and competes in the video game industry through its Xbox platform. According to Microsoft's 2006 annual report, the company's revenues grew from $36.8 billion in 2004 to over $44.3 billion in 2006, an annual growth rate of approximately 10 percent. According to Microsoft's footnotes to its financial statements:

> Revenue is recognized when persuasive evidence of a sales arrangement exists, delivery has occurred, the fee is fixed or determinable, and collectibility is probable . . . . Revenue for retail products and products licensed to original equipment manufacturers is recognized as products are shipped, with a portion of the revenue recorded as **unearned** (emphasis added) due to undelivered elements including free post-delivery telephone support and the right to receive unspecified upgrades/enhancements.

Microsoft's 2006 balance sheet disclosed the following amounts for its unearned revenue:

(in millions)	2005	2006
Short-term unearned revenue	$7,502	$ 9,138
Long-term unearned revenue.	1,665	1,764
Total unearned revenue	$9,167	$10,902

Although not inconsistent with generally accepted accounting principles, many investment professionals view Microsoft's practice of deferring the recognition of a portion of the revenue from its retail products and OEM-licensed products as a form of rear-end loading of revenues. Rear-end loading of revenues—that is, postponing the income statement recognition of certain revenues until a later fiscal period—reduces the total level of revenues currently recognized, and thus, reduces currently reported operating income.

Analysts critical of Microsoft's revenue reporting argue that the practice creates an earnings reserve on the company's balance sheet, enabling the firm to manage its reported earnings and consistently meet or exceed Wall Street's earnings' expectations. Microsoft has met or exceeded the Street's earnings' expectations for 17 consecutive years. Wall Street pundits also note that the practice of revenue deferral enables Microsoft to appear less profitable, and hence, less monopolistic—an important feature as the company appeals the anti-competitiveness ruling brought against it in 2004 by the European Union Committee on Competition.

In this chapter, we explore the important accounting construct of revenue recognition. In the eyes of most investment professionals, there is no accounting policy decision more important than the selection of an appropriate revenue recognition method. The importance of this policy decision stems from the relationship of operating revenue to firm value—operating revenues are the key driver of firm value!

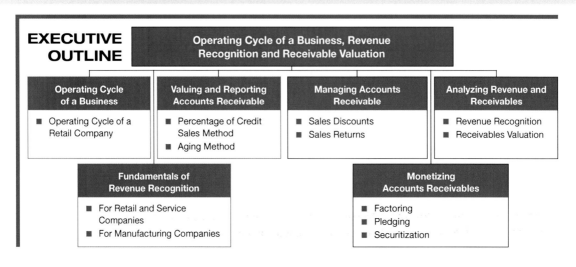

OPERATING CYCLE OF A BUSINESS

Almost all businesses have an identifiable cycle of activities that reflect the ongoing operations of the business. This repetitive cycle of events is commonly referred to as the **operating cycle** of the business. Exhibit 5.1 presents, for example, the operating cycle of a typical retail operation. It reveals that retail businesses buy inventory ready for sale to their customers, then sell the inventory, and finally, collect cash following the sales transaction.

Illustrative of this cycle are the operating cycles of **Wal-Mart** and **Daimler-Chrysler**, both international retail businesses. (Daimler-Chrysler Corporation is, technically, a manufacturing company; however, the company maintains a network of dealers that specialize in the sale and maintenance of Daimler-Chrysler products. We are referring here to that retail network of dealers.) Wal-Mart, for example, uses its available cash to buy inventory for sale to its customers; but, because the products that Wal-Mart sells are relatively inexpensive, and because Wal-Mart's business strategy is to be a low-cost, low profit margin, but high volume business, all of its sales transactions are in cash or using a debit/credit card. In short, Wal-Mart does not extend credit to its customers. Daimler-Chrysler, on the other hand, operates in the highly competitive automotive industry and sells a relatively expensive product to its customers, most of whom could not afford to buy a car or truck for cash. Thus, Daimler-Chrysler, through its financing subsidiary, arranges for most of its customers to buy its products on credit. As these examples reveal, depending upon the relative cost of a product, the financial capability of a business' customers, and the competitiveness of a given business environment, a business will (or will not) sell its products or services to its customers on credit.

In this chapter, we explore the various ways that businesses can recognize their operating revenues, and if they extend credit to their customers, the risks and attendant costs associated with this important business practice.

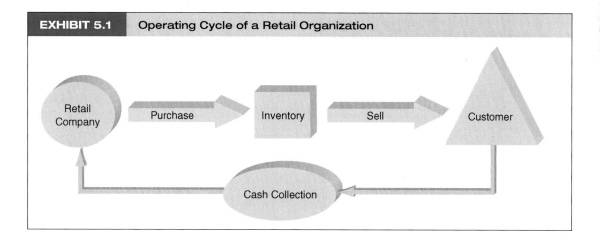

EXHIBIT 5.1 **Operating Cycle of a Retail Organization**

FUNDAMENTALS OF REVENUE RECOGNITION

Revenue refers to the inflow of assets (such as cash, accounts receivable, or bartered assets) to a business that occurs as a direct consequence of providing goods or services to customers. In Chapter 2, the topic of revenue recognition was introduced. At that time, we said that revenue could be **recognized**—that is, revenue could be reported on the income statement as having been earned—at the point in time at which a company provides goods or services to its customers and when collectability of any unpaid cash from the customer is reasonably assured.

Recognizing revenue is a significant economic event for a business. It signifies that the business has successfully performed some activity such as selling a product or providing a service. In the view of most investment professionals, recognizing revenue is the most important event affecting a business since it indicates the market's acceptance of the firm's product or service. Since revenue recognition increases shareholders' wealth, it is considered to be the primary driver of firm share price, and thus, the key driver of firm value.

When revenue is recognized and matched with the expenses incurred to produce the revenue, net income (loss) results. In Chapter 2, the financial data of the Russian River Valley Winery was used to illustrate how financial statements could be produced from a series of economic events and transactions. In that illustration, the winery recognized revenue from the sale of its wine at the time that its wines were sold to the company's customers (when legal ownership of the wine passed from the winery to the customer). But the winery could have recognized its revenue at other points in time, for example when the wine was delivered, if delivery occurred after the sale, or at the point of cash collection, if customers were allowed to purchase the wine on credit.

In essence, the key business conditions that must be satisfied before a firm may recognize revenue include: (1) the revenue must be earned; and (2) the revenue must be realized or realizable. The first condition refers to the fact that the company must satisfy its obligations under the terms of any sales agreement. The second condition refers to the fact that the company has been paid or can reasonably expect to be paid. While these conditions may seem relatively clear cut, inaccurate revenue recognition is by far the leading cause for U.S. Securities and Exchange Commission (SEC) enforcement actions against U.S. exchange-listed companies. The revenue recognition inaccuracies range from differences of opinion regarding the application of revenue recognition rules to outright fraud. We will have more to say about this problem later in this chapter.

The large number of inaccurate, usually aggressive or premature, revenue recognition practices adopted by firms led the SEC to issue explicit guidance regarding the recognition of revenue in Staff Accounting Bulletin (SAB) 101. According to SAB 101, the following criteria must be satisfied before revenue can be recognized by a business: (1) persuasive evidence of a sales arrangement must exist; (2) delivery of the product or service must occur; (3) the seller's price to the buyer is fixed or determinable; and (4) collectability of any unpaid cash is reasonably assured.

Unfortunately, numerous grey areas arise within the interpretation of exactly when to recognize revenue. A partial list of the controversial issues include: (1) exactly what constitutes persuasive evidence of a sales arrangement; (2) consignment sales; (3) a right-of-product return policy exists; (4) the product is complete and paid for but not yet delivered; (5) the seller receives nonrefundable fees;(6) the seller acts as a middleman between the retailer and the customer; and, (7) the sale involves a barter transaction. Appendix 5B to this chapter provides an analysis of these controversial issues.

To illustrate just a few of these controversies, Exhibit 5.2 depicts six possible points in time when revenue might be recognized by a business enterprise. Moving from right to left, these points represent a continuum of increasing risk that the amount of revenue recognized will subsequently prove to be in error. For instance, if revenue is recognized before production of a product even begins (see the far left end of the continuum in Exhibit 5.1), there is a very high probability that the amount of recorded revenue will not actually be earned. Many events may occur before the product is ultimately produced, sold, and delivered to the final consumer that could change its final selling price, and thus, the appropriate amount of revenue to be recognized.

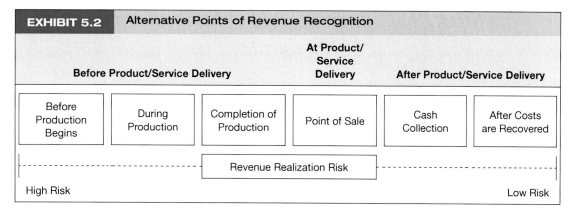

EXHIBIT 5.2 **Alternative Points of Revenue Recognition**

			At Product/Service Delivery	
Before Product/Service Delivery				**After Product/Service Delivery**
Before Production Begins	During Production	Completion of Production	Point of Sale	Cash Collection	After Costs are Recovered

Revenue Realization Risk

High Risk   Low Risk

Consider the case of a jewelry manufacturer that uses diamonds and gold in its finished products. If the jeweler recognizes revenue for a ring that has not even been produced, the jeweler would have to be very certain that the price of diamonds and gold would not change, that the cost of labor would remain stable, and that the ring would be sufficiently attractive that the jeweler would have no trouble finding a buyer at the planned selling price. But one or all of these assumptions is likely to be false, and hence, revenue (and net income) is likely to be incorrectly reported. Thus, the first point on the left—before production begins—is too early to recognize revenue even if the company has a guaranteed purchase commitment from a customer at a specified purchase price (such as a signed purchase contract). The company has yet to *earn* the revenue and therefore cannot recognize the revenue.

The second point, when the company is actively producing inventory for sale, indicates that the risk of being able to produce the product has been at least partially resolved. The risks that remain, however, include finding a buyer for the product at the anticipated selling price and collecting the full purchase price in cash, among others.

At the third point, production of the product is complete, and thus, the risk of production has been eliminated; but, the risk that remains is that a buyer will need to be found who is willing to pay the specified selling price. If a purchase order from a customer is received, this would indicate that the customer is convinced of the product's value, and thus, it may seem that revenue recognition could be justified. This is not the case, however, since the earning process has not been completed. Until delivery takes place and the risks of ownership transfer to the buyer, revenue cannot be recognized.

At the fourth point, the point of sale, all of the risks of successful production have been resolved and a final consumer has been identified. At this point, the principal remaining risks are that of cash collection, assuming that a business allows its customers to buy its goods and services on credit, and the risk of customer dissatisfaction, assuming that a business offers its customers the opportunity to return unwanted or defective goods. For these businesses, there is the risk that some customers will be unable or unwilling to pay for previously purchased goods and services, as well as the risk that some products will be returned. While the point of delivery is the customary point at which revenue is properly recognized, questions remain as to whether the revenue has been earned and whether collection is reasonably assured. If a right-of-return policy exists or if collection is not assured, it is premature to recognize the entire revenue amount. In such cases, companies must establish certain allowances or reserves to provide for the contingency that the product will be returned or will not be paid for. We illustrate such reserves later in the chapter.

At the fifth point, the point of cash collection, all revenue realization risks have been eliminated except for product-return risk. The product has been successfully produced; a final customer has been identified; and, the expected cash has been received. The remaining risks at this stage involve customer dissatisfaction and inflation. In the case of customer dissatisfaction, if a business maintains a policy of allowing customers to return unwanted and/or defective products, the risk of product return will persist until any product-return-guarantee period has expired. With respect to inflation, a business must be able to generate sufficient cash flow from its sales to replace its sold inventory; otherwise, it will be unable to survive in the long-term. In most situations, this business risk is unavoidable and is simply a matter of degree; however, a carefully constructed product pricing policy which links retail prices to expected rates of inflation can successfully manage inflation risk.

At the final point, recognizing revenue after product replacement costs have been recovered, there are no revenue realization risks remaining unless the company's product-return-guarantee period has not yet expired. Also, at this point, all business risks have been successfully encountered. But, is it necessary for a business to wait until this point in time is reached before recognizing its revenue? Definitely not! Generally accepted accounting practice around the world provides considerable flexibility to companies to select the point of revenue recognition that makes the most economic sense for a given business model. This flexibility is possible because the accrual accounting system has built-in mechanisms that allow the measurement and reporting of any remaining revenue realization risks (such as bad debts, sales returns, etc.). Thus, it is possible to recognize revenue at a point in time with some remaining revenue risk so long as these risks are estimable and reported in the financial statements.

Revenue Recognition by Retail and Service Companies

Most retail businesses buy goods completely manufactured and ready for sale to the final consumer, whereas service companies provide a service to the final customer. For these businesses, the selection of a revenue recognition method is usually limited to the following two options:

* Point of sale
* Point of cash collection

Global retail companies like **Wal-Mart** typically recognize revenue at the point of sale (which coincides with product delivery) because they rarely grant credit to their customers. Wal-Mart customers pay with cash, debit card, credit card, or by writing a check. For those retail businesses or service companies, such as the accounting firm **Ernst and Young**, which do grant credit to their customers, point of sale is still the most common method of revenue recognition *unless* there is significant doubt regarding the debt-paying ability of a customer. When account payment is uncertain, companies may instead chose to recognize revenue at the point of cash collection, or what is commonly called the **installment method.**

Under the installment method of revenue recognition, revenue is recognized only to the extent of any cash received. For instance, if a used car dealer sells an automobile to a customer with poor credit (who is unable to obtain bank financing for the purchase), the dealer may chose to recognize the revenue from the transaction on an installment basis. To illustrate, assume that the dealer sold a car for $15,000 that had a cost basis to the dealer of $12,000. Under the terms of the purchase agreement, the customer made an initial down payment of $1,500 (ten percent of the purchase price) and signed a promissory **note receivable** requiring nine additional monthly payments of $1,500.

> **Accounts receivable** refer to short-term (usually 30, 60, or 90 days in duration) credit arrangements that are typically interest-free. **Notes receivable**, on the other hand, refer to credit which is longer term (perhaps as long as three to five years), for large amounts, and consequently, likely to involve interest charges.

Under the installment method, the car dealer will recognize only the initial down payment of $1,500 as revenue and record cost of goods sold of $1,200 (ten percent of $12,000). As each monthly payment is received, the dealer will recognize $1,500 in revenue and $1,200 in cost of goods sold, yielding an apparent profit of $3,000 ($15,000 − $12,000) after all cash payments have been received. Since receipt of the entire $15,000 is in doubt because of the customer's poor credit history, the dealer appropriately only recognizes revenues and costs to the extent of the cash received. However, because the dealer financed the customer's purchase over a nine-month period, there is a hidden opportunity cost to the dealer equal to the time value of money. (If you are unclear about the time value of money, please read the appendix at the end of this textbook.) If the dealer has a cost of borrowing of, say, one percent per month, the opportunity cost implicit in the transaction is $651.00, calculated as follows:

Amount financed by customer.	$13,500
Less: Present value of 9 payments of $1,500 @ 1%: $1,500 × 8.566. . . .	(12,849)
Opportunity cost	$ 651

Thus, the dealer's real profit is only $2,349 ($3,000 − $651). To recover such opportunity costs, businesses that sell their product on credit over extended periods (such as greater than 90 days) often charge their customers interest on any unpaid balances. We will have more to say about the concept of opportunity costs in Chapter 9.

Revenue Recognition by Manufacturing Companies

Manufacturing companies take one or more raw materials and produce a product. To allow these companies to focus on the task of producing a product, most manufacturers do not sell directly to the final consumer of their products but rather sell to retailers who specialize in product distribution. For example, General Motors manufactures cars and trucks but does not sell these products directly to the final consumer. Instead, GM sells its cars and trucks to a network of dealers who specialize in retailing to consumers.

For most manufacturers, revenue recognition will occur at the point of product delivery or the point of cash collection if collection is uncertain. In some industries, manufacturers produce goods under contract when production may span several fiscal periods. In these situations, special rules apply that allow revenue recognition either during production or after production when the product is complete. Companies that manufacture a product under contract include such firms as Boeing, one of the world's leading manufacturers of commercial aircraft, and General Dynamics Corporation, one of the world's leading manufacturers of defense systems. Since the cost of the products sold by these companies is quite large, they manufacture a product only after a purchase contract has been signed by the customer and a deposit customarily paid, principally to help minimize their business risk.

To illustrate the financial effects of these alternative revenue recognition approaches, consider data for ProFlight Inc., a manufacturer of private corporate jets. ProFlight signed a contract to build five jets over a two year period for TransGlobal Airlines. Under the contract, ProFlight will receive total revenues of $10 million and anticipates that its cost to build the planes will equal $8 million, yielding a gross profit of $2 million. Data regarding the contract is presented in Exhibit 5.3.

Exhibit 5.3 reveals that in 2004, ProFlight completed 20 percent of the work required under the contract, sent an invoice for $1 million to TransGlobal, and received a payment of $500,000. In 2005, ProFlight completed the remaining 80 percent of the project on budget at $8 million in total costs, delivered the five planes, sent an invoice for the remaining $9 million to TransGlobal, and received a $4.5

million payment. In early 2006, after completing flight testing of the aircraft, TransGlobal remitted the final $5 million in cash to ProFlight.

EXHIBIT 5.3	Revenue Recognition by a Company Manufacturing Under Contract		
	2004	2005	2006
Percentage of Work Completed	20%	80%	
Costs incurred	$2,000,000	$6,000,000	—
Progress billings	1,000,000	9,000,000	—
Cash collected	500,000	4,500,000	$5,000,000

Revenue Recognition during Production. If ProFlight recognizes revenue as production of the planes proceeds, it will recognize revenue on the basis of the amount or percentage of work actually completed each period. According to Exhibit 5.3, ProFlight completed 20 percent of the work in 2004 and the remaining 80 percent in 2005. This would suggest that ProFlight should recognize $2 million as revenue (20 percent of $10 million) in 2004 and $8 million as revenue (80 percent of $10 million) in 2005. This method of revenue recognition is commonly referred to as the **percentage of completion method**—that is, revenue is recognized in proportion to the amount of work actually completed each fiscal period.

In the spreadsheet below, ProFlight records revenues of $2 million in 2004 and costs of production of $1.6 million (20 percent of $8 million). Of the $2 million in revenue, only $1 million is actually billed to the customer; the remaining $1 million is accounted for as an unbilled account receivable. (An unbilled account receivable is an internal billing for revenue which, for contractual reasons, is not sent to a customer for payment.) During 2004, ProFlight collected $500,000 on account and acquired $2 million in production materials which it paid for at year-end. The remaining $400,000 in production material not recognized as a cost of production on the income statement is carried on ProFlight's balance sheet as an asset, called production-in-progress.

In 2005, ProFlight records the remaining $8 million in revenue, collects $4.5 million in cash, and records $6.4 million in production costs (80 percent of $8 million). In 2006, ProFlight collects the remaining $5 million in cash.

ProFlight Inc. Spreadsheet					=	Liabilities	+	Equity
	Assets							
	Cash	Account Receivable	Production-in-Progress	Unbilled Accounts Receivable		Accounts Payable		Retained Earnings
2004								
Contract signing		0				0		0
Acquire production items on credit			2,000,000			2,000,000		
Bill customer		1,000,000		1,000,000				2,000,000 (revenue)
Collect cash	500,000	−500,000						
Record production costs			−1,600,000					−1,600,000 (cost of production)

continued

ProFlight Inc. Spreadsheet

	Assets				= Liabilities	+ Equity
	Cash	Account Receivable	Production- in- Progress	Unbilled Accounts Receivable	Accounts Payable	Retained Earnings
Pay bills	−2,000,000				−2,000,000	
End-of-year balance.	−1,500,000	500,000	400,000	1,000,000	0	400,000
2005						
Acquire production items on credit.			6,000,000		6,000,000	
Bill customer.		9,000,000		−1,000,000		8,000,000 (revenue)
Collect cash	4,500,000	−4,500,000				
Record production costs			−6,400,000			−6,400,000 (cost of production)
Pay bills	−6,000,000				−6,000,000	
End-of-year balance.	−3,000,000	5,000,000	0	0	0	2,000,000
2006						
Collect cash	5,000,000	5,000,000				
End-of-year balance.	2,000,000	0	0	0	0	2,000,000

Revenue Recognition at Completion of Production. If ProFlight recognizes its revenue, costs of production, and hence gross profit when the project is complete, no revenues or expenses will be reported on the income statement until 2005. (ProFlight will consider the contract to be satisfied upon delivery of the planes at the end of 2005; TransGlobal Airlines, however, considers the contract to be complete after successful flight testing of the aircraft in 2006.)

Since no revenue is recognized in 2004, the $1 million billed to TransGlobal in 2004 will be accounted for as **deferred revenue**, a liability account on ProFlight's balance sheet. When the project is complete at the end of 2005, the deferred revenue will then be considered earned, and the balance in the deferred revenue account will be transferred to the revenue account on the income statement. Similarly, the $2 million spent on production costs in 2004 will be accounted for as **production-in-progress**, an asset account on ProFlight's balance sheet until the project is complete, at which time the balance in the production-in-progress account is transferred to the cost-of-production account on the income statement. As a consequence, no profit is recognized in 2004 and instead is deferred until 2005 when all work is completed. This method of revenue recognition is called the **completed contract method**, and the events using this revenue recognition approach are presented in ProFlight's spreadsheet below.

ProFlight Inc. Spreadsheet

	Assets			= Liabilities		+ Equity
	Cash	Accounts Receivable	Production- in-Progress	Accounts Payable	Deferred Revenue	Retained Earnings
2004						
Contract signing.						0
Acquire production items on credit.			2,000,000	2,000,000		

continued

ProFlight Inc. Spreadsheet							
	Assets			=	Liabilities		+ Equity
	Cash	Accounts Receivable	Production-in-Progress		Accounts Payable	Deferred Revenue	Retained Earnings
Bill customer.		1,000,000				1,000,000	
Collect cash	500,000	−500,000					
Pay bills	−2,000,000				−2,000,000		
End-of-year balance.	−1,500,000	500,000	2,000,000		0	1,000,000	0
2005							
Acquire production items on credit.			6,000,000		6,000,000		
Bill customer.		9,000,000				9,000,000	
Collect cash	4,500,000	−4,500,000					
Pay bills	−6,000,000				−6,000,000		
Recognize revenue.						−10,000,000	10,000,000 (revenue)
Record cost of production			−8,000,000				−8,000,000 (cost of production)
End-of-year balance	−3,000,000	5,000,000	0		0	0	2,000,000
2006							
Collect cash	5,000,000	−5,000,000					
End-of-year balance	2,000,000	0	0		0	0	2,000,000

A Comparison of Performance: Percentage of Completion and Completed Contract. Exhibit 5.4 presents a comparison of gross profit for ProFlight under the two alternative revenue recognition methods. The results are equal, in total, however the percentage of completion method spreads the gross profit between 2004 and 2005, whereas the completed contract recognizes all the gross profit in the year of completion.

EXHIBIT 5.4	Comparison of Gross Profit under Percentage of Completion and Completed Contract Revenue Recognition		
	2004	2005	2006
Percentage of completion	$400	$1,600	$0
Completed contract	0	2,000	0

VALUING AND REPORTING ACCOUNTS RECEIVABLE

Companies extend credit to current and potential customers when the expected revenues from these incremental sales exceed the costs associated with extending the credit—specifically, when the incremental revenues exceed the time value of money of the credit sale and the potential cost of any uncollectible accounts. Businessmen and women know that some customers won't pay for their credit purchases but they just don't know which ones. If they did, they would certainly avoid extending credit to these

BUSINESS PERSPECTIVE: REVENUE RECOGNITION

AMR Corporation is the parent company of American Airlines, American Eagle Airlines, and TWA Airlines. According to the company's footnotes to its financial statements, passenger ticket sales are initially recorded as a component of "air traffic liability," a current liability on the balance sheet (equivalent to deferred or unearned revenue); and, subsequently, the air traffic liability is recognized as revenue on the income statement at the time that flight service is provided. Alternative revenue recognition policies that could have been considered by the airline company include:

- Revenue recognition at the time of flight reservation
- Revenue recognition at the time of passenger ticketing
- Revenue recognition at the time of flight service

Recognition at the time of flight reservation is not generally accepted in that although AMR's final customer has been identified and the amount of revenue to be recognized is known, no service has yet been provided by the company. Recognition at the time of passenger ticketing, on the other hand, which coincides with the point of sale and the point of cash collection, may seem to be a realistic alternative. Revenue recognition guidelines under SAB No. 101, however, require that any revenue be earned before it can be recognized. Since AMR does not earn its revenue until it has provided air transportation to its customers, AMR appropriately defers the recognition of its revenue until the time of flight service. According to AMR's 2002 annual 10-K report filing with the U.S. Securities and Exchange Commission, the amount of recognized revenue and deferred revenue for 2001 and 2002 was as follows:

(in millions)	2002	2001
Passenger revenue recognized	$15,772	$17,158
Passenger revenue deferred	2,614	2,763

Investment professionals would be concerned by the trend in AMR's reported and deferred revenues—both figures declined from 2001 to 2002. Undoubtedly, this trend was a direct consequence of the airline tragedy associated with September 11, 2001 and the subsequent reluctance of individuals to utilize airline travel as a mode of transportation.

customers! Companies can reduce the risk of bad debts, however, by acquiring information about their customers from credit information intermediaries such as **Dun and Bradstreet**. For a fee, Dunn and Bradstreet will supply information about a customer's past credit history and will use credit scoring techniques to predict the likelihood that a customer will pay for goods and services on a timely basis.

Despite the fact that a company might not know by the end of a fiscal period with certainty what its credit losses associated with its current period's revenue are going to be, the matching principle nonetheless requires that an estimate of these losses be made to facilitate a full matching of revenue and expenses on the income statement. There are a variety of methods available to help businesses estimate their expected credit losses. The two most widely used methods are the **percentage-of-credit sales method** and the **aging method**.[1]

---

[1] A third approach is the **direct write-off-method**, in which no estimate of credit losses is matched with current revenue. Instead, the actual accounts receivable write-off is reported on the income statement as a bad debt expense in the period in which non-collectability is confirmed. The direct write-off method is not GAAP because it fails to match the cost of extending credit to customers in the same period in which the corresponding revenue is recognized.

In Practice 5.1 *Revenue Recognition Method: A Glimpse of a Sample of Fortune 1000 Companies*   The following table identifies the method used by a sample of 131 Fortune 1000 companies to account for revenue under long-term contracts. Over 64 percent of the firms surveyed used the percentage-of-completion method:

Accounting Method	Number	Percentage
Percentage of completion	84	64
Units of delivery	41	31
Completed contract	6	5
Total	131	100

Source: 2006 Accounting Trends & Techniques

Percentage of Credit Sales Method

Under the percentage-of-credit sales method, a business estimates its expected future credit losses as a function of the relationship between its historical credit losses and its historical credit sales. The percentage of historical credit losses divided by historical credit sales is multiplied with current period credit sales to estimate a business' expected future credit losses. The principal limitations of this approach are that it fails to capture the changing payment patterns of customers in a timely manner and it lacks the estimation precision provided by the aging method.

To demonstrate the percentage-of-credit sales method, assume that the Savanna Company recognized $600,000 of credit sales during the current fiscal period. Further, assume that Savanna's management has determined from prior experience that approximately three percent of all credit sales eventually must be written off due to collection failure. Since bad debts resulting from collection failure are a cost of doing business, it is necessary to match this expense with current period revenue. Consequently, Savanna will recognize a bad debt expense in the amount of $18,000 (3 percent of $600,000) on its income statement in the current period. Savanna will also establish a contra-account—the Allowance for Uncollectible Accounts—on its balance sheet to reflect the amount of the outstanding receivables that are not expected to be collected. We will discuss this contra-account more fully shortly; but, what is important to note is that Savanna's management recorded their estimate of the expected bad debt exepnse in the current period rather than waiting until a future period at which time they will know with certainty which receivables are uncollectible and should be written off.

Savanna Company Spreadsheet					
Assets		=	**Liabilities**	+	**Equity**
Accounts Receivable	Allowance for Uncollectible Accounts				Retained Earnings
600,000					600,000
	−18,000				−18,000

Aging Method

A more refined approach to credit loss estimation, and consequently, the most widely used approach, is the Aging Method. Under the Aging Method, a business first categorizes its outstanding accounts receivable according to how much time has elapsed since the credit sale took place. Then, using historical customer payment data to estimate the probability of payment (and hence, the probability of non-payment), the estimated probabilities of non-payment are multiplied with the outstanding receivable age category balance to arrive at the expected credit loss. To illustrate this method, consider data for Pan American Enterprises.

Pan American Enterprises Inc. sells its internationally recognized wine on credit to bars and restaurants throughout the United States. The company's credit terms require customers to pay their bills within 30 days of a transaction. The chief financial officer (CFO) of Pan American is concerned about the possibility of bad debts arising when customers fail to pay for previously purchased inventory. The CFO realizes that bad debts may occur but offering the company's customers credit has generated much higher sales and profit levels.

Exhibit 5.5 shows that credit sales for Pan American Enterprises were $3.2 million in 2004, of which Pan American collected $2.85 million in cash. In Pan American's spreadsheet, this information is reported as an increase in retained earnings (via revenue) and an increase in accounts receivable in the amount of $3.2 million, and an increase in cash and a decrease in accounts receivable in the amount of $2.85 million.

EXHIBIT 5.5	Pan American Enterprises, Inc.			
Year		Credit Sales	Accounts Receivable (year-end)	Bad Debt Write-Off
2004		$3,200,000	$350,000	—
2005		5,300,000	800,000	$11,500

Pan American Enterprises Spreadsheet				
		Assets		Equity
2004	Cash	Accounts Receivable	Allowance for Uncollectible Accounts	Retained Earnings
Sales.		3,200,000		3,200,000
Cash collections.	2,850,000	−2,850,000		
End-of-year balance.	2,850,000	350,000	0	3,200,000

Even if Pan American Enterprises screens its customers carefully, it is unlikely that the entire $350,000 of outstanding accounts receivable at year-end 2004 will be collected. Further, prior to the preparation of an income statement for 2004, the matching principle requires that the cost of extending credit to its customers—that is, the **bad debt expense**—be estimated and matched with the sales revenue for 2004.

To estimate Pan American's bad debt expense using the aging method, an aging schedule of Pan American's accounts receivable is prepared and is presented in Exhibit 5.6. This exhibit shows that, at year-end 2004, $145,000 in receivables have been outstanding for less than 30 days, $100,000 outstanding for 31 to 60 days, $70,000 for 61 to 90 days, $20,000 for 91 to 120 days, and $15,000 for over 120 days.

Many companies consider receivables over 120 days old to be worthless, and consequently, remove these receivables from the balance sheet to avoid overstating the realizable value of accounts receivable. Worthless receivables are usually turned over to a collection agency to pursue collection.

An analysis of Pan American's past customer payment experience is then used to estimate the amount that will be uncollected from each category. As shown in Exhibit 5.6, the CFO's analysis of prior credit customer payment behavior found that 0.5 percent of accounts 30 days or less fail to pay, one percent of accounts that are 31 to 60 days old fail to pay, and that as much at 20 percent of accounts outstanding for more than 120 days end up in default. The total amount that is not expected to be collected is the sum of the amounts in each category times the percentage estimated to be uncollectible.

For example, $725 (0.5 percent times $145,000) of the less than 30-days accounts is expected to be uncollectible. For the total outstanding receivable balance of $350,000 as of year-end 2004, $10,925 is expected to be uncollectible.

EXHIBIT 5.6	Aging of Accounts Receivable				
		December 31, 2004		December 31, 2005	
Period Outstanding	Estimated Uncollectible Percentage	Outstanding Receivable Balance	Estimated Bad Debt	Outstanding Receivable Balance	Estimated Bad Debt
30 days or less	0.5%	$145,000	$ 725	$400,000	$ 2,000
31–60 days	1.0%	100,000	1,000	200,000	2,000
61–90 days	6.0%	70,000	4,200	100,000	6,000
91–120 days	10%	20,000	2,000	75,000	7,500
More than 120 days . . .	20%	15,000	3,000	25,000	5,000
Total		$350,000	$10,925	$800,000	$22,500

To record the results of the aging analysis, Pan American will establish a contra-account—the **Allowance for Uncollectible Accounts**—on its balance sheet to reflect the amount of the outstanding receivables that are not expected to be collected. The allowance for uncollectible accounts is a reserve for future expected losses resulting from uncollectible credit sales. Despite the fact that the future losses cannot be known with certainty at year-end, the matching principle nonetheless requires that an attempt be made to estimate those losses, recognizing that the estimate may prove incorrect as additional information is obtained. Thus, $10,925 will be the balance in the allowance for uncollectible accounts and this contra-account is subtracted from the total outstanding receivable balance on Pan American's balance sheet to arrive at the **net realizable value** ($350,000 − $10,925 = $339,075) of the outstanding accounts receivable. It is the net realizable value of Pan American's accounts receivable that will be included in the firm's total assets.

Since 2004 was Pan American Enterprises' first year of operations, the beginning balance in the allowance account is $0. Thus, $10,925 is the amount necessary to bring the allowance account to the required amount of $10,925, and hence, it is also the amount of the bad debt expense reported on Pan American's income statement for the period. In the spreadsheet below, the bad debt expense reduces retained earnings by $10,925 and the allowance for uncollectible accounts decreases by the same amount. Since the allowance account is an offset to the accounts receivable account, this transaction effectively reduces the balance of accounts receivable. Under this approach, accounts receivable are not reduced directly because the allowance account is just an estimate of Pan American's expected future credit losses.

	Pan American Enterprises Spreadsheet				
		Assets			Equity
2004		Cash	Accounts Receivable	Allowance for Uncollectible Accounts	Retained Earnings
Credit sales.			3,200,000		3,200,000
Cash collections.		2,850,000	−2,850,000		
Recognize bad debt expense.				−10,925	−10,925
End-of-year balance.		2,850,000	350,000	−10,925	3,189,075

Pan American's abbreviated income statement for 2004 discloses sales revenue less the bad debt expense of $3,189,075 (see Exhibit 5.7, Panel A), and Pan American's balance sheet at December 31, 2004 reflects an accounts receivable balance, net of the allowance for uncollectible accounts, of $339,075, representing the net cash that Pan American expects to collect from its credit customers (see Exhibit 5.7, Panel B).

EXHIBIT 5.7	Selected Financial Data

Panel A

Pan American Enterprises Inc.
Income Statement (abbreviated)

	2004
Sales revenue.	$3,200,000
Less: Bad debt expense.	10,925
Net income.	$3,189,075

Panel B

Pan American Enterprises Inc.
Balance Sheet

	2004
Accounts receivable.	$ 350,000
Less: Allowance for uncollectible accounts.	10,925
Accounts receivable, net	$ 339,075

In early 2005, Pan American Enterprises received information from a number of its credit customers that they would be unable to pay their outstanding unpaid bills. As a consequence, Pan American's CFO immediately wrote off the identified uncollectible accounts receivable, which totaled $11,500. In the spreadsheet below, the write off of uncollectible accounts is executed by reducing accounts receivable by $11,500 and adjusting the allowance for uncollectible accounts for an equivalent amount. Recall that the allowance account represents a reserve for expected future losses from uncollectible credit sales. When Pan American received information that the expected credit losses were no longer uncertain, the CFO immediately removed both the uncollectible receivables from the balance in accounts receivable and an equivalent amount from the reserve for such losses. In this particular case, however, Pan American underestimated its actual 2004 credit

---

In Practice 5.2 *Balance Sheet Caption: A Glimpse of a Sample of Fortune 1000 Companies* The following table identifies the caption used by a sample of 600 Fortune 1000 companies on their balance sheets to describe the allowance for uncollectible accounts:

Doubtful Account Captions	Number	Percentage
Allowance for doubtful accounts	325	54.2
Allowance.	141	23.5
Allowance for uncollectible accounts.	25	4.2
Allowance for losses.	13	2.1
Reserve for doubtful accounts.	17	2.8
Other.	4	.07
Receivables shown net	23	3.8
No reference to doubtful accounts.	52	8.7
Total	600	100.0

Source: 2006 Accounting Trends & Techniques

losses by $575 ($11,500 − $10,295), and thus, will need to correct this understatement of the 2004 bad debt expense in its 2005 financial statements. Notice also that the actual write-off of $11,500 in accounts receivable in 2004 is simply a housekeeping adjustment. No expense is recognized at this time as the expense had already been recognized at the time that the initial estimate was made (at year-end 2004). In addition, the net accounts receivable balance remains unchanged as an equal amount is removed both from accounts receivable and from the allowance for uncollectible accounts.

According to Exhibit 5.5, Pan American Enterprises generated credit sales of $5.3 million during 2005 and received cash payments from customers totaling $4,838,500. At year-end, the outstanding balance in accounts receivable for the company totaled $800,000. The aging schedule (see Exhibit 5.6) revealed that Pan American could suffer bad debt losses of as much as $22,500. However, given that the credit losses for 2004 had been understated by $575, Pan American will need to correct this situation in 2005 by increasing the allowance for uncollectible accounts and the bad debts expense by a total of $23,075 ($22,500 + $575).

Pan American Enterprises Spreadsheet				
		Assets		Equity
2005	Cash	Accounts Receivable	Allowance for Uncollectible Accounts	Retained Earnings
Beginning balance	2,850,000	350,000	−10,925	3,189,075
Write off uncollectible accounts.		−11,500	11,500	
Credit sales.		5,300,000		5,300,000
Cash collections.	4,838,500	−4,838,500		
Recognize bad debt expense.			−23,075	−23,075
End-of-year balance.	7,688,500	800,000	22,500	8,466,000

Pan American's abbreviated income statement for 2005, presented in Exhibit 5.8 (Panel A), shows sales revenue less the bad debt expense of $5,276,925, while Pan American's balance sheet (Panel B) shows net receivables at December 31, 2005 of $777,500. The company's use of the aging method insures that a full matching of revenue and expenses, including an estimate of the bad debt expense, occurs on the company's income statement, and that the expected realizable value of the outstanding accounts receivable is correctly reflected on the company's balance sheet.

EXHIBIT 5.8	Selected Financial Data	
Panel A		
	Pan American Enterprises Inc. Income Statement	
		2005
Sales revenue.		$5,300,000
Less: Bad debt expense.		23,075
Net income.		$5,276,925
Panel B		
	Pan American Enterprises Inc. Balance Sheet	
		2005
Accounts receivable.		$ 800,000
Less: Allowance for uncollectible accounts.		22,500
Accounts receivable, net		$ 777,500

MANAGING A COMPANY'S INVESTMENT IN RECEIVABLES

When a company extends credit to its customers by permitting them to buy goods and services on credit, the company is, in effect, making an investment in accounts receivable. Like any investment, an investment in accounts receivable should generate returns to the company that are sufficiently large to justify the risks associated with the investment—that is, the gross profit resulting from the incremental credit sales must exceed the cost of extending credit. The principal costs of extending credit to customers include the cost of the goods or services if a customer fails to pay for their credit purchases and/or the time value of money (the opportunity cost) when a customer takes a long time to pay.

Sales Discounts

By extending credit to customers, a company is effectively lending to its customers on an interest-free basis for the period of time that the account receivable is outstanding. To maximize the return on a company's investment in accounts receivable, and thus, the firm's overall profitability, it is important to keep the duration of these interest-free loans as short as possible. One way that companies attempt to manage account receivable **duration** is by giving customers an incentive to pay quickly. That incentive usually takes the form of a price discount. For instance, some companies offer their customers **credit terms** or **trade terms** of 2/10, n/30. The term "2/10" indicates that if a customer pays their bill within ten days of purchase, they will be given a two percent reduction in the gross purchase price of the purchased items. The term "n/30"—pronounced "net 30"—indicates that if the customer fails to take advantage of the quick-payment incentive, the full purchase price is expected within 30 days of the sales transaction. The specific credit terms used by a company are usually dictated by the competitive conditions that characterize a given industry. Thus, in less competitive industries, terms of 2/10, n/30 are common, whereas in highly competitive industries, more generous trade terms of 3/10, n/90 may be required.

When a customer takes advantage of a quick-pay incentive, this price reduction is called a **sales discount** and is reported on the income statement as a deduction from gross revenue. The resulting amount is called **net revenue** or net sales. In accounting terminology, the sales discount account is a contra-revenue account.

To illustrate, consider a credit sale of $1,000 with trade terms of 2/10, n/30. For a customer who pays her bill in full within the ten day period, the final purchase price will be reduced to $980 ($1,000 less two percent of $1,000). This is shown in the spreadsheet below. In contrast, a customer who pays after the ten day "quick pay" window has expired will be expected to pay the full $1,000, and payment is expected not later than 30 days after the original sale transaction.

	Assets		=	Liabilities	+	Equity
	Cash	Accounts Receivables				Retained Earnings
Credit sales.		1,000				1,000
Cash collections.	980	−1,000				−20
Totals	980	0				980

When customers fail to take advantage of existing quick-pay incentives, the seller is faced with another dilemma: The longer a receivable remains unpaid, the lower the real profit on the sale because of the time value of money. Thus, well-managed companies usually pay considerable attention to their

receivable collection period to help monitor this potential problem area. As discussed in Chapter 4, the receivable collection period is calculated as follows:

$$\text{Receivable collection period} = \frac{\textbf{365 days}}{\textbf{Net sales/Account receivable balance}}$$

To illustrate the use of this financial ratio, consider the following data for the **Robert Mondavi Corporation**, a well-known beverage and wine company in the United States:

(in thousands of dollars)	2002	2003
Net sales.	$463,587	$504,615
Accounts receivable (net).	$ 92,555	$104,555
Receivable collection period	$\dfrac{365}{(\$463,587/\$92,555)} = 72.9$ days	$\dfrac{365}{(\$504,615/\$104,555)} = 75.6$ days

The data suggest that the average Mondavi credit customer took 72.9 days and 75.6 days, respectively, to pay for their credit purchases in 2002 and 2003. If Mondavi's credit terms are 2/10, n/60, then some of its customers have greatly exceeded the company's payment terms. How would Mondavi benefit if the average payment period were reduced to 60 days? With an average payment period of 60 days and the same level of revenue, Mondavi would have reported outstanding receivables of only $76,206 and $82,950 at year-end 2002 and 2003, respectively:

(in thousands of dollars)	2002	2003
Revised receivable balance	$\dfrac{60 \times \$463,587}{365} = \$76,206$	$\dfrac{60 \times \$504,615}{365} = \$82,950$
Increase in cash	$92,555 − $76,206 = **$16,349**	$104,555 − $82,950 = **$21,605**

The reduction in Mondavi's outstanding accounts receivable balance and the associated reduction in the receivable collection period would have resulted in an increase in the company's operating cash flows by $16.349 million and $21.605 million in 2002 and 2003, respectively. What could Mondavi do with the extra cash? Some possibilities would be to pay down interest-bearing debt, increase dividends, or invest in new operating assets.

Sales Returns

Many companies allow their customers to return unwanted and/or defective products for a cash or credit refund or for store credit. Like the bad debts expense, the amount of customer returns may not be known with certainty until well after the completion of a fiscal period. To insure that a business' revenue is not overstated, managers must estimate the expected future customer returns at the end of each fiscal period before an income statement can be prepared. Like the bad debt expense, customer returns are typically estimated on the basis of recent historical business experience.

The amount of any expected sales returns are reported in a contra-revenue account, the **sales returns** account, on the income statement as well as in a contra-asset account on the balance sheet, called the **allowance for sales returns,** if the original sale was on credit. Like the allowance for uncollectible accounts, the allowance for sale returns is a reserve for future losses associated with product returns and is subtracted from the balance in accounts receivable to arrive at the net realizable value of accounts receivable.

Sales returns can be a serious problem in some businesses. The most effective way to manage this problem is through a program of continuous quality control of manufacturing processes to insure the production of high quality goods, as well as a diligent assessment of customer needs and preferences to insure that a company's products are meeting or exceeding customer needs and expectations.

MONETIZING ACCOUNTS RECEIVABLE TO MANAGE OPERATING CASH FLOW

In addition to collecting accounts receivable as a means to generate operating cash, a business can also sell its receivables to an outside buyer, use the receivables as collateral in a borrowing arrangement, or securitize its receivables. Collectively, these actions are referred to as "monetizing" a company's accounts receivable. Each of these cash-management options is considered below.

> Monetizing is the process of converting a non-cash asset into cash. In the case of accounts and notes receivable, these assets may be converted into cash by selling or factoring, by borrowing against the value of the asset (pledging), or by securitization through the creation of an SPE or SPV.

Factoring

The process of selling accounts and notes receivable is called **factoring**. Many financial institutions have divisions devoted exclusively to buying accounts and notes receivable from businesses which need cash quickly and are unable to wait for customer payment on outstanding credit transactions. Factors convert a business' receivables into cash at their face value less a service charge and a charge for the time value of money. The service charge for factoring varies considerably depending upon the degree of collection risk assumed by the factor. Receivables which are sold **with recourse** means that if a factor is unable to collect on a particular account or note receivable, the factor has the right to return the uncollectible receivable to the seller and recover its money directly from the seller. In this case, the factor assumes no collection risk, and thus, the factor's service fee is likely to be low, ranging, for example, from five to ten percent of the face value of the sold receivables.

When receivables are sold **without recourse**, the factor assumes all risk of collection and thus will charge a considerably higher fee (such as 12 to 15 percent or more) to compensate for the potential bad debt expense associated with any uncollectible receivables. When accounts and notes receivable are sold without recourse, the factor is unable to recover any uncollected amounts from the seller. To help estimate the extent of the assumed collection risk, factors frequently ask companies that sell their receivables to provide them with a copy of their aging schedule.

Because factoring is an expensive financing option for most businesses, it is only used when less expensive options (such as pledging) are unavailable. For instance, a business with a 15 percent gross profit margin which sells its receivables to a factor charging a ten percent service fee (sold with recourse) would see its profit margin on these sales decline by 67 percent!

Pledging

Another way that businesses can use their accounts and notes receivable to expedite operating cash inflows is to use the receivables as collateral to obtain bank financing, usually in the form of working capital financing. Although the business typically retains ownership of its pledged receivables, as well as the responsibility and risk of collecting the receivables, the cash flow from account and note collection is usually "pledged" to pay the principal and debt service charges associated with such a loan. Pledging receivables is a common form of financing for most businesses because it is a lower cost option than factoring.

Securitization

A third approach to monetize accounts and notes receivable is to sell the receivables to a private legal entity created by a company for the exclusive purpose of buying its receivables. Entities established for this purpose are called **special purpose entities (SPEs)** or **special purpose vehicles (SPVs)**.

For example, **General Motors (GM) Corporation** disclosed in its annual report the following:

> GM and GMAC use off-balance sheet special purpose entities (SPEs) where the economics and sound business principles warrant their use. The principal use of the SPEs occurs in connection with the securitization and sale of financial assets generated in the ordinary course of business. The assets securitized and sold by GMAC consist principally of mortgages and retail loans secured by vehicles sold through GM's dealer network. The assets sold by GM consist of trade receivables. The use of qualifying SPEs enables GM and GMAC to access the highly liquid and efficient market for the sale of these types of financial assets.

In essence, an SPE or SPV acts like a company-owned factor. The SPE borrows money from investors or from a financial services company and then uses the borrowed funds to buy accounts and notes receivable from its parent company. The advantage of securitization over pledging is that the parent company does not increase its leverage. Because of complex accounting rules, the borrowings of an SPE or SPV remain off-balance sheet to its parent company. The advantage of securitization over external factoring is that the cost of factoring to a company-sponsored SPE is less than would normally be incurred when selling receivables to an independent, unaffiliated factor. We will have more to say about SPEs and SPVs, along with a newer creation, **variable interest entities (VIEs)**, in Chapter 8.

ANALYZING OPERATING REVENUE AND RECEIVABLES

Since security prices are sensitive to earnings' news, some managers resort to the use of questionable accounting practices as a means to favorably impact their firm's share price. Two common approaches used by some managers to manage their company's reported earnings involve over-estimating the amount of earned revenue and under-estimating the amount of expected credit losses on accounts and notes receivable.

Revenue Recognition Policy

In the case of revenue, it is not uncommon to find that some companies have recognized revenue on the income statement before it is appropriate—that is, before goods or services have been delivered to the customer and/or where cash collection is doubtful. Recognizing revenue prematurely is often referred to as front-end loading. Consider, for example, the case of **MicroStrategy, Inc.** MicroStategy is a publicly-held provider of business intelligence software ("data-mining" software) that enables firms to analyze their proprietary data to reveal trends about their business, and consequently, manage themselves more effectively. In early 2000, the shares of MicroStrategy traded at $333 per share, but fell to $140 per share in mid-March 2000 after announcing that the company would restate its operating results for 1999 and 2000 to comply with new SEC accounting guidelines on revenue reporting (see Appendix 5B to this chapter). MicroStrategy had reported its revenue for software service contracts at the time the contracts were signed, even though the contracts provided for services to be delivered over many future fiscal periods. In essence, the company front-loaded revenue that should have been deferred until the future services were actually delivered to the customer. The company originally reported 1999 earnings of $0.16 per share, but the firm's EPS were subsequently restated to a loss of $0.44 per share. By April 2000, MicroStrategy's share price had fallen to $33 per share, a decline of 90 percent.

While it is far more common to observe aggressive or premature revenue recognition, some firms actually attempt to delay the recognition of some of their company's revenue flows (see "Microsoft Corporation: Managing earnings to meet Wall Street earnings' expectations" at the beginning of this chapter). Investment professionals frequently assume that a company which delays the recognition of some of its revenue, or what is often referred to as rear-end loading of revenue, is attempting to create a revenue reserve on the balance sheet (ie. the Deferred Revenue account) to enable the firm to more readily meet or exceed future Wall Street earnings' expectations. To help evaluate whether a firm is engaging in either front-end loading or the rear-end loading of revenues, some investment professionals calculate a financial ratio called the cash conversion ratio, defined as cash sales divided by accrual sales (see Chapter 3). When the cash conversion ratio gets significantly below (above) one, it may indicate the presence of front-end (rear-end) loading of revenue.

Receivable Valuation Policy

In the case of receivable valuation, some managers intentionally understate the cash collection risk associated with their accounts and notes receivable as a means to minimize the bad debts expense and, in so doing, boost the level of currently reported earnings. Consider, for example, the case of **Fairfield Communities, Inc.**, a U.S.-based developer of time-share resorts. Fairfield sells the annual right to vacation at any of the company's resorts for the duration of a buyer's lifetime. The purchase price is typically financed with a down payment of 15 percent and a seven year, non-recourse note receivable for the balance. An analysis of Fairfield's allowance for uncollectible accounts reveals that Fairfield's expected credit losses amounted to only 4.7 percent of time-share revenue, as contrasted with the industry average of seven to nine percent. Some investment professionals allege that Fairfield understated its expected credit losses on its notes receivable as a means to "pump up" its earnings by understating the allowance for uncollectible accounts, and hence, understating its bad debt expense on the income statement.

In a similar situation, although its gross accounts receivable at year-end 2002 and 2003 were essentially unchanged at $2.6 billion, **Nortel Networks Corporation** reduced its allowance for doubtful accounts from $517 million in 2002 to just $256 million in 2003. In essence, the company's allowance for doubtful accounts as a percentage of gross accounts receivable declined from nearly 20 percent in 2002 to just ten percent in 2003. The decline in Nortel's allowance for doubtful accounts was accompanied by an equivalent $261 million increase in pre-tax net income. Most investment professionals viewed Nortel's decline in its allowance for bad debts, the corresponding decline in its bad debts expense, and the related increase in pre-tax net income suspiciously, causing the company's share price to fall to record low levels.

To help evaluate whether a company is managing its bad debts expense as a means to positively impact its current net earnings, and also overstate the realizable value of its outstanding receivables, some investment professionals calculate a financial ratio of the allowance for uncollectible accounts divided by gross accounts receivable. In the case of Nortel Networks, this ratio declined by 50 percent, from

20 percent ($517/$2,600) in 2002 to just 10 percent ($256/$2,600) in 2003. A decline of this magnitude in just one year would suggest that the financial fortunes of Nortel's credit customers, and hence, their account payment behavior, dramatically improved from 2002 to 2003, an unlikely scenario given the shortness of the time period involved.

ETHICS PERSPECTIVE

While **Enron** and **WorldCom** have dominated recent discussions of corporate fraud, arguably one of the most egregious frauds in U.S. history is the **Equity Funding Corporation of America**. Equity Funding began operations in the 1960s as a financial services business which sold life insurance policies to individuals, and then later resold the policies to other insurance firms. The company began with an investment of only $10,000; however, by 1973, the firm was reported to be managing over $1 billion in assets. As it later turned out, most of these assets were fictitious. Equity Funding would write insurance policies on non-existent individuals and then resell these policies at a profit. Those involved in the fraud grew as fast as the fraudulent revenue, with nearly 150 employees in the company doing such things as creating fake birth certificates to support the fraudulent insurance policies. Later, some rogue employees began "killing" some of the phony policyholders to collect their death benefits. The fraud was eventually uncovered when a disgruntled employee blew the whistle on the scheme. Such bold behavior was a natural consequence where the culture of deception created at the top of the organization was so open. It is often stated that the ethical culture of a business is derived from the "tone at the top."

REVIEW PROBLEM

The Arcadia Company bid on a multi-year contract to construct the new hockey arena for The Phoenix Coyotes. The contract required that construction begin not later than January 1, 2003 and be completed not later than December 31, 2005. Arcadia won the contract with a bid of $720 million. During the three-year period 2003 to 2005, the company incurred the following construction costs:

	Construction Costs	Percentage of Project Completed
2003	$144 million	30%
2004	144 million	30
2005	192 million	40
Total	$480 million	100%

Under the terms of the contract, The Arcadia Company was entitled to bill the city of Glendale, Arizona, for 25 percent of the total bid ($180 million) upon completion of 30 percent of the planned project. Thus, at the end of 2003, and again at the end of 2004, Arcadia sent progress billings to, and was paid by, the City of Glendale in the amount of $180 million. At the end of 2005, after receiving all necessary occupancy approvals, The Arcadia Company billed the City of Glendale for the remaining $360 million.

Required

Prepare income statements for The Arcadia Company for 2003, 2004, and 2005 assuming that the company recognizes revenue from the Coyote arena contract (a) on the cash basis, (b) on the completed contract basis, and (c) on the percentage-of-completion basis.

Solution

a. Cash basis:

(in millions)	2003	2004	2005	Total
Revenue	$180	$180	$360	$720
Less: Construction costs	144	144	192	480
Net income	$ 36	$ 36	$168	$240

b. Completed contract basis:

(in millions)	2003	2004	2005	Total
Revenue	$0	$0	$720	$720
Less: Construction costs	0	0	480	480
Net income	$0	$0	$240	$240

c. Percentage-of-completion basis:

(in millions)	2003	2004	2005	Total
Revenue	$216[1]	$216[1]	$288[2]	$720
Less: Construction costs	144	144	192	480
Net income	$72	$72	$96	$240

[1]$720 million x 30% = $216 million.
[2]$720 million x 40% = $288 million.

EXECUTIVE SUMMARY

This chapter investigated the important concepts of revenue recognition and receivable valuation. We saw that depending upon the particular business circumstances encountered, a company could recognize its operating revenue at the point of sale and delivery, during the production process, at the end of the production process, or at the point of cash collection if collection was in doubt. We also saw that when businesses allow their customers to buy their products on credit, certain additional costs are likely to be encountered, specifically the opportunity cost of not immediately collecting the promised cash and the potential losses when an account is uncollectible. Approaches to manage these costs were discussed; in addition, approaches to monetize a firm's accounts and notes receivable were considered.

As a validation of your understanding of the content of this chapter, you should now be able to:

- Explain how service, retail and manufacturing companies recognize their operating revenue.
- Explain how revenue is recognized under the completed contract and percentage of completion methods.
- Explain how accounts receivables are valued and how the allowance for uncollectible accounts and bad debt expense are estimated.
- Explain why the effective management of accounts receivable is important for a business.

In Chapter 6, we examine various inventory valuation approaches used by companies to measure the cost of their products sold and the inventory remaining on hand.

KEY CONCEPTS AND TERMS

APPENDIX 5A: Recording Operating Revenue and Receivables using the Debit and Credit Paradigm

In this appendix, the traditional approach to recording accounting transactions—that is, the debit and credit paradigm—is followed to illustrate how the journal entries for the operating revenue and receivables for ProFlight Inc. and for Pan American Enterprises, Inc. would be recorded by these enterprises. The information used in this appendix is taken directly from the content of Chapter 5. To facilitate your understanding of the transactions, asset accounts are labeled with an (A), liability accounts with an (L), shareholders' equity accounts with an (SE), and revenue or expense accounts with an (R) or an (E), respectively.

Revenue Recognition Transactions: ProFlight Inc.

ProFlight Inc., a manufacturer of private corporate jets, signed a contract to build five jets over a two-year period for TransGlobal Airlines. Under the terms of the contract, ProFlight will receive total revenue of $10 million and anticipates that its cost to build the planes will total $8 million. During 2004, ProFlight completed 20 percent of the work, sent an invoice for $1 million to TransGlobal, and received a cash payment of $500,000. During 2005, ProFlight completed the remaining 80 percent of the work on budget, delivered the five planes, sent an invoice for the remaining $9 million to TransGlobal and received a $4.5 million cash payment. In 2006, after completing flight testing of the aircraft, TransGlobal remitted the final $5 million in cash to ProFlight. Journal entries are presented to reflect ProFlight's accounting transactions under the percentage-of-completion method and the completed contract method of revenue recognition.

Percentage-of-Completion Method.   Under the percentage-of-completion approach to revenue recognition, ProFlight will recognize its operating revenue and expenses on the basis of the amount of work actually completed each fiscal period (20 percent in 2004 and 80 percent in 2005). Consequently, the journal entries for ProFlight for the period 2004 through 2006 would appear as follows:

Date	Accounts	Debit	Credit
2004	No entry is required at contact signing		
	Production-in-progress (A)...............................	2,000,000	
	Accounts payable (L)...............................		2,000,000
	To record the acquisition of production material on credit.		
	Accounts receivable (A)	1,000,000	
	Unbilled accounts receivable (A)	1,000,000	
	Retained earnings (R)...............................		2,000,000
	To recognize revenue based on a 20 percent work completion: *20% × $10,000,000.*		
	Cash (A)	500,000	
	Accounts receivable (A).............................		500,000
	To record the collection of cash on the billed account receivable.		
	Retained earnings (E)...................................	1,600,000	
	Production-in-progress (A)..........................		1,600,000
	To record the consumption of production material—that is, cost of goods sold—related to the revenue recognized, 20 percent of $8 million.		
	Accounts payable (L)	2,000,000	
	Cash (A)		2,000,000
	To record the payment of accounts payable for production materials.		
2005	Production-in-progress (A)..............................	6,000,000	
	Accounts payable (L)...............................		6,000,000
	To record the acquisition of production material on credit to complete the contract.		
	Accounts receivable (A)	9,000,000	
	Unbilled accounts receivable (A)		1,000,000
	Retained earnings (R)...............................		8,000,000
	To record the completion of the contract, the remaining revenue and final customer billing.		
	Cash (A)	4,500,000	
	Accounts receivable (A).............................		4,500,000
	To record the collection of cash on billed accounts receivable.		
	Retained earnings (E)..................................	6,400,000	
	Production-in-progress (A)..........................		6,400,000
	To record the consumption of production material— that is, the cost of goods sold—related to the revenue recognized in 2005, 80 percent of $8 million.		
	Accounts payable (L)	6,000,000	
	Cash (A)		6,000,000
	To record the payment of accounts payable.		
2006	Cash (A)	5,000,000	
	Accounts receivable (A).............................		5,000,000
	To record the collection of cash on billed accounts receivable.		

Completed Contract Method. Under the Completed Contract approach, ProFlight will defer the recognition of any operating revenue or expenses until the contract is fully satisfied at the end of 2005. Consequently, the journal entries for ProFlight for the period 2004 through 2006 would appear as follows:

Date	Accounts	Debit	Credit
2004	No entry is required at contact signing		
	Production-in-progress (A)...............................	2,000,000	
	Accounts payable (L).............................		2,000,000
	To record the acquisition of production materials on credit.		
	Accounts receivable (A)	1,000,000	
	Deferred revenue (L).............................		1,000,000
	To record progress billing sent to customer.		
	Cash (A)	500,000	
	Accounts receivable (A)...........................		500,000
	To record cash collected on billed account receivable.		
	Accounts payable.....................................	2,000,000	
	Cash (A).......................................		2,000,000
	To record payment of accounts payable related to production material.		
2005	Production-in-progress (A).............................	6,000,000	
	Accounts payable (L).............................		6,000,000
	To record the acquisition of production material on credit.		
	Accounts receivable (A)	9,000,000	
	Deferred revenue (L).............................		9,000,000
	To record progress billing sent to customer.		
	Cash (A)	4,500,000	
	Accounts receivable (A)		4,500,000
	To record cash collection on billed account receivable.		
	Accounts payable (L)	6,000,000	
	Cash (A).......................................		6,000,000
	To record payment of accounts payable related to production material.		
	Deferred revenue (L).................................	10,000,000	
	Retained earnings (R)............................		10,000,000
	To recognize revenue associated with contract completion.		
	Retained earnings (E)	8,000,000	
	Production-in-progress (A).........................		8,000,000
	To recognize the cost of goods sold associated with contract completion.		

Accounting for Receivables: Pan American Enterprises, Inc.

Pan American Enterprises, Inc. sells its internationally recognized wine on account to bars and restaurants throughout the United States. The company's credit terms require customers to pay their bills within 30 days of a transaction. During 2004 and 2005, Pan American Enterprises experienced the following accounting events:

Year	Credit Sales	Cash Collections	Estimated Bad Debt	Bad Debt Write-Off
2004	$3,200,000	$2,850,000	$10,925	$ —
2005	5,300,000	4,838,500	22,500	11,500

Using the debit/credit paradigm, Pan American Enterprises would record the following journal entries to reflect this accounting information:

Date	Accounts	Debit	Credit
2004	Accounts receivable (A)	3,200,000	
	Retained earnings (R).		3,200,000
	To record credit sales for 2004.		
	Cash (A)	2,850,000	
	Accounts receivable (A)		2,850,000
	To record collections on credit sales.		
	Retained earnings (E)	10,925	
	Allowance for Uncollectible Accounts (CA)		10,925
	To record the estimated bad debt expense and establish the allowance for future account write-offs.		
2005	Allowance for Uncollectible Accounts (CA)	11,500	
	Accounts receivable (A)		11,500
	To write off uncollected accounts receivable that have proven to be worthless.		
	Accounts receivable (A)	5,300,000	
	Retained earnings (R).		5,300,000
	To record credit sales for 2005.		
	Cash (A)	4,838,500	
	Accounts receivable (A)		4,838,500
	To record cash collections on credit sales.		
	Retained earnings (E)	23,075	
	Allowance for Uncollectible Accounts (CA))		23,075
	To record the estimated bad debt expense of $22,500 for 2005 and to record the under-estimated expense of $575 for 2004.		

To validate your understanding of the above journal entries, create T-accounts for each of the accounts, post the journal entry amounts to the appropriate T-accounts, and create account totals. Your T-account balances should reconcile with the balances reported in the chapter.

APPENDIX 5B: Revenue Recognition: SAB No. 101

Although the general criteria regarding revenue recognition is quite straightforward—the revenue must be earned and the collection of cash realized or realizable—revenue recognition issues dominate SEC enforcement actions involving exchange-traded companies. SEC Staff Accounting Bulletin (SAB) No. 101 on revenue recognition in financial statements was written to provide guidance for those situations in which a straightforward interpretation was not obvious. Below are key questions and answers extracted from SAB No. 101.

General Guidance on Revenue Recognition

Revenue should not be recognized until it is realized or realizable and earned. Revenue is generally realized or realizable and earned when all of the following criteria are met:

- Persuasive evidence of a sales arrangement exists.
- Delivery has occurred or services have been rendered.
- The seller's price to the buyer is fixed or determinable; and,

- Cash collectibility is reasonable assured.

Persuasive Evidence of a Sales Arrangement

Facts: Company A has product available to ship to Company B prior to the end of the period. It is customary for Company A to enter into a written sales agreement that requires the signature of the buyer company. Company B places a verbal order stating that it is highly likely that the contract will be approved one week after the end of the fiscal period. Company A ships the goods and Company B received the goods prior to the end of the period.

Question and Response: May Company A recognize revenue in the current period? It would not be appropriate to recognize revenue until the signed sales agreement is received since this is the general business practice of Company A. The signed agreement represents persuasive evidence of an agreement.

Facts: Company A enters into an arrangement with Customer B to deliver products to Customer B on a consignment basis. Title does not pass from Company A to Customer B until Customer B consumes the product. Company A delivers the product to Customer B under the terms of the arrangement.

Question and Response: May Company A recognize revenue upon delivery of its product to Customer B? No, consignment arrangements do not qualify for revenue recognition until a sale occurs. Revenue recognition is not appropriate since Company A retains the risks and rewards of ownership and title did not pass to Customer B.

Another characteristic in a transaction that will likely preclude revenue recognition, even if title has passed, is if the buyer has a right-of-product return. In general, under this set of circumstances, revenue recognition will be precluded until the right-of-return period has expired.

Delivery and Performance

Facts: Company A receives a purchase order for products it has in stock, however, the customer is unable to take delivery at this time.

Question and Response: Can Company A recognize revenue if it either segregates the inventory in its own warehouse or ships to a third-party warehouse if Company A retains title to the product? Generally, no; delivery is not considered to have taken place until the customer has taken title and assumed the risks and rewards of ownership. This interpretation includes layaway sales where a seller takes a nonrefundable deposit and holds the merchandise for later pickup by the customer. Further, revenue should not be recognized, even after delivery, if uncertainty exists regarding customer acceptance. Uncertainty exists, for example, if the customer has the right to test the product or require additional services subsequent to delivery.

Facts: Companies often require up-front, nonrefundable fees from its customers. Examples include a lifetime membership fee in a health club or an activation fee by a wireless telephone provider.

Question and Response: When should the revenue related to nonrefundable, up-front fees be recognized? Deferral of revenue recognition is appropriate unless the up-front fee is in exchange for delivered products or the performance of services that represent the culmination of a separate earnings process. Health club membership fees or activation fees by wireless telephone providers generally do not qualify for immediate revenue recognition.

Fixed or Determinable Sales Price

Facts: Company B is a discount retailer that generates revenue from annual membership fees it charges customers to shop at its stores and from the sale of products at a discount price to those customers. The membership arrangements with retail customers require the customer to pay the entire membership fee at the start of the arrangement. The customer has the unilateral right to cancel the arrangement at any time during its term and receive a full refund of the initial fee.

Question and Response: May Company B recognize revenue for the membership at the beginning of the membership period? No; the earnings process is not complete and the ability of the member to receive a refund raises an uncertainty as to whether the fee is fixed or determinable. A company's contracts may include provisions for the customer to cancel or terminate early. In addition, side agreements may be present providing additional rights for the customer. Provisions of this type raise questions as to whether the sales price is fixed or determinable. The sales price is neither fixed nor determinable until cancellation privileges expire. If the cancellation privilege expires ratably over a stated time period, the sales price is considered to become determinable ratably over the stated period.

Other Issues

Facts: Company A operates an internet site from which it sells the products of other companies. Company A receives orders, processes credit card payments, and passes the order to Company B which possesses the product. Company B then ships the product to the ultimate customer. The product is sold for $175, of which Company A retains a $25 commission.

Question and Response: Should Company A report revenue on a gross basis as $175 with a corresponding $150 cost of sales or report revenue on a net basis of $25? Company A should report revenue on a net basis unless it takes title to the product and assumes the risks and rewards of ownership.

DISCUSSION QUESTIONS

Q5.1 **Revenue Recognition Criteria.** MicroStrategy, Inc. is a software company that sells its services to other companies under multi-year contracts (on average for three years). The contracts call for a minimum fee, paid monthly, and additional fees when the services provided exceed certain levels. The chief operating officer (COO) of MicroStrategy is uncertain when the most appropriate time is to recognize the revenue from such contracts: (a) at the time of contract signing; (b) monthly, when billings are sent to customers; or (c), when the contract is complete and all services have been rendered. Discuss the criteria that should be considered in reaching this accounting policy decision. What would you recommend to MicroStrategy's COO?

Q5.2 **The Materiality Concept.** The materiality concept is a financial statement disclosure guideline used by most businesses to help determine when a particular account balance or economic event should be separately disclosed in a firm's financial statements. Unfortunately, there are no generally accepted guidelines for determining when an amount is material. Assume that you are the chief operating officer of a company generating $100 million in revenue, $10 million in net income, and $150 million in total assets. Discuss the materiality standard that you believe would be appropriate for such a business. Be prepared to justify your decision.

Q5.3 **Accrual Accounting, Accounts Receivable, and Cash Flow.** A well-known poem about accounting was written by H.S. Bailey, Jr. and published in 1975 in *Publishers Weekly*:

> *Though my bottom line is black, I am flat upon my back.*
> *My cash flows out and customers pay slow.*
> *The growth of my receivables is almost unbelievable.*
> *The result is certain—unremitting woe!*
> *And I hear the banker utter an ominous low mutter—"Watch cash flow."*

Discuss the message that Mr. Bailey was trying to convey through this poem.

Q5.4 **Revenue Recognition, the Matching Principle, and the Bad Debt Expense.** Urcarco, Inc. is a publicly-held used-car dealer that has defined its market niche as customers with a low or no credit rating. In some years, Urcarco's repossession rate has run as high as 40 percent of all vehicles sold. Discuss how Urcarco should recognize revenue from vehicle sales and how it should estimate its bad debt expense.

Q5.5   **Revenue Recognition in the Air Transportation Industry.** U.S. Airways recognizes revenue from airline ticket sales when a customer takes a flight or not later than one year from the date of sale (flight coupons have a useful life of one year from the date of purchase). Discuss the alternative revenue recognition policy options available to U.S. Airways.

Q5.6   **Managing Earnings and the Bad Debt Expense.** Total Networks, Inc. reported gross accounts receivable of $1.2 billion in 2005 and an allowance for doubtful accounts of $300 million. In 2006, the company's gross accounts receivable declined slightly to $1.1 billion and its allowance for doubtful accounts likewise declined to $150 million. Calculate the ratio of the allowance for doubtful accounts divided by gross accounts receivable for 2005 and 2006. Discuss how Total networks, Inc. might be managing its earnings.

Q5.7   **Sales Channel Stuffing.** On April 14, 2006, *The Wall Street Journal* carried an article headlined "Research in Motion Skeptics Pipe Up." The article concerned **Research in Motion Ltd** (RIM), the manufacturer of the Blackberry, a handheld device to send and receive e-mail. One week earlier, RIM had disappointed investors with a weaker-than-expected revenue forecast for the current quarter. In the one week period following the revenue announcement, RIM's share price declined 9.5 percent.

        The Wall Street Journal article expressed new concerns about RIM's financial performance. RIM generates revenue two ways:

1.   70 percent of its revenue comes from sales of the Blackberry device; and,
2.   30 percent of its revenue comes from the sale of subscriptions to the wireless network that supports the Blackberry.

Of concern to Wall Street analysts was the fact that a widening gap was beginning to build between the number of new Blackberry network subscribers and the number of Blackberry devices shipped to retailers. In the latest reporting period, RIM reportedly shipped 1.12 million Blackberries, while new network subscribers totaled only 625,000, a difference of about 495,000. According to the company, the "gap" between units shipped and new network subscribers for the prior three quarters, respectively, were 475,000, 335,000, and 248,000.

        Discuss whether RIM is engaging in "channel stuffing." (Note: Channel stuffing refers to the practice of shipping unwanted and unsolicited goods to retailers, usually with a guarantee to allow the return of any unsold goods.) Why is channel stuffing of concern to analysts and investors?

Q5.8   **Sales Forecasts and Share Prices.** In early 2006, the **Bausch & Lomb Company** halted shipments of its ReNu contact lens product and recalled from retailers any unsold containers of its contact lens solution. The contact lens-cleaning solution had been linked to an increasing number of serious eye infections caused by a fungus. ReNu products generated about $45 million in 2005 sales for Bausch & Lomb, but analysts predicted a wider decline in sales in related products as well. For 2006, equity analysts predicted that the company might lose $75 million to $100 million in lens-solution sales, or about 4.6 percent of the firm's total projected sales for 2006. Shares of Bausch & Lomb declined over $8 per share, or 15 percent, in response to the product recall.

        Discuss the relationship between revenue forecasts and security prices. Did the capital market overreact to the Bausch & Lomb news about ReNu?

Q5.9   **Revenue Recognition by Software Companies.** Microsoft, Inc. recognizes revenue from its licensed software products at the "time of sale" or "time of installation." Despite receiving such revenue in cash, Microsoft defers the recognition of a portion of its software revenue. The deferred portion represents the value of any future software upgrades that might be distributed free-of-charge, as well as the value of any technical support services provided free-of-charge during the software warranty period. Discuss Microsoft's revenue recognition policy. Do you agree with Microsoft's policy choice? Discuss the company's possible motivation for adopting this revenue recognition approach.

Q5.10   **Revenue Recognition by Aircraft Manufacturers.** Airbus and Boeing are the world's two largest manufacturers of commercial and military aircraft. Each company requires a deposit of as much as $100 million per aircraft prior to the start of construction of an airplane, which may take as long as nine months to complete. Airbus and Boeing also receive periodic progress payments from their customers as certain aircraft construction milestones are met. Typically, ten percent of an airplane's purchase price is withheld by the buyer until flight-testing is complete and title of the aircraft is transferred to the buyer. The average cost of a commercial aircraft is approximately $350 million. Discuss the possible approaches to revenue recognition that Boeing and Airbus might adopt. Which approach do you prefer? Why?

Q5.11   **(Ethics Perspective) Ethics and the Tone at the Top.**   Discuss what is meant by the "tone at the top" and why it is important. Further, discuss whether you feel it is ethical to be a whistle blower.

⊘ **indicates that check figures are available on the book's Website.**

EXERCISES

E5.12   **Revenue Recognition Policy Decisions.**   Consider the following independent situations:

1.   An international health club sells lifetime memberships costing $1,500 which allow the purchaser unlimited use of any of the club's 300 facilities around the world. The initiation fee may be paid in 36 monthly installments, with a two percent interest charge on any unpaid balance.

2.   Global Motors, Inc. has always offered a limited, 36-month warranty on its cars and trucks, but to counter the significant competition in the industry, the company has come to the conclusion that it must do something more. With that in mind, the company developed a new warranty program: For a $1,500 payment at the time of purchase, a customer can buy a seven-year warranty that will cover replacement of almost all parts and labor. The purchased warranty expires at the end of seven years or when the customer sells the vehicle, whichever occurs first.

3.   Arcadia Promotions Inc. sells coupon books that give the holder a ten percent discount at any of 50 participating merchants. The buyer of the coupon book pays $25 for the book but can realize up to $500 in savings. Arcadia convinces merchants to participate in the program at no cost, arguing that participation will build customer traffic and will create the opportunity for repeat business from the coupon book-holders.

4.   Luxury Furniture Inc. sells household furniture under installment purchase contracts. The contracts usually carry interest rates of 16 percent or more a year. When the company accumulates $500,000 of contracts with at least a year or more to go, it sells the contracts to a finance company on a non-recourse basis. Luxury Furniture continues to service the contracts and is paid a service fee. If a contract is uncollectible, Luxury Furniture turns it over to a collection agency and has no further responsibility for it. In January, Luxury sold contracts with a face value of $1 million and received $1.06 million in cash from the finance company.

5.   Community News, Inc. prints and distributes a weekly newspaper throughout the city. Local stores order a certain number of the papers each week and pay for them on delivery. Community News always takes back any unsold papers and gives the merchant a credit toward future purchases.

For each of these situations, describe the revenue recognition policy that you believe that the company should follow, explaining the basis for your recommendation.

E.5.13   **Revenue Recognition.**   The Longo Corporation contracted with The Davis Company to manufacture various metal component parts that would be assembled by Longo before resale to Longo's customers. Longo placed its most recent order with Davis for 10,000 parts in December 2006. Because of existing work commitments, however, Davis indicated that work on the Longo order could not commence until January 2007, with an expected delivery date of February 2007. Davis provides its customers with trade credit terms of 2/10, n/30, and thus, didn't expect to be paid the contract price of $100,000 by Longo until March 2007.

In which month should Davis Company recognize the $100,000 in revenue from the Longo order? Why?

⊘ E5.14 **Analyzing Accounts Receivable.** The following information is taken from the 2006 annual report of The Lincoln Electric Company.

Balance Sheet (amounts in thousands)	2005	2006
Accounts receivable, net of the allowance for uncollectible accounts of $2,460 and $2,700, respectively	$79,500	$75,390

Calculate the ratio of the allowance for uncollectible accounts divided by gross accounts receivable for 2005 and 2006. Did this ratio increase from 2005 to 2006? If so, what does that indicate? The bad debt expense on Lincoln Electric's 2006 income statement did not equal $2,700. What might explain this?

E5.15 **Analyzing Accounts Receivable.** The following information is taken from the 2006 annual report of the Couche Corporation.

Balance Sheet	2005	2006
Accounts receivable, net of the allowance for uncollectible accounts of $4,500 and $4,100, respectively	$125,650	$132,500

Calculate the ratio of the allowance for uncollectible accounts divided by gross accounts receivable. Did this ratio decrease from 2005 to 2006? If so, what does that indicate? The bad debt expense on the Couche Corporation's 2006 earnings statement did not equal $4,100. What might explain this?

E5.16 **Accounting for Quick-Pay Incentives.** Charles Smith, Inc. is a manufacturer of small office equipment. Smith transacts most of its business on credit and offers its customers credit terms of 2/10, n/30. On July 1, Smith shipped an order valued at $120,000 to a customer and shipped a second order valued at $80,000 to another customer on July 10. Payment was received on the July 1st order on July 6, but payment on the July 10th order was not received until August 15. Calculate total sales, the sales discount, and net sales for Charles Smith, Inc. for July. Why do companies like Smith, Inc. offer sales discounts to their customers? Why are sales discounts valuable to the customers of Smith, Inc.?

E5.17 **Preparing an Aging Schedule.** M. Beall Inc. uses the aging method to estimate the company's bad debt expense. Mike Beall, the president of the company, collected information about the company's outstanding accounts receivable and their probability of collection:

Account Age	Amount	Probability of Non-Collection
0–30 days.	$725,000	0.5%
31–60 days.	275,000	1.5
61–90 days.	170,000	2.5
91–120 days.	100,000	4.0
Over 120 days	40,000	20.0

Calculate the expected bad debt expense for M. Beall, Inc., the total balance in accounts receivable, and the net realizable value of the company's accounts receivable.

E5.18 **Preparing an Aging Schedule.** D. Wilcoxson, Inc. uses the aging method to estimate its bad debts. Dave Wilcoxson, the chief executive officer of the company, collected the following information about the company's outstanding accounts receivable and their probability of collection:

Account Age	Amount	Probability of Non-Collection
0–30 days..	$1,087,500	0.3%
31–60 days...	412,500	1.0
61–90 days...	255,000	1.5
91–120 days..	150,000	3.0
Over 120 days	60,000	15.0

Calculate the expected bad debt expense for D. Wilcoxson, Inc., the total balance in accounts receivable, and the net realizable value of the company's accounts receivable.

E5.19 **Analyzing Accounts Receivable.** The following information is taken from the 2005 annual report of Coca-Cola Enterprises, Inc.:

(amounts in millions)	2004	2005
Net sales..	$18,158	$18,706
Accounts receivable (net)............................	1,884	1,802

Calculate the receivable turnover ratio and the receivable collection period for 2004 and 2005. How much additional cash flow from operations could Coca-Cola Enterprises generate in 2005 if it could reduce its receivable collection period to just 30 days?

E5.20 **Analyzing Accounts Receivable.** The following information is taken from the 2006 annual report of The Mann Corporation:

(all amounts in millions)	2005	2006
Net sales..	$26,258	$25,649
Accounts receivable (net)............................	4,684	4,883

Calculate the receivable turnover ratio and the receivable collection period for 2005 and 2006. How much additional cash flow from operations could The Mann Corporation generate in 2006 if it could reduce its receivable collection period to 60 days?

E5.21 **Analyzing Accounts Receivable.** The following information is taken from the 2006 annual report of The Mayfair Corporation:

(in thousands)	2005	2006
Net sales..	$8,753	$8,550
Accounts receivable (net)............................	2,342	2,442

Calculate the receivable turnover ratio and the receivable collection period for 2005 and 2006. How much additional cash flow from operations could The Mayfair Corporation generate in 2006 if it could reduce its receivable collection period to 80 days?

E5.22 **Revenue Policy Change: Software Service Contracts.** Computer Associates, Inc. is a software company that designs, develops, installs, and services business software for manufacturing companies. Typically, Computer Associates provides its services over a multi-year period. Beginning in 2000, the company changed its method of recognizing revenue under its multi-year service contracts. Originally, Computer Associates recognized all contract revenue at the time that a contract was signed; however, beginning in 2000, the company decided to recognize contract revenue on a pro-rata basis over the life of each multi-year contract.

1. How will the change in revenue recognition policy affect the following items on the financial statements of Computer Associates?
   - a. Revenue
   - b. Total assets
   - c. Cash flow from operations
   - d. Total liabilities
2. Do you agree with the policy change implemented by Computer Associates? Why?

E5.23 **Revenue Policy Change: Retail Company.** Retailers like **Dillard's**, **Wal-Mart**, and **Nordstrom's** allow their customers to buy goods on layaway plans. Under a layaway arrangement, a customer makes payments over time on selected merchandise to a retailer who holds the merchandise until all payments are received. Until recently, **Wal-Mart** recorded the revenue under a layaway arrangement as a customer made payments (as cash was received), but recently changed its revenue recognition policy such that no revenue would be recorded until the full purchase price had been paid and until the customer took possession of the merchandise.

1. How will the change in Wal-Mart's layaway revenue recognition policy affect the following financial statement items?
   - a. Revenue
   - b. Total assets
   - c. Cash flow from operations
   - d. Total liabilities
2. Do you agree with Wal-Mart's policy change? Why?

PROBLEMS

⊘ P5.24 **Installment Basis versus Point-of-Sale Revenue Recognition.** The Apollo Company is a catalog-based retailer that began operations in 2005. The following describes Apollo's operations for 2005 and 2006:

	2005	2006
Sales (all on account)	$400,000	$600,000
Cash collections from customers		
On 2005 sales	180,000	220,000
On 2006 sales	—	240,000
Cash purchases of merchandise inventory	360,000	480,000
Merchandise inventory-on-hand (year-end)	120,000	228,000
Operating expenses (other than inventory)	64,000	88,000

Required

1. Prepare an income statement for each year assuming that Apollo recognizes revenue using the point-of-sale method and assuming that all operating expenses are paid in cash.
2. Prepare an income statement for each year assuming that Apollo recognizes revenue using the installment method and assuming that all operating expenses are paid in cash.

P5.25 **Revenue Recognition and Income Measurement.** At the beginning of 2006, Roy Herberger, the owner of a large agricultural concern, had no inventories on hand. During 2006, however, his company produced 80,000 bushels of corn, 100,000 bushels of soybeans, and 160,000 bushels of wheat. Upon completion of the harvest, Herberger sold one-half of each of his crops at the following prices: corn, $4.50 per bushel; soybeans, $3.25 per bushel; and wheat, $2 per bushel. At year-end, the remaining half of the crop was unsold.

To operate the company, Herberger incurred costs during 2006 of $370,000. The commodity price quotations reported in the *Wall Street Journal* at year-end 2006 revealed that the current market price per bushel for each of the crops was as follows: corn, $5 per bushel; soybeans, $3.47 per bushel; and wheat, $2.20 per bushel. Presented on next page is the balance sheet for R. Herberger, Inc., as of January 1, 2006:

R. Herberger, Inc.			
Balance Sheet			
As of January 1, 2006			
Assets		**Liabilities & Shareholders' Equity**	
Cash.	$ 75,000	Liabilities.	$ 0
Land	400,000	Shareholders' equity:	
Building & equipment $750,000		Capital stock	$650,000
Less: Accumulated		Retained earnings	225,000
depreciation. . . . . (350,000)	400,000		
Total assets.	$875,000	Total equities	$875,000

Required

Prepare an income statement and balance sheet for the company as of December 31, 2006, assuming that revenue is recognized on the basis of (a) the actual quantity of bushels sold and (b) the actual quantity of bushels produced.

P5.26 **Revenue Recognition.** At the beginning of 2006, John Cornell decided to quit his job as a construction company supervisor and formed his own residential housing construction company. When he resigned, he had a contract to build a custom home at a price of $400,000. The full price was payable in cash when the house was completed.

By year-end 2006, Cornell's new company Luxury Homes, Inc. had spent $50,000 for labor, $107,740 for materials, and $3,800 in miscellaneous expenses in connection with the construction of the new home. Cornell estimated that the project was 70 percent complete at year-end. In addition, construction materials on hand at year-end 2006 had cost $2,600.

During the year, Luxury Homes, Inc., had also purchased a small house for $95,000, spent $32,000 fixing it up, and then sold it on November 1, 2006 for $175,000. The buyer paid $25,000 down and signed a note for the remainder of the balance due. The note called for interest payments only at a rate of 12 percent per year, with a lump-sum payment for the outstanding balance payable at the end of 2008. John's wife, Karen, kept the accounting records for Luxury Homes, Inc., and on December 31, she prepared the following statement:

Luxury Homes, Inc.			
Where We Stand at Year-End			
Assets		**Debts and Owners' Capital**	
Cash	$ 21,000	Accounts payable.	$ 44,600
Materials.	2,600	Owners' investment	242,540
Renovation contract receivable	150,000	Sale of renovated house.	175,000
Construction in progress	161,540		
Cost of renovated house	127,000		
Total assets.	$462,140	Total debts & owners' capital	$462,140

After reviewing the statement, John and Karen got into a discussion concerning the level of revenue the company had earned during the year. John argued that all of the revenue from the sale of the renovated home, along with 70 percent of the expected revenue from the new construction contract, had been earned. Karen, on the other hand, maintained that the revenue on the renovation project should be recognized only to the extent of the cash actually collected and that no revenue should be recognized on the new home construction until it was completed and available for occupancy. John and Karen agreed that there were four possible alternative approaches to measuring the company's revenue:

1. Report the entire amount of renovation revenue and a proportionate amount of the new construction contract revenue.
2. Report the entire amount of renovation revenue but none of the new construction contract revenue.
3. Report the renovation revenue in proportion to the amount of cash received and the new construction contract revenue in proportion to the amount of work completed.
4. Report the renovation revenue in proportion to the amount of cash received but none of the new construction contract revenue.

Required

Prepare the balance sheets and income statements that would result under each of the four approaches. Which set of statements do you believe best reflects the results of Luxury Homes, Inc. for 2006? Why?

⊘ P5.27 **Completed Contract Method versus Percentage-of-Completion Method.** The Miller Company won a contract to build a shopping center at a price of $240 million. The following schedule details the estimated and actual costs of construction and the actual cash collections under the contract:

	Estimated (Actual) Costs of Construction	Cash Collections From Customer
2004	$ 40,000,000	$ 48,000,000
2005	60,000,000	60,000,000
2006	70,000,000	60,000,000
2007	30,000,000	72,000,000
	$200,000,000	$240,000,000

Required

1. Prepare an income statement for the Miller Company for each year assuming that the company recognizes revenue under the completed contract method.
2. Prepare an income statement for the Miller Company for each year assuming that the company recognizes revenue under the percentage-of-completion method.
3. Which set of income statements best reflects the actual performance of the Miller Company? Why?

P.5.28 **Revenue Recognition under Long-Term Construction Contracts.** In June 2004, Biltmore Construction Company (BCC) was hired by the City of Phoenix, Arizona to assist in constructing its new Trade Center complex. The construction agreement called for work to begin no later than August 2004 and required Biltmore to construct the concrete frame for the complex. Under the terms of the three year contact, BCC was to receive a total of $10 million in cash payments from the City of Phoenix, to be paid as follows: 25 percent when the project was 30 percent complete, 25 percent when the project was 60 percent complete, and the remaining 50 percent, when the project was fully complete. The contract required that BCC's completion estimates be certified by an independent engineering consultant *before* any cash progress payments would be made.

In preparing its bid, Biltmore estimated that the total cost to complete the project would be $8.3 million, assuming no cost overruns. During the first year of the contract, BCC incurred actual costs of $2.49 million, and on June 30, 2005, the engineering firm of J. Graham & Associates determined that the project had attained a 30 percent completion level. (BCC's fiscal year ran from July 1 to June 30.) In the following year, BCC incurred actual costs of $3.1 million, and on June, 30, 2006, the firm of J. Graham & Associates determined that the project had attained at least a 60 percent completion level. By May 2007, BCC had completed the remainder of the project. Actual costs incurred during the year to June 30, 2007, amounted to $3.11 million. The firm received a certification for the fully completed work.

Required

1. Assuming that BCC had no other sources of revenue or expenses, determine the level of profits to be reported for the years ended June 30, 2005, 2006, and 2007, using the following revenue recognition methods:
   a. Percentage of completion
   b. Completed contract
   c. Cash basis
2. Which set of results best reflect the economic performance of the company over the period 2005-2007? Why?

P5.29 **Revenue Recognition: R & D Company.** Wind Technology, Inc., is an independent research laboratory that undertakes contractual research for a variety of corporate and governmental clients. In January 2004, scientists at Wind Technology began work on a number of projects involving wind-power generation. During 2004, costs incurred in these efforts amounted to $363,000. In May 2005, promising results emerged and were reported to the U.S. Department of Energy. Development costs incurred in 2005 through the end of May totaled $204,000.

At this point, Wind Technology tried to secure a government contract to support the remainder of the research effort. The Department of Energy (DOE) was reluctant to commit substantial sums until further tests had been completed. Nonetheless, to ensure that it retained access to the new technology, the DOE gave Wind Technology a seed grant of $50,000 to help support continuation of the studies. This grant carried a stipulation that the DOE would retain the right to acquire the results, patents, and copyrights from the research any time on or before December 31, 2006 for $2.4 million.

Further testing proved favorable, although additional development costs incurred in 2005 amounted to $325,000 and to $210,000 in 2006. On December 28, 2006, the DOE exercised its right and agreed to purchase the results, patents, and copyrights from the lab. As previously agreed, the DOE paid Wind Technology $300,000 immediately, with the remainder of the contract price payable in seven equal annual installments beginning on December 31, 2007 through December 31, 2013. On March 1, 2007, Wind Technology delivered all scientific and legal documents, test results, and samples to the DOE offices in Washington, D.C.

Required

Evaluate the facts and determine when Wind Technology, Inc., should recognize the various revenue streams associated with its work on this project: a) the $2.4 million contract proceeds; b) the $50,000 seed grant; and c) the interest implicit in the seven year deferred payment (assume a discount rate of ten percent).

P5.30 **Revenue Recognition: Natural Resource Company.** In January 2006, the Western Canadian Oil & Gas Company was formed to explore for oil and gas in the western provinces of Canada. During the first year of operations, the following events occurred:

1. Spent $2 million cash to drill two oil wells that resulted in the discovery of a reserve estimated to contain 400,000 recoverable barrels of oil. It was estimated that Western would incur costs of $5.50 per barrel to extract and ship the oil to its customers.
2. Extracted 80,000 barrels of oil.
3. Sold 70,000 barrels of oil at a price of $20 per barrel.
4. Collected $1.8 million in cash from customers.
5. Paid $440,000 cash for extraction and shipping costs.

Required

Calculate the amount of (a) revenue and (b) net income that Western would report under each of the following four revenue recognition approaches in 2006:

1. Sales basis (revenue is recognized as oil is sold).
2. Production basis (revenue is recognized as oil is produced).
3. Discovery basis (revenue is recognized as oil is discovered).
4. Cash basis (revenue is recognized as cash is collected).

P5.31 **Revenue Restatement: Software Development Company.** Software, Inc. is a developer and manufacturer of innovative software products for laptop computers. The company follows a policy of recognizing all revenue from product sales at its internet website at the time of sale; however, for products sold through various retail outlets (such as Office Depot and CompUSA), revenue is deferred and subsequently recognized as earned in the following year. The company's justification for deferring the recognition of revenue for sales through retail outlets is that its products may sit on the retail shelves for months before a final sale occurs, delaying the start of the warranty and technical support period. Presented below are revenue data for Software, Inc. for the period 2003 to 2006:

(in millions)	2003	2004	2005	2006
Revenue (as reported on the income statement)...	$1,000	$1,200	$1,400	$1,600
Deferred revenue (as reported on the balance sheet)	200	400	600	800
Gross profit (80%)	800	960	1,120	1,280

Required

1. Assume that all revenue (both online sales and sales through retail outlets) should be recognized at the point of sale. How much (a) revenue and (b) gross profit would Software, Inc. report for the years 2003-2006?
2. Why would Software, Inc. want to defer the recognition of revenue from its product sales to retail outlets? Do you agree with this policy? Why or why not?

⊘ P5.32 **Aging of Accounts Receivable.** The Miller Company's accounts receivable reveal the following balances by age category:

Age of Account	Receivable Balance
0–30 days...	$ 800,000
31–60 days..	180,000
61–90 days..	80,000
91–120 days...	40,000
	$1,100,000

The Allowance for Uncollectible Accounts has an existing positive balance of $34,200. The company's internal auditors suggest that the following percentages be used to estimate the amount of outstanding receivables that will eventually prove to be uncollectible.

0-30 days	0.5%
31-60 days	1.0
61-90 days	10.0
91-120 days	70.0

Required

1. Calculate the projected new balance for (a) the Allowance for Uncollectible Accounts and (b) the Bad Debts Expense.
2. Why is there an existing balance of $34,200 in the Allowance for Uncollectible Accounts? What could be inferred if the existing balance in the Allowance for Uncollectible Accounts was a negative balance of $34,200?

P5.33 **Aging of Accounts Receivable.** The following data were taken from the Accounts Receivable account of Panama Products Company as of December 31, 2006:

Receivable Age Classification	Receivable Balance Outstanding	Probability of Non-Collection
0–10 days..................................	$100,000	1.0%
11–30 days................................	60,000	1.5
31–60 days................................	30,000	3.0
61–90 days................................	27,500	5.0
91–120 days..............................	11,000	7.5
Over 120 days	2,000	100.0

A balance of $1,000 existed in the Allowance for Uncollectible Accounts account as of the beginning of the year.

Required
Assume that the Panama Products Company follows a policy of writing off as uncollectible any account receivable older than 120 days. Determine the amount of Bad Debt Expense to be recorded at year-end 2006 by the company.

P5.34 **Accounts Receivable Analysis.** Kate Miller owned a dance studio in Los Angles, California. Students could buy access to the dance classes by paying a monthly fee. Unfortunately, many of Kate's students were struggling actors and actresses who lacked the ability to pay their bills in a timely manner. And, although the students were expected to pay for classes in advance, Kate had begun offering credit to many of her students to grow her business. This, however, had put Kate in a serious liquidity problem as revealed by the growing balance in the studio's outstanding accounts receivable:

Age Classification	Accounts Receivable Outstanding Balance	Historical Estimate of Non-Collection
0–30 days..........................	$44,000	4%
31–60 days.........................	31,000	8
61–90 days.........................	22,000	12
91–120 days........................	13,000	14
121–150 days.......................	9,000	20
> 150 days	5,000	50

Kate's accountant, Matt Thomas, had tried to help her get a handle on the studio's accounts receivable problem, but to little avail. One trick he had successfully used in the past to make Kate realize the seriousness of the problem was to overestimate the extent of Kate's bad debt problem; consequently, there currently existed a balance in the Allowance for Uncollectible Accounts totaling $2,700.

Required
1. The first step to help get Kate's business back on track is to write off all receivables having a very low probability of collection (those accounts over 150 days). What balance sheet accounts will be affected, and in what amount, when Matt executes this action?
2. Prepare an aging of Kate's remaining accounts receivable. What balance should be in the Allowance for Uncollectible Accounts account?
3. Kate is in need of an immediate cash infusion and Matt has advised her to sell some of her receivables. A local bank has offered her two alternatives:
   a. Factor $40,000 of "current" receivables (0–30 days old) on a non-recourse basis at a flat fee of eleven percent of the value of the receivables sold.

b. Factor $40,000 of "current" receivables on a recourse basis at a flat fee of six percent of the value of the receivables sold.

Which option should Kate choose? Why?

P5.35 **Factoring versus Pledging of Accounts Receivable.** Global Markets, Inc. was experiencing a shortage of cash. Consequently, the President was considering two options to provide an immediate inflow of cash. The first option was to obtain a 60-day loan from a local bank using its outstanding receivables as collateral. Under the loan agreement, Global Markets would be charged 13 percent annual interest on the outstanding loan and would pledge receivables equal to 122 percent of the loan amount (a loan-to-value ratio of 82 percent). The second option was to sell $2 million of the company's accounts receivable on a non-recourse basis. The factoring cost would amount to 15.5 percent of the value of the factored receivables.

Required:

Compare the cost under each financing option. Which option is best for the company? Why?

P5.36 **Analyzing Trade Receivables.** Pam Herberger, President of DFW Farm Services, had a problem. Although in the past the company's credit customers had paid their bills in a timely fashion, an increasing percentage had started to fall behind on their payments. The following is the company's accounts receivable data:

Age Classification of Accounts Receivable	Account Balance Outstanding	Recent Estimate of the Probability of Collection
0–30 days	$ 4,000,000	96%
31–60 days	3,000,000	88
61–90 days	2,000,000	80
91–120 days	1,000,000	75
> 121 days	500,000	60
	$10,500,000	

Required

1. What amount of the outstanding accounts receivable total of $10.5 million is expected to be uncollectible?

2. Last year, Pam had written off one account of $100,000 after learning that the customer had filed for bankruptcy. Pam had recently been informed by an attorney for the customer that she would indeed receive the $100,000 in about 60 days. What action is necessary to re-establish this account receivable?

3. Because of a cash flow problem, Pam has decided to factor $4 million of current accounts receivable on a non-recourse basis at a fee of 12 percent of the value of the receivables sold. Alternatively, she is also considering borrowing an equivalent amount at a cost of eight percent interest for three months. Which option is best? Why?

P5.37 **Improving Cash Flow through Receivable Management.** UTStarcom, Inc. designs, manufacturers, and sells telecommunication equipment, and provides services associated with their installation, operation, and maintenance in China, India, Korea, and Vietnam. During 2005, the company's share price traded as high as $23 per share; but, in January, 2005, the company disclosed that it would file its Form 10-K with the U.S. Securities and Exchange Commission late due to material internal control problems identified by its independent auditor, PriceWaterhouseCoopers. One of the identified concerns related to the company's recording of revenue and the related accounts receivable. In response, the company's share price sank to $6 per share. Presented on next page are selected financial information from UTStarcom's 2004 annual report:

	2004	2003
Net sales.	$2.56 billion	$1.78 billion
Accounts receivable (net).	0.81 billion	0.37 billion

Required

1. Calculate UTStarcom's receivable collection period for 2003 and 2004. Is the company's receivable management decreasing in quality, improving, or about the same?
2. If the company could improve its receivable collection period to the industry average of 60 days, how much additional cash flow from accounts receivable would have been generated in 2003 and 2004?

P5.38 **(Appendix 5A) Recording the Bad Debt Expense using the Debit/Credit Paradigm.** Holcombe Inc. uses the aging method to estimate the company's bad debt expense. Travis Holcombe, president of the company, collected information about the company's outstanding accounts receivable and their probability of collection:

Account Age	Amount	Probability of Non-Collection
0–30 days.	$725,000	0.5%
31–60 days.	275,000	1.5
61–90 days.	170,000	2.5
91–120 days.	100,000	4.0
Over 120 days	40,000	20.0

Required

Calculate the expected bad debt expense for Holcombe Inc., and prepare the journal entry to record the estimate using the debit/credit paradigm. Assume that one-half of the estimated bad debts prove to be uncollectible. Prepare the journal entry to write off the uncollectible accounts receivable. If $1,000 of the previously written off uncollectible receivables is found to be collectible, what entry would be needed to reinstate the accounts receivable on the books of Holcombe Inc.?

P5.39 **(Appendix 5A) Recording Revenue and Expenses using the Debit/Credit Paradigm.** RJ Miller Company won a contract to build a shopping center at a price of $240 million. The following schedule details the estimated and actual costs of construction and the actual cash collections under the contract:

	Estimated (Actual) Costs of Construction	Cash Collections From Customer
2004	$ 40,000,000	$ 48,000,000
2005	60,000,000	60,000,000
2006	70,000,000	60,000,000
2007	30,000,000	72,000,000
	$200,000,000	$240,000,000

Required

1. Prepare the journal entries to record the revenue and expenses for RJ Miller Company for 2004 through 2007 assuming that the company recognizes revenue under the completed contract method.
2. Prepare the journal entries to record the revenue and expenses for RJ Miller Company for 2004 through 2007 assuming that the company recognizes revenue under the percentage-of-completion method.

CORPORATE ANALYSIS

CA5.40 **The Procter and Gamble Company.** The 2005 annual report of the Procter and Gamble Company (P & G) is available at www.pg.com/annualreports/2005/pdf/pg2005annualreport.pdf. After reviewing P & G's annual report, respond to the following questions:

   a. When does P & G recognize revenue from its product sales?

   b. In the Management Discussion and Analysis section, the company highlights its financial targets. What percentage sales growth is targeted by the company? Assuming that this target is met for 2006, what level of sales will the company achieve? What was the company's growth in sales in 2004 and 2005? Do the new sales targets indicate that sales growth is increasing or decreasing?

   c. When does P & G recognize its sales discounts and sales returns?

   d. Calculate P & G's receivable turnover ratio and receivable collection period for 2004 and 2005. Are these ratios improving?

   e. Assume that P & G's allowance for uncollectible accounts was $180 million at year-end 2004 and $205 million at year-end 2005. Calculate the ratio of the allowance for uncollectible accounts-to-gross accounts receivable for 2004 and 2005. Did this ratio improve from 2004 to 2005? If so, what does that indicate?

   f. Using your forecast of net sales for 2006 from question (b), and your 2005 receivable turnover ratio from question (d), forecast the balance of accounts receivable for 2006 (assuming that receivable turnover remains the same from 2005 to 2006).

   g. If P & G can increase its receivable turnover in 2006 from 13.6 to 14.0, driving the receivable collection period down from 26.8 days to only 26.0 days, how much additional cash will become available?

CA5.41 **Internet-based Analysis.** Consider a publicly-held company whose products you are familiar with. Some examples might include:

Company	Product	Corporate Website
• **Johnson & Johnson Company**	• Band-Aids	• www.jnj.com
• **Microsoft Corporation**	• Windows XP software	• www.microsoft.com
• **Nokia Corporation**	• Cellular phones	• www.nokia.com
• **Intel Corporation**	• Pentium processors	• www.intel.com
• **Kimberly-Clark Corporation**	• Kleenex	• www.kimberly-clark,com

Access the company's public website and search for its most recent annual report. (Some companies will provide access to their financial data through an "investor relations" link, while others will provide a direct link to their "annual reports.") After locating your company's most recent annual report, open the file and review its contents. After reviewing the annual report for your selected company, prepare answers to the following questions:

   1. Identify whether the company is a retailer, a manufacturer, or a service-provider.

   2. Review the company's "Summary of Significant Accounting Principles." When does the company recognize its operating revenue? Can you identify an alternative method to recognize its operating revenue? If so, describe the alternative approach.

   3. Review the company's balance sheet and related footnotes. Identify the gross accounts receivable and the allowance for uncollectible accounts for each of the last two years. Calculate the ratio of the allowance for uncollectible accounts divided by the gross accounts receivable for each of the last two years. Is this ratio increasing or decreasing? Why?

   4. Calculate the company's receivable turnover and receivable collection period for each of the last two years. Is the receivable collection period increasing or decreasing? What might explain this increase or decrease?

   5. Calculate the company's cash collections from sales for each of the last two years. Using this calculation, compute the company's cash conversion ratio (cash collections from sales divided by net sales). Is the cash conversion ratio increasing or decreasing? Is the cash conversion ratio at an acceptable level?

Chapter Six

Operating Expenses, Inventory Valuation and Accounts Payable

TAKEAWAYS

When you complete this chapter, you should be able to:

1. Explain how inventory is valued using FIFO, LIFO, and the weighted-average cost method and how the resulting cost of goods sold is matched with revenue.
2. Describe why the lower-of-cost-or-market method is sometimes used to value ending inventory and how this method affects reported net income.
3. Explain what the inventory reserve is and how a LIFO-inventory liquidation can artificially increase a company's gross and net profit.
4. Describe how accounts payable are valued and how the payment of these payables can be managed to positively impact a firm's operating cash flow.

Where have we been?	Where are we?	Where are we going?
In Chapter 5, we found that companies may recognize their operating revenue at many different points in time—during production, at the completion of production, when goods are sold or delivered, or when goods are paid for. We also learned that when companies allow their customers to buy goods and services on credit, it creates a number of risks for the company. For example, there is the risk that some customers will take a long time to pay for their credit purchases and the risk that some customers won't pay at all. Chapter 5 explored the various ways that generally accepted accounting principles attempt to measure these risks and reflect them in a firm's financial statements.	In Chapter 6, we continue the examination of the important accounting concept called "matching." Specifically, this chapter investigates the various ways that companies can value their inventory available for sale and match their cost of goods sold with operating revenue from the sale of those goods. We will see that managers are faced with a number of inventory valuation and matching choices: specific identification, FIFO, LIFO, and weighted-average cost. Just which valuation/matching method is chosen can have a dramatic effect on a company's reported performance. Consequently, the chapter illustrates why the inventory valuation method choice is often linked to corporate income tax and income reporting considerations.	In Chapter 7, our exploration of the accounting concept of matching operating revenue and operating expenses continues; however, the focus shifts to matching the cost of long-lived assets such as buildings, machinery, equipment, patents, and intellectual property rights with the revenue that these assets produce. For these assets, matching is accomplished by the use of an allocation method that systematically distributes the acquisition cost of an asset over the periods that the asset produces operating revenue. This allocation process is called depreciation when referring to plant and equipment, amortization when referring to intangible assets, and depletion when referring to natural resources.

GENERAL MOTORS CORPORATION   Symbol: GM

General Motors Corporation is the world's second largest automaker. Founded in 1908 in Detroit, Michigan, GM manufactures its cars and trucks in 33 countries. In 2006, the company sold 9.1 million cars and trucks under the following brands: Buick, Cadillac, Chevrolet, GMC, GM Daewoo, Holden, HUMMER, Opel, Pontiac, Saab, Saturn, and Vauxhall.

GM is considered to be a capital intensive company with a capital intensity ratio of 0.18—that is, the company's investment in property, plant, equipment and intangible assets represents 18 percent of total assets. Besides its significant investment in property, plant and equipment, GM maintains a sizeable investment in inventory to service its worldwide network of GM dealers. GM's investment in inventory represented 3 percent and 7 percent of total assets in 2004 and 2005, respectively. A major challenge for GM's management team is to keep its investment in inventory as low as possible without damaging its ability to effectively service its dealer network.

According to the company's 2005 annual report, GM's investment in inventory totaled $14.354 billion, $12.247 billion, and $10.960 billion in 2005, 2004, and 2003, respectively. The company's inventory turnover for these same three fiscal years was 11.92, 13.06, and 13.90, respectively, representing an inventory-on-hand period of 30.6 days, 27.9 days, and 26.3 days. By way of comparison, the average inventory turnover for the automobile industry in 2005 was 12.8 times, representing an industry inventory-on-hand period of 28.5 days. For Toyota, the recognized efficiency leader in the industry, the inventory turnover for 2005 was 35 times, representing an inventory-on-hand period of just 10 days. The GM data clearly indicate a deteriorating trend in the management of GM's inventory, leading to an increase in the amount and cost of funds tied up in inventory on hand. Not surprisingly, GM's net income also declined over this same three year period, from $3.8 billion in 2003, to $2.8 billion in 2004, to a loss of over $10.6 billion in 2005.

In this chapter, we investigate the important accounting construct of matching and examine the various ways that companies like GM can match the cost of constructing their inventory with the revenue produced when the inventory is sold. In the case of GM, the company used the last-in, first-out (LIFO) method to account for 67 percent of its U.S. inventory and the first-in, first-out (FIFO) method to account for the remaining 33 percent.

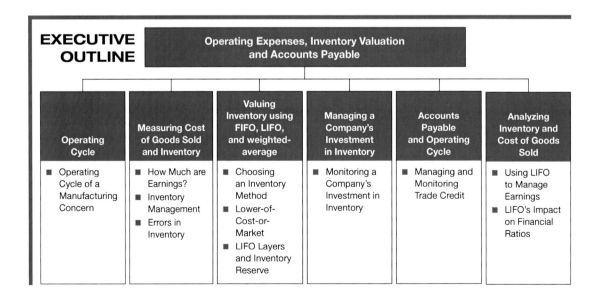

EXECUTIVE OUTLINE

Operating Expenses, Inventory Valuation and Accounts Payable

Operating Cycle	Measuring Cost of Goods Sold and Inventory	Valuing Inventory using FIFO, LIFO, and weighted-average	Managing a Company's Investment in Inventory	Accounts Payable and Operating Cycle	Analyzing Inventory and Cost of Goods Sold
■ Operating Cycle of a Manufacturing Concern	■ How Much are Earnings? ■ Inventory Management ■ Errors in Inventory	■ Choosing an Inventory Method ■ Lower-of-Cost-or-Market ■ LIFO Layers and Inventory Reserve	■ Monitoring a Company's Investment in Inventory	■ Managing and Monitoring Trade Credit	■ Using LIFO to Manage Earnings ■ LIFO's Impact on Financial Ratios

OPERATING CYCLE OF A MANUFACTURER

Most businesses have an identifiable cycle of activities that reflects the day-to-day operations of the business. This cycle is known as its operating cycle. Exhibit 6.1, for instance, presents the operating cycle of a typical manufacturing company. In Chapter 5, we illustrated the operating cycle for a typical retail or service company (see Exhibit 5.1). In the case of a retailer, the business acquires inventory ready for sale and then sells the inventory to its customers. Initially, the inventory is carried as an asset on the retailer's balance sheet, but upon its sale, the cost of the inventory is transferred from the balance sheet to the cost of goods sold on the income statement, to be matched with the operating revenue produced by the sale. The inventory is subsequently replaced by cash, or an account receivable if sold on credit, on the balance sheet.

In the case of a manufacturing firm, the operating cycle is more complex. A manufacturing company begins its operating cycle with the purchase of raw material, which then enters its production process. During the production process, the raw material is altered by the production-line workers and manufacturing equipment, yielding what is known as work-in-process inventory. When the production process is complete, the ready-for-sale inventory is called finished goods inventory. As in the case of a retail company, the manufacturer's finished goods inventory (as well as its raw material and work-in-process inventory) is considered to be an asset on the balance sheet. Upon the sale of the finished goods inventory, the cost of the sold inventory is transferred to cost of goods sold on the income statement and replaced by cash or accounts receivable on the balance sheet.

In this chapter, we will focus on the operating cycle of two companies—Home Heating Oil Co. and the Arizona Ice Cream Company Inc. We will see that one of the key operating expenses for each of these retailers is the cost of goods sold. In subsequent chapters, we will consider some of the other typical operating expenses of such businesses—depreciation expense, employee compensation expense, interest expense, and income tax expense, among others.

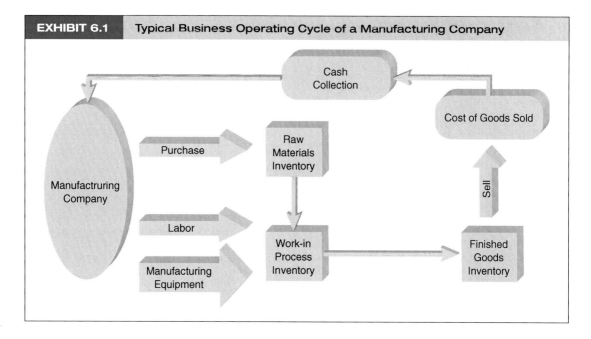

EXHIBIT 6.1   Typical Business Operating Cycle of a Manufacturing Company

MEASURING COST OF GOODS SOLD AND ENDING INVENTORY

Case Illustration: How Much are Earnings?

Home Heating Oil Inc. purchases heating oil from a major oil company and then resells and delivers the oil to its retail customers. The company began its first month of operations by acquiring one barrel of heating oil at a cost of $10 on January 1. It purchased another barrel of oil on January 12 for $16. On January 20, Home Heating sold one barrel for $25, by which time the wholesale price of heating oil had risen to $22 per barrel. This sequence of events is shown on the time-line below:

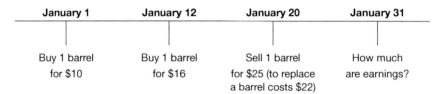

The chief executive officer (CEO) of Home Heating wondered exactly how much profit the company had made during the month of January and what value should be assigned to the barrel of oil that remained in inventory at the end of the month. After some review, the CEO concluded that there were four possible ways to compute the company's earnings and to value its ending inventory. Applying the four methods produced gross profit for the business that ranged from a high of $15 to a low of $3 and ending inventory valuations that ranged from $22 to $10 per barrel (see Exhibit 6.2). The CEO wondered if the company could choose any of the four methods. Method Four appeared to be the best choice for income tax purposes since taxable earnings would be only $3, whereas Method One would be more likely to impress the company's shareholders since earnings for the month would be $15.

EXHIBIT 6.2	Alternative Inventory Valuation Methods: Home Heating Oil, Inc.			
	Method 1	Method 2	Method 3	Method 4
Income statement				
Revenue	$25	$25	$25	$25
Cost of goods sold.	10	16	13	22
Gross profit.	$15	$ 9	$12	$ 3
Balance sheet				
Inventory.	$16	$10	$13	$22

To the CEO, the answer seemed clear: Use Method Four on the company's income tax return and Method One in the annual report to shareholders. That way Home Heating would pay low income taxes but report high earning to its shareholders! The last idea sounded particularly appealing to the CEO whose year-end bonus was linked to reported earnings, and consequently, his personal income would be positively impacted.

Fortunately, Home Heating's chief financial officer (CFO) set the CEO straight about the constraints the company faced when selecting an inventory valuation method for the company's income tax return and when selecting a method for use in its audited financial reports to shareholders. Although methods one, two, and three are acceptable under generally accepted accounting practice (GAAP) in the United States, Method Four is not. Method Four—using the replacement cost to value inventory—could be used in some countries including Mexico, Australia, and the United Kingdom, but it was not GAAP in the U.S.[1]

The CFO informed Home Heating's CEO that Method One was known as **FIFO**—first-in, first-out—and as the name suggests, this approach assumes that the first units purchased are the first units sold, so Home Heating's cost of goods sold for January would be $10. The units remaining on hand are the units purchased more recently so the company's ending inventory would be $16, the cost of the last unit purchased on January 12. Method Two was known as **LIFO**—last-in, first-out. This method assumes that the units purchased most recently, the $16 unit purchased on January 12, are the first units sold. Hence, the unit in ending inventory would be the $10 unit purchased on January 1. Use of the LIFO method would result in reduced income taxes but there was a hitch—in the United States, the Internal Revenue Service required businesses that used LIFO for income tax purposes to also use LIFO in the preparation of their audited financial reports to shareholders. This is known as the **LIFO conformity rule**. The CFO noted that this requirement would put a crimp in the CEO's desire to pay low taxes *and* report high earnings to shareholders. He would have to choose! LIFO also appeared to have the undesirable effect of reporting a low value for ending inventory ($10) on the balance sheet—a value that was considerably less than it would cost ($22) the business to buy a similar unit at the end of the month. Method Three, the **average cost method**, caused the unit sold and the unit in inventory to both be valued at $13, the average of the $10 and $16 purchase prices. Method Four, the **replacement cost method**, valued both the unit sold and the unit on hand at the inventory's replacement cost of $22.

Home Heating's CFO also informed the CEO that there was another option available to the company—the specific identification method. Under the specific identification method, if the CEO could identify exactly which barrel of heating oil was sold on January 20—the barrel purchased on January 1 or the barrel purchased on January 12—then the actual price of the identified barrel would be charged to cost of goods sold and the cost basis of the remaining barrel would also be known. Not surprisingly, the CEO could not clearly identify which barrel of oil was purchased on which date since the barrels were identical in appearance, content, and quality. Observing that the specific identification method was impractical for some companies, this option was discarded by both the CEO and CFO.

> The specific identification approach tends to be used by manufacturers (such as Boeing) which produce a limited number of high-value products. For companies that produce in large volume, the additional record-keeping costs associated with this method are rarely justified.

After much debate, the CEO selected LIFO as the company's inventory valuation method. He decided that he would explain to shareholders that the operating cash flow saved by using LIFO for income tax purposes would enable the firm to pay more dividends, make additional investments in long-term assets, and reduce debt. That should keep the shareholders happy enough to pay him a large bonus!

Inventory Management Systems

In addition to selecting an inventory valuation method, one of the decisions that must be made by the CEO of a company like Home Heating Oil Inc. is the type of inventory management system that will be used to keep track of the inventory purchased, sold, and on hand. The choice involves two types of systems—periodic and perpetual.

---

[1] A key reporting convention followed under U.S. GAAP, and the GAAP of many countries, is the historical cost convention, which stipulates that all assets be initially valued at their original or historical cost. Methods One, Two, and Three are consistent with this convention, whereas Method Four, which relies on the inventory's *future* replacement cost, is not.

As the name implies, a **periodic system** periodically updates such information as the cost and quantity of inventory on hand, but only when new goods are purchased and when a physical count of the on-hand inventory is undertaken. A periodic system presumes that management does not need minute-by-minute (or even daily) information regarding the quantity of inventory on hand or its cost. The deficiency of this system is that reliable information about a company's inventory available for sale is only periodically available. For this reason, it is rarely used by well-run businesses because knowing how much inventory is available for sale is important for managers who try to provide the best possible service to their customers.

A **perpetual system**, on the other hand, updates a firm's inventory data after every purchase *and* every sale, providing a constant source of reliable information about the cost and quantity of goods available for sale. Perpetual systems are informationally superior to periodic inventory systems, but they are also more costly. In today's competitive marketplace, however, even small companies can realize the benefits of a perpetual system given the low cost of computer equipment and inventory management software.

A good way to understand the strengths and weaknesses of each inventory management system is by considering some illustrative inventory data. Assume that Home Heating Oil, Inc. experienced the following events:

January 1	Purchased 100 barrels of oil at $10 per barrel, for a total expenditure of $1,000.
January 3	Sold 50 barrels at $15 per barrel, for a total sale of $750.
January 15	Purchased 100 barrels at $13 per barrel, for a total expenditure of $1,300.
January 20	Sold 125 barrels at $15 per barrel, for a total sale of $1,875.
January 30	Physically counted the available inventory, determining that 25 barrels were on hand.

Under a periodic system, the managers of Home Heating would not know exactly how many barrels of oil were on hand and available for sale until January 30, following a physical count of the inventory. Although a periodic system does capture information concerning units purchased, it does not record the cost of the sold units until a physical count of the inventory on hand verifies the quantity actually available. Thus, a periodic system records the quantities added to inventory on January 1 and January 15, but does **not** record the quantities removed from inventory on January 3 and January 20 until a physical count is executed on January 30. Hence, if an additional order for 30 barrels had been received on January 22 for delivery on January 25, Home Heating's managers would not have had the necessary information to know whether the company could satisfy the order because they lacked the knowledge as to how many barrels were actually on hand.

Under a perpetual system, however, the quantity of on-hand inventory is updated after every purchase and sale transaction. Thus, the system is perpetually updating itself so as to constantly provide current information about the quantity and cost of goods available for sale. Under a perpetual system, if an additional order for 30 barrels were received on January 22, Home Heating's manager could easily access the inventory management system to verify that the quantity on hand was insufficient to service the order. In this case, Home Heating's managers would find that there were only 25 barrels on hand, and thus, that five more barrels would first need to be ordered.

Even though a perpetual system provides up-to-the-minute information regarding inventory quantities, it is still important for a company to periodically physically count its inventory on hand. Almost all types of inventory are subject to damage, deterioration and theft, and a physical count is the best way to identify the existence and magnitude of these problems.[2]

---

[2] Retailer's like **Dillard's**, **Nordstrom's**, and **Wal-Mart** typically do a physical count of their merchandise inventory at least once a year, and more commonly, twice a year. To avoid interrupting normal daily sales activities, physical counts are usually executed at night, after store closing hours.

Errors in Inventory Count

A physical inventory count serves as the basis to determine the quantity and value of ending inventory, along with the cost of goods sold for firms utilizing a periodic inventory system. In addition, the inventory count serves as a confirmation of the ending inventory balance for firms employing a perpetual inventory system. If the inventory value computed from the physical count differs from the inventory records maintained under the perpetual system, the company will adjust its records to match the physical count.

It should be noted that any amount needed to adjust ending inventory will affect not only inventory on the balance sheet but also cost of goods sold, and therefore net income on the income statement. Consider the case of the Home Store Company, a retail hardware store. Home Store maintains a perpetual inventory system and shows an ending inventory balance of $2,550 as of December 31, 2005. A physical count of the inventory on December 31, however, reveals that the actual inventory on hand is only $2,325, perhaps due to inventory breakage or theft. To recognize the inventory loss, it is necessary to enter a charge of $225 to cost of goods sold and a reduction of $225 to inventory (see the company's spreadsheet below). Note that this adjustment affects not only income in 2005—a reduction of $225—but will also affect 2006 in an opposite direction. This results because the ending inventory of $2,325 in 2005 becomes the beginning inventory in 2006.

Home Store Company Spreadsheet			
	Assets	=	Equity
2005	Inventory		Retained Earnings
Pre-count balance	2,550		
Adjust to physical count.	(225)		(225)
Ending balance.	2,325		(225)

To see how an error in ending inventory affects net income in two different years, consider again the Home Store Company. Assume that instead of determining the ending inventory to be $2,325, several items were double counted and the ending 2005 inventory was determined to be $2,700. Keep in mind that inventory is first reported on the balance sheet as an asset and then removed from the balance sheet and charged as cost of goods sold to the income statement when the inventory is sold. This provides a matching of the revenue from a sale with the expense of the inventory sold as required by GAAP. The basic formula to partition inventory expenditures between the inventory account and the cost of goods sold is as follows:

Beginning inventory
+ Purchases
= Goods available for sale
− Ending inventory
= Cost of goods sold

As can be seen from this basic formula, goods available for sale are partitioned into either ending inventory, an asset on the balance sheet, or cost of goods sold, an expense on the income statement. If the ending inventory count is erroneously too high (low), then cost of goods sold will be erroneously too low (high). Further, ending inventory in one year becomes the beginning inventory for the next year. Since goods available for sale includes beginning inventory, any error in the previous year is carried forward and results in an error in cost of goods sold of equal magnitude, but opposite direction, the following year.

VALUING INVENTORY USING FIFO, LIFO, AND WEIGHTED-AVERAGE—A CLOSER LOOK

Arizona Ice Cream Company, Inc. retails ice cream in large order sizes in Phoenix, Arizona. The current year is the company's first year of operations. The retail sales price of a ten gallon bucket of ice cream is $20. The company has a sophisticated bar code scanner system that enables the company to operate a perpetual inventory system in each of its ten retail outlets.

When ice cream is sold to a customer at one of its stores, the inventory system automatically updates the company's inventory records. It also sends a purchase order to a supplier when inventories fall to pre-determined levels. The system records the cost of goods sold based on the specific inventory method the company uses, although Arizona Ice Cream Company (AICC) has not decided whether to use FIFO, LIFO, or the weighted-average cost method.

> The weighted-average cost method differs from the average cost method in that each inventory price is weighted by the quantity of units purchased at a given price, whereas the average cost method calculates a simple average of the various inventory purchase prices without regard to the quantities purchased. The weighted-average cost method is widely regarded as being informationally superior to the average cost method, and consequently, is used by most firms not electing to adopt FIFO or LIFO. The weighted-average cost method is often simply referred to as the "average cost method" in many corporate financial reports.

During the year, AICC made purchases of ice cream on September 5, October 22, November 15, and December 30 at prices that ranged from $10 to $15 per bucket. AICC purchased a total of 10,000 buckets of ice cream at an aggregate cost of $128,500. AICC also sold inventory on September 20, November 4, December 22, and December 31. Total sales amounted to $160,000 (8,000 buckets at $20 per bucket). How much profit did AICC make on its sales and what was the value of its ending inventory?

If AICC uses FIFO to value its inventory, and thus match the cost of goods sold with its revenue, the results under a perpetual system would appear as presented in Exhibit 6.3. (We suggest that you work through the values in the columns labeled "FIFO Cost of Goods Sold" and "FIFO Ending Inventory" in Exhibit 6.3 to insure that you understand how these values are calculated.) Using the FIFO perpetual method, AICC's cost of goods sold is $98,500, and gross profit is $61,500 ($160,000 − $98,500). Thus, the value of the 2,000 buckets of ice cream remaining in inventory for future sale is $30,000 ($128,500 − $98,500).

In Practice 6.1 *Income Statement Caption: A Glimpse of a Sample of Fortune 1000 Companies* The following table identifies the caption for cost of goods sold used on the income statement for a sample of 600 Fortune 1000 companies. The preferred label is "cost of sales:"

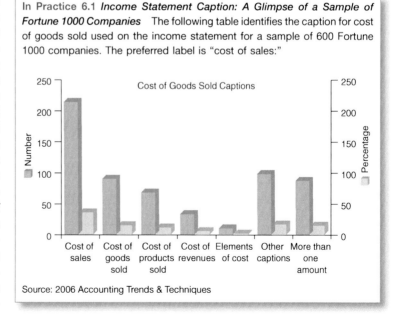

Source: 2006 Accounting Trends & Techniques

EXHIBIT 6.3	Valuing Inventory and Cost of Goods Sold using FIFO					
Date	Purchases (# buckets)	Purchase Price (per bucket)	Total Cost	Sales (# buckets)	FIFO Cost of Goods Sold	FIFO Ending Inventory
Sep 5	1,000	$10	$ 10,000			1,000 @ $10
Sep 20				800	800 @ $10 $ 8,000	200 @ $10
Oct 22.	2,500	12	30,000			200 @ $10
						2,500 @ $12
Nov 4				2,600	200 @ $10 30,800	100 @ $12
					2,400 @ $12	
Nov 15	4,500	13	58,500			100 @ $12
						4,500 @ $13
Dec 22				3,400	100 @ $12 44,100	1,200 @ $13
					3,300 @ $13	
Dec 30	2,000	15	30,000			1,200 @ $13
						2,000 @ $15
Dec 31				1,200	1,200 @ $13 15,600	2,000 @ $15
Total	10,000		$128,500	8,000	$98,500	$30,000

If, on the other hand, AICC uses LIFO, the results under a perpetual system would appear as presented in Exhibit 6.4. Under the LIFO perpetual method, AICC's cost of goods sold is $101,200, and gross profit is $58,800 ($160,000 − $101,200). The value of the 2,000 buckets of ice cream remaining in inventory for future sale is $27,300 ($128,500 − $101,200).

EXHIBIT 6.4	Valuing Inventory and Cost of Goods Sold using LIFO					
Date	Purchases (# buckets)	Purchase Price (per bucket)	Total Cost	Sales (# buckets)	LIFO Cost of Goods Sold	LIFO Ending Inventory
Sep 5	1,000	$10	$10,000			1,000 @$ 10
Sep 20				800	800 @ $10 $ 8,000	200 @$ 10
Oct 22.	2,500	12	$30,000			2,500 @ $12
						200 @ $10
Nov 4				2,600	2,500 @ $12 31,000	100 @ $10
					100 @ $10	
Nov 15	4,500	13	$58,500			4,500 @ $13
						100 @ $10
Dec 22				3,400	3,400 @ $13 44,200	1,100 @ $13
						100 @ $10
Dec 30	2,000	15	$30,000			2,000 @ $15
						1,100 @ $13
						100 @ $10
Dec 31				1,200	1,200 @ $15 18,000	800 @ $15
						1,100 @ $13
						100 @ $10
Total	10,000		$128,500	8,000	$101,200	$27,300

The operating revenue that AICC would recognize from selling 8,000 buckets at $20 per bucket is $160,000 regardless of whether the company uses FIFO or LIFO. However, the cost of goods sold under FIFO and LIFO varies ($98,500 versus $101,200, respectively) as a consequence of the different inventory cost flow assumptions that characterize FIFO and LIFO. As a result, AICC's gross profit varies under the different inventory methods, as follows:

	FIFO	LIFO
Revenue	$160,000	$160,000
Cost of goods sold.	(98,500)	(101,200)
Gross profit.	$ 61,500	$ 58,800

Similarly, even though the quantity of inventory on hand for AICC is the same at the end of the year, (2,000 buckets), the reported value of the ending inventory under FIFO versus LIFO varies ($30,000 and $27,300, respectively):

	FIFO	LIFO
Inventory.	$30,000	$27,300

The gross profit for Arizona Ice Cream Company is highest under FIFO and lowest under LIFO. This outcome will occur when the cost of inventory is increasing. In this instance, the cost of AICC's inventory purchases increased from $10 to $12 to $13 per bucket, and finally to $15 per bucket. If, on the other hand, inventory costs are decreasing, LIFO will yield the highest gross profit and FIFO the lowest. If prices are perfectly stable, there will be no difference in the cost of goods sold or ending inventory under any of the methods.

But what if AICC decided to use the weighted-average cost method instead?[3] The results for the weighed-average cost method under a perpetual system are presented in Exhibit 6.5. Under this approach, AICC's cost of goods sold is $100,018, about midway between the cost of goods sold under FIFO and LIFO. The value of AICC's ending inventory is $28,482, again about midway between the value of ending inventory under FIFO and ending inventory under LIFO. Finally, gross profit is $59,982, about midway between FIFO gross profit of $61,500 and LIFO gross profit of $58,800. (Were you able to verify each of these figures by working through the two right-most columns of Exhibits 6.3, 6.4, and 6.5?) In essence, while FIFO and LIFO yield values representing the ends of a continuum, the weighted-average cost method yields results which fall somewhere in the middle of that continuum.

Choosing an Inventory Method

With the diversity of cost of goods sold and ending inventory values provided under FIFO, LIFO, and the weighted-average cost method, how do managers decide which method is "best" for their company? In many cases, the inventory method deci-

> Under U.S. Department of the Treasury regulations, if a company uses LIFO to obtain the income tax-sheltering benefits provided by the LIFO method, it must also use LIFO in its audited financial statements, which helps explain why LIFO became the industry standard in the U.S. automobile industry and many other U.S. industries.

---

[3] The CEO and CFO decided that use of the specific identification method by Arizona Ice Cream Company, Inc. was not practical since the appearance, content, and quality of the buckets of ice cream were indistinguishable, and in any case, the additional record-keeping cost associated with the specific identification method did not appear justified.

EXHIBIT 6.5		Valuing Inventory and Cost of Goods Sold using Weighted-Average				
Date	Purchases (# buckets)	Purchase Price (per bucket)	Total Cost	Sales (# buckets)	Weighted-Average Cost of Goods Sold	Weighted-Average Ending Inventory
Sep 5	1,000	$10	$ 10,000			1,000 @ $10
Sep 20				800	800 @ $10 $ 8,000	200 @ $10
Oct 22	2,500	$12	30,000			2,700 @ $11.852*
Nov 4				2,600	2,600 @ $11.852 30,815	100 @ $11.852
Nov 15	4,500	$13	58,500			4,600 @ $12.975*
Dec 22				3,400	2,400 @ $12.975 44,115	1,200 @ 12.975
Dec 30	2,000	$15	30,000			3,200 @ $14.241*
Dec 31				1,200	1,200 @ $14.241 17,088	2,000 @ $14.241
Total	10,000		$128,500	8,000	$100,018*	$28,482*

*(Rounded)

sion is driven by the prevailing industry standard. For instance, the industry standard in the United States' automobile industry is LIFO; and thus, investment professionals expect to observe car and truck manufacturers using this inventory valuation method. If they observed otherwise, it might be a "red flag" raising concern about a company's reported financial results.

GLOBAL PERSPECTIVE

In some countries, the inventory method decision is constrained by the allowable generally accepted practice. For instance, in the United Kingdom, LIFO is not GAAP and consequently is never used in that country in audited financial statements. In some settings, the operating environment faced by a business drives the inventory method decision. In Japan, for example, auto and truck manufacturers use FIFO even though LIFO is generally accepted, because this industry has been able to implement just-in-time (JIT) inventory management techniques. For companies able to operate in a "lean manufacturing" environment, the inventory method decision has little impact on reported results because the required investment in inventory is kept to a minimum. In countries whose economies are characterized by high rates of inflation, several variants of LIFO may also be GAAP: HIFO, highest-in, first-out, and NIFO, next-in, first-out. Neither HIFO nor NIFO is acceptable under U.S. GAAP.

In some companies, the inventory method decision is linked to the physical flow of inventory through the business. Companies that supply perishable food products to hotels and restaurants, for example, frequently use FIFO. It is noteworthy, however, that it is not a requirement that the selected inventory method reflect the actual flow of goods through a business. A supermarket selling perishable food products can use LIFO or the weighted-average cost method even though store managers encourage customers to buy on a FIFO basis to minimize losses associated with the tendency of food products to spoil. The prevailing economic environment is also a contributing factor to the inventory method decision. In inflationary environments, LIFO is preferred over FIFO because it more effectively matches inflated selling prices with inflated inventory costs. Finally, for some firms, the inventory method selection is driven by a desire to report higher (or lower) earnings. For companies desiring to report the highest level of reported income, the FIFO method is often selected, at least when inventory costs are increasing. On the other hand, for firms desiring to constrain the level of reported (or taxable) earnings, the LIFO method is often adopted.

In Practice **6.2** *Inventory Method: A Glimpse of a Sample of Fortune 1000 Companies* The following table identifies the inventory method used by a sample of 600 Fortune 1000 companies. Also shown for the LIFO firms is the extent of LIFO usage. The FIFO method was predominantly used by the sampled firms:

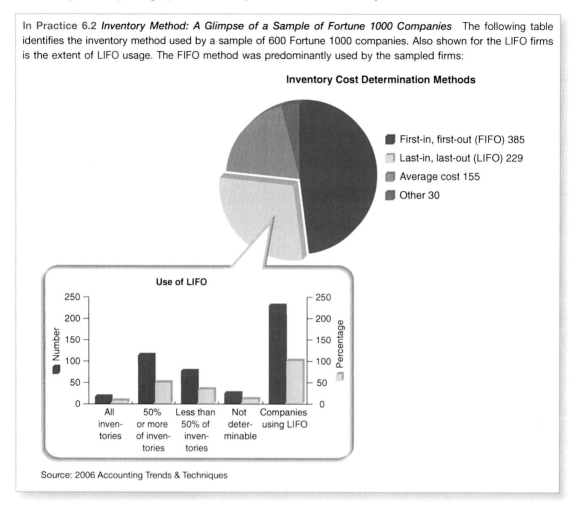

Inventory Cost Determination Methods

- First-in, first-out (FIFO) 385
- Last-in, last-out (LIFO) 229
- Average cost 155
- Other 30

Source: 2006 Accounting Trends & Techniques

Once a company has selected a particular inventory valuation method, does the company have to use that same method for all of its inventories? No. Companies that manufacture and/or sell multiple products may chose to use LIFO for one product, FIFO for another, and weighted-average for a third, although this is rarely done. Recall that at the beginning of this chapter, General Motors disclosed that it used LIFO to account for 67 percent of its U.S. inventories, with the remainder accounted for using FIFO. Can a company change its method of inventory valuation? Under certain circumstances, yes, they can. GAAP provides companies with considerable flexibility. Not only can a company choose between five different inventory valuation methods (average cost, FIFO, LIFO, specific

An important principle of accounting is the consistency principle which stipulates that whenever possible, a business should utilize a consistent set of accounting policies from one fiscal period to the next. When companies change their accounting policies (such as a LIFO to FIFO switch), the analysis of financial statements is adversely impacted because a change in accounting policy is likely to induce variance in the reported accounting numbers unrelated to a firm's actual performance. For this reason, voluntary corporate accounting policy changes are widely regarded as a "red flag" by investment professionals.

identification, and weighted-average cost), but GAAP permits a LIFO company, for example, to switch to FIFO. Companies are encouraged, however, to be consistent from year to year in the accounting methods they apply in their financial reporting. Companies are allowed to switch methods if they can justify why a switch will provide a more meaningful financial statement presentation. Changing inventory valuation methods, however, is often viewed as a "red flag" by investment professionals that worry that such voluntary accounting policy changes may be motivated more by a desire to manage earnings than to use the most appropriate accounting method. In addition, the Internal Revenue Service, under Revenue procedure 92–20, require taxpayers who have changed from LIFO to another method to wait five years before re-adopting LIFO unless extraordinary circumstances can be shown.

Lower-of-Cost-or-Market (LCM)

Under U.S. and IASB GAAP, companies are required to ensure that the value of ending inventory carried on the balance sheet is recorded at an amount that does not exceed its current replacement cost. This principle reflects the desire to ensure that asset values are never overstated (although they are sometimes understated, for example as a consequence of the use of the historical cost convention). Under this practice, if the current replacement cost of inventory is less than its recorded book value, the company must write the value of its inventory down to its lower replacement cost. If, however, the replacement cost is higher than its recorded book value, the inventory is not written up to the higher value but remains valued at its

> The LCM method reflects the conservatism principle of accounting, namely that losses should be recognized as soon as they are identified (even if unrealized), whereas gains should be recognized only after they are realized.

cost. This convention is called the **lower-of-cost-or-market (LCM) method** and is an excellent illustration of the conservative bias of U.S. GAAP and the GAAP of many countries—losses on inventory are recognized immediately, even if the inventory is unsold, but gains are not.

To illustrate the application of the LCM method, assume that AICC's CFO determined that the replacement cost of the company's ice cream was $14 per bucket at year-end. With 2,000 buckets in inventory, the replacement cost of AICC's inventory at December 31 would be $28,000 ($14 × 2,000). If AICC used FIFO, the LCM convention would require the company to write its ending inventory down by $2,000 ($30,000 less $28,000). No write-down would be required if AICC used LIFO because its ending inventory would be stated at its LIFO cost of $27,300, which is lower than its replacement cost of $28,000. AICC's application of LCM under FIFO is demonstrated in the following spreadsheet:

> In some countries (such as the United Kingdom), it is permissible to write the value of ending inventory up to the inventory's current replacement cost; however, this practice is not widespread throughout the world.

Arizona Ice Cream Company Spreadsheet					
Assets	=	Liabilities	+	Equity	
Inventory				Retained Earnings	
Inventory write-down to LCM.	30,000 (2,000) 28,000				Cost of goods sold (2,000)

When an end-of-period write-down of inventory is necessary, the adjustment is usually recorded as a component of cost of goods sold on the income statement; that is, both inventory and retained earnings are reduced by the amount of the LCM write-down. If the amount of the write-down is material in amount, however, it may be necessary to disclose the inventory write-down on the income statement as a separate line item (such as loss on inventory write-down) as a consequence of the materiality principle.

One consequence of the LCM method is that while the immediate financial statement effect of an inventory write-down is to reduce current earnings by the amount of the inventory write-down, the future effect may be to inflate earnings. For example, if AICC maintains its selling price of $20 per bucket, the LCM adjustment will lower current profit by $2,000, but raise future profit by the same amount when the inventory on hand is ultimately sold in some future period. In effect, the LCM method may shift the profit on some future sales from one period to the next, when the inventory is ultimately sold.

LIFO Layers and the Inventory Reserve

As noted above, the value of AICC's ending inventory is highest under FIFO and lowest under LIFO because the cost of inventory purchases is increasing. Comparing the calculated cost basis of AICC's ending inventory on December 31 under the two methods reveals the following:

LIFO Ending Inventory	FIFO Ending Inventory
800 @ $15	
1,100 @ $13	
100 @ $10	2,000 @ $15
$27,300	$30,000

These figures illustrate that the entire FIFO ending inventory is valued at the most recent purchase price of $15 per bucket, whereas less than half of the LIFO inventory is valued at $15 per bucket. The LIFO ending inventory reflects a blend of purchase prices—100 buckets at $10, 1,100 buckets at $13, and 800 buckets at $15. These differing prices are referred to as **LIFO price layers** and AICC has three such layers. Since the LIFO method assumes that the most recently purchased inventory is the first inventory to be sold, it is not unusual for a company like AICC to have multiple LIFO price layers, often reflecting prices from several prior fiscal periods. As a consequence, when inflation is present, the value of ending inventory under LIFO may be much lower than its current replacement cost or its FIFO cost.

Concerned that the LIFO method may produce misleading ending inventory values—that is, that the ending inventory (and hence, current assets) under LIFO may be materially undervalued relative to its current replacement value, and consequently, that comparability with non-LIFO firms may be impaired— accounting standard-setters require that companies using LIFO disclose the value of the **inventory reserve** in their footnotes. The inventory reserve is a measure of the difference ($2,700) between the replacement cost of a company's ending inventory ($30,000) and the LIFO cost of its ending inventory ($27,300). The disclosure of the inventory reserve in a company's footnotes is important because it enables financial statement users to use the LIFO reserve to determine the fair market value of LIFO ending inventory ($30,000) by simply adding the value of the reserve ($2,700) to the value of the reported LIFO ending inventory. Notice that adding the inventory reserve to the value of LIFO ending inventory effectively restates the value of the ending inventory from the LIFO method to the FIFO method.

Disclosure of the inventory reserve is also significant because it enables investment professionals to restate AICC's gross profit under LIFO ($58,800) to estimate what gross profit would have been had FIFO ($61,500) been used instead. The inventory reserve is a cumulative measure of the difference between the LIFO cost of ending inventory and the current replacement cost of the inventory. This amount may accumulate over multiple periods as prices rise and as a company maintains certain minimum quantities of inventory on hand to service the needs of its customers. It is possible to disaggregate this accumulated amount on a period-by-period basis by calculating the change in the reserve from one period to the next. The change in the value of the inventory reserve from one fiscal period to the next is a good estimate of the difference between LIFO cost of goods sold and FIFO cost of goods sold on a period-by-period basis. Thus, adding the **change** in the inventory reserve to the LIFO gross profit yields an estimate of FIFO gross profit:[4]

Gross profit under LIFO	$58,800
Add: increase in inventory reserve ($2,700 − $0)	+2,700
Gross profit under FIFO	$61,500

To illustrate the potential misstatement in the value of ending inventory that can result under LIFO, In Practice 6.3 presents inventory data for ten U.S. companies having large inventory reserves. Consider, for example, **ExxonMobil Corporation** (see bolded area in In Practice 6.3). This company's ending inventory is valued at $7.904 billion under LIFO. Under FIFO, this same inventory would be valued at $12.104 billion ($7.904 + $4.2). If ExxonMobil's inventory reserve at the beginning of the period had been $3.0 billion, the change in the reserve for the period would equal $1.2 billion ($4.2 − $3.0), and this would suggest that the company's FIFO earnings before income taxes would have been $16.305 billion ($15.105 + $1.2), as compared to just $15.105 billion under LIFO.

As a concluding point, since ExxonMobil used LIFO for income tax purposes, we can infer that ExxonMobil has deferred approximately $1.26 billion in income taxes, assuming a 30 percent effective tax rate ($4.2 billion × 30 percent = $1.26 billion). Although ExxonMobil may ultimately pay these income taxes at some point in the future, in the interim, the U.S. government has effectively provided the company with $1.26 billion in interest-free financing.

In Practice 6.3 *Ten U.S. Companies with the Largest Inventory Reserves (in millions of dollars)*

	Ending Inventory	Cost-of-Goods Sold	Earnings Before Income Taxes	LIFO Reserve	Inventory Reserve/ Ending Inventory
ExxonMobil Corp.	$ 7,904	$143,833	$15,105	$4,200	53.14%
Caterpillar Inc.	2,925	13,583	805	1,923	65.74
General Motors Corp.	20,221	130,942	601	1,814	8.97
ChevronTexaco Corp	2,948	76,809	3,931	1,580	53.60
Deere & Co.	1,506	9,365	(64)	1,004	66.68
DaimlerChrysler AG	14,913	101,576	(589)	981	6.58
Ford Motor Co.	6,191	143,484	(5,453)	905	14.62
Philip Morris Co. Inc.	8,923	31,944	8,566	700	7.84
General Electric Co.	10,290	97,958	14,128	676	6.57
Walgreen Co.	3,482	17,780	886	638	18.31

*Based on data for fiscal year 2002.

---

[4] If the inventory reserve decreases (increases) during the period, it is necessary to subtract (add) the decrease (increase) from the LIFO gross profit to compute FIFO gross profit.

Liquidating LIFO Layers

Most companies have a number of operating objectives that they strive to meet. For example, a common corporate goal is to maximize shareholder wealth (maximize share price) while being a good member of the local community. Achieving these goals may involve trying to produce the highest quality product or service at the lowest price, being attentive to customer needs, providing a healthy work environment for employees, being environmentally-friendly, and trying to save on income taxes. Another goal may be to meet profit expectations as set by the board of directors, by Wall Street financial analysts, or by institutional investors.

Sometimes it is impossible to meet internal or external earnings expectations by increasing sales, and thus, managers may look for other ways to increase net income (such as cutting costs). One temporary profit-enhancing approach used by some managers of LIFO-accounted companies is the liquidation of LIFO price layers. Liquidating a LIFO price layer has the effect of lowering the reported cost of goods sold, and hence, raising gross profit because a lower cost of inventory is effectively matched with revenue.

To illustrate this phenomenon, consider again the case of the Arizona Ice Cream Company. AICC's LIFO price layers consist of the following:

LIFO Price Layers

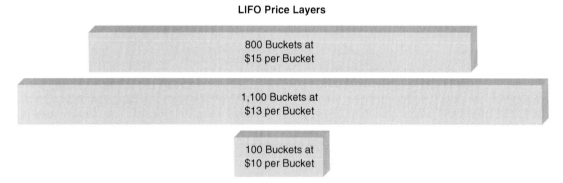

800 Buckets at $15 per Bucket

1,100 Buckets at $13 per Bucket

100 Buckets at $10 per Bucket

AICC's managers could decide to temporarily cease replacing its inventory when units are sold and instead liquidate its current inventory. At the current retail price of $20 per bucket, AICC's gross margin on its 800 buckets costing $15 is $5 per bucket. But AICC's gross margin increases to $7 per bucket if the 1,100 buckets costing $13 are sold, and its gross margin increases to $10 per bucket if the 100 buckets costing $10 are sold.

In essence, by liquidating the LIFO price layers that have a lower cost basis, AICC is able to lower its cost of goods sold, and consequently, boost its gross profit and net income. It is important to observe, however, that these LIFO price-layer liquidations produce what is commonly called **phantom profit** because although gross profit is increased, cash flow is not. (Remember that AICC's selling price remains constant at $20 per bucket.) In fact, the operating cash flow from LIFO price-layer liquidations is actually reduced as a consequence of the additional income taxes that must be paid on the phantom profits generated by these sales.

To illustrate the phenomenon of the phantom profit associated with a LIFO-price-layer liquidation, consider the data presented in In Practice 6.4. This exhibit presents inventory reserve data for 28 companies, all of which lost money. Consider, for example, **Deere & Co.** which reported a loss of $64 million (see bolded area in In Practice 6.4). Notice also that Deere reported a LIFO inventory reserve of over $1 billion. If Deere's managers had decided to liquidate the various LIFO price layers reflected in its inventory reserve of $1 billion, it could have completely eliminated its loss for the year and even reported a substantial profit!

The 28 firms listed in the In Practice 6.4 illustration all used LIFO (at least for some inventories), reported negative earnings before extraordinary items, and had an inventory reserve that exceeded the

In Practice 6.4 *Inventory Reserve Data*

($ millions)	Inventory	Total Assets	Earnings Before Extraordinary Items	Inventory Reserve
Allegheny Technologies Inc..............	$ 508.4	$ 2,643.2	$ (25.2)	$ 77.2
Amcon Distributing Co.	29.8	99.2	(1.8)	3.8
Bassett Furniture Industries	32.2	301.4	(2.6)	17.6
Boise Cascade Corp..................	653.0	4,934.0	(42.5)	52.5
Brush Engineered Materials	109.1	423.8	(10.3)	25.7
Castle (A M) & Co....................	134.8	327.4	(5.1)	40.0
Columbus McKinnon Corp.............	89.7	524.3	(6.0)	7.0
Community Distributors Inc..............	34.0	89.6	(1.8)	4.1
DaimlerChrysler AG	14,912.7	184,415.7	(589.3)	980.9
Deere & Co.........................	1,505.7	22,663.1	(64.0)	1,004.0
Eagle Food Centers Inc................	56.6	200.0	(4.1)	8.4
Eastman Chemical Co.................	659.0	6,086.0	(179.0)	288.0
Hartmarx Corp......................	149.6	455.4	(13.9)	32.9
Honeywell Intl Inc.	3,355.0	24,266.0	(99.0)	116.0
Lennox Intl Inc......................	281.2	1,794.0	(42.4)	49.1
McRae Industries-CL A	13.8	39.0	(0.6)	0.8
Mestek Inc.........................	64.6	259.5	(2.2)	6.8
Mueller (Paul) Co....................	9.6	54.8	(1.4)	5.9
Nyer Medical Group	4.7	12.6	(0.3)	0.4
Olin Corp..........................	223.2	1,219.1	(9.5)	58.0
Omnova Solutions Inc.................	56.7	639.1	(6.7)	18.1
Pantry Inc.	81.7	950.0	(2.7)	13.9
Ruddick Corp.	212.5	940.0	(0.7)	23.5
Solutia Inc.........................	303.0	3,408.0	(59.0)	113.0
Stanadyne Auto Corp.	32.7	273.1	(1.4)	2.0
Swiss Army Brands Inc................	34.8	114.1	(3.2)	4.8
Timken Co..........................	429.2	2,533.1	(41.7)	152.0
United States Steel Corp...............	870.0	8,337.0	(218.0)	410.0

Source: *Compustat*

magnitude of their negative earnings. Thus, all of these firms could have reported positive earnings instead of a loss by liquidating their inventory reserves, but they chose not to do so! Can you think of any reason why these companies chose to behave this way? If you thought about the fact that all of these firms would have faced significantly higher income taxes, you are probably correct!

MANAGING A COMPANY'S INVESTMENT IN INVENTORIES

When a business holds large quantities of inventory to service its customers' needs, the business is required to invest its cash not only to purchase and/or manufacture the inventory, but also for warehousing and insurance on the inventory. To help minimize these costs, some businesses have devised methods for reducing the quantity of inventory that they must maintain to support their customers' purchases. For example, supply chain management techniques integrate a company's information system with those of its suppliers so that

BUSINESS PERSPECTIVE: GENERAL MOTORS CORPORATION

General Motors Corporation (GM) discloses the following information about inventories in its annual report:

December 31 (in millions)	2002	2001
Productive material, work-in-process, and supplies	$ 4,915	$ 5,069
Finished product and service parts	6,859	6,779
Total inventories at FIFO.	11,774	11,848
Less: LIFO allowance.	(1,807)	(1,814)
Total inventories at LIFO.	$ 9,967	$10,034

Inventories are generally stated at cost, which is not in excess of market. The cost of approximately 84 percent of U.S. inventories is determined by the last-in, first-out (LIFO) method. Generally, the cost of all other inventories is determined by either the first-in, first-out (FIFO) or average cost methods.

Although GM does not use the label "inventory reserve," the disclosed value of the company's LIFO inventory reserve (called the "LIFO allowance") is reported to be approximately $1.8 billion in both 2001 and 2002 (see bolded area in table). Accordingly, if GM had used FIFO to value all of its inventories, GM's aggregate pre-tax profit would have been $1.8 billion higher. As a consequence of using LIFO for principally all of its U.S. inventories, GM has deferred taxation on these potential profits and has effectively received an interest-free loan from the U.S. government equivalent to $540 million (assuming an effective tax rate of 30 percent).

inventory can be delivered just-in-time or JIT. JIT inventory delivery helps reduce a company's investment in the quantity of inventory on hand, along with the related costs of warehousing and insurance.

For those businesses unable to use JIT techniques, the investment in inventory must be carefully monitored to avoid over-stocking and damaging profits. One method used by investment professionals to assess how effectively a company is managing its investment in inventory is the **inventory-on-hand period** (365 days/[cost of goods sold / cost of inventory on hand]), which measures the average number of days required to sell the existing on-hand inventory. This ratio is one of many useful measures of a firm's liquidity, as well as a firm's effectiveness in controlling its investment in inventory.

To illustrate the positive impact of JIT on inventory costs and the use of the inventory-on-hand ratio as an inventory quantity monitoring tool, consider data for Dell Computer in Exhibit 6.6. Beginning

EXHIBIT 6.6	Illustration of the Effects of Just-in-Time Inventory Management									
	Del Computer Corporation (dollars in millions) Fiscal Year Ending									
	1/30/94	1/29/95	1/28/96	2/2/97	2/1/98	1/29/99	1/28/00	2/2/01	2/1/02	1/31/03
Net sales.	$2,873	$3,475	$5,296	$7,759	$12,327	$18,243	$25,265	$31,888	$31,168	$35,404
Sales growth.		21.0%	52.4%	46.5%	58.9%	48.0%	38.5%	26.2%	(2.3%)	13.6%
Inventories	$ 220	$ 293	$ 429	$ 251	$ 233	$ 273	$ 391	$ 400	$ 278	$ 306
Total assets.	1,140	1,594	2,148	2,993	4,268	6,877	11,471	13,670	13,535	15,470
Cost of goods sold. . . .	2,440	2,737	4,229	6,093	9,605	14,137	20,047	25,445	25,661	29,055
Inventory-on-hand period (in days)	32.95	39.07	37.03	15.04	8.85	7.05	7.12	5.74	3.95	3.84

in 1996, Dell began introducing JIT techniques into its operations and was able to reduce its inventory-on-hand period from 37 days in 1996 to only 15 days in 1997. Dell continued to refine its inventory management practices, and as a consequence, reduced its inventory-on-hand period to less than four days by 2002. If Dell had not introduced JIT into its operating system, the company would have required an investment in inventory-on-hand in 2003 of nearly $3 billion (based on the 1996 inventory-on-hand ratio of 37 days) versus the $306 million actually on hand at the beginning of 2003. The opportunity cost savings created by Dell by using JIT are enormous! Assuming a cost of inventory financing of only five percent, Dell saved over $130 million in inventory financing costs in 2003 alone.

ACCOUNTS PAYABLE AND A COMPANY'S OPERATING CYCLE

Because of competitive market conditions, most businesses permit their customers to buy goods and services on credit. As a consequence, the sale of inventory is usually accompanied by the creation of an account (or note) receivable by the seller and an account (or note) payable by the purchaser.

In Chapter 5, we observed that most businesses try to constrain the amount of time that their customers take to pay their bills by offering quick-pay incentives. Credit terms such as "2/10, n/30" indicate that if the buyer pays a bill within ten days of the original transaction date, they will receive a two percent reduction in the purchase price; but, if payment is not made within the ten day quick-pay window, then full payment is expected within 30 days of the transaction. As a practical matter, taking advantage of such price discounts can be very valuable to a buyer. A two percent price discount, when annualized, is equivalent to an opportunity cost of 36 percent ($365/20 \times .02$). Thus, a customer would be better off obtaining bank financing at interest rates exceeding 25 percent to take advantage of such price discounts. But what happens if a customer's payment is not received within 30 days of the transaction date?

> Businesses grant credit to other businesses who are their customers, although they rarely grant credit to individuals who are the final consumer of their products or services. In this latter case, payment by cash, check, or debit/credit card is normally expected when the product or service is provided. When credit is extended to a business-customer, **accounts payable** refer to relatively immaterial, short-term, non-interest bearing credit balances. When the credit period exceeds 90 days or the amount involved is material, it is usually represented by an interest bearing debt contract called a **note payable**.

Technically, failure to pay an outstanding accounts payable within the allotted period indicates that a buyer has violated the implied credit agreement with the seller and is in technical default. At this point most sellers start contacting their customers by mail, e-mail, or by telephone, suggesting that payment would be greatly appreciated. And, in some cases, the seller may begin charging interest on the unpaid account payable balance.

Some customers intentionally violate the credit terms of their suppliers as a way to preserve their operating cash, particularly if there are no interest charges for doing so. In essence, these customers look to the credit provided by their suppliers as a source of interest-free financing for their own operations. One measure of the extent to which a firm utilizes this form of vendor financing is the **days' payable period**. This ratio indicates the average number of days that a company normally takes to pay its outstanding accounts payable:

$$\text{Days' payable period} = \frac{365}{[\text{Cost of goods sold/Accounts payable}]}$$

Some companies use the days' payable period as a component of their credit-granting review process. Customers that have historically taken a long time to pay for their credit purchases may be poor future credit risks. Comparing a customer's historical days' payable period with a seller's credit terms provides an easy approach to identify whether a customer is likely to pay for its credit purchases in a timely manner.

ANALYZING INVENTORY AND COST OF GOODS SOLD

In this chapter, we examined the various ways that businesses calculate their cost of goods sold and the value of their ending inventory. We learned that over 38 percent of U.S. public companies elect to use the LIFO method for this purpose. Since LIFO results in a lower taxable net income when input costs are rising, as compared to FIFO and weighted-average cost, we can speculate that the widespread usage of LIFO is linked to the income tax sheltering afforded by the method, along with the U.S. Department of Treasury's LIFO conformity rule.

Despite LIFO's tax advantage, and the related positive impact on firm operating cash flow, some investment professionals charge that the method has a "dark side." For instance, some professionals allege that, as a consequence of LIFO's tax advantage, the method creates a "hidden earnings reserve" on the balance sheet in the form of under-valued ending inventory. The value of that earnings reserve on a pre-tax basis is, of course, the value of the LIFO inventory reserve that must be disclosed in the footnotes to the financial statements. Some investment professionals allege that LIFO-accounted firms can draw down on their LIFO earnings reserve when additional income is needed to meet Wall Street earnings' expectations. While this is all true, it must be remembered that when a firm liquidates its LIFO earnings reserve—that is, when a firm liquidates it LIFO price layers—the amount of the LIFO liquidation profits must be disclosed in the footnotes to the financial statements. So, it is a simple matter for a professional, as part of their due diligence review, to read the inventory footnote, determine the amount of LIFO liquidation profit, and restate a firm's net income as if the liquidation had not occurred.

LIFO liquidation profits are often derisively referred to as phantom profit because such profits do not result in a corresponding increase in a firm's cash flow from operations. In fact, a firm which liquidates its LIFO inventory reserve will reduce its operating cash flow as a consequence of the additional income taxes due on the LIFO liquidation profits.

Another LIFO-related concern expressed by some investment professionals is that the method causes distortions in many of the popular financial ratios used to evaluate firm performance. For example, the LIFO method causes cost of goods sold to be overstated and the value of ending inventory to be understated relative to a FIFO-accounted firm, assuming increasing inventory costs. And, as a consequence, a firm's inventory turnover ratio will be overstated and the inventory-on-hand period understated. Similarly, since net income under LIFO will be lower than net income under FIFO, some professionals worry that the return on sales, the return on assets, and the return on equity will be artificially mis-stated. Fortunately, using the techniques discussed in this chapter, it is possible to restate a firm's cost of goods sold and its pre-tax net income on the income statement and the ending inventory on the balance sheet to their approximate values as if FIFO had been used instead of LIFO. By making these financial statement restatements, it is possible to develop restated financial ratios that will facilitate inter-firm comparisons of performance.

ETHICS PERSPECTIVE

One of the distinguishing characteristics of a profession is a code of ethics that its members are required to follow. The accounting profession is no exception. In order to be granted a certified public accounting (CPA) certificate it is necessary to not only pass a competency exam but also an ethics exam. One reason for this requirement may be the public trust that is associated with membership in a profession and the fact that it is often difficult for a consumer to judge the quality of the service provided. This is certainly true regarding an audit, and is likely true regarding such services as tax planning and investing. Ultimately, the public's belief in how competently and ethically a profession performs will determine its ability to dictate how it does business. Prior to the **Enron** and **WorldCom** scandals, the accounting profession was largely self-policed by its own internal organization, the American Institute of Certified Public Accountants (AICPA), which monitored the quality of the work of its members. Because of the profession's loss of credibility as a result of these corporate audit failures, the profession is now subject to oversight by the Public Company Accounting Oversight Board (PCAOB), a governmental organization.

REVIEW PROBLEM

Part A.

The Walgreen Company is the United States' largest drugstore chain, operating over 4,500 retail outlets in the U.S. and Puerto Rico. According to Walgreen's financial statements (see Review Problem Exhibit in part 3 below for the company's financial statements), the company values its inventory using the lower of last-in, first-out (LIFO) cost or market basis. The company footnotes also disclose that:

> Included in inventory are product costs and inbound freight. Cost of sales is primarily derived based upon point-of-sale scanning information with an estimate for shrinkage. At year-end 2004 and 2003, inventories would have been greater by $736.4 million and $729.7 million, respectively, if they had been valued on a lower of first-in, first-out (FIFO) cost or market basis.

Thus, Walgreen's inventory reserve as of year-end 2004 and 2003 was $736.4 million and $729.7 million, respectively, and the change in the company's inventory reserve from 2003 to 2004 was $6.7 million ($736.4 − $729.7).

Required

1. What would Walgreen's earnings before income tax provision have been (in millions) at year-end 2004 if the Walgreen Company had used FIFO to value its inventory?

   Answer

LIFO earnings before income tax provision (see Panel A of Review Problem Exhibit)	$2,176.3
Add: Change in inventory reserve (as reported in Walgreen's footnote disclosures)	+6.7
Earnings before income tax provision assuming use of FIFO	$2,183.0

2. What would Walgreen's disclose on its balance sheet at year-end 2004 as the value of its inventory (in millions) if the company had used FIFO instead of LIFO?

   Answer

Inventory (see Panel B of Review Problem Exhibit)	$4,738.6
Add: Inventory reserve	+736.4
Inventory assuming use of FIFO.	$5,475.0

3. How much did the Walgreen Company save in income taxes (in millions) in 2004 by using LIFO to value its inventory?

Answer

Walgreen's effective tax rate for 2004: $816.10 ÷ $2,176.30 = 37.5%	
Inventory reserve data	
Inventory reserve (2004).	$736.4
Less: Inventory reserve (2003).	(729.7)
Change in the reserve	$ 6.7
Income tax savings in 2004: $6.7 × 37.5% = $2.51 million.	

REVIEW PROBLEM EXHIBIT	**Financial Statement Disclosures: Walgreen Company**		
Panel A. Consolidated Statement of Earnings (in millions)	**2004**	**2003**	**2002**
Net sales.	$37,508.20	$32,505.40	$28,861.10
Costs and deductions			
Cost of sales.	(27,310.40)	(23,706.20)	(21,076.10)
Selling, occupancy and administration	(8,055.10)	(6,950.90)	(5,980.80)
Interest income.	17.30	10.80	6.90
Other income	16.30	29.60	6.20
Earnings before income tax provision	2,176.30	1,888.70	1,637.30
Income tax provision	(816.10)	(713.00)	(618.10)
Net earnings.	$ 1,360.20	$ 1,175.70	$ 1,019.20

Panel B. Consolidated Balance Sheets (in millions)		**2004**	**2003**
Cash and cash equivalents		$ 1,695.50	$ 1,268.00
Accounts receivable, net		1,169.10	1,017.80
Inventories		4,738.60	4,202.70
Other current assets.		161.20	102.50
Total current assets		7,764.40	6,609.00
Property and equipment, at cost, less accumulated			
depreciation and amortization.		5,446.40	4,940.00
Other non-current assets		131.30	107.80
Total assets.		$13,342.10	$11,656.80
Trade accounts payable.		$ 2,641.50	$ 2,407.80
Accrued expenses and other liabilities.		1,370.50	1,157.80
Income taxes		65.90	105.80
Total current liabilities.		4,077.90	3,671.40
Deferred income taxes		327.60	228.00
Other non-current liabilities		708.60	561.70
Total non-current liabilities		1,036.20	789.70

continued

continued from previous page

REVIEW PROBLEM EXHIBIT	Financial Statement Disclosures: Walgreen Company	
Panel B. Consolidated Balance Sheets (in millions)	**2004**	**2003**

Shareholders' equity		
Common stock, $.078125 par value; authorized		
3.2 billion shares, issued 1,025,400,000 in 2004		
and 1,024,908.276 in 2003	80.10	80.10
Paid-in capital	632.60	697.80
Retained earnings	7,591.60	6,417.80
Treasury stock at cost, 2,107,263 shares in 2004	(76.30)	—
Total shareholders' equity	8,228.00	7,195.70
Total liabilities and shareholders' equity.	$13,342.10	$11,656.80

4. What was Walgreen's inventory-on-hand period for 2004? 2003?

   Answer

   $$\text{LIFO Inventory-on-hand period} = \frac{365}{\text{Cost of sales/Inventory}}$$

   2004: $\dfrac{365}{(\$27,310.40/\$4,738.60)} = 63.4 \text{ days}$

   2003: $\dfrac{365}{(\$23,706.20/\$4,202.70)} = 64.7 \text{ days}$

5. Would Walgreen's inventory-on-hand period change if the company had used FIFO to value its inventory instead of LIFO?

   Answer

   FIFO Inventory-on-hand period for 2004

   $$\frac{365}{[(\$27,310.40 + \$6.7)/(\$4,738.60 + \$736.4)]} = 73.2 \text{ days}$$

6. What was Walgreen's days' payable period ratio for 2004? 2003?

   Answer

   $$\text{Days' Payable Period Ratio} = \frac{365}{\text{Cost of sales/Accounts Payable}}$$

   2004: $\dfrac{365}{(\$27,310.40/\$2,641.50)} = 10.4 \text{ days}$

   2003: $\dfrac{365}{(\$23,706.20/\$2,407.80)} = 9.9 \text{ days}$

Part B.

The Arcadia Company is uncertain whether it should utilize the first-in, first-out (FIFO) method or the last-in, first-out (LIFO) method to account for its inventory. The company's controller decided that she would compare the financial results under the two approaches as a way to reach a decision regarding which method to adopt. Data for the first two months of operations were as follows:

	Units	Unit Cost	Total
January			
Beginning inventory..	6,000	$2.00	$ 12,000
Purchases: Jan. 5	10,300	2.00	20,600
Jan. 20	29,300	2.10	61,530
			$ 94,130
Sales: Jan. 25	38,400		
February			
Beginning inventory..	7,200		
Purchases: Feb. 8..	28,200	2.20	$ 62,040
Feb. 23..	15,300	2.60	39,780
			$101,820
Sales: February 27	40,700		
Ending inventory..	10,000		

Required

a. Calculate the cost of goods sold for January and February for The Arcadia Company using both FIFO and LIFO.

b. Assume that revenue for the two-month period totaled $300,000. What inventory valuation method would you recommend that the company adopt? Why?

Solution

a. Cost of goods sold:

				Costs of Goods Sold
FIFO				
January	6,000 units	@	$2.00	$12,000
	10,300 units	@	2.00	20,600
	22,100 units	@	2.10	46,410
				$79,010
February..	7,200 units	@	$2.10	15,120
	28,200 units	@	2.20	62,040
	5,300 units	@	2.60	13,780
Total				$169,950
LIFO				
January	29,300 units	@	$2.10	$ 61,530
	9,100 units		2.00	18,200
				79,730
February..	15,300 units	@	$2.60	39,780
	25,400 units	@	2.20	55,880
Total				$175,390

b. If the goal of the management of The Arcadia Company is to report the highest gross profit, the company should adopt the FIFO method:

	FIFO	LIFO
Revenues	$300,000	$300,000
Less: Cost of goods sold	(169,950)	(175,390)
Gross profit.	$130,050	$124,610

If, however, the goal of the management of The Arcadia Company is to report the lowest gross profit, perhaps to minimize taxable net income, the company should adopt the LIFO method.

EXECUTIVE SUMMARY

This chapter examined the important accounting issue of how to match operating revenue and operating expenses—specifically, how to match the cost of goods and services sold with the revenue produced by the sale of those goods and services. A number of inventory costing methods were considered—FIFO, LIFO, and the Weighted-average cost method. Just which method a company adopts was shown to have a dramatic effect on reported gross profit and net income. Finally, the chapter illustrated that the choice of an inventory costing method was often linked to income tax and income reporting considerations.

As a validation of your understanding of the content of this chapter, you should now be able to:

- Explain how inventory is valued using FIFO, LIFO, and the weighted-average cost method and how the resulting cost of goods sold is matched with revenue.
- Explain why the lower-of-cost-or-market method is sometimes used to value ending inventory and how this method affects reported net income.
- Explain what the inventory reserve is and how a LIFO inventory liquidation may artificially increase a company's gross and net profit.
- Explain how accounts payable are valued and how the payment of these payables can be managed to positively impact a firm's operating cash flow.

In Chapter 7, our investigation of the matching concept continues; however, in the next chapter, the focus shifts to matching the cost of such long-lived assets as plant and equipment, intangible assets, and natural resources with the operating revenue produced by these assets.

KEY CONCEPTS AND TERMS

Accounts payable, 6.19
Conservatism principle, 6.13
Consistency principle, 6.12
Days' payable period, 6.19
Finished goods inventory, 6.3
First-in, first-out (FIFO), 6.5
Highest-in, first-out (HIFO), 6.11
Historical cost convention, 6.5
Inventory-on-hand period, 6.18

Inventory reserve, 6.14
Last-in, first out (LIFO), 6.5
LIFO conformity rule, 6.5
Lower-of-cost-or-market method
    (LCM), 6.13
LIFO price layers, 6.14
Next-in, first-out (NIFO), 6.11
Notes payable, 6.19
Operating cycle, 6.3

Operating expense, 6.3
Periodic system, 6.6
Perpetual system, 6.6
Phantom profit, 6.16
Raw material inventory, 6.3
Replacement cost method, 6.5
Specific identification method, 6.5
Weighted-average cost method, 6.8
Work-in-process inventory, 6.3

APPENDIX 6A: Recording Cost of Goods Sold and Inventory using the Debit and Credit Paradigm

In this appendix, the traditional approach to recording accounting transactions—that is, the debit and credit paradigm—is used to illustrate how the journal entries for the cost of goods sold and inventory for the Arizona Ice Cream Company, Inc. would be recorded. Since the journal entries are similar under FIFO, LIFO, and the weighted-average cost method (only the recorded amounts differ), we assume that the company adopts the FIFO method to value its cost of goods sold and ending inventory (see Exhibit 6.3).

Arizona Ice Cream Company, Inc: Recording Inventory Transactions

During the year, Arizona Ice Cream Company, Inc. (AICC) made the following cash purchases of ice cream:

Date	Amount	Cost per Bucket	Total Cost
September 5.	1,000	$10	$ 10,000
October 22	2,500	12	30,000
November 15	4,500	13	58,500
December 30	2,000	15	30,000
	10,000		$128,500

AICC also sold 8,000 buckets of ice cream at a retail price of $20 per bucket for total operating revenue of $160,000. All sales were in cash and the sales occurred on the following dates:

Date	Number of Buckets Sold
September 20.	800
November 4	2,600
December 22	3,400
December 31	1,200
	8,000

At year-end, the AICC's CEO determined that the replacement cost of the company's inventory of 2,000 buckets of ice cream was $28,000 ($14 per bucket x 2,000 buckets).

The above financial data would be recorded as follows:

Date	Accounts	Debit	Credit
Sep 5	Inventory (A)	10,000	
	Cash (A)		10,000
	To record the cash purchase of 1,000 buckets.		

continued

continued from previous page

Date	Accounts	Debit	Credit
Sep 20	Cash (A) . . . . Retained earnings (R). . . . . *To record the cash sale of 800 buckets.*	16,000	16,000
	Retained Earnings (E). . . . . Inventory (A). . . . . *To record the cost of goods sold on 800 buckets.*	8,000	8,000
Oct 22	Inventory (A) . . . . Cash (A) . . . . *To record the cash purchase of 2,500 buckets.*	30,000	30,000
Nov 4	Cash (A) . . . . Retained Earnings (R) . . . . *To record the cash sale of 2,600 buckets.*	52,000	52,000
	Retained Earnings (E). . . . . Inventory (A). . . . . *To record the cost of goods sold on 2,600 buckets.*	30,800	30,800
Nov 15	Inventory (A) . . . . Cash (A) . . . . *To record the cash purchase of 4,500 buckets.*	58,500	58,500
Dec 22	Cash (A) . . . . Retained Earnings (R) . . . . *To record the cash sale of 3,400 buckets.*	68,000	68,000
	Retained Earnings (E). . . . . Inventory (A). . . . . *To record the cost of goods sold on 3,400 buckets.*	44,100	44,100
Dec 30	Inventory (A) . . . . Cash (A) . . . . *To record the cash purchase of 2,000 buckets.*	30,000	30,000
Dec 31	Cash (A) . . . . Retained Earnings (R) . . . . *To record the cash sale of 1,200 buckets.*	24,000	24,000
	Retained Earnings (E). . . . . Inventory (A). . . . . *To record the cost of goods sold on 1,200 buckets.*	15,600	15,600
Dec 31	Retained Earnings (E). . . . . Inventory (A). . . . . *To record the Lower-of-cost-or-market write-down of inventory.*	2,000	2,000

Summary

To validate your understanding of the above journal entries, create a series of T-accounts and enter the data from AICC's various transactions. Your final T-account balances should reflect the following totals:

Account	Debit	Credit
Inventory.	28,000	
Cost of goods sold.	100,500	
Revenue		160,000

DISCUSSION QUESTIONS

Q6.1 **Consistency Principle.** The consistency principle svtipulates that when a company begins using a given inventory valuation method (FIFO, LIFO, or the weighted-average cost method), the company should continue to use that method to prepare its financial statements until such time as its senior management, with concurrence from the firm's independent auditors, conclude that another method would more fairly present the company's financial condition and performance. Discuss why the consistency principle is important to investors and shareholders. If a company changes its method of accounting for its inventory, how will that change be disclosed in its financial statements?

Q6.2 **Physical Inventory Counts.** Although physically counting a business' inventory is integral to the periodic system of inventory recordkeeping, it is not an explicit component of the perpetual system. Nonetheless, most well-run businesses do annually (and sometimes, semi-annually) conduct a physical count of their inventory. Discuss why physically counting a company's inventory is considered to be "best practice" regardless of which inventory recordkeeping system is utilized.

Q6.3 **Inventory Valuation Method Changes and Share Prices.** Voluntary accounting policy changes are said to be "unintended signals" about the financial health and future prospects of a firm from management to a firm's shareholders. Discuss how and why you would expect the capital markets to react to news that a company was voluntarily changing its inventory valuation policy from (a) LIFO to FIFO and from (b) FIFO to LIFO.

Q6.4 **Lower-of-Cost-or-Market Method.** The lower-of-cost-or-market method (LCM) is often referred to as "a one-way street" because under LCM, ending inventory values may be written down to a lower replacement value but are never written up when the expected replacement cost exceeds the inventory cost basis. What accounting principle is reflected in the application of LCM? What accounting principle is violated by the application of LCM? Discuss whether you think that LCM should be modified to become a "two-way street," allowing both inventory value write-ups and write-downs.

Q6.5 **Earnings Management and Inventory Valuation.** Investment professionals frequently develop concerns that earnings management may be present when they observe that a firm has voluntarily changed its inventory valuation policy from LIFO to FIFO. Similar concerns arise when the capital market discovers that a firm using LIFO is liquidating its inventory price layers. Discuss why these two financial statement disclosures might indicate the presence of earnings management. Discuss when these disclosures might not indicate the presence of earnings management.

Q6.6 **LIFO Inventory Reserve.** The LIFO inventory reserve is a measure disclosed in a company's footnotes and reveals the difference between the current value of a company's ending inventory and the LIFO-value of its ending inventory. Discuss why and how this measure is useful to shareholders and investment professionals as they evaluate the financial condition and performance of a company that uses LIFO inventory valuation.

Q6.7 **LIFO and Earnings Management.** Some investment professionals refer to LIFO inventory valuation as an "earnings management" tool, suggesting that LIFO allows a company to create a hidden earnings reserve on a company's balance sheet, to be used in later periods to help meet Wall Street earnings expectations. Discuss why this assertion might be true and how to measure the size of a company's "hidden LIFO earnings reserve."

Q6.8 **Inventory Valuation Policy Change.** Riverwood International Corporation, a leading provider of paperboard, announced the following:

> During the fourth quarter of 2002, the Company changed its inventory valuation method from the last-in, first-out method to the first-in, first-out (FIFO) method as the Company determined that over time, FIFO more closely matches the Company's revenues with its costs.

Discuss why, and under what conditions, FIFO might enable Riverwood International to "more closely match" its costs with its revenue.

Q6.9   **LIFO Layer Liquidations.**   During 2004 and 2005, **Alleghany Technologies Incorporated** disclosed that:

> . . . inventory usage resulted in liquidations of LIFO inventory quantities. The inventories were carried at lower costs prevailing in prior years as compared to the cost of current purchases. The effect of these LIFO liquidations was to decrease the cost of sales by $2.8 million in 2005 and by $0.6 million in 2004.

Discuss why a liquidation of LIFO inventory quantities would reduce a company's cost of goods sold. Does this event indicate that a firm is attempting to manage its earnings? Why or why not?

Q6.10   **Inventory Write-Down.**   *The Financial Times* reported that **Delphi, Inc.**, a manufacturer of automotive parts, would take a $100 million write-down of its inventory to reflect reduced demand for some of its products. The write-down was part of the company's efforts to restructure its money-losing operations. Discuss what accounting principle is being followed by Delphi when it implements the inventory write-down. Discuss how the write-down will affect the company's financial statements. Discuss how the write-down will affect the company's inventory turnover ratio and its inventory-on-hand period. Could an inventory write-down be used to manage earnings? If so, how?

Q6.11   **(Ethics Perspective) Code of Ethics.**   It has been argued that to be classified as a professional one must offer services to the public rather than simply be an employee of an organization. As such, most employees of an organization, including accountants that are not CPAs, are not subject to their profession's ethical code of conduct. We have seen, however, that serious breaches of the public trust can result from the unethical conduct of some of these "professional" employees. Examples of such breaches include faulty construction in the city of Boston "Big Dig" and the current scandal involving back-dated employee stock options. Do you feel that professionals working for an organization should be bound by the same code of ethical conduct as their colleagues that serve the public directly?

☑ **indicates that check figures are available on the book's Website.**

EXERCISES

E6.12   **Compute the Missing Inventory Values.**   The following information was disclosed in the 2006 annual report of The Arcadia Company.

	2006	2005	2004
Beginning inventory	$?	$?	$11,560
Purchase of inventory	45,850	?	42,640
Inventory available for sale	?	?	54,200
Ending inventory	?	9,655	?
Cost of goods sold	13,600	42,480	43,715

Fill in the missing values.

☑ E6.13   **Calculating FIFO Inventory Values.**   The Mann Corporation began operations in 2005. Information relating to the company's purchases of inventory and sales of products for 2005 and 2006 are presented below.

2005				
January 1	Purchase	200 units	@	$10 per unit
April 1	Sold	120 units	@	$25 per unit
July 1	Purchase	100 units	@	$14 per unit
September 1	Sold	130 units	@	$25 per unit

continued

continued from previous page

2006				
January 1	Purchase	100 units	@	$16 per unit
April 1.	Sold	80 units	@	$30 per unit
July 1	Purchase	100 units	@	$18 per unit
September 1	Sold	100 units	@	$35 per unit

Calculate the FIFO cost of goods sold and ending inventory for 2005 and 2006 assuming use of (a) the periodic method and (b) the perpetual method.

E6.14 **Calculating LIFO Inventory Values.** The Mann Corporation began operations in 2005. Information relating to the company's purchases of inventory and sales of products for 2005 and 2006 are presented below.

2005				
February 1	Purchase	200 units	@	$10 per unit
May 1.	Sold	120 units	@	$25 per unit
August 1.	Purchase	100 units	@	$14 per unit
October 1.	Sold	130 units	@	$25 per unit
2006				
February 1	Purchase	100 units	@	$16 per unit
May 1.	Sold	80 units	@	$30 per unit
August 1.	Purchase	100 units	@	$18 per unit
October 1.	Sold	100 units	@	$35 per unit

Calculate the LIFO cost of goods sold and ending inventory for 2005 and 2006 assuming use of (a) the periodic method and (b) the perpetual method.

E6.15 **Calculating Weighted-Average Cost Inventory Values.** The Mann Corporation began operations in 2005. Information relating to the company's purchases of inventory and sales of products for 2005 and 2006 are presented below.

2005				
March 1	Purchase	200 units	@	$10 per unit
June 1	Sold	120 units	@	$25 per unit
September 1	Purchase	100 units	@	$14 per unit
November 1.	Sold	130 units	@	$25 per unit
2006				
March 1	Purchase	100 units	@	$16 per unit
June 1	Sold	80 units	@	$30 per unit
September 1	Purchase	100 units	@	$18 per unit
November 1.	Sold	100 units	@	$35 per unit

Calculate the weighted-average cost of goods sold and ending inventory for 2005 and 2006 assuming use of (a) the periodic method and (b) the perpetual method.

E6.16 **FIFO versus LIFO: Ratio Analysis.** Presented below is financial data for two companies that are identical in every respect except that Company X uses the FIFO method to value its inventory and Company Z uses the LIFO method to value its inventory. Using this data, calculate the following ratios: return on sales, inventory turnover, inventory-on-hand period, and current ratio. Which of the two companies is the best investment opportunity? Why?

	Company X	Company Z
Sales.	$100,000	$100,000
Cost of goods sold.	47,500	56,400
Net income.	29,000	18,600
Inventory.	$ 19,000	$ 8,600
Current assets	64,000	53,600
Current liabilities.	21,000	21,000

⊘ **E6.17** **Inventory Management.** The following financial information is taken from the 2005 annual report of Intel Corporation:

(amounts in millions)	2005	2004
Net revenues	$38,826	$34,209
Cost of goods sold.	15,777	14,463
Ending inventories	3,126	2,621

Using the above data, calculate the company's inventory turnover, inventory-on-hand period, and gross profit percentage for 2004 and 2005. Is the company's inventory management improving? Intel uses FIFO to value its inventory; would these ratios look better if the company used LIFO instead? Why?

E6.18 **LIFO to FIFO Change.** In 2002, **Riverwood International Corporation** announced that it would change its inventory valuation method from last-in, first-out (LIFO) to first-in, first-out (FIFO). The company also disclosed that the inventory valuation policy change would have a "positive impact on gross profit by $12.6 million." Presented below is Riverwood International's originally reported (using LIFO) financial results for 2002:

(in millions)	2002
Net sales.	$298,731
Gross profit.	49,766
Income from operations	10,201

Describe the financial effects of this policy change on the company's income statement, balance sheet, and statement of cash flow. Does the inventory method change materially impact the company's reported income from operations?

E6.19 **Ratio Analysis: Alternative Inventory Valuation Methods.** Exhibits 6.3, 6.4, and 6.5 in Chapter 6 present the financial results of the Arizona Ice Cream Company, Inc. using FIFO, LIFO, and the weighted-average cost method, respectively. Using this data, complete the following table for the company:

	FIFO	LIFO	Wt. Average
Inventory turnover	_____	_____	_____
Inventory-on-hand period.	_____	_____	_____
Gross margin percentage.	_____	_____	_____

Under which inventory valuation method does the company's performance appear most favorable? Using which inventory valuation method does the company's performance appear least favorable?

E6.20 **LIFO Reserve: Restating Financial Statements.** The following information is taken from the 2005 annual report of the **Walgreen Company**:

(in millions)	2005	2004
Cost of goods sold..	$30,414	$27,310
Net income before tax	2,456	2,160
Ending inventory..	5,593	4,739
Inventory reserve	804	736

The Walgreen Company uses LIFO to value its inventory. Restate the company's financial results for 2005 assuming the use of the FIFO method. Assume an effective tax rate of 30 percent.

E6.21 **Calculating the Days' Payable Period.** The following information is taken from the 2005 annual report of **Coca-Cola Enterprises, Inc.**:

(amounts in millions)	2005	2004
Net revenue	$18,706	$18,158
Cost of goods sold..	11,185	10,771
Inventories	786	763
Accounts payable...	2,639	2,708

Using this information, calculate the accounts payable turnover ratio and the days' payable period for 2004 and 2005. Is Coca-Cola Enterprises taking longer to pay its accounts payable to its suppliers? Do the ratios indicate that the company's credit risk is increasing? Why or why not?

E6.22 **Restating Financial Data: FIFO versus LIFO.** The following information was disclosed in the 2005 annual report of the **Alleghany Technologies Inc.**:

(in millions)	2005	2004
Sales...	$3,540	$2,733
Cost of goods sold..	2,890	2,488
Net income before tax	307	20
Inventory...	607	513

In addition, the company's footnotes revealed:

The effect of using the LIFO methodology to value inventory, rather than FIFO, increased cost of sales in 2005 and 2004 by $45.8 million and $112.2 million, respectively.

Calculate Alleghany Technologies cost of goods sold, net income before income tax, and ending inventory for 2005 assuming the use of FIFO rather than LIFO. The company's LIFO reserve declined from 2004 to 2005; what does that indicate?

E6.23 **LIFO Layer Liquidations and Net Income.** The following information is taken from the 2006 annual report of The Claremont Corporation:

(in millions)	2006	2005
Net income before tax	$360	$20

The company uses the LIFO method to value its inventory. In addition, the footnotes to the company's annual report revealed that, during 2006 and 2005, inventory usage resulted in liquidations of LIFO inventory quantities, and the effect of these liquidations was to reduce the cost of goods sold by $28 million and $6 million in 2006 and 2005, respectively. Calculate the company's net income before tax assuming that the LIFO inventory liquidations had not occurred. Discuss why the incremental profit from a LIFO-layer liquidation is often referred to as "phantom profit."

PROBLEMS

P6.24 **Calculating the Value of Ending Inventory and Cost of Goods Sold: Periodic Method.** Keystone Consolidated, Inc. is a leading manufacturer of steel products. The following inventory data relates to the firm's production during the first quarter of 2006:

Date of Purchase	Tons of Raw Steel Purchased	Purchase Price per Ton	Total Cost
Jan. 1	500	$40	$20,000
Jan. 15	700	35	24,500
Feb. 7	200	33	6,600
Feb. 21	450	30	13,500
March 15	350	42	14,700
	2,200		$79,300

At the end of the first quarter of 2006, Keystone's internal auditors determined that 1,700 tons of raw steel had been processed and sold.

Required
1. Calculate the cost-of-steel processed and sold during the quarter under each of the following methods, assuming use of a periodic inventory management system:
   a. FIFO
   b. LIFO
   c. Weighted-average
2. Assume that the replacement cost per ton is $39 at the end of the quarter. What amount should Keystone's ending inventory be valued at on its March 31 balance sheet under each of the following methods:
   a. FIFO
   b. LIFO
   c. Weighted-average

P6.25 **Calculating the Value of Ending Inventory and Cost of Goods Sold: Perpetual Method.** Consider the following inventory data for the first two months of the year for CompX International:

	Total Units	Unit Cost	Total Cost
Beginning inventory on hand			
January 1	60,000	$2.00	$120,000
Purchases during month			
January 5	103,600	2.00	207,200
January 20	293,900	2.10	617,190
	457,500		$944,390
Sales of inventory			
January 25	383,900		
Beginning inventory at			
February 1	73,600		
Purchases during month			
February 8	282,200	2.20	620,840
February 23	153,500	2.60	399,100
	509,300		
Sales of inventory			
February 27	407,600		
Ending Inventory	101,700		

Required
1. Calculate the cost of goods sold and ending inventory for January and February under each of the following methods, assuming use of a perpetual inventory management system:
   a. FIFO
   b. LIFO
   c. Weighted-average
2. Assume that the replacement cost of CompX International's ending inventory is $2.05 per unit on January 30 and $2.35 per unit on February 28. Calculate the value of the ending inventory for January and February under each of the following methods:
   a. FIFO
   b. LIFO
   c. Weighted-average

P6.26 **Calculating the Value of Ending Inventory and Cost of Goods Sold: Periodic Method.** Amalgamated Sugar Company processes raw sugar beets into sugar. The following information relates to the company's operations during the last quarter of 2006.

Date		Amount	Cost per Ton
Oct. 1	Inventory-on-hand	1,000,000 tons	$.10 per ton
Oct. 15	Sugar processed	300,000 tons	$.09 per ton
Oct. 30	Sugar processed	300,000 tons	$.08 per ton

continued

Date		Amount	Cost per Ton
Nov. 12	Sugar processed	200,000 tons	$.09 per ton
Nov. 28	Sugar processed	200,000 tons	$.08 per ton
Dec. 10	Sugar processed	100,000 tons	$.07 per ton
Dec. 29	Sugar processed	100,000 tons	$.07 per ton
Sales of processed sugar for the quarter totaled: 2 million tons			

Required

1. Complete the following table at year-end 2006 assuming that Amalgamated uses a periodic inventory management system:

Method	Cost of Good Sold	Ending Inventory
FIFO		
LIFO		
Weighted-average		

2. Complete the above table at year-end 2006 assuming that the replacement cost of processed sugar is $.085 per ton at year-end.

P6.27 **Calculating the Value of Ending Inventory and Cost of Goods Sold: Perpetual Method.** Amalgamated Sugar Company processes raw sugar beets into sugar. The following information relates to the company's operations during the last quarter of 2006.

Date		Amount	Cost per Ton
Oct. 1	Inventory-on-hand	1,000,000 tons	$.10 per ton
Oct. 15	Sugar processed	300,000 tons	$.09 per ton
Oct. 30	Sugar processed	300,000 tons	$.08 per ton
Nov. 12	Sugar processed	200,000 tons	$.09 per ton
Nov. 28	Sugar processed	200,000 tons	$.08 per ton
Dec. 10	Sugar processed	100,000 tons	$.07 per ton
Dec. 29	Sugar processed	100,000 tons	$.07 per ton
Sales of Processed Sugar (in tons)			
Nov. 10	. . . .	1,200,000	
Dec 12	. . . .	800,000	

Required

1. Complete the following table at year-end 2006 assuming that Amalgamated uses a perpetual inventory management system:

Method	Cost of Good Sold	Ending Inventory
FIFO		
LIFO		
Weighted-average		

2. Complete the above table at year-end 2006 assuming that the replacement cost of processed sugar at year-end is $0.085 per ton.

⊘ **P6.28** **Calculating the Value of Ending Inventory and Cost of Goods Sold: Lower-of-Cost-or-Market Method.** The following inventory data is taken from the financial records for 2006 of Fernandez, Inc., a personal computer software manufacturer.

	No. of Units	Unit Cost	Total Cost
Beginning inventory (Jan. 1)......................	160,000	$1.00	$160,000
Purchases: May 5	60,000	1.50	90,000
Sept. 3	60,000	2.00	120,000
Total available for sale	280,000		$370,000
Less: Sales*	250,000		?
Ending inventory (Dec. 31)......................	30,000		?
Jan. 1, 2007 expected replacement cost per unit		1.40	

*Sales in 2006	No. of Units Sold
Feb 3...	120,000
Jun. 30.......................................	30,000
Oct. 5..	100,000
	250,000

Required
1. Complete the following table for 2006.

		Periodic		Perpetual	
	Method	**Ending Inventory**	**Cost of Goods Sold**	**Ending Inventory**	**Cost of Goods Sold**
A.	FIFO				
B.	LIFO				
C.	Weighted-average				

2. Which inventory method would you recommend that Fernandez, Inc. use for income tax purposes? Why?
3. Which method would you recommend that Fernandez, Inc. use for accounting purposes if the company operates in a highly inflationary environment? Why?
4. Which method would you recommend that Fernandez, Inc. use for accounting purposes if the company operates in a deflationary environment? Why?

P6.29 **Restating Inventory Values using the LIFO Inventory Reserve.** Presented below are the condensed financial statements of Global Enterprises, Inc. The company's inventory is valued using LIFO. The company's footnotes reveal that the LIFO reserve was as follows.

Year	LIFO Reserve (in thousands)
2005	$2,266
2006	2,152

Also, the footnotes indicate that net reductions in inventory levels resulted in a liquidation of LIFO layers amounting to $163,000 in 2005 and $114,000 in 2006.

Global Enterprises, Inc. Condensed Balance Sheet		
($ thousands)	**2005**	**2006**
Assets		
Quick assets	$ 7,327	$ 7,754
Inventory	3,029	3,158
Total current assets	10,356	10,912
Noncurrent assets	11,259	12,376
Total assets	$21,615	$23,288
Liabilities and Shareholders' equity		
Current liabilities	$ 8,153	$ 8,688
Long-term liabilities	3,099	3,162
Total liabilities.	11,252	11,850
Shareholders' equity	10,363	11,438
Total liabilities and shareholders' equity	$21,615	$23,288

Global Enterprises, Inc. Condensed Income Statement		
($ thousands)	**2005**	**2006**
Sales of products	$26,500	$26,797
Cost of goods sold.	(24,095)	(24,248)
Other income	312	450
Income taxes	(900)	(975)
Net earnings.	$ 1,817	$ 2,024

Required:
1. Restate the company's financial statements for 2006 assuming the use of FIFO instead of LIFO.
2. Compare the tax consequences of using LIFO versus FIFO in 2006, and for all prior years. (Assume an effective tax rate of 33 percent.)

P6.30 **Restating Inventory Values Using the LIFO Inventory Reserve.** Presented below are the condensed financial statements of The Mann Corporation. The footnotes to the financial statements reveal that the company uses LIFO to account for the cost of its inventory. In addition, the footnotes also reveal that the value of the company's LIFO reserve was as follows:

Year	LIFO Reserve (in thousands)
2004	$2,940
2005	2,481
2006	2,082

The Mann Corporation Condensed Balance Sheet		
($ thousands)	**2005**	**2006**
Assets		
Current assets (excluding inventory)	$1,260.0	$1,524.0
Inventory	2,505.0	2,625.0
Noncurrent assets	4,303.5	4,998.0
Total assets.	$8,068.5	$9,147.0
Liabilities and shareholders' equity		
Current liabilities	$1,990.5	$2,542.5
Noncurrent liabilities	1,480.5	1,456.5
Total liabilities.	3,471.0	3,999.0
Common stock	265.5	270.0
Retained earnings	4,332.0	4,878.0
Total liabilities and shareholders' equity.	$8,068.5	$9,147.0

The Mann Corporation Condensed Income Statement		
($ thousands)	**2005**	**2006**
Sales.	$11,419.5	$12,897.0
Cost of goods sold.	9,258.0	10,435.5
Selling, general and administrative expenses	1,072.5	1,266.0
Income taxes	351.0	348.0
Net income.	$ 738.0	$ 847.5

Required
1. Restate the company's income statements for 2005 and 2006 to reflect the use of FIFO instead of LIFO. Assume an effective tax rate of 35 percent.
2. Restate the company's balance sheets as of year-end 2005 and 2006 to reflect the use of FIFO instead of LIFO.
3. Calculate the following ratios for each year under FIFO and LIFO:
    a. Current ratio
    b. Inventory turnover
    c. Inventory-on-hand period
    d. Total debt-to-shareholders' equity

⊘ P6.31 **Restating Inventory Values using the LIFO Inventory Reserve: International.** BASF is an international manufacturer of chemical and derivative products, headquartered in Germany. The company is best known for its advertising slogan: "We don't make a lot of the products that you buy, we make a lot of the products that you buy better!" Presented below is selected information from BASF's recent annual report.

BASF, Inc.
Condensed Balance Sheet

(millions of Deutsche Marks)

Assets	2004	2003	Liabilities & Shareholders' Equity	2004	2003
Inventory.............	6,500	6,200	Liabilities.............	25,270	24,520
Other current assets....	13,560	13,900	Capital stock	7,460	7,180
Noncurrent assets	20,300	18,900	Retained earnings	7,630	7,300
Total	40,360	39,000	Total	40,360	39,000

BASF, Inc.
Condensed Statement of Earnings

(millions of Deutsche Marks)	2004	2003
Revenues	40,570	41,900
Cost of goods sold..............................	27,650	28,240
Gross profit....................................	12,920	13,660
Other expenses	11,760	12,425
Income taxes	300	620
Net earnings...................................	860	615

The footnotes to the company's financial statements revealed that BASF values most of its inventory using LIFO. The LIFO reserve was approximately DM 600 million and DM 300 million, respectively, at year-end 2004 and 2003.

Required
1. If BASF had used FIFO instead of LIFO to value its inventory, what value would have been reported for 2004 for the following accounts:
    a.   Ending inventory   c.   Net income before tax
    b.   Cost of goods sold   d.   Retained earnings
2. How much additional income tax would the company have paid if it had used FIFO instead of LIFO to value its inventory?

P6.32   **Inventory Valuation and Earnings.**   Dominick Portet Wines Inc. began operations in 2004 to import fine wines from Australia to the U.S. Sales and purchase information is provided below.

	2004	2005	2006
Sales.....................	170 units	220 units	300 units
Purchases................	250 units at $10 each	200 units at $8 each	? units at $15 each
LIFO ending inventory	80 units at $10	60 units at $10	

Assume that Portet Wines uses the LIFO method of inventory valuation. The purchase amount for 2006 has been left blank because Portet Wines has not yet decided the total number of units to purchase during the year. (Assume that all sales occur on the last day of the year, after all purchases for the year have been made. The company's year-end is December 31.)

Required
1. How many units should be purchased in 2006 if the firm's objective is to maximize reported income for the year?
2. Compute the cost of goods sold for 2006 assuming the number of units computed in (1) is purchased.
3. How many units should be purchased in 2006 if the firm's objective is to minimize income taxes for the year?
4. Compute the cost of goods sold for 2006 assuming the number of units computed in (3) is purchased.
5. Assume Portet Wines uses FIFO instead of LIFO and the company purchased just enough units to meet sales demand. What would the cost of goods sold be in 2006? Assume that FIFO ending inventory is equal to 80 units at $10 in 2004 and 60 units at $8 in 2005.

P6.33   **Inventory Valuation and Earnings.**   New South Wales, Inc. began operations in 2004 as an importer of Australian beer to the U.S. Sales and purchase information is provided below.

	2004	2005	2006
Sales....................	250 units	150 units	300 units
Purchases................	300 units at $15 each	200 units at $12 each	? units at $17 each
LIFO inventory	50 units at $15	50 units at $15	_____
		50 units at $12	

Assume New South Wales, Inc. uses the LIFO method of inventory valuation. The purchase amount for 2006 has been left blank because the company has not yet decided the total number of units to purchase during the year. (Assume that all sales occur on the last day of the year, after all purchases for the year have been made. The company's year-end is December 31.)

Required
1. How many units should be purchased in 2006 if the firm's objective is to minimize income taxes for the year?
2. Compute the cost of goods sold for 2006 assuming the number of units computed in (1) is purchased.
3. How many units should be purchased in 2006 if the firm's objective is to maximize reported income for the year?
4. Compute the cost of goods sold for 2006 assuming the number of units computed in (3) is purchased.

⊘ P6.34   **Inventory Valuation and Earnings.**   Santiago, Inc. began operations in 2004 as an importer of fine Chilean wine to the U.S. Sales and purchase information is provided below.

	2004	2005	2006
Sales....................	250 units	140 units	300 units
Purchases................	300 units at $10 each	200 units at $15 each	? units at $20 each
Ending Inventory	50 units at $10 each	50 units at $10 each	_____
		60 units at $15 each	

Santiago, Inc. uses the LIFO method of inventory valuation. The purchase amount for 2006 has been left blank because the company has not yet decided the total number of units to purchase during the year. (Assume that all sales occur on the last day of the year, after all purchases for the year have been made. The company's year-end is December 31.)

Required

1. How many units should be purchased in 2006 if the firm's objective is to minimize income taxes for the year?
2. Compute the cost of goods sold for 2006 assuming that the number of units computed in (1) is purchased.
3. How many units should be purchased in 2006 if the firm's objective is to maximize reported income for the year?
4. Compute the cost of goods sold for 2006 assuming that the number of units computed in (3) is purchased.

P6.35 **FIFO versus LIFO: Ratio Analysis.** Presented below are the financial statements of two companies that are identical in every respect except the method of valuing their inventories. The method of valuing inventory is LIFO for the LIFO Company and FIFO for the FIFO Company.

Comparative Income Statements	FIFO Company	LIFO Company
Sales.	$20,000,000	$20,000,000
Less: Cost of goods sold	9,200,000	11,280,000
Gross profit.	10,800,000	8,720,000
Less: Operating expenses	5,000,000	5,000,000
Net income before tax	$ 5,800,000	$ 3,720,000

Comparative Balance Sheets		
Assets		
Cash	$ 3,000,000	$ 3,000,000
Receivables	6,000,000	6,000,000
Inventory.	3,800,000	1,720,000
Total current assets	12,800,000	10,720,000
Total noncurrent (net)	20,000,000	20,000,000
Total	$32,800,000	$30,720,000
Liabilities and Equities		
Current liabilities.	$ 4,200,000	$ 4,200,000
Noncurrent liabilities.	9,000,000	9,000,000
Total liabilities	13,200,000	13,200,000
Total shareholders' equity	19,600,000	17,520,000
Total	$32,800,000	$30,720,000

Required

Using the two sets of financial statements, calculate the following ratios for each firm:

1. Current ratio
2. Inventory turnover ratio
3. Inventory-on-hand period
4. Return on total assets
5. Total debt-to-total assets
6. Long-term debt-to-shareholders' equity
7. Gross margin ratio
8. Return on sales
9. Return on shareholders' equity
10. Earnings per share (assume 2 million shares outstanding)

Based on the above ratios, which company represents the best investment opportunity? The best acquisition opportunity? The best lending opportunity? Why?

P6.36   **Evaluating Firm Performance using FIFO and LIFO.**   **Target Corporation** is a general merchandise retailer, comprised of three operating segments: Target, Mervyn's, and Marshall Field's. Target, an upscale discount chain located in 47 states, contributed 84 percent of the firm's 2003 total revenues. Mervyn's, a middle-market promotional department store located in 14 states in the West, South and Midwest, contributed nine percent of total revenues. Marshall Field's (including stores formerly named Dayton's and Hudson's), a traditional department store located in eight states in the upper Midwest, contributed six percent of total revenues. Using selected parts of Target Corp.'s. 2003 10-K report, answer the questions below. (The year 2003 refers to the year ending February 1, 2004. The effective tax rate is 40 percent.)

Required
1.   Was 2003 a good year or a bad year for Target Corporation? Why?
2.   Target Corporation accounts for inventory and the related cost of goods sold using the Last-in, first-out (LIFO) method. Inventory is stated at the lower of LIFO cost or market. The cumulative LIFO inventory reserve was $52 million and $64 million at year-end 2003 and 2002, respectively.
    a.   Estimate the income before income taxes in 2003 assuming the company used FIFO to value its inventory?
    b.   Estimate Target's cumulative tax payments through February 1, 2004 assuming the company had used FIFO to value its inventory instead of LIFO.

Target Corp. Consolidated Balance Sheet		
($ millions)	02/01/04	02/02/03
Cash and cash equivalents	$ 758	$ 499
Accounts receivable, net of allowance for doubtful		
accounts of $399 and $261, respectively	5,565	3,831
Inventory.	4,760	4,449
Other.	852	869
Total current assets	11,935	9,648
Property and equipment.	—	—
Land	3,236	2,833
Buildings and improvements	11,527	10,103
Fixtures and equipment	4,983	4,290
Construction-in-progress	1,190	1,216
Accumulated depreciation	(5,629)	(4,909)
Property and equipment, net	15,307	13,533
Other.	1,361	973
Total assets.	$28,603	$24,154
Liabilities and shareholders' investment		
Accounts payable.	$ 4,684	$ 4,160
Accrued liabilities	1,545	1,566
Income taxes payable	319	423
Current portion of long-term debt and notes payable	975	905
Total current liabilities.	7,523	7,054
Long-term debt	10,186	8,088
Deferred income taxes and other.	1,451	1,152
Shareholders' investment.	—	—

continued

continued from previous page

Target Corp. Consolidated Balance Sheet		
($ millions)	02/01/04	02/02/03
Common stock—Authorized 6,000,000,000 shares, $.0833 par value; 909,801,560 shares issued and outstanding at February 1, 2004	76	75
Additional paid-in-capital.	1,256	1,098
Retained earnings	8,107	6,687
Accumulated other comprehensive income.	4	—
Total shareholders' investment.	9,443	7,860
Total liabilities and shareholders' investment.	$28,603	$24,154

Target Corp. Consolidated Statements of Income			
In millions except per share amounts for period	2003	2002	2001
Sales.	$42,722	$39,114	$36,310
Net credit card revenues	1,195	712	541
Total revenues	43,917	39,826	36,851
Cost of goods sold.	29,260	27,143	25,214
Gross Profit	14,657	12,683	11,637
Expenses	—	—	—
Selling, general and administrative expense	9,416	8,461	7,928
Credit card expense.	765	463	290
Depreciation and amortization	1,212	1,079	940
Interest expense.	588	473	426
Earnings before income taxes	2,676	2,207	2,053
Provision for income taxes.	1,022	839	789
Net earnings.	$ 1,654	$ 1,368	$ 1,264
Basic earnings per share	1.82	1.52	1.40
Diluted earnings per share	1.81	1.50	1.38

P6.37   **Evaluating Firm Performance using FIFO and LIFO.**   OshKosh B'Gosh, Inc. designs, sources, and markets apparel primarily for the children's wear and youth wear markets. In addition to the Company's wholesale business, the company also operates a chain of 137 domestic OshKosh B'Gosh branded stores, including 129 factory outlet stores, three showcase stores, and five strip mall stores. Using selected parts of OshKosh B'Gosh, Inc.'s 2002 10-K report, answer the questions below. The company's fiscal year is a 52/53 week year ending on the Saturday closest to December 31. The effective tax rate is 40 percent.

Required
1. What was the amount of purchases of merchandise inventory in 2002?
2. Assuming all inventory purchases are on account, estimate the amount of cash paid for inventory in 2002?
3. OshKosh reports that inventory is stated at the lower-of-cost-or-market. LIFO is the method used to value virtually all inventories. The replacement cost of inventory exceeds the LIFO cost by $11,983 and $11,381 at December 30, 2002 and January 1, 2002, respectively.

      a.   Estimate the income before income taxes in 2002 assuming the company had used FIFO to value its inventory?

      b.   Estimate retained earnings at December 30, 2002 assuming the company had used FIFO to value its inventory.

  4. How much inventory would Oshkosh have on hand on December 30, 2003 assuming sales grew ten percent in 2003, the company maintained the same inventory-on-hand-period in 2003 as in 2002, and the gross margin percentage was 45 percent in 2003?

	2002
Sales.	$453,062
Cost of goods sold.	262,638
Actual inventory	53,185
Inventory-on-hand period.	73.91 days

Oshkosh B'Gosh, Inc. Consolidated Statements of Cash Flows			
In thousands for period ended	12/30/02	01/01/02	01/02/01
Cash flows from operating activities	—	—	—
Net income.	$32,217	$32,448	$29,335
Adjustments to reconcile net income to net cash			
provided by operating activities	—	—	—
Depreciation	7,154	7,093	8,776
Amortization	834	965	630
(Gain) loss on disposal of assets.	(1,195)	96	160
Deferred income taxes	850	2,000	(300)
Compensation earned under restricted stock plan.	233	—	—
Income tax benefit from stock option exercises	432	650	550
Benefit plan expense, net of contributions	(14)	2,550	(880)
Changes in operating assets and liabilities:	—	—	—
Accounts receivable	(13,652)	7,494	(730)
Inventory	(4,690)	17,089	2,642
Prepaid expenses and other current assets	(1,108)	88	403
Accounts payable	4,571	2,631	(2,635)
Accrued liabilities	2,966	(2,472)	4,840
Net cash provided by operating activities	28,598	70,632	42,791
Cash flows from investing activities.	—	—	—
Additions to property, plant and equipment	(8,550)	(7,148)	(11,420)
Proceeds from disposal of assets	1,954	691	3,054
Sale of investments, net	—	1,989	6,200
Changes in other assets	592	(1,703)	(71)
Net cash used in investing activities	(6,004)	(6,171)	(2,237)
Cash flows from financing activities.	—	—	—
Principal from long-term borrowings	—	44,000	—
Dividends paid	(2,397)	(3,113)	(3,187)
Net proceeds from issuance of common shares.	767	813	780
Repurchase of common shares.	(10,218)	(110,376)	(37,618)
Other	—	(1,000)	—

continued

continued from previous page

Oshkosh B'Gosh, Inc. Consolidated Statements of Cash Flows			
In thousands for period ended	12/30/02	01/01/02	01/02/01
Net cash used in financing activities	(11,848)	(69,676)	(40,025)
Net increase (decrease) in cash and cash equivalents	10,746	(5,215)	529
Cash and cash equivalents at beginning of year	9,093	14,308	13,779
Cash and cash equivalents at end of year	$19,839	$ 9,093	$14,308
Supplementary disclosures	—	—	—
Cash paid for interest	4,105	512	224
Cash paid for income taxes	16,630	19,182	20,112

Oshkosh B'Gosh, Inc. Consolidated Statements of Income			
In thousands except per share amounts for period ended	12/30/02	1/1/02	1/2/01
Net sales	$453,062	$429,786	$423,232
Cost of products sold	262,638	249,592	257,700
Gross profit	190,424	180,194	165,532
Selling, general and administrative expenses	143,012	133,977	124,798
Royalty income, net	(8,257)	(7,435)	(8,186)
Operating income	55,669	53,652	48,920
Other income (expense)	—	—	—
Interest expense	(5,148)	(1,469)	(399)
Interest income	946	1,092	871
Miscellaneous	1,326	(88)	(67)
Other income (expense)—net	(2,876)	(465)	405
Income before income taxes	52,793	53,187	49,325
Income taxes	20,576	20,739	19,990
Net income	$ 32,217	$ 32,448	$ 29,335
Net income per common share	—	—	—
Basic	2.61	2.01	1.54
Diluted	2.58	1.99	1.52

P6.38 **Ethical Dilemma (Part 1).** Reggie Lewis started to work for MiniScribe Corporation, a leading supplier of hard-disk drives, in early 1987. Reggie was particularly excited to be working for one of the top growth companies in the electronics industry and was looking forward to rapid career advancement with MiniScribe. Almost immediately after beginning work at the company, Reggie felt the pressure for sales growth from the senior management, particularly from Mr. Wiles, the chairman of the board and chief executive officer (CEO). Reggie learned that Mr. Wiles came to MiniScribe as its CEO in early 1985 in a financial agreement with Hambrecht & Quist, a venture capital firm. At that time, MiniScribe, a high growth company, was in a severe liquidity crisis and Mr. Wiles, who had a proven track record for turning around ailing companies, was brought in to fix MiniScribe's liquidity problem. However, it turned out that Mr. Wiles was more than interested in merely turning the company around. Instead, he wanted to be remembered as "the man who made MiniScribe into a billion-dollar company," which was a rather ambitious goal for a company with sales of $124 million in 1984. Since Mr. Wiles' arrival at MiniScribe, sales objectives had become the company's driving force, and achieving sales targets became a company-wide obsession. This obsession, along with Wiles' aggressive management style, created a "pressure cooker environment." The environment, however, produced remarkable results. The company returned to profitability shortly after Wiles' arrival. Sales increased by 50 percent in two years, with a reported net income of $22.7 million in 1986.

During the first few months Reggie worked at the corporate controller's office, he found some of MiniScribe's revenue recognition practices troublesome. Specifically, MiniScribe booked sales at the time goods were shipped. On the surface this practice seemed entirely consistent with the revenue recognition principles Reggie had learned in his accounting courses. However, in order to increase reported sales MiniScribe shipped quantities of goods at year-end that were far in excess of the amounts ordered by customers. Furthermore, despite this practice, Reggie noticed that MiniScribe booked sales returns and allowances of only approximately 1 percent of total sales while 4 percent to 10 percent was typical in the industry. Finally, Reggie was very uncomfortable with MiniScribe's practice of "bill and hold." MiniScribe owned several warehouses around the country and in Canada as "just-in-time" suppliers for distributors. Under a bill and hold transaction, MiniScribe booked sales when goods were shipped to the warehouses rather than when they were shipped to customers. Consequently, MiniScribe was able to increase sales by simply shipping goods to its own warehouses. These aggressive accounting practices helped MiniScribe report sales of $362 million in 1987, a 95-percent increase over the previous year. Growth was so rapid that Electronic Business Magazine named MiniScribe one of the top growth companies in the electronics industry. Reggie reviewed the relevant literature regarding revenue recognition and concluded that the above practices were not consistent with generally accepted accounting principles. He decided to discuss this with his superior in the corporate controller's office. However, he was told that MiniScribe's practices were consistent with GAAP and common in the industry. At the end of the conversation, he was also reminded how important it was for everyone at MiniScribe to be a team player.

Required
1. What is the authoritative literature that Reggie Lewis should have reviewed in judging whether MiniScribe's revenue recognition practices were consistent with GAAP? Based on your review of the literature, do you agree with Reggie or his superior?
2. Assume you are in Reggie's position. What would you do in the above situation? Explain in detail the rationale that supports your decision. As a part of your explanation, include a discussion of the major stakeholders of the company who would be affected by your decision.

(Source: AICPA Case No. 96-07.)

P6.39 **Ethical Dilemma (Part 2).** Several months later, Mr. Wolfe, corporate controller of MiniScribe, was replaced by Mr. Huff. With the arrival of the new controller, Reggie was hopeful that corrective actions would be taken to straighten out the company's problematic revenue recognition practices before financial statements were released. However, Reggie was disappointed to see that, despite the change in controllership, the company continued to be aggressive in accounting practices and often went to great lengths to increase its sales and profits. The company dramatically increased the shipments of inventory to its warehouses and recorded those shipments as sales. The company also accumulated scrap that had been written off the company's books, and, instead of discarding it, repackaged it and counted it as good inventory. Furthermore, millions of dollars of false inventory were generated by packaging bricks as finished products and shipping them to distributors at the end of the year. In addition, Reggie learned in conversations with his colleagues that Owen Taranto, the Chief Financial Officer, was creating a software program called "Cook Book" to produce false sales transactions. While clearly troubled by "Cook Book," he also heard that some of his superior officers had even gone as far as breaking into the company's auditors' trunks to obtain copies of the list of inventory items that had been test-counted by the auditors, so that they could inflate the number of inventory items that the auditors had not sampled. Reggie sadly learned that a substantial number of company personnel knowingly assisted with the tactics used to conceal the inventory shortfall and to inflate the reported profits. Reggie also discovered that the Board of Directors was restructured by Mr. Wiles to include a majority of directors who either worked for or were otherwise affiliated with Mr. Wiles and the Hambrecht & Quist group. Furthermore, the Audit Committee of the Board of Directors usually met only twice a year and had never challenged management's financial representations. Witnessing all these fraudulent reporting practices, Reggie felt that he should so something.

Required

1. What were the possible courses of action for Reggie Lewis? Assume you are in Reggie's position, which course of action would you take?
2. As an employee-accountant, was Reggie legally or professionally obligated to blow the whistle about what was happening at MiniScribe? Did Reggie have an ethical obligation to blow the whistle?
(Source: AICPA Case No. 96-07.)

P6.40   (Appendix 6A) Recording Inventory and the Cost of Goods Sold using the Debit/Credit Paradigm.   The following information was disclosed in the 2006 annual report of The Arcadia Company.

	2006	2005
Beginning inventory	$ 9,655	$10,485
Purchase of inventory.	45,850	41,650
Ending inventory.	41,905	9,655
Cost of goods sold.	13,600	42,480

Required

Prepare the journal entries to record (1) the purchase of inventory and (2) the cost of goods sold for The Arcadia Company for 2005 and 2006.

P6.41   (Appendix 6A) Recording Inventory and the Cost of Goods Sold using the Debit/Credit Paradigm.   The following information was disclosed in the 2006 annual report of The Claremont Company.

	2006	2005
Beginning inventory	$20,970	$11,560
Purchase of inventory.	83,300	42,640
Ending inventories	19,310	20,970
Cost of goods sold.	84,960	33,230

Required

Prepare the journal entries to record (1) the purchase of inventory and (2) the cost of goods sold for The Claremont Company for 2005 and 2006.

CORPORATE ANALYSIS

CA6.42   **The Procter and Gamble Company.**   The 2005 annual report of the **Procter and Gamble Company** (P & G) is available at www.pg.com/annualreports/2005/pdf/pg2005annualreport.pdf. After reviewing P & G's annual report, respond to the following questions:

1. How does P & G value its inventory? What costs does P & G include in its cost of products sold? Do you agree with these policy decisions? How much of P & G's total assets are represented by its inventory?
2. Calculate P & G's inventory turnover ratio, inventory-on-hand period, accounts payable turnover ratio, and days' payable period for 2004 and 2005. What can you conclude from these ratios?
3. Assume that P & G's cost of inventory financing is five percent, the company needs to maintain an inventory of about $5,006 in 2006 (as in 2005), the effective tax rate is 30 percent, and that in 2006,

the company is able to raise its inventory turnover rate to (a) 6.5 times or (b) 7.0 times. How much financing costs would be saved under each scenario? How much would net income and the cash flow from operations increase as a result of the improvement in the inventory turnover?

CA6.43 **Internet-Based Analysis.** Consider a publicly-held company whose products you are familiar with. Some examples might include:

Company	Product	Corporate Website
• **Johnson & Johnson Company**	• Band-Aids	• www.jnj.com
• **Microsoft Corporation**	• Windows XP software	• www.microsoft.com
• **Nokia Corporation**	• Cellular phones	• www.nokia.com
• **Intel Corporation**	• Pentium processors	• www.intel.com
• **Kimberly-Clark Corporation**	• Kleenex	• www.kimberly-clark.com

Access the company's public website and search for its most recent annual report. (Some companies will provide access to their financial data through an "investor relations" link, while others will provide a direct link to their "annual reports.") After locating your company's most recent annual report, open the file and review its contents. After reviewing the annual report for your selected company, prepare answers to the following questions.

1. What method does the company use to account for its inventory? Do you agree with the company's selection of its inventory valuation method? Calculate the inventory as a percentage of total assets. Did the percentage increase or decrease over the last two years?
2. Calculate the inventory turnover ratio and the inventory-on-hand period for each of the last two years? Is the inventory-on-hand period increasing or decreasing? What might explain the change in the inventory-on-hand period?
3. Calculate the days' payable period for each of the last two years. Is the company paying its accounts payable faster or slower? What might explain this change?

Chapter Seven

Long-Lived Fixed Assets, Intangible Assets, and Natural Resources

TAKEAWAYS

When you complete this chapter you should be able to:

1. Explain how the acquisition cost of a long-lived asset is determined.

2. Describe why the matching of depreciation, depletion, and amortization expense with operating revenue is important.

3. Explain how depreciation is calculated using the straight-line, the double-declining balance, and the units-of-production methods.

4. Define what an asset impairment is and how impairments are reflected in financial statements.

Where have we been?	Where are we?	Where are we going?
In Chapter 6, the important conceptual issue of matching the operating revenue and operating expenses of a business enterprise was considered. Specifically, the various ways that companies can match the cost of their sold inventory with the revenue produced by the sale was investigated. Inventory valuation methods such as FIFO, LIFO, and the weighted-average cost method were discussed and illustrated. Just which method is used was shown to have a dramatic effect on a company's gross profit and its reported value of ending inventory. Finally, the reasons why a company selects one inventory valuation method versus another were considered.	In this chapter, the acquisition, use, and accounting for investments in long-lived fixed assets, intangible assets, and natural resources is investigated. We continue our exploration of the concept of matching by focusing on how the cost of these long-lived assets can be matched with the operating revenue produced by these assets over their expected useful lives. Various depreciation methods such as straight-line, double-declining balance, and the units-of-production method are explored, as are amortization and depletion methods that distribute the cost of an intangible asset or a natural resource over an asset's expected useful life. The issues of asset sales, impairment, and revaluation are also considered.	In Chapter 8, the strategic decision to invest in other companies is investigated. The motivation for these intercorporate investments, as well as the accounting for them, is considered. We will see that when companies acquire a small fraction of the equity ownership of another company, these investments are frequently accounted for at their fair market value. Investments involving 20 to 50 percent of the outstanding equity shares are accounted for using the equity method, and investments involving a controlling interest (greater than 50 percent ownership), usually involve consolidation accounting. Finally, issues concerning the accounting for investments in foreign companies, joint ventures, and special purpose entities are also examined.

AMERICA ONLINE, INC.   Symbol: AOL

In 1992, America Online, Inc. (AOL) went public and within three years grew ten-fold to become the leader in interactive computer services in the United States. AOL's share price had risen dramatically over this same time period, from an initial public offering price of $11.50 per share to over $70 per share in November 1995.

A *Newsweek* magazine article featuring AOL jokingly editorialized that "one of AOL's hidden assets is the brilliant accounting decision to treat its marketing and R&D costs as capital items rather than as expenses" (October 30, 1995). According to AOL's 1995 annual report, the company capitalized as an asset on its balance sheet:

* Product development costs, or the costs incurred for the production of computer software used in the sales of AOL's interactive services; and,
* Deferred subscriber acquisition costs, or the costs related to the solicitation of prospective clients for the company's interactive services.

The company also disclosed that it amortized its product development costs (PDC) and deferred subscriber acquisition costs (DSAC) over 60 months and 24 months, respectively.

By year-end 1995, AOL's balance sheet disclosed capitalized PDC and DSAC totaling $18.9 million and $77.2 million, respectively; and, collectively, these two costs exceeded the company's cumulative earned income by over $130 million. (Although AOL had reported positive earnings from 1992 to 1994, the company reported a net loss of $33.6 million in 1995, creating an accumulated deficit of $33 million in retained earnings.)

In response to criticism from Wall Street investment professionals regarding the company's treatment of PDC and DSAC as assets, AOL wrote off over $96 million of these "assets" in 1996. The Wall Street investment community questioned whether the PDC and DSAC expenditures truly represented an asset of the business. The financial community was pleased to see AOL adopt a more appropriate accounting treatment of its PDC and DSAC as AOL's share price was bid up substantially in the weeks following the asset write-offs. The new accounting treatment provided a more transparent presentation of the company's performance, enabling investment professionals to measure and predict the company's sustainable earnings with greater certainty. The AOL case provides additional evidence that Wall Street analysts tend to discount the shares of those companies suspected of using questionable accounting practices.

In 2000, AOL merged with the Time Warner Company to form AOL Time Warner. Since the merger, the value of AOL has declined from $226 billion to just $20 billion. In this chapter, we investigate the acquisition, use, and accounting for investments in long-lived fixed assets, intangible assets, and natural resources. We will see that the key issues surrounding these assets are (1) how to the match their acquisition cost with the revenue generated by their use, and (2) the continuing asset value that should be reported on a company's balance sheet.

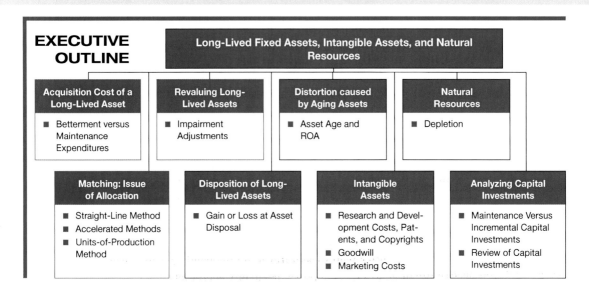

ACQUISITION COST OF A LONG-LIVED ASSET

When an asset is initially acquired by a business, it is generally-accepted accounting practice globally to **capitalize** the acquisition cost of the asset—that is, to place the value of the asset on the company's balance sheet at the asset's acquisition cost. This accepted practice reflects the historical cost principle discussed in Chapter 2. Frequently, an asset's **acquisition** cost includes more than just its listed purchase price; it may also include sales tax on the purchase price, transportation costs from the seller to the buyer's location, as well as a number of ancillary costs. As a general rule, all expenditures necessary to purchase an asset, transport the asset to the buyer's place of business, and place the asset into a revenue-producing state may be capitalized to the balance sheet as part of an asset's acquisition cost. For example, if use of an acquired asset requires special employee training, these training costs may be capitalized to the balance sheet (although they frequently are not) as part of the asset's acquisition cost. In addition, if installation of the asset requires modification of the buyer's facilities (such as the installation of higher voltage electrical wiring or reinforced flooring), these costs may also be capitalized to the balance sheet as part of the asset's acquisition cost because they are necessary to get the acquired asset to a revenue-producing state.

Some businesses self-construct the assets they utilize in their business. For example, automotive and truck manufacturers typically "retool" their production lines every three to five years. Retoolings often coincide with the introduction of a new model or the redesign of existing models. The cost of retooling is quite expensive, frequently involving billions of dollars. Rather than outsource these production-line changes, the automotive companies often undertake the retooling themselves. Consequently, the costs incurred during the retooling process are capitalized to the automotive company's balance sheet as a component of the plant and equipment account.

The interest charges on any borrowed funds used to finance the retooling can also appropriately be capitalized to the balance sheet as part of the production-line cost during the period of retooling. However, once the retooling process is complete, the interest charges may no longer be capitalized as part of the cost of the asset, and instead, must thereafter be expensed. When borrowing costs are capitalized, it is accepted practice to disclose the amount of the capitalized interest charges in the company's footnotes. Many investment professionals question the economic rationale behind the practice of capitalizing interest charges, preferring to see all financing costs expensed in the fiscal period in which they are incurred (recognizing the income statement deduction in the same fiscal period as the cost is incurred). Disclosure of the amount of capitalized interest costs in the footnotes to the financial statements enables these professionals to restate a company's financial statements as if the interest charges had been expensed, rather than capitalized.

Betterment versus Maintenance Expenditures

After an asset has been placed in service, it is not uncommon to incur expenditures related to the asset's continued use. Some of these expenditures involve routine maintenance of the asset (such as an oil change on a company truck) which is necessary to obtain the normal productive output from the asset. As a consequence, routine maintenance expenditures are expensed on the income statement in the fiscal period in which they are incurred. Other expenditures may be non-routine, however, and consequently, may be more appropriately accounted for by capitalizing them to the balance sheet as part of the cost of an asset. For example, a factory with an expected useful life of 50 years may require a new roof every twenty years. The cost of replacing the factory roof is not a maintenance expense, but instead, is typically considered to be a betterment or improvement. Betterment expenditures are frequently material in amount and either (1) extend the productive life of an asset, (2) improve the quality and/or quantity of an asset's output, or

---

BUSINESS PERSPECTIVE: CAPITALIZE VERSUS EXPENSE

WorldCom Inc. was a discount long-distance telephone service provider founded in 1995 with the merger of Williams Telecommunications Group Inc. and LDDS Inc. By 2002, WorldCom had become the United States' second largest long-distance telephone company through more than 60 mergers and acquisitions. In 2003, a U.S. Securities and Exchange Commission complaint alleged that WorldCom changed its accounting for the cost of land-lines leased from such companies as **AT&T** and **SBC**, among others. Originally, the line costs—that is, the charges paid by WorldCom for access to other telephone company networks—were expensed to match the company's operating expenses with its operating revenue. However, beginning in 2000, WorldCom began inappropriately capitalizing these costs to its corporate balance sheet as an asset. An investigation by WorldCom's auditors **KPMG** revealed that as much as $7 billion in line costs may have been inappropriately capitalized to enable the struggling company to report positive earnings. The accounting change was masterminded to buoy WorldCom's sagging share price. In July, 2002, WorldCom filed for bankruptcy, the largest in U.S. corporate history. In March 2005, former WorldCom CEO Bernard Ebbers was convicted of conspiracy to commit fraud by falsifying WorldCom's financial results, securities fraud by misleading investors and the public about WorldCom's true financial condition, and making false filings with the U.S. Securities and Exchange Commission that misrepresented WorldCom's financial position. In late 2005, Mr. Ebbers was sentenced to 25 years in prison; he began serving his prison sentence in September, 2006.

Could an astute financial analyst have identified the pending WorldCom disaster? It is very likely that a rigorous financial analysis and review of WorldCom's financial statements would have provided analysts with "red flags" regarding the company's financial problems. For instance, WorldCom's **fixed asset turnover ratio**—that is, its net sales divided by net fixed assets—declined over the period 2000 to 2002 from 0.31 to a mere 0.19, a drop of nearly 40 percent, as the amount of capitalized land-line costs increased. A decline of this magnitude should have raised concern among the investment professionals that followed the company.

---

(3) reduce the operating expenses associated with the asset. As a consequence, betterments are capitalized to the balance sheet, to be depreciated over the asset's remaining expected useful life.

The identification of just which expenditures are maintenance expenditures versus those which are betterments is often quite ambiguous. Since this accounting decision can have a significant impact on a business' current earnings, these decisions are carefully reviewed by a firm's CFO in conjunction with its independent auditor. An expenditure which is capitalized to the balance sheet does not reduce current earnings, whereas an expenditure which is expensed reduces current pre-tax profit. Managers who are compensated on the basis of reported earnings prefer to capitalize as many expenditures as can be justified to avoid the adverse effect on net income (and their compensation) caused by expensing such outlays.

MATCHING: A QUESTION OF ALLOCATION

Once the acquisition cost of a long-lived asset has been determined, the next accounting issue to be confronted is "how best to allocate the capitalized cost of the asset over its expected productive life?" The process of allocating the capitalized cost of a fixed asset over its expected useful life is commonly referred to as **depreciation**, whereas the process of allocating the acquisition cost of an intangible asset over its productive life is called **amortization**. **Depletion**, on the other hand, refers to the allocation of the acquisition and development costs of a natural resource over its expected productive life. **Fixed assets** include such tangible assets as property, plant and equipment, whereas **intangible assets include research and development costs, marketing costs, goodwill, and the intellectual property rights represented by** copyrights and patents. Natural resources include such assets as standing timber, oil and gas reserves, iron ore, coal, and uranium mines.

The significance of the allocation process for long-lived assets arises as a consequence of the matching concept—that is, the desire to match a company's operating revenues with **all** of the costs incurred to generate that revenue. Long-lived assets, by their nature, have the capacity to generate operating revenue over many years, and consequently, it is necessary to arrive at a logical and systematic way to distribute the capitalized value of these assets against the future revenue generated by their use.

For most long-lived fixed assets, it is difficult to know with certainty in what amount, or when, an asset's future revenue stream is going to occur since operating revenue is dependent on so many externalities such as product demand, competition, changing customer tastes, and innovation, among others. Consequently, given the ambiguity surrounding the revenue streams associated with such assets, the accounting community has developed a number of "logical and systematic" allocation schemes that have become accepted as GAAP. In the case of fixed assets, these generally-accepted allocation approaches include:

- Straight-line method
- Accelerated methods
  - ○ Double-declining balance
- Production-based methods
  - ○ Units-of-production

In the case of intangible assets, amortization using the straight-line method is almost universally practiced worldwide. And, in the case of natural resources, the use of the units-of-production depletion approach is considered to be "best practice."

Straight-Line Method

The straight-line method of depreciation (and amortization) allocates the capitalized cost of an asset equally over an asset's expected productive life using the following formula:

$$\text{Operating expense for the period} = \frac{1}{n}\,(\text{Acquisition cost} - \text{Residual value})$$

where n equals the asset's expected useful life in months or in years. The useful life of an asset is the length of time that the asset is expected to be productive for the company (to produce revenue for the company). This length of time is generally shorter than the actual physical life of the asset. For example, a computer may have a ten-year physical life; however, the useful life of the computer is likely to be much shorter, perhaps only four years or less, because of technological improvements in the area of information technology. The estimated amount that the computer could be sold for at the end of its useful life is called the asset's residual value or scrap value.

If, for example, the asset to be depreciated is a truck having an expected useful life of five years, costing $30,000, and with an expected residual value of $4,000 at the end of its five year useful life, the annual straight-line depreciation charge would be $5,200 (1/5[30,000 − 4,000]). Thus, in each of the asset's five years, a constant amount ($5,200) would be matched against the revenue produced by the truck. An implicit assumption underpinning the straight-line method is that an asset's productive capacity is approximately equal during each period of its useful life. Over the expected five year useful life of the truck, the depreciation charges will aggregate to $26,000 (five years × $5,200 per year), representing the **depreciable cost** of the asset. The residual value of the asset ($4,000) should not be depreciated since this is the expected value that the asset can be sold for when retired from use.

How is depreciation calculated when an asset is acquired part way though a fiscal period? In recognition of the reality that depreciation expense is just an estimate of the value of an asset that is consumed or used up in a given fiscal period, most companies employ a practice known as the half-year convention. Under this convention, no matter when an asset is acquired during a fiscal year, only one-half year of depreciation expense is taken in the first year of use. An alternative application of the half-year convention used by some companies is that when an asset is acquired during the first six months of the year, the asset is assumed to have been acquired on the first day of the year and thus a full year of depreciation expense is taken. For assets acquired anytime during the second six months of the fiscal year, only one-half year of the first year's depreciation expense is taken.

When a company records its depreciation expense for the period, retained earnings is reduced by the amount of the expense and an equivalent amount is subtracted from the book value of the asset. However, instead of reducing the asset account directly, the current depreciation charge is placed in a contra-asset account called **accumulated depreciation**, which is then subtracted from the asset account. The asset's remaining **book value** ($24,800) is calculated as the acquisition cost ($30,000) minus the accumulated depreciation ($5,200) to date. In the case of the truck, this information is illustrated in the spreadsheet below.

		Assets		=	Liabilities	+	Equity
	Cash	Truck	Accumulated Depreciation				Retained Earnings
Acquire asset	−30,000	30,000					
Depreciate asset			−5,200				−5,200 (depreciation expense)

The convention of using the accumulated depreciation account to record the depreciation taken on an asset stems from a desire to preserve an asset's original acquisition cost while also disclosing its current book value. Comparing an asset's acquisition cost to its book value reveals the relative age of an asset and consequently, how soon the asset will need to be replaced. For example, the ratio of book value-to-acquisition cost for our $30,000 truck after one year of use yields a ratio of 83 percent ($24,800/$30,000), suggesting that only 17 percent of the asset has been consumed to date, and thus, that the asset will not need to be replaced for some years in the future. Knowing the relative age of a business' assets is useful as managers and investment professionals try to forecast a company's future cash flow needs.

Accelerated Methods

Accelerated depreciation methods, as the name implies, are allocation methods that cause an asset to be depreciated at a rate faster than the straight-line rate (the depreciation rate under the straight-line method is $1/n$). **The double-declining balance** method is an accelerated method, yielding the fastest write off of any of the generally-accepted depreciation methods. Under this approach, the annual depreciation expense is calculated as follows:

The double-declining balance (DDB) method is part of a family of declining-balance depreciation methods. The depreciation rate for DDB is $2/n$, where n is the asset's expected useful life. But other rates are also permissible (such as $1.5/n$, $1.25/n$, etc.) so long as they do not exceed the DDB rate of $2/n$.

$$\text{Operating expense for the period} = \frac{2}{n} (\text{Book value})$$

where n equals the asset's expected useful life in months or in years.[1]

In the case of the truck with a five year life, costing $30,000, and with a residual value of $4,000, double-declining depreciation would be calculated as follows:

	Depreciation Expense	Double-Declining Balance Calculations	Book Value
Year 1	$12,000	2/5 × ($30,000)	$18,000
Year 2	7,200	2/5 × ($30,000 − $12,000)	10,800
Year 3	4,320	2/5 × ($30,000 − $12,000 − $7,200)	6,480
Year 4	1,240	1/2 × ($26,000 − $23,520)	5,240
Year 5	1,240	1/2 × ($26,000 − $23,520)	4,000
	$26,000		4,000

The double-declining balance method depreciates the truck so rapidly that by the end of Year 3, the remaining book value is only $6,480. Continuing to use the declining balance formula would cause the truck to be depreciated below its expected resale value of $4,000. Consequently, at this point, the declining balance process is typically abandoned, and thereafter, a straight-line approach is utilized, with the remaining depreciable cost of $2,480 ($6,480 − 4,000) spread equally over the remaining two years of the truck's useful life (see Exhibit 7.1).

As a practical matter, if the salvage value of an asset is unknown, the declining-balance formula would be consistently applied over the asset's useful life. It is noteworthy that all generally accepted depreciation methods incorporate an asset's expected residual value in the calculation of the annual (or periodic) depreciation expense except the double-declining balance method, which does not consider the asset's expected salvage value for purposes of calculating the periodic depreciation expense other than determining the book value where no additional depreciation will be recorded.

Units-of-Production Method

For some assets, calculating depreciation as a function of time (such as straight-line) may not be relevant since the expected useful life of certain assets is more closely linked to their actual usage than the passage of time. For example, some equipment manufacturers have determined that their products have a reasonably well-defined useful life as measured by the number of machine-hours they are likely to run or the

---

[1] A second, but less widely used, accelerated depreciation method is the **sum-of-the-years' digits method**. The sum-of-the-years' digits (SYD) may be calculated as follows: $\text{SYD} = n(n + 1)/2$, where n is the asset's expected useful life. For an asset costing $30,000, with a useful life of five years (SYD = 15) and residual value of $4,000, the depreciation expense under this method would be calculated as follows:

	Depreciation Expense	Calculation
Year 1	$ 8,667	5/15 × ($30,000 − $4,000)
Year 2	6,933	4/15 × ($30,000 − $4,000)
Year 3	5,200	3/15 × ($30,000 − $4,000)
Year 4	3,467	2/15 × ($30,000 − $4,000)
Year 5	1,733	1/15 × ($30,000 − $4,000)
	$26,000	

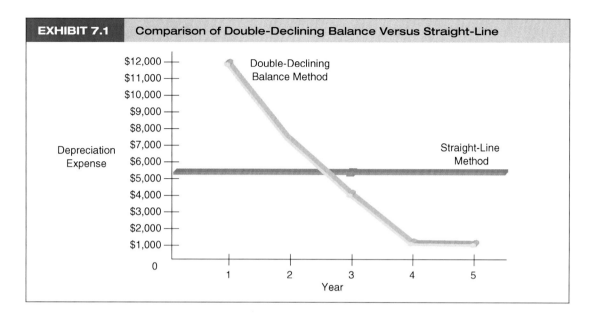

| EXHIBIT 7.1 | Comparison of Double-Declining Balance Versus Straight-Line |

number of units they are likely to produce. For instance, the manufacturer of our truck costing $30,000 may believe that, based upon engineering statistics and actual utilization data, the truck's useful life is best defined in terms of expected miles to be driven (such as most truck leases are defined in terms of a maximum allowable mileage). Under these circumstances, the use of an output-based allocation method, such as the units-of-production method, may yield superior matching results.

Under the **units-of-production method**, the periodic depreciation charge is calculated as follows:

$$\text{Operating expense for the period} = \frac{\text{Output consumed this period}}{\text{Total estimated lifetime output}} (\text{Acqusition cost} - \text{Residual value})$$

If the truck is expected to be driven an aggregate of 100,000 miles before replacement, and the actual mileage driven is 28,000 miles in Year 1, 25,000 miles in Year 2, 20,000 miles in Year 3, and 15,000 and 12,000 miles in Years 4 and 5, respectively, the units-of-production depreciation would be calculated as follows:

	Depreciation Expense	Units-of-Production Calculation
Year 1	$ 7,280	$\frac{28,000}{100,000} \times (\$30,000 - \$4,000)$
Year 2	6,500	$\frac{25,000}{100,000} \times (\$30,000 - \$4,000)$
Year 3	5,200	$\frac{20,000}{100,000} \times (\$30,000 - \$4,000)$
Year 4	3,900	$\frac{15,000}{100,000} \times (\$30,000 - \$4,000)$
Year 5	3,120	$\frac{12,000}{100,000} \times (\$30,000 - \$4,000)$
	$26,000	

In Practice 7.1 *Depreciation Method: A Glimpse of a Sample of Fortune 1000 Companies* The following table identifies the depreciation method used by a sample of 600 *Fortune 1000* companies. Over 98 percent of the surveyed firms reported using the straight-line method for some or all of their depreciable assets:

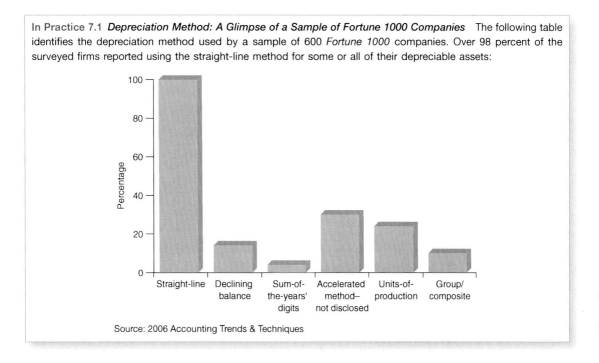

Source: 2006 Accounting Trends & Techniques

Like the straight-line method, units-of-production depreciation incorporates an asset's expected residual value, and consequently, only allocates the truck's depreciable cost of $26,000 ($30,000 − $4,000) over its expected five year life.

The process of allocating the cost of an asset over its useful life is done solely for the purpose of matching the acquisition cost of the asset with the revenue generated by the asset's use. The purpose is not to align the asset's balance sheet value—its book value—with the actual market value of the asset. It will only be by coincidence that an asset's book value will ever equal the market value of the asset at any time other than the point of initial purchase. It should also be noted that accumulated depreciation is nothing more than a running total offset to the acquisition cost of the asset. This account does not represent a fund of money that can be used for asset replacement as is sometimes thought by those who lack an understanding of accounting. Finally, be sure to observe that each depreciation method will result in the same total depreciation over an asset's useful life—only the amount of the periodic depreciation charge will differ between the methods.

Choosing a Depreciation Method

Given the variety of depreciation approaches that are considered GAAP, how does the management of a company decide which method to use to depreciate its assets? Although GAAP permits the use of a combination of depreciation methods—that is, some assets may be depreciated using the straight-line method while others may be depreciated using double-declining balance or the units-of-production method—most companies tend to use one allocation approach for all of their depreciable assets, particularly in their publicly-disclosed financial statements.

In the U.S., the depreciation method most commonly used in audited financial statements is the straight-line method. The popularity of the straight-line method in the U.S. appears linked to several considerations. First, for capital-intensive companies, the depreciation expense is one of the largest operating expenses (if not the largest) deducted against operating revenue. The straight-line method holds that expense stable, thereby enabling management to know with certainty a significant component of the operating expenses that they will need to cover each fiscal period. Some managers feel that this knowledge allows them to focus on other important issues when making operating decisions. Second, some investment professionals allege that companies attempt to "smooth" their reported earnings on the presumption that earnings stability is highly valued by the capital market (smooth earnings represent certainty, and hence, less risk). The straight-line method is thought to facilitate income smoothing because it provides a stable level of depreciation deductions over the life of an asset. Finally, relative to the accelerated methods, the straight-line method provides smaller depreciation deductions against operating revenues, especially in the early years of an asset's life (see Exhibit 7.1). For companies concerned about reporting the highest possible earnings, the straight-line method tends to facilitate this financial reporting objective.

GLOBAL PERSPECTIVE

Outside the U.S., the depreciation method choice is usually driven by other considerations. For example, in Germany and Japan, income tax considerations cause most public companies to prefer accelerated methods for financial statement purposes. While in the U.S. it is common for public companies to maintain multiple sets of financial data (such as one set of accounting data for managers, one set for shareholders, and one set for taxation purposes), the governments of Germany and Japan use the audited financial reports distributed to shareholders as the basis for assessing income taxes for German and Japanese businesses. Thus, managers in these countries face a dilemma: Use straight-line depreciation to report higher profits to shareholders and pay higher income taxes, or use an accelerated method to reduce the tax burden but show lower profits to shareholders! Managers facing this dilemma tend to prefer the preservation of their operating cash flow by using accelerated depreciation methods that lower earnings, and hence, lower income tax payments.

For U.S. income tax purposes, companies must follow a depreciation system called the modified accelerated cost recovery system (MACRS). This system specifies how, and the rate at which, various assets must be depreciated. The MACRS system provides very generous depreciation deductions which approximate the depreciation charges experienced under an accelerated method. We will have more to say about MACRS in Chapter 10.

Accounting Policy Changes

Under the GAAP of most countries, companies are permitted to change the estimated useful life of a depreciable asset, its expected residual value, or the particular depreciation method in use. Frequent accounting policy changes, however, are normally not observed because it is well known that investment professionals regard any type of voluntary accounting policy change suspiciously, possibly indicating an attempt by management to "manage" reported earnings through the accounting policy change. Empirical evidence indicates that when a company's earnings increase as a consequence of an accounting policy change (such as a switch from double-declining balance depreciation to straight-line depreciation), a firm's share price will tend to fall as the equity market speculates that such a change may forebode adverse future corporate news.[2] In essence, the capital market appears to "second guess" the motivation behind voluntary corporate accounting policy changes. If the policy change results in an increase in accounting earnings, the market appears to infer that management is attempting to cover up

---

[2] D. Dharam and B. Lev, "The Valuation of Consequences of Accounting Changes," *Journal of Accounting, Auditing and Finance,* (1993).

BUSINESS PERSPECTIVE: DEPRECIATION DISCLOSURES

Financial statement disclosures of the H.J. Heinz Company for its fixed assets are presented below. The data reveals that Heinz uses the straight-line method to depreciate these assets (see footnote information). Since land is generally not depreciated, the depreciation expense of $213.968 million reported in Heinz's 2001 consolidated income statement relates only to the company's buildings and equipment. Is it possible to estimate the average age of Heinz's buildings and equipment and their expected useful lives?

The aggregate cost of Heinz's depreciable assets in 2001 is $3.826 billion ($878.028 + $2,947.978). Since the company uses the straight-line method, if we assume a zero residual value, the expected useful life of these assets can be estimated by dividing their aggregate cost by the depreciation expense for 2001 ($3.826 billion/$213.968 million), yielding an average expected useful life of nearly 18 years. With respect to the remaining useful life of the company's buildings and equipment, dividing the accumulated depreciation balance at year-end 2001 by the assets' aggregate capitalized cost ($1,712/$3,826) indicates that approximately 45 percent of the assets' expected useful lives have been used up, leaving 55 percent, or approximately 9.9 years (55 percent × 18 years), of remaining useful life. Thus, we can conclude that at the current rate of depreciation, Heinz will not need to replace these long-lived productive assets for almost ten years.

The H.J. Heinz Company **Consolidated Balance Sheet**		
Property, plant and equipment (in thousands)	**2001**	**2000**
Land	$ 54,774	$ 45,959
Buildings and leasehold improvements	878,028	860,873
Equipment, furniture and other	2,947,978	3,440,915
	3,880,780	4,347,747
Less: Accumulated depreciation	1,712,400	1,988,994
Net property, plant and equipment	$2,168,380	$2,358,753
Consolidated Income Statement		
(in thousands)		
Depreciation expense.	$ 213,968	$ 219,255

Footnote disclosure

Land, buildings and equipment are recorded at cost. For financial reporting purposes, depreciation is provided on the straight-line method over the estimated useful lives of the assets. Expenditures for new facilities and improvements that substantially extend the capacity or useful life of an asset are capitalized. Ordinary repairs and maintenance are expensed as incurred. When property is retired or disposed, the cost and related depreciation are removed from the accounts.

poor expected future operating performance. If, on the other hand, an accounting policy change results in a decrease in accounting earnings, the market appears to infer that the firm's operating performance is expected to exceed management's projections, and consequently, the policy change is intended to "bank" some of the excess earnings for use in future periods (creating an earnings reserve to help meet future Wall Street earnings' expectations).

There are three types of **accounting policy changes** permitted under GAAP: entity, estimate, and method. An **entity change** occurs when a company acquires, merges with, or divests itself of another company, such as a subsidiary or division. In this case, the consolidated reporting entity is changed, and consequently, changes in the reported consolidated financial results are clearly imminent. To help financial statement users understand the effects of an entity change, companies are required to include pro forma financial data in their annual report—that is, data "as if" the entity change had not occurred—to enable statement users to evaluate the consolidated entity's performance independent of the entity change. The presentation of such pro forma information is normally required for only one year following an entity change.

An **estimate change**, on the other hand, is a change in an existing accounting estimate used by a firm in the preparation of its financial statements. Common financial statement estimates include the estimated bad debt expense, estimated sales returns, the estimate of an asset's residual value, and the estimated useful life of an asset. When a firm changes one of its estimates, the financial impact of the estimate change on the firm's net earnings must be disclosed in the company's footnotes. Consider, for example, the case of **Valley National Gas, Inc.** In 1998, the company changed its estimate of the remaining expected useful life of its plant and equipment from 12 to 30 years. The change had the effect of reducing the company's annual depreciation expense by $2.3 million and increasing the company's net income after tax by $1.3 million. The change in accounting estimate raised Valley National's earnings per share by $0.14 per share, or approximately 80 percent.

Estimate changes like the Valley National expected useful life change are executed on a **prospective basis**; that is, no attempt is made to restate the historical financial statements of the company for the financial effects of the change. For instance, if after two years of depreciating a truck costing $30,000, with a residual value of $4,000 and expected useful life of five years using the straight-line method, it is determined that the truck will last eight years in total, no change is made to the depreciation expense taken in years one and two. Instead, the remaining depreciable cost of the truck of $15,600 ($26,000 − $10,400) will be spread over the new remaining expected useful life of six years (8 years − 2 years). Consequently, the new depreciation expense will be $2,600 per year ($15,600/6 years), as compared to the original annual depreciation expense of $5,200.

Finally, a **method change** occurs when, for example, a firm changes its depreciation approach from double-declining balance depreciation to straight-line depreciation or when a company switches from LIFO to FIFO. Unlike estimate changes which are executed on a prospective basis, accounting method changes are executed on a **retroactive basis**—that is, a company re-computes its depreciation expense, and hence its net income, under the new method for all prior periods and then restates all affected financial statements. (An exception to the practice of retroactive restatement for an accounting method change is a method change from FIFO to LIFO, which is executed on a prospective basis.) Since it would be impractical and very expensive for a company to issue new historical financial statements to shareholders reflecting the restated results, only the financial statements for those years included in the latest annual report are restated for the effect of the method change, and a lump-sum adjustment for all prior years is made to current earnings on the income statement. The lump-sum adjustment to reflect the prior-period financial effect of the method change is often labeled the **cumulative prior period effect of an accounting policy change.** Like unusual and extraordinary items, the cumulative prior-period financial effect resulting from an accounting method change should not be considered as part of a company's sustainable earnings—it is a one-time, non-recurring event (it is part of transitory earnings). Beginning in 2006 in the U.S., the cumulative prior period effect of an accounting policy change will be reported as an adjustment to retained earnings on the statement of shareholders' equity and no longer on the income statement as a component of current net income.[3]

As noted previously, accounting estimate and method changes are viewed skeptically by the capital market. Available empirical evidence, for example, suggests that a company's share price will tend to

---

[3] See Financial Accounting Statement No. 154.

fall when a firm changes from an income-reducing method to an income-enhancing method (such as a switch from double-declining balance depreciation to straight-line depreciation). Similarly, when a firm changes from an income-enhancing method to an income-reducing method (such as a FIFO to LIFO change), the company's share price will tend to increase.[4]

> Voluntary accounting policy changes are characterized by some investment professionals as an "unintended signal" from the management of a company to the capital market regarding the company's future operating prospects. This characterization of accounting policy changes reflects what has become known as signaling theory.

REVALUING LONG-LIVED ASSETS

Two constructs that underpin the GAAP of most developed countries are the historical cost concept and conservatism. The former stipulates that the assets of a business should initially be valued at their historical acquisition cost, and the latter that the expected losses of a business should be recorded as soon as they are identified, while gains should not be recorded until they are actually realized. As a consequence of these concepts, accepted accounting practice in the U.S., for example, requires downward revaluations of all assets (such as the lower-of-cost-or-market rule for inventory) whereas upward asset revaluations are only selectively permitted. As will be seen in Chapter 8, marketable securities are often carried at their current market value, and thus, may be revalued upward or downward to reflect changes in their fair market value. But, this asset group is an exception to the general rule under U.S. GAAP. (A second exception to this generally-accepted practice occurs when one company acquires another company. As will be seen in Chapter 8, the assets and liabilities of acquired entities are revalued to their fair market value at the time of acquisition.)

Long-lived assets, however, may only be written down in value, and this may occur in two situations. First, downward value adjustments are periodically recorded as depreciation expense to reflect the consumption of a long-lived asset associated with the ongoing operations of a business. Second, when the future revenue-generating capacity of an asset declines unrelated to the depreciation process, the diminishment in value is recorded in the firm's income statement as an impairment loss. An asset is said to be "impaired" when it is no longer expected to produce previously anticipated levels of revenue or cash flow. For example, if consumer demand for a product declines, the revenue-producing capacity of the long-lived assets used to produce the product, such as plant and equipment, is said to be impaired unless the assets can be utilized in the production of some alternative product. Consider the case of AMR Corporation, the parent company of American Airlines, American Eagle Airlines, and TWA Airlines. Following the aircraft hijacking associated with the September 11, 2001, New York City terrorist attacks, AMR determined that the revenue-producing capacity of its fleet of aircraft had been impaired as consumer and business air travel declined significantly. Lacking an ability to convert its fleet of commercial aircraft to alternative revenue-producing activities, AMR took a $1.24 billion impairment charge at year-end 2001 and a second impairment charge of $0.66 billion at year-end 2002.

In some countries, such as the United Kingdom, Australia, and New Zealand, when an asset appreciates in value, it is permissible to revalue the asset upward to reflect its appreciation in value. These upward revaluations may be executed annually and are reported in the financial statements by increasing the appreciated asset's balance sheet value and by increasing a

> The use of annual asset revaluations in the U.K. and elsewhere reflects the commitment of standard-setters in these countries to the market-value model of accounting, in which all assets and liabilities are valued at their fair market value on the balance sheet.

---

[4] Dharam and Lev, (1993), loc. cit.

shareholders' equity account called the **asset revaluation reserve** for the amount of the appreciation in asset value. The asset revaluation reserve is analogous to the "Unrealized gain/loss on available-for-sale securities" account found under U.S. GAAP that will be discussed in Chapter 8. These accounts represent unrealized wealth changes for a business and are reported as part of shareholders' equity on the balance sheet of the business because the wealth change has not yet been realized.

SALE OR RETIREMENT OF LONG-LIVED ASSETS

When long-lived assets are first acquired, they are recorded at their acquisition cost following the historical cost convention. These assets are then depreciated over their expected useful lives in order to properly match the asset's acquisition cost with the revenue that the asset contributes to a business. When an asset is eventually sold or retired, it is necessary to remove the asset's remaining book value from the company's books. Any difference between the proceeds from the sale of an asset and the remaining book value of the asset is recorded as a gain if the proceeds exceed the book value or as a loss if the proceeds are less than the book value. To illustrate, assume that Savanna Corporation sells a truck and receives $15,000. Further, assume that the truck was originally purchased for $60,000 and has accumulated depreciation to date of $50,000. Since the proceeds of $15,000 exceed the asset's remaining book value of $10,000 ($60,000 − $50,000), Savanna will record a $5,000 gain on the sale. This is shown in spreadsheet format below. Observe that not only is the original cost of the asset removed from the balance sheet at the time of sale but so too is any accumulated depreciation related to the retired asset.

			Savanna Corporation Spreadsheet				
		Assets		=	**Liabilities**	+	**Equity**
	Cash	**Truck**	**Accumulated Depreciation**				**Retained Earnings**
Acquire asset	−60,000	60,000					
Depreciate asset.			−50,000				−50,000 (depreciation expense)
Sell asset	15,000	−60,000	50,000				5,000 (gain on sale)

DISTORTION CAUSED BY AGING ASSETS

Since the book value of a long-lived asset declines as the asset ages, a reduction in book value can cause a distortion in some financial ratios when they are compared across time for a given company. For example, if we assume that the productivity of an asset does not vary much during its early life, the return on assets (ROA) ratio will increase simply because the denominator of the ratio—total assets—decreases over time.

To illustrate, assume that Savanna Corporation purchases a single asset for $1,100,000 that is estimated to have a ten-year life and a salvage value of $100,000. Further assume that Savanna reports constant net income of $120,000 per year, including the annual $100,000 depreciation expense on its only asset. The return on assets ratio, defined as net income divided by ending total assets, will be 12 percent for the first year ($120,000/$1,000,000). After six years, however, the book value of the asset will have declined to $500,000 and Savanna's ROA will have climbed to 24 percent, twice as high as the first year. Recall that net income has remained constant and Savanna is still operating with the same asset. The doubling of Savanna's ROA is simply a function of the reduction in book value resulting from the annual depreciation charge on the asset. Results such as this can provide perverse incentives to managers, preventing them from making needed capital investments to replace their aging assets. The following table illustrates how the aging of long-lived assets can distort such important performance metrics as the ROA ratio:

	01/01/01	12/31/01	12/31/02	12/31/03	12/31/04	12/31/05	12/31/06
Book value	$1,100,000	$1,000,000	$900,000	$800,000	$700,000	$600,000	$500,000
Depreciation		100,000	100,000	100,000	100,000	100,000	100,000
Net income		120,000	120,000	120,000	120,000	120,000	120,000
ROA		12%	13.3%	15%	17.1%	20%	24%
Asset age (in years) . . .		1	2	3	4	5	6

INTANGIBLE ASSETS

Intangible assets refer to those long-lived revenue-producing assets that lack physical qualities. Examples include the intellectual property rights associated with copyrights and patents, goodwill associated with merger and acquisition transactions, and, under some circumstances, research and development costs and marketing costs.

Research and Development Costs, Patents, and Copyrights

The accounting treatment of research and development (R&D) costs is globally quite diverse. Under U.S. GAAP, all R & D is expensed when occurred. Under IASB accounting, however, research costs are expensed, whereas development costs may be capitalized when a commercially viable output is evident and market demand for the product is likely. Under Brazilian GAAP, on the other hand, all R&D is capitalized.

Exceptions to the general practice of expensing all R&D under U.S. GAAP exist in the computer software industry for subsequent generations of a software program (such as Microsoft Windows XP) and in the oil and gas industry for exploration and development costs. The cost of second and third generation software enhancements and natural resource exploration/development costs may be capitalized to corporate balance sheets.

The conservative treatment of R&D under U.S. GAAP causes several notable problems for public companies with active R&D programs. In the pharmaceutical industry, for example, although billions of dollars may be spent on the development of a new drug, almost none of the massive R&D expenditure associated with new drug discoveries is capitalized to pharmaceutical company balance sheets since most (if not all) of the costs have been previously expensed as R&D. However, when a drug company purchases the property rights to a new drug from another company, the cost of the purchased patent is capitalized to the acquirer's balance sheet and subsequently amortized over the drug's expected useful life, but in any case not in excess of the patent's remaining legal life. Amortization of copyrights, patents, and capitalized R&D universally follows the straight-line method.

BUSINESS PERSPECTIVE: INTANGIBLE ASSET DISCLOSURES

Presented below are the financial statement disclosures of the Bristol-Myers Squibb Company (BMS) for its intangible assets. Consistent with U.S. GAAP, BMS expenses its research and development costs, amounting to over $2.2 billion in 2002 and 2003, on its income statement (see bolded area in Panel A). As a consequence, the cost of any internally-developed pharmaceutical products does not appear on BMS' balance sheet. However, for those drug-related intangible assets purchased from other pharmaceutical or biotechnology companies, the cost of the acquired asset less any amortization taken to date is capitalized on BMS' balance sheet (see Panel B). BMS' footnotes also reveal that the company amortizes its intangible assets on a straight-line basis over their expected useful lives, ranging from three to 17 years. In short, BMS' investment in pharmaceutical assets is materially understated on its balance sheet as only those drug-related intangible assets purchased from other entities are reported on its balance sheet under U.S. GAAP.

Intangible Asset Disclosures: Bristol-Myers Squibb Company		
Panel A Consolidated Statement of Earnings		
Year Ended December 31 (in millions)	**2003**	**2002**
Net sales.	$20,894	$18,106
Cost of products sold.	7,592	6,532
Marketing, selling and administration	4,660	4,124
Advertising and product promotion	1,416	1,143
Research and development.	2,279	2,206
Acquired in-process research and development	—	169
Provision for restructuring and other items	26	14
Litigation charges, net	199	659
Gain on sales of businesses/product line	—	(30)
Asset impairment charge for investment in ImClone	—	379
Equity in net income from affiliates	(151)	(80)
Other expense, net.	179	229
Total expenses	16,200	15,345
Earnings from continuing operations before minority interest and income taxes	4,694	2,761
Provision for income taxes.	1,215	391
Minority interest, net of taxes.	373	303
Earnings from continuing operations	3,106	2,067
Discontinued operations		
Net earnings.	—	32
Net gain on disposal	—	38
Net earnings.	$ 3,106	$ 2,137

continued

Goodwill

The concept of goodwill may mean different things in different parts of the world. In France, for instance, goodwill may refer to a firm's positive corporate image as evidenced by how desirable the firm's products are perceived to be by consumers (a positive brand image). As a consequence, under French GAAP,

continued from previous page

BUSINESS PERSPECTIVE: INTANGIBLE ASSET DISCLOSURES

Panel B Footnotes Disclosures: Intangible Assets by Major Asset Class December 31 (in millions)	2003	2002
Patents/Trademarks	$ 253	$ 214
Licenses	248	554
Technology	1,783	1,783
	2,284	2,551
Less accumulated amortization	552	647
Net carrying amount	$1,732	$1,904

Amortization expense for other intangible assets (the majority of which is included in costs of products sold) for the years ended December 2003, 2002, and 2001 was $227 million, $269 million, and $116 million, respectively.

companies may capitalize internally-generated goodwill on the balance sheet as an asset, along with an increase in a parallel shareholders' equity account called the asset revaluation reserve. In the U.S. and most developed countries, however, goodwill only arises as a consequence of a merger or acquisition. When one corporate entity acquires a second corporate entity at a price exceeding the acquiree's fair market value of identifiable net assets, the excess of the purchase price over the acquiree's fair market value is capitalized to the acquiror's consolidated balance sheet as goodwill. (Negative goodwill arises when a firm acquires another corporate entity for less than the acquiree's reported book value. When negative goodwill occurs, it is frequently written off against the book value of the acquiree's long-lived assets, and consequently, is rarely seen on consolidated financial statements.)

Acquisition goodwill in the U.S. is not subject to amortization, but instead, is evaluated annually for any impairment or diminishment in value. In the event of an impairment, a reduction in the goodwill account is recorded along with an "impairment loss" on the income statement. For example, as a consequence of the terrorist attacks of September 11, 2001, AMR Corporation determined that its entire $1.4 billion of goodwill relating to prior acquisitions had been impaired. Consequently, in 2002, AMR recorded a one-time, non-cash goodwill impairment charge against net earnings of $988 million, net of tax benefits of $363 million, to write off all of the company's goodwill associated with prior acquisitions (such as TWA Airlines). We will have more to say about goodwill in Chapter 8.

The process to evaluate capitalized goodwill for value impairment under U.S. GAAP is a two-step procedure. In the first step, the amount of goodwill associated with each prior corporate acquisition is first identified. The current fair market value of the previously acquired corporate entity is then calculated and compared to the investor's book value of the acquired entity. In the event that the acquired entity's book value exceeds its current market value, preliminary evidence exists that a goodwill impairment has occurred. In the second step, the investor-company estimates the value of the goodwill associated with each prior acquisition as if the acquired entity were acquired at its current market value. Any goodwill is then written down if the new market value is less than the goodwill's book value. As a consequence of the two-step procedure followed under U.S. GAAP to evaluate the current value of goodwill, goodwill impairment write-downs are rare and are likely to occur only in those cases in which an acquisition was materially over-priced or when an extraordinary externality impacts a business (such as AMR and the terrorist attack of 2001).

Marketing Costs

As a general rule, all advertising and marketing costs are expensed when incurred under U.S. GAAP and the GAAP of most countries. This conservative treatment of these operating expenditures stems from an inability to determine whether an advertising campaign has been successful, and if so, an inability to predict when the resulting increase in product sales associated with the advertising will occur. Thus, lacking reliable information about "when" and "how much," U.S. GAAP and the GAAP of most countries recommends, but does not require, that advertising and marketing costs be expensed against operating revenue in the period in which the costs are incurred.

Occasionally, exceptions to this generally-accepted practice may arise. Consider, for example, the case of **HCI Direct Inc.** HCI was engaged in the direct mail and internet marketing, manufacturing and distribution of hosiery products in Canada, the United States, and the United Kingdom. HCI capitalized its cost of soliciting customers to its balance sheet as an asset called "deferred customer acquisition costs." (Note the similarity between the treatment of customer acquisition costs by HCI and American Online Inc., as discussed at the beginning of this chapter.) By year-end, 2000, HCI had deferred customer acquisition costs totaling $47.5 million on its balance sheet, representing approximately 34 percent of its total assets. Including HCI's marketing expenditures in its income statement as an operating expense would have caused the company to report a loss of $54.3 million. In 2002, HCI filed for bankruptcy. In essence, the capitalization of its marketing costs allowed HCI to maintain a façade of corporate viability until 2002.

NATURAL RESOURCES

Natural resources include such assets as standing timber, oil and gas reserves, iron ore, coal, and uranium mines. When these assets are purchased from other natural resource companies, they are reported on the balance sheet at their acquisition cost. Alternatively, when these assets are internally developed by a resource company, several valuation approaches are available: the **full cost method** and the **successful efforts method**. Under the full cost method, all costs associated with the exploration for, and development of, natural resource assets are capitalized to the natural resource account on the balance sheet. Under this method, even the costs of unsuccessful exploration activities are capitalized to the balance sheet under the philosophy that the identification of new natural resource reserves is a speculative activity involving some inherent failure. In contrast, under the successful efforts method, only the costs associated with successful exploration and development activity are capitalized to the balance sheet. The cost of any unsuccessful activity is immediately expensed against net income.

Both the full cost and the successful efforts methods are generally accepted, and thus, both are available for use by managers of natural resource companies. In practice, however, only small resource companies tend to use the full cost method, whereas larger companies tend to utilize the successful efforts method. Can you think of a reason why small firms would prefer to use the full cost method?[5]

---

[5] If you thought about the adverse effect on net income associated with the successful efforts method, you are correct. Small firms have difficulty raising exploration and development capital, and this fund-raising effort is made more difficult if the firm reports little or no earnings. The full cost method capitalizes all exploration and development costs, making it more likely that a small firm will be able to report positive earnings, thus increasing its chances of raising future exploration and development capital.

To illustrate the difference between these two approaches, consider the case of an energy company involved in the exploration and development of oil and gas wells. Assume that the energy company owns the rights to explore for oil and gas on a given site and anticipates drilling four exploratory wells at a cost of $1 million each. The company's exploration program yielded two successful wells and two unsuccessful (or "dry") wells. Under the full cost method, the entire $4 million spent on drilling the four exploratory wells would be capitalized to the company's balance sheet, whereas under the successful efforts method, only $2 million, representing the cost of the two successful wells, may be capitalized. The $2 million cost associated with the unsuccessful wells would be expensed on the income statement.

Depletion

Depletion refers to the allocation of the capitalized cost of a natural resource over its productive life. Unlike depreciation, there is only one generally accepted depletion approach, the units-of-production method. This method is procedurally similar to the units-of-production depreciation method used by some companies to depreciate their machinery and equipment. Under units-of-production depletion, the first step is to estimate the number of units—barrels of oil, tons of ore, or board feet of timber—likely to be produced by a well, mine, or tract of timber. Next, a depletion rate per unit is determined by dividing the capitalized resource cost by the asset's expected total output in barrels, tons, or board feet. For example, if the estimated number of tons of ore to be extracted from a mine is two million and the mine's original cost, less estimated residual value, is $10 million, the depletion rate per ton of extracted ore would be $5.00 ($10 million/2 million tons). If, during the first year of operations, 20,000 tons of ore are extracted, the depletion expense for the year would be $100,000, or $5.00 times 20,000 tons.

ANALYZING CAPITAL INVESTMENTS

The accrual basis of accounting is one of the principal constructs underlying the financial statements of all companies that are going concerns. For these companies, investment professionals, lenders, and shareholders expect to see recurring investments in new property, plant and equipment (P,P&E) and intangible assets. If these types of capital investments were not routinely observed, there would exist concern regarding the sustainability of a firm's cash flow and operating earnings. The amount of a company's capital investment is readily identifiable from the investing activities section of the statement of cash flow. These cash outflows are usually segmented by financial statement users into two categories—maintenance capital expenditures which are intended to maintain a business' existing productive capacity and incremental capital expenditures which are designed to increase a business' productive capacity. To help assess the relative amount of each type of capital investment, investment professionals usually estimate the amount of maintenance capital investment by the level of the current depreciation expense, although this estimation approach fails to consider the effect of inflation on the replacement cost of such long-lived assets. Any capital investment in excess of the current period depreciation expense is consequently assumed to represent incremental capital investment.

For firms which do not follow a policy of regularly replacing their long-lived, revenue-producing assets, investment professionals require an approach to estimate the relative age of a firm's depreciable assets, and consequently, to estimate how soon a significant cash outlay will be required to finance the replacement of these assets. In this situation, the ratio of accumulated depreciation divided by gross property, plant and equipment is a good indicator of the percentage of a firm's capital assets which have been consumed by operations to date. Subtracting the percentage of consumed capital assets from 100 percent yields the relative percentage of the assets' remaining productive life. Finally, multiplying the percentage of estimated remaining useful life times the average life expectancy of a firm's capital assets yields an estimate of the number years before a major capital asset refinancing will be required. Estimating the amount and timing of any major capital investments is important when estimating firm value. As we will see in Chapter 12, the calculation of firm value assumes regular capital asset replacement.

When conducting a due diligence review of the financial statement disclosures associated with a firm's capital investments, important issues to consider include not only the age of the existing capital investments, how soon the existing assets will need to be replaced, and whether a firm follows a program of regular asset replacement, but it should also include a consideration of the following questions:

- What depreciation accounting policy has the firm chosen to depreciate its capital assets (straight-line or double-declining balance) and is the method consistent with the industry standard? If not, what rationale does the firm offer for its use of the selected method?
- Has the company changed any of its depreciation or amortization policy components (such as the method of depreciation or amortization, the estimate of expected useful life, or the expected residual value), and if so, what explanation did the company offer for the policy change? Did the policy change bring the firm's accounting procedures more (or less) into compliance with the industry norm?
- For companies that engage in significant research and development expenditures (such as pharmaceutical and technology companies), does the company have any unreported capital investments in such intangible assets as patents and copyrights?
- Is the company capitalizing any expenditures that would more properly be accounted for as an operating expense, and if so, should the financial statements be restated for these amounts?
- Is the company taking regular capital investment write-downs as "restructuring costs," perhaps to lower the annual depreciation expense and positively impact firm value?
- Is the company capitalizing significant amounts of interest costs associated with the self-construction of capital assets? And if so, is a financial statement restatement appropriate to facilitate firm benchmarking?

The answers to most of the above questions provide financial statement users with evidence regarding the quality of a firm's earnings and assets—an important investigative topic when evaluating firm value. A firm which undertakes regular capital investment write-downs as a means to lower its recurring depreciation charge, or what has become known as "taking a bath," is generally considered by investment professionals to have a lower quality of earnings and assets than a firm which does not resort to such discretionary accounting (see the reference to the Eastman Kodak Company on page 3.19). Similarly, a company which does not inappropriately capitalize its operating expenses to the balance sheet as a capital investment is considered to have a higher quality of earnings and assets than a company that does (see the WorldCom Inc. Business Perspective on page 7.4). Where sufficient information exists regarding the financial statement impact of these discretionary accounting policy decisions—for example, the amount of capitalized interest is reported in the footnotes to the financial statements—it is possible for financial statement users to undertake a financial restatement to compensate for any questionable accounting policy decisions. Otherwise, financial statement users will need to consider alternative approaches to account for these risks when developing an assessment of firm value (such as by increasing the discount rate used to discount a firm's future operating cash flows).

ETHICS PERSPECTIVE

Publicly-listed companies are under constant pressure to meet the earnings' expectations of Wall Street analysts. It has been argued that this pressure induces some managers to focus too much attention on short-term corporate profitability. Many accounting policy choices can be made to enhance short-term profits at the expense of future profits. One such choice is the estimate of an asset's expected useful life. The longer the estimated useful life, the lower the current year depreciation, and hence, the higher current year profits will be. A longer estimated useful life, however, also means that the total depreciable cost of the asset will be spread over a greater number of years, thereby increasing future profits as well. Given the significant impact of this and other accounting estimates on reported corporate earnings, an integral part of the annual audit process for a firm involves a review of these estimates by a firm's independent auditor.

REVIEW PROBLEM

The Arcadia Company is contemplating a large capital investment of $32 million in new production-line equipment which is expected to have a useful life of six years and a residual value of $2 million at retirement. The company's controller is uncertain whether the equipment should be depreciated using the straight-line method or the double-declining balance method. The CEO suggested that a decision be made only after comparing the financial effects of the two methods.

Required

a. Prepare a depreciation schedule for The Arcadia Company for the new equipment assuming (1) use of the straight-line method and (2) use of the double-declining balance method.

b. The Arcadia Company expected net income, exclusive of depreciation expense, to be $6 million each year for the next six years. Which depreciation method would you recommend to the CEO? Why?

Solution

a. Depreciation schedule

	Straight-Line Method	Double-Declining Balance Method
Year 1	$ 5,000,000	$10,665,600
Year 2	5,000,000	7,110,756
Year 3	5,000,000	4,740,741
Year 4	5,000,000	3,160,652
Year 5	5,000,000	2,161,126
Year 6	5,000,000	2,161,126
Total	$30,000,000	$30,000,000
Book value	$ 2,000,000	$ 2,000,000

b. If The Arcadia Company earns net income, exclusive of depreciation expense, of $6 million per year, its net income after depreciation expense but before income taxes would be as follows:

	Straight-Line Method	Double-Declining Balance Method
Year 1	$1,000,000	$(4,665,600)
Year 2	1,000,000	(1,110,756)
Year 3	1,000,000	1,259,259
Year 4	1,000,000	2,839,348
Year 5	1,000,000	3,838,874
Year 6	1,000,000	3,838,873
Total	$6,000,000	$ 6,000,000

The analysis reveals that The Arcadia Company will report substantial losses in Years 1 and 2 under the double-declining balance method, turning profitable in Year 3 and thereafter, effectively rear-end loading the firm's profitability into Year 3 through Year 6. The straight-line method, however, enables the company to report a smooth earnings stream throughout the six year period. Although there are certain income tax advantages associated with rear-end loading its taxable income, the CEO is likely to prefer the stable earnings under the straight-line method for the company's financial reports to shareholders.

EXECUTIVE SUMMARY

This chapter investigated the accounting for long-lived fixed, intangible, and natural resource assets. Various depreciation methods used to match the cost of these long-lived assets with the operating revenue they produce were explored: straight-line, double-declining balance, and units-of-production. In addition, the issues of amortization of intangible assets and depletion of natural resources were examined. Finally, the accounting for asset sales, asset impairments and asset revaluations were also investigated.

As a validation of your understanding of the content of this chapter, you should now be able to:

- Explain how the acquisition cost of a long-lived asset is determined.
- Explain why the matching of depreciation, depletion, and amortization expense with operating revenue is important.
- Explain how depreciation is calculated using the straight-line method, the units-of-production method, and the double-declining balance method.
- Explain what an asset impairment is and how such impairments are reflected in corporate financial statements.

In the next chapter, the accounting for intercorporate investments is considered, to include the equity method and consolidation accounting.

KEY CONCEPTS AND TERMS

Accelerated method, 7.6
Accounting policy change, 7.10
Accumulated depreciation, 7.6
Acquisition cost, 7.3
Amortization, 7.4

Asset revaluation reserve, 7.14
Betterment expenditure, 7.3
Book value, 7.6
Capitalize, 7.3
Capitalized interest, 7.3

Conservatism, 7.13
Cumulative prior period effect of an
  accounting policy change, 7.12
Depletion, 7.4
Depreciable cost, 7.6

APPENDIX 7A: Recording Investments in, and Sales of, Long-Lived Assets using the Debit and Credit Paradigm

In this appendix, the traditional approach to recording accounting transactions—that is, the debit and credit paradigm—is used to illustrate the journal entries for the acquisition, depreciation, and retirement of long-lived assets. Data for the current illustration follows the example in the chapter and assumes the use of straight-line depreciation:

A truck having an expected useful life of five years and a resale value of $4,000 upon retirement is purchased for $30,000 cash at the beginning of the year (BOY). At the end of the five year period, the truck is sold for $4,500. Note: End of the year is represented by (EOY).

Illustrative Journal Entries

Date	Accounts	Debit	Credit
Year 1 (BOY)	Truck (A) . . . . Cash (A) . . . . *To record the cash purchase of an asset.*	30,000	30,000
Year 1 (EOY)	Retained Earnings (E) . . . . Accumulated Depreciation (CA) . . . . *To record the annual depreciation expense on the truck.*	5,200	5,200
Year 2 (EOY)	Retained Earnings (E) . . . . Accumulated Depreciation (CA) . . . . *To record the annual depreciation expense on the truck.*	5,200	5,200
Year 3 (EOY)	Retained Earnings (E) . . . . Accumulated Depreciation (CA) . . . . *To record the annual depreciation expense on the truck.*	5,200	5,200
Year 4 (EOY)	Retained Earnings (E) . . . . Accumulated Depreciation (CA) . . . . *To record the annual depreciation expense on the truck.*	5,200	5,200
Year 5 (EOY)	Retained Earnings (E) . . . . Accumulated Depreciation (CA) . . . . *To record the annual depreciation expense on the truck.*	5,200	5,200

continued

continued from previous page

Date	Accounts	Debit	Credit
Year 5 (EOY)	Cash (A) . . . . Accumulated Depreciation (CA). . . . . Retained Earnings (G) . . . . Truck (A). . . . . *To record the sale of the truck for $4,500, the gain (G) on sale of $500, and the removal of the truck and related accumulated depreciation from the financial records.*	4,500 26,000	500 30,000

DISCUSSION QUESTIONS

Q7.1 **Brand Names.** **Williams-Sonoma, Inc.** is a specialty retailer of products for the home. The retail segment of the company's business sells products through its four retail concepts: Williams-Sonoma, Pottery Barn, Pottery Barn Kids, and Hold Everything. The direct-to-customer segment sells similar products through its six direct-mail catalogs (Williams-Sonoma, Pottery Barn, Pottery Barn Kids, Pottery Barn Bed + Bath, Hold Everything, and Chambers) and three e-commerce websites. Williams-Sonoma stores offer a wide selection of culinary and serving equipment, including cookware, cookbooks, cutlery, informal dinnerware, glassware, and table linens. In addition, these stores carry a variety of quality foods, including a line of Williams-Sonoma food products, such as gourmet coffees and pasta sauces. The Williams-Sonoma brand name is well known in the U.S. Discuss why the company doesn't report its brand name as an asset on its balance sheet. Is the company's brand name reflected anywhere in its financial statements?

Q7.2 **Depreciation, Depletion and Amortization: The Matching Concept.** Depreciation, depletion, and amortization are allocation processes that distribute the acquisition cost of an asset to the many periods of the asset's expected useful life. Discuss how these processes reflect the matching principle and why they are important to the measurement of corporate profitability.

Q7.3 **Advertising Costs: Capitalize or Expense?** The **Johnson and Johnson Company** discloses in its annual report that "costs associated with advertising are expensed in the year incurred and are included in selling, marketing and administrative expenses" on the income statement. Discuss why the expensing of advertising costs is considered to be "best practice." Can an argument be made that advertising costs should be capitalized?

Q7.4 **Revaluation of Long-lived Assets.** The Thunderbird Corporation was founded in 1947 on a decommissioned military installation that had been purchased from the U.S. government for a price of $1. Today, that same land carries a fair market value of $70 million. Consistent with the historical cost principle, The Thunderbird Corporation continues to value the land at its original purchase price of $1 plus the cost of any improvements (such as roadways, lights, and drainage). Discuss the financial statement problems created by the historical cost principle for entities like The Thunderbird Corporation that have significant investments in long-lived appreciating assets (such as land). Should these companies be allowed to revalue these assets? Why? How would a land revaluation be reflected in the financial statements?

Q7.5 **Capitalization of Interest Costs and Earnings Quality.** Under U.S. GAAP, a company may capitalize any interest costs associated with borrowings used in the self-construction of a business asset. Any capitalized interest is added to the cost basis of the asset and then depreciated over the expected useful life of the asset. Some investment professionals question the appropriateness of interest capitalization, observing that the interest costs associated with general corporate borrowings are expensed when paid and are not capitalized. These professionals allege that interest capitalization is a form of rear-end loading of expenses, and when material in amount, draws into question the quality of a firm's reported earnings. Discuss the validity of these arguments.

Q7.6 **Changing Depreciation Methods.** The **Tomoegawa Paper Company Ltd.** (TPC) is a well-known public company headquartered in Tokyo, Japan. In TPC's 2005 annual report, the company revealed that it had changed its method of depreciating its fixed assets from the straight-line method to the declining-balance method. Discuss the various financial effects of this accounting policy change on TPC's 2005 financial statements. Why do you think the company made this voluntary accounting policy change?

Q7.7 **Changing the Estimated Useful Life of a Long-lived Asset.** McCormick & Company revealed in its 2004 annual report that it had changed the estimated useful life of certain capitalized software costs from five to eight years. Discuss the effect of this accounting policy change on the company's 2004 financial statements. How would you expect the capital markets to react to this voluntary accounting policy change?

Q7.8 **Exploration and Development Costs in the Natural Resource Industry.** Under U.S. GAAP, research and development costs are expensed as incurred; however, in the natural resource industry, the cost of finding and developing natural resources may be capitalized to the balance sheet under the full cost and successful efforts methods. Are these methods inconsistent with the general treatment of research and development costs under U.S. GAAP? If so, why? What explanation can you offer for this inconsistency in accounting treatment of similar outlays under U.S. GAAP?

Q7.9 **Asset Impairments.** Under U.S. GAAP, an asset which is "impaired" should be written down in value, with an equivalent loss taken on the income statement. Discuss how you would determine whether an asset's value was impaired or not.

Q7.10 **Capitalized Interest and Cash Flow.** Under U.S. GAAP, the interest cost associated with borrowings used in the self-construction of a business asset may be capitalized to the balance sheet as part of the self-constructed asset's cost basis. As a consequence, the cash outflow for capitalized interest are reported as part of the cash flow from investing on the statement of cash flow. The interest cost associated with general corporate borrowings, however, is reported on the income statement, and thus, as part of the cash flow from operations. Discuss whether the practice of interest capitalization misstates a company's cash flow from operations.

Q7.11 **Depreciation, Depletion, Amortization and Cash Flow.** Users of financial statements often describe depreciation expense, depletion expense, and amortization expense as "sources of operating cash flows." Discuss the accuracy of this assertion.

Q7.12 **R & D Failure and Share Prices.** On December 2, 2006, Pfizer Inc. announced that it was immediately discontinuing clinical trials of its Torcetrapib drug. Recent clinical results showed that patients taking the drug suffered a higher incident of heart attacks than patients taking a placebo. Pfizer reported that it had spent over $1 billion on the development of the drug, which had been expected to be a "blockbuster" for the pharmaceutical company. Pfizer's share price fell 11percent, or nearly $2.90 per share, following the announcement. Discuss the financial statement impact of the announcement to discontinue clinical trials for Torcetrapib. Discuss why Pfizer's share price declined by 11 percent following the announcement. Discuss the impact of this decision on Pfizer's financial statements.

Q7.13 **(Ethics Perspective) Depreciation Policy Choices to Manage Short-term Profits.** Do you feel that there are any ethical issues involved when management decides to extend the depreciable life of its long-lived assets in order to increase the firm's current net income to a level that meets analysts' expectations?

⊘ **indicates that check figures are available on the book's Website.**

EXERCISES

⊘ E7.14 **Determining the Cost of an Asset.** Omar Corporation paid $200,000 for a tract of land that had an old gas station on it. The gas station was demolished at a cost of $20,000 and a new warehouse was constructed on the site at a cost of $550,000. In addition, several other costs were incurred:

Legal fees (associated with the purchase of the land)	$35,000
Architect fees (associated with the new warehouse)	42,000
Interest on the construction loan (for the new warehouse)	18,000

What value should be assigned to (a) the tract of land and (b) the new warehouse? Why?

E7.15 **Determining the Cost of an Asset.** Keystone, Inc. replaced its truck-and-dolley system of moving inventory around its plant with a computer-controlled conveyor system. The costs associated with this equipment replacement were as follows:

Purchase price of conveyor system	$1,200,000
Book value of truck-and-dolley system	40,000
Installation cost of new conveyor system	75,000

The truck-and-dolley system was sold for scrap for $60,000. What value should be capitalized to the balance sheet of Keystone, Inc. as the cost basis of the new conveyor system? Why?

E7.16 **Calculating Repair and Maintenance Expense.** The Camelback Cement Company made the following expenditures relating to its plant and equipment:

* Overhauled several machines at an aggregate cost of $175,000 to improve the efficiency of the equipment over its remaining useful life.
* Replaced a broken drive-shaft on a forklift at a cost of $30,000.
* Completed regularly scheduled repairs at a cost of $75,000.
* Installed a foam roof on the plant over the existing-but-leaking flat-rolled roof at a cost of $200,000.

What amount should be expensed as repairs and maintenance? Why?

E7.17 **Computing Depreciation Expense.** Equipment costing $290,000, with an expected scrap value of $30,000 and an estimated useful life of five years, was purchased on January 1, 2006. Calculate the depreciation expense for years 2006 to 2010 using (a) the straight-line method and (b) the double-declining balance method. Which method would you prefer to use for (a) income tax purposes and (b) financial reporting purposes? Why?

E7.18 **Full Cost versus Successful Efforts Method.** During 2006, The Alberta Oil & Gas Company began an exploration project in Montana. The company had paid $500,000 for the drilling rights on a tract of 500 acres of land. The company then spent another $40,000 building roads and containment ponds. The project called for eight exploratory wells to be drilled at an expected cost of $100,000 per well. The first six wells drilled were found to be "dry" (lacking commercially viable quantities of oil or gas); however, both the seventh and eighth wells drilled contained commercially-viable quantities of oil condensate. Consequently, two additional development wells were drilled at a cost of $120,000 per well. Calculate the capitalized cost of Alberta's oil reserves under (a) the full cost method and (b) the successful efforts method.

E7.19 **Calculating Accelerated Depreciation.** Equipment costing $640,000, with an expected useful life of twelve years and an expected salvage value of $20,000, was purchased on January 1, 2006. Calculate the depreciation expense for the first five years (2006 to 2010) using (a) the sum-of-the-years' digits method and (b) the double-declining balance method. Which method would you prefer to use for (a) income tax purposes and (b) financial reporting purposes? Why?

E7.20 **Calculating Units-of-Production Depreciation.** Swift Trucking Company purchased a long-haul tractor-trailer for $400,000 on March 1, 2006. The expected useful life of the tractor-trailer rig was eight years or 500,000 miles. Salvage value was estimated to be $40,000. During the first five years of use, the rig logged the following usage in miles:

2006	80,000 miles
2007	75,000 miles
2008	80,000 miles
2009	76,000 miles
2010	60,000 miles
Total	371,000 miles

Calculate the depreciation expense to be taken on the tractor-trailer for each year (2006 through 2010) using (a) the units-of-production method and (b) the straight-line method. Which method gives you the highest total depreciation charges over the five-year period?

E7.21   **Analyzing Non-Current Asset Disclosures.**   The following are financial data taken from the 2005 annual report of **The Johnson and Johnson (J & J) Company:**

(amounts in millions)	2005	2004
Net sales.	$50,514	$47,348
Gross property, plant and equipment.	19,716	18,664
Accumulated depreciation	8,886	8,228
Intangible assets (net).	6,185	5,979

Calculate the following ratios for 2004 and 2005: intangible asset turnover, fixed asset turnover, accumulated depreciation divided by gross fixed assets. What do the trends in these ratios reveal about J & J?

⊘ E7.22   **Analyzing Non-Current Asset Disclosures.**   The following are financial data taken from the 2005 annual report of **Pfizer, Inc:**

(amounts in millions)	2005	2006
Net sales.	$51,298	$52,516
Gross property, plant and equipment.	26,617	26,919
Accumulated depreciation	(9,527)	(8,534)
Intangible assets (net).	27,786	33,251

Calculate the following ratios for 2005 and 2006: intangible asset turnover, fixed asset turnover, accumulated depreciation divided by gross fixed assets. What do the trends in these ratios reveal about Pfizer?

E7.23   **Calculating the Depletion Expense.**   Herberger Oil & Gas Company paid $10 million for the drilling rights to a 1,000 acre tract of land near Midland, Texas. On the basis of several exploratory wells that had cost an aggregate of $400,000 to drill, petroleum engineers estimated that the tract of land might contain as much as 500,000 barrels of oil. Four additional development wells were drilled at a cost of approximately $200,000 each. Calculate the depletion expense for the first year assuming that 100,000 barrels are extracted. Calculate the depletion expense for the second year assuming that 150,000 barrels are extracted. What is the cost basis of the remaining reserves at the end of the second year?

E7.24   **Intangible Assets.**   During 2005, Intelligencia Inc. was incorporated as a research and development company in the biotechnology industry. The company incurred the following costs relating to various intangible assets:

1.   The company incurred $125,000 in organization costs associated with its incorporation.
2.   During 2005, the company completed work on a research project and filed for a patent. The research work had cost $450,000 and the patent filing cost $30,000.
3.   Shortly after receiving the patent, it was challenged in court by another biotechnology company. Intelligencia won the case, protecting its patent, but incurred legal fees of $200,000.
4.   The company purchased a patent from another biotechnology company for $700,000. Unfortunately, this patent was also challenged in court and Intelligencia lost the case, incurring legal fees of $175,000.

Should the above costs be capitalized to the balance sheet as an intangible asset or expensed on the income statement in 2005? Why or why not?

⊘ **E7.25** **Changing the Estimated Life of a Depreciable Asset.** On January 1, 2006, The Claremont Company purchased a 100-ton press for $750,000. The equipment had an estimated useful life of ten years and a salvage value of $30,000. The company decided to depreciate this equipment using the straight-line method. After eight years of trouble-free use, The Claremont Company concluded that it would be able to utilize the equipment for up to a total of 14 years; and consequently, at the end of year eight, changed its estimate of the equipment's expected life to 14 years, adding four more years to the asset's remaining useful life. Calculate the depreciation expense on the equipment in years eight and nine.

PROBLEMS

P7.26 **Calculating Depreciation.** The Miller Company purchased a new headquarters building on January 1 at a cost of $40 million. The building is expected to last 20 years, at which time its residual value is expected to be $5 million.

Required

Calculate the depreciation expense for each of the first three years on the new headquarters building using each of the following methods:

1. Straight-line
2. Double-declining balance

P7.27 **Calculating Depreciation.** The Amphlett Corporation started business with the following long-lived assets:

- 20,000 square foot office building purchased for $1 million, having an expected life of 20 years and a residual value of $100,000.
- 20 personal computers costing $1,000 each, with an expected useful life of four years and no salvage value.
- Four automobiles costing $18,000 each, with an expected useful life of six years and a salvage value of $2,000 each.
- Miscellaneous office furniture costing $20,000, with an expected useful life of ten years and no expected salvage value.

Required

Calculate the depreciation expense for each of the above long-lived assets in years one and two, using each of the following methods:

1. Straight-line
2. Double-declining balance

P7.28 **Capitalize versus Expense.** On September 1, 2003, *The Financial Times* reported that China Unicom, a leading Chinese telecom company, had capitalized to its balance sheet the cost of customer handset subsidies (the difference between the cost of the handset and the price charged to retain customers). Observers suggested that the subsidies should have been charged against income at the time the customer purchased the handset rather than capitalized to the company's balance sheet.

Required

If China Unicom switched from capitalizing and amortizing handset subsidies to immediately expensing them (for reporting to shareholders only), indicate how the following financial statement items would be affected:

1. Operating expenses   4. Liabilities
2. Assets   5. Operating revenue
3. Cash flow from operations

P7.29   **Intangible Assets.**   Global Music Enterprises, Inc. had a balance sheet loaded with intangible assets—copyrights on music, goodwill from various prior acquisitions, and internet customer lists purchased from other online music retailers. During 2005, several accounting policy decisions were required regarding various intangible asset-related expenditures.

Required
What accounting policy should be adopted for the following expenditures? Why?

1. Legal fees incurred while successfully defending a copyrighted song.
2. Advertising costs intended to create customer goodwill.
3. Purchase of online customer lists from Amazon.com.
4. Legal fees incurred to successfully defend Global's CEO from a sexual harassment lawsuit.
5. Legal fees incurred to unsuccessfully defend a copyrighted song and lyrics.

P7.30   **Betterment versus Maintenance Expenditures.**   During 2006, Graham International made the following expenditures relating to plant, machinery, and equipment:

- Completed regularly scheduled repairs at a cost of $250,000.
- Overhauled several stamping machines at a cost of $500,000 to improve production efficiency.
- Replaced a broken cooling pump on a 100-ton press at a cost of $25,000.

Required
Identify which expenditures should be expensed as a maintenance expense or capitalized as a betterment outlay.

⊘ P7.31   **Depletion Expense.**   In 2005, Ottawa Oil Corporation paid $40 million for a partial interest in a Canadian oil field with proven reserves. The company's share of the future production was capped at eight million barrels.

Required

1. Assuming that the oil field attains its expected future output, calculate Ottawa's depletion charge per barrel.
2. If in 2006, Ottawa's share of the field's total production amounts to two million barrels, what is the firm's depletion expense for 2006?
3. Go to the following Internet website www.ips.gov and locate Publication 535 "Business Expenses." Section 10 of this publication is entitled "Depletion." Read this section to determine how oil and gas companies in the U.S. calculate their depletion expense for U.S. income tax purposes. How does this tax practice compare to U.S. GAAP?

P7.32   **Estimating Depreciation Expense and Book Value.**   Equipment costing $29,000, with a scrap value of $5,000 was purchased on January 1, 2005 by Global Communications, Inc. The estimated useful life of the equipment was four years and it was expected to generate 80,000 finished units of production. Units actually produced were 14,000 in 2005 and 20,000 in 2006.

Required
Complete the following table.

	Depreciation Expense		Net Book Value	
Depreciation Method	**2005**	**2006**	**12/31/05**	**12/31/06**
Straight-line				
Double-declining balance.				
Units-of-production				

P7.33 **Successful Efforts versus Full Cost Method.** **Barrett Oil and Gas Company** was about to embark on a 50 well exploration program in Texas and Louisiana. The CEO estimated that the average cost to drill a well would run $800,000 per well, with a resulting success ratio of 60 percent (30 wells were expected to yield commercially viable quantities of oil while 20 wells were expected to be commercially unproductive). In aggregate, the CEO estimated that the 30 successful wells would yield ten million barrels of oil, to be extracted at the following rates.

| | | Estimated Per Barrel | |
| | | | |
Year	Production (in barrels)	Selling Price	Lifting Cost
2005	1,000,000	$30	$5
2006	1,500,000	30	5
2007	1,500,000	35	6
2008	2,500,000	40	7
2009	3,500,000	45	8
	10,000,000		

The CEO of Barrett Oil and Gas Company was concerned about how the accounting for the exploration project would affect the firm's overall reported results.

Required
Assume that this is the company's only exploration project. Prepare the firm's income statements and balance sheets for 2005 through 2009 assuming the use of:

1. The full cost method
2. The successful efforts method

P7.34 **Impairment of Long-Lived Assets: Goodwill.** **Titanium Metals Corporation (TIMET)** is one of the world's leading producers of titanium sponge and titanium melted and mill products, used principally in the manufacture of commercial and military aircraft. The economic slowdown in the United States and other regions of the world in the latter part of 2001 and the September 11, 2001, terrorist attacks combined to negatively impact commercial air travel in the U.S. and abroad throughout 2002. These factors caused TIMET's sales to decline approximately 25 percent from 2001 to 2002, and its net loss to increase from $42 million to over $111 million, respectively.

In addition, the company adopted SFAS No. 142, "Goodwill and Other Intangible Assets," on January 1, 2002. Under SFAS No. 142, goodwill is subject to a two-step impairment test performed annually. According to TIMET's 2002 annual report:

> The company determined that the implied value of its recorded goodwill was zero. Accordingly, the company recorded a non-cash goodwill impairment charge of $44.3 million, representing the entire balance of the company's recorded goodwill at January 1, 2002.

Required

1. What are the financial effects on TIMET's financial statements (income statement, balance sheet, statement of cash flow) associated with its goodwill impairment write-off?
2. TIMET has substantial borrowings secured by its U.S. assets. Under these credit agreements, the company is subject to a number of debt covenants. How would the goodwill impairment and related write-off affect the company's ability to meet its debt covenants?

P7.35 **Accounting for Goodwill: International.** Presented below is the 2001 consolidated balance sheet of **Kingfisher Plc.** Kingfisher is a world-wide retailer headquartered in the United Kingdom. During 2001, Kingfisher made a number of acquisitions resulting in the creation of £266.8 million of goodwill. According to the company's annual report, acquisition goodwill is capitalized to the balance sheet and annually reviewed for any impairment in value. During 2001, the company wrote down the value of its goodwill by £2.3 million due to an impairment in its value.

Kingfisher Plc **Consolidated Balance Sheet**		
(£ millions)		**2001**
Fixed assets		
Goodwill		264.5
Other intangible assets.		2.8
Total intangible assets		267.3
Tangible assets.		2,885.4
Investments in joint ventures		
Share of gross assets	105.1	
Share of gross liabilities.	(94.9)	10.2
Investments in associates		11.2
Other investments		45.0
Total investments		66.4
		3,219.1
Current assets		
Development work in progress.		69.0
Stocks		1,465.4
Debtors due within one year		608.8
Debtors due after more than one year		144.1
Securitised consumer receivables	321.0	
Less: non-recourse secured notes.	(247.4)	73.6
Investments		311.7
Cash at bank and in hand		241.2
		2,913.8
Creditors		
Amounts falling due within one year		(2,726.0)
Net current assets		187.8
Total assets less current liabilities		3,406.9
Creditors		
Amounts falling due after more than one year		(768.8)
Provisions for liabilities and charges		(21.8)
		2,616.3
Capital and reserves		
Called up share capital.		170.0
Shares premium account		237.7
Revaluation reserve		395.4
Non-distributable reserves.		146.3
Profit and loss account.		1,301.2
Equity shareholders' funds		2,250.6
Equity minority interests.		365.7
		2,616.3

Required

1. Assume that Kingfisher amortized its acquisition goodwill over 20 years instead of its current accounting treatment. How would the company's 2001 financial statement data change?
2. Consider the following three alternative methods to account for goodwill:
   - *a.* Capitalize goodwill to the balance sheet and annually review for an impairment in value.
   - *b.* Capitalize goodwill to the balance sheet and annually amortize over its expected life.
   - *c.* Write off goodwill against shareholders' equity.

   As a manager of a publicly-held company, which method would you prefer? Why?

P7.36 **Intangible Assets: Customer Acquisition Costs.** YP.Net, Inc. is in the business of providing Internet-based yellow page advertising space on www.Yellow-Page.Net and www.YP.Net. The company's website enables internet users to search through these "yellow page" listings and is used by businesses and consumers attempting to locate a business and/or service provider in response to a user's specific search criteria. The company's primary source of revenue is its offer of "preferred" listings to businesses for a monthly fee (currently $17.95). As of September 30, 2002, the company had approximately 106,439 "preferred" listing advertisers who had subscribed to this enhanced advertising service.

Customer Acquisition Costs represent the direct response marketing costs that are incurred as the primary method by which customers subscribe to the company's services. The company capitalizes and amortizes the costs of direct-response advertising on a straight-line basis over eighteen months, the estimated average period of retention for new customers.

Selected information from YP.Net, Inc.'s 2002 10-K report is presented below:

YP Net Inc. Consolidated Balance Sheet	
	09/30/02
Customer acquisition costs, net.	$ 1,418,227
Total assets.	10,561,638
Retained earnings	4,965,309
Total stockholders' equity	$ 9,135,832

YP Net Inc. Consolidated Statements of Income		
For Period Ended	9/30/02	9/30/01
Net revenues	$13,232,743	$15,084,917
Income before income taxes	3,450,489	3,042,728
Net income.	3,696,463	1,812,281

YP Net Inc. Consolidated Statements of Cash Flow		
For Period Ended	09/30/02	09/30/01
Net income.	$3,696,463	$1,812,281
Adjustments to reconcile net income to net cash provided by operating activities.		
Depreciation and amortization.	581,290	603,426
Changes in assets and liabilities:		
Customer acquisition costs	(1,224,983)	37,654

Required

1. How much would YP.Net's total assets be at September 30, 2002, if the company had always expensed its customer acquisition costs?
2. If YP.Net had always expensed its customer acquisition costs (for shareholder reporting purposes only), would its cash flow from operations in 2002 be higher, the same, or lower? Why?
3. What would YP.Net's income before income taxes be in 2002 if the company had always expensed its customer acquisition costs (for shareholder reporting purposes only)?
4. Estimate the amount of customer acquisition costs, net of amortization, on YP.Net's balance sheet at September 30, 2001.
5. What accounting arguments might the company provide to justify its current policy of capitalizing its customer acquisition outlays?

P7.37 **Intangible Assets: Deferred Subscriber Acquisition Costs.** Muzak LLC is the leading provider of business music programming in the United States. Together with its franchisees, it has a market share of approximately 60 percent of the U.S. business locations currently subscribing to business music programming. The company provides products to numerous types of businesses including specialty retailers, restaurants, department stores, supermarkets, drug stores, financial institutions, hotels, health and fitness centers, business offices, manufacturing facilities, and medical centers, among others. Clients typically enter into a non-cancelable five year contract that renews automatically for at least one additional five-year term unless specifically terminated at the initial contract expiration date. The average length of service for a client is approximately twelve years.

The company reports that direct sales commissions incurred in connection with acquiring new customers are capitalized to the balance sheet as **deferred subscriber acquisition costs** and are then amortized on a straight-line basis over the life of the client contract or five years, whichever is shorter.

Selected information from Muzak's 2002 annual report is presented below:

Muzak LLC Consolidated Balance Sheet—selected items		
In thousands	12/31/02	12/31/01
Deferred subscriber acquisition costs, net...................	$ 41,410	$ 37,442
Total assets......................................	474,195	495,942

Muzak LLC Consolidated Statements of Income—selected items			
In thousands for period ended	12/31/02	12/31/01	12/31/00
Revenues.....................................	—	—	—
Music and other business services	$162,999	$150,472	$138,167
Equipment and related services..................	54,757	52,889	53,981
	217,756	203,361	192,148
Loss before income taxes and extraordinary item.....	(30,985)	(44,741)	(44,020)
Income tax benefit	(956)	(595)	(1,082)
Loss from operations before extraordinary item	(30,029)	(44,146)	(42,938)
Extraordinary loss.............................	—	—	(1,418)
Net loss	$ (30,029)	$ (44,146)	$ (44,356)

Muzak LLC			
Consolidated Statements of Cash Flow—selected items			
In thousands for period ended	**12/31/02**	**12/31/01**	**12/31/00**
Cash flows from operating activities	—	—	—
Net loss	$(30,029)	$(44,146)	$(44,356)
Amortization of deferred subscriber acquisition costs. .	12,387	9,516	5,786
Deferred subscriber acquisition costs	(16,355)	(16,404)	(18,371)
Net cash provided by (used in) operating activities	$ 31,589	$ 38,035	$ (3,456)

Required

1. How much did Muzak record as the expenditure of cash for deferred subscriber acquisition costs in 2002?
2. How much would the company's total assets be at December 31, 2002, if the company had always expensed its subscriber acquisition costs?
3. If Muzak had always expensed its expenditures for subscriber acquisition costs in its financial statements to shareholders, would the cash flow from operations be higher, the same, or lower? Why?
4. What would the company's loss before income taxes be in 2002 if Muzak had always expensed its expenditures for subscriber acquisition costs?
5. Estimate the amount of total deferred subscriber acquisition costs, net of amortization, on Muzak's balance sheet at December 31, 2000.

P7.38 **Intangible Assets: Deferred Customer Acquisition Costs.** HCI Direct, Inc. is engaged in the direct mail and Internet marketing, manufacturing and distribution of hosiery products to consumers throughout North America and the United Kingdom. The company markets women's sheer hosiery through a continuous product shipment or "continuity" program. The company's continuity program involves promoting to customers a free offer or a specially priced introductory hosiery offer, the acceptance of which enrolls customers in the program and results in additional shipments of hose on a regular and continuous basis upon payment of a prior shipment.

Deferred customer acquisition costs consist of marketing costs associated with the initial shipment to a customer and similar costs associated with the re-solicitation of previously canceled customers. These costs are capitalized and amortized on an accelerated basis based upon the estimated current year revenue in proportion to the expected future revenue generated by these customers. Approximately 58 percent of these costs are amortized in the first twelve months, 71 percent within 18 months, and 80 percent within 24 months.

Selected information from HCI Direct Inc.'s 2000 annual report is presented below:

HCI Direct, Inc.		
Abbreviated Consolidated Balance Sheet		
In thousands	**12/31/00**	**12/31/99**
Deferred customer acquisition costs	$ 47,447	$ 56,203
Total assets.	142,262	155,612
Retained earnings (accumulated deficit)	(127,355)	(122,722)

Abbreviated Consolidated Statements of Income			
In thousands for period ended	**12/31/00**	**12/31/99**	**12/31/98**
Net revenues	$230,626	$259,881	$198,681
Operating income.	10,985	39,890	38,080
(Loss) Income before (benefit) provision for income taxes.	(6,784)	20,990	21,519
Net (loss) income	(4,633)	12,228	13,464

Abbreviated Consolidated Statements of Cash Flow			
In thousands for period ended	12/31/00	12/31/99	12/31/98
Operating activities.	—	—	—
Net (loss) income	$(4,633)	$12,228	$13,464
Adjustments to reconcile net income to net cash			
provided by operating activities.	—	—	—
Depreciation and amortization.	3,814	3,599	3,405
Amortization of deferred customer acquisition costs	56,220	45,376	32,134
(Increase) decrease in operating assets	—	—	—
Accounts receivable	6,734	(17,411)	(7,596)
Payments for deferred customer acquisition costs.	(47,464)	(59,306)	(47,188)

Required

1. How much did HCI spend on deferred customer acquisition costs in 2000?
2. What would income before the provision for income taxes be in 2000 if HCI had always expensed its expenditures for customer acquisition costs?
3. Estimate the amount of total deferred customer acquisition costs on HCI's balance sheet at December 31, 1998.
4. If HCI had always expensed its expenditures for customer acquisition costs, would the cash flow from operations be higher, the same, or lower? Why?
5. What accounting arguments could HCI make to justify its policy of capitalizing and amortizing customer acquisition costs?

P7.39 **(Appendix 7A) Recording Investments in, and Sales of, Long-lived Assets using the Debit/Credit Paradigm.** At the beginning of 2005, The Beall Corporation purchased a warehouse for $10 million and immediately made certain necessary renovations to the facility which cost $2 million. The chief financial officer of the company decided to depreciate the new warehouse using the straight- line method over a 20 year expected useful life, assuming no salvage value at the end of the 20 year period. After two years of use, Beall received an offer to sell the warehouse for $17 million and accepted the offer.

Required
Prepare the journal entries to record (1) the purchase and renovation of the warehouse, (2) the depreciation expense on the warehouse for the first two years, and (3) the sale of the warehouse.

P7.40 **(Appendix 7A) Recording Investments in, and Sales of, Long-lived assets using the Debit/Credit Paradigm.** On January 1, 2006, West Virginia Coal Company purchased the mining rights to a tract of farm land for $1.4 million. The company then constructed necessary roads and slurry ponds at a cost of $400,000. Geologists for the company estimated that the land contained 20,000 tons of coal. During 2006, the company extracted and sold 10,000 tons of coal for $1.2 million. At year-end, the company received an offer to sell the remaining coal reserves from the Kingwood Coal Company for a price of $2,000,000, which it accepted.

Required
Prepare the journal entries to record (1) the purchase of the mining rights and the construction of roads and slurry ponds, (2) the sale of 10,000 tons of coal, (3) the depletion of the coal reserves, and (4) the sale of the remaining coal reserves.

CORPORATE ANALYSIS

CA7.41 **The Procter and Gamble Company.** The 2005 annual report of **The Procter and Gamble Company** (P & G) is available at www.pg.com/annualreports/2005/pdf/pg2005annualreport.pdf. After reviewing P & G's annual report, respond to the following questions:

1. What percentage of P & G's total assets is represented by its net property, plant and equipment in 2004 and 2005? What percentage of P & G's total assets is represented by its net goodwill and other intangible assets in 2004 and 2005? Which category of non-current assets is larger? Calculate the capital intensity ratio for 2004 and 2005? (Recall that in Chapter Four, the capital intensity ratio was defined as the sum of fixed assets plus intangible assets divided by total assets.) Is P & G a capital-intensive company?

2. Calculate the fixed asset turnover ratio and the intangible asset turnover ratio for 2004 and 2005. What do these ratios tell you about P & G's operations?

3. How much depreciation expense and amortization expense was taken in 2004 and 2005? What depreciation method does P & G use? What is the relative age of P & G's fixed assets (what percentage of the assets has been used up and what percentage remains available)?

4. What is P & G's target for capital spending each year? What is P & G's sales growth target? If P & G's exactly achieves its sales growth target in 2006, how much capital spending might occur?

5. How much goodwill did P & G acquire in 2005? How much intangible assets did the company acquire in 2005?

CA7.42 **Internet-based Analysis.** Consider a publicly-held company whose products you are familiar with. Some examples might include:

Company	Product	Corporate Website
• **Johnson & Johnson Company**	• Band-Aids	• www.jnj.com
• **Microsoft Corporation**	• Windows XP software	• www.microsoft.com
• **Nokia Corporation**	• Cellular phones	• www.nokia.com
• **Intel Corporation**	• Pentium processors	• www.intel.com
• **Kimberly-Clark Corporation**	• Kleenex	• www.kimberly-clark.com

Access the company's public website and search for its most recent annual report. (Note: Some companies provide access to their financial data through an "investor relations" link, while others provide a direct link to their "annual reports.") After locating your company's most recent annual report, open the file and review its contents. After reviewing the annual report for your selected company, prepare answers to the following questions:

1. How does the company depreciate its property, plant and equipment (P, P&E)? Calculate the ratio of the accumulated depreciation divided by gross P, P&E for the past two years. How old are the company's P, P&E assets? What percentage of their useful life remains?

2. Does the company have any intangible assets? If so, what are they? What percentage of total assets do they represent?

3. Did the company invest in new P, P&E or new intangible assets during the past two years? If so, in what amount?

4. Calculate the total asset turnover, the P, P&E turnover, and the intangible asset turnover for each of the past two years. Are these turnover ratios increasing or decreasing? What might explain these trends?

Chapter Eight

Other Corporate Entities, Joint Ventures, and Mergers and Acquisitions

TAKEAWAYS

When you complete this chapter you should be able to:

1. Explain why companies acquire ownership interests in other businesses.
2. Describe how to account for investments in debt and equity securities, including the application of the equity method and consolidation accounting.
3. Explain the accounting for joint ventures and special purposes entities.
4. Describe the foreign currency issues that arise with investments in foreign companies.

Where have we been?	Where are we?	Where are we going?
In Chapter 7, the important business decision of investing in long-lived assets was considered. Specifically, the chapter examined the measurement and financial statement disclosure of strategic investments in such long-lived assets as property, plant and equipment, such intangible assets as copyrights and patents, and such natural resources as coal, natural gas, and oil. The chapter also investigated various depreciation methods, including straight-line, double-declining balance, and units-of-production. Finally, the amortization of intangible assets and the depletion of natural resources were considered.	In this chapter, we continue our examination of corporate investment decisions, specifically investigating how and why companies invest in other companies. We will see that companies buy shares in other companies for strategic reasons that vary from a desire to be a passive investor without exerting significant influence on the management of the investee-firm, to a desire to acquire active management control of a business. When companies acquire a small fraction (less than 20 percent) of the outstanding equity shares of another company, such investments are accounted for using mark-to-market accounting. Investments of 20 to 50 percent of the outstanding shares are accounted for using the equity method. And, investments in which the investor-company gains control of an investee's operating decisions (over 50 percent ownership) are accounted for using consolidated financial statements. Finally, we investigate the financial statement issues that arise when a company obtains a significant ownership interest in a foreign entity.	Chapter 9 begins an exploration of the strategic financing decisions of companies. Specifically, this chapter examines how and why companies finance their operations and their capital investments with debt. It examines how to calculate the value of bonds and notes, the accounting for and the financial statement disclosure of capital and operating leases, and the calculation of the weighted average cost of debt of a business.

In 2000, Foster's Group Ltd. of Australia made a tender offer for all of the outstanding shares of U.S.-based Beringer Wine Estate Holdings Inc. The offer price of $55.75 per share represented a premium of more than 60 percent above Beringer's share price 30 days prior to the announcement. With the assumption of $370 million of Beringer debt, the investment was valued at $1.17 billion.

According to Foster's, the Beringer acquisition "would create a global premium wine company." (In 2005, Foster's purchased Southcorp Ltd. to create the world's second largest winemaker.) The company's filing with the U.S. Securities and Exchange Commission disclosed that for some time, Foster's had pursued a corporate strategy of expanding its core beverage operations by acquisition. In 1996, for example, Foster's acquired Mildara Blass Ltd., one of Australia's largest premium wine companies. Subsequently, Foster's established a goal of acquiring a significant U.S. wine company in order to expand its operations on a global basis. Foster's intended to use Beringer's extensive North American distribution capabilities to expand the sales of its Mildara Blass unit, and to similarly expand Beringer's export sales by using Mildara Blass' distribution channels in Australia, Asia and Europe. In essence, the motivation for the acquisition was linked to revenue synergies that Foster's hoped to create by combining the distribution channels of the two companies.

On the day of the merger announcement, Foster's share price dropped from $4.40 to $4.10 per share while the Australian Stock Exchange All Ordinaries Index, a broad-based index of stocks listed on the exchange, remained unchanged. Foster's share price eventually recovered to trade at $4.23 per share 30 days after the announcement. Thus, Foster's shareholders did not appear to view the Beringer acquisition as value creating as evidenced by Foster's relatively stable share price around the transaction announcement date.

Today, Foster's produces, markets and exports the world's leading portfolio of premium wine brands, including Penfold's, Wolf Blass, Rosemont, Lindemans, Saltram, Seppelt, Wynns and Yellowglen from Australia, Beringer, Etude, Stag's Leap, and Chateau Souvrain from North America, Matua Valley and Secret Stone from New Zealand, and Castella de Gabiano from Italy. The company also produces and distributes a number of well known brands of beer, to include Crown Lager, Victoria Bitter, and Carlton Draught. The company's flagship international beer brand, Foster's Lager, is ranked in the top 10 international brands. The company's shares trade on the Australian Stock Exchange under the symbol FGL.

In this chapter, we examine the investment decisions of companies like Foster's. Specifically, we examine why and how they invest in other companies. We will see that companies invest in other companies for a variety of reasons and that the accounting for these investments is driven largely by the size of the ownership interest acquired.

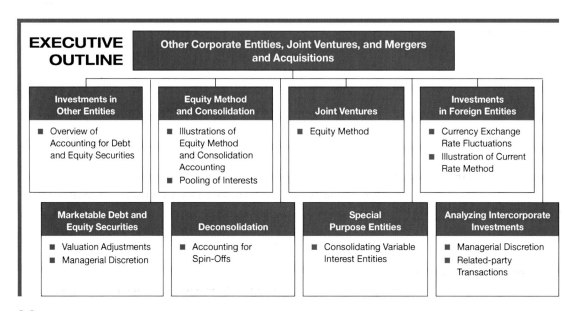

INVESTMENTS IN OTHER ENTITIES

Transactions such as the Foster's/Beringer acquisition are a regular part of corporate life as companies buy and sell the shares of other businesses. The amount of shares acquired varies from relatively small amounts to 100 percent of the outstanding shares as in the case of the Beringer takeover. When a company acquires a relatively small percentage of the outstanding shares of another entity (less than 20 percent), it usually indicates an expectation that the investment will provide an acceptable rate of return on idle corporate funds and also that the investor-company does not intend to take an active role in the day-to-day management and running of the investee.

When a company acquires a significant stake in another company—20 to 100 percent—it is usually because the investor-company desires to exercise an active role in the investee's business activities and affairs. Gaining control of the business affairs of another company may be of considerable economic value to an investor. For instance, it may enable an investor to generate incremental operating profit from cost savings and/or operating revenue enhancements. Operating cost/revenue synergies may be created by eliminating excess productive capacity, dropping unprofitable products, or generating incremental product sales. The Foster's/Beringer transaction is an example of an acquisition intended to create such synergies. An investor-company may also acquire a significant stake in an investee in order to oust an inefficient management team or because the investor believes that the investee's shares are temporarily undervalued and present an opportunity to profit from the capital market mis-pricing of the investee's shares. The combination of two companies may also be justified on financing grounds—one or both firms may have unused debt capacity capable of providing low-cost financing for growth of the combined entity. Finally, an investor may acquire shares in an investee to gain access to various skills, technology or resources that would be more expensive to obtain in other ways.

Overview of Accounting for Debt and Equity Securities

Investments in debt and equity securities in which the shareholding is relatively small—less than 20 percent of the outstanding voting shares for equity investments—are referred to as marketable debt and equity securities. Provided that a ready market exists for trading these securities—such as the New York Stock Exchange or the NASDAQ—a special accounting treatment known as mark-to-market accounting is allowed. For most assets, GAAP requires that a company carry its assets at their historical cost, with reductions for value impairments and depreciation. The general argument is that while the resulting historical cost number may lack a degree of relevance, it is reliable. Mark-to-market accounting is an exception to this generally-accepted practice and allows assets to be written up or down to their current market value. This accounting is permitted because a ready resale market exists such that an investment's current value can be reliably ascertained.

Marketable debt and equity securities which may be sold at any time to take advantage of price changes are called trading securities. As shown in Exhibit 8.1, these investments are valued at their market value on the balance sheet, with any unrealized gain (loss) in a security's value included directly in the investor's net income. An unrealized gain (loss) is an increase (decrease) in the value of an asset which has not yet been sold. When the asset is sold, the gain (loss) is said to be "realized."

Alternatively, investments in debt and equity securities that management intends to hold for the long term but which, under the right circumstances management might liquidate are referred to as available-for-sale securities. As shown in Exhibit 8.1, these investments are also valued on the balance sheet at their market value but for these investments, any unrealized gain (loss) in value is reported in a

EXHIBIT 8.1	Overview of Accounting for Debt and Equity Securities	
Ownership Interest	**Equity Securities**	**Debt Securities**
Less than 20 percent	*Marketable Equity Securities* Trading securities • Valued at market value on balance sheet • Unrealized gain/loss included in income • Dividends included in income Available-for-sale • Valued at market value on balance sheet • Unrealized gain/loss included as a component of equity on balance sheet • Dividends included in income	*Marketable Debt Securities* Trading securities • Valued at market value on balance sheet • Unrealized gain/loss included in income • Interest revenue included in income Available-for-sale • Valued at market value on balance sheet • Unrealized gain/loss included as a component of equity on balance sheet • Interest revenue included in income Held-to-maturity • Valued at amortized cost on balance sheet • Interest revenue included in income
Between 20 and 50 percent	**Equity Method** • Investment in Equity Affiliate valued at cost plus share of earnings less share of dividends on balance sheet • Proportionate share of affiliate's earnings included in income of investor-company	

Greater than 50 percent	**Consolidation Accounting**
	• On parent-company books; investment is accounted for using the equity method.
	• Upon consolidation:
	  • Assets and liabilities of subsidiary are added to those of parent, with Investment in Equity Affiliate eliminated and minority interest shown on balance sheet
	  • Transactions between parent and subsidiary are netted out
	  • Revenue and expenses of subsidiary are combined with those of parent-company, with minority interest in subsidiary's income deducted from consolidated earnings	

separate shareholders' equity account on the balance sheet. For companies using U.S. GAAP, the unrealized gains (losses) on available-for-sale securities are considered to be part of Other Comprehensive Income, a category of yet-to-be-realized wealth increases or decreases disclosed in the shareholders' equity section of the balance sheet. We will have to say more about Other Comprehensive Income in Chapter 11.

Debt securities which management intends to hold until maturity are referred to as **held-to-maturity debt securities**. These investments are valued at their **amortized cost**—that is, the original purchase price of the debt plus (minus) the amortization of any purchase discount (premium). We will have more to say about the amortization of purchase discounts (premiums) on debt instruments in Chapter 9.

GLOBAL PERSPECTIVE

In lesser developed countries where there are not actively traded markets for debt and equity securities, and thus not readily available or reliable market prices, the valuation of marketable debt and equity securities is often at the original **cost** of the investment. In some developed countries, a variant of the market value approach called **lower-of-cost-or-market** is used. Under the lower-of-cost-or-market method, a security is valued at the lower of two values—its current market value or its original cost. When a security's market value falls below its cost, the security is written down to the lower amount and the unrealized loss is reported in current income. Although unrealized losses (gains) may be included as income for accounting purposes, they are not reported as income for income tax purposes until the asset is sold and the loss (gain) realized.

Investments in equity securities wherein the investor-company can exercise significant influence over an investee's operating policies but which are not sufficiently large to represent voting control—between 20 and 50 percent of the outstanding voting shares—are accounted for using the equity method. Under the equity method (see Exhibit 8.1), the Investment in Equity Affiliate account on the balance sheet is reported at its original cost plus a proportionate share of the affiliate's earnings or losses less a proportionate share of any dividends paid by the affiliate. The investor-company is also permitted to include its ownership interest in the affiliate's earnings (or loss) as part of its current income on the income statement in an account called equity in the earnings (loss) of an unconsolidated affiliate.

> When preparing a statement of cash flow for an investor-company, it is customary to (1) subtract (add) the "equity in the earnings (loss) of an unconsolidated affiliate" and (2) subtract (add) any unrealized gains (losses) on trading securities from net income when calculating the cash flow from operations, and instead, to reflect these amounts as components of the cash flow for investing.

Finally, investments in equity securities in which an investor-company establishes voting control over an affiliate—over 50 percent ownership—are accounted for using consolidation accounting. Under consolidation accounting, the operating results of the affiliated company are combined with those of the investor. Thus, shareholders in the investor-company receive a single set of financial statements representing a combination of both the investor and affiliate-company financial results. Affiliate companies in which an investor-company owns more than 50 percent of the outstanding voting shares are often referred to as "subsidiaries."

ILLUSTRATION OF ACCOUNTING FOR MARKETABLE DEBT AND EQUITY SECURITIES

To illustrate the accounting for, and the financial statement disclosures associated with, marketable debt and equity securities, we refer to the investing activities of The New South Wales Trading Company, Inc. In 2005, The New South Wales Trading Company (NSWT) raised $50 million in cash from an initial public offering of its common shares. The company planned to use most of the cash to establish a chain of fast food restaurants specializing in Australian cuisine. Since the company's planned capital investments would take place over a three year period, NSWT decided to temporarily invest some of its cash in debt and equity securities having a high degree of liquidity. The company settled on three investments:

Investment	Acquisition Date	Acquisition Cost	Classification	Market Value at December 31, 2005
(1) Qantas Inc. 10% Notes due in 2008....................	September 2005	$10 million	Held-to-Maturity	$9.8 million
(2) 100,000 shares of BHP Inc. common stock..............	November 2005	6.1 million	Trading	6.8 million
(3) 200,000 shares of Coles Inc. common stock..............	December 2005	8.4 million	Available-for-sale	8.2 million

In September 2005, NSWT invested $10 million in **Qantas Inc.** 10 percent notes. The company planned to hold the notes until 2008 when they matured and the principal of $10 million repaid. The notes paid $1 million in interest income (10 percent of $10 million) on December 31 each year. The notes were classified by NSWT's chief financial officer (CFO) as **held-to-maturity debt securities.**

In November 2005, NSWT invested $6.1 million in 100,000 shares of **BHP Inc.** common stock at $61 per share. Since BHP was a growth company, it paid no dividends to its shareholders. NSWT's CFO thought the shares were substantially undervalued, and consequently, placed an order to sell the BHP shares when they hit $80 per share. BHP's shares were classified by the CFO as **trading securities.**

In December 2005, NSWT purchased 200,000 shares of **Coles Inc.** common stock at $42 per share for a total cost of $8.4 million. Like BHP, Coles had a policy of paying no dividends. The NSWT CFO thought the shares were fairly valued but that NSWT would sell them in the unlikely event that the Coles shares traded above $50 per share. The Coles shares were classified as **available-for-sale securities.**

The accounting for the acquisition of the three securities is illustrated in the spreadsheet in Exhibit 8.2, Panel A. The investment in Qantas Inc. Notes reduces cash by $10 million and increases held-to-maturity debt securities by $10 million. The investments in BHP and Coles common shares reduces cash by $6.1 and $8.4 million, respectively, and increases trading equity securities and available-for-sale equity securities by $6.1 and $8.4, respectively.

EXHIBIT 8.2	**Accounting for Marketable Debt and Equity Securities**

The New South Wales Trading Company, Inc. Spreadsheet

Date (in thousands)	Cash	Held-to-Maturity Debt Securities	Trading Equity Securities	Available-for-Sale Equity Securities	Common Stock	Retained Earnings	Unrealized Gain (Loss) on Available-for-Sale Securities
		Assets — Investments			= Equity		
Sept. 1, 2005	50,000				50,000		
Panel A							
(1) Sep. 2005	−10,000	10,000					
(2) Nov. 2005	−6,100		6,100				
(3) Dec. 2005	−8,400			8,400			
Panel B							
(1) Dec. 31, 2005	1,000					1,000	
(2) Dec. 31, 2005			700			700	
(3) Dec. 31, 2005				−200			−200
Dec. 31, 2005.........	26,500	10,000	6,800	8,200	50,000	1,700	−200

Year-End Valuation Adjustments

At the end of 2005, NSWT must consider several important events concerning its investments. These are shown in Exhibit 8.2, Panel B. First, NSWT received an interest payment of $1 million on the Qantas Notes, increasing cash and retained earnings (interest income) by $1 million. Second, the market value at year-end of NSWT's investments differed from their acquisition cost.

Since the Qantas notes are held-to-maturity securities, they are valued at their acquisition cost, requiring no downward adjustment to their market value of $9.8 million. NSWT's trading securities (BHP shares), however, must be valued at their market value with any gain (loss) in value taken into income. NSWT's trading securities have a market value of $6.8 million versus an acquisition cost of $6.1 million. Thus, the trading equity securities account is increased by $700,000 to reflect its market value of $6.8 million and retained earnings is increased by $700,000 to reflect the unrealized gain includable as current income. *(N1)*

The market value of the Coles shares, however, is just $8.2 million versus an acquisition cost of $8.4 million; consequently, this investment must be written down to market value with the unrealized loss reported as a component of shareholders' equity. Recording the unrealized loss reduces available-for-sale securities by $200,000 and reduces the shareholders' equity account Unrealized Gain (loss) on Available-for-Sale-Securities by $200,000. The shareholders' equity account Unrealized Gain (loss) on Available-for-Sale Securities is classified as a component of Other Comprehensive Income under U.S. GAAP.

Following these end-of-year adjustments, NSWT's balance sheet at year-end 2005 is presented in Exhibit 8.3. The balance sheet shows NSWT's investment in held-to-maturity debt securities at cost and its investments in trading and available-for-sale securities at their market value. Shareholders' equity reflects the unrealized loss on available-for-sale securities and the unrealized gain on the trading securities. NSWT's

EXHIBIT 8.3	Financial Statement Disclosures: Marketable Debt and Equity Securities

The New South Wales Trading Company, Inc.
Balance Sheet

($ thousands)	Dec. 31, 2005
Cash	$26,500
Investments	
Held-to-maturity debt securities	10,000
Trading equity securities	6,800
Available-for-sale equity securities	8,200
Total Assets	$51,500
Shareholders' Equity	
Common stock	$50,000
Retained earnings	1,700
Other Comprehensive income	
Unrealized loss on available-for-sale securities	(200)
Shareholders' equity	$51,500

The New South Wales Trading Company, Inc.
Partial Income Statement

($ thousands)	Dec. 31, 2005
Interest income	$ 1,000
Unrealized gain on trading equity securities	700
Net income	$ 1,700

partial income statement for the year is also presented in Exhibit 8.3. It shows the interest income of $1 million and the $700,000 of unrealized gain on trading securities.

Managerial Discretion

One might question why there is an inconsistent treatment of unrealized gains and losses between trading and available-for-sale securities. The difference in treatment coincides with the expected length of the holding period for the two investment categories—a relatively short holding period for trading securities and an uncertain holding period for available-for-sale securities. It could be argued that unrealized gains and losses should never be included in current income since the amount ultimately realized on a sale could be much different than the amount recognized in the current period. In fact, large swings in market values, over which management has no control, may distort current period performance as measured by net income. This argument is the principal reason why unrealized gains and losses for available-for-sale securities are classified as Other Comprehensive Income on the balance sheet rather than as income on the income statement. Trading securities, on the other hand, are expected to be sold within a relatively short time frame. Hence, large changes in market value are much less likely to occur; and consequently, recognizing these unrealized gains and losses on the income statement in the current period is considered justifiable.

By classifying the shares of BHP Inc. as trading securities rather than as available-for-sale, the unrealized gain of $700,000 is included in NSWT's earnings rather than as a component of shareholders' equity on the balance sheet. Similarly, classifying the shares in Coles Inc. as available-for-sale rather than as trading securities causes the unrealized loss of $200,000 to be included in shareholders' equity and not in NSWT's current earnings. Perhaps NSWT's CFO anticipated this situation and strategically classified these securities to cause the most favorable impact on reported firm performance. Such a conclusion implies that the CFO has an ability to forecast future share prices, a talent that might lead the CFO to resign his current position and become a professional stock picker. Yet, such strategic decision-making is more plausible in the CFO's decision to sell securities. If a boost in earnings is required for a given year, perhaps because operating profit has fallen short of analysts' expectations, NSWT's CFO might be inclined to sell the available-for-sale securities, enabling an otherwise unrealized gain that would flow to shareholders' equity to manifest itself as a realized gain in current earnings. In some circles, such behavior is known as "cherry picking"—that is, selectively selling securities to include realized gains but not losses in a firm's current earnings. According to U.S. regulators, the **Federal National Mortgage Association** (also known as Fannie Mae), a publicly-held company chartered by the U.S. Congress to provide financing for home mortgages, did just that. The Office of Federal Housing Enterprises Oversight charged in 2005 that Fannie Mae violated GAAP by pursuing an accounting policy which allowed it to keep the best mortgage-backed securities and to sell less-attractive ones to investors, a practice that became known as "keep the best, sell the rest."[1]

EQUITY METHOD AND CONSOLIDATION ACCOUNTING

To illustrate the accounting for the acquisition of a significant shareholding—20 to 100 percent of a company's shares—we examine three scenarios involving the financial statement disclosures of Savanna Inc. and Waterloo Inc. Summary financial information for the two companies is provided in Exhibit 8.4. Savanna Inc. is the larger company in terms of assets—$150 million for Savanna versus $100 million for Waterloo.

To simplify the illustration, we assume that (1) all revenue, expenses and dividends are paid in cash; (2) there are no income taxes; (3) interest on long-term debt is ignored; (4) neither company initially holds

---

[1] *The Wall Street Journal*, "Fannie Mae Accused of Rule Breaking", April 7, 2005.

EXHIBIT 8.4	Summary Financial Data for Savanna Inc. and Waterloo Inc.

Pre-Investment Balance Sheet
As of January 1

($ millions)	Savanna Inc.	Waterloo Inc.
Cash.	$ 50	$ 20
Inventory.	100	80
Total assets.	$150	$100
Long-term debt	$ 50	$ 80
Common stock.	100	20
Liabilities & shareholders' equity	$150	$100

Income Statement
Year Ending December 31

($ millions)	Savanna Inc.	Waterloo Inc.
Revenue	$200	$100
Expenses	170	90
Net income.	$ 30	$ 10
Dividend	$ 0	$ 5

debt or equity securities in the other; and, (5) Savanna pays no dividend during the year while Waterloo pays a $5 million cash dividend. Finally, we assume that there are no inter-company sales transactions between the two companies.

Case 1: Savanna Inc. acquires 40 percent of the common shares of Waterloo Inc for $8 million on January 2; the fair market value of Waterloo's net assets equals their book value of $20 million ($100 million in assets minus $80 million in liabilities).

Since Savanna's investment of $8 million is equal to 40 percent of the fair value of Waterloo's net assets (40 percent of $20 million), there is no goodwill associated with the Waterloo investment. Goodwill is the excess of the purchase price of an investment over the fair market value of the purchased identifiable net assets.[2] The size of Savanna's investment in Waterloo's shares (40 percent) indicates that Savanna desires a significant but not controlling interest in Waterloo's operating decisions. As a consequence, Savanna should use the equity method to

Consolidation accounting requires that prior to the combination of financial results, any profits on inter-company sales between related companies be eliminated. This requirement stems from the accounting principle that only profit from arms-length transactions be included in the income statement; that is, it is inappropriate to include the profit on a sale between two divisions of the same company in the consolidated results. In some circumstances, the profit on transactions between a parent-company and an *unconsolidated* affiliate may be included in the consolidated income statement, but this situation (if material) must be disclosed in the footnotes to the consolidated financial statements as a related-party transaction.

---

[2] There are many reasons why an acquiring company will pay an amount in excess of the fair value of an acquiree's identifiable assets, thus requiring an amount to be recorded as goodwill. The acquiring firm may believe that there are synergies that can be realized upon the acquisition, or alternatively, that certain "unidentified assets" such as technological know-how or managerial talent may be present in the acquired firm. Consequently, it should not be concluded that the existence of goodwill in an acquisition implies that the acquiring firm simply erroneously paid too much for an acquiree.

account for its investment in Waterloo. Savanna's accounting for its investment under the equity method is summarized below and is displayed in the spreadsheet in Exhibit 8.5:

1. On January 2, Savanna decreases Cash by $8 million for its investment in Waterloo and also increases the Investment in Equity Affiliate account by $8 million.
2. During the year, Savanna reports its earnings as an increase in Cash of $30 million and an increase in Retained Earnings of $30.
3. During the year, Savanna reports its 40 percent share of Waterloo's earnings, or $4 million (40 percent of $10 million), as an increase in the Investment in Equity Affiliate of $4 million and as an increase in Retained Earnings of $4 million (equity in the earnings of an unconsolidated affiliate). Under the equity method, Savanna reports a portion of Waterloo's earnings as both a source of earnings on its own income statement and as an increase in its investment in Waterloo on its balance sheet. If Waterloo had reported a loss instead of a profit, Savanna would report its ownership share of Waterloo's loss on its income statement and as a reduction in the investment account on its balance sheet.
4. During the year, Savanna reports its 40 percent share of Waterloo's cash dividend, or $2 million (40 percent of $5 million), by increasing Cash by $2 million and decreasing the Investment in Equity Affiliate by $2 million. Under the equity method, the payment of a dividend by an affiliate is treated as a reduction in (or liquidation of) the investment and not as a source of earnings. In effect, the affiliate's dividend is accounted for by the parent company (Savanna) as a return of investment, not a return on investment.

> A dividend that is considered to be a return of capital, rather than a return on capital, is called a liquidating dividend.

EXHIBIT 8.5	Accounting for an Investment using the Equity Method: Case 1

Savanna, Inc. Spreadsheet

		Assets		=	Liabilities	+	Equity	
Events ($ millions)	Cash	Inventory	Investment in Equity Affiliate		Long-term Debt		Common Stock	Retained Earnings
January 1	50	100			50		100	0
(1) Acquire shares in Waterloo.	−8		8					
(2) Savanna's earnings for year	30							30
(3) 40% share of Waterloo's earnings.			4					4
(4) 40% share of Waterloo's dividends	2		−2					
December 31.	74	100	10		50		100	34

The balance sheet for Savanna on January 2 after the initial investment in Waterloo's common shares and at the end of the year are shown in Exhibit 8.6. Savanna's Investment in Equity Affiliate increases from $8 million at the time of the investment to $10 million at the end of the year. The income statement for Savanna is also shown in Exhibit 8.6 and reveals that Savanna's earnings include not only its own net earnings of $30 million, but also Savanna's 40 percent share of Waterloo's earnings ($4 million).

EXHIBIT 8.6	Financial Statement Disclosures: Case 1

Savanna, Inc.
Balance Sheet

($ millions)	January 2	December 31
Cash.	$ 42	$ 74
Inventory.	100	100
Investment in equity affiliate.	8	10
Total assets.	$150	$184
Long-term debt	$ 50	$ 50
Common stock.	100	100
Retained earnings	0	34
Liabilities & shareholders' equity	$150	$184

Savanna, Inc.
Income Statement

($ millions)	December 31
Revenue	$200
Expenses	170
Operating income.	30
Equity in the earnings of unconsolidated affiliate.	4
Net income.	$ 34

It may seem strange at first to see Savanna increasing its investment account for a portion of Waterloo's earnings, even if they are not received, and then decreasing the investment account for any dividends actually received. There is, however, logic behind this accounting treatment. Savanna's investment account represents its percentage ownership interest in Waterloo's shareholders' equity. Savanna initially paid an amount exactly equal to its percentage share of Waterloo's equity, so the investment account equaled 40 percent of $20 million or $8 million. During the year Waterloo reported net income of $10 million and paid dividends of $5 million. These amounts increase Waterloo's shareholders' equity (retained earnings) by $10 million and decrease its retained earnings by $5 million. Correspondingly, Savanna's investment account was increased by 40 percent of these amounts, $4 million minus $2 million, or $2 million. At year-end, Waterloo's shareholders' equity totals $25 million and Savanna's investment account is 40 percent of this amount, or $10 million. You may wish to try to replicate this reconciliation between Savanna's investment account and Waterloo's shareholders' equity for Case 2.

Case 2: Savanna acquires 80 percent of Waterloo's common shares for $16 million; the fair market value of Waterloo Inc.'s net assets equals their book value of $20 million.

Since the purchase price of $16 million is equal to 80 percent of the fair value of Waterloo's net assets (80 percent of $20 million), no goodwill is associated with the Waterloo investment. The size of Savanna's investment indicates that it has

Although it is generally true that when a company acquires a majority shareholding in another, the investor will report its financial results with those of the subsidiary on a consolidated basis, the presentation of consolidated financial statements is not required in every country (such as India). Consolidated financial statements are intended to help investors avoid the problem of information overload (giving investors too much financial information to comprehend).

In Practice 8.1 *Equity in the earnings of an unconsolidated affiliate* Care should be exercised when analyzing the income statements of investor-firms reporting affiliate earnings under the equity method since these earnings are often not received in cash. An analysis of public-company filings in 2005 found many companies reported earnings from affiliate-companies in excess of the cash dividends received from these affiliates. Moreover, in several cases, the affiliate-company earnings accounted for over half of the investor-firms' reported net income:

Company	Unremitted portion of unconsolidated affiliate-company earnings as reported under equity method ($ millions)	Consolidated income before extraordinary items and discontinued operations ($ millions)
Thomas Properties Group	$ 18.40	$ 0.64
Bexil Corp.	7.92	1.40
General Growth Properties, Inc.	259.26	63.87
Firstcity Financial Corp.	12.21	8.08
Macerich Co.	88.24	68.19
United Capital Corp	9.19	12.27
Regency Centers Corp.	62.49	101.07
Tennessee Gas Pipeline Co.	50.00	82.00

Source: Standard and Poor's Compustat

acquired a controlling interest in Waterloo's business, and therefore, Savanna should consolidate Waterloo's financial results. Savanna will initially account for its investment in Waterloo using the equity method on its *unconsolidated* financial statements and then prepare consolidated financial statements at the end of the fiscal period by making various consolidating adjustments. We follow that approach in this illustration. Savanna's initial accounting for its investment under the equity method is summarized below and in the spreadsheet in Exhibit 8.7:

1. On January 2, Savanna decreases Cash by $16 million for its cash investment in Waterloo and increases the Investment in Equity Affiliate account by $16 million.

2. During the year, Savanna reports its earnings as an increase in Cash of $30 million and an increase in Retained Earnings of $30 million.

3. During the year, Savanna reports its 80 percent share of Waterloo's earnings, or $8 million, as an increase in the Investment in Equity Affiliate by $8 million and an increase in Retained Earnings by $8 million (equity in the earnings of unconsolidated affiliate).

4. During the year, Savanna reports its 80 percent share of Waterloo's cash dividend, or $4 million, by increasing Cash by $4 million and decreasing the Investment in Equity Affiliate by $4 million.

The financial statements for Savanna and Waterloo at December 31 are shown in Exhibit 8.8. Waterloo's assets of $105 million reflect its beginning assets of $100 million plus earnings for the year of $10 million less the dividends paid to its shareholders of $5 million. Since Savanna owns 80 percent of Waterloo's common shares, it must report its financial results and those of Waterloo on a consolidated basis. Thus, Waterloo's assets of $105 million are added to Savanna's assets. Similarly, Waterloo's $80 million of long-term debt are added to Savanna's liabilities. However, to avoid overstating the total consolidated assets and liabilities, certain adjusting (eliminating) entries are required. First, the Investment in Equity Affiliate ($20 million) must be removed from the consolidated balance sheet to avoid double-counting

EXHIBIT 8.7	Accounting for an Investment using the Equity Method: Case 2

Savanna, Inc. Spreadsheet

	Assets			=	Liabilities	+	Equity	
Events ($ millions)	Cash	Inventory	Investment in Equity Affiliate		Long-term Debt		Common Stock	Retained Earnings
January 1.	50	100	0		50		100	0
(1) Acquire shares in Waterloo.	−16		16					
(2) Savanna's earnings for year.	30							30
(3) 80% share of Waterloo's earnings.			8					8
(4) 80% share of Waterloo's dividends	4		−4					
December 31.	68	100	20		50		100	38

some of Waterloo's assets. This amount is offset against 80 percent of Waterloo's common stock ($16 million) and 80 percent of Waterloo's retained earnings ($4 million). Second, the remaining 20 percent of Waterloo's common stock and retained earnings not legally owned by Savanna belong to another group of shareholders' whose claim on Waterloo's net assets, valued at $5 million (20 percent of $20 million plus 20 percent of $5 million), is known as the **minority interest** since Savanna is the majority shareholder. Minority interest refers to the portion of a subsidiary's net assets not owned by the parent-company. Under consolidation accounting, 100 percent of an affiliate's assets and liabilities are consolidated with those of the parent-company (Savanna) even though legal ownership may be less than 100 percent. The process of consolidating all of a subsidiary's assets and liabilities even though legal ownership is less than 100 percent is known as **full consolidation**.

> The **minority interest** account is disclosed on the credit side of the consolidated balance sheet, listed after long-term debt but just prior to shareholders' equity. This balance sheet classification reflects the ambiguity surrounding the nature of this account. Technically, the minority interest account is neither an obligation of the consolidated entity nor a shareholding in the parent-company. It is a claim on the net assets of the consolidated subsidiary. For purposes of financial statement analysis, however, most investment professionals regard minority interest as a component of debt for purposes of calculating such ratios as the debt-to-equity ratio and the total debt-to-total assets ratio.

By adding across the left three columns, we arrive at Savanna's consolidated balance sheet in Exhibit 8.8, Panel A. The consolidated balance sheet shows that the net assets of $143 million ($273 million in assets less $130 million in long-term debt) are equal to the $138 million of Savanna's equity claims plus the $5 million in claims by the minority shareholders.

Savanna's consolidated income statement is shown in Exhibit 8.8, Panel B. All of Waterloo's operating revenue and operating expenses are added to those of Savanna despite the fact that Savanna legally owns only 80 percent of Waterloo. To avoid double counting Waterloo's earnings, it is necessary to eliminate the $8 million of Equity in the Earnings of Unconsolidated Affiliate and to subtract the 20 percent share of Waterloo's earnings, or $2 million (20 percent of $10 million), attributable to the claims of the minority shareholders. Savanna's consolidated financial statements in Exhibit 8.8 reflect what is commonly referred to as **purchase accounting** or the **purchase method**.

EXHIBIT 8.8	Financial Statement Disclosures: Case 2			

Panel A: Balance Sheet ($ millions)	Equity Method Savanna Inc. December 31	Waterloo Inc. December 31	Adjustments	Consolidated Savanna Inc. December 31
Cash	$ 68	$ 25		$ 93
Inventory.	100	80		180
Investment in equity affiliate.	20	0	−$20	0
Total assets.	$188	$105	−$20	$273
Long-term debt	$ 50	$ 80		$130
Minority interest in consolidated subsidiary. . .			$ 5	5
Common stock.	100	20	−20	100
Retained earnings	38	5	−5	38
Liabilities and shareholders' equity	$188	$105	−$20	$273

Panel B: Income Statement ($ millions)	Equity Method Savanna Inc. December 31	Waterloo Inc. December 31		Consolidated Savanna Inc. December 31
Revenue	$200	$100		$300
Expenses	(170)	(90)		(260)
Operating income.	30	10		40
Equity in the earnings of unconsolidated affiliate	8	—	−$ 8	
Minority interest in the earnings of consolidated subsidiary.	—	—	−2	(2)
Net income.	$ 38	$ 10	−$10	$ 38

Notice in Panel B of Exhibit 8.8 that the $38 million of net income reported by Savanna under the equity method is the same as the consolidated net income reported under consolidated accounting. This illustrates that consolidation accounting and the equity method produce similar income statement results. This is not true, however, for the balance sheet: Total assets and long-term debt are higher under consolidation accounting than under the equity method. In fact, Savanna would report a long-term debt-to-equity ratio of 0.94 ($130 million divided by $138 million) under consolidation accounting but a ratio of only 0.36 ($50 million divided by $138 million) under the equity method.

The equity method enables a parent-company to engage in what is commonly referred to as off-balance-sheet financing—that is, avoiding the disclosure of a subsidiary's debt on the parent-company balance sheet. By maintaining an equity holding of 50 percent or less, a company is permitted to use the equity method to account for its intercorporate investments. Under U.S. GAAP, and that of many countries, parent-companies are required to disclose the aggregate assets, liabilities, revenue and expenses of equity affiliates in the parent-company footnotes. Does it matter if a subsidiary's debt is disclosed in the footnotes rather than reported on the parent's balance sheet? If investors are reasonably astute they should be able to make the necessary adjustments to the parent's unconsolidated balance sheet to derive "as if" consolidated financial statements which reflect the debt of the subsidiary. Nevertheless, some managers go to great lengths to keep debt off the consolidated balance sheet, presumably under the belief that financial statement users don't make full and complete adjustments for off-balance-sheet debt. By keeping such debt off the balance sheet, these managers hope to make their companies appear less risky, and thus, positively impact the company's credit rating and the share price of the company's stock.

Case 3: Savanna acquires 100 percent of Waterloo's common shares for $25 million; the book value of Waterloo's assets and liabilities equal their fair market value except inventory, which has a current value of $82 million versus a book value of $80 million. Thus, the fair market value of Waterloo's net assets is $22 million ($20 million plus $2 million representing the understatement of inventory).

Savanna's acquisition of 100 percent of Waterloo's shares indicates that Savanna should prepare consolidated financial statements. Further, since Savanna paid $25 million for an investment having a fair value of $22 million, goodwill in the amount of $3 million is present in the Waterloo acquisition. Finally, since Waterloo's inventory has a fair value of $82 million but a book value of only $80 million, Savanna must increase, or "step-up," the value of Waterloo's inventory by $2 million before the consolidated balance sheet is prepared. Under purchase accounting, the assets and liabilities of an acquiree are written-up (or down) to current value prior to the preparation of the consolidated financial statements.

As in Case 2, Savanna will initially account for its investment in Waterloo using the equity method, and at the end of the fiscal period, prepare consolidated financial statements. Savanna's equity method accounting for its investment in Waterloo is summarized below and in the spreadsheet in Exhibit 8.9:

1. On January 2, Savanna increases the Investment in Equity Affiliate account by $25 million and decreases Cash for an equivalent amount.

2. During the year, Savanna reports its earnings for the year as an increase in Cash of $30 million and an increase in Retained Earnings of $30 million.

3. During the year, Savanna reports its 100 percent share of Waterloo's earnings, or $10 million, as an increase in the Investment in Equity Affiliate account and as an increase in Retained Earnings of $10 million (equity in the earnings of unconsolidated affiliate).

4. During the year, Savanna reports its 100 percent share of Waterloo's cash dividend, or $5 million, by increasing Cash by $5 million and decreasing the Investment in Equity Affiliate by $5 million.

EXHIBIT 8.9	Accounting for an Investment using the Equity Method: Case 3					
	Savanna, Inc. Spreadsheet					
	Assets			= Liabilities	+	Equity
Events ($ millions)	Cash	Inventory	Investment in Equity Affiliate	Long-term Debt	Common Stock	Retained Earnings
January 1	50	100	0	50	100	0
(1) Acquire shares in Waterloo.	−25		25			
(2) Savanna's earnings for year.	30					30
(3) 100% share of Waterloo's earnings.			10			10
(4) 100% share of Waterloo's dividends	5		−5			
December 31.	60	100	30	50	100	40

The balance sheets for Savanna and Waterloo at December 31 are shown in Exhibit 8.10, Panel A. The purchase price of $25 million exceeds the fair value of Waterloo's net assets of $20 million, with the excess of $5 million represented by a $2 million step-up in the value of Waterloo's inventory and goodwill in the amount of $3 million. As before, the Investment in Equity Affiliate of $30 million is eliminated against Waterloo's common stock of $20 million, retained earnings of $5 million, the creation of goodwill for $3 million and the inventory write-up of $2 million. Consolidated financial statements are presented in Exhibit 8.10.

EXHIBIT 8.10	**Financial Statement Disclosures: Case 3**			
Panel A: Balance Sheet ($ millions)	**Equity Method Savanna, Inc December 31**	**Waterloo Inc. December 31**	**Adjustments**	**Consolidated Savanna, Inc. December 31**
Cash.	$ 60	$ 25		$ 85
Inventory.	100	80	$ 2	182
Investment in equity affiliate.	30	0	−30	0
Goodwill.	—	—	3	3
Total assets.	$190	$105	−$25	$270
Long-term debt	$ 50	$ 80	—	$130
Common stock.	100	20	−$20	100
Retained earnings	40	5	−5	40
Liabilities & shareholders' equity	$190	$105	−$25	$270
Panel B: Income Statement ($ millions)	**Equity Method Savanna, Inc December 31**	**Waterloo Inc. December 31**		**Consolidated Savanna, Inc. December 31**
Revenue	$200	$100		$300
Expenses	170	90		260
Operating income.	30	10		40
Equity in earnings of unconsolidated affiliate	10	—	−$10	—
Net income.	$ 40	$ 10	−$10	$ 40

Pooling-of-Interests Accounting

For business combinations concluded prior to July 1, 2001, some companies had an option under U.S. GAAP to account for a merger using pooling-of-interests accounting rather than purchase accounting, if certain conditions were met (such as the transaction was executed by an exchange of voting shares). Referring to the data from Case 3, under pooling-of-interests accounting, the Investment in Equity Affiliate and Savanna's issued shares would have been valued at only $20 million—the book value of Waterloo at the time of the investment—even though Savanna's shares may have had a fair market value of $25 million. Pooling-of-interests accounting treatment was controversial and was sometimes referred to as "dirty pooling." One argument for ending the use of pooling accounting was the difficulty involved in comparing companies that engaged in different consolidation accounting practices. Perhaps the most controversial issue, however, was the claim that companies could "buy earnings" through pooling accounting. Under purchase accounting, an acquiring company can only recognize income from an acquired company for the portion of the year in which the combination is in effect. Under pooling accounting, however, an acquiring company could recognize an entire year of the acquired company's earnings, even for transactions occurring as late as the last day of the year! In addition, goodwill was not recorded under pooling accounting. While pooling-of-interests accounting is no longer allowed in the United States, its effects are still present on the financial statements of many companies that executed pooling-of-interests' transactions prior to 2001.

DECONSOLIDATION

Just as firms consolidate the financial statements of their majority-owned subsidiaries, they must reverse this process when their ownership interest falls below 50 percent. The **deconsolidation** process most commonly occurs when a parent company sells a business division or distributes its ownership shares to its existing shareholders. The distribution of ownership of a business division from a company to its shareholders is called a **spin-off** and is usually executed as a tax-free distribution.

Consider, for example, the 1998 spin-off of Associates First Financial by the **Ford Motor Company**. Ford distributed its 81 percent ownership stake in Associates First Financial to its Ford Class A and Class B shareholders. The spin-off reduced Ford's net worth by one-third (the book value of the net assets transferred to the newly-formed Associates Company), and Ford's share price declined from $65.50 per share prior to the spin-off to $43.75 post-spin-off. The decline in Ford's share price ($21.75) represented the opening fair market value of the distributed shares of the new Associates Company. Following the spin-off, the Associates Company, a consumer-finance company, was able to be exchange-traded as a separate corporate entity from Ford. Following the announcement of the spin-off, Ford's share price rose 18 percent, suggesting that the equity market perceived the transaction to be a value-enhancing decision for Ford Company shareholders. Spin-offs are a mechanism by which companies, like the Ford Motor Company, can create value for their shareholders when the consolidated entity is mis-valued by the capital market. Conglomerates, like Ford, which are made up of a variety of businesses, often trade at a discount from their aggregate fair market value. This discount is known as the **conglomerate discount**.

The accounting for a spin-off is executed like a reverse pooling-of-interest—that is, the book value of the division's assets and liabilities are removed from the consolidated balance sheet and placed on a new, separate unconsolidated balance sheet representing the new corporate entity. Parent-company shareholders receive shares in the spun-off entity in proportion to their ownership interest in the parent, and subsequently, can trade the shares of the newly created corporate entity separately from the parent-company.

ACCOUNTING FOR JOINT VENTURES

In some cases, a business may establish a **joint venture** with another company to produce a product or provide a service. These ventures are often quite effective because each company typically has some unique skill, knowledge or resource that makes it more efficient to partner with another company than to attempt the undertaking alone. These partnering arrangements are often established as separate corporate entities in which each partner owns 50 percent of the venture's equity, although owning exactly 50 percent is not a necessary condition to establish a joint venture. Since each partner owns half of the joint venture's equity, these ventures are accounted for using the equity method.

GLOBAL PERSPECTIVE

Another approach used to account for joint ventures in some countries is partial consolidation. Under partial consolidation, a parent company only consolidates its ownership interest in a joint venture's assets, liabilities, revenue and expenses. Unlike full consolidation, in which 100 percent of a subsidiary's net assets and net revenue are consolidated, partial consolidation consolidates only the legally-owned percentage of assets, liabilities, revenue, and expenses. As a consequence, there are no minority interest accounts on the consolidated financial statements under partial consolidation. In the U.S., partial consolidation for unincorporated joint ventures is practiced in only a few industries (such as the mining industry).

For example, the Starbucks Coffee Company disclosed in its annual report that it had entered into two joint ventures to produce and distribute Starbucks-branded products. The North American Coffee Partnership is a 50/50 joint venture with the Pepsi-Cola Company to produce and distribute bottled Frappuccino coffee drink, whereas the Starbucks Ice Cream Partnership is a 50/50 joint venture with Dreyer's Grand Ice Cream Inc. to produce and distribute premium ice creams. Starbucks accounts for these investments using the equity method. The Company's share of joint venture income ($15.1 million in 2000) is included as "Joint Venture Income" on Starbucks' consolidated income statement (not shown). Starbucks' balance sheet is presented in Exhibit 8.11, Panel A, and shows the company's investment in its joint ventures as a line item in the non-current assets section (see bolded area in Exhibit 8.11). Starbucks provides additional information about its joint ventures in the footnotes to its financial statements in Panel B, Exhibit 8.11. The exhibit reveals that Starbucks' investment in its joint ventures was increased by its share of the joint venture income ($15.1 million) and additional capital contributions ($8.4 million) that the company made to the joint venture during 2000, but was decreased by the dividends paid by the joint venture to Starbucks ($14.2 million).

ACCOUNTING FOR SPECIAL PURPOSE ENTITIES

Special purpose entities (SPEs) or special purpose vehicles (SPVs) refer to a separate legal entity created by a parent company along with other independent investors for a legitimate business purpose. Under U.S. GAAP, an SPE or SPV need not be consolidated by a parent company if certain conditions are met. The reporting rules governing these entities have recently been revised, including a new label for this type of entity, variable interest entity or VIE.

Companies that sell goods or services on credit, for example, often create an SPE to buy outstanding accounts receivable from the parent company. In essence, the SPE acts like a financial services company, borrowing from the investment community to then buy accounts receivable from the parent company. Because of complex accounting rules, SPEs may be accounted for by the parent company using the equity method even though the parent-company may own a majority of the SPE's equity shares (up to 90 percent under U.S. GAAP).

Unfortunately, the accounting rules that permitted majority-owned SPEs to remain unconsolidated were integral to several high profile corporate scandals, notably the Enron Corporation case. It is now known that Enron made extensive use of SPEs, largely as an off-balance sheet financing tool. An examination of Enron's footnotes concerning its unconsolidated equity affiliates reveals that Enron had extensive off-balance sheet debt (see Business Perspective on page 8.20). What was not revealed in Enron's footnotes

EXHIBIT 8.11	Financial Statement Disclosures: Joint Ventures

Panel A

Starbucks Coffee Company
Consolidated Balance Sheet

($ thousands)	Oct. 1, 2000	Oct. 3, 1999
Cash and cash equivalents	$ 70,817	$ 66,419
Short-term investments	61,336	51,367
Accounts receivable, net of allowances of $2,941 and $1,227, respectively	76,385	47,646
Inventories	201,656	180,886
Prepaid expenses and other current assets	20,321	19,049
Deferred income taxes, net	29,304	21,133
Total current assets	459,819	386,500
Joint ventures	52,051	42,718
Other investments	3,788	25,342
Property, plant and equipment, net	930,759	760,289
Other assets	25,403	23,474
Goodwill, net	21,311	14,191
Total assets	$1,493,131	$1,252,514

Panel B

Starbucks Coffee Company
Footnote Disclosures

	Joint Ventures
Balance: October 3, 1999	$42,718
Allocated share of income	15,139
Distributions from joint ventures	(14,279)
Capital contributions	8,473
Balance: October 1, 2000	$52,051

was the extent to which Enron was contingently liable for much of the debt of its unconsolidated SPEs. The alleged abuses of SPEs led the FASB to revisit the reporting rules governing these entities. The FASB had trouble defining an SPE and instead defined a broader category of entity called a variable interest entity, or VIE. Many former SPEs that previously escaped consolidation are now required to be consolidated under the new accounting rules.[3] Specifically, a VIE must be consolidated with the sponsoring parent-company if the VIE is not independent from the sponsoring company and does not have sufficient capital to operate separately from the sponsoring company. If there is more than one sponsoring company, the VIE should be consolidated with the sponsoring company that will absorb the majority of the VIE's expected losses or receive a majority of the VIE's expected residual returns.

The following are excerpts from the footnotes of the Ford Motor Company from its 2005 financial statements regarding its VIEs:

> Note 1. **Principles of Presentation and Consolidation** Our financial statements include consolidated majority-owned subsidiaries and, beginning July 1, 2003, consolidated Variable Interest Entities ("VIEs")

---

[3] See FASB Interpretation No. 46 (revised December 2003) FIN46R, Consolidation of Variable Interest Entities.

of which we are the primary beneficiary. Affiliates that we do not consolidate, but over whose operating and financing policies we have significant influence are accounted for using the equity method.

Note 17. **Variable Interest Entities** We consolidate VIEs of which we are the primary beneficiary. The liabilities recognized as a result of consolidating these VIEs do not represent additional claims on our general assets; rather, they represent claims against the specific assets of the consolidated VIEs. Conversely, assets recognized as a result of consolidating these VIEs do not represent additional assets that could be used to satisfy claims against our general assets. Reflected in our December 31, 2005, balance sheet are $5.5 billion of VIE assets related to VIEs that were consolidated.

BUSINESS PERSPECTIVE: SPE DISCLOSURES

Enron's abbreviated balance sheet at December 31, 2000, is presented below. The balance sheet reveals that Enron disclosed $8.55 billion of long-term debt and $5.294 billion of Investments in and Advances to Unconsolidated Equity Affiliates at year-end 2000. The use of this last account indicates that Enron used the equity method to account for its unconsolidated SPEs (see bolded area).

Enron Corporation **Abbreviated Balance Sheet**		
December 31 ($ millions)	**2000**	**1999**
Assets		
Current assets		
Total current assets	$30,381	$ 7,255
Investments & other assets		
Investments in & advances to unconsolidated equity affiliates	5,294	5,036
Assets from price risk management activities	8,988	2,929
Goodwill.	3,638	2,799
Other	5,459	4,681
Total investments & other assets	23,379	15,445
Property, plant & equipment (net).	11,743	10,681
Total assets.	$65,503	$33,381
Liabilities & shareholders' equity		
Total current liabilities.	$28,406	$ 6,759
Long-term debt.	8,550	7,151
Total deferred credits & other liabilities	13,759	6,471
Minority interests	2,414	2,430
Company-obligated preferred securities of subsidiaries	904	1,000
Total shareholders' equity	11,470	9,570
Total liabilities & shareholders' equity	$65,503	$33,381

Enron's footnotes provide summarized balance sheet information about its unconsolidated SPEs and reveal that its SPEs held $9.717 billion of related long-term debt. In simple terms, consolidating Enron's SPEs would have added another $9.717 billion of assets and long-term debt to Enron's consolidated balance sheet and consequently, increased Enron's reported debt-to-equity ratio from 0.75 ($8,550/$11,470) to 1.59 ($8,550 + $9,717)/$11,470—an increase of more than 100 percent! As is now known, an important objective in Enron's use of the equity method to account for its many SPEs was to keep the massive debt held by its unconsolidated SPEs off its consolidated balance sheet so that investors and investment professionals would perceive Enron to be less risky than it really was. Even such knowledgeable risk-rating agencies as Moody's and Standard & Poor's failed to correctly identify the financial risk inherent in Enron's financial arrangements. Enron filed for bankruptcy in late 2001.

ACCOUNTING FOR INVESTMENTS IN FOREIGN ENTITIES

With increasing globalization, even small companies now consider manufacturing and/or selling their goods and services abroad. Many U.S. companies, for example, have located manufacturing plants in Mexico and Asia to take advantage of large pools of skilled but relatively inexpensive labor. Another reason that companies locate their operations in other countries is to take advantage of natural currency hedges that exist when receipts from product sales and outlays for production costs are denominated in the same currency. A **currency hedge** is an attempt by a company to avoid the potential losses that may accompany an exchange rate movement between two currencies.

Currency Exchange Rate Fluctuations

A company may locate a sales office in a foreign country or it may establish an entire operating subsidiary that operates relatively autonomously from the parent-company. One of the issues that must be addressed when locating a production and/or sales organization in another country is the resulting exposure to currency exchange rate fluctuations. If, for instance, a manufacturing facility is built in Mexico by a U.S. company, the value of the Mexico-based business to the U.S. parent company will rise and fall as the exchange rate between the U.S. dollar and the Mexican peso rises and falls. Currency exchange rate problems do not exist between countries in which the currencies are pegged to one another, as for example between the U.S. and Guatemala or Panama.

Before any consolidated financial statements which include the results of foreign-based subsidiaries can be prepared, the financial results of any foreign subsidiary must first be converted from its local currency into the currency of the parent company. Under U.S. GAAP and the GAAP of most countries, the **current rate method** is used to translate the foreign-currency denominated financial statements of foreign subsidiaries that are self-contained business units.

Under the current rate method, a foreign subsidiary's assets and liabilities are translated at the current or closing exchange rate as of the balance sheet date while shareholders' equity is translated at the historical exchange rate when the subsidiary

> The financial results of foreign subsidiaries that are not self-contained are usually translated using the temporal method. Under the temporal method, monetary assets and liabilities are translated at the current or closing exchange rate, whereas non-monetary assets and liabilities are translated at historical exchange rates.

was established. Income statement items, on the other hand, are translated at the average exchange rate for the fiscal period. Any foreign currency translation gains/losses—that is, any changes in the translated value of the foreign subsidiary assets and liabilities over the fiscal period—are reported as a component of shareholders' equity and do not flow through to the income statement. Foreign currency translation gains (losses) represent unrealized wealth changes, much like the unrealized gains (losses) on available-for-sale securities. And, as a consequence, the accumulated balance of any foreign currency translation gains (losses) are reported on the balance sheet as a component of Other Comprehensive Income under U.S. GAAP.

Illustration of Current Rate Method: Jimbo Inc.

Jimbo Inc., is a U.S.-based manufacturer and distributor of food preparation equipment. To take advantage of growth opportunities outside the U.S., the company established a self-contained operating subsidiary in Mexico. The Mexican subsidiary—Jimbo de Mexico SA de CV—was established on January 1 when the exchange rate was 10 pesos to $1. At the inception of the Mexican subsidiary, its balance sheet appeared as follows:

Jimbo de Mexico Balance Sheet January 1			
(P millions)			
Cash..........................	P1,500	Long-term debt	P 900
Accounts receivable..............	300	Common stock....................	900
Total assets.....................	P1,800	Liabilities & shareholders' equity	P1,800

How would Jimbo de Mexico report its balance sheet in U.S. dollars on January 1? Exhibit 8.12, Panel A, shows Jimbo de Mexico's balance sheet in Mexican pesos and in U.S. dollars. The company's assets and liabilities are translated at the current exchange rate of 10 pesos per dollar while shareholders' equity is translated at the historical exchange rate, which in this instance is also 10 pesos per dollar.

EXHIBIT 8.12	Translating Balance Sheets: Current Rate Method

Panel A. Pre-devaluation

	Jimbo de Mexico Balance Sheet		
(in millions)	January 1 (Mexican pesos)	Exchange Rate (pesos per $1)	January 1 (U.S. dollars)
Cash......................................	P1,500	10	$150
Accounts receivable........................	300	10	30
Total assets...............................	P1,800		$180
Long-term debt	P 900	10	$ 90
Common stock............................	900	10	90
Cumulative foreign currency translation adjustment......................	0		0
Liabilities & shareholders' equity	P1,800		$180

Panel B. Post-devaluation

	Jimbo de Mexico Balance Sheet		
(in millions)	January 2 (Mexican pesos)	Exchange Rate (pesos per $1)	January 2 (U.S. dollars)
Cash......................................	P1,500	15	$100
Accounts receivable........................	300	15	20
Total assets...............................	P1,800		$120
Long-term debt	P 900	15	$ 60
Common stock............................	900	10	90
Cumulative foreign currency translation adjustment......................	0		(30)
Liabilities & shareholders' equity	P1,800		$120

Now assume that on January 2, the Mexican peso depreciated to an exchange rate of 15 pesos per U.S. dollar. How would Jimbo de Mexico report its balance sheet in U.S. dollars following the devaluation? Jimbo de Mexico's post-devaluation balance sheet in U.S. dollars is shown in Exhibit 8.12, Panel B. After the devaluation, the company's assets and liabilities are translated at the new current exchange rate of 15 pesos per U.S. dollar while shareholders' equity is translated at the historical rate of 10 pesos per U.S. dollar. The cumulative foreign currency translation adjustment (CTA) of negative $30 million is required to ensure that the translated balance sheet actually balances. The CTA represents the exposure that Jimbo's shareholders suffered from the currency devaluation on their investment in Jimbo de Mexico. The $30 million unrealized loss is equal to the equity investment in Jimbo de Mexico times the change in the exchange rate [900 million pesos $\times$ (1/10–1/15)].

The foreign currency translation account may carry either a negative (net unrealized loss) or positive (net unrealized gain) balance. The account balance will increase or decrease each period in response to the changing exchange rate between the currency of the country of the parent and the currency of the country of the subsidiary. The balance at any point in time represents the gain (loss) that could be realized by the parent-company if the foreign subsidiary were sold for a price equivalent to its current book value, with the net proceeds from the sale repatriated back to the parent's currency.

ANALYZING INTERCORPORATE INVESTMENTS

The analysis of intercorporate investments—that is, an investment by one corporate entity in the equity of a second corporate entity—presents analytical challenges for financial statements users at several different levels. First, the managerial discretion that is required in the designation of marketable securities as being either trading securities or available-for-sale securities presents a significant opportunity for earnings' management. If, for example, the chief financial officer (CFO) of an investor-company anticipates that an investee-company is likely to sustain operating losses that might adversely affect its market value, the CFO might selectively classify the investment as available-for-sale to avoid the potential negative income statement effect associated with an unrealized loss if the investment were classified as a trading security. Similarly, if the CFO anticipates an upward share price movement in the value of an investee-company, the CFO might selectively designate the investment as a trading security to enable any unrealized gain to flow through to the investor-company's income statement and positively impact its reported earnings. In this latter case, financial statement users would be wise to recall the definition of sustainable earnings from Chapter 3—sustainable earnings exclude any one-time or non-operating events such as an unrealized gain on a trading security.

Second, with respect to equity method-accounted intercorporate investments, which include an investment in an unconsolidated affiliate, joint venture, or special purpose entity, some investment professionals regard the equity method as a form of off-balance sheet financing. Under the equity method, an investor-company adjusts its carrying value for an investee-company for its proportionate share of the investee's operating earnings, losses, and dividends paid; but, the investor-company is not required to account for its implicit ownership interest in any changes in the level of debt financing of the investee. As a consequence, an investee may significantly increase its use of leverage, often for the express purpose of transferring the borrowed funds to the investor-company, but the investor is not required to reflect the increased investee borrowing on its own financial statements. The favorable accounting treatment associated with the debt of an equity method-accounted investee was at the root of Enron Corporation's extensive use of off-balance sheet special purpose entities.

A final consideration in the analysis of intercorporate investments is the issue of related-party transactions—that is, the profit or loss generated by transactions between two entities that are related by virtue of existing cross-firm equity investments. Although the elimination of any intercompany transactions among consolidated entities is required under existing GAAP, the financial effects of any intercompany transactions between an investor-company and an unconsolidated affiliate company are permitted to be included in the consolidated financial statements. Where such intercompany transactions are material in amount, details of the transactions must be disclosed in the footnotes to the financial statements. With this information, financial statement users are empowered to decide whether (or not) to restate the consolidated financial statements to eliminate the financial effects of these related-party transactions prior to assessing the value of a firm.

ETHICS PERSPECTIVE

The Enron scandal was arguably the most complex financial fraud ever uncovered in the U.S. Somewhat surprisingly, it was not Enron's external auditors, Arthur Anderson, or U.S. regulators that are credited with exposing the company's accounting improprieties. Instead, it was an Enron employee, Sherron Watkins, who stepped forward to warn that Enron would "implode in a wave of accounting scandals." It is often whistle blowers such as Sherron Watkins at Enron and Cynthia Cooper at WorldCom that have the necessary knowledge to expose these financial frauds. Inside knowledge, unfortunately, is not always enough to get whistle blowers to come forward with the information to expose corporate wrongdoing. Some corporate managers have made exposing fraud very costly to the whistle blower through threats, intimidation, and character attacks. The Sarbanes-Oxley Act, passed into law in 2002, recognized the value of having a system in place such that employees would be more likely to report corporate wrongdoing. Provisions under Section 307 of the legislation make it easier for an employee to report items in a confidential matter while Section 806 prohibits retaliation by a company against any employee reporting questionable activities.

REVIEW PROBLEM

The Arcadia Company made an offer to purchase all of the outstanding shares of The Claremont Company at a price of $10 per share, or an aggregate of $22 million. Immediately prior to the purchase offer, the balance sheets of the two companies appeared as follows:

	The Arcadia Company	The Claremont Company
Assets		
Cash.	$ 26,000,000	$ 2,000,000
Inventory.	12,000,000	7,000,000
Fixed assets, net	50,000,000	15,000,000
Intangible assets	30,000,000	18,000,000
Total Assets	$118,000,000	$42,000,000
Liabilities		
Accounts payable.	$ 7,000,000	$ 4,000,000
Bonds payable	25,000,000	19,000,000
Total	32,000,000	23,000,000

continued

continued from previous page

	The Arcadia Company	The Claremont Company
Shareholders' Equity		
Capital stock	56,000,000	14,000,000
Retained earnings	30,000,000	5,000,000
Total	86,000,000	19,000,000
Total liabilities and shareholders' equity.	$118,000,000	$42,000,000

During its due diligence review, Arcadia determined that while the liabilities of The Claremont Company were fairly valued, the reported value of Claremont's inventory was understated by $1,000,000 as a consequence of using the LIFO method and the intangible assets of The Claremont Company were overstated by $4,000,000 because an impairment in the value of certain intangible assets that had not yet been recorded in the company's financial statements.

Required

a. Calculate the value of the goodwill implicit in the offer price of $22 million.
b. Prepare the unconsolidated balance sheet of The Arcadia Company immediately following a successful acquisition of 100 percent of the outstanding shares of The Claremont Company.
c. Prepare the consolidated balance sheet for The Arcadia-Claremont Company assuming a successful acquisition offer.

Solution

a. Goodwill

Purchase price		$22,000,000
Less: Fair market value		
Book value	$19,000,000	
Add: Inventory understatement	1,000,000	
Less: Intangible asset impairment	(4,000,000)	
		(16,000,000)
Goodwill		$ 6,000,000

b. Unconsolidated balance sheet

The Arcadia Company Unconsolidated Balance Sheet				
Assets			**Liabilities & Shareholders' Equity**	
Cash	$ 4,000,000[1]		Accounts payable	$ 7,000,000
Inventory	12,000,000		Bonds payable	25,000,000
Investment in Claremont Co.	22,000,000		Total	32,000,000
Fixed assets, net	50,000,000		Shareholders' equity	
			Capital stock	56,000,000
Intangible assets	30,000,000		Retained earnings	30,000,000
Total	$118,000,000		Total liabilities & equity	$118,000,000

[1] Cash: $26,000,000 − $22,000,000 = $4,000,000.

c. Consolidated balance sheet

The Arcadia Company Consolidated Balance Sheet			
Assets		**Liabilities & Shareholders' Equity**	
Cash	$ 6,000,000	Accounts payable	$ 11,000,000
Inventory	20,000,000	Bonds payable	44,000,000
Investment in Claremont Co.	0	Total	55,000,000
Fixed assets, net	65,000,000	Shareholders' equity	
		Capital stock	56,000,000
Intangible assets	44,000,000	Retained earnings	30,000,000
Goodwill	6,000,000	Total	86,000,000
Total	$141,000,000	Total liabilities & equity	$141,000,000

EXECUTIVE SUMMARY

This chapter examined the accounting for investments in other corporate entities. We considered why such investments are made and how they are accounted for. In general, small equity investments (0 to 20 percent) are accounted for at their current market value. Investments representing 20 to 50 percent of the outstanding equity are accounted for using the equity method, as are most joint ventures and special purpose entities; and, investments involving a controlling equity interest (greater than 50 percent) are accounted for using consolidated accounting.

As a validation of your understanding of the content of this chapter, you should now be able to:

- Explain why companies acquire ownership interests in other businesses.
- Understand how to account for investments in debt and equity securities, including the application of the equity method and consolidation accounting.
- Understand the accounting for joint ventures and special purposes entities.
- Understand the foreign currency issues that arise with investments in foreign companies.

In Chapter 9, we begin an exploration of corporate financing decisions, specifically how companies finance their operations and capital investments using debt.

KEY CONCEPTS AND TERMS

Arms-length transaction, 8.9
Available-for-sale securities, 8.3
Conglomerate discount, 8.17
Consolidation accounting, 8.5
Currency hedge, 8.21
Current rate method, 8.21
Cumulative foreign currency
　translation adjustment, 8.23
Deconsolidation, 8.17
Equity in the earnings (loss) of an
　unconsolidated affiliate, 8.5
Equity method, 8.5
Full consolidation, 8.13

Goodwill, 8.9
Held-to-maturity debt securities, 8.4
Information overload, 8.11
Joint ventures, 8.17
Liquidating dividend, 8.10
Lower-of-cost-or-market, 8.5
Marketable debt and equity
　securities, 8.3
Mark-to-market accounting, 8.3
Minority interest, 8.13
Off-balance sheet financing, 8.14
Other Comprehensive Income, 8.4
Partial consolidation, 8.18

Pooling-of-interests
　accounting, 8.16
Purchase accounting, 8.13
Related-party transaction, 8.9
Revenue synergies, 8.2
Special purpose entities, 8.18
Special purpose vehicle, 8.18
Spin-off, 8.17
Temporal method, 8.21
Trading securities, 8.3
Unrealized gains (losses), 8.3
Variable interest entity, 8.18

APPENDIX 8A: Recording Investments in Other Corporate Entities using the Debit and Credit Paradigm

In this appendix, the traditional approach to recording accounting transactions—that is, the debit and credit paradigm—is used to illustrate the journal entries associated with the various investments made by The New South Sales Trading Company, Inc. and by Savanna, Inc. Please refer to the content of Chapter 8 for additional information regarding these transactions (see Exhibits 8.2 through 8.12).

Accounting for Marketable Debt and Equity Securities: The New South Wales Company Inc.

In August 2005, The New South Sales Trading Company, Inc. raised $50 million from an initial public offering (IPO) of its common shares. The company decided to temporarily invest some of its IPO cash in various debt and equity securities having a high degree of liquidity. These events are recorded below:

Date	Accounts	Debit	Credit
Aug 2005	Cash (A)	50,000,000	
	Common Stock (SE)		50,000,000
	To record the sale of common stock for $50 million.		
Sep 2005	Investment in Qantas Inc. 10% Notes (A)	10,000,000	
	Cash (A)		10,000,000
	To record the purchase of held-to-maturity debt securities.		
Nov 2005	Investment in BHP, Inc. Common Stock (A).....................	6,100,000	
	Cash (A)		6,100,000
	To record the investment in trading equity securities.		
Dec 2005	Investment in Coles Inc. Common Stock (A)	8,400,000	
	Cash (A)		8,400,000
	To record the investment in available-for-sale equity securities.		

At the end of 2005, the CFO of The New South Sales Trading Company, Inc. determined that the Qantas notes were worth $9.8 million, the BHP common shares worth $6.8 million, and the Coles Inc. common shares worth $8.2 million. In addition, the CFO observed that Qantas Inc. had made an interest payment of $1 million on its notes on December 31, 2005. This information would be recorded as follows:

Date	Accounts	Debit	Credit
Dec 31, 2005	Cash (A)	1,000,000	
	Retained Earnings (I)		1,000,000
	To record interest income I on the Qantas notes.		
	Investment in BHP Inc. common stock (A)...................	700,000	
	Retained Earnings (G)		700,000
	To record the gain of $700,000 on trading equity securities.		
	Unrealized Loss on Available-For-Sale Securities (SE)	200,000	
	Investment in Coles Inc. Common Stocks (A)..............		200,000
	To record the decline in market value on available-for-sale securities.		

To verify your understanding of these transactions, create a series of T-accounts for the affected accounts, post the amounts to the T-accounts, and calculate a year-end balance. Your results should reveal the following balances:

Assets		Shareholders' Equity	
Cash	$26,500,000	Common stock	$50,000,000
Investments		Retained earnings	1,700,000
Qantas notes	10,000,000	Other Comprehensive Income	
BHP common stock.	6,800,000	Unrealized loss on available-	
Coles common stock.	8,200,000	for-sale securities	(200,000)
Total	$51,500,000	Total	$51,500,000

Equity Method and Consolidated Accounting: Savanna, Inc.

Case 1. Savanna Inc. acquires 40 percent of the common shares of Waterloo Inc. for $8 million at the beginning of 2005. At year-end, Savanna reports cash earnings of $30 million; Waterloo reports cash earnings of $10 million; and, Waterloo pays its shareholders a cash dividend of $5 million. These transactions would be recorded as follows on Savanna's books:

Date	Accounts	Debit	Credit
Jan 2005	Investment in Waterloo Inc. (A). . . . . Cash (A) . . . . *To record the initial investment in Waterloo Inc.*	8,000,000	8,000,000
Dec 2005	Cash (A) . . . . Retained Earnings (SE) . . . . *To record Savanna's cash earnings of $30 million.*	30,000,000	30,000,000
	Investment in Waterloo Inc. (A). . . . . Retained Earnings (I) . . . . *To record Savanna's 40 percent share of Waterloo's $10 million in earnings.*	4,000,000	4,000,000
	Cash (A) . . . . Investment in Waterloo Inc. (A) . . . . *To record Savanna's 40 percent share of Waterloo's $5 million dividend payment.*	2,000,000	2,000,000

Case 2. Savanna Inc. acquires 80 percent of Waterloo's common shares for $16 million in January 2005; the fair market value of Waterloo's net assets equals their book value of $20 million (no goodwill is implicit in the investment). At year-end, Savanna reports cash earnings of $30 million; Waterloo reports cash earnings of $10 million; and, Waterloo pays its shareholders a cash dividend of $5 million. Because of its majority shareholding, Savanna prepares consolidated financial statements at year-end. These transactions would be recorded as follows on Savanna's books:

Date	Accounts	Debit	Credit
Jan 2005	Investment in Waterloo Inc. (A). . . . . Cash (A) . . . . *To record Savanna's acquisition of a 80 percent shareholding in Waterloo Inc.*	16,000,000	16,000,000

continued

continued from previous page

Date	Accounts	Debit	Credit
Dec 2005	Cash (A) . . . . Retained Earnings (SE) . . . . *To record Savanna's cash earnings of $30 million.*	30,000,000	30,000,000
	Investment in Waterloo Inc. (A). . . . . Retained Earnings (I) . . . . *To record Savanna's 80 percent ownership interest in Waterloo earnings of $10 million.*	8,000,000	8,000,000
	Cash (A) . . . . Investment in Waterloo (A). . . . . *To record Savanna's 80 percent ownership interest in Waterloo's dividend payment of $5 million.*	4,000,000	4,000,000
	Cash (A) . . . . Inventory (A). . . . . Investment in Waterloo (A). . . . . Minority Interest (L/SE). . . . . Long-Term debt (L) . . . . *To consolidate Waterloo's net assets with those of Savanna and to establish the minority interest account.*	25,000,000 80,000,000	20,000,000 5,000,000 80,000,000

(The journal entries for Case 3 are not presented here. You may wish to create these entries using the contents of Exhibits 8.9 and 8.10)

DISCUSSION QUESTIONS

Q8.1   **Accounting for Marketable Securities.**   Marketable securities are classified under U.S. GAAP as either trading securities or available-for-sale securities. Regardless of their classification, marketable securities are accounted for at their current market value using mark-to-market accounting. Discuss why mark-to-market accounting is superior to accounting for marketable securities at their historical cost. Should mark-to-market accounting be adopted to account for all assets on the balance sheet? Why or why not?

Q8.2   **Equity Method versus Consolidated Reporting.**   The equity method is often described as a "one-line consolidation." Discuss the similarities of the equity method and consolidated reporting. Discuss how these methods differ in their financial statement presentation.

Q8.3   **Minority Interest.**   The minority interest account arises on consolidated financial statements when a parent-company owns less than 100 percent of the voting shares of a subsidiary. On the consolidated balance sheet, the minority interest account is customarily listed between the liabilities and the shareholders' equity sections. Discuss whether the minority interest account on the balance sheet constitutes a component of debt or equity.

Q8.4   **Other Comprehensive Income.**   Other Comprehensive Income (OCI) appears as a subsection of shareholders' equity on the balance sheet. Discuss the components of OCI. What information does the OCI convey to financial statement users about the financial health of a business?

Q8.5   **Cumulative Foreign Currency Translation Adjustment.**   The cumulative foreign currency translation adjustment (CTA) account appears on the balance sheet as a component of Other Comprehensive Income. The CTA account may have either a positive (credit) or negative (debit) balance. Discuss the financial implications when the CTA account balance is negative and when it is positive.

Q8.6   **Goodwill.**   In 1989, **PepsiCo Inc.** acquired three international franchise-food operations—Pizza Hut, Taco Bell, and Kentucky Fried Chicken. PepsiCo paid an aggregate of $3.4 billion for the three businesses, which had been valued by investment professionals to be worth, in aggregate, $400 million. As a consequence, PepsiCo recorded $3.0 billion of goodwill on its consolidated balance sheet associated with the acquisitions. Discuss why PepsiCo may have been willing to pay so much above the fair market value of the three businesses.

Q8.7   **Negative Goodwill.**   Negative goodwill is said to arise in an acquisition transaction when an acquiror pays less that the acquiree's book value to purchase the company. Under U.S. GAAP, negative goodwill is charged off against the tangible assets of an acquiree prior to consolidation, thereby potentially eliminating all (or most) of the negative goodwill. Discuss the circumstances that might lead to the presence of negative goodwill in an acquisition transaction.

Q8.8   **Accounting for Long-term Investments.**   In 2006, **CKX, Inc.**, a New York sports entertainment company, paid $50 million for an 80 percent ownership interest in G.O.A.T. LLC. (G.O.A.T. stands for "Greatest of All Time" and is a business which licenses the name and image of former boxing champion Mohammad Ali.) The remaining 20 percent of G.O.A.T. LLC is owned by the Ali Trust. Recent financial statements reveal that the gross revenue of G.O.A.T. averages $5 million annually, giving the LLC an estimated fair-market value of $30 million. Discuss how CKX's investment in G.O.A.T. LLC should be accounted for. How should the Ali Trust account for its 20 percent ownership interest in G.O.A.T.?

Q8.9   **Mergers, Acquisitions and Share Price.**   In 2006, **Danaher, Inc.** announced its intent to acquire Sybron Dental Specialties, Inc., a manufacturer of dental products. Danaher indicated that it had agreed to pay $47 per share for all of Sybron's outstanding shares. The cash tender offer, which included the assumption of $200 million of Sybron debt, was valued at $2 billion. In response to the acquisition announcement, Danaher's shares increased by 1.3 percent. Discuss how the capital market responds to merger and acquisition announcements, and specifically, the message implied by the market's response to Danaher's announcement of its planned acquisition of Sybron. What was the equity value of Sybron implicit in the transaction?

Q8.10   **Acquisition Bidding and the Winner's Curse.**   **Aztar Corporation** is an operator of casinos and hotels. The company's flagship properties are the Tropicana Hotel & Casino located in Las Vegas, Nevada and in Atlantic City, New Jersey. In early 2006, Aztar's common shares were trading at $29 per share. On March 12, 2006, Pinnacle Entertainment Inc. made a tender offer to buy all of Aztar's outstanding common shares for $38 per share, a premium of 31 percent above Aztar's market price. Two weeks later, Ameristar Casinos, Inc. made a competing tender offer to buy Aztar's outstanding shares at a price of $43 per share. On April 15, 2006 Columbia Sussex Corporation made an unsolicited offer to buy Aztar at $47 per share, a premium of over 62 percent above Aztar's share price before the bidding competition began. Then, on April 28, 2006, Pinnacle raised its bid to $48 per share, followed immediately by a $50 per share bid by Columbia Sussex. Finally, on May 10, 2006, Pinnacle again raised its bid for Aztar to $51 per share, only to again be out bid by Columbia which offered $53 per share. Some industry analysts described the bidding war for Aztar as an example of "The Winner's Curse," a situation in auction-like settings in which the winner is the entity which most over-values the item being bid on, and thus, winning the final bid actually signals that the winner has lost as a consequence of over-paying for the item.

Discuss whether you think the Aztar bidding war is an example of The Winner's Curse. Does the significantly higher bid by Columbia Sussex of $53 per share indicate that the market for Aztar's common stock prior to the bidding war was inefficient? Why would Columbia Sussex be willing to pay such a significant premium ($24 per share) for Aztar's shares?

Q8.11   **Goodwill Impairment.**   On February 27, 2006, **Vodafone**, the United Kingdom-based telecommunications company, announced that it would write off $49 billion in goodwill associated with its $192 billion acquisition of Germany's Mannesmann in 2000. Discuss how Vodafone will account for the write-off and why the company decided to make this adjustment to its goodwill account. How do you think the capital market reacted to this news announcement, and why?

Q8.12   **Divesting Long-term Investments.**   **BAE Systems**, Europe's largest defense company, announced that it was selling its 20 percent shareholding in Airbus, Europe's largest aircraft manufacturer, to EADS, the

Franco-German aerospace company that already owned 80 percent of Airbus. The CEO of BAE Systems stated that Airbus had been an excellent investment but "we believe that now is the right time for us to divest our Airbus shareholding to allow us to concentrate on our core strategy." BAE's cost basis of its investment in Airbus was believed to be $4.3 billion, with a current market value of approximately $7.8 billion. Prior to 2001, at which time BAE and EADS purchased their shareholdings in Airbus, the passenger aircraft manufacturer had been structured as a "consortium" whose assets were held by national companies in the United Kingdom, France, Germany, and Spain. Discuss how Airbus might have been accounted for prior to 2001. Following the sale of Airbus to BAE and EADS in 2004, how would each firm's investment in Airbus have been accounted for? Estimate BAE's gain on the divestiture of its Airbus shareholding.

Q8.13 **De-Merger and Share Prices.** In early 2006, Henry Silverman, chairman and CEO of Cendant Corporation, announced that the company's board of directors had approved the de-merger of Cendant into four operating companies—Avis Budget (a vehicle rental company composed of Avis, Budget, and Budget Truck), Wyndham Worldwide (a lodging company composed of such hotels and resort chains as Wyndham Resorts, Ramada Inn, Howard Johnson, and others), Realogy (a real estate franchise company composed of Century 21, Coldwell Banker, and Sotheby's, among others), and Travel Distribution (a travel company composed of Orbitz.com, CheapTickets.com, and RatesToGo.com, among others). Under the split-up plan, Wyndham Worldwide and Realogy would be de-merged by a public offering of shares, whereas Avis Budget and Travel Distribution would be spun-off to existing Cendant shareholders.

The reason for the de-merger, according to Silverman, was that Cendant's earnings were not being properly reflected in its share price. "We were among the 100 most profitable companies in America in 2004, yet we were somewhere in the 300s in terms of market value." Discuss the reasons why Cendant's share price in 2004 may not have reflected its earnings in 2004. If the de-merger is successful, what should happen to the share price of the four operating companies? Why?

Q8.14 **Poison-Pill Defense.** Following a series of hostile acquisitions in the global steel industry, **Nippon Steel Corporation** announced the implementation of a "poison-pill" plan designed to fend off any hostile takeover bids of the Japanese steel company. Under the plan, if a hostile buyer attempts to acquire a stake of 15 percent or more in the company, the steelmaker's shareholders would be allowed to double the number of shares they own for a nominal amount. Executives of Nippon Steel indicated that adoption of the plan was aimed at fending off potential acquirers who might damage the firm's corporate value. Market analysts expressed concern that the poison-pill defense would adversely affect the firm's share price. Discuss how Nippon's poison-pill defense could prevent an unwanted takeover bid and why the plan might actually hurt the company's share price.

Q8.15 **Goodwill Impairment and Debt Covenants.** The October 12, 2006, edition of The Wall Street Journal carried an article entitled "Expedia Might Trip Debt Covenant." The article revealed that the share price of **Expedia Inc.**, an online travel company, had recently declined by 33 percent following the company's spin-off from its parent company IAC/InterActive Corporation. IAC/InterActive had acquired Expedia several years earlier in an acquisition that involved $5.9 billion in goodwill.

When Expedia was spun-off by its parent, the $5.9 billion in goodwill associated with the acquisition was downloaded from the consolidated balance sheet to Expedia's balance sheet. Further, a provision in Expedia's $1 billion borrowing arrangement required that the company maintain a shareholders' equity of $5.4 billion. With the decline in its share price to $16 per share, the company's market capitalization had dropped to just $5.2 billion. The company's book value at the time was just $5.8 billion. Discuss what action the company should take with respect to its $5.9 billion in acquisition goodwill. What are the consequences of those actions?

Q8.16 **(Ethics Perspective) Whistle Blowing.** Whistle blowers often question themselves as to whether they are doing the "right thing." Terms such as "snitch" and "tattletale" are often associated with an individual who exposes wrongdoing. Do you believe that it is ethical to report questionable activity as an anonymous whistle blower, especially if you do not completely understand the events you are reporting?

⊘ **indicates that check figures are available on the book's Website.**

EXERCISES

E8.17 **Accounting for Marketable Securities.** **Microsoft Inc.** maintains a large investment in marketable securities (principally fixed income securities) valued at approximately $42 billion as of the beginning of the year. During the year, the securities produced investment income (dividends and interest income) totaling $2 billion. At year-end, the portfolio of marketable securities had appreciated to $43.5 billion. Calculate the income statement effect of the marketable securities if (a) the entire portfolio is classified as trading securities and (b) the entire portfolio is classified as available-for-sale securities. How much of the income in (a) and (b) is subject to current income taxation?

E8.18 **Accounting for Short-term Investments.** The **Claremont Corporation** invests its excess cash in low risk, dividend-paying equity securities until such funds are needed to support operations. At the beginning of the year, the company's portfolio consisted of the following securities:

Company	Cost Basis
Bristol-Myers Squibb (BMS)..	$ 75,000
Johnson and Johnson (JNJ)..	55,000
Pfizer, Inc. (PFE)..	110,000
Total	$240,000

At year-end, the market values of the three securities were as follows: BMS $82,000; JNJ $53,000; and PFE $100,000. Calculate the income statement effect of the company's short-term investments assuming: (a) all securities are classified as trading; (b) all securities are classified as available-for-sale; (c) BMS and JNJ are classified as trading, while PFE is classified as available-for-sale.

E8.19 **Comprehensive Income.** The following financial data is taken from the annual report of **The Carlton Company**:

(in thousands)	Year 1	Year 2	Year 3
Net income...................................	$20,493	$21,450	$21,846
Other comprehensive income (loss)...............			
Net unrealized gain (loss) on available-for-sale			
securities...............................	(138)	219	33
Cumulative foreign currency translation			
adjustment............................	630	(549)	(96)
Comprehensive income	$20,985	$21,120	$21,783

Explain (a) what "comprehensive income" is and how it differs from net income, (b) what happened to the value of The Carlton Company's available-for-sale securities each year, and (c) what caused the cumulative foreign currency translation adjustment to increase or decrease each year.

E8.20 **Comprehensive Income.** The following financial data is taken from the 2005 annual report of **Bristol-Myers Squibb Company**:

(in millions)	2003	2004	2005
Net earnings......................................	$3,106	$2,388	$3,000
Other comprehensive income			
Foreign currency translation	233	208	(270)

continued

continued from previous page

(in millions)	2003	2004	2005
Deferred gain (loss) on derivatives			
qualifying as hedges	(171)	(51)	325
Minimum pension liability adjustment	(36)	(93)	(6)
Available-for-sale securities.	23	(1)	(22)
Comprehensive income	$3,155	$2,451	$3,027

Explain (a) what "comprehensive income" is and how it differs from net income, (b) what happened to the company's available-for-sale securities in 2003, 2004, and 2005, and (c) what happened to cause the foreign currency translation balance to increase or decrease over the three-year period.

⊘ E8.21   **Available-for-Sale Securities.**   The 2005 annual report of the **Bristol-Myers Squibb Company** (BMS) reveals that the company maintains a large investment in marketable securities;

(in millions)	2004	2005
Marketable securities	$3,794	$2,749

The footnotes to the company's financial statements report:

> The Company accounts for marketable securities in accordance with SFAS No. 115, "Accounting for Certain Investments in Debt and Equity Securities." The Company determined the appropriate classification of all marketable securities was "available-for-sale" at the time of purchase.

Further, the company's statement of cash flow reveals that sales of marketable securities in 2005 produced a positive cash flow of $1,043. Did the company's remaining portfolio of marketable securities experience a gain or loss in value in 2005, and in what amount? How did the company account for that gain or loss?

E8.22   **Available-for-Sale Securities.**   The 2005 annual report of **Pfizer, Inc.** (PFE) reveals that the company maintains a significant investment in short-term investments:

(in millions)	2004	2005
Short-term investments	$18,085	$19,979

During the year, the company purchased short-term investments (net of sales of short-term investments) totaling $1,261. Did the company's portfolio of short-term investments experience a gain or a loss during 2005, and in what amount? Assuming all of Pfizer's short-term investments are classified as available-for-sale securities, how did the company account for the gain or loss in 2005?

E8.23   **Long-term Equity Investments.**   The 2005 annual report of the **Bristol-Myers Squibb** (BMS) Company discloses the following amounts on its consolidated statement of earnings:

(in millions)	2003	2004	2005
Equity in net income of affiliates.	$151	$273	$334

On the company's statement of cash flow, the following amounts appear as a subtraction from net earnings under the Cash Flow from Operating Activities:

(in millions)	2003	2004	2005
Undistributed income of affiliates.	$66	$7	$50

Calculate the amount of cash dividends received by BMS from its affiliates in 2003, 2004, and 2005. Assume that BMS neither sold nor purchased any equity interest in its affiliates in 2003, 2004, or 2005. What happened to the balance sheet value of the "investment in equity affiliates" account in 2003, 2004, and 2005?

⊘ E8.24 **Long-term Equity Investments.** The annual report of The Arcadia Company discloses the following amounts on its consolidated statement of income:

	2004	2005	2006
Equity in earnings of unconsolidated affiliates........	$350	$415	$520

Further, on Arcadia's consolidated balance sheet, it reports the following amounts for its investment in its unconsolidated affiliates:

	2004	2005	2006
Investment in unconsolidated affiliates	$10,500	$10,715	$10,950

Calculate the amount of cash dividends received by The Arcadia Company from its unconsolidated affiliates in 2005 and 2006. Calculate the adjustment to net income that appears on Arcadia's statement of cash flow in 2005 and 2006 for "undistributed earnings of unconsolidated affiliates."

E8.25 **Equity Method.** The balance sheet of The Miller Corporation disclosed a long-term investment in the common shares of The Mann Corporation valued at $350,000 as of December 31, 2006. The investment had been purchased by the Miller Corporation in January, 2003. Further, the following financial information from The Mann Corporation is available:

Year	Net Income (loss)	Dividends Paid
2003	$ (30,000)	$ -0-
2004	120,000	50,000
2005	150,000	60,000
2006	200,000	80,000

Determine how much The Miller Corporation paid for its investment in Mann common shares in January 2003 assuming that the investment represents a 25 percent ownership interest.

⊘ E8.26 **Equity Method.** On January 1, 2005, The Miller Corporation purchased 300,000 shares of The Mayfair Corporation for $5.7 million. The investment represented 25 percent of The Mayfair Corporation's outstanding common shares. During 2005, Mayfair reported net earnings of $2.25 million and paid a cash dividend of $0.15 per share. During 2006, Mayfair reported a net loss of $180,000 and again paid a dividend of $0.15 per share. Calculate the book value of Miller's investment in Mayfair as of December 31, 2005 and December 31, 2006.

E8.27 **Equity Method.** On January 2, 2005, Winstead & Company purchased 1,000,000 shares of the Secrest Company for $32.0 million. The investment represented 40 percent of the outstanding common shares of The Secrest Company. During 2005, Secrest reported net earnings of $1.05 per share and paid a cash dividend of $0.35 per share. During 2006, Secrest reported net earnings of $1.50 per share and paid a cash dividend $0.40 per share. Calculate the book value of Winstead's investment in Secrest as of December 31, 2005 and December 31, 2006.

E8.28   **Equity Method.**   The Coca-Cola Company accounts for its investment in its unconsolidated affiliate Coca-Cola Enterprises, Inc. (CCE) using the equity method. Coca-Cola's 2005 annual report disclosed the book value of its 36 percent ownership interest in CCE as follows:

(in millions)	2004	2005
Equity investment in Coca-Cola Enterprises	$1,569	$1,731

During 2005, CCE reported net income of $514 million. Calculate the amount of dividends paid by CCE to Coca-Cola in 2005. What disclosure will appear in Coca-Cola's Operating Activities section of its 2005 statement of cash flow regarding its investment in CCE?

E8.29   **Accounting for Joint Ventures.**   Starbucks Corporation and PepsiCo formed a joint venture to produce and distribute bottled Frappuccino coffee drink throughout North America. Assume that the 50/50 joint venture had a book value on the consolidated balance sheet of Starbucks Corporation of $90 million and $70 million at year-end 2004 and 2003, respectively. Further, assume that on Starbucks' 2004 statement of cash flow, the company disclosed an adjustment to net income for the PepsiCo joint venture as follows:

	2004
Equity in income of joint venture	$(18,000,000)

Calculate the joint venture's total earnings and total cash dividends for 2004.

PROBLEMS

P8.30   **Accounting for Marketable Equity Securities.**   Tim Propp, CFO of Thunderbird, Inc. invested some of the firm's excess cash in the common shares of what he thought were three undervalued securities. At year-end, he reviewed how the portfolio of securities had done.

Security Name	Cost Basis	Market Value at Year-End	Classification
Microsoft Corporation	$100,000	$122,000	Trading security
Pfizer, Inc..	75,000	73,000	Trading security
Boeing, Inc.	50,000	48,000	Available-for-sale security
	$225,000	$243,000	

Required
1.   Calculate the value that would be assigned to the portfolio of securities on Thunderbird's balance sheet at year-end.
2.   Calculate the income statement effect of the portfolio of securities at year-end.
3.   Calculate the income statement effect of the portfolio of securities at year-end assuming all securities are classified as available-for-sale.

P8.31   **Accounting for Marketable Equity Securities.**   Among the various responsibilities of the Chief financial Officer (CFO) of the Amphlett Corporation was the management and oversight of the firm's cash reserves. During the year, the CFO had invested some of the firm's excess cash in what she thought were three under-valued stocks. All of the securities were classified as available-for-sale. At year-end, she reviewed how the portfolio of investments had done.

Investment	Cost Basis	Market Value at Year-End
Bristol-Myers-Squibb, Inc.	$ 50,000	$ 42,000
Titanium Metals, Inc.	50,000	55,000
Zila, Inc.	50,000	80,000
	$150,000	$177,00

Required
1. Calculate the value that would be assigned to the portfolio of marketable equity securities on the balance sheet of The Amphlett Corporation at year-end under each of the following approaches:
   a. Cost
   b. Lower-of-cost-or-market
   c. Market value
2. How will the disclosure on the year-end balance sheet change if the entire portfolio is classified as "trading securities" versus "available-for-sale securities"?

P8.32 **Accounting for Equity Investments: Equity Method.** At the beginning of the year, the Carlton and United Brewery (CUB) of Melbourne, Australia purchased a 30 percent ownership interest in the Icehouse Brewery of Brisbane, Australia. The investment had cost $30 million. At year-end, The Icehouse Brewery declared and paid cash dividends to shareholders totaling $800,000, after reporting earnings of $5 million.

Required
1, Calculate the income statement effect of CUB's investment in Icehouse Brewery as of year-end.
2. Calculate the book value of CUB's equity investment in Icehouse Brewery at year-end.
3. Calculate the book value of CUB's equity investment in Icehouse Brewery at year-end assuming that Icehouse reported a loss of $3 million (instead of a profit of $5 million) and still paid its dividend of $800,000.

⊘ P8.33 **Equity Method.** At mid-year, National Steel Fabricators, Inc. purchased a 35 percent ownership interest in Keystone Consolidated, Inc. for $40 million. At year-end, Keystone reported an operating loss of $6 million, of which only $2 million related to the second half of the year. Despite the operating loss, Keystone paid its regular quarterly dividend of $1 million in both the third and fourth quarters.

Required
1. Calculate the income statement effect for National Steel at year-end associated with its investment in Keystone.
2. Calculate the book value that National Steel should record on its balance sheet for its investment in Keystone at year-end.

P8.34 **Purchase Accounting.** ABC Inc. purchased all of the outstanding common shares of XYZ Inc. for $100 million. At the time of the acquisition, the fair value of XYZ was $80 million. Presented below are the condensed balance sheets for ABC and XYZ immediately prior to the acquisition:

(in millions)	ABC Inc.	XYZ Inc.
Assets.	$150	$100
Liabilities.	$ 30	$ 20
Shareholders' equity	120	80
Total	$150	$100

Required
Prepare ABC's (a) unconsolidated balance sheet immediately after making the equity investment in XYZ and (b) the consolidated balance sheet immediately following the acquisition.

P8.35 **Purchase Accounting.** MTF, Inc. acquired all of the outstanding shares of KMF, Inc. by means of a share exchange valued at $50 million. At the time of the acquisition, the fair market value of KMF was $40 million. Presented below are the condensed balance sheets for MTF, Inc. and KMF, Inc. immediately prior to the acquisition:

Balance Sheet	KMF, Inc.	MTF, Inc.
Assets.	$50 million	$70 million
Liabilities.	$10 million	$20 million
Shareholders' equity	40 million	50 million
Total	$50 million	$70 million

Required
1. Prepare the unconsolidated balance sheet for MTF immediately after making the investment in KMF.
2. Prepare the MTF-KMF consolidated balance sheet following the acquisition.

P8.36 **Consolidated Reporting: Restating Financial Statements.** At year-end 2005, Aussie Products International, Inc. (API) acquired the net assets of Kiwi Inc. (KI) by issuing 1.9 million shares of API common shares in exchange for all of the voting shares of KI. Because of the nature of the transaction, API had accounted for the acquisition as a pooling-of-interests, and accordingly, included in the consolidated financial statements the book value of Kiwi's net assets as follows:

Kiwi, Inc.	
Assets.	$70 million
Liabilities.	(38 million)
Net worth	$32 million

At the time of the transaction, API's common shares were trading at $50 per share. Further, at the time of the transaction, the fair market value of KI's net assets was $35 million (the book value of KI's assets were understated by $3 million, although its liabilities were all fairly valued).

Required
1. Calculate the total market value of the API shares given to KI shareholders.
2. Calculate the value of goodwill inherent in the transaction assuming that purchase accounting was used.
3. Assuming purchase accounting was used, how would the acquisition affect API's unconsolidated balance sheet?

P8.37 **Purchase Accounting.** Graham Inc. acquired all of the outstanding shares of Mahoney Inc through an exchange of common shares. The aggregate market value of the Graham shares distributed to the Mahoney shareholders was $400,000. Further, at the time of the exchange, the fair value of Mahoney's net assets was equal to their book value, except for Mahoney's property and equipment which was appraised at $540,000. Presented below are the pre-acquisition balance sheets of the two companies:

Preacquisition Balance Sheets	Graham Inc	Mahoney Inc
Cash	$ 60,000	$ 10,000
Accounts receivable (net)	140,000	80,000
Inventory (FIFO)	220,000	120,000
Property and equipment (net)	800,000	500,000
Other assets	40,000	20,000
	$1,260,000	$730,000
Accounts payable	$ 100,000	$ 25,000
Other current liabilities	100,000	15,000
Bonds payable	240,000	350,000
Common stock (no par value)	500,000	250,000
Retained earnings	320,000	90,000
	$1,260,000	$730,000

Required

Prepare the consolidated balance sheet for the new company immediately following the transaction using purchase accounting.

P8.38 **Purchase Accounting.** After an intense period of negotiation, Global Enterprises Corporation agreed to purchase all of the outstanding common shares of The Carlton Corporation. The agreed upon price was $294 million, payable in Global Enterprise shares. According to the agreement, Global Enterprises would issue one share of its common stock in exchange for each share of The Carlton Corporation. Following the exchange, The Carlton Corporation would become a wholly-owned subsidiary of Global Enterprises. At the time of the negotiations, the market price of Global Enterprises' shares was $24.50 per share. Presented below are the pre-acquisition balance sheets of Global Enterprises and The Carlton Corporation:

Preacquisition Balance Sheets	Global Enterprises Corporation	The Carlton Corporation
Assets		
Cash	$ 80,000,000	$ 25,000,000
Short-term investments	50,000,000	35,000,000
Accounts receivable (net)	75,000,000	50,000,000
Inventory (LIFO)	190,000,000	95,000,000
Property & equipment (net)	380,000,000	230,000,000
Other assets	45,000,000	15,000,000
Total assets	$820,000,000	$450,000,000
Liabilities & Shareholders' Equity		
Accounts payable	$ 95,000,000	$ 75,000,000
Other current liabilities	40,000,000	30,000,000
Bonds payable	110,000,000	—
Other long-term debt	75,000,000	125,000,000
Common stock ($10 par)	120,000,000	—

continued

continued from previous page

Preacquisition Balance Sheets	Global Enterprises Corporation	The Carlton Corporation
Common stock ($5 par)	—	60,000,000
Capital in excess of par value	70,000,000	20,000,000
Retained earnings	310,000,000	140,000,000
Total liabilities & shareholders' equity	$820,000,000	$450,000,000

As part of Global Enterprises' due diligence, the company determined that while the liabilities of The Carlton Corporation were fairly valued, some of the company's assets were not fairly valued. The fair value of Carlton's assets were as follows:

Asset	Fair Market Value	Under/(Over) Statement
Cash	$ 25,000,000	$ –0–
Short-term investments	45,000,000	10,000,000
Accounts receivable (net)	35,000,000	(15,000,000)
Inventory (LIFO)	130,000,000	35,000,000
Property & equipment (net)	280,000,000	50,000,000
Other assets	0	(15,000,000)
Total	$515,000,000	$65,000,000

Required
Prepare the consolidated balance sheet immediately following the acquisition using purchase accounting.

P8.39 **Equity Investments: International.**   Aussie Steaks Inc. operates a chain of steak restaurants in the U.S. On January 1, 2005, the company had $500 million in assets.

On January 1, 2005, the company acquired 25 percent of the shares of Sun Devil Burgers, a hamburger chain of 200 outlets, for $10 million in cash. At the time of the acquisition, Sun Devil had total assets of $100 million and total liabilities of $60 million. In 2005, Sun Devil reported net income of $12 million and paid cash dividends of $4 million.

On March 6, 2006, the company established Zaijian Burgers, a wholly-owned self-sustaining Chinese subsidiary, with cash of RMB24 million. The Chinese RMB (renmimbi) is the functional currency for Zaijian Burgers. The exchange rate at the time the subsidiary was established was RMB8 per $1. Immediately, after the subsidiary was established the exchange rate changed to RMB12 per $1. Aussie Steaks and its affiliates have a December 31 year-end.

Required
1.   What amount will Aussie Steaks Inc. report on its January 1, 2005 balance sheet with regard to its investment in Sun Devil Burgers following the acquisition?
2.   What amount will Aussie Steaks Inc. report on its December 31, 2005 balance sheet with regard to its investment in Sun Devil Burgers?
3.   What is the amount of total assets that Zaijian Burgers will show on its balance sheet in U.S. dollars on March 6, 2006?
4.   What is the amount of the cumulative foreign currency translation adjustment that Aussie Steaks will report on its consolidated balance sheet on March 6, 2006, following the exchange rate change?

⊘ **P8.40** **Equity Investments: International.** On January 1, 2005, Tradiciones, Inc. established Tradiciones de Mexico, a wholly-owned, self-sustaining Mexican subsidiary with assets valued at 48 million pesos. The peso is the functional currency for Tradiciones de Mexico. The exchange rate at the time that the subsidiary was established was Ps8 per $1. On January 2, 2005, after the subsidiary was established, the exchange rate changed to Ps6 per $1.

Required
1. What is the amount of total assets that Tradiciones de Mexico will show on its balance sheet in U.S. dollars on January 1, 2005 (before the exchange rate change)?
2. What is the amount of the cumulative foreign currency translation adjustment that Tradiciones, Inc. will report on its balance sheet on January 2, 2005, after the exchange rate change?
3. At December 31, 2005, Tradiciones de Mexico reported the information below. Did the Mexican peso appreciate, remain unchanged, or depreciate against the U.S. dollar?

In millions of dollars	Common Stock	Other Comprehensive Income	Retained Earnings	Total
Net income.			100	100
Other comprehensive income-foreign currency translation adjustment		(5)		(5)

P8.41 **Equity Investments: International.** Emu Ale Inc. operates a chain of pubs in the U.S. On January 2, 2005, the company had $500 million in assets.

On January 2, 2005, the company acquired 100 percent of the shares of Penfold's Inc., a wine bar chain with 50 outlets, for $60 million in cash. At the time of the acquisition, Penfold's Inc. had total assets of $100 million and total liabilities of $50 million. The fair value of Penfold's net assets approximated their book value.

On September 1, 2005, Emu established Emu de Mexico, a wholly-owned, self-sustaining Mexican subsidiary, with assets valued at 150 million pesos. The peso is the functional currency for Emu de Mexico. The exchange rate at the time the subsidiary was established was Ps10 per $1. Immediately after the subsidiary was established, the exchange rate changed to Ps15 per $1. Emu and its affiliates have a December 31 year-end.

Required
1. What would Emu Ale's consolidated total assets be on January 2, 2005 following the Penfold acquisition?
2. What is the amount of total assets that Emu de Mexico will show on its balance sheet in U.S. dollars on September 1, 2005 (before the exchange rate change)?
3. What is the amount of the cumulative foreign currency translation adjustment that Emu Ale will report on its consolidated balance sheet after the exchange rate change?

P8.42 **Consolidated versus Unconsolidated Reporting.** Global Enterprises Corporation (GE) is a manufacturing company whose principal products are microwave ovens, refrigerators, and conventional ovens. The company had a long history of selling high-quality, high-priced home appliances; however, recent reductions in the price of competitor products forced GE to consider ways to provide assistance to its customers to help them buy its products. As a consequence, GE started its own finance subsidiary, the GE Acceptance Corporation (GEAC), to assist customers in financing their purchases.

GE Corporation is also associated with three other companies. It holds an 80 percent interest in Scrub-All, a company that makes automatic dishwashers. GE purchased the interest in Scrub-All because the company's product line complemented its own items and the products were a quality that GE would have had difficulty duplicating. Further, to ensure a steady supply of chrome parts for its appliances, GE obtained a ten percent interest in the common stock of Acme Chrome Company. Well over 50 percent of Acme's sales were attributed to purchases by GE and Scrub-All. Further, to compete in the low-end market for various appliances, GE formed a joint venture (Spotless Appliance) with Whirlwind Products Co. to produce low cost appliances. The following is a summary of GE's subsidiaries, affiliates, and equity investments:

GE Acceptance Corporation. GEAC is a wholly-owned subsidiary that purchases consumer notes from its parent, GE Corporation. GEAC borrows funds from several banking institutions on a medium and long-term basis and uses the margins between the short-term interest rates on the consumer notes and the rates on its medium and long-term liabilities to cover its overhead costs. The parent company (GE) guarantees all of the borrowings of GEAC.

Scrub-All Company. With an ownership interest of 80 percent of the common stock of Scrub-All, GE controls the strategic policies of Scrub-All Company through an interlocking board of directors. Scrub-All, like GE, sells its consumer notes to GEAC.

Acme Chrome Company. To guarantee a steady supply of chrome parts, GE purchased a ten percent interest in Acme Chrome Company. Over the years, a strong relationship had developed between GE and Acme. For example, Acme schedules the production run of its other customers around the production needs of GE and Scrub-All.

Spotless Appliance Company. Both GE Corporation and Whirlwind Products Company (an otherwise unrelated company) contributed half of the funds necessary to start Spotless Appliance Company. Spotless Appliance Company makes low-end appliance models that are sold under the Spotless trade name or are labeled with various department store names.

GE Corporation
Consolidated Statement of Financial Position
December 31, 2005

Assets	
Current assets	$ 37,500,000
Notes receivable	58,000,000
Investment in Spotless Appliance at equity (50%)	1,750,000
Investment in Acme Chrome Company (10%) at market	5,600,000
Other assets	101,500,000
Goodwill	3,200,000
Total assets	$207,550,000
Liabilities and Shareholders' Equity	
Current liabilities	$ 31,500,000
Long-term liabilities	102,100,000
Minority interest	7,500,000
Common stock	15,000,000
Retained earnings	51,450,000
Total liabilities and shareholders' equity	$207,550,000

Scrub-All Company
Statement of Financial Position
December 31, 2005

Assets	
Current assets	$16,400,000
Other assets	52,600,000
Total assets	$69,000,000

continued

continued from previous page

Scrub-All Company Statement of Financial Position December 31, 2005	
Liabilities and Shareholders' Equity	
Current liabilities.	$13,350,000
Long-term liabilities	18,150,000
Common stock.	12,000,000
Retained earnings	25,500,000
Total liabilities and shareholders' equity.	$69,000,000

Acme Chrome Company Statement of Financial Position December 31, 2005	
Assets	
Current assets	$14,750,000
Other assets	36,250,000
Total assets.	$51,000,000
Liabilities and Shareholders' Equity	
Current liabilities.	$ 5,000,000
Long-term liabilities	15,000,000
Common stock.	18,750,000
Retained earnings	12,250,000
Total liabilities and shareholders' equity	$51,000,000

GE Acceptance Corporation Statement of Financial Position December 31, 2005	
Assets	
Current assets	$ 8,000,000
Notes receivable.	58,000,000
Other assets	6,500,000
Total assets.	$72,500,000
Liabilities and Shareholders' Equity	
Current liabilities.	$ 5,000,000
Long-term debt	47,100,000
Common stock ($1 par)	10,000,000
Retained earnings	10,400,000
Total liabilities and shareholders' equity.	$72,500,000

*$3,000,000 of the current liabilities is a promissory note to GE Corporation. GE Corporation accounts for this as a long-term receivable in other assets.

Spotless Appliance Company
Statement of Financial Position
December 31, 2005

Assets	
Current assets	$ 8,500,000
Other assets	16,000,000
Total assets	$24,500,000
Liabilities and Shareholders' Equity	
Current liabilities	$ 3,000,000
Long-term debt	18,000,000
Common stock ($1 par)	6,000,000
Retained earnings	(2,500,000)
Total liabilities and shareholders' equity	$24,500,000

Required

1. Why are the investments in Acme Chrome and Spotless Appliance Companies shown on the GE Corporation consolidated balance sheet while the investments in Scrub-All and GEAC are omitted?

2. What is meant by the carrying value "at equity" for the investment in Spotless Appliance Company on GE's consolidated balance sheet?

3. Why is the investment in Acme Chrome Company shown "at market"?

4. Explain the Goodwill account on GE's consolidated balance sheet. To what company is this account related?

5. What is meant by "minority interest" on GE's consolidated balance sheet? To which company is this account related? Is this a liability or a shareholders' equity account?

6. What are GE Corporation's current ratio, total debt-to-equity ratio, and total debt-to-total asset ratio? Are these ratios correct?

7. How would the consolidated balance sheet of GE Corporation appear if Spotless Appliance Company were consolidated? Would you recommend consolidation for Spotless?

8. How will the ratios calculated in question (6) change after the consolidation of Spotless Appliance? Can an argument be made for consolidating Acme Chrome Company with the GE Corporation?

P8.43 **Consolidating Financial Statements.** The General Electric Company (GE) engages in the development, manufacture, and marketing of various products for the generation, transmission, distribution, control, and utilization of electricity. The company operates through eleven business segments: Advance materials, commercial finance, consumer finance, consumer and industrial products, Energy, Equipment, Healthcare, Infrastructure, Insurance, NBC Universal, and Transportation. GE is only one of six U.S. industrial companies earning a AAA rating from Standard & Poor's rating agency.

Presented below are the 2004 financial statements for GE and its financial services subsidiary, General Electric Capital Services (GECS). Any transactions between GE and GECS have been eliminated from the data.

Statement of Financial Position		
	GE 2004	GECS 2004
Assets		
Cash and equivalents.	$ 3,155	$ 12,367
Investment securities	413	135,152
Current receivables	14,533	—
Inventories	9,589	189
Financing receivables, net	—	282,467
Insurance receivables, net	—	25,971
Other GECS receivables.	—	14,134
Property, plant and equipment, net	16,756	46,578
Investment in GECS.	53,755	—
Intangible assets, net	54,720	28,520
All other assets.	38,123	72,949
Total assets.	$191,044	$618,327
Liabilities and Shareholders' Equity		
Short-term borrowings	$ 3,409	$154,843
Accounts payable, principally trade accounts	11,013	17,104
Progress collections and price adjustments accrued	3,937	—
Dividends payable	2,329	—
All other current costs and expenses accrued.	17,569	—
Long-term borrowings	7,625	206,499
Insurance liabilities, reserves and annuity benefits	—	140,902
All other liabilities	23,561	25,744
Deferred income taxes	3,616	10,798
Total liabilities.	73,059	555,890
Minority interest in equity of consolidated affiliates.	7,701	8,682
Common stock (10,586,358,000 shares outstanding at year-end 2004)	669	1
Accumulated gains (losses), net		
Investment securities.	2,268	2,345
Currency translation adjustment	6,929	5,183
Cash flow hedges	(1,223)	(1,354)
Minimum pension liabilities	(657)	(150)
Other capital.	24,265	12,370
Retained earnings	90,795	35,360
Less common stock held in treasury	(12,762)	—
Total shareholders' equity	110,284	53,755
Total liabilities and shareholders' equity.	$191,044	$618,327

Statement of Earnings		
	GE 2004	GECS 2004
Revenues		
Sales of goods	$52,260	$ 2,840
Sales of services	29,954	—
Other income	1,076	—
Earnings of GECS before accounting changes	8,161	—
GECS revenues from services	—	67,936
Total revenues	91,451	70,776
Costs and Expenses		
Cost of goods sold.	39,999	2,741
Cost of services sold	19,368	—
Interest and other financial charges	979	11,372
Insurance losses and policyholder and annuity benefits	—	15,844
Provision for losses on financing receivables	—	3,888
Other costs and expenses	12,001	26,840
Minority interest in net earnings of consolidated affiliates	538	390
Total costs and expenses	72,885	61,075
Earnings before income taxes	18,566	9,701
Provision for income taxes.	(1,973)	(1,540)
Net earnings.	$16,593	$ 8,161

Required:
1. Prepare the consolidated balance sheet and consolidated income statement for the **General Electric Company** for 2004.
2. Using your results from question one, calculate the following ratios for GE on (a) an unconsolidated basis and (b) a consolidated basis. What ratios are most affected by the consolidation of GECS with GE?
   - Return on sales
   - Return on assets
   - Return on equity
   - Asset turnover
   - Total debt-to-total assets
   - Total debt-to-shareholders' equity
   - Times-interest-earned ratio

P8.44 (Appendix 8A) Recording Marketable Equity Securities Transactions using the Debit/Credit Paradigm. **Microsoft Inc.** maintains a large investment in marketable securities (principally fixed income securities) valued at approximately $42 billion as of the beginning of the year. During the year, the securities produced investment income (dividends and interest income) totaling $2 billion. At year-end, the portfolio of marketable securities had appreciated to $43.5 billion.

Required
Using journal entries, record (1) Microsoft's purchase of the securities at the beginning of the year, (2) the receipt of $2 billion in investment income during the year, and (3) the appreciation of the portfolio by $1.5 billion at the end of the year. Assume that the entire portfolio is classified as "trading securities."

P8.45 (Appendix 8A) Recording Equity Method Transactions using the Debit/Credit Paradigm. On January 1, 2005, The Miller Corporation purchased 300,000 shares of The Mayfair Corporation for $5.7 million. The investment represented 25 percent of The Mayfair Corporation's outstanding common shares. During

2005, Mayfair reported net earnings of $2.25 million and paid a cash dividend of $0.15 per share. During 2006, Mayfair reported a net loss of $180,000 and again paid a dividend of $0.15 per share.

Required

Using journal entries, record (1) The Miller Corporation's initial investment in The Mayfair Corporation and (2) the appropriate entries for 2005 and 2006 assuming that The Miller Corporation uses the equity method to account for its investment in Mayfair.

CORPORATE ANALYSIS

CA8.46 **The Procter and Gamble Company.** The 2005 annual report of The Procter and Gamble Company (P & G) is available at www.pg.com/annualreports/2005/pdf/pg2005annualreport.pdf. After reviewing P & G's annual report, respond to the following questions:

a. P & G's consolidated balance sheet reveals that the company had $1.744 billion ($1.660 billion) of investment securities at June 30, 2005 (2004). What percentage of total current assets is represented by the investment securities in 2004 and 2005? What percentage of total assets is represented by the investment securities? How does P & G classify the investment securities—trading or available-for-sale? How does P & G account for the unrealized gains and losses on the investment securities?

b. In September 2003, P & G acquired a controlling interest in Wella, and in June 2004, signed a Domination and Profit Transfer Agreement giving P & G 100 percent operating control of Wella. How much did P & G pay in 2003 for Wella? How much ownership interest did P & G buy in 2003? How was the acquisition financed? How much did P & G pay in 2004 for the Domination and Profit Transfer Agreement? How was it financed? What was the final total purchase price for Wella?

c. In January 2005, P & G entered into an agreement to acquire The Gillette Company. How much did P & G agree to pay for Gillette? How would the transaction be financed? Why is the acquisition considered to be tax-free? How will the acquisition be accounted for?

d. P & G's consolidated balance sheet reveals that the company has $19.816 billion ($19.610 billion) in goodwill as of June 30, 2005 (2004). What percentage of total assets does goodwill represent in 2004 and 2005? Does P & G amortize its goodwill? If so, over what period? If not, why not? Did P & G recognize an impairment in its goodwill in either 2004 or 2005? How much goodwill was involved in the Wella acquisition? What percentage of the total Wella acquisition price was goodwill?

CA8.47 **General Electric Company.** General Electric Company (GE) is the parent-company of General Electric Capital Services Inc. (GECS). GECS, in turn, is the parent-company of General Electric Capital Corporation and GE Insurance Solutions Corporation. Because of the diverse nature of the businesses reflected in the operations of GE and GECS, GE presents its financial statements in two formats—a fully consolidated format (including the results of GE, GECS, and all other majority-owned entities) and a partially consolidated format (excluding the results of GECS). In GE's partially-consolidated financial statements, the investment in GECS is accounted for using the Equity Method.

a. Presented below are the partially-consolidated income statements and balance sheets for GE and GECS for 2005. Using this information, prepare the fully-consolidated financial statements for GE for 2005.

b. What significant differences do you notice about GE's financial statements on a partially-consolidated basis versus a fully-consolidated basis?

Statement of Earnings
For the years ended December 31

($ millions)	GE 2005	GECS 2005
Revenues		
Sales of goods	$ 57,378	$ 2,528
Sales of services	33,052	—
Other income	1,764	—
GECS earnings from continuing operations.	9,141	—
GECS revenues from services	—	56,769
Total revenues	101,335	59,297
Costs and Expenses		
Costs of goods sold	43,870	2,369
Cost of services sold	20,945	—
Interest and other financial charges	1,432	14,308
Investment contracts, insurances losses and insurance		
annuity benefits	—	5,674
Provision for losses on financing receivables	—	3,841
Other costs and expenses	13,279	22,658
Minority interest in net earnings of consolidated affiliates	784	202
Total costs and expenses	80,310	49,502
Earnings from continuing operations before income		
taxes and accounting changes.	21,025	10,245
Provision for income taxes.	(2,750)	(1,104)
Earnings form continuing operations before		
accounting changes	18,275	9,141
Earning (loss) from discontinued operations, net of taxes	(1,922)	(1,922)
Net earnings	$ 16,353	$ 7,219

Statement of Financial Position
At December 31

($ millions)	GE 2005	GECS 2005
Assets		
Cash and equivalents.	$ 2,015	$ 7,316
Investment securities	461	52,706
Current receivables	15,058	—
Inventories	10,315	159
Financing receivables—net	—	286,639
Other GECS receivables.	—	19,060
Property, plant and equipment—net	16,504	51,024
Investment in GECS	50,815	—
Intangible assets—net	57,839	23,887
All other assets.	36,752	52,058
Assets of discontinued operations.	—	46,756
Total assets.	$189,759	$540,605

continued

continued from previous page

Statement of Financial Position At December 31		
($ millions)	GE 2005	GECS 2005
Liabilities and Shareholders' Equity		
Short-term borrowings.	$ 1,127	$157,672
Accounts payable, principally trade accounts	11,870	13,133
Progress collections and price adjustment accrued	4,456	—
Dividends payable	2,623	—
All other current costs and expenses accrued.	18,436	—
Long-term borrowings	9,081	204,397
Investment contracts, insurance liabilities and		
insurance annuity benefits.	—	45,722
All other liabilities	23,273	17,453
Deferred income taxes	3,733	12,597
Liabilities of and minority interest in discontinued operations	—	36,568
Total liabilities.	74,599	487,542
Minority interest in equity of consolidated affiliates.	5,806	2,248
Common stock (10,484,268,000 shares outstanding		
at year-end 2005	669	1
Accumulated gains (losses)—net.		
Investment securities.	1,831	1,754
Currency translation adjustments	2,532	2,287
Cash flow hedges	(822)	(813)
Minimum pension liabilities	(874)	(179)
Other capital.	25,227	12,386
Retained earnings	98,117	35,379
Less common stock held in treasury	(17,326)	—
Total shareholders' equity	109,354	50,815
Total liabilities and shareholders' equity.	$189,759	$540,605

CA8.48 **Internet-based Analysis.** Consider a publicly-held company whose products you are familiar with. Some examples might include:

Company	Product	Corporate Website
• **Johnson & Johnson Company**	• Band-Aids	• www.jnj.com
• **Microsoft Corporation**	• Windows XP software	• www.microsoft.com
• **Nokia Corporation**	• Cellular phones	• www.nokia.com
• **Intel Corporation**	• Pentium processors	• www.intel.com
• **Kimberly-Clark Corporation**	• Kleenex	• www.kimberly-clark.com

Access the company's public website and search for its most recent annual report. (Note: Some companies provide access to their financial data through an "investor relations" link, while others provide a direct link to their "annual reports.") After locating your company's most recent annual report, open the file and review its contents. After reviewing the annual report for your selected company, prepare answers to the following questions:

1. Does the company have any short-term investments or marketable securities? If so, are they trading securities or available-for-sale securities? Over the past year, did the company experience any unrealized gain or losses on its marketable securities? If so, in what amount?
2. Does the company have any unconsolidated affiliates or joint ventures? If so, how are they accounted for? Did the unconsolidated affiliates or joint ventures produce a profit or loss last year?
3. Does the company have any consolidated subsidiaries? If so, how many? Does the company own 100 percent of all of its consolidated subsidiaries? How were you able to determine this?
4. Does the company have any goodwill from prior acquisitions? How does the company account for its goodwill? Has the goodwill been impaired in either of the last two years? If so, what amount was the impairment?

Chapter Nine

Debt Financing: Bonds, Notes, and Leases

TAKEAWAYS

When you complete this chapter you should be able to:

1. Explain how bonds and notes are valued and reported in financial statements.
2. Describe how companies account for debt when it is retired before its maturity.
3. Explain the difference between a capital lease and an operating lease and how each are reported in financial statements.
4. Discuss how and why companies manage the amount of debt reported on their balance sheets.

Where have we been?	Where are we?	Where are we going?
Chapter 8 examined how and why companies invest in one another. We saw that for small equity investments (those involving less than 20 percent of the ownership of a business), mark-to-market accounting is used to value these equity investments for purposes of disclosure on corporate balance sheets. For investments involving 20 to 50 percent of firm ownership, the equity method is used; and, for investments constituting a majority ownership (51 to 100 percent), consolidation accounting is usually adopted. Finally, the accounting and reporting issues that arise with investments in foreign corporations, joint ventures, and special purpose entities were considered.	In this chapter, we begin an exploration of the strategic financing decisions of companies. We examine how companies finance their operations and asset purchases using bonds, notes, and leases. We will see that debt financing is reported on corporate balance sheets using the present value approach. We will also examine how companies account for the retirement of their debt when it is no longer needed to finance their operations. We consider how and why some firms lease their long-term revenue-producing assets. Finally, we consider how to calculate the weighted-average cost of debt for a business and how and why some companies attempt to manage the amount of their reported debt.	In Chapter 10, we continue our investigation of the various forms of corporate debt. Specifically, we consider the difference between commitments and contingent liabilities and how to identify when retirement obligations are fully funded or not. The topic of deferred income tax liabilities is investigated and how and why this liability increases and decreases. Finally, we examine how financial instruments and derivatives are valued and reported in corporate financial statements.

John W. Nordstrom used his stake from the Alaska gold rush to open a small shoe store in Seattle, Washington in 1901. This small store has since grown into an upscale department store chain with 156 U.S. and 32 international stores, along with both catalog and internet sales. The company is perhaps best known for its legendary reputation for top-rate customer service. In addition to its reputation for pleasing the customer, the company has also garnered a reputation for its treatment of its employees. Nordstrom is a Hall of Fame member of *Fortune* magazine's "100 Best Companies to Work For."

An examination of Nordstrom's balance sheet reveals that the company's largest single asset is its investment in land, buildings and equipment, valued at nearly $1.8 billion as of fiscal year-end 2006. Nordstrom financed these assets, along with other major assets such as nearly $1 billion of inventory, with a combination of debt and equity. The company's balance sheet reports debt totaling almost $3 billion and shareholders' equity of slightly over $2 billion, representing a total debt-to-equity ratio of 1.35.

Does the Nordstrom balance sheet portray a complete picture of the company's use of financing? Many investment professionals would say "no," and that to better understand how Nordstrom finances its assets, financial statement users need to dig into the footnotes to the financial statements. In particular, it is important to understand Nordstrom's use of off-balance-sheet financing. Nordstrom entered into various operating leases for the land and building for many of its 188 stores. Generally accepted accounting principles allow Nordstrom to omit this form of financing, along with the corresponding leased assets, from its corporate balance sheet. The company's footnotes reveal that it is committed to over $680 million in future lease payments associated with these leases as of January 2006. Failing to include these leased assets and lease liabilities in an analysis of the company's financial statements, however, can cause serious distortion to such important financial indicators as the debt-to-equity ratio and the return on assets ratio.

In this chapter, we consider various debt financing strategies and products, including the use of lease financing, available to companies like Nordstrom's. In addition, we discuss a methodology that can aid in the analysis of corporate financial statements which rely on off-balance-sheet debt financing.

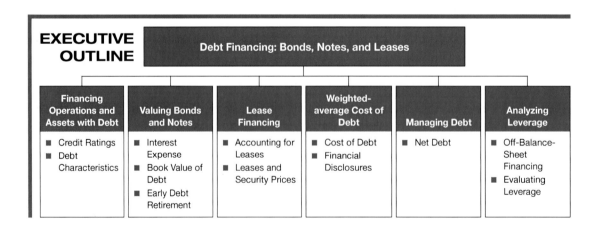

FINANCING OPERATIONS AND ASSETS WITH DEBT: BONDS AND NOTES

Most businesses finance at least a part of their operations with debt. One of the reasons for this is that debt financing is always a cheaper form of financing than equity. Since creditors assume less risk than equity investors, it is appropriate that the expected rate of return to be earned by creditors should be less than the expected rate of return to be earned by shareholders. Remember that shareholders may lose all of their investment if a business fails, whereas creditors are likely to lose only part, if any, of their investment because they have first claim on any assets of the business.

The specific source of debt financing available to a borrower will depend on the desired length of the borrowing period, the amount of the borrowing, and the riskiness of the borrower. Small firms, for example, are considered to be riskier than larger, established firms. A sustained history of operating performance makes lenders more comfortable with a firm's ability to repay debt, and small firms tend to lack a history of operating experience. Further, small firms tend to borrow smaller amounts, and since investment bankers are unlikely to engage in public debt offerings of less than $100 million, small borrowings are typically sourced from a single, private lender. Thus, most small firms have access to only a limited set of lenders, to include local financial institutions, business development companies, the Small Business Administration, friends and family, and in some cases, private equity and venture capital firms.

Larger, established firms, on the other hand, have many borrowing options, including financial institutions, insurance companies, pension funds, as well as the public debt market. Just which lending segment is likely to be accessed is a function of the desired length of the borrowing period, also called the loan **duration**. Banks and similar financial institutions prefer to limit their risk exposure to loans involving durations of one day to five years, whereas the public debt market is typically the source for borrowings of five to 20 years. Finally, borrowings involving durations greater than 20 years tend to be sourced from insurance companies and pension funds, which have the capacity and desire to place funds with borrowers for extended periods of time.

The public debt market is composed of two similar lending products (among others)—bonds and notes. **Bonds** are publicly-issued financial instruments that promise to pay the bondholder interest over the life of the investment, usually ten to 20 years, and make a lump-sum principal repayment at maturity. **Notes** are similar instruments but have shorter maturities, usually one to ten years, and are frequently privately placed with large institutional investors or financial institutions. Bonds and notes often have the following common features:

> Companies may also access the very short-term commercial paper market. **Commercial paper** refers to unsecured corporate loans that are typically 30 to 180 days or less in duration.

- No voting rights at the annual shareholders' meeting.
- An **indenture agreement** that specifies covenants, often based on accounting ratios, which may restrict the borrower's ability to pay dividends, issue additional debt, undertake mergers and acquisitions, or sell assets.
- A **trustee**, such as a bank or trust company, which administers the provisions of the indenture agreement and acts as an independent party to protect the interests of the lenders.
- Priority in receiving interest and principal repayments over any payments to common and preferred shareholders, such as dividends or payments in liquidation.

Bonds and notes may be **secured**—that is, the lender has a priority claim on specific assets of the borrower in the event of default—or **unsecured** (having no claim on specific assets in the event of a default). Unsecured debt, also known as **debentures**, may be **subordinated**—that is, the claim of the unsecured debtholder has a lower priority, or is "junior" to, the claims of secured creditors. **Unsubordinated** or senior debt has a priority claim equivalent to that of suppliers who hold the accounts payable of a firm, and thus, typically hold a claim against specific operating assets (such as inventory) of a business.

Bonds and notes may also be **convertible** into the common shares of the borrower. Convertible bonds and notes carry a share conversion ratio indicating the number of common shares to be received in the event of conversion and are convertible at the option of the debtholder (usually, however, only after some portion of the debt duration has expired). Some bonds and notes are **callable** at the option of the borrower. A callable bond or note is one that may be mandatorily redeemed or retired prior to maturity. Callable bonds or notes are also often convertible to provide debtholders with an option to either accept cash if the bond or note is called or to convert the bond or note into the common shares of the borrower. Finally, some bonds are commodity-based in which the principal repayment is indexed to the price of a commodity like gold, silver, or oil, often with an option to receive the commodity instead of cash at maturity.

Credit Ratings

Publicly-issued bonds and notes carry a **credit-risk rating** indicating the likelihood that the borrower will make all interest and principal payments on a timely basis. (Non-public debt is often unrated.) Credit rating agencies such as *Moody's* and *Standard & Poor's* make a qualitative assessment of the probability of default of a bond or note using a letter rating system as follows:

Credit Risk	Moody's	Standard & Poor's
Investment Grade.	Aaa1, Aaa2, Aaa3 Aa1, Aa2, Aa3 A1, A2, A3 Baa1, Baa2, Baa3	AAA+, AAA, AAA− AA+, AA, AA− A+, A, A− BBB+, BBB, BBB−
Junk	Ba1, Ba2, Ba3 B1, B2, B3 Caa1, Caa2, Caa3 Ca1, Ca2, Ca3 C1, C2, C3 D	BB+, BB, BB− B+, B, B− CCC+, CCC, CCC− CC+, CC, CC− C+, C, C− D

Recall that there is a positive relationship between risk and reward—that is, the higher the credit risk associated with a debt contract, the higher the expected return. Thus, bonds and notes rated Aaa1 or AAA+ will carry a low interest rate because available evidence indicates that there is a very low probability of default by these investment-grade borrowers. Junk bonds and notes (especially ones rated D, which are in default), on the other hand, should be avoided by investors who have a low tolerance for risk. **Junk bonds**, also known as high-yield bonds, have a significantly higher probability of default, and thus, carry higher rates of interest.

How do *Moody's* and *Standard & Poor's* arrive at a borrower's credit rating? The process is lengthy but the financial statement analysis skills discussed in Chapter 4 are an integral part of the process. Additionally, these organizations use proprietary bankruptcy predictions models, such as the Z-score and Zeta Analysis, to help identify a borrower's probability of default.[1]

VALUING BONDS AND NOTES

Under U.S. GAAP, and the GAAP of most developed countries, liabilities are valued at their **present value**. (See the appendix at the end of this book for a review of present value concepts.) Exceptions to this rule include such current liabilities as accounts payable, accrued expenses payable and dividends payable, and

---

[1] E. Altman, "Financial Ratios, Discriminant Analysis and the Prediction of Corporate Bankruptcy," *Journal of Finance*, September 1968; E. Altman, R. Haldeman, and P. Narayanan, "Zeta Analysis: A New Model to Identify Bankruptcy Risk of Corporation," *Journal of Banking and Finance*, 1977.

such long-term liabilities as deferred income tax liabilities, which will be discussed in Chapter 10. Since the present value of an account payable due in 30, 60, or 90 days is extremely close to its maturity value, discounting of these short-term obligations is not required on practical grounds—that is, there is very little difference between the present value and the future value of a liability payable in 30, 60, or 90 days. For long-term obligations, however, there can be a substantial difference between the present value of the debt—that is, how much cash would be required to pay the obligation off today—and its future settlement value. Consider, for instance, Jacob De Haven's $450,000 loan to the revolutionary army of General George Washington in 1777 (see the appendix at the end of this book). At five percent interest, the settlement or **maturity value** of the De Haven loan would cost the U.S. government over $32 billion today!

To calculate the present value of a bond or note, it is necessary to know the following facts:

* The maturity value and maturity date of the debt.
* The coupon, or stated, rate of interest on the debt.
* The number of interest payment, or compounding, periods.
* The yield, or effective, rate of interest on the debt.

The **coupon rate** is the cash rate of interest on a debt instrument whereas the **yield rate** is the effective, or market, rate of interest. The coupon rate is used only to determine the periodic cash flow paid as interest to the bondholder or noteholder. The yield rate, on the other hand, is used to discount both the periodic cash interest payments and the lump-sum repayment of principal at maturity.

To illustrate the valuation of, and accounting for, bonds and notes, consider the following scenario:

On January 1, 2005, **Midwestern Airlines Inc.** issued $100 million face value (maturity value) of mortgage notes with an annual coupon rate of eight percent and a maturity of ten years. The notes pay interest on June 30 and December 31 of each year. At the time the notes were issued, the market yield rate of interest on equivalent risk-rated notes was ten percent. Five years later, on December 31, 2009, the market yield rate of interest on equivalent-risk-rated notes increased to twelve percent.

Ignoring any transactions costs associated with selling the notes to the investing public, which may average one to three percent of the value of the issued debt, the Midwestern Airlines notes would generate proceeds of $87.548 million when sold. But how was this value calculated? There are two cash flow streams associated with a bond or note—a lump-sum payment of principal at maturity and the periodic payment of interest. In the case of the Midwestern Airlines' notes, the payment of $100 million in principal will occur in ten years, or 20 compounding periods, on December 31, 2014. Further, with an annual coupon rate of eight percent and interest paid semi-annually on June 30 and December 31, noteholders will receive an annuity of 20 payments of $4 million each ([$100 million × 8 percent]/2).

Thus, the present value of the Midwestern notes on the date of issuance is the sum of (1) the present value of $100 million to be paid in ten years, compounded semi-annually, discounted at five percent per period (½ of ten percent) and (2) the present value of a 20 period annuity of $4 million per period, also discounted at five percent. Hence:

> When discussing debt, it is common practice to convert percentages to **basis points**. One percent, for instance, is equal to 100 basis points. Thus, an interest rate of four percent may be referred to as 400 basis points. The basis point system permits a more precise description of interest rates.

> It is important to observe that both the periodic cash interest payments and the lump-sum principal payment are discounted at the same yield rate over the same number of periods. The appropriate discount rate is the market yield rate at the time of debt issuance.

Present value of $100 million in 20 periods @ 5%: $100 million × 0.377	=	$37.700 million
+ Present value of $4 million per period for 20 periods @ 5%: $4 million × 12.462	=	49.848 million
Present value of notes		$87.548 million

The present value factors of 0.377 and 12.462 were obtained from Tables 1 and 2 in the appendix at the end of this book (n = 20; i = 0.05).

Since the Midwestern Airlines' notes carried a coupon rate of only four percent per period (one-half of eight percent) while investors were expecting five percent (one-half of ten percent), perhaps to compensate investors for the higher credit risk associated with the airline company, the notes would, of necessity, be sold at a discount from their face value of $100 million. If the selling price of the notes was not discounted (or lowered), investors would be unwilling to buy the notes and would instead seek out other higher yielding investments. The discount of $12.452 million ($100 million − $87.548 million) equals the amount of additional income demanded by investors to earn an effective rate of return of five percent per period over the twenty periods. If investors hold the notes until maturity, they will receive the $12.452 million as part of the lump-sum payment of the $100 million maturity value. Thus, over the life of the notes, investors will receive a total of $180 million—that is, $87.548 million as a return *of* investment and $92.452 million in interest income ($80.0 million + $12.452 million) as a return *on* their investment.

On January 1, 2005, when the $100 million face value of notes are sold, Midwestern Airlines will show an increase in cash of $87.548 million, an increase in notes payable for the future value of the debt of $100 million, and a decrease in the **note discount** account in the amount of $12.452 million (see Midwestern's spreadsheet in Exhibit 9.1). The note discount account is a **contra-liability** account; it is subtracted from the notes payable account to arrive at the book value of the debt. It is rare to see the note discount account on the face of a corporate balance sheet because these amounts are typically netted out against the maturity value of the debt.

EXHIBIT 9.1	Accounting for Bonds and Notes

Midwestern Airlines, Inc. Spreadsheet	Assets	=	Liabilities		+	Equity
($ millions)	Cash		Notes Payable	Note Discount		Retained Earnings
2005						
Issue notes on January 1	87.548		100.000	−12.452		
Pay interest on June 30	−4.000			0.3774		−4.3774 (interest expense)
Pay interest on December 31	−4.000			0.3963		−4.3963 (interest expense)
2009						
Retire notes on December 31	−85.24		−100.00	7.72		7.04 (gain on early retirement)

Since bond investors demanded an annual rate of return of ten percent but the Midwestern Airlines' notes were only offering eight percent, why didn't Midwestern just change the coupon rate to enable the notes to be sold at their full face value of $100 million? Before any debt or equity securities can be sold in the U.S. capital market, the issuing company must register the securities with the U.S. Securities and Exchange Commission. This requirement is intended to protect investors by insuring that all publicly-issued securities meet certain disclosure standards. As part of the registration statement for the debt securities, called a prospectus, the issuing company must contractually establish certain characteristics of the security—the amount to be borrowed, the length of the borrowing period, the purpose of the borrowing, the method of repayment, and the coupon rate, among other things. Thus, once registered, an issuing company is unable to change its coupon rate, or any other security features reported in the filing, even if the goal is to meet or satisfy investor expectations. As the registration statement becomes the equivalent of a binding contract, the only characteristic of the debt instrument that can be altered to meet changing investor expectations is the security's actual selling price, which is not part of the firm's registration statement.

In the case of the Midwestern Airlines' notes, the selling price of the notes was lowered—that is, the notes were sold at a discount from their face value—to enable investors to earn the higher expected rate of return. If, on the other hand, investors had demanded only a six percent rate of return (or three percent per compounding period), the Midwestern Airlines' notes would have been sold at a price above their face value—that is, the notes would have been sold at a premium.[2] Finally, in that rare instance in which the rate of return demanded by investors is exactly equal to the coupon rate provided by a bond or note, the debt instruments will sell at a price exactly equal to their par or face value.

> As a general rule, companies issuing debt set the offered coupon rate slightly below the expected market yield rate so that the bonds or notes will sell at a small discount from their face value. This practice is undertaken principally for marketing purposes.

Interest Expense

On June 30, 2005, Midwestern Airlines will make its first cash payment of $4 million to its noteholders. But how much interest expense did Midwestern incur during this first six month period? Interest expense, or the cost of debt financing, is calculated by multiplying the yield rate on the debt (five percent in this case) times the book value of the debt as of the beginning of the fiscal period; hence,

$$\text{Interest expense} = 5\% \times \$87.548 \text{ million} = \$4.3774 \text{ million}$$

Midwestern's interest expense of $4.3774 million exceeds its actual cash payment of $4.0 million by $0.3774 million. The excess of $0.3774 million represents the portion of the $12.452 million note discount that is allocated to the period January 1, 2005 to June 30, 2005. The $12.452 million to be paid to noteholders on December 31, 2014, represents the additional interest necessary to enable the investors to earn a ten percent rate of return on the Midwestern notes and must be allocated over the twenty interest payment periods. It would be inappropriate and distortive to the financial statements to consider the entire $12.452 million payment as interest expense in the year paid (2014).

The process of allocating a bond discount (or bond premium) over the various interest compounding periods is called amortization. Amortizing a discount (or premium) using the present value tables from the appendix to this book is called the effective interest method. Discounts and premiums may also be amortized in a straight-line fashion, but only if this method does not differ materially from the effective interest method. The straight-line method is not widely used among public companies; and, in any case, straight-line amortization of discounts (premiums) is not recognized as economically meaningful in modern financial theory.

---

[2] With a coupon rate of eight percent, a yield rate of six percent, and semi-annual compounding, the Midwestern Airlines' notes would sell for $114.908 million, a premium of $14.908 million. Can you verify this calculation using Tables 1 and 2 in the appendix to this book?

Exhibit 9.2 presents an **amortization schedule** for the Midwestern Airlines' notes. It details the periodic cash interest payments of $4 million (Column 1), Midwestern's interest expense on a period-by-period basis (Column 2), the amortization of the note discount on a period-by-period basis (Column 3), the remaining balance of the note discount (Column 4), and the book value of the notes (Column 6). Observe that Column 6 is equal to Column 5, the face value of the notes, minus Column 4, the unamortized note discount.

EXHIBIT 9.2		Note Amortization Schedule (in millions)*						
(Principal = $100; Coupon rate = 8%; Yield rate = 10%)								
Date	Period	Cash Flow (1)	Interest Expense[1] (2)	Amortized Note Discount[2] (3)	Note Discount[3] (4)	Face Value of Notes (5)	Book Value of Notes (6)	Market Value of Notes
12/31/05	0	$ 87.55			$12.46	$100.00	$ 87.55	
06/30/05	1	4.00	$4.38	0.38	12.08	100.00	87.92	
12/31/05	2	4.00	4.40	0.40	11.68	100.00	88.32	
06/30/06	3	4.00	4.42	0.42	11.26	100.00	88.74	
12/31/06	4	4.00	4.44	0.44	10.82	100.00	89.18	
06/30/07	5	4.00	4.46	0.46	10.38	100.00	89.62	
12/31/07	6	4.00	4.48	0.48	9.90	100.00	90.10	
06/30/08	7	4.00	4.51	0.51	9.39	100.00	90.61	
12/31/08	8	4.00	4.53	0.53	8.86	100.00	91.14	
06/30/09	9	4.00	4.56	0.56	8.31	100.00	91.69	
12/31/09	10	4.00	4.58	0.58	7.72	100.00	92.28	$ 85.24
06/30/10	11	4.00	4.61	0.61	7.11	100.00	92.89	
12/31/10	12	4.00	4.64	0.64	6.46	100.00	93.54	
06/30/11	13	4.00	4.68	0.68	5.79	100.00	94.21	
12/31/11	14	4.00	4.71	0.71	5.08	100.00	94.92	
06/30/12	15	4.00	4.75	0.75	4.33	100.00	95.67	
12/31/12	16	4.00	4.78	0.78	3.55	100.00	96.45	
06/30/13	17	4.00	4.82	0.82	2.72	100.00	97.28	
12/31/13	18	4.00	4.86	0.86	1.86	100.00	98.14	
06/30/14	19	4.00	4.91	0.91	0.95	100.00	99.05	
12/31/14	20	4.00	4.95	0.95	0.00	100.00	100.00	
12/31/14	20	100.00						100.00

*Figures are rounded to two decimal places.
[1] Column 2 = Column $6_{t-1} \times 5$ percent
[2] Column 3 = Column 2 − Column 1
[3] Column 4 = Column 4_{t-1} − Column 3_t

On December 31, 2005, Midwestern Airlines must make its second cash payment of $4 million to its noteholders. But how much interest expense did Midwestern incur from June 30 to December 31, 2005? Using the formula to calculate the periodic interest expense (Interest expense = Yield rate × Book value of debt as of the beginning of the period), Midwestern's interest expense for the second compounding period is calculated as follows:

$$\text{Interest expense} = 5\% \times \$87.9254 \text{ million} = \$4.3963 \text{ million}$$

Be sure to observe that on June 30, the book value of the notes is now $87.9254 million ($100 − $12.452 + $0.3774), and thus, the interest expense for the second interest payment period is $4.3963 million. The cash interest payment of $4 million is unchanged, and thus, the discount amortization for the second period is $0.3963 million. After considering the discount amortization, the book value of the Midwestern notes at December 31, 2005 is $88.3217 million (see bolded area in Exhibit 9.2), or $87.9254 million plus $0.3963 million.

Market Rates of Interest and the Book Value of Debt

Implicit in the Midwestern Airlines illustration is the assumption that the book value of the notes equals their present value and that the yield rate of interest on the Midwestern notes remains constant over time. In reality, market yield rates are constantly changing in the public debt market to reflect changing investors' expectations regarding the economic and political conditions of the local, national, and global economy. For financial statement purposes, however, the changing market perceptions and related changing market yield rates are ignored. On the financial statements of Midwestern, the $100 million notes are reported as if the yield rate on the notes remains a constant ten percent. But what will happen to the actual market value of the Midwestern notes if the market rate of interest demanded by investors increases to, say, twelve percent on December 31, 2009 (with ten interest payment periods remaining)?

Using the formula to calculate the present value of a debt instrument, the market value of the Midwestern notes would be $85.24 million, calculated as follows:

Present value of $100 million in 10 periods @ 6%: $100 million × 0.558	=	$55.80 million
+ Present value of $4 million per period for 10 periods @ 6%: $4 million × 7.360	=	29.44 million
Market value of notes		$85.24 million

The book value of the notes on Midwestern's balance sheet, however, remains $92.28 million, reflecting the assumption that the company's cost of debt is unchanged at ten percent (see bolded area in Exhibit 9.2).

The new market value of the Midwestern notes ($85.24 million) demonstrates an important relationship between the market value of fixed interest rate debt instruments and market rates of interest: As market rates of interest increase (decrease), the fair value of debt instruments with a fixed rate of return will decline (increase) to compensate investors for the changing time value of money. Since the coupon rate of interest on the Midwestern notes must remain fixed at four percent per period, but investors are now demanding a yield rate of six percent per period (one-half of twelve percent), the market price of the notes must decline to enable investors to earn the higher expected market rate of return. If the market price of the Midwestern notes did not adjust downward to enable investors to earn their expected rate of return, investors would be unwilling to buy the notes.

Early Debt Retirement

Businesses sometimes find that they no longer need their existing debt financing, perhaps because the business has been successful at generating operating cash flow or because their current debt is at a higher rate than current market rates and refinancing can lower the firm's cost of debt financing. When this situation arises, firms will sometimes prepay, or retire, their outstanding interest-bearing debt.

Returning to the Midwestern Airlines illustration, assume that the company decides to retire all of its outstanding eight percent notes on December 31, 2009. As indicated above, the market value of the notes is $85.24 million assuming a prevailing market yield rate of twelve percent, whereas the book value is $92.28 million (see bolded area in Exhibit 9.2). Ignoring transaction costs that may be necessary to facilitate the note repurchase, Midwestern will pay $85.24 million to retire the debt early. Thus, the company's cash will decline by $85.24 million, notes payable will decline by $100 million, the note discount account will increase by $7.72 million ($100 million − $92.28 million) and retained earnings will increase by $7.04 million ($92.28 million − $85.24 million). By retiring the notes early, Midwestern will record a gain on early debt retirement of $7.04 million (see the Midwestern spreadsheet in Exhibit 9.1), largely as a consequence of the increase in the market rate of interest from ten to twelve percent.

Gains and losses on financing transactions like the early retirement of bonds or notes require special consideration when analyzing a company's income statement. These one-time gains or losses should not be considered as part of a firm's recurring or sustainable earnings. If material in amount, the gains or losses should be separately disclosed on the income statement; however, if immaterial, the gains or losses will need to be identified by financial statement users through a review of the footnotes and then removed from any estimate of sustainable earnings. During the preparation of a statement of cash flow, it is customary to remove any gains or losses from financing transactions (such as the early retirement of debt) from the cash flow from operations, and instead, reflect these gains or losses as part of the cash flow from financing.

Zero-Coupon Bonds and Notes

The public market for bonds and notes is made up of many investors and institutions with diverse risk preferences. Some investors prefer debt instruments that pay regular interest payments, whereas others are willing to forego the regular receipt of interest in exchange for a higher rate of return. Zero-coupon bonds and notes are designed with this latter group of investors in mind.

As the name implies, **zero-coupon bonds** and notes have no coupon rate, and thus, pay no periodic cash interest payment. Instead, the regular but unpaid interest is added to the principal value of the bond (or note) and is paid as a lump sum at maturity. Zero-coupon bonds are important financing tools for companies with limited current cash flow since the issuing company is not required to pay the regular debt servicing associated with traditional interest-bearing bonds or notes.

To illustrate the valuation of, and accounting for, zero-coupon bonds and notes, consider the following scenario:

On January 1, 2005, **Midwestern Airlines, Inc.** issued $100 million face value of zero-coupon mortgage notes with a maturity of ten years (in 2014), with semi-annual compounding. At the time of issuance, the market yield rate on equivalent risk-rated debt instruments was twelve percent.

Assuming no transaction costs, how much would Midwestern Airlines receive from the sale of the notes? Unlike interest-bearing notes, the Midwestern zero-coupon notes have only one cash flow stream to discount, namely the lump-sum payment of principal in 2014. Using the present value formula, the proceeds from the sale of the notes would be $31.2 million, calculated as follows:

> Zero-coupon bonds and notes pay no regular interest payments to investors, and thus, are considered to be riskier investments than interest-bearing bonds and notes. As a consequence, zero-coupon debt may carry returns as much as 200 basis points higher than interest-bearing debt. The higher returns reflect the opportunity cost that must be borne by investors who purchase zero-coupon debt.

Present value of $100 million in 20 periods @ 6%: $100 million × 0.312 = $31.2 million

Thus, the Midwestern zero-coupon notes would be sold at a discount of $68.8 million ($100 million − $31.2 million). The discount of $68.8 million represents the periodic cash interest payments to be paid to an investor at maturity plus interest on those unpaid amounts, assuming a six percent return per period compounded over 20 periods.

Although Midwestern will not make any interest payments until 2014, the company will still report its implicit interest expense on its mortgage notes on its income statement. On June 30, 2005, for example, the company's effective cost of borrowing is $1.872 million, or six percent times $31.2 million. Although the interest is unpaid, it is added to the book value of the notes. Thus, the zero-coupon notes are said to be valued at their accreted value—that is, the original issue price plus any accrued-but-unpaid interest. On June 30, 2005, for example, the accreted value of the zero-coupon notes is $33.072 million ($31.2 million + $1.872 million).

For the six-month period ended December 31, 2005, Midwestern's cost of borrowing on the notes is $1.984 million ($33.072 million × 6 percent), and this amount would be reported as interest expense on Midwestern's income statement. Further, the accreted value of the notes at year-end 2005 will be reported as $35.06 million ($33.072 million + $1.984 million) on the airline's balance sheet.

> The tax effect of zero-coupon bonds is essentially tax-neutral. The unpaid interest expense is tax deductible to the issuing firm but is taxable income to the buyer of the bonds in the period in which the interest is effectively earned, not the period when it is received.

In general, the tax-treatment of zero-coupon bonds and notes follows the accounting treatment—that is, the implicit interest on the debt is tax deductible by Midwestern in the period incurred, not when paid at maturity. Thus, zero-coupon bonds have two cash flow advantages: (1) the periodic interest cost remains unpaid until maturity, and (2) the unpaid periodic interest cost is currently tax-deductible, providing an immediate interest tax shield to the issuing company.

BUSINESS PERSPECTIVE: CENTURY BONDS

In 1996, International Business Machines Corporation (IBM) made financing history in the U.S. debt market by launching the largest ever issue of 100-year debentures, or what are now known as century bonds. Prior to the IBM debt placement, 21 companies had issued century bonds in the U.S. capital market but none were as large as the $850 million IBM offering. The development of the century bond was patterned after the 1894 sale of $87.3 million (U.S. dollar equivalent) of gold bonds by the Imperial Government of Russia. A unique feature of the Russian gold bonds was that redemption was only by lottery drawing, conducted at the pleasure of the Russian government, causing some pundits to refer to the bonds as "perpetuity bonds" or "permanent debt."

IBM's century bond placement was possible because of the low, stable interest rate environment that characterized the U.S. debt market, as well as the significant demand for very long-term investment products by pension funds and insurance companies. The yield on the IBM century bonds was only ten to 20 basis points higher than the yields on comparable 30-year bonds. (Note: One hundred basis points equal one percentage point of interest.) One adverse aspect of the IBM bonds was that the U.S. Treasury Department had threatened to rule that the bonds were a form of "permanent capital," and consequently, disallow the tax deductibility of interest charges on grounds that the interest payments were equivalent to dividend payments, which are not tax deductible under U.S. tax statutes. In 1997, the U.S. Treasury Department enacted tax regulations that eliminated the tax deductibility of any interest payments on debt instruments after 40 years (such as during the last 60 years of the IBM century bonds).

LEASE FINANCING

Leasing has become one of the most frequently utilized financing strategies for acquiring business assets. Office buildings, equipment, airplanes, trucks—almost any business asset—can be leased.

Companies lease assets for a variety of reasons. Some firms lease because they lack sufficient cash to purchase an asset—bank financing, for example, often requires a substantial down payment. Other firms lease because they have a poor credit rating and are too risky to secure bank financing. Financially healthy companies, on the other hand, often lease because they have better alternatives for investing their cash. And, some companies lease to avoid locking in to technology that may soon become outdated. Finally, some firms lease to take advantage of the special accounting treatment accorded certain types of leases. Leasing, however, is not without certain disadvantages. For instance, the interest rates implicit in some leases may be higher than typical long-term borrowing rates. The bottom-line, however, is that the decision to lease an asset is a strategic financing decision with both pros and cons.

Accounting for Leases

Leasing is a vehicle for financing the short or long-term use of an operating asset. In most countries, leases are classified into two categories—capital leases and operating leases. A capital lease is an asset purchase agreement involving a deferred payment plan; and, as such, the operating asset acquired under a capital lease and the related obligation to make lease payments are capitalized to the lessee's balance sheet. (The lessor accounts for the leased asset as if it is sold to the lessee.) An operating lease, on the other hand, represents a contractual relationship wherein the lessor provides temporary access to the leased asset to the lessee. Because access to the leased asset under an operating lease is conditional (it is contingent on its future availability), accounting standards do not require that the leased asset or the related obligation to make lease payments be capitalized to the lessee's balance sheet. Critics of the accounting for operating leases contend that this accounting treatment effectively provides a form of off-balance-sheet financing for the lessee in that the lessee gains access to the productive capacity of the leased asset but is not required to report the future payments needed to finance that access on its balance sheet. Critics also observe that the accounting for operating leases effectively understates a lessee's true debt position, possibly leading to inefficiencies in the public and private debt markets. A U.S. Securities and Exchange Commission study in 2004 found that of 200 publicly-held companies analyzed, 77 percent had off-balance operating leases, valued at approximately $1.25 billion.

The criteria used to identify when a lease is a capital lease varies from country to country. Under current lease accounting rules in the United States, for example, a lease must be reported as a capital lease if *any* of the following conditions apply to the lease:

- The lease agreement transfers legal ownership of the leased asset to the lessee by the end of the lease term.
- The lease agreement contains a "bargain purchase" option—that is, the lessee has the right to buy the leased asset at a price less than its fair market value.
- The lease term is 75 percent or more of the leased asset's remaining economic life.
- The present value of the minimum contractual lease payments is equal to or greater than 90 percent of the leased asset's fair market value.[3]

The evaluation as to whether a lease is a capital or operating lease is made at the inception of a lease. If a lease is determined to be a deferred purchase contract (a capital lease), capitalization of both the leased asset and a lease liability ensues. Otherwise, the lease is accounted for as a contingent liability, and the

---

[3] Many leases contain "escalation clauses" linking the actual lease payment to the level of revenues generated by the leased asset. Thus, while the minimum contractual lease payment is known at the time of lease signing, the actual lease payment cannot be known until the level of future revenue is determined.

existence, key terms, and characteristics of the operating lease agreement are disclosed in the footnotes to the financial statements but not on the face of the balance sheet. We will have more to say about contingent liabilities in Chapter 10.

On the lessee's income statement, the cost of an operating lease is disclosed as a lease expense, whereas for a capital lease, the income statement effect is reported as depreciation on the capitalized leased asset and interest expense on the capitalized lease liability. It is rare that the lease expense under an operating lease will equal the sum of the depreciation expense plus the interest expense under a capital lease in any given year largely as a consequence of the allocation assumption inherent in most depreciation methods. Over the duration of the entire lease period, however, the total expense will be the same regardless of how a lease is accounted for. On the statement of cash flow, the cash flow effect of the two lease forms is identical each year because the cash flow effect, the lease payment, is equivalent under both lease forms.

To illustrate the similarities and differences between an operating lease and a capital lease, consider the case of Midwestern Airlines Inc. which entered into a ten-year lease agreement for flight equipment having a fair market value of $100 million and an implicit interest rate of ten percent per year. The annual lease payments are $16.27 million and are paid annually at the end of each year. (A constant set of payments made at the end of each period is referred to as an **ordinary annuity** or an **annuity-in-arrears**.) The leased equipment had an expected remaining useful life of 13 years.

Capital Lease. Although the Midwestern Airlines' lease agreement does not provide for a transfer of ownership at any time during the life of the lease or provide the lessee with a bargain purchase option, there are two reasons why this lease should be accounted for as a capital lease. First, the length of the lease period (ten years) exceeds 75 percent of the leased asset's remaining economic life of 13 years (75 percent × 13 years = 9.75 years). Second, the present value of the minimum contractual lease payments is greater than 90 percent of the equipment's fair market value. In fact, the present value of the lease payments is $100 million, which is exactly 100 percent of the equipment's fair market value. (Can you verify that the present value of ten payments of $16.27 million at ten percent interest is $100 million?)

Assuming treatment as a capital lease, the value of the leased flight equipment will be capitalized to Midwestern's balance sheet as a long-term asset at its present value of $100 million, with a lease liability for the same amount also reflected on the balance sheet. This information is illustrated in Midwestern Airlines' spreadsheet in Exhibit 9.3. At the end of the first year of the lease, a cash payment for $16.27 million is made, reducing cash by $16.27 million, the lease liability by $6.27 million, and retained earnings by $10 million representing interest expense on the outstanding lease liability ($100 million × 10 percent). In addition, depreciation expense on the capitalized asset must be recorded. Assuming use of the straight-line method, a useful life of ten years (the life of the lease agreement), and a zero residual value since the leased asset reverts back to the lessor at the end of the lease period, the depreciation expense would amount to $10 million ($100 million/10 years).

A lease **amortization schedule** for Midwestern Airlines is presented in Exhibit 9.4. Consider, for example, Year Two of the Midwestern equipment lease (see bolded area in Exhibit 9.4). According to the amortization schedule, Midwestern's lease payment of $16.27 million in Year Two will reduce the lease

> When discounting the future minimum lease payments under a capital lease, the appropriate discount rate is the interest rate implicit in the lease agreement. The rate implicit in a lease is not always known, however, and thus, it is accepted practice to use a firm's incremental cost of borrowing (the rate at which the firm could borrow an equivalent amount of money given its existing debt structure) to discount the lease payments. When the incremental cost of debt is unknown, a firm's weighted-average cost of debt or an inferred rate based upon a firm's credit rating (if known) can be used.

EXHIBIT 9.3	Accounting for a Capital Lease					

Midwestern Airlines Inc. Spreadsheet		Assets		=	Liabilities	+	Equity
($ millions)	Cash	Equipment	Accumulated Depreciation	Lease Liability	Retained Earnings
Year 1					
Lease signing		100.00		100.00	
Lease payment	−16.27			−6.27	−10.00 (interest expense)
Recognize depreciation expense			−$10.00		−10.00 (depreciation expense)
End-of year	−16.27	100.00	−10.00	93.73	−20.00
Year 2					
Lease payment	−16.27			−6.90	−9.37 (interest expense)
Recognize depreciation expense			−10.00		−10.00 (depreciation expense)
End-of-year	−32.74	100.00	−20.00	86.82	−19.37

liability by $6.9 million, with the remainder of the payment ($9.37 million) applied as interest expense ($93.73 million $\times$ 10 percent). This information is recorded in Midwestern's spreadsheet in Exhibit 9.3.

Operating Lease. If the Midwestern Airlines' equipment lease is accounted for as an operating lease, no asset or liability is capitalized to the company's balance sheet. The annual lease payment of $16.27 million is recorded on the income statement as a lease expense and as a reduction in cash on the balance sheet. This is shown in Midwestern's spreadsheet in Exhibit 9.5.

As Exhibit 9.4 reveals, the total cash outflow for the Midwestern Airlines' lease is $162.75 million over the ten-year life of the lease, regardless of whether the lease is accounted for as an operating lease or as a capital lease. The total expenses deducted against revenues over the life of the lease are also equivalent ($162.75 million) under either lease accounting treatment. The key financial statement difference between the two types of leases involves the balance sheet disclosure—capital leases are reported on Midwestern's balance sheet as an asset and as a form of debt, whereas operating leases are not.

Lease Accounting and Security Prices

Although the annual cash outflow of $16.27 million for Midwestern Airlines is the same under each lease treatment, the periodic balance sheet and income statement effects differ. Under the operating lease, Midwestern's lease expense totals $16.27 million each year, whereas under a capital lease the lease-related expenses total $20 million in Year 1 and $19.37 million in Year 2, respectively. On the balance sheet, a capital lease requires the creation of an asset and liability, whereas the operating lease does not. Do the financial statement differences associated with the accounting for operating leases and capital leases affect the perceived riskiness of a firm? And, do the financial statement differences between the two lease forms affect security prices? Available empirical research suggests that investors **do** include the financial risk associated with off-balance-sheet operating leases in their assessment of share prices, indicating that capital market participants are not misled by the differing accounting treat-

EXHIBIT 9.4	Lease Amortization Schedule

Ten year lease with implicit interest rate of 10 percent per year;
straight-line depreciation of leased asset

						Total Expenses Under	
Year	Lease Balance[1] (1)	Interest Expense[2] (2)	Principal Reduction[3] (3)	Lease Payment (4)	Asset Depreciation (5)	Operating Lease	Capital Lease
0.......	$100.00						
1.......	93.73	$10.00	$ 6.27	$ 16.27	$ 10.00	$ 16.27	$ 20.00
2.......	86.82	9.37	6.90	16.27	10.00	16.27	19.37
3.......	79.23	8.68	7.59	16.27	10.00	16.27	18.68
4.......	70.88	7.92	8.35	16.27	10.00	16.27	17.92
5.......	61.69	7.09	9.19	16.27	10.00	16.27	17.09
6.......	51.69	6.17	10.11	16.27	10.00	16.27	16.17
7.......	40.47	5.16	11.12	16.27	10.00	16.27	15.16
8.......	28.25	4.05	12.23	16.27	10.00	16.27	14.05
9.......	14.80	2.82	13.45	16.27	10.00	16.27	12.82
10.......	0.00	1.48	14.80	16.27	10.00	16.27	11.48
Total	$0.00	$62.75	$100.00	$162.75	$100.00	$162.75	$162.75

[1] Column 1 = Column 1_{t-1} − Column 3
[2] Column 2_t = Column 1_{t-1} × 10%
[3] Column 3_t = Column 4 − Column 2

EXHIBIT 9.5	Accounting for an Operating Lease

Midwestern Airlines Inc. Spreadsheet	Assets	=	Equity
($ millions)	Cash		Retained Earnings
Year 1			
Lease payment.........................	−16.27		−16.27 (Lease expense)
End-of-year...........................	−16.27		−16.27
Year 2			
Lease payment.........................	−16.27		−16.27 (Lease expense)
End-of-year...........................	−32.54		−32.54

ment of the two lease forms.[4] Stated alternatively, capital market participants see the two lease forms as economically-equivalent forms of asset financing.

Concerned about the financial statement effect of the accounting for leases on some companies' reported debt, the FASB decided to explore whether all non-cancelable leases should be accounted for as capital leases. To illustrate the basis for the FASB's concern, In Practice 9.1 presents data for five publicly-held retail businesses that rely extensively on operating leases to finance their access to retail space. The In Practice data reveals, for example, that **Circuit City Stores** has off-balance-sheet operating

---

[4] K. Ely, "Operating Lease Accounting and the Market's Assessment of Equity Risk," *Journal of Accounting Research* (1995).

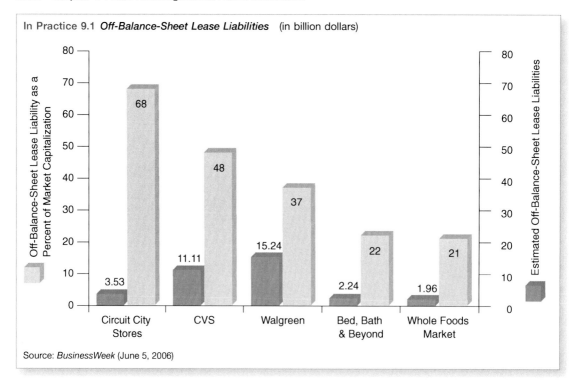

In Practice 9.1 *Off-Balance-Sheet Lease Liabilities* (in billion dollars)

Source: *BusinessWeek* (June 5, 2006)

lease liabilities valued at $3.53 billion, equivalent to 68 percent of the firm's total market capitalization. Consequently, failure to consider Circuit City's operating leases when valuing the company would cause a serious overstatement of the firm's share price.

CALCULATING THE WEIGHTED-AVERAGE COST OF DEBT

A firm's cost of borrowing will vary with the amount to be borrowed, the duration of the borrowing, the purpose of the borrowing, the firm's existing debt structure, and whether or not the debt is secured. In general, short-term debt is less costly than longer-term debt as risk is a function of the duration of a borrowing. Similarly, a highly leveraged firm will find it increasingly more costly to add additional debt than a less highly leveraged firm, as the cost of any new debt is related to the amount of existing debt (existing credit risk). Finally, the larger the proposed borrowing amount, the higher the cost as the amount of risk assumed by a lender is greater.

To help investment professionals and managers estimate the cost of any new debt financing, it is accepted practice in many countries to disclose in the footnotes to the financial statements a firm's **weighted-average cost of debt** for both its short-term and long-term debt. The weighted-average cost of debt is calculated by averaging a firm's various interest rates, weighted by the amount of debt outstanding at the various rates.

To illustrate, consider data for The Claremont Company Inc. presented in Exhibit 9.6. The company has five debt issuances outstanding, with effective interest rates ranging from six percent to nine and one-

In Practice 9.2 *Long-Term Leases: A Glimpse of a Sample of Fortune 1000 Companies* The following table identifies the types of leases disclosed by a sample of 600 *Fortune 1000* companies. The data reveal that 53 percent of the surveyed firms use operating leases exclusively:

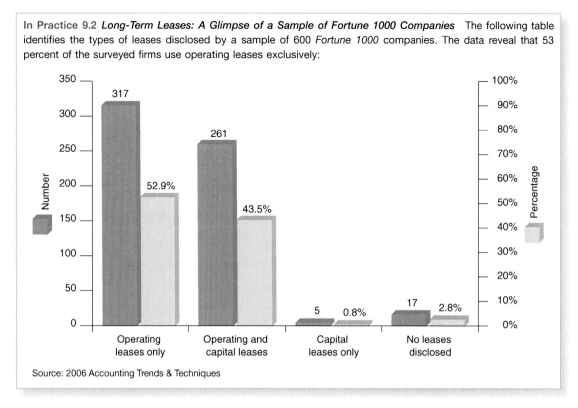

Source: 2006 Accounting Trends & Techniques

EXHIBIT 9.6	Calculating the Weighted-average Cost of Debt
The Claremont Company Inc.	
Amount of Borrowing	**Interest Rate**
$100 million.	7.50%
75 million.	6.30
50 million.	6.00
200 million.	8.00
500 million.	9.50
$925 million.	
Average	7.46
Weighted-average	8.51

half percent. The simple average of the five interest rates is 7.46 percent, but the weighted average is 8.51 percent. If The Claremont Company needed to finance its future growth with debt, at what rate would the company most likely be able to borrow the needed funds?

Although the company's borrowing rate would be contingent on the length of the borrowing and whether it was secured, a good estimate of The Claremont Company's cost of future borrowing would be its weighted-average cost of existing debt (8.51 percent), which reflects the firm's existing capital structure.

MANAGING REPORTED DEBT

One of the metrics used to measure a firm's solvency, and hence, its credit risk, is the amount of a business' net debt. **Net debt** is the amount of debt outstanding after subtracting the value of any liquid assets immediately available to repay a business' debt. Thus, net debt is the amount of debt that a firm expects to repay from future operating cash flows, asset sales, equity issuances, or debt refinancing, and is calculated as follows:

$$\text{Net debt} = \text{Total debt} - \text{Liquid assets}$$

Because of the importance of net debt as an indicator of financial health, especially business solvency, some firms have attempted to manage the level of their reported net debt. Consider, for example, the case of **Parmalat SpA**, an Italian dairy company. In late 2003, the company filed for bankruptcy after revealing that it had massively under-reported its outstanding net debt. The accounting fraud had apparently been executed over a decade, without detection by the firm's external auditors, **Grant Thorton**.

> **Liquid assets**, or quick assets, include a firm's cash and cash equivalents, short-term marketable securities, and accounts receivables. These current assets are readily convertible into cash at values that closely approximate their book value.

According to the Italian company's investigative auditor, **PricewaterhouseCoopers**, Parmalat under reported its net debt position by approximately $16 billion. The under-reporting was achieved by overstating the amount of liquid assets on its balance sheet, specifically by overstating the amount of cash on hand and retaining worthless accounts receivable on the company's balance sheet.

Another way that some companies manage the amount of debt disclosed on their balance sheet is through the use of off-balance-sheet financing. **Off-balance-sheet financing** refers to the various ways that a company can gain access to productive operating assets while not disclosing the obligation to pay for that access on its balance sheet. Examples of off-balance-financing discussed thus far include the use of operating leases to finance operating assets and the use of the equity method to account for unconsolidated affiliates, joint ventures, and special purpose entities. We will have more to say about other forms of off-balance-sheet debt in Chapter 10.

ANALYZING A COMPANY'S USE OF LEVERAGE

The first thing that a financial statement user should consider when analyzing a firm's debt financing is whether the reported financial statement numbers accurately reflect the firm's use of leverage. As discussed in this chapter, GAAP provides business managers with the opportunity to finance the acquisition of a firm's operating assets with leases and avoid any balance sheet recognition of the lease liability provided that the lease qualifies as an operating lease. As a consequence, GAAP provides managers with a perverse incentive to structure their company's lease financing to satisfy the criteria for operating-lease accounting. This does not preclude the financial statement user, however, from undertaking various financial statement adjustments to place these obligations on the balance sheet, especially where it is determined that the amount of debt involved is material. U.S. GAAP requires that a company financing its assets with operating leases disclose sufficient information in the footnotes to permit a financial statement user to value the off-balance-sheet debt and to capitalize any lease obligations, along with the corresponding leased assets, on a firm's balance sheet.

Operating lease obligations, however, are only one of several off-balance-sheet financing arrangements that should to be considered as part of any financial statement due diligence. In Chapter 8, for example, we examined how the use of the equity method enables parent-companies to report only the net assets

BUSINESS PERSPECTIVE: LEASE DISCLOSURES

AMR Corporation is the parent company of American Airlines, American Eagle Airlines, and TWA Airlines. AMR uses leases to gain access to a variety of passenger airline equipment (principally aircraft). The company's 2002 annual report disclosed the following information with respect to its capital and operating leases:

AMR leases various types of aircraft equipment and airport property. The future minimum lease payments required under capital leases, together with the present value of such payments, and future minimum lease payments required under operating leases that have initial or remaining non-cancelable lease terms in excess of one year were:

Year Ending (in millions)	Capital Leases	Operating Leases
2003	$ 254	$ 1,521
2004	299	1,216
2005	233	1,158
2006	235	1,089
2007	179	1,038
2008 and thereafter	1,113	10,296
	2,313	$16,318
Less amount representing interest	(736)	
Present value of minimum lease payments	$1,577	

AMR's abbreviated balance sheet is presented below and reveals that the company has $19.694 billion ($18.258 + $1.436) invested in equipment and property as of year-end 2002, of which $1.436 billion was financed using capital leases. This total fails to include, however, the $16.318 billion that AMR expects to pay in the future for equipment and property financed using operating leases. AMR's lease disclosures reveal that the company relies extensively on operating leases as a form of financing. Only $1.577 billion ($1.422 + $0.155) is disclosed on AMR's 2002 balance sheet as leasing-related debt, and this amount represents less than nine percent of the firm's total future minimum lease payments ($16.318 + $2.313 = $18.631). If AMR's operating leases were accounted for as capital leases (the leased assets and lease liabilities were capitalized to the balance sheet), how much additional debt would be added to AMR's balance sheet?

($ millions)	2002	2001
AMR Corporation		
Abbreviated Consolidated Balance Sheets		
Current assets	$ 4,937	$ 6,571
Equipment and property (net)	18,258	17,988
Equipment and property under capital leases	2,410	2,821
Less: Accumulated depreciation	(974)	(1,154)
	1,436	1,667
Other assets	5,636	6,615
Total assets	$30,267	$32,841
Current liabilities	$ 7,240	$ 7,512
Long-term debt, less current maturities	10,888	8,310
Obligations under capital leases		
Less current obligations (155 and 216 in 2002 and 2001, respectively)	1,422	1,524
Other liabilities	9,760	10,122
Shareholders' equity	957	5,373
Total liabilities and shareholders' equity	$30,267	$32,841

continued

continued from previous page

BUSINESS PERSPECTIVE: LEASE DISCLOSURES

Assuming that the interest rate implicit in AMR's operating leases is ten percent, the present value of the company's future minimum lease payments under its operating leases is $8.584.96 billion, calculated as follows:

Future Minimum Lease Payments Under Operating Leases (millions)	Present Value Factor (10%)	Present Value Of Minimum Lease Payments (millions)
$ 1,521	0.909	$ 1,382.60
1,216	0.826	1,004.42
1,158	0.751	869.66
1,089	0.683	743.79
1,038	0.621	644.60
1,038	0.564	585.43
1,038	0.513	532.49
1,038	0.467	484.75
1,038	0.424	440.11
1,038	0.386	400.67
1,038	0.350	363.30
1,038	0.319	331.12
1,038	0.290	301.02
1,038	0.263	272.99
954	0.239	228.01
$16,318		$8,584.96

AMR's lease disclosures (see footnote information) report the first five years of minimum lease payments along with a summation of the minimum lease payments for all years following the fifth year. In order to compute the present value of the future lease payments, we assume that the minimum lease payment from year five remains constant for the following years (years 6 through 14 in this example) with any remainder to be paid in the final year. Excluding AMR's operating leases, the company's long-term debt at year-end 2002 totaled $22.225 billion ($10.888 + $1.422 + $0.155 + $9.760). Including the present value of AMR's operating leases on the company's balance sheet brings the company's total long-term debt position to $30.810 billion ($22.225 + $8.585), an increase of 39 percent. These figures reveal the extent to which AMR relies on the use of operating leases as a form of debt financing, but also the extent to which the company uses off-balance-sheet financing to gain access to its operating assets: Nearly 28 percent ($8.585 ÷ $30.810) of AMR's long-term debt is carried off-balance-sheet! As a consequence, failure to consider AMR's operating leases as a form of debt financing materially understates the firm's total use of leverage.

of an affiliate company, rather than fully reporting the affiliate's assets and liabilities. We also learned that the equity method was principally used to account for joint ventures and special purpose entities (SPE), enabling the parent-company of such entities to keep any debt off the parent's balance sheet. In Chapter 10, additional off-balance-sheet liabilities, such as commitments and contingencies, are examined. We will see that, like operating lease obligations, the key elements of these potential obligations are disclosed in the footnotes to the financial statements; and consequently, it is possible for financial statement users to determine whether to include this risk-related information in any assessment of a firm's use of leverage.

In Chapter 4, we examined several financial ratios that can prove useful when evaluating a firm's use of leverage, to include the long-term debt-to-total assets ratio and the long-term debt-to-shareholders' equity ratio. Both of these ratios provide information regarding a firm's use of debt financing relative to its use of equity financing. As a general rule, debt financing can be used to enhance shareholder returns so long as the firm is able to earn a return on its borrowed funds that exceeds its cost of borrowing the funds; thus, for most firms, the use of debt financing provides a good approach to build shareholder value. For some firms, however, increasing levels of debt financing will destroy shareholder value, especially when excessive debt levels impair management's operational flexibility. A final ratio that can help assess whether a firm has excessive levels of debt is the interest coverage ratio. By comparing a firm's current level of debt service charges with its operating earnings, the financial statement user can develop an informed opinion regarding a firm's liquidity and its solvency.

ETHICS PERSPECTIVE

Numerous reasons were cited in this chapter as to why some firms use leasing as a financing approach for acquiring capital assets. One reason is the managerial desire to avoid disclosing the operating lease liability on a company's balance sheet. It can be argued that there should not be any difference to financial statement users whether a lease obligation appears on the face of the balance sheet or is disclosed in the footnotes to the financial statements. As demonstrated in this chapter, it is a simple procedure for financial statement users to adjust the balance sheet for this type of off-balance-sheet debt. Nonetheless, many managers behave as if they believe that financial statement users will not undertake the necessary financial statement adjustments to develop a complete assessment of a firm's debt exposure. Available evidence, however, indicates that financial markets are not fooled by off-balance-sheet financing, and instead, market participants appear to incorporate this information in their assessments of the risk premium associated with public companies utilizing off-balance-sheet financing.

REVIEW PROBLEM

The Arcadia Company issued $50 million of five-year bonds on January 2, 2006. The bonds carried an annual coupon rate of six percent, with interest paid semi-annually, and were issued at a time when similar risk-rated securities were yielding eight percent. Within twelve months of the debt issuance, however, market yield rates had risen to ten percent.

Required

a. Calculate the proceeds from the five-year debt offering on January 2, 2006.
b. Calculate the interest expense for the Arcadia Company on June 30, 2006 and on December 31, 2006.
c. Calculate the market value of the five-year bonds on December 31, 2006.
d. If the Arcadia Company elects to retire the bonds on December 31, 2006, how much gain (loss) would the company recognize?
e. Is the decision to retire the bonds on December 31, 2006 a good decision?

Solution

a. Proceeds of debt offering:

Present value of $50 million in 10 periods @ 4%: $50,000,000 × 0.67556	=	$33,778,000
+ Present value of $1,500,000 per period for 10 periods @ 4%: $1,500,000 × 8.111	=	12,166,350
Proceeds		$45,944,350

b. Interest expense:

June 30: $45,944,350 × .04	=	$1,837,774
December 31: ($45,944,350 + $377,774) × .04	=	$1,851,285

c. Market value:

Present value of $50 million in 8 periods @ 5%: $50,000,000 × 0.67684	=	$33,842,000
+ Present value of $1,500,000 per period for 8 periods @ 5%: $1,500,000 × 6.46321	=	9,669,482
Market value		$43,511,482

d. Gain on retirement:

Book value of bonds	$45,944,350
Discount amortization (06/30/06).	337,774
Discount amortization (12/31/06).	351,285
Book value (12/31/06)	46,633,409
Less: Market value.	(43,511,482)
Gain on early retirement.	$ 3,121,927

e. The Arcadia Company will recognize a gain of $3,121,927 on the debt retirement as a consequence of the decline in the market value of the bonds, associated with the market interest rate increase from eight to ten percent. Thus, if the debt is no longer needed to finance the operations of the company, the decision would be a good decision.

EXECUTIVE SUMMARY

This chapter investigated the strategic financing decision of companies, specifically how companies finance their operations and asset purchases with bonds, leases, and notes. We saw that most liabilities were valued at their present value. We also examined how and why some firms lease their long-term revenue-producing assets. Finally, we illustrated how to calculate the weighted-average cost of debt of a company. In Chapter 10, our investigation of debt financing continues with a consideration of commitments and contingent liabilities, retirement obligations, deferred income tax liabilities, and financial instruments and derivatives.

As a validation of your understanding of the content of this chapter, you should now be able to:

- Explain how bonds and notes are valued and reported in corporate financial statements.
- Explain how a company accounts for debt when it is retired before its maturity.
- Explain the difference between a capital lease and an operating lease and how each are reported in the financial statements.
- Explain how and why companies manage the amount of debt reported on their corporate balance sheets.

KEY CONCEPTS AND TERMS

Accreted value, 9.11	Annuity-in-arrears, 9.13	Bond payable, 9.3
Amortization, 9.7	Basis point, 9.5	Callable bond, 9.4
Amortization schedule, 9.8	Bond, 9.3	Capital lease, 9.12

APPENDIX 9A: Recording Debt Financing Transactions using the Debit and Credit Paradigm

In this appendix, the traditional approach to recording accounting transactions—that is, the debit and credit paradigm—is used to illustrate how the journal entries associated with the issuance of various debt instruments by Midwestern Airlines, Inc. would be recorded. Specifically, the accounting for interest-bearing notes, zero-coupon notes, and operating and capital leases is illustrated.

Accounting for Notes

On January 1, 2005, Midwestern Airlines, Inc. issued $100 million face value (maturity value) of mortgage notes with an annual coupon rate of eight percent and a maturity of ten years. The notes pay interest on June 30 and December 31 of each year. At the time the notes were issued, the market yield rate on equivalent risk-rated instruments was ten percent. Five years later, on December 31, 2009, the market yield rate on equivalent risk-rated securities had increased to twelve percent. No longer needing the debt financing, Midwestern Airlines decided to retire all of its outstanding debt on December 31, 2009. (Please refer to the chapter for the calculation of the following values.)

Date	Accounts	Debit	Credit
Jan 5, 2005	Cash (A) . . . . Note discount (CL) . . . . Notes payable (L) . . . . *To record the issuance of $100 million in notes at a discount.*	87,548,000 12,452,000	 100,000,000

Jun 30, 2005	Retained earnings (E) . . . .
	    Cash (A) . . . .
	    Note discount (CL) . . . .
	To record the payment of interest on the notes.
		4,377,400	
			4,000,000
			377,400

Dec 31, 2005	Retained earnings (E) . . . .
	    Cash (A) . . . .
	    Note discount (CL) . . . .
	To record the payment of interest on the notes.
		4,396,300	
			4,000,000
			396,300

(Interest payment entries similar to those presented above would be recorded for 2006, 2007, 2008, and 2009. Appropriate values for the entries can be obtained from the Note Amortization Table in Exhibit 9.2)

Dec 31, 2009	Notes payable (L)	100,000,000	
	Cash (A)		85,240,000
	Note discount (CL)		7,720,000
	Retained earnings (G)		7,040,000
	To record the early retirement of the notes at a gain.		

Assume now that on January 1, 2005, Midwestern Airlines, Inc. issued $100 million face value of zero-coupon mortgage notes, having a maturity of ten years with semi-annual compounding. At the time of issuance, the yield rate on equivalent risk-rated debt securities was twelve percent. (Please refer to the chapter for the calculation of the following values.)

Jan 1, 2005	Cash (A)	31,200,000	
	Note discount (CL)	68,800,000	
	Notes payable (L)		100,000,000
	To record the issuance of $100 million in zero-coupon notes.		
Jun 30, 2005	Retained earnings (E)	1,872,000	
	Note discount (CL)		1,872,000
	To record the interest expense implicit in the zero-coupon notes.		
Dec 31, 2005	Retained earnings (E)	1,984,000	
	Note discount (CL)		1,984,000
	To record the interest expense implicit in the zero-coupon notes.		

Accounting for Leases

Midwestern Airlines entered into a ten-year lease agreement for flight equipment having a fair market value of $100 million and an implicit interest rate of ten percent per year. Annual lease payments of $16.27 million are paid at the end of each year. The leased equipment had an expected remaining useful life of 13 years.

If the lease is accounted for as an operating lease, the following transactions would be recorded:

Date	Accounts	Debit	Credit
Year 1 (BOY)	No entry is recorded at the time of lease signing.		
Year 1 (EOY)	Retained earnings (E)	16,270,000	
	Cash (A)		16,270,000
	To record the annual lease payment and lease expense.		
Year 2 (EOY)	Retained earnings (E)	16,270,000	
	Cash (A)		16,270,000
	To record the annual lease payment and lease expense.		

(Equivalent journal entries would be recorded each year until the lease agreement expires at the end of ten years.) If the lease is accounted for as a capital lease, the following transactions would be recorded:

Year 1 (BOY)	Leased equipment (A)	100,000,000	
	Lease liability (L)		100,000,000
	To record the signing of a capital lease agreement.		

continued

Year 1 (EOY)	Retained earnings (E) . . . . Lease liability (L) . . . . Cash (A) . . . . *To record annual lease payment, debt reduction, and interest* *expense.*	10,000,000 6,270,000	16,270,000
	Retained earnings (E) . . . . Accumulated depreciation (CA) . . . . *To record the depreciation expense on the leased equipment.*	10,000,000	10,000,000
Year 2 (EOY)	Retained earnings (E) . . . . Lease liability (L) . . . . Cash (A) . . . . *To record annual lease payment, debt reduction, and interest* *expense.*	9,370,000 6,900,000	16,270,000
	Retained earnings (E) . . . . Accumulated depreciation (CA) . . . . *To record annual depreciation expense on the leased equipment.*	10,000,000	10,000,000

DISCUSSION QUESTIONS

Q9.1   **Financing with Debt versus Equity.**   It is commonly understood that the cost of financing a business' asset purchases with debt is cheaper than financing those purchases with equity. Discuss why debt financing is cheaper than equity financing. Is there a set of circumstances when the cost of debt financing would exceed the cost of equity financing? If so, when?

Q9.2   **Credit Ratings.**   In 2005, The **General Motors Corporation** (GM) reported a net less of $10.6 billion. Moreover, the automobile manufacturer had been losing U.S. market share to increasing competition from Japanese automakers. In response, Standard & Poor's rating service indicated that it was reviewing whether to lower GM's debt rating from its current B rating (five levels below investment grade status). Standard & Poor's also reported that it was "putting GM's debt on its CreditWatch list with negative implications" because the automaker disclosed that as much as $3 billion in lease obligations could be subject to possible covenant violations that might cause an acceleration of debt repayment. The credit-rating agency also expressed concern that the company's recent disappointing performance might affect the firm's access to its $5.6 billion standby credit facility. Discuss why credit ratings are important to a company like GM. Discuss the consequences to a company when it violates its existing debt covenants.

Q9.3   **Credit Ratings.**   In early 2006, The **General Motors Corporation** (GM) took significant steps to improve its deteriorating financial condition. Besides downsizing its workforce and closing certain inefficient plants, the company also sold its ownership interest in several of its subsidiaries. For instance, GM sold its equity stake in Japan's Isusu Motors for $300 million and sold a majority shareholding in its financing subsidiary, General Motors Acceptance Corporation (GMAC), for $14 billion. In response to these GM actions, U.S. credit-rating agencies took the following actions:

- Fitch, Inc. revised its outlook on GMAC's bonds to "positive."
- Standard & Poor's reported that it might raise the ratings on GMAC's bonds from BB to BB+.
- Moody's indicated that it might downgrade the GMAC bonds.

Discuss why a favorable credit rating is important to a company like GM. Do you agree with Moody's response (a possible credit-rating downgrade) to the GM actions? Why?

Q9.4   **Long-Term Debt Disclosures.**   The **Johnson & Johnson Company** reported the following borrowings in its 2005 annual report:

Borrowing (dollars in millions)	Amount	Effective Rate (%)
3.00% zero-coupon convertible debenture, due 2020	$ 202	3.00
4.95% debentures, due 2033.	500	4.95
3.80% debentures, due 2013.	500	3.82
6.95% notes, due 2029	293	7.14
6.73% debentures, due 2023.	250	6.73
6.625% notes, due 2009	199	6.80
Industrial revenue bonds	31	3.90
Other	55	—
Total	$2,030	
Less: Current portion	(13)	
	$2,017	

Discuss the difference between a "note" and a "debenture." Of Johnson and Johnson's (J&J) total long-term borrowings of $2,017, what amount will appear as a current liability and what amount will appear as a non-current liability? Were the 3.80% debentures, due 2013, originally sold at a discount, at their par value, or at a premium? Why? Were the 6.95% notes, due 2029, originally sold at a discount, at their par value, or at a premium? Why? Which of J&J's borrowings were sold at their par value? How do you know this?

Q9.5 **Selling Bonds at a Discount, at Par, and at a Premium.** It is widely accepted that bonds may sell at a discount from their par value, at their par value, or at a premium above their par value. Discuss why, and under what circumstances, a bond would sell at a discount, at its par value, and at a premium.

Q9.6 **Accounting for Bonds at a Constant Yield Rate.** When bonds are sold by a company, they are recorded on the issuing firm's financial statements at their selling price. This price reflects the yield rate on the date of sale for equivalent risk-rated debt instruments. Although the market yield rate for a given bond may fluctuate widely in the debt market, the changing market rate is ignored for accounting purposes; and instead, the debt instrument remains on the financial statements of the issuing company at the yield rate prevailing at the time of sale. Discuss the implications of this accounting treatment. Do you believe that bond values should be periodically revised to reflect a changing interest-rate environment? Why or why not?

Q9.7 **Why do Companies Lease?** Leasing is a common form of asset financing. Discuss why leasing is such a popular form of financing for many businesses.

Q9.8 **Operating Leases and Market Efficiency.** Many businesses use operating leases as a method to finance their operating assets. One of the frequently stated reasons for the popularity of operating leases (as opposed to capital leases) is that operating leases are carried off-balance-sheet—that is, operating leases are a form of off-balance-sheet financing. Discuss whether you think the capital market is "efficient" with respect to operating leases. Stated alternatively, discuss whether you believe that the capital market treats operating leases as off-balance-sheet debt or as on-balance sheet debt. Be prepared to justify your answer.

Q9.9 **Zero-Coupon Convertible Debentures.** In 2000, ALZA Corporation, a wholly-owned subsidiary of the Johnson and Johnson (J&J) Company, sold zero-coupon convertible debentures at a price of $551.26 per $1,000 principal amount at maturity. The twenty-year debentures were also convertible into J&J s shares. Discuss the reasons why ALZA might issue zero-coupon convertible debentures. Estimate the yield to maturity on the debentures.

Q9.10 **Converting Notes Payable into Common Stock.** In 2006, US Airways Group announced that more than 99 percent of its convertible senior notes had been converted into the airline's common stock. The $112 million of 7.5 percent notes, due 2009, had been called for redemption and noteholders had been given six weeks to either convert the notes into common stock or redeem the notes for approximately $1,050 in cash per $1,000 of notes. The notes were convertible into 34.376 shares of US Airways stock, which had recently been trading at $36 per share. Why did the US Airways noteholders convert their notes into the airline's common stock? Why hadn't they converted their notes earlier? Explain how a conversion of debt into common stock might benefit US Airways Group.

Q9.11 **Collateralized Debt Obligations.** Collateralized debt obligations (CDOs) are bonds issued by a bank, real estate investment trust, or financial institution, which are backed by loans collateralized by commercial real estate (such as shopping malls, hotels, office buildings). In short, CDOs represent an interest in a pool of real estate loans and mortgages. Discuss why a bank, real estate investment trust, or financial institution would sell CDOs instead of issuing debentures backed by the firm's credit rating.

Q9.12 **Debt-for-Equity Exchange.** The May 9, 2006, edition of the *Wall Street Journal* carried the following headline:

Accounting Gain Masks UAL Loss of $306 Million

The related article explained that **UAL Corporation**, parent company of United Airlines, reported first quarter net income of almost $23 billion thanks to a $24 billion gain from "discharging its obligations to unsecured creditors in exchange for giving them 115 million UAL common shares." Without the non-cash gain, UAL would have reported a net loss of $306 million. UAL emerged from bankruptcy in February 2006. UAL common shares traded at $39 per share prior to the May 9, 2006 announcement. Discuss the financial effects of UAL's exchange of its stock for its unsecured debt. What was the market value of the UAL stock given to creditors? What was the book value of the UAL debt?

Q9.13 **(Ethics Perspective) Avoiding the Recording of Leases on Balance Sheet.** Why do you suppose that managers desire to keep debt off the balance sheet even when they know that the obligation will be fully disclosed in the footnotes? Do you feel that it is ethical to choose to lease an asset rather than to purchase the asset if the only reason for the accounting policy choice is to avoid the balance sheet recognition of the lease obligation?

⊘ **indicates that check figures are available on the book's Website.**

EXERCISES

E9.14 **Coupon Rates, Yield Rates, and Bond Issuance Prices.** The relation between a bond's coupon rate and yield rate is known to influence a bond's issuance price. Presented below are coupon rates and yield rates for a selection of corporate bonds. Identity whether each bond was sold at a discount, at its par value, or at a premium, and explain why.

Bond	Coupon Rate	Yield Rate
A....................	7.5%	7.55%
B....................	8.1	8.0
C....................	6.0	6.0
D....................	4.5	4.4
E....................	9.0	9.15

⊘ E9.15 **Calculating Bond Issuance Prices.** Presented below are annual coupon rates, yield rates, and expected duration for a series of debentures. Calculate the issuance price for each debenture assuming that the face value of each bond is $1,000 and that interest is paid semi-annually.

Bond	Coupon Rate	Yield Rate	Duration
A....................	4.0%	6.0%	5 years
B....................	10.0	8.0	6 years
C....................	6.0	6.0	10 years
D....................	0.0	8.0	15 years
E....................	8.0	10.0	10 years

E9.16   **Bond Discounts and Effective Interest Rates.**   During 2005, the Mayfield Corporation issued $400 million of zero-coupon debentures, due in 2015. The proceeds of the bond sale totaled approximately $182.56 million. Assuming semi-annual compounding, estimate the effective interest rate on the zero-coupon debentures. Calculate the interest expense incurred by the Mayfield Corporation during the first year that the debt was outstanding.

☑ E9.17   **Calculating the Fair Value of Debt.**   The Longo Corporation issued $50 million maturity value in notes, carrying a coupon rate of six percent, with interest paid semi-annually. At the time of the note issue, equivalent risk-rated debt instruments carried yield rates of eight percent. The notes matured in five years.

Calculate the proceeds that Longo Corporation will receive from the sale of the notes. How will the notes be disclosed on Longo's balance sheet immediately following the sale? Calculate the interest expense for Longo Corporation for the first year that the notes are outstanding. Calculate the balance sheet value of the notes at the end of the first year.

E9.18   **Building a Note Amortization Table.**   Valcor Inc. issued $100 million maturity value of three-year notes, which carried a coupon rate of four percent and which paid interest semi-annually. At the time of the note sale, equivalent risk-rated debt instruments carried a yield rate of six percent. Develop a note amortization table for Valcor's four percent, three-year notes.

E9.19   **Accounting for Bonds Sold at a Discount.**   The Biltmore National Bank raised capital through the sale of $100 million face value of eight percent coupon rate, ten-year bonds. The bonds paid interest semi-annually and were sold at a time when equivalent risk-rated bonds carried a yield rate of ten percent.

Calculate the proceeds that The Biltmore National Bank received from the sale of the eight percent bonds. How will the bonds be disclosed on Biltmore's balance sheet immediately following the sale? Calculate the interest expense on the bonds for the first year that the bonds are outstanding. Calculate the book value of the bonds at the end of the first year.

E9.20   **Market Yield Rates and Bond Values.**   Smith & Company issued $80 million maturity value of five-year bonds, which carried a coupon rate of six percent, with interest paid semi-annually. At the time of the debt offering, equivalent risk-rated bonds were yielding eight percent. One year after the five-year bond offering, yield rates had risen to ten percent; but, by the second anniversary of the bond sale, the yield rate on similarly risk-rated debt instruments had dropped to only four percent.

Calculate the proceeds from the sale of the six percent, five-year bonds. Calculate the book value of the bonds after one year and after two years. Calculate the market value of the bonds after one year and after two years. What is the relationship between market yield rates and bond values?

☑ E9.21   **Accounting for Notes issued at a Premium.**   The Longo Corporation issued $50 million maturity value of eight percent coupon rate notes, with interest paid semi-annually. At the time of the note issuance, equivalent risk-rated debt instruments carried a yield rate of six percent. The notes matured in five years.

Calculate the proceeds that the Longo Corporation would receive from the sale of the notes. How will the notes be reported on Longo's balance sheet immediately following the sale? Calculate the interest expense on the notes for the first year. Calculate the book value of the notes at the end of the first year.

E9.22   **Issuing Zero-Coupon Bonds.**   On July 28, 2000, **ALZA Corporation** completed a private placement of Zero-coupon Convertible Subordinated Debentures. The zero-coupon debentures were issued at a price of $551.26 per $1,000 principal amount at maturity. Although the zero-coupon bonds paid no periodic interest payments, interest was assumed to be compounded semi-annually. The bonds mature in 2020.

Estimate the yield rate on the zero-coupon bonds at the time of issuance. Why would ALZA Corporation issue non-interest-bearing bonds? Why would ALZA attach a conversion feature to the zero-coupon bonds? Calculate ALZA's implicit interest expense for the first year.

E9.23   **Retiring Debt Early.**   Smith & Company issued $80 million maturity value of five-year bonds, which carried a coupon rate of six percent and paid interest semi-annually. At the time of the offering, the yield rate for equivalent risk rated securities was eight percent. Two years later, market yield rates had risen to ten percent, and since the company no longer needed the debt financing, executives at Smith & Company decided to retire the debt.

Calculate the gain or loss that Smith & Company will incur as a consequence of retiring the debt early. Is the early retirement of the debt a good decision? What factors should be considered in making this decision?

E9.24 **Operating Leases.** The **Johnson and Johnson Company** disclosed in its 2005 annual report that it leases various vehicles and machinery using operating lease agreements. According to its footnotes the minimum payments required under the non-cancelable operating lease agreements were as follows:

Year Ending ($ millions)	Operating Leases
2006	$162
2007	142
2008	119
2009	103
2010	88
After 2010	151
Total	$765

If the interest rate implicit in each of the lease agreements is eight percent, what is the present value of the company's non-cancelable lease payments? Johnson and Johnson's long-term debt-to-equity ratio at year-end 2005 was 8.1 percent ($2,565/$31,813). If the company's operating leases were accounted for as capital leases instead of operating leases, how would the firm's long-term debt-to-equity ratio change?

E9.25 **Capitalizing Operating Leases.** The following information is taken from the 2005 annual report of the **Walgreen Company**:

(in millions)	2005
Total assets.	$14,609
Total liabilities	5,719
Shareholders' equity	8,890
Minimum future non-cancelable lease payments under operating leases	
2006	$ 1,390
2007	1,436
2008	1,396
2009	1,370
2010	1,347
Thereafter	17,173
Total	$24,112

Assume that the cost of debt implicit in the company's operating leases is eight percent. Calculate the present value of Walgreen's operating leases at year-end 2005. Calculate the company's total liabilities-to-total assets ratio and its total debt-to-shareholders' equity ratio for 2005 (a) with and (b) without considering the company's operating leases. Does the presence of operating leases impact a firm's financial risk?

E9.26 **Capital Lease versus Operating Lease.** **Maximum Electronics Inc.** is a retail chain of discount electronic stores throughout the southwest United States. Maximum leases a fleet of 200 trucks to deliver purchases to its customers. The annual lease payment per truck totals $5,000 and the interest rate implicit in the lease is eight percent. On January 1, 2006, Maximum renewed its truck fleet lease under the same terms for a five-year period. Assume that the truck lease should be accounted for as a capital lease. What value should be capitalized to Maximum's balance sheet for the leased assets and lease liability on January 1, 2006.

Assume that the trucks will be depreciated on a straight-line basis with no salvage value. Compare the financial statement effects over the five-year lease period assuming the lease is accounted for as (a) an operating lease and as (b) a capital lease. Which approach provides the greatest tax benefits? Why?

PROBLEMS

P9.27   **Debt Valuation: Interest-Bearing Debentures.**   At the beginning of the year, Global Minds Inc. issued $100 million (maturity value) of 20 year debentures. The debentures carried a four percent per period coupon rate, were subject to semi-annual compounding and had been issued at a time when the yield rate was six percent per period.

Required
1.   Calculate the proceeds received by Global Minds when the bonds were sold.
2.   Explain why the Global Minds bonds were sold at a discount.
3.   Calculate the market value of the bonds if, after ten years, the market yield rate is ten percent per period.
4.   Calculate the cost of retiring the Global Minds bonds after 15 years assuming that the market yield rate is ten percent per period at the time of retirement. Does the retirement result in a gain or loss?

P9.28   **Debt Valuation: Zero-Coupon Debentures.**   At the beginning of the year, KMF Inc. issued $100 million (maturity value) of 15 year, zero-coupon debentures, at a time when the yield rate was six percent per period. The KMF, Inc. bonds would be subject to semi-annual compounding.

Required
1.   Calculate the proceeds to be received by KMF Inc. when the bonds are sold.
2.   Calculate the cost to repurchase and retire the bonds after five years assuming that the market yield rate at that time is eight percent per period. Is the early retirement of debt a good decision in this set of circumstances? What factors did you consider in reaching your decision?

P9.29   **Debt Retirement.**   MTF Inc. is a manufacturer of electronic components for facsimile equipment. The company financed the expansion of its production facilities by issuing $100 million of ten-year bonds carrying a coupon rate of eight percent with interest payable annually on December 31. The bonds had been issued on January 1. At the time of the issuance, the market rate of interest on similar risk-rated instruments was six percent.

Two years later, the market rate of interest on comparable debt instruments had climbed to twelve percent. The CEO of MTF realized that this might be an opportune time to repurchase the bonds, particularly because an unexpected surplus of cash made the outstanding debt no longer necessary.

Required
1.   Calculate the proceeds received by the company when the debt was initially sold.
2.   Calculate the interest expense for each of the two years that the bonds were outstanding.
3.   Calculate the amount of cash needed to retire the debt after two years assuming a market yield rate of twelve percent.

⊘ P9.30   **Note Valuation.**   Lowe's Company Inc. reported that in on April 1, 2001, the company issued $500 million principal value of unsecured 5.375 percent Senior Notes due April 1, 2006. Presented below are excerpts from Lowe's 2002 annual report:

Lowe's Company Inc.
Consolidated Statements of Income

In Thousands For Period Ended	2/3/02	1/28/01	1/29/00
Net Sales	$22,111,108	$18,778,559	$15,905,595
Cost of Sales	15,743,267	13,487,791	11,525,013
Gross Margin	6,367,841	5,290,768	4,380,582
Expenses			
Selling, General and Administrative.	3,913,355	3,348,060	2,772,428
Store Opening Costs	139,870	131,825	98,448
Depreciation.	516,828	408,618	337,359
Interest.	153,537	120,825	84,852
Nonrecurring Merger Costs	—	—	24,378
Total Expenses	4,723,590	4,009,328	3,317,465
Pretax Earnings	1,644,251	1,281,440	1,063,117
Income Tax Provision	600,989	471,569	390,322
Net Income.	$ 1,023,262	$ 809,871	$ 672,795

Long-term debt (in 000s)	February 3, 2002	January 28, 2001
5.375% Senior Notes Due April 1, 2006	$ 500,000	$ 0
Total long-term debt.	$3,734,011	$2,697,669

Required
1. Were the notes sold at a discount, a premium, or at par? Why?
2. How much interest expense did the company record on October 1, 2001 with regard to the Notes, assuming semi-annual compounding?
3. How much would the Notes have been sold for if the market rate of interest at the time of sale had been six percent per year?
4. Moody's reports that the notes were rated as **Ba1.**
   a. If the rating had been Ba3 instead, would the yield rate on the bonds have been lower, higher, or the same?
   b. If the notes had been secured, would the yield rate have been lower, higher, or the same?
5. The company reported that the fair market value of the company's 5.375 percent Senior Notes was $511 million on February 3, 2002. If the company repurchased all of the Notes on February 3, 2002, how much gain (loss) would it record?

P9.31 **Note Valuation.** The **Lincoln Company** is a multinational manufacturer of electrical equipment and components. Selected financial information is provided below:

	Consolidated Statements of Income		
For Period Ended (In millions)	**2005**	**2004**	**2003**
Net sales.	$9,682.00	$9,597.60	$7,819.00
Operating income.	523.20	1,089.40	1,079.70
Interest expense	(253.00)	(255.30)	(183.50)
Other income (expense), net	(6.80)	35.80	3.10
Minority interests	(20.10)	(39.30)	(29.10)

continued

Consolidated Statements of Income			
For Period Ended (In millions)	**2005**	**2004**	**2003**
Earnings before income taxes	243.30	830.60	870.20
(Benefit) provision for income taxes	(2.90)	284.40	307.10
Earnings from continuing operations	246.20	546.20	563.10
Discontinued operations (net of tax)	—	123.20	28.00
Net earnings	$ 246.20	$ 669.40	$ 591.10

Abbreviated Consolidated Balance Sheet		
(in millions)	**2005**	**2004**
Total assets.	$11,063.70	$11,052.60
Long-term debt	2,900.70	1,540.40
Shareholders' equity	3,916.60	3,481.20
Total liabilities and stockholders' equity.	$11,063.70	$11,052.60

Note 8–Long-Term Debt and Credit Facilities		
(in millions)	**2005**	**2004**
5.75% Notes Due 2007.	$ 600.00	$ 0
Total long-term debt.	$2,900.70	$1,540.40

Required

1. The company reported that on February 1, 2005, the company issued $600 million of 5.75 percent secured notes due February 1, 2007.

   a. Were the notes sold at a discount, a premium, or at par value?

   b. How much interest expense did the company record on August 1, 2005, assuming semi-annual compounding?

   c. How much would the company have raised through the sale of the notes if the market rate of interest had been six percent per year?

2. Moody's reports that the notes were rated **A3**.

   a. If the rating had been A1 instead, would the yield rate have been higher, lower, or the same?

   b. If the notes had been unsecured, would the yield rate have been higher, lower, or the same?

   c. The company reports that the fair market value of the company's long-term debt at December 31, 2005 was $2,996.70. If the company repurchased all of the outstanding long-term debt on December 31, 2005, how much gain (loss) would be recognized?

   d. Assume Moody's only used the long-term debt-to-equity ratio and the interest coverage ratio in making its rating decision. Would the rating on the 5.75 percent notes have been higher, the same, or lower if the notes had been issued in 2004 instead of 2005?

P9.32 **Note Valuation.** **Seaquest Wholesale Corporation** began operations in 1983 in Seattle, Washington. Selected information from Seaquest's 2005 Annual Report is provided below:

Long-term Debt (dollars thousands)	09/02/2005	09/02/2004
7.125% Senior Notes due January 2009	$300,000	$300,000
Zero-coupon convertible subordinated notes due February 2017	489,659	473,005

On January 15, 1999, the Company issued $300 million of 7.125 percent Senior Notes due January 15, 2009. Interest on the notes was payable semi-annually on January 15 and July 15. At September 2, 2005, the fair value of the 7.125 percent Senior Notes, based on market quotes, was approximately $317,460,000.

On February 19, 2001, the Company completed the sale of $900 million principal amount at maturity Zero-coupon Subordinated Notes (the "Notes") due February 19, 2017. The Notes resulted in gross proceeds to the Company of $449,640,000. The Notes are convertible into a maximum of 20,438,180 shares of Seaquest common shares at a conversion price of $22.00 per share. None of the Notes were converted during 2005. The fair value of the Zero-coupon Subordinated Notes at September 2, 2005, based on market quotes, was approximately $755,615,000.

Required

1. Consider the 7.125 percent Senior Notes.
   a. How much cash did the company receive when the Senior Notes were issued on January 15, 1999?
   b. How much interest expense was recorded at the time of the first interest payment, assuming semi-annual compounding?
   c. If the company were to repurchase the remaining Notes on September 2, 2005, would the company report a gain or loss on the transaction. What is the amount of the gain or loss?
   d. Compared to the market rate on equivalent-risk bonds on January 15, 1999, was the yield rate on the Senior Notes on September 2, 2001 higher, lower, or the same?
2. Consider the Zero-coupon Subordinated Notes.
   a. What is the amount of the liability that Seaquest would have reported on its balance sheet on February 19, 2001?
   b. If the company were to repurchase the remaining Notes on September 2, 2005, would the company report a gain or loss on the transaction. What is the amount of the gain or loss?
   c. Compared to the market rate of interest on equivalent-risk bonds on February 19, 2001, was the yield rate on the zero-coupon bonds on September 2, 2001 higher, lower, or the same?
   d. Under what condition would noteholders convert their notes to common shares?
   e. How much interest expense was reported for the Notes for the year ending September 2, 2005?
   f. What was the approximate market rate of interest on the Notes on February 19, 2001?

P9.33 **Valuing a Lease.** On January 1, the president of KMF Inc. signed an eight year lease agreement for retail space at a lease rate of $50,000 per year. During the negotiations, the president had learned that the lessor had built an implicit borrowing cost of ten percent per year into the lease contract. The agreement called for the lease payments to be made annually at the beginning of each year. Hence, the first payment of $50,000 was made immediately after the lease agreement was signed on January 1.

Required

1. Assume that the lease agreement is to be accounted for as a capital lease by KMF. How will the lease commitment be reflected on the company's financial statements? At what value?
2. At the beginning of the second year of the lease, what financial effects will be recorded in the financial statements of KMF? At the beginning of the third year?

⊘ P9.34 **Lease Accounting.** On January 1, 2005, Durant Inc. entered into a non-cancelable ten-year lease for cooking equipment with a fair value of $100 million and requiring annual year-end lease payments. The company's year-end is December 31.

Required

1. If the implicit interest rate on the lease is eight percent, what is the annual lease payment?
2. Assuming that the lease is accounted for as a capital lease, what financial effects will be recorded in the financial statements with regard to the lease on January 1, 2005?
3. Assuming that the lease is accounted for as a capital lease, what financial effects will be recorded with regard to the lease on December 31, 2005 (at the end of the first year)?
4. What are the total expenses associated with the lease in 2006 (the second year) if it is accounted for as an operating lease? As a capital lease?

P9.35 **Lease Accounting.** On January 1, 2005, Longo Inc. entered into a non-cancelable 15-year lease for cooking equipment with a fair value of $150 million and requiring annual year-end lease payments. The company's year-end is December 31.

Required
1. If the implicit interest rate on the lease is twelve percent, what is the annual lease payment?
2. Assuming that the lease is accounted for as a capital lease, what financial effects will be recorded in the financial statements with regard to the lease on January 1, 2005?
3. Assuming that the lease is accounted for as a capital lease, what financial effects will be recorded with regard to the lease on December 31, 2005 (at the end of the first year)?
4. What are the total expenses associated with the lease in 2006 (the second year) if it is accounted for as an operating lease? As a capital lease?

P9.36 **Lease Accounting.** On January 1, 2005, **Famous Restaurants Inc.** entered into a non-cancelable twelve year lease for cooking equipment with a fair value of $300 million and requiring annual year-end lease payments. The company's year-end is December 31.

Required
1. If the implicit interest rate on the lease is eight percent, what is the annual lease payment?
2. Assuming that the lease is accounted for as a capital lease, what financial effects will be recorded in the financial statements with regard to the lease on January 1, 2005?
3. Assuming that the lease is accounted for as a capital lease, what financial effects will be recorded with regard to the lease on December 31, 2005 (at the end of the first year)?
4. What are the total expenses associated with the lease in 2006 (the second year) if it is accounted for as an operating lease? As a capital lease?

P9.37 **Capitalizing Operating Leases.** **Global Telecommunications Inc.** leases a substantial quantity of its noncurrent assets under both capital and operating leases with an average life of ten years. As of year-end 2005, for example, the company had leased more than 30 percent of its noncurrent assets and the obligations associated with those leases represented nearly 50 percent of the company's total long-term debt.

Presented below are condensed financial statements for the company. The company's footnotes also revealed that at year-end 2005, the minimum lease commitments under non-cancelable leases were:

Year	Capital Leases	Operating Leases	Total
2005	$ 57,876	$ 16,610	$ 74,486
2006	50,753	15,443	66,196
2007	42,721	14,441	57,162
2008	35,620	12,669	48,289
2009	24,410	10,580	34,990
2010 and thereafter	17,213	49,220	66,433
Minimum lease payments	228,593	$118,963	$347,556
Less: Amount representing interest	(47,388)		
Present value of future lease payments	$181,205		

Interest rates on capital lease obligations on a weighted-average basis approximate 12 percent.

Global Telecommunications, Inc. Condensed Balance Sheet	
	2005
Assets	
Current assets	$228,428
Noncurrent assets	631,970
Total assets.	$860,398
Liabilities and Shareholders' equity	
Current liabilities.	$185,540
Deferred income taxes.	34,058
Long-term debt	400,018
Shareholders' equity	240,782
Total liabilities and shareholders' equity.	$860,398

Required
1. Calculate the present value of the company's operating leases.
2. Restate the company's balance sheet assuming that all operating leases are capitalized.
3. Calculate the:
    a. Long-term debt-to-shareholders' equity ratio.
    b. Total debt-to-total assets ratio, both with and without the capitalization of the operating leases. How would the company's debt rating be affected if all leases (both capital and operating) were capitalized to the balance sheet?

P9.38 **(Appendix 9A) Recording Debt Financing Transactions using the Debit/Credit Paradigm.** During 2006, the Mayfield Corporation issued $100 million of zero-coupon debentures, due in 2016. The proceeds of the bond sale totaled approximately $45.64 million, assuming the bonds were sold to yield 4 percent per period.

Required

Using journal entries, record (1) the proceeds from the sale of the Mayfield bonds in 2006 and (2) the interest expense to be recognized on the bonds at the end of the first six month period.

P9.39 **(Appendix 9A) Recording Lease Financing Transactions using the Debit/Credit Paradigm.** Maximum Electronics Inc. is a retail chain of discount electronic stores throughout the southwest United States. Maximum leases a fleet of 200 trucks to deliver purchases to its customers. The annual lease payment per truck totals $5,000 and the interest rate implicit in the lease is eight percent. On January 1, 2006, Maximum renewed its truck fleet lease under the same terms for a five-year period.

Required
1. Assume that the fleet lease should be accounted for as a capital lease. Using journal entries, record the leased assets and lease liability on January 1, 2006.
2. Assume that the trucks will be depreciated on a straight-line basis with no salvage value. Using journal entries, record the depreciation expense on the leased assets and the interest expense and debt payment on the lease liability on December 31, 2006.

CORPORATE ANALYSIS

CA9.40 **The Procter and Gamble Company.** The 2005 annual report of the **Procter and Gamble Company** (P & G) is available at www.pg.com/annualreports/2005/pdf/pg2005annualreport.pdf. After reviewing P & G's annual report, respond to the following questions.

    a. Calculate P & G's total debt-to-total assets ratio for 2004 and 2005. Is the company principally debt or equity financed? What is the trend in P & G's use of debt financing? What was P & G's short-term and long-term weighted-average cost of debt? What is the trend in P & G's cost of borrowing?

    b. Calculate P & G's return on assets for 2004 and 2005. Is the company's financing strategy sound? What is P & G's short-term and long-term credit rating? Does P & G have an "investment grade" rating or a "junk grade" rating.

    c. P & G reports in its Management Discussion & Analysis that "total debt increased by $3.49 billion in 2005 to $24.33 billion." What is the composition of P & G's "total debt?" Why would P & G issue notes denominated in British pounds, EU euros, Japanese yen, Swiss francs, as well as in U.S. dollars? Is P & G subject to any debt covenants under its various borrowings? If so, what are the covenants and is the company satisfying the covenants?

    d. Does P & G use operating leases to finance any of its operating assets? If so, what are the future minimum operating lease payments for 2006, 2007, 2008, 2009, 2010, and thereafter? Calculate the present value of P & G's operating leases assuming an implicit cost of borrowing of five percent? Is P & G's use of operating leases material?

CA9.41 **Internet-based Analysis.** Consider a publicly-held company whose products you are familiar with. Some examples might include:

Company	Product	Corporate Website
• **Johnson & Johnson Company**	• Band-Aids	• www.jnj.com
• **Microsoft Corporation**	• Windows XP software	• www.microsoft.com
• **Nokia Corporation**	• Cellular phones	• www.nokia.com
• **Intel Corporation**	• Pentium processors	• www.intel.com
• **Kimberly-Clark Corporation**	• Kleenex	• www.kimberly-clark.com

Access the company's public website and search for its most recent annual report. (Some companies provide access to their financial data through an "investor relations" link, while others provide a direct link to their "annual reports.") After locating your company's most recent annual report, open the file and review its contents. After reviewing the annual report for your selected company, prepare answers to the following questions:

1. Calculate the total debt-to-total assets ratio for the past two years. Is the company principally debt-financed or equity-financed? Do you agree with this strategic decision?

2. Review the company's long-term debt footnote. What kinds of debt –bonds, notes, zero-coupon bonds—does the company have outstanding? Are the debt instruments denominated in U.S. dollars? If not, why not?

3. What is the company's weighted-average cost of debt? What is the company's return on assets? Can the company use leverage effectively?

4. Does the company use leases to finance any of its assets? If so, what kind of leases—operating or capital—does the company use?

5. Calculate the company's interest coverage ratio for the past two years. What is the trend in this ratio? Why? What is your assessment of the company's liquidity and solvency? What did you base your opinion on?

Chapter Ten

Commitments and Contingent Liabilities, Deferred Tax Liabilities, and Retirement Obligations

TAKEAWAYS

When you complete this chapter you should be able to:

1. Explain the difference between a commitment and a contingent liability.
2. Describe deferred income tax liabilities and why this account increases and decreases.
3. Explain how employee retirement obligations are valued and disclosed.
4. Describe how financial instruments and derivatives are valued and reported in corporate financial statements.

Where have we been?	Where are we?	Where are we going?
Chapter 9 investigated the strategic financing decisions of companies by examining several important forms of debt financing—bonds, notes, and leases. We discovered that debt instruments were reported on the balance sheet using the present value approach. The chapter also examined how to account for early debt retirements, as well as how to calculate the weighted-average cost of debt for a business. Finally, the differences between operating and financing leases were considered, along with how those differences were manifested in their financial statement disclosure.	In this chapter, we continue our investigation of corporate debt. Specifically, we investigate the difference between commitments and contingent liabilities and explore why some investment professionals view these items as a form of off-balance-sheet debt. The topic of deferred income tax liabilities and why and how this account increases and decreases is also considered. Finally, the chapter examines how employee retirement obligations are valued and reported in corporate financial statements, and in an appendix to the chapter, how financial instruments and derivatives are valued and disclosed.	In Chapter 11, we complete our investigation of corporate financing decisions by examining how companies raise capital through equity financing. Share issuances and retirements and free share distributions (stock dividends and stock splits) are investigated. Finally, we examine the various components of Other Comprehensive Income and the controversial topic of employee stock options.

Wal-Mart Stores Inc., with its motto of "Low prices, always," has used its low price strategy to fuel tremendous growth. Sam Walton, the company founder, opened the first Wal-Mart store in 1962 and incorporated the business as *Wal-Mart Stores Inc.* in 1969, by which time it had expanded to 38 stores. As of January 2007, Wal-Mart was the world's largest retailer with 1,074 Wal-Mart Discount Stores, 2,257 Wal-Mart Supercenters, 112 Neighborhood Markets, 579 Sam's Clubs in the U.S., and over 2,700 stores in fourteen countries outside the U.S.

The company refers to its employees as "associates." In addition, Wal-Mart stores in the U.S. and Canada have designated "greeters," whose role is to welcome shoppers at the store entrance and play a role in inventory loss prevention. It has been reported that 80 percent of U.S. residents shop at Wal-Mart at least once a year. Each week, 100 million customers visit a Wal-Mart store, or roughly one in every three Americans. While Wal-Mart may be cheered by consumers for its low prices, others are more critical of the company. Wal-Mart has been criticized and sued by community groups, trade unions, and environmental groups for, among other things, its extensive foreign product sourcing, treatment of employees and product suppliers, environmental policies, use of public subsidies, and store impacts on local communities and businesses. One such lawsuit alleges that female employees were discriminated against in pay and promotions. The following description of the lawsuit appeared in the company's 2006 annual report:

> "The Company is a defendant in Dukes v. Wal-Mart Stores Inc., a class-action lawsuit commenced in June 2001 and pending in the United States District Court for the Northern District of California. The case was brought on behalf of all past and present female employees in all of the Company's retail stores and warehouse clubs in the United States. The complaint alleges that the Company engaged in a pattern and practice of discriminating against women in promotions, pay, training and job assignments. The complaint seeks, among other things, injunctive relief, front pay, back pay, punitive damages, and attorneys' fees. Following a hearing on class certification on September 24, 2003, on June 21, 2004, the District Court issued an order granting in part and denying in part the plaintiffs' motion for class certification. . . . . . . The class as certified currently includes approximately 1.6 million present and former female associates.
>
> If the Company is not successful in its appeal of class certification, or an appellate court issues a ruling that allows for the certification of a class or classes with a different size or scope, and if there is a subsequent adverse verdict on the merits from which there is no successful appeal, or in the event of a negotiated settlement of the litigation, the resulting liability could be material to the Company. The plaintiffs also seek punitive damages which, if awarded, could result in the payment of additional amounts material to the Company. However, because of the uncertainty of the outcome of the appeal from the District Court's certification decision, because of the uncertainty of the balance of the proceedings contemplated by the District Court, and because the Company's liability, if any, arising from the litigation, including the size of any damages award if plaintiffs are successful in the litigation or any negotiated settlement, could vary widely, the Company cannot reasonably estimate the possible loss or range of loss which may arise from the litigation."

Presented below is the liabilities section of Wal-Mart's 2006 balance sheet. Where does Wal-Mart disclose the potentially massive legal liability associated with the class-action lawsuit?

Liabilities and shareholders' equity (amounts in millions)	
Commercial paper	$ 3,754
Accounts payable	25,373
Accrued liabilities	13,465
Accrued income taxes	1,340
Long-term debt due within one year	4,595
Obligations under capital leases due within one year	299
Total current liabilities	48,826
Long-term debt	26,429
Long-term obligations under capital leases	3,742
Deferred income taxes and other	4,552
Minority interest	1,467
Commitments and contingencies	—

continued

If you guessed that the lawsuit is disclosed under "commitments and contingencies" with a zero balance, you are correct. Under U.S. GAAP, a company is required to record its potential litigation exposure only if the company concludes that it is highly probable that it will lose the ruling and if the amount of any potential award can be reasonably estimated. As noted above, Wal-Mart is unable to reasonably estimate the possible loss from this lawsuit, and consequently, the company is not required to record a liability for its potential loss.

In this chapter, we examine the important category of potential liabilities called commitments and contingencies, along with two other corporate obligations, deferred income tax liabilities and employee retirement obligations. In Appendix 10B we examine another potential obligation—financial instruments and derivatives.

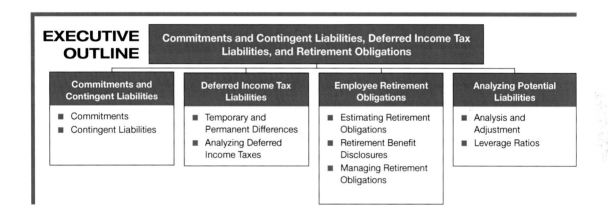

EXECUTIVE OUTLINE	**Commitments and Contingent Liabilities, Deferred Income Tax Liabilities, and Retirement Obligations**			
	Commitments and Contingent Liabilities	**Deferred Income Tax Liabilities**	**Employee Retirement Obligations**	**Analyzing Potential Liabilities**
	■ Commitments ■ Contingent Liabilities	■ Temporary and Permanent Differences ■ Analyzing Deferred Income Taxes	■ Estimating Retirement Obligations ■ Retirement Benefit Disclosures ■ Managing Retirement Obligations	■ Analysis and Adjustment ■ Leverage Ratios

COMMITMENTS AND CONTINGENT LIABILITIES

In the day-to-day running of most businesses, it is common for the managers of a company to execute **executory contracts** on behalf of the business. An executory contract is an agreement that calls for some form of future performance by both parties to the agreement, often involving an exchange of assets. For example, the CFO of a company may sign a **purchase commitment** with one of a company's key suppliers, committing the firm to buy certain quantities of raw materials in the future. Since financial statements portray "what is" or "what has been" and not "what will be," executory contracts and the related future obligation to perform associated with them are not reported in the financial statements, although they are frequently described in the footnotes to the financial statements.

In accounting language, executory contracts are referred to as **commitments**—that is, an unexecuted contract in which the amount of the pending obligation is *relatively certain*. Examples include bank lines-of-credit, operating leases, purchase commitments, and take-or-pay contracts. In the case of a bank **line-of-credit**, when a borrower draws down on a credit line, the executory component of the contract is executed and the amount of the borrowing must be reported on the borrower's balance sheet, along with the amount of borrowed cash. Similarly, in the case of a purchase agreement, as soon as the promised product is delivered, a contractual obligation to pay the supplier is created and must be recorded on the face of the purchaser's balance

> A **line-of-credit** is a guaranteed loan, which may be used by a borrower in whole or in part. The borrower pays a fee to gain access to the line-of-credit and pays interest on any borrowed amounts.

sheet, along with the newly acquired inventory. Until those events occur, however, the obligation to buy the goods at some point in the future or the obligation to repay un-borrowed funds under a line-of-credit need only be disclosed in the footnotes to the financial statements.

In Practice 10.1 *Commitments and Contingencies: A Glimpse of a Sample of Fortune 1000 Companies* The following table identifies the types of commitments and loss contingencies disclosed by a sample of 600 *Fortune 1000* companies. As can be seen, debt covenant restrictions represent the most frequently disclosed commitment, while litigation is the most frequently disclosed source of loss contingency:

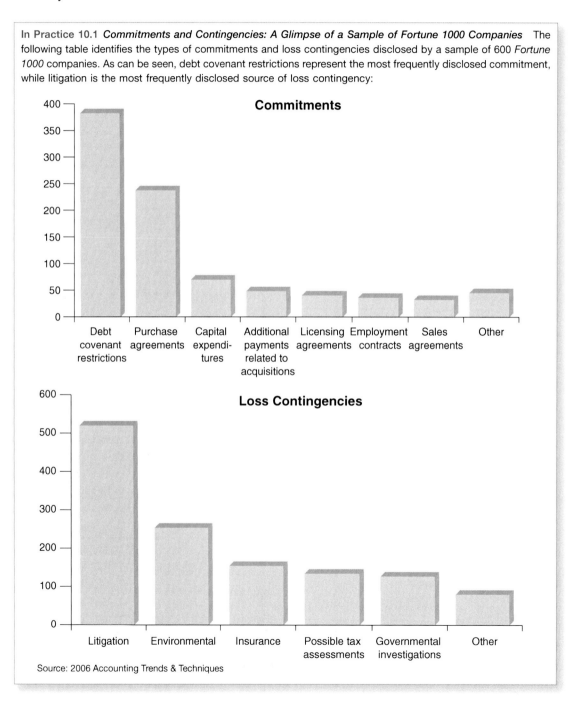

Source: 2006 Accounting Trends & Techniques

Closely related to commitments are contingent liabilities—that is, an obligation contingent upon the occurrence of some future event in which the amount of the pending obligation is *relatively uncertain*. Examples include the financial settlement of a pending lawsuit, loan guarantees, and the potential reimbursement associated with accounts receivable sold with recourse. In the case of an account receivable sold with recourse, the seller of an account receivable is uncertain what its future reimbursement obligation to a factor will be until the factor tries, and fails, to collect on a specific account receivable. Similarly, in the case of a pending lawsuit, until a court verdict is rendered in which the defendant-firm is judged to have damaged the plaintiff and an award to the plaintiff is assessed, there is uncertainty as to whether an award will occur and how large the award will be.

How and where contingencies are disclosed in corporate financial statements is determined based on the probability of occurrence of the future event and whether an amount can be reliably estimated. Gain contingencies, such as winning a financial settlement in a lawsuit, are almost never accrued on the financial statements and are rarely even disclosed in the footnotes. Instead, gain contingencies are normally only recognized when they are realized. Loss contingencies, on the other hand, are usually disclosed and may also be accrued on the financial statements under certain circumstances. If a loss contingency has a high probability of occurrence and can be reliably estimated, it must be accrued as a liability on the balance sheet. If, however, a loss contingency has a high probability of occurrence but the amount cannot be estimated, or the probability of occurrence is only reasonable, the contingency must be disclosed via the footnotes but not accrued on the financial statements. Finally, if the probability of occurrence of a loss is deemed to be only remote, then the contingency can be ignored. It should be noted that existing accounting standards do not provide detailed definitions as to what level of probability is considered high, reasonable, or remote. Therefore, a business' management team has considerable discretion as to which contingencies are accrued, disclosed, or simply ignored. Often legal considerations also figure into the financial statement disclosure decision where management may feel it is safer to disclose a loss contingency in the footnotes even if they truly feel the contingency is remote.

The commonality of commitments and contingent liabilities is that if and when a specific future event occurs, the firm will face an economic obligation, in most cases involving the payment of cash. Commitments and contingent liabilities are most commonly disclosed in the footnotes to the financial statements, especially if they are material in amount. They constitute an important source of information about a firm's future credit risk and cash flow obligations, and they should be carefully considered by investors and shareholders as they evaluate the future financial well-being of a company (as they conduct their due diligence).

BUSINESS PERSPECTIVE: MICROSOFT CORPORATION

In 1998, the European Union's Commission on Competition began an investigation of Microsoft Corporation alleging that the firm failed to disclose information which would enable competitors to fully connect with Microsoft products, the firm engaged in discriminatory product pricing, and the firm improperly bundled certain products to forestall competition. According to Microsoft's footnotes to its 2003 annual report, the Commission could impose "fines in an amount as large as ten percent of worldwide annual revenue" if the company was found guilty of the allegations. Microsoft's 2003 financial statement disclosures illustrate the contingent nature of this potential loss, which could have reached as much as $3.2 billion based on 2003 sales. At the time of Microsoft's 2003 annual report preparation, the EU Commission had not reached a decision on the case. Microsoft's management must have felt that any potential award was either not highly probable or could not be reliably estimated; hence, the potential liability for the fines was carried off-balance-sheet in Microsoft's footnotes. In early 2004, the EU Competition Commission found against Microsoft and fined the company 497.2 million euros ($611 million). Thereafter, Microsoft carried a provision for future litigation settlement on its balance sheet as a liability pending its appeal of the EU commission decision and related fine.

DEFERRED INCOME TAX LIABILITIES

One frequently hears that firms "keep more than one set of books." This statement is often erroneously interpreted to indicate that a firm is doing something unethical, illegal, or at best, "shady." Quite the contrary, most firms are forced to maintain two sets of accounting records since the rules governing financial accounting, as determined by GAAP, differ in many respects from the rules governing the calculation of taxable income, as determined in the United States by the Internal Revenue Code. It should not be surprising that there are significant differences between the measurement of net income under GAAP and the measurement of taxable income under Internal Revenue Code (IRC) tax regulations. The motivation for developing effective accounting standards differs from that associated with legislating tax policies. The goal of the FASB and the IASB, for example, is to develop accounting practices that enable firms to measure and report their financial performance to investors and lenders in a "fair" manner. Tax regulations, on the other hand, are enacted by elected and appointed governmental officials to raise revenues and to achieve various public policy objectives, such as encouraging investment in R&D or in new capital assets. In most cases, the difference in pretax net income created by these differing accounting practices and income tax regulations is only temporary, and over time, the financial effect of any differences is eliminated. In essence, over the life of a business, the amount of income taxes actually paid to the taxation authority should (and in most cases, do) equal the aggregate income tax expense reported for financial statement purposes.

U.S. corporate income tax rates vary as a function of the level of taxable income. For 2006, those rates were as follows:

Taxable Income	Tax Rate %
0 to $50,000	15
$50,001 to $75,000	25
$75,001 to $10 million . .	34
Over $10 million	35

The question that then arises is "What amount should be reported as the income tax expense on a firm's income statement?" Should it be the amount of tax appearing on the firm's income tax return based on taxable income, or should it be the estimated tax expense based on net earnings calculated under GAAP? In the U.S., GAAP requires that a firm compute its accounting income tax expense based on its GAAP earnings so as to properly match its reported income tax expense with its revenues from the same period. Unfortunately, this creates some confusion since the reported accounting tax expense is unlikely to equal a firm's income tax liability according to the Internal Revenue Service (IRS). The discrepancy between GAAP income and taxable income can arise from two types of policy differences—permanent and temporary differences. Permanent differences are GAAP-IRC differences that never reconcile. Examples of permanent differences include the interest from municipal bonds that is included in GAAP net income but which is excluded from IRC taxable income and the payment of fines on illegal activities which are not deductible for income tax purposes but which are recorded as a business expense on a firm's corporate income statement. Temporary differences, on the other hand, are timing differences between GAAP and taxable income that reverse over time, and hence, eventually fully reconcile. An example of a temporary difference is the income difference created by using straight-line depreciation for accounting purposes and MACRS depreciation for income tax purposes (see Chapter 7).

The deferred income tax account is used to reconcile the timing differences between a firm's tax expense based on its GAAP earnings and the taxes actually paid to the U.S. Department of Treasury based on IRS regulations. Recall from Chapter 2 that one of the disciplines imposed on the balance sheet is that it must always balance, and the deferred income tax account helps satisfy this requirement. The Deferred Income Tax account is the cumulative, after-tax effect of the difference between a firm's income tax expense reported in its income statement and the income taxes actually paid that result from the accounting/tax policy differentials that may arise in the measurement of net income for some businesses. Examples of these accounting/tax policy differentials include the following:

Income Statement Item	Accounting and Tax Policy Differences	
	Accounting Policy	Tax Policy
• Revenue	• Percentage-of-completion	• Completed contract
• Bad debt expense	• Expense estimated using an aging schedule	• Estimates not permitted; tax deduction based on actual receivable write-offs.
• Depreciation expense	• Straight-line method	• Modified accelerated cost recovery system (MACRS).
• Warranty expense	• Expense estimated based on historical experience	• Estimates not permitted; tax deduction based on actual payments for warranty repairs.
• Gain (loss) in value of trading marketable securities	• Unrealized gain (loss) recognized under mark-to-market accounting	• Unrealized gains (losses) not recognized until gain (loss) is realized

To illustrate how temporary differences between a firm's accounting income tax expense and the income taxes actually paid may arise, consider the case of Arcadia Inc. Arcadia purchased a piece of equipment costing $100,000, having an expected useful life of eight years, but with an uncertain residual value at retirement. Under the Modified Accelerated Cost Recovery System (MACRS) used to depreciate all business assets for U.S. income tax purposes, depreciable assets are first classified into a "life category" (such as a three-year asset, a five-year asset, etc). Each asset life category then specifies how much depreciation may be taken on the asset in any year. If we assume that Arcadia's equipment qualified for depreciation as a five-year asset,[1] it would be depreciated at the following established MACRS rates:

MACRS Depreciation	
Five Year Asset	Depreciation Percentage
1st Year.	20.00%
2nd Year	32.00
3rd Year	19.20
4th Year	11.52
5th Year	11.52
Residual value	5.76
	100.00%

If Arcadia depreciates the asset using the straight-line method for financial statement purposes over its expected useful life of eight years, and assuming no salvage value at retirement, the depreciation expense for accounting and income tax purposes would be as follows:

---

[1] Although the expected useful life of Arcadia's asset was eight years, for MACRS purposes it qualified as a five-year asset. This is not unusual as the rapid write off of assets for income tax purposes has been found to be an effective economic stimulus promoting business investment in new capital assets.

| | Depreciation Expense | | | |
	Accounting: Straight-line	Tax: MACRS	Temporary Difference	Cumulative Temporary Difference
1st Year.	$ 12,500	$ 20,000	$ 7,500	$ 7,500
2nd Year	12,500	32,000	19,500	27,000
3rd Year	12,500	19,200	6,700	33,700
4th Year	12,500	11,520	(980)	32,720
5th Year	12,500	11,520	(980)	31,740
6th Year	12,500	5,760	(6,740)	25,000
7th Year	12,500	0	(12,500)	12,500
8th Year	12,500	0	(12,500)	0
	$100,000	$100,000		

Notice that the depreciation expense taken under the MACRS system for income tax purposes exceeds the straight-line depreciation charge for accounting purposes in years 1 through 3; but, beginning in Year 4, the depreciation expense for accounting purposes exceeds the MACRS depreciation deduction. Over the life of the asset, the total depreciation expense reported for accounting and tax purposes is the same ($100,000), but the amount reported in any given year differs—and hence, the notion of a temporary difference. Exhibit 10.1 presents a graphical comparison of Arcadia's depreciation expense for accounting and income tax purposes. The shaded area in Exhibit 10.1 represents the temporary difference between the accounting and tax depreciation expense that will arise over the life of the asset as a consequence of the differing depreciation treatments.

EXHIBIT 10.1 A Comparison of Depreciation Expense: Accounting Versus MACRS

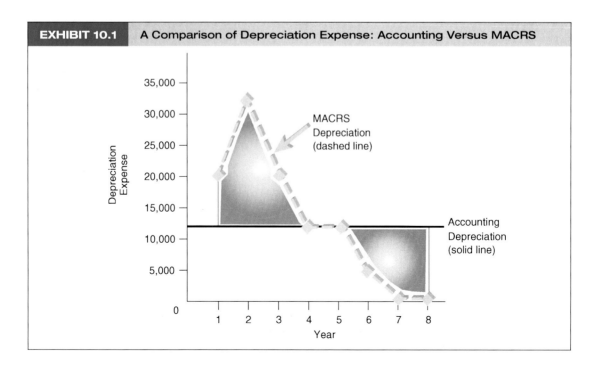

If Arcadia's pretax income before depreciation expense is $60,000 each year, the company's pretax income after depreciation and its subsequent income tax expense, assuming a 25 percent tax rate, for accounting and tax purposes is presented in Exhibit 10.2. At the end of Year 1, Arcadia Inc. will make a cash payment of $10,000 to the IRS for its current year income taxes and will report an income statement deduction for its current tax expense of $11,875. To bring the financial statements into balance, it is necessary to create a deferred income tax liability of $1,875 on the company's balance sheet. Thus, Arcadia's **deferred income tax liability** represents the future taxes *to be paid* on the incremental income ($47,500 − $40,000 = $7,500) that has been reported to the shareholders of the company *but not yet* reported to the taxation authorities.

EXHIBIT 10.2	Calculating the Deferred Income Tax Liability				
	Pretax Income* After Depreciation		Tax Expense (25%)		Deferred Income Tax Liability
	Accounting	Tax	Accounting	IRS	
1st Year.	$ 47,500	$ 40,000	$11,875	$10,000	$1,875
2nd Year	47,500	28,000	11,875	7,000	6,750
3rd Year	47,500	40,800	11,875	10,200	8,425
4th Year	47,500	48,480	11,875	12,120	8,180
5th Year	47,500	48,480	11,875	12,120	7,935
6th Year	47,500	54,240	11,875	13,560	6,250
7th Year	47,500	60,000	11,875	15,000	3,125
8th Year	47,500	60,000	11,875	15,000	0
	$380,000	$380,000	$95,000	$95,000	

*Pretax net income before depreciation is $60,000 annually.

At the end of Year 2, Arcadia will make a cash payment of $7,000 to the IRS for its current income taxes. On the other hand, Arcadia will report an income statement deduction for its current period income tax expense of $11,875. To bring Arcadia's financial statements into balance, it is necessary to increase the deferred income tax liability by $4,875, for a cumulative total of $6,750 (see bolded area in Exhibit 10.2). By the end of Year 2, Arcadia has disclosed $27,000 ($7,500 + $19,500) in incremental net income to its shareholders that has not yet been reported to the IRS.

At the end of Year 3, Arcadia will make a cash payment of $10,200 for its current income taxes, while reporting an income statement deduction for its income tax expense of $11,875. To bring its financial statements into balance, Arcadia will increase its Deferred Income Tax liability by $1,675, for a total cumulative deferred income tax liability at the end of Year 3 of $8,425. By the end of Year 3, Arcadia has reported $33,700 in additional net income to its shareholders that has not yet been reported to the IRS for which it will eventually pay future taxes of $8,425 ($33,700 × 25 percent).

At the end of Year 4, the temporary differences created in Years 1, 2 and 3 begin to reverse. (Observe in Exhibit 10.1, for example, that the MACRS line dips below the straight-line depreciation line.) Arcadia will make a cash payment of $12,120 to the IRS for its current period income taxes, but will show an income statement deduction for its income tax expense of only $11,875. As a consequence, the Deferred Tax Income liability account is reduced by $245, and thus, the cumulative deferred income tax liability at the end of Year 4 declines to $8,180. These financial effects are summarized in Arcadia's spreadsheet in

Exhibit 10.3 (see bolded area). At the end of Year 4, the amount of income reported to Arcadia's shareholders but not yet reported to the IRS declines to $32,720.

EXHIBIT 10.3	Accounting for Deferred Income Taxes					
Arcadia Inc. Spreadsheet		Assets	=	Liabilities	+	Equity
		Cash		Deferred Income Taxes		Retained Earnings
Year 1		−$10,000		$1,875		−$11,875 (tax expense)
Year 2		−7,000		4,875		−11,875
Year 3		−10,200		1,675		−11,875
Year 4		−12,120		−245		−11,875
Year 5		−12,120		−245		−11,875
Year 6		−13,560		−1,685		−11,875
Year 7		−15,000		−3,125		−11,875
Year 8		−15,000		−3,125		−11,875
Total		−$95,000		$ 0		−$95,000

The decline in the Deferred Income Tax liability account continues in Years 5, 6, 7, and 8 as the cash income taxes paid to the IRS grow relative to the income tax expense reported on Arcadia's income statement. This result occurs because the MACRS depreciation is heavily loaded into Years 1, 2, and 3 of the asset's life, and then dramatically declines to zero in Years 7 and 8, causing increasing amounts of Arcadia's net income to be exposed to income taxes in Years 4 through 8. In essence, MACRS provides a depreciation tax shield in the early years of the asset's life, and thereafter, increasingly exposes the company's income to taxation (see shaded areas in Exhibit 10.1).

By the end of Year 8, Arcadia's cumulative income reported to shareholders and to the IRS will total $380,000; and, the cumulative income taxes actually paid and the aggregate accounting tax expense will total $95,000 (see Exhibit 10.3). Thus, over the life of Arcadia's equipment, the differences in taxable income caused by using different depreciation approaches for income tax and accounting purposes are eliminated, reflecting their temporary nature.

When a company experiences an operating loss, IRS regulations allow the company to carry such losses back up to two years to offset any previously taxed income and obtain a refund of any previously paid income taxes. In the event that the operating loss is large enough to more than offset taxable earnings of the previous two years, the excess operating loss may be carried forward up to 20 years to reduce future income taxes. **Tax-loss carryforwards** and **tax-loss carrybacks** are found in the tax provisions of most countries; however, the length of the carryback/carryforward period varies dramatically between countries. The potential future tax savings associated with tax-loss carryforwards are usually disclosed in the footnotes to the financial statements because of their importance in estimating future operating cash flows.

Analyzing Deferred Income Taxes

The Arcadia Inc. illustration shows how one policy differential involving the depreciation of equipment affects not only a company's income statement but its balance sheet as well. These policy differences do not, however, affect the statement of cash flow as the amount of cash paid for income taxes is unchanged (it is based on the actual income taxes paid to the IRS).

Deferred income taxes can result from many accounting and tax policy differences, thus potentially creating both deferred income tax liabilities, as illustrated above, and **deferred income tax assets**. In general, the existence of a large deferred income tax liability is often viewed favorably by investment professionals who recognize that the balance of the deferred income tax liability effectively represents an interest-free loan from the taxation authorities. Financing a business with interest-free debt creates considerable shareholder value.

Deferred income tax liabilities are common on the financial statements of many U.S. corporations. In fact, a recent study by the U.S. General Accounting Office of the income taxes actually paid by U.S. corporations for the period 1989 to 2000, revealed that 63 percent of the companies paid no income taxes at all![2] Thus, for the majority of U.S. firms, most, (and sometimes all) of the income tax expense reported on corporate income statements is effectively deferred, creating a substantial future obligation, as well as considerable interest-free financing from the U.S. Department of Treasury.

Unlike most long-term corporate debt, deferred income tax liabilities are not discounted; instead, they are valued at their future expected settlement value and not their present value. It is not possible to use the present value approach to value these liabilities since the exact date of their payment is unknown (payment of a deferred income tax liability depends upon the future performance of the firm, which of course, is unknown.)

GLOBAL PROSPECTIVE

The amount of deferred income taxes reported on the balance sheet of multinational corporations varies dramatically from country to country. In the U.S., the U.K., and Canada, where significant accounting/tax policy differentials may exist, the deferred income tax obligation of large, mature companies may be substantial. However, in Germany and Japan, the amount of permitted accounting/tax policy differentials is constrained, and as a consequence, the deferred income tax obligation of companies from these countries is frequently immaterial in amount.

Some analysts use the information contained in a company's income tax footnote to gain insight into the degree of discretion that management has used in its financial reporting. One measure of the degree of how aggressive a company's accounting policy choices have been is the **conservatism ratio**, defined as reported income before income taxes divided by taxable income. The theory behind this ratio is that firms will choose to delay paying their income taxes as long as it is legally possible and will, therefore, make accounting policy choices that accelerate expenses and defer revenues in reporting taxable income, the denominator of the ratio. Thus, the more the ratio exceeds one, the more aggressive a firm's financial reporting can be assumed to be.

Pretax net income, the numerator in the conservatism ratio, can be taken directly from a company's income statement. Taxable income, on the other hand, must be computed from information contained in the income tax footnote, as follows:

$$\text{Taxable income} = \text{Current year tax liability/Effective tax rate}$$

Utilizing data from **Kohl's** fiscal year 2002 footnote disclosures, (see Business Perspective) we see that the current year income tax liability is $337,671 thousand ($300,128 + $37,543) and the effective tax rate is 37.8 percent. Taxable income is, consequently, $893,310 thousand ($337,671/37.8 percent). Since pretax net income on the income statement is reported to be $1,034,379 thousand, Kohl's conservatism ratio is 1.16 ($1,034,379/$893,310). Given the proximity of Kohl's conservatism ratio to 1.0, we can conclude that Kohl's reports its income on a relatively conservative basis.

---

[2] *Wall Street Journal,* April 7, 2004.

BUSINESS PERSPECTIVE: DEFERRED INCOME TAX DISCLOSURES

Kohl's Corporation operates approximately 500 specialty department stores throughout the United States. The company's consolidated balance sheet for the years ended 2002 and 2003 are presented below. The balance sheets reveal that Kohl's reports deferred income taxes both as an asset and as a liability (see bolded areas). Combining the deferred income tax asset and the deferred income tax liability reveals that Kohl's had a net deferred income tax liability of $115,258 thousand ($171,951 − $56,693) and $61,936 thousand ($114,228 − $52,292), respectively, in 2003 and 2002. These amounts are clearly material in amount, representing approximately three to five percent of Kohl's outstanding obligations.

Kohl's Corporation
Consolidated Balance Sheet

For Year Ended ($ thousands)	February 1, 2003	February 2, 2002
Current assets		
Cash and cash equivalents	$ 90,085	$ 106,722
Short-term investments	475,991	229,377
Accounts receivable trade, net of allowance for doubtful		
accounts of $20,880 and $17,780.	990,810	835,946
Merchandise inventories	1,626,996	1,198,307
Deferred income taxes.	56,693	52,292
Other.	43,519	41,400
Total current assets	3,284,094	2,464,044
Property and equipment, net	2,739,290	2,199,494
Favorable lease rights, net	180,420	174,860
Goodwill	9,338	9,338
Other assets	102,361	81,850
Total assets.	$6,315,503	$4,929,586
Liabilities and Shareholders' Equity		
Current liabilities		
Accounts payable.	$ 694,748	$ 478,870
Accrued liabilities	315,630	259,598
Income taxes payable	142,150	125,085
Current portion of long-term debt	355,464	16,418
Total current liabilities.	1,507,992	879,791
Long-term debt	1,058,784	1,095,420
Deferred income taxes.	171,951	114,228
Other long-term liabilities	64,859	48,561
Shareholders' equity		
Common stock $0.01 par value, 800,000,000 shares authorized, ...		
337,332,102 and 335,138,497 shares issued, respectively	3,373	3,351
Paid-in capital	1,082,277	1,005,169
Retained earnings	2,426,267	1,782,886
Total shareholders' equity	3,511,917	2,791,406
Total liabilities and shareholders' equity.	$6,315,503	$4,929,586

continued

continued from previous page

BUSINESS PERSPECTIVE: DEFERRED INCOME TAX DISCLOSURES

Kohl's Corporation
Consolidated Statements of Income

Fiscal Year Ended ($ thousands)	February 1, 2003	February 2, 2002	February 3, 2001
Net sales.	$9,120,287	$7,488,645	$6,151,990
Cost of merchandise sold	5,981,219	4,923,520	4,056,140
Gross margin	3,139,068	2,565,125	2,095,850
Operating expenses			
Selling, general and administrative	1,817,968	1,527,476	1,282,360
Depreciation and amortization.	191,439	151,965	121,786
Goodwill amortization	—	5,200	5,200
Pre-opening expenses.	39,278	30,509	35,189
Total operating expenses	2,048,685	1,715,150	1,444,535
Operating income.	1,090,383	849,975	651,315
Other expense (income)			
Interest expense	59,449	57,351	49,332
Interest income	(3,440)	(7,240)	(3,131)
Income before income taxes	1,034,374	799,864	605,114
Provision for income taxes	390,993	304,188	232,966
Net income.	$ 643,381	$ 495,676	$ 372,148

Income Tax Note
Deferred income taxes consist of the following

($ thousands)	February 1, 2003	February 2, 2002
Deferred tax liabilities		
Property and equipment.	$193,273	$133,844
Deferred tax assets		
Merchandise inventories	39,369	38,156
Accrued and other liabilities.	27,796	23,398
Accrued step rent liability.	10,850	10,354
	78,015	71,908
Net deferred tax liability	$115,258	$ 61,936

Components of the provision for income taxes follows

Fiscal Year ($ thousands)	2002	2001	2000
Current federal	$300,128	$258,195	$204,989
Current state.	37,543	28,782	27,550
Deferred	53,322	17,211	427
	$390,993	$304,188	$232,966

continued

continued from previous page

BUSINESS PERSPECTIVE: DEFERRED INCOME TAX DISCLOSURES

The provision for income taxes differs from the amount that would be provided by applying the statutory U.S corporate tax rate due to the following items

Fiscal Year	2002	2001	2000
Provision at statutory rate	35.0%	35.0%	35.0%
State income taxes, net of federal tax	2.9	3.1	3.4
Goodwill amortization.	—	0.2	0.3
Other.	(0.1)	(0.3)	(0.2)
Provision for income taxes.	37.8%	38.0%	38.5%
Amounts paid for income taxes	$ 274,724	$218,831	$ 85,063

The footnotes to Kohl's financial statements reveal the sources of the company's net deferred tax liability. The income tax footnote data reveals that Kohl's accounting/tax policy differential involving depreciation on its property and equipment resulted in a deferred income tax *liability* of $193.273 million as of fiscal year 2002; however, its accounting/tax policy differentials involving inventory and accrued expenses resulted in a deferred income tax *asset* of $78.015 million as of fiscal year 2002. In essence, Kohl's tax treatment of inventory and accrued expenses was less tax-advantaged than was its tax treatment of depreciation.

Kohl's income statement reports a fiscal year 2002 provision for income taxes—income tax expense—of $390,993 thousand on pretax income of $1,034,374 thousand. The increase in the net deferred income tax liability of $53,322 thousand ($115,258 − $61,936) from fiscal year 2001 to fiscal year 2002 represents the amount of Kohl's current period income tax expense that will be paid at a later date. Thus, Kohl's cash payments to federal and state taxation agencies for 2003 amounted to $337,671 thousand ($390,993 - $53,322), although by fiscal year 2002, only $320,606 thousand ($337,671 − [$142,158 − $125,085]) had actually been paid. Kohl's income tax expense of $390,993 thousand on pretax income of $1,034,374 thousand yields an effective income tax rate of 37.8 percent, which differs from the U.S. statutory income tax rate of 35 percent rate largely as a consequence of state income taxes.

EMPLOYEE RETIREMENT OBLIGATIONS

An important employment benefit offered by many businesses to attract and retain qualified employees is the availability of retirement benefits. Foremost among retirement benefits is a pension plan wherein an employee receives a continuous stream of income after retirement from active employment. There are two types of retirement benefit plans—**defined-benefit plans** and **defined-contribution plans**. Under both types of plans, funds contributed to a retirement plan are managed by an independent **trustee** who invests the funds on behalf of the employees. At retirement, the employee gains access to any contributed funds and earnings thereon, to be used as retirement income or to pay for dental, health, or life insurance during the post-employment period. Any funds contributed by an employer to a retirement trust account are considered to be owned by the employees and not the contributing company. Thus, these retirement plan payments are not carried on the balance sheet of the contributing firm as an asset under U.S. GAAP.

In some businesses, the cost of retirement benefits is paid in full by the employer, whereas in others, employees pay the cost in whole or in part. A plan in which an employer pays for all benefits is called **noncontributory**; a plan in which the employee pays some or all of the cost is called **contributory**. Our focus is on those non-contributory or partial-contributory retirement plans in which the employer pays all or part of the cost of the plan, and thus, may retain some obligation to its employees upon their retirement.

Under a defined-contribution plan, an employer commits to pay a specified amount into a retirement plan on behalf of each employee. The employer makes no guarantees regarding the ultimate benefit the employee will receive upon retirement; the only guarantee is the amount contributed into the plan. The employee, therefore, assumes all of the risk under this type of plan in which the final payout will be largely determined by how much the pension funds contributed by the employer earn in their respective investments. The accounting for a defined contribution plan is straight-forward. The employer simply reduces cash and records a pension expense when a contribution is made. Defined contribution plans are often supplemented by other retirement programs such as a 401(k) plan that permits the employee to make tax-deferred contributions to their own retirement plans.

> In the event that an employer overfunds a retirement plan, the firm retains the right to revert the over-funded assets back to the contributing firm. Reverted retirement plan assets, however, are subject to significant income and excise taxes at the time of reversion which effectively discourages firms from reclaiming any surplus contributions.

Under a defined-benefit plan, an employer commits to provide each employee with a specific level of future income or compensation upon retirement based on a pension formula. The formula is usually based on years of service and the salary the employee earns at the time of retirement. Since retirement benefits are linked directly to an employee's current employment, the cost associated with the future retirement benefit is considered to be part of an employee's total compensation, and thus, part of a business' current wage expense. However, since the retirement benefit may not be paid for many years, it is necessary to estimate the future cost of the benefit and then discount the estimated future cost to its present value. It is the present value of the future retirement cost that must be funded by a firm, or if unfunded, reported on the firm's balance sheet as an obligation. Unfortunately, the estimation of a firm's future retirement obligation, and correspondingly, its current expense, is much more complex with defined benefit plans. Consider that, at a minimum, the calculation involves estimates of (1) the length of service for the employee until retirement, (2) the employee's future salary at retirement, (3) the number of years the employee will live beyond retirement to collect pension benefits, (4) the amount of earnings that will be earned by contributions made to the plan, and (5) an appropriate interest rate to discount these amounts to a present value. This is no small task and usually requires the assistance of outside experts such as actuaries. A key difference between the defined contribution plan and the defined benefit plan is the shift of risk from the employee to the employer. Whereas under the defined contribution plan the employer simply agrees to make certain contributions but does not guarantee any future payout, under the defined benefit plan the employer agrees to provide certain defined future benefits. Largely due to this future uncertainty and the increased costs of defined benefit plans, many employers are abandoning defined benefit plans.

For many years, employers were not required to contribute funds to fund the estimated pension obligation of a defined-benefit plan. In fact, some firms intentionally under-funded their plans and subsequently went out of business, leaving the employees without their promised benefits. The government enacted the Employee Retirement Income Securities Act (ERISA) in 1974 to prevent these abuses. ERISA mandates certain minimum levels of funding; however, it is quite likely that a defined-benefit plan can be under-funded at any point in time and still be within compliance with ERISA funding requirements. In addition to the minimum funding requirements mandated by ERISA, additional employee protection is provided by the Pension Benefit Guarantee Corporation (PBGC), which provides federal insurance for defined benefit plans and assumes funding responsibility for pension plans of insolvent employers.

Estimating Retirement Obligations and Their Cost

Under U.S. GAAP, and that of many countries, the cost of any currently earned retirement benefits must be expensed and funded in the period in which those benefits are earned. The amount that should be expensed is the present value of the future benefit. The primary pension plan components that need to be calculated to estimate the pension obligation and the related pension expense include:

- The service cost, which represents the increase in the pension obligation from an additional year of employee service.
- The interest cost, which represents the increase in the pension obligation from an additional year of accrued interest. This cost results from the discounting process in which the present value of the pension obligation increases since it is now one year closer to the date on which an employee is expected to retire and begin receiving benefits.
- The investment return, which is the increase in the pension assets earned by the fund trustee on any contributed funds.

In the past, nearly all pension reporting occurred off-balance-sheet in the footnotes to the financial statements. This has recently changed with the introduction of a new FASB standard effective in 2007 which requires the recording of the actual funding status of a pension plan on the corporate balance sheet. In addition to the actual funding status, required disclosures consist of details regarding the pension obligation and the fair value of the plan assets. The difference between these two figures represents the funding status of the pension plan.[3]

Retirement Benefit Disclosures

To understand the financial statement disclosures relating to retirement benefits, it is necessary to understand several key concepts:

- **Plan assets at fair value**—the market value of the retirement plan assets held by the retirement plan trustee. The balance of this account is increased (decreased) by investment gains (losses), increased by new contributions, and decreased by any benefits paid to retirees.
- **Projected benefit obligation (PBO)**—the present value of the future retirement plan benefits earned by employees assuming some rate of future salary increase. The balance of the PBO is increased by service costs and interest costs and decreased by benefits paid to retirees. The balance may also be changed for plan amendments and actuarial adjustments.
- **Benefit Cost**—the current period matching of the increase in compensation expense attributed to the pension plan with the service provided by employees in the current period. This cost is increased by service and interest costs and decreased by the expected return on plan investments. The expense is also adjusted for the amortization of deferred amounts that were not currently recognized in earnings of prior periods. Note that GAAP allows the use of expected rather than actual investment earnings in the calculation of benefit cost. The rationale behind this choice is to prevent large swings in current income resulting from investment return volatility.

---

[3] A complete discussion of pension accounting is beyond the scope of this textbook. This topic is covered in more detail in intermediate accounting texts. The authoritative source for U.S. pension accounting, prior to its recent overhaul, is contained in SFAS 87, "Employers' Accounting for Pensions". The most recent pension accounting reporting rules are contained in SFAS 158.

An illustration of the typical corporate pension plan disclosures, as reported by the Procter and Gamble Company, is presented in the following Business Perspective.

BUSINESS PERSPECTIVE: RETIREMENT OBLIGATION DISCLOSURES

According to the financial statement footnote disclosures of the **Procter & Gamble Company (P & G)**, the company's retirement obligation at year-end 2005 totaled $8.705 billion, composed of $3.079 billion of retirement benefits-other-than pensions and $5.626 billion of pension benefits. With respect to the funding status of P & G's retirement plans, the footnotes reveal that the company has failed to fund $3.433 billion ($3.054 + $0.379) of its total retirement obligation (pension plus other benefits) as of year-end 2005 (see bolded area).

The Procter and Gamble Company		
($ millions)	2005 Pension Benefits	2005 Other Retiree Benefits
Change in projected benefit obligation		
Benefit obligation at beginning of year.	$4,616	$2,400
Service cost	162	67
Interest cost	241	146
Participant's contributions	18	33
Amendments	45	
Actuarial loss	807	566
Acquisitions	(7)	
Special termination benefits.		2
Currency translation	(35)	9
Benefit payments	(221)	(144)
Projected benefit obligation at end of year	$5,626	$3,079
Change in plan assets		
Fair value of plan assets at beginning of year	$2,263	$2,843
Actual return on plan assets.	201	(44)
Employer contributions	310	11
Participants' contributions	18	33
Currency translation	1	1
Benefit payments	(221)	(144)
Fair value of plan assets at end of year	2,572	2,700
Funded status.	($3,054)	($ 379)

While P & G's retirement accounts were under-funded by $3.433 billion, only $1.338 billion ($1.323 billion of pension benefits and $15 million of retirement benefits-other-than pensions) is recognized as a liability on its 2005 balance sheet (see bolded area). This results because GAAP allows various components of the liability to be smoothed into the calculation over many years rather than requiring immediate recognition. Under the new FASB standard, the entire $3.433 billion of under-funding would appear as a liability on the balance sheet.

continued

continued from previous page

BUSINESS PERSPECTIVE: RETIREMENT OBLIGATION DISCLOSURES

The Procter and Gamble Company		
($ millions)	2005 Pension Benefits	2005 Other Retiree Benefits
Calculation of net amount recognized		
Funded status at end of year	($3,054)	($379)
Unrecognized net actuarial loss	1,641	606
Unrecognized transition amount	9	
Unrecognized prior service cost.	(81)	(242)
Net amount recognized	($1,323)	($ 15)

In addition to disclosure of the funding status of the retirement plans, P&G's footnote disclosures also detail the net benefit expense for 2005 that is a component of P&G's 2005 net income. The primary components of this expense are service and interest costs, partially offset by the expected return on plan assets. Note that P&G follows GAAP rules and uses expected returns rather than actual returns so as to avoid large annual swings in investment earnings. The new FASB pension reporting standard does not change the way this expense is computed or recognized.

The Procter and Gamble Company		
($ millions)	2005 Pension Benefits	2005 Other Retiree Benefits
Service cost	$162	$ 67
Interest cost	241	146
Expected return on plan assets	(185)	(333)
Amortization of deferred amounts	6	(22)
Curtailment and settlement loss.	13	
Recognized net actuarial loss	31	1
Dividends on ESOP preferred stock.		(73)
Net periodic benefit cost (credit)	$268	($214)

GAAP requires that the major assumptions used in the above calculations be fully disclosed in the footnotes. These assumptions include discount rates, expected rates of return on plan assets, and the anticipated annual increases in employee compensation rates.

The Procter and Gamble Company		
($ millions)	2005 Pension Benefits	2005 Other Retiree Benefits
Assumptions used to determine benefit obligations		
Discount rate	4.5%	5.1%
Rate of compensation increase	2.8	
Assumptions used to determine net periodic benefit cost		
Discount rate	5.2	6.1
Expected return on plan assets	7.2	9.5

Managing Retirement Obligations

Companies have resorted to two discretionary actions in an effort to minimize the magnitude of their reported retirement obligations disclosed in corporate financial statements:

- Use a higher-than-justified discount rate to measure the present value of their retirement benefits (a higher discount rate lowers the present value of the benefit).
- Use a higher-than-justified rate of return to estimate the future return on plan assets (a higher assumed rate of return lowers the amount of future funding required to meet a plan's obligations).

The effect of these two actions is to lower the size of any funding insufficiency, and thus, to lower the retirement obligation to be reported on a firm's balance sheet. A higher discount rate, however, will have an undetermined effect on the benefit expense through the interest cost component. A higher discount rate will result in a smaller obligation being multiplied by a higher interest rate; and, the ultimate effect could be a higher or lower interest cost.

Consider, for example, IBM Corporation, one of the largest computer equipment manufacturers in the world. In 2000, IBM raised the assumed rate of return on its pension plant assets from 9.5 to 10.0 percent. This increase lowered its pension expense in 2001 and 2002 by five percent, causing an equal increase in pretax net income. Was the rate of return increase justified? Apparently not in that the U.S. Securities and Exchange Commission warned U.S. companies in 2002 that, based on historical returns on equity and debt securities, it would challenge companies that used rate of return assumptions above nine percent. As a consequence, the rate of return assumptions utilized by U.S. corporations (such as IBM) to forecast the returns on their plan assets fell to 8.4 percent in 2003.[4]

Appendix 10A to this chapter contains an illustration of the computations needed to compute the funding status and the benefit cost of a hypothetical defined benefit pension plan.

BUSINESS PERSPECTIVE: A TIME BOMB WAITING TO EXPLODE

According to a report released in 2007 by The Center For Government Analysis, California faces serious future problems because of its under-funded public retirement systems. California has approximately 130 public pension plans, the biggest being California Public Employees Retirement System (CalPERS) and California State Teachers Retirement System (CalSTRS). As of 2004, nearly 3,500,000 people were covered by these plans. During the fiscal year 2003–04, over $20.1 billion was paid to retired California public employees, while the total state income tax revenue was $37.7 billion. This is nearly double the $10.2 billion paid in 1997–98. The funding status of these plans has also deteriorated substantially. The plans had an actuarial surplus in 1997–08. The combined retirement systems in California had an actuarial deficit of approximately $50.9 billion in 2003–04! These figures are not that surprising when one looks at how lavish these plans are relative to those in the private sector. In many systems, government employees can retire at 50 after working only 14 years and receive pension benefits equivalent to over 40% of their working salary.

ANALYZING OTHER POTENTIAL LIABILITIES

In this chapter, we examined several potential liabilities. As was noted in Chapter 9, it is the responsibility of financial statement users to first determine whether a company's balance sheet adequately portrays the extent of a firm's use of leverage; and, if not, whether any financial statement adjustments should be undertaken.

---

[4] "Pumped-up Pension Plays", *BusinessWeek*, October, 25, 2004.

In Practice 10.2 *Pension Plan Assumptions: A Glimpse of a Sample of Fortune 1000 Companies*   The following table identifies various pension plan assumptions for defined benefit plans as reported by a sample of 600 *Fortune 1000* companies. As can be seen, 428 of the surveyed firms reported having a defined benefit plan. Also note the range in the assumptions used by these firms, with the expected rate of return on plan assets ranging from a low of 4.5 percent or less to a high of 10 percent:

Amount (%)	Discount Rate	Expected Rate of Return	Rate Of Compensation Increase
4.5 or less.	10	2	345
5.	29	1	25
5.5.	182	1	7
6.	185	10	7
6.5.	13	4	
7.	1	22	
7.5.		37	1
8.		98	
8.5.		175	2
9.		52	
9.5.		5	
10.		1	
10.5.			
11 or greater.			
Not disclosed	8	20	41
Companies Disclosing Defined Benefit Plans	428	428	428

Source: 2006 Accounting Trends & Techniques

GAAP provides corporate managers with considerable discretion regarding the balance sheet presentation of contingent liabilities. While these potential liabilities may not appear on the balance sheet, they are usually disclosed in the footnotes to the financial statements. Consequently, the financial statement user must use their judgment as to whether a balance sheet adjustment is needed to provide a better portrayal of a firm's debt exposure to these potential liabilities.

Deferred income taxes, for example, while often appearing as a liability on the balance sheet, require additional consideration because this "liability," unlike traditional accounting liabilities, does not represent an amount owed to anyone. It is simply a reconciling item between the income taxes payable to the IRS based on taxable income and the income tax provision based on GAAP income appearing on a company's income statement. Assuming that a firm is a going-concern and continues to replace its depreciable assets, it is quite likely that a firm's deferred income tax liability will remain outstanding for many future periods. As a consequence, many investment professionals feel that the proper value to assign to any deferred income tax liability is zero, since liabilities are valued at their present value and the present value of an indefinitely-deferred amount is close to zero.

Prior to the recently enacted FASB standard on employee retirement obligations, most pension liabilities appeared off-balance-sheet; and consequently, extensive footnote disclosures were required to aid financial statement users in assessing a firm's debt exposure to its employees. Beginning in 2007, this type of footnote review will no longer be as critical since the new pension reporting standard requires that the full extent of pension plan under or over-funding be disclosed on the face of the balance sheet. Nonetheless, when conducting a financial review of fiscal years prior to 2007, some pension footnote due diligence is required to evaluate a firm's pension liability exposure under the prior pension plan accounting rules. In additional, it is prudent for financial statement users to consider whether the pension assumptions reported in the footnotes, including the discount rate, the estimated rate of wage increase, and the expected return on plan assets, are reasonable.

Chapter 9 discussed three ratios that are helpful when analyzing a firm's use of leverage. Those ratios include the long-term debt-to-total assets ratio, the long-term debt-to-shareholders' equity ratio, and the interest coverage ratio. These ratios can be useful for assessing a firm's solvency, with the caveat that it may be necessary to modify the level of reported debt for any material off-balance-sheet obligations reported in the footnotes.

ETHICS PERSPECTIVE: DIFFERENT SETS OF BOOKS

Many firms maintain multiple sets of financial data for income tax purposes and for financial reporting purposes because of different rules governing GAAP-based financial reporting and income tax reporting governed by the U.S. Internal Revenue Code. No one should question a firm's ethical standards for maintaining these multiple sets of books since the firms are simply complying with external reporting requirements. In addition to the record keeping required for GAAP financial reporting and tax reporting, firms often keep a third set of books for their own internal use. This supplemental financial reporting is often used for internal decision-making and for incentive compensation contracts. Unlike GAAP reporting and income tax reporting, the assumptions used for internal reporting purposes are rarely, if ever, disclosed to individuals outside the firm to protect a firm's competitive market position.

REVIEW PROBLEM

The Glendale Water Company is a retailer of water-softening equipment used principally in residential facilities. An entire system costs $3,600 including installation. The Glendale Water Company requires a down payment of $1,200 for those customers deciding to pay for the system over 24 months (in equal monthly installments of $100). Approximately one-half of the company's customers pay for the system in full at the time of installation. For accounting purposes, Glendale recognizes the revenue from the sale of a system when installation of the system is complete, regardless of whether a customer pays in full or over 24 months. For income tax purposes, however, Glendale uses the installment basis to recognize the revenue from the sale of a system. The revenue streams for accounting and income tax purposes for a single system appear as follows. The cost of a complete system, including installation is $900.

	Accounting	Income Tax
Year 1	$3,600	$2,400
Year 2	0	1,200
Total	$3,600	$3,600

Required

Assume that The Glendale Water Company has an effective tax rate of 30 percent. Illustrate the accounting for the sale of a system occurring on January 1 using a spreadsheet approach. Your spreadsheet should assume that the system is financed over a 24 month period; hence, remember to consider the deferred income tax effect.

Date	Cash	Accounts Receivable	Inventory	=	Deferred Income Taxes	+	Retained Earnings	
		Assets		**=**	**Liabilities**	**+**	**Equity**	
Year 1								
Jan 1........	$1,200	$2,400					$3,600	(R)
			-$900				-900	(E)
Feb 1	100	-100						
Mar 1	100	-100						
Apr 1........	100	-100						
May 1	100	-100						
Jun 1........	100	-100						
Jul 1	100	-100						
Aug 1	100	-100						
Sep 1	100	-100						
Oct 1........	100	-100						
Nov 1	100	-100						
Dec 1	100	-100						
Dec 31	-540				$270[1]		-810	(E)
EOY	$1,860	$1,200	-$900		$270		$1,890	
Year 2								
Jan 1........	100	-100						
Mar 1	100	-100						
Apr 1........	100	-100						
May 1	100	-100						
Jun 1........	100	-100						
Jul 1	100	-100						
Aug 1	100	-100						
Sep 1	100	-100						
Oct 1........	100	-100						
Nov 1	100	-100						
Dec 1	100	-100						
Dec 31	-270				-270[2]			
EOY	$2,790	$ 0	-$900		$ 0		$1,890	

1. Calculation of the Deferred Income Tax Liability for Year 1:

	Accounting	Income Tax	Deferred Income Tax
Revenue	$3,600	$2,400	
Less: Cost of goods sold	900	600	
Pretax income	$2,700	$1,800	
Income tax (30%)	810	540	$270
Net income	$1,890	$1,260	

2. Calculation of the Deferred Income Tax Liability for Year 2:

	Accounting	Income Tax	Deferred Income Tax
Revenue	$0	$1,200	
Less: Cost of goods sold	0	300	
Pretax income	$0	$900	
Income tax (30%)	0	270	−$270
Net income	$0	$ 630	$ 0

EXECUTIVE SUMMARY

This chapter concludes our investigation of corporate liabilities. Specifically, we examined the valuation and financial statement disclosure of such potential obligations as commitments and contingent liabilities, deferred income tax liabilities, unfunded retirement obligations, and financial derivatives (see Appendix 10B). In Chapter 11, we consider the shareholders' equity section of the balance sheet and examine how companies raise capital through the sale of equity instruments.

As a validation of your understanding of the content of this chapter, you should now be able to:

- Explain the difference between a commitment and a contingent liability.
- Explain deferred income tax liabilities and why this account increases and decreases.
- Explain how employee retirement obligations are valued and disclosed.
- Explain how financial instruments and derivatives are valued and reported in corporate financial statements (see Appendix 10B).

KEY CONCEPTS AND TERMS

Commitment, 10.3
Conservatism ratio, 10.11
Contingent asset, 10.5
Contingent liability, 10.5
Contributory plan, 10.14
Counterparty, 10.28

Current funding, 10.16
Deferred income taxes, 10.11
Deferred income tax asset, 10.11
Deferred income tax liability, 10.11
Defined-benefit plan, 10.14
Defined-contribution plan, 10.14

Depreciation tax shield, 10.10
Executory contract, 10.3
Financial instruments, 10.27
Funding status, 10.27
Gain contingency, 10.5
Interest cost, 10.24

APPENDIX 10A: Illustration of Pension Accounting

George in the only employee of Solo Inc. George is getting on in years and has decided to work for Solo because of the defined benefit pension plan he was offered as part of his compensation package. He has agreed to work for five years before he retires. Solo determined from a medical examination that George took for employment purposes that he will only live for five years after retirement. The pension plan guarantees that for each year he works for Solo, George will receive $1,000 at the end of each year during his retirement. In other words, if George works five years, he will receive $5,000 a year during each year of his five-year retirement. Solo discounts its future obligations at six percent to compute a present value. Further, Solo estimates that it will be able to earn a rate of return of twelve percent on its pension plan assets. Finally, Solo has decided to contribute $3,315 at the end of each year that George works for Solo.

Service cost represents the pension cost attributable to the company service that George provides each year that he works for Solo. Service cost is computed as the present value of each future benefit attributed to the current year's service. For George, this will amount to $1,000 for each of five years following retirement. The service cost computation is illustrated in the diagram below.:

Service Cost Computation										
Year of Service					Year of Retirement					
1	2	3	4	5	1	2	3	4	5	
$3,337					$1,000	$1,000	$1,000	$1,000	$1,000	
	$3,537				1,000	1,000	1,000	1,000	1,000	
		$3,749			1,000	1,000	1,000	1,000	1,000	
			$3,974		1,000	1,000	1,000	1,000	1,000	
				$4,212	1,000	1,000	1,000	1,000	1,000	

The diagram shows that the service cost for the first year of George's employment is $3,337. This represents the present value of an annuity of $1,000 for five years starting five years from the present. The service cost increases each year because the present value calculation is computed using an annuity starting date one year sooner.

The projected benefit obligation (PBO) represents the present value of the entire amount of future benefits, not just the benefits from one year of service. Therefore, the PBO calculation considers not just the current year's service, but also all prior year's service that has been performed. To take the prior year's service into account, Solo calculates an interest cost on each year's prior service.

Since the pension benefit obligation is computed following each year of service, there isn't any interest cost the first year. For the second year, the interest cost is computed as the prior year's accumulated service cost multiplied by the interest rate. For Solo, this will be $200 calculated as $3,337 × .06. For the third year, the interest cost will be $424 calculated as $212 for year one service (($3,337 + $200) × .06) and $212 for year two service ($3,537 × .06).

In a similar manner, year four interest cost will be $675 calculated as $225 for year one service (($3,337 + $200 + $212) × .06) plus $225 for year two service (($3,537 + $212) × .06) plus $225 for year three service ($3,749 × .06). The computation of the interest cost is illustrated in the diagram below:

	Interest Cost Computation				
	Interest Cost For Year				
Cost attributed to year	1	2	3	4	5
1.........................		$200	$212	$225	$238
2.........................			212	225	238
3.........................				225	238
4.........................					238
Total	$0	$200	$424	$675	$954

For our simple defined benefit plan, the projected benefit obligation at the end of each year is simply the prior year ending balance plus the sum of the service and interest costs for the current year, as shown below:

	Projected Benefit Obligation				
	Year of Service				
	1	2	3	4	5
Beginning balance	$ 0	$3,337	$ 7,074	$11,247	$15,896
Service cost	3,337	3,537	3,749	3,974	4,212
Interest cost	0	200	424	675	954
Total	$3,337	$7,074	$11,247	$15,896	$21,062

Solo elects to contribute to the pension plan $3,315 at the end of each year of George's employment. Solo expected to earn twelve percent each year on the invested funds; however, things did not go so well, with actual earnings of only eight percent. This leads to a total of $19,448 for the fair value of the plan assets at the end of George's five-year employment. The details of the plan assets are shown below:

	Plan Assets At Fair Value				
	Year of Service				
	1	2	3	4	5
Beginning balance	$ 0	$3,315	$ 6,895	$10,762	$14,938
Contribution	3,315	3,315	3,315	3,315	3,315
Earnings	0	265	552	861	1,195
Total	$3,315	$6,895	$10,762	$14,938	$19,448

The actual funding status of the pension plan is simply the difference between the projected benefit obligation and the fair value of plan assets. If the plan assets at fair value exceed the projected benefit obligation, the pension fund is over-funded; otherwise, it is under-funded. Solo is under-funded by $1,614 at the beginning of George's retirement as shown below:

Pension Plan Funding Status					
	Year of Service				
	1	2	3	4	5
Plan assets at fair value	$3,315	$6,895	$10,762	$14,938	$19,448
Projected benefit obligation	3,337	7,074	11,247	15,896	21,062
Funding status	$ (22)	$ (179)	$ (485)	$ (958)	$ (1,614)

Prior to a new FASB pension accounting standard, effective in 2007, even though the pension plan is under-funded by amounts ranging from $22 to $1,614, these amounts would not appear on Solo's balance sheet. To deter-mine the recognized amounts, we first needed to determine the yearly benefit cost that will appear on the income statement. For Solo, the **pension benefit cost** consists of the annual service cost and interest cost, less the *expected* plan earnings using the expected rate of twelve percent rather than the actual rate of eight percent. These amounts are shown below.

Pension Benefit Cost					
	Year of Service				
	1	2	3	4	5
Service cost	$3,337	$3,537	$3,749	$3,974	$4,212
Interest cost	0	200	424	675	954
Expected return	(0)	(398)	(827)	(1,291)	(1,793)
Total	$3,337	$3,339	$3,346	$3,357	$3,374

Solo would then recognize a net liability as the recognized expense less the cash contributed. This is shown below in spreadsheet format:

	Assets	=	Liabilities	+	Equity	
Year	Cash		Pension Liability		Retained Earnings	
1	(3,315)		22		(3,337)	Pension expense
2	(3,315)		24		(3,339)	Pension expense
3	(3,315)		31		(3,346)	Pension expense
4	(3,315)		42		(3,357)	Pension expense
5	(3,315)		59		(3,373)	Pension expense
Totals	(16,575)		178		(16,753)	

Actual versus Recognized Net Pension Obligation					
	Year of Service				
	1	2	3	4	5
Actual funding status	$(22)	$(178)	$(485)	$(958)	$(1,614)
Recognized net obligation	(22)	(46)	(77)	(119)	(178)
Difference	$ 0	$(132)	$(408)	$(839)	$(1,436)

In the case of Solo's pension, the reason for the difference between the actual **funding status** and the recognized pension obligation is due to the lower-than-expected actual returns on plan assets. The actual returns are used to compute the actual funding status since the actual returns are what are included in the fair value of plan assets. In contrast, the expected returns are used to calculate the recognized benefit cost, and hence the recognized net obligation. For more complex pensions, many other items can cause a difference between recognized and actual funding status. It is not at all unusual for the recognized net obligation to be much smaller than the actual funding status even though the firm is complying with GAAP. For example, Ford Motor Company recognized a net asset on its 2005 balance sheet for its pensions of approximately $5.5 billion even though Ford's pensions were under-funded by nearly $11 billion! For this reason, it is quite important for a reader of the financial statements to go beyond the actual statements and carefully review the footnotes, where the details regarding a company's pension plans are disclosed.

The new pension accounting standard, SFAS 158, requires that the actual funding status of a pension plan appear as either an asset, if over-funded, or a liability, if under-funded, on a company's balance sheet. The corresponding adjustment required to keep the balance sheet in balance is to Accumulated Other Comprehensive Income in the shareholders' equity section of the balance sheet. The income statement presentation does not change under the new standard.

APPENDIX 10B: Financial Instruments and Derivatives

As businesses have come under increasing pressure from shareholders to maximize firm value, more and more firms have begun utilizing exotic financial contracts to minimize the risk of business losses and maximize the likelihood of business gains. Examples of such contracts include financial instruments and derivative securities.

Financial instruments are financial contracts which impose an obligation on a business that uses these instruments to exchange cash (or some other financial asset) under potentially unfavorable conditions. (Not all financial instruments are obligations, some are assets. We restrict our consideration to those financial instruments that impact a firm's credit risk.) Examples include repurchase or repo agreements, forward purchase agreements for securities or commodities, and various hybrids of these instruments. For example, a business with excess cash, desiring to maximize its return on its excess cash, might purchase a portfolio of bonds from a brokerage firm under a repurchase agreement. During the term of the **repo agreement**, often six months to one year, the business receives interest income from its investment in the portfolio of bonds. However, at the end of the agreement, the business is obligated to sell the portfolio of bonds back to the brokerage firm at their original purchase price; and, as a consequence, the buyer is protected from any loss due to a decline in the principal value of the bond investment. Both parties to the repo agreement, however, are exposed to market risk—that is, the risk that the market value of the portfolio of bonds could be greater than or less than the amount that the purchaser originally paid for them. If the bond portfolio declines in value because of an increase in market interest rates, the brokerage firm loses while the purchaser gains. On the other hand, if the portfolio gains in value, the brokerage firm gains and the purchaser loses. A repo agreement is, in effect, a **zero-sum game**—one party gains what the other party loses! Why would a company engage in a repo arrangement? In an attempt to maximize the return on its excess cash, and thus, maximize shareholder value.

Derivative financial instruments are financial contracts that derive their value from some other asset or index. Examples include options, forward contracts, futures contracts, and interest rate swaps. For example, to illustrate the mechanics of an **interest rate swap**, assume that Firm A has an outstanding note payable with a face value of $100,000 that bears interest at the rate of 7 percent, payable annually on December 31. Firm A has the option of repaying the note anytime prior to its maturity in five years; however, the amount of the repayment will be determined based on the market value of the note at the time of repayment. Firm A is worried that interest rates may fall and cause the value of the note to increase. Firm Z also has an outstanding note payable with a face value of $100,000 with payments due annually on December 31. In contrast to the Firm A note, Firm Z's note has a variable interest rate based on the prime lending rate. Firm Z is concerned that its cash flow will be harmed if interest rates increase, causing its interest payments to increase. To mitigate these risks, Firm Z may negotiate a contract to swap or exchange its interest payments with Firm A. This is typically accomplished through a swap dealer such as a bank that serves as a intermediary to bring together the two **counterparties** to the swap transaction. Under a swap arrangement, Firm A assumes responsibility for the payment of Firm Z's variable rate interest payment, whereas Firm Z assumes responsibility for the payment of Firm A's fixed rate interest payment. As a consequence of the swap, Firm Z locks in a fixed rate to protect its cash flow and Firm A will have a variable rate interest payment whose cash flow changes will be offset by the change in the fair value of its outstanding note. Interest rate swaps are derivative instruments because they derive their value from movements in the general corporate borrowing rate. Like repo agreements, interest rate swaps are a zero-sum game in which one party gains while the other party loses.

Financial instruments like repurchase agreements and derivative financial instruments like interest rate swaps may constitute significant obligations for a company. Under U.S. GAAP, these instruments are accounted for by valuing the instruments at their fair market value. Since the instrument's fair market value may increase or decrease over time as economic conditions change, the firms that are party to the instrument may experience a wealth increase or decrease. Under U.S. GAAP, these wealth changes are not currently reportable as income on the income statement so long as the instruments are outstanding (the gains (losses) remain unrealized). However, since the unrealized wealth change does affect the overall value of a business, the wealth change must be disclosed as a component of shareholders' equity on the balance sheet. Unrealized gains and losses on derivative instruments are reported as a component of Other Comprehensive Income on U.S. financial statements. We will have more to say about unrealized gains and losses on derivative securities in Chapter 11. Under IASB GAAP, however, the unrealized gain (loss) on financial instruments **is** reported on the income statement rather than on the balance sheet as under U.S. GAAP. This divergence in practice between U.S. and IASB GAAP reflects the IASB's commitment to the use of market-value based accounting.

DISCUSSION QUESTIONS

Q10.1 **Contingent Liability Accounting.** In 2006, **Merck & Company** was sued by the survivors of a plaintiff who had died of a heart attack while taking Merck's painkiller drug Vioxx. A jury found the company guilty and awarded the plaintiff's estate $4.5 million in damages. In a similar case, Merck was found not liable by the courts for a second plaintiff's death. By mid-2006, more than 9,600 Vioxx-related cases were pending in the U.S. courts. According to *CFO Magazine,* Merck's potential Vioxx-related liability was somewhere between $5 billion and $50 billion. Discuss how Merck should disclose the $4.5 lawsuit award and the 9,600 pending Vioxx-related cases in its 2006 annual report.

Q10.2 **Debt Covenants and Going-Concern Exceptions.** The May 2, 2006 edition of *The Financial Times* carried the following leading story headline:

Auditors to Warn over Sea Containers

The related article reported that **Sea Containers Ltd.**, a Bermuda-based container leasing and passenger transport company, remained unable to file its 2005 financial statements with the U.S. Securities and Exchange Commission. The company reported that while it expected to receive an unqualified auditor's opinion on its 2005 financial report, it also "anticipated that there would be a paragraph (in the auditor's report) raising substantial doubt about (the company's) ability to continue as a going concern." In March of 2006, Sea Containers disclosed to the public that it had violated some of its debt covenants when it wrote off $500 million of its leasing business, causing the firm's net worth to drop below required covenant minimums. Discuss why a violation of an existing debt covenant might cause an auditor to issue a going-concern exception about Sea Containers.

Q10.3 **Pension Accounting and Debt Covenants.** In 2006, the Financial Accounting Standards Board adopted a new pension accounting standard which required that, effective year-end 2007, pension and retirement-benefit plan surplus and deficit funding be disclosed on corporate balance sheets as an asset or liability, respectively. The new accounting standard, however, might adversely affect the ability of some businesses to satisfy their debt covenants on existing loan agreements. Consider, for example, **Electronic Data**

Systems (EDS), which faced a debt covenant of a required minimum level of $6.42 billion in shareholders' equity. (EDS's shareholders' equity was $7.5 billion.) Under the new FASB pension accounting standard, EDS would be required to add $1.08 billion to its liabilities due to a pension plan funding deficit and also reduce its shareholders' equity to exactly the covenant minimum of $6.42 billion. Discuss how EDS should respond to the new pension accounting with respect to its creditors.

Q10.4　**Accounting for Pending Lawsuits.**　On April 13, 2006, Bausch & Lomb Inc. pulled its ReNu contact lens solution from suppliers' shelves over mounting concerns that the product was linked to over 100 cases of a rare fungal eye infection (Fusarium Keratitis) that could lead to corneal damage and required corneal transplant. In a statement released on April 14, 2006, the Federal Food and Drug Administration indicated its support for the product recall/removal while the Center for Disease Control investigated Bausch & Lomb's production facilities for possible contamination. On May 9, 2006, the law firm of Weitz & Luxenberg filed a lawsuit against Bausch & Lomb on behalf of a Philadelphia client who was diagnosed with Fusarium Keratitis after using the ReNu product. Discuss how Bausch & Lomb should disclose the pending lawsuit in its 2006 annual report. Discuss the financial effects to Bausch & Lomb's financial statements associated with the ReNu product recall/removal.

Q10.5　**Interpreting Deferred Income Tax Assets.**　The following information was taken from the 2005 annual report of Microsoft Inc.:

(in millions)	2004	2005
Current assets		
Deferred income taxes.	$1,701	$2,097
Non-current assets		
Deferred income taxes.	3,621	3,808
Total	$5,322	$5,905

A review of the footnotes to Microsoft's annual report reveals that the two major accounting policies affecting its deferred income taxes were (1) the accounting for unearned revenue and (2) the accounting for its portfolio of trading securities. When Microsoft sells a software product, it defers a portion of the revenue received to cover the cost of future technical service and free upgrades that may be provided during the warranty period. Discuss how Microsoft's accounting for unearned revenue and its accounting for its portfolio of trading securities could result in the creation of a deferred income tax asset. Discuss the difference between a current deferred income tax asset and a non-current deferred income tax asset.

Q10.6　**Interpreting Deferred Income Tax Liabilities.**　The following information is taken from the 2005 annual report of Coca-Cola Enterprises, Inc.:

(in millions)	2004	2005
Long-term Deferred Income Tax Liability.	$5,338	$5,106

The footnotes to the company's annual report reveal that the primary contributor to its deferred income tax liability was its accounting for franchise licenses. According to Coca-Cola Enterprises' Summary of Significant Accounting Policies:

> We do not amortize our goodwill and franchise license intangible assets. Instead, we test these assets for impairment annually.

Discuss why and how the company's accounting for franchise licenses results in a deferred income tax liability. The long-term deferred income tax liability declined by $232 million from 2004 to 2005; what does this decline suggest?

Q10.7 **Analyzing the Funding Status of a Pension Plan.** The following information is taken from the 2005 annual report of **Coca-Cola Enterprises, Inc.:**

Pension plans (in millions)	2005	2004
Benefit obligations (at end of year).	$2,904	$2,576
Fair value of plan assets.	2,221	1,810

Discuss whether Coca-Cola Enterprises' (CCE) pension plans are fully funded at year-end 2004 and 2005. Did the company's funding improve from 2004 to 2005? The footnotes reveal that CCE changed the discount rate that it used to discount its benefit obligations from 5.8 percent in 2004 to 5.4 percent in 2005; how would this change likely impact the value of CCE's benefit obligation?

Q10.8 **Changing Pension Plan Assumptions.** The 2005 annual report of The **Johnson and Johnson Company** (J&J) disclosed the following information:

U.S. Retirement Plans	2002	2003	2004	2005
Discount rate	6.75%	6.00%	5.75%	5.75%
Expected long-term rate of return on plan assets	9.00	9.00	9.00	9.00
Rate of increase in compensation levels	4.50	4.50	4.50	4.50

Between 2002 and 2005, J&J lowered the discount rate used to calculate the present value of its projected benefit obligation from 6.75 percent to 5.75 percent, while it maintained the expected rate of return on plan assets at nine percent. Discuss how a lowering of the assumed discount rate while maintaining the expected rate of return on plan assets would impact J & J's pension obligations. Why would J&J lower the discount rate on its projected benefit obligation?

Q10.9 **Discounting Deferred Income Tax Liabilities.** Deferred income tax liabilities arise because of differences in the policies used to account for revenue and expenses for financial reporting purposes versus the policies utilized to report revenue and expenses for income tax purposes. For instance, revenue might be recognized for financial reporting purposes at the point of sale, whereas for income tax purposes, revenue might be recognized at the point of cash collection using the installment method. It is generally accepted practice to discount liabilities to their present value for purposes of presentation on the balance sheet. Discuss why deferred income tax liabilities are not valued on corporate balance sheets at their present value.

Q10.10 **(Appendix B) Interest Rate Swaps.** The 2005 annual report of The **Home Depot Inc.** revealed the following information regarding its derivative securities:

> At January 29, 2006, the Company had several outstanding interest rate swaps accounted for as fair value hedges, with a notional amount of $475 million that swap fixed rate interest on the Company's $500 million 5 3/8 percent Senior Notes for variable interest rates equal to LIBOR plus 30 to 245 basis points and expire on April 1, 2006. At January 29, 2006, the fair market value of these agreements was a liability of $1 million, which is the estimated amount that the Company would have paid to settle similar interest rate swap agreements at current interest rates.

Assume that Home Depot swaps its fixed rate interest payment on its $500 million 5 3/8 percent notes for variable interest rate payments equal to LIBOR (London Interbank Offered Rate) plus 50 basis points. Describe the financial effects of the swap for Home Depot. At what LIBOR rate does Home Depot benefit from the swap? At what LIBOR rate does Home Depot lose from the swap? Discuss what is meant by a "zero-sum game."

Q10.11   **Underfunded Retirement Obligations and Firm Valuation.**   In its 2005 annual report, The Johnson and Johnson Company disclosed that its employee retirement obligations were underfunded by $2.063 billion at year-end 2005. And, of this amount, only $475 million was reported on the company's balance sheet, leaving the remainder ($1.588 billion) as an off-balance-sheet liability. Discuss whether the off-balance sheet portion of J&J's underfunded retirement obligation should be considered when calculating the value of Johnson and Johnson's capital stock.

Q10.12   **(Ethics Perspective) Multiple Sets of Books.**   As noted in the ethics perspective at the end of this chapter, firms routinely maintain separate sets of books for their financial reporting and their tax reporting. Can you think of any reason why a firm would be justified in keeping a third, internal set of books? Do you feel that it is ethically acceptable to not fully disclose to shareholders how a company's internal books differ from those used for external reporting purposes?

⊘ indicates that check figures are available on the book's Website.

EXERCISES

E10.13   **Calculating Deferred Income Taxes.**   The Sample Corporation prepared the following income statements and income tax returns for 2003 through 2006.

Income Statement	2003	2004	2005	2006
Sales.	$1,000	$1,000	$1,000	$1,000
Operating expenses	650	650	650	650
Pretax net income	350	350	350	350
Provisions for income taxes	140	140	140	140
Net income	$ 210	$ 210	$ 210	$ 210

Income Tax Return	2003	2004	2005	2006
Sales.	$1,000	$1,000	$1,000	$1,000
Operating expenses	900	900	400	400
Taxable income	$100	$100	$600	$600
Income tax payable	40	40	240	240
After-tax net income.	$ 60	$ 60	$ 340	$ 340

Calculate the balance in the company's deferred income tax liability account at the end of each year. Assume that the time value of money is ten percent per year; calculate the implicit value of the company's tax deferral strategy.

E10.14   **Calculating Deferred Income Taxes.**   ProFlight, Inc. used the percentage-of-completion method to recognize revenue for financial reporting purposes but the completed contract method to recognize revenue for income tax purposes. The company's income statements for financial reporting purposes and for income tax purposes are presented below:

Percentage-of-Completion Accounting	2004	2005
Revenue	$2,000,000	$8,000,000
Cost of production	1,600,000	6,400,000
Pretax net income	$ 400,000	$1,600,000

Completed Contract Accounting	2004	2005
Revenue	$0	$10,000,000
Cost of production	0	8,000,000
Pretax net income	$0	$ 2,000,000

Assume an effective tax rate of 35 percent; calculate the accounting tax expense, the income tax payable, and the deferred income taxes for 2004 and 2005. Assume a time value of money of ten percent; calculate the implicit value of ProFlight's tax deferral strategy.

⊘ E10.15 **Deferred Income Taxes and Changing Tax Rates.** The Waterloo Company uses straight-line depreciation accounting in its corporate financial reports but MACRS depreciation accounting for income tax purposes. In 2005, Waterloo reported taxable income to the IRS totaling $130,000 and pretax net income to its shareholders of $160,000. MACRS depreciation expense for 2005 totaled $70,000, while straight-line depreciation was only $40,000. Assume an effective tax rate of 35 percent for 2005; calculate Waterloo's deferred income taxes for the year. Is the company's deferred income tax effect for 2005 an asset or a liability? If the income tax rate was lowered to 30 percent, how much will the company's deferred income taxes for 2005 change? Explain the change in deferred income taxes.

E10.16 **Reporting the Provision for Income Taxes.** Smith & Sons Company presented the following information in the income tax footnote in its 2005 annual report:

Note 13. Income Taxes Provision for income taxes includes the following (in thousands)

	2005
Current payable	
U.S.	$4,026
Foreign.	438
Deferred	
U.S.	2,880
Foreign.	(174)
Total	$7,170

How much tax expense did Smith & Sons report on its income statement in 2005? How much of the reported income tax expense was paid currently and how much was deferred to a future period for payment? What is implied by the negative foreign deferred income taxes of $174?

E10.17 **Analyzing Retirement Fund Obligations.** The following information is taken from the 2005 annual report of The **Johnson and Johnson Company** (J&J):

(amounts in millions)	2004	2005
Projected benefit obligation	$10,171	$8,941
Plan assets at fair value	8,108	7,125
Net amount recognized in the company's balance sheet (as a liability).	475	288

Calculate the amount that J&J's retirement fund obligations are underfunded as of year-end 2004 and 2005. How much of the underfunding is reported on the company's balance sheet? Is the unreported portion of the underfunded pension obligation an example of an off-balance-sheet liability? If so, how might you restate J&J's balance sheet to fully reflect its pension debt as is now required under a new FASB pension accounting standard?

⊘ E10.18 **Analyzing Retirement Fund Obligations.** The following information is taken from the 2005 annual report of the **Intel Corporation**:

(amounts in millions)	2005	2004
Projected benefit obligation	$903	$546
Plan assets at fair value	568	283
Net amount recognized in the company's balance sheet (as a liability).	190	219

Calculate the amount that Intel's retirement fund obligations are underfunded as of year-end 2004 and 2005. How much of the underfunding is reported on Intel's balance sheet? Is the unreported portion of the under-funded pension obligation an example of an off-balance-sheet liability? If so, how would you restate Intel's balance sheet to fully reflect its pension debt as is now required under a new FASB pension accounting standard?

E10.19 **Analyzing Retirement Fund Obligations.** The following information is taken from the 2005 annual report of the **Bristol-Myers Squibb Company (BMS)**:

(amounts in millions)	2005	2004
Projected benefit obligation	$5,918	$5,481
Plan assets at fair value	5,017	4,602
Net amount recognized in the company's balance sheet (as a net asset).	1,229	1,215

Calculate the amount that BMS' retirement fund obligations are underfunded as of year-end 2004 and 2005. How much of the underfunding is reported on the company's balance sheet? Is the unreported portion of the underfunded pension obligation an example of an off-balance-sheet liability? If so, how could you restate BMS' balance sheet to fully reflect its pension debt as is now required under a new FASB pension accounting standard?

E10.20 **(Appendix 10B) Analyzing Foreign Currency Hedges.** The Arizona Company, a U.S.-based manufacturer, ordered a piece of equipment from Sonora Inc., a Mexico-based supplier, agreeing to pay 200,000 Mexican pesos upon delivery of the equipment in three months time. At the time of the contract signing, the exchange rate between the U.S. dollar and the Mexican peso was 10P:$1. With concerns about a weakening U.S. dollar, The Arizona Company decided to hedge its currency exposure by purchasing a forward foreign exchange contract from a local bank. The forward contract committed The Arizona Company to pay $20,300 in three months in exchange for 200,000 pesos.

What was the forward foreign exchange rate implicit in the contract (assuming no transaction costs)? If the foreign exchange rate in three months was 9.5P:$1, how much did The Arizona Company save by purchasing the currency hedge? If the foreign exchange rate in 3 months was 9.0P:$1, how much did the company save by purchasing the currency hedge? Was the decision to hedge the foreign exchange exposure a good decision?

E10.21 **(Appendix 10B) Analyzing Interest Rate Swaps.** The Phoenix Company purchases a piece of equipment from the Anthem Company by issuing a three-year note with a face value of $100,000. The two companies agree that the interest rate on the note will be pegged to LIBOR (London InterBank Offering Rate), which was currently eight percent, and would be reset at the end of each year for the following year.

Because of concerns about raising interest rates, The Phoenix Company arranged an interest rate swap with its local bank. Under the swap agreement, The Phoenix Company agreed to pay the bank eight percent annually for the three-year period, thus swapping its potentially variable-rate interest payment for a fixed-rate payment. Calculate the value of The Phoenix Company's loss over the three-year swap assuming that LIBOR drops to six percent at the end of the first year and remains there until the end of the swap agreement. Calculate the value of The Phoenix Company's gain over the three-year swap assuming that LIBOR goes to ten percent at the end of the first year and remains there until the end of the swap agreement.

E10.22 **(Appendix 10B) Analyzing Forward Commodity Contracts.**   The Portet Wine Company holds 20,000 gallons of wine in inventory at year-end. The company expects to age the wine for another six months before selling it as bulk wine. Given uncertainties surrounding the economic conditions in six months, Portet Wine Company decided to purchase a forward commodity contract in which it promised to sell the 20,000 gallons of wine in six months at a total fixed price of $3.2 million.

Ignoring transaction costs, what was the forward price per gallon of wine implicit in the commodity contract? If the purchase price per gallon of bulk wine in six months is $170 per gallon, was the decision to purchase a forward commodity contract a good decision? If so, why? If not, why not?

PROBLEMS

P10.23 **Legal Proceedings: Patent Infringement.**   Bristol-Myers Squibb Company (BMS) engages in the discovery, development, license, manufacture, marketing, distribution and sale of pharmaceutical and other health care products. Selected financial information for the company is as follows:

	2004	2003
Revenue	$19.4 billion	$20.9 billion
Net income	2.4 billion	3.1 billion
Total assets.	30.4 billion	27.5 billion
Total liabilities	20.2 billion	17.7 billion

BMS' 2004 annual report disclosed the following information in its footnotes:

> **Legal Proceedings and Contingencies**   Various lawsuits, claims, proceedings and investigations are pending against the Company and certain of its subsidiaries. In accordance with SFAS No. 5, *Accounting for Contingencies,* the Company records accruals for such contingencies when it is probable that a liability will be incurred and the amount of loss can be reasonably estimated. These matters involve antitrust, securities, patent infringements, the Employee Retirement Income Security Act of 1974, as amended (ERISA), pricing, sales and marketing practices, environmental, health and safety matters, product liability and insurance coverage. The most significant of these matters are described on next page.

> **Plavix Litigation**   The Company's U.S. territory partnership under its alliance with Sanofi is a plaintiff in three pending patent infringement lawsuits instituted in the U.S. District Court for the Southern District of New York. Plaintiffs' infringement position is based on defendants' filing of their Abbreviated New Drug Application (ANDA) with the FDA, seeking approval to sell generic clopidogrel bisulfate prior to the expiration of the composition of matter patent in 2011. Plavix is currently the Company's largest product ranked by net sales. Net sales of Plavix were approximately $3.3 billion and $2.5 billion for the years ended December 31, 2004 and 2003, respectively. Loss of market exclusivity of Plavix and the subsequent development of generic competition would be material to the Company's sales of Plavix and results of operations and cash flows and could be material to its financial condition and liquidity.

Required
1. Historically, the loss of patent protection on a brand name pharmaceutical product has resulted in a 70 percent decline in product sales. Assuming that (a) BMS' patent protection on Plavix is lost as of the beginning of 2005, (b) revenue and earnings for 2005 would, in the absence of the loss of patent protection, have equaled those of 2004, and (c) the after-tax margin on Plavix is 60 percent, estimate BMS' revenue and earnings for 2005. How material are these financial effects?
2. BMS' Plavix patent is carried on its balance as an intangible asset valued at $120 million. In the event of patent protection loss, how should the company reflect this in its financial statements?
3. How should the capital market react to (a) the disclosure that a patent infringement suit involving Plavix had been filed against BMS and (b) the disclosure that the suit had been lost (won)?

P10.24   Commitments: Loan Guarantees.   Microsoft Corporation engages in the development, manufacture, licensing, and support of a wide range of computer software products. The company also operates in the Internet marketplace with its MSN.com Internet service and in the PC games market with its Xbox video game console and games. Microsoft's 2004 annual reported revealed the following footnote disclosure regarding its off-balance-sheet commitments:

> We have unconditionally guaranteed the repayment of certain Japanese yen denominated bank loans and related interest and fees of Jupiter Telecommunication, Ltd., a Japanese cable company (Jupiter). These guarantees arose on February 1, 2003 in conjunction with the expiration of prior financing arrangements, including previous guarantees by us. As part of Jupiter's new financing agreement, we agreed to guarantee repayment by Jupiter of the loans of approximately $51 million. The guarantees are in effect until the earlier of repayment of the loans, including accrued interest and fees, or February 1, 2009. The maximum amount of the guarantees is limited to the sum of the total due and unpaid principal amounts, accrued and unpaid interest, and any other related expenses. If we were required to make payments under the guarantees, we may recover all or a portion of those payments upon liquidation of Jupiter's assets. The proceeds from such liquidation cannot be accurately estimated due the multitude of factors that would affect the valuation and realization of the proceeds in the event of liquidation.

Required
1. If Jupiter Telecommunication, Ltd. were to fail, forcing Microsoft Corporation to repay its debt, how would the payment be reflected in Microsoft's financial statements?
2. At year-end 2004, Microsoft reported net income of $5.3 billion, total assets of $81.7 billion, and total liabilities of $16.8 million. Is the Jupiter loan guarantee material in amount? If not, why do you think Microsoft disclosed the guarantee in its annual report?

P10.25   Loss Contingency: Lawsuit Award.   Microsoft Corporation is a leading designer and retailer of PC software applications. In its 2003 annual report, the company disclosed that the European Union Competition Commission had filed suit against it alleging antitrust violations:

> The European Commission has instituted proceedings in which it alleges that we have failed to disclose information that our competitors claim they need to interoperate fully with Windows 2000 clients and servers and that we have engaged in discriminatory licensing of such technology, as well as improper bundling of multimedia playback technology in the Windows operating system. The remedies sought, though not fully defined, include mandatory disclosure of our Windows operating system technology, either the removal of Windows Media technology from Windows or a "must carry" obligation requiring OEMs to install competitive media players with Windows, and imposition of fines in an amount that could be as large as ten percent of our worldwide annual revenue. We deny the European Commission's allegations and intend to contest the proceedings vigorously.

Based on 2003 reported revenue of $32.2 billion, Microsoft could suffer fines of as much as $3.22 billion. In Microsoft's 2004 annual report, the company disclosed that the EU Competition Commission had found it guilty of the alleged violations:

> On March 25, 2004, the European Commission announced a decision in its competition law investigation of Microsoft. The Commission concluded that we infringed European competition law by refusing to provide our competitors with licenses to certain protocol technology in the Windows server operating systems and by including streaming media playback functionality in Windows desktop operating systems. The Commission ordered us to make the relevant licenses to our technology available to our competitors and to develop and make available a version of the Windows desktop operating system that does not include specific software relating to media playback. The decision also imposed a fine of 497 million euros, which resulted in a charge of 497 million euros ($605 million). We filed an appeal of the decision to the Court of First Instance on June 6, 2004 and will seek interim measures suspending the operation of certain provisions of the decisions. We contest the conclusion that European competition law was infringed and will defend our position vigorously.

Required
1. How should Microsoft account for the EU Competition Commission lawsuit in its 2003 annual report? Why?

2. How should Microsoft account for the imposed fine of $605 million in its 2004 report? Why?
3. How would the capital markets react to an announced lawsuit like that filed by the EU Competition Commission in 2003? How would the capital markets react to the announcement that such a lawsuit had been lost and a fine imposed?

P10.26 **Deferred Income Taxes: Bad Debt Expense Policy.** Claremont Enterprises, Inc. started operations in early 2004. During the first year of operations, Claremont generated sales of $3.2 million, and at year-end, had $350,000 in outstanding accounts receivable. Using collection estimates provided by its controller, the company estimated that its bad debt expense for 2004 would be $10,925.

During its second year of operations, Claremont generated sales of $5.3 million, and at year-end, had $800,000 in outstanding accounts receivable. Using an aging schedule, the controller estimated that Claremont's bad debt expense for 2005 would be $22,500. In June of 2005, Claremont received confirmation that one of its outstanding accounts receivable in the amount of $11,500 had gone into bankruptcy, and thus would not be collected.

In discussions with the firm's independent auditor, the CFO of Claremont Enterprises learned that while an estimate of expected uncollectible accounts was permitted for purposes of preparing its U.S. GAAP-based annual report, the U.S. Treasury Department only allowed firms to deduct actual, known uncollectible accounts for purposes of preparing their income tax returns.

Required
Prepare a schedule showing the company's income tax expense, its income tax payable, and its deferred income tax balance for 2004 and 2005. Assume an effective tax rate of 30 percent and that Claremont has no other expenses other than the bad debt expense. Do you agree with the tax policy of the U.S. Treasury Department regarding the treatment of bad debts? Why or why not?

P10.27 **Deferred Income Taxes: Depreciation Accounting Policy.** At the start of 2004, the Miller Company acquired a $100,000 piece of equipment that was to be depreciated on a straight-line method basis for financial statement purposes but on an accelerated depreciation basis for income tax purposes. The Miller Company employed a half-year convention under which only one-half of the first year's depreciation expense would be taken regardless of when an asset was purchased and placed in service. The company also followed the accounting practice that if the level of accelerated depreciation charges fell below the level of straight-line depreciation charges (such as in 2007 in the schedule below), the company would switch from accelerated depreciation to a straight-line approach. The company's CFO prepared the following depreciation schedule for financial statement and income tax purposes.

	Straight-Line Depreciation	Accelerated Depreciation
2004	$ 8,333	$ 16,667
2005	16,666	27,778
2006	16,667	18,519
2007	16,667	12,347
2008	16,667	8,230
2009	16,667	8,230
2010	8,333	8,230
	$100,000	$100,000

Required
Assuming a 30 percent effective tax rate, prepare a schedule illustrating the deferred income tax effects for 2004 to 2010 associated with this asset.

P10.28 **Deferred Income Taxes: Natural Resource Accounting Policy.** The Herberger Oil & Gas Company explored for and developed oil and gas wells in Texas, Louisiana, and Oklahoma. Presented below are the company's income statements for the five-year period 2002 through 2006 under the successful efforts method and the full cost method. Herberger Oil & Gas used the successful efforts method for purposes of preparing its income tax return but the full cost method for purposes of preparing its audited financial statements for its equity investors.

Income Statement under the Successful Efforts Method						
(in millions)	2002	2003	2004	2005	2006	Total
Revenues	$30.0	$45.0	$52.5	$100.0	$157.5	$385.0
Less						
Lifting costs	5.0	7.5	9.0	17.5	28.0	67.0
Exploration costs	16.0	0.0	0.0	0.0	0.0	16.0
Interest expense	4.0	4.0	3.0	2.0	1.0	14.0
Depletion expense	2.4	3.6	3.6	6.0	8.4	24.0
Income before tax	$ 2.6	$29.9	$36.9	$ 74.5	$120.1	$264.0

Income Statement under the Full Cost Method						
(in millions)	2002	2003	2004	2005	2006	Total
Revenues	$30.0	$45.0	$52.5	$100.0	$157.5	$385.0
Less						
Lifting costs	5.0	7.5	9.0	17.5	28.0	67.0
Exploration costs	0.0	0.0	0.0	0.0	0.0	0.0
Interest expense	4.0	4.0	3.0	2.0	1.0	14.0
Depletion expense	4.0	6.0	6.0	10.0	14.0	40.0
Income before tax	$17.0	$27.5	$34.5	$ 70.5	$114.5	$264.0

Required

Assuming an effective tax rate of 30 percent, calculate the deferred income tax effect for Herberger Oil & Gas Company for the five year period 2002-2006.

P10.29 **(Appendix 10B) Interest Rate Swaps.** In 2005, Global Enterprises (GE) acquired MNC Inc. As part of the acquisition, GE assumed responsibility for MNC's $150 million of eight percent, senior notes. Global Enterprises subsequently guaranteed the senior notes to avoid having them called by the lender (the sale of MNC triggered an immediate redemption covenant in the note indenture). To hedge its interest rate risk associated with the senior note guarantee, Global Enterprises entered into the following three-year reverse swap arrangement:

> The Company entered into a three-year reverse interest rate swap beginning June 1, 2005 and ending June 1, 2008. Under the terms of the swap, the Company receives a fixed interest payment of 4.9 percent and pays six-month LIBOR* for the prior six months on $150 million. The effect of the swap is to convert the first three years of the eight percent senior notes from a fixed rate obligation to a floating rate obligation (composed of a fixed payment of 3.1 percent plus a floating payment based on six-month LIBOR for the prior six months). The swap agreement increased the company's interest expense by $1 million in 2006 and reduced its interest expense by $1.2 million in 2005. *(LIBOR = London Interbank Offered Rate)

Required

1. Describe the financial effects of the reverse swap for Global Enterprises.
2. Under what LIBOR rate does Global Enterprises gain from the swap? Under what LIBOR rate does Global Enterprises lose?
3. How should GE account for this interest rate swap on its financial statements?

P10.30 **(Appendix 10B) Foreign Exchange Contracts.** The financial statements of **MNE Corporation** revealed the following:

> The Company operates internationally and is exposed to fluctuations in currency values. The fluctuations can increase the costs of financing and operating the business.
>
> The Company manages this risk to acceptable limits through the use of derivatives to create offsetting positions in foreign currency markets. The Company views derivative financial instruments as risk management tools and is not party to any leveraged derivatives.
>
> The notional amounts of derivative contracts do not represent the amounts exchanged by the parties, and thus are not a measure of the exposure of the Company through its use of derivatives. The amounts exchanged by the parties are normally based on the notional amounts and other terms of the derivatives, which relate to exchange rates. The value of derivatives is derived from those underlying parameters and changes in the relevant rates.
>
> At December 31, 2004, the Company had $139 million notional principal amount of outstanding currency swap contracts to hedge its foreign net assets, which were terminated in 2005.
>
> Foreign currency commitment and transaction exposures are managed at the operating unit level as an integral part of the business and residual exposures that cannot be offset to an insignificant amount are hedged. Hedged items include foreign currency denominated receivables and payables on the balance sheet, firm purchase orders and firm sales commitments.
>
> At December 31, the Company had the following amounts related to foreign exchange contracts hedging foreign currency transaction and firm commitments:

In millions of dollars	2005	2004
Notional amount		
Buy contracts.	$1,747	$1,928
Sell contracts.	1,062	780
Gains and losses explicitly deferred as a result of		
hedging firm commitment		
Gains deferred	$ 14	$ 14
Losses deferred	(69)	(14)
	$ (55)	$ 0

Required

1. Why does MNE Corporation use foreign exchange derivatives? What is the likely form of these derivatives?
2. What is the "notional amount" of a derivative?
3. How are the gains/losses on MNE's foreign exchange derivatives accounted for?

P10.31 **(Appendix 10B) Interest Rate Swaps.** The **Proctor & Gamble Company** is a U.S.-based multinational enterprise that manufactures and markets a range of consumer products worldwide. The company's annual report discloses that:

> The Company is exposed to market risk, including changes in interest rates, currency exchange rates and commodity prices. To manage the volatility relating to these exposures, the Company nets the exposures to take advantage of natural offsets and enters into various derivative transactions for the remaining exposures. The Company does not hold or issue derivative financial instruments for trading purposes.
>
> **Interest rate management** The Company's policy is to manage interest cost using a mix of fixed and variable rate debt. To manage this mix in a cost-efficient manner, the Company enters into interest rate swaps in which the Company agrees to exchange, at specified intervals, the difference between fixed and variable interest amounts calculated by reference to an agreed-upon notional principal amount. These swaps are designed to hedge underlying debt obligations. For qualifying hedges, the interest rate differential is reflected as an adjustment to interest expense over the life of the swaps. The following table presents information for all interest rate instruments. The notional amount does not necessarily represent amounts exchanged by the parties, and, therefore, is not a direct measure of the Company's exposure

to credit risk. The fair value approximates the cost to settle the outstanding contracts. The carrying value includes the net amount due to counterparties under swap contracts, currency translation associated with currency interest rate swaps and any marked-to-market value adjustments of instruments.

June 30	2004	2003
Notional amount.	$2,149	$1,488
Fair value	7	(54)
Carrying value	28	(28)
Unrecognized loss	$ (21)	$ (26)

Although derivatives are an important component of the Company's interest rate management program, their incremental effect on interest expense for 2004 and 2003 were not material. *(The company's interest charges for 2004 totaled about $550 million.)*

Required
1. Describe Proctor and Gamble's strategy involving its use of interest rate swaps.
2. Identify the notional amount, carrying value, and fair value of the company's swap contracts as of year-end 2004. What is the difference between these values?
3. Was the company's use of interest rate swaps effective in 2003 and 2004?
4. How does the company account for its unrecognized loss of $26 million in 2003 and $21 million in 2004 on its swap contracts?

◆ P10.32 **Retirement Obligations: Funding Status.** Global Enterprises Inc. (GE) is a multinational company based in the United States. The company maintains private pension plans for its employees worldwide. Presented below is information from GE's 2005 annual report regarding its U.S. pension plans.

U.S. Plans ($ millions)	Plan Assets Exceed Accumulated Benefits		Accumulated Benefits Exceed Plan Assets	
	2005	2004	2005	2004
Actuarial present value of benefit obligations				
Vested	$(468)	$(452)	$(2)	$(14)
Nonvested	(10)	(18)	—	4
Accumulated benefit obligation	(478)	(470)	(2)	(10)
Effect of projected future				
compensation levels	(59)	(61)	—	(12)
Projected benefit obligation	(537)	(531)	(2)	(22)
Plan assets at fair value	803	645	—	5
Plan assets in excess of (less than)				
projected benefit obligation.	266	114	(2)	(17)
Unrecognized net loss (gain)	(255)	(60)	(1)	—
Unrecognized prior service cost.	20	14	—	11
Unrecognized net transition obligation.	3	8	—	(2)
Post September 30 contributions	—	1	—	—
(Accrued) prepaid pension cost at				
December 31	$ 34	$ 77	$(3)	$ (8)

During 2005, GE's total pension expense was $10 million and was fully funded. In addition, the company earned $200 million on its plan assets due to a strong U.S. stock market.

Required
1. Identify the following values for 2005:

      a.   Total projected benefit obligation (PBO)

      b.   Total pension plan assets

      Using the PBO as a standard, was GE's U.S. pension plan over or underfunded as of year-end 2005? If overfunded, where do the excess pension plan assets appear on GE's financial statements?

  2.   How much cash was paid by the pension plan to GE's former employees in 2005?

  3.   How much is GE's "minimum pension liability" for 2005? Where is the minimum pension liability disclosed on GE's balance sheet? Do you agree with this disclosure? Why?

  4.   What adjustments to GE's balance sheet would be necessary to bring the company's pension accounting disclosures into compliance with the new FASB pension accounting standard?

P10.33   **Retirement Obligations Funding Status.**   MNC Inc. is a worldwide manufacturer of plastic parts. The company's pension disclosures in its 2005 report were as follows:

> **Employee Benefit Plans**   The Company has defined benefit and defined contribution retirement plans for its employees. The defined benefit pension plans pay benefits to employees at retirement using formulas based on a participant's years of service and compensation. The funded status of the defined benefit plans is as follows:

($ thousands)	2005	2004
Assets available for benefits.	$287,482	$247,783
Projected benefit obligation		
Vested	(244,050)	(182,005)
Nonvested	(17,938)	(12,696)
Total accumulated benefit obligation.	(261,988)	(194,701)
Effect of projected future compensation increases	(45,164)	(30,203)
Total actuarial projected benefit obligation	(307,152)	(224,904)
Assets (less than) in excess of projected obligation	$ (19,670)	$ 22,879
Consisting of amounts to be offset against (charged to) future pension costs		
Remaining assets in excess of obligation existing at adoption of SFAS 87 in 1986.	$ 5,598	$ 6,777
Unrecognized actuarial (loss) gain due to differences in assumptions and actual experience	(15,977)	8,974
Unrecognized prior service cost	6,262	7,199
Accrued pension costs.	(15,553)	(71)
	$ (19,670)	$ 22,879

> The actuarial present value of the accumulated benefit obligation and the projected benefit obligation was calculated using a discount rate of 7.25 percent in 2005 and 8.0 percent in 2004, and the rate of increase in future compensation levels used was 5.5 percent each year. The expected long-term rate of return on assets was 10.0 percent in 2005 and 9.0 percent in 2004. The plan invests primarily in marketable securities and time deposits.

Required

  1.   Identify the following values of 2004 and 2005:

      a.   Projected benefit obligation (PBO)

      b.   Pension plan assets

      Is MNC's defined benefit plan over or under-funded relative to its PBO? What financial statement adjustment would be required to fully reflect MNC's pension asset/debt position on its balance sheet?

  2.   What was the financial effect on MNC's PBO in 2005 when it lowered its discount rate from 8.00 percent in 2004 to 7.25 percent in 2005? What was the financial effect on MNC's plan assets in 2005 when it raised its expected long-term rate of return from nine percent in 2004 to ten percent in 2005? Do you agree with these changes?

P10.34   **Retirement Obligations: An Overfunded Plan.**   The **General Electric Company** (GE) engages in the development, manufacture, and marketing of various products for the generation, transmission, distribution and utilization of electricity through the world. The company sponsors over 30 U.S. and non-U.S. pension plans, with over 600,000 plan participants. The company's 2004 annual report reveals the following information about the company's pension plans:

	Principal Pension Plans			
Actuarial Assumptions	**2004**	**2003**	**2002**	**2001**
Discount rate	5.75%	6.00%	6.75%	7.25%
Compensation increases	5.00	5.00	5.00	5.00
Expected return on assets	8.50	8.50	8.50	9.50

Funding Policy   The funding policy for the GE Pension Plan is to contribute amounts sufficient to meet minimum funding requirements as set forth in employee benefit and tax laws plus such additional amounts as we may determine to be appropriate. We have not made contributions to the GE Pension Plan since 1987. We will not make any contributions to the GE Pension Plan in 2005; any GE contribution to that plan would require payment of excise taxes and would not be deductible for income tax purposes.

	Principal Pension Plans	
Projected Benefit Obligation (in millions)	**2004**	**2003**
Balance at January 1	$37,827	$33,266
Service costs for benefits earned.	1,178	1,213
Interest cost on benefit obligations	2,199	2,180
Participant contributions	163	169
Plan amendments	—	654
Actuarial loss	969	2,754
Benefits paid	(2,367)	(2,409)
Acquired plans	—	—
Exchange rate adjustments and other	—	—
Balance at December 31	$39,969	$37,827

	Principal Pension Plans	
Fair Value of Assets (in millions)	**2004**	**2003**
Balance at January 1	$43,879	$37,811
Actual gain on plan assets	4,888	8,203
Employer contributions	102	105
Participant contributions	163	169
Benefits paid	(2,367)	(2,409)
Acquired plans	—	—
Exchange rate adjustments and other	—	—
Balance at December 31	$46,665	$43,879

Required
1.   What is the funding status of GE's principal pension plans in 2003 and 2004? How should this be reflected in GE's financial statements?
2.   GE indicates that it has not contributed to its pension plan since 1987; why?

3. Given GE's actuarial assumptions and the fact that the plan is currently overfunded, is it likely that GE will ever have to contribute to the plan again? Why?
4. How does pension plan overfunding affect firm value?

CORPORATE ANALYSIS

CA10.35 **The Procter and Gamble Company.** The 2005 annual report of The Procter and Gamble Company (P & G) is available at www.pg.com/annualreports/2005/pdf/pg2005annualreport.pdf. After reviewing P & G's annual report, respond to the following questions.

a. Describe P & G's outstanding commitments and contingencies as of June 30, 2005. Does the company consider these commitments and contingencies to be material?

b. P & G lists its income tax expense for 2005 as $3.182 billion. What was the company's effective tax rate for 2005 and how much of the tax expense of $3.182 billion was deferred? P & G discloses deferred income taxes of $1.081 billion as a current asset and deferred income taxes of $2.894 billion as a non-current liability on its 2005 balance sheet. What is the difference between these two accounts (what do they represent)? Why is an increase in P & G's deferred income tax liability consistent with the fact that the company's fixed assets grew from 2004 to 2005?

c. Describe some of P & G's financial instruments and derivatives that it uses to management it various business risks.

d. Describe P & G's postretirement benefit plans for its employees. Evaluate the funding status of the company's defined benefit pension plan in 2005. Is the plan fully-funded relative to the projected benefit obligation (PBO)? If not, how underfunded is this plan relative to the PBO? How much of the underfunding is reported on P & G's balance sheet and how much is carried off-balance-sheet?

CA10.36 **Internet-based Analysis.** Consider a publicly-held company whose products you are familiar with. Some examples might include:

Company	Product	Corporate Website
• Johnson & Johnson Company	• Band-Aids	• www.jnj.com
• Microsoft Corporation	• Windows XP software	• www.microsoft.com
• Nokia Corporation	• Cellular phones	• www.nokia.com
• Intel Corporation	• Pentium processors	• www.intel.com
• Kimberly-Clark Corporation	• Kleenex	• www.kimberly-clark.com

Access the company's public website and search for its most recent annual report. (Some companies provide access to their financial data through an "investor relations" link, while others provide a direct link to their "annual reports.") After locating your company's most recent annual report, open the file and review its contents. After reviewing the annual report for your selected company, prepare answers to the following questions:

1. Review the company's commitments and contingent liabilities footnote. Describe the company's existing commitments. Is the company involved in any litigation? If so, what kind?
2. Does the company have any pension or retirement plans for its employees? If so, are they defined benefit plans or defined contribution plans? Are the plans underfunded or overfunded? If so, by what amount?
3. Does the company use derivatives to hedge its business risks? If so, what kinds of derivatives does it use and what kinds of business risks are being hedged?
4. Does the company have any deferred income taxes on its balance sheet? If so, are the deferred income taxes an asset or a liability? Is the amount of the deferred income tax asset or liability increasing or decreasing? What might explain this increase or decrease?

Chapter Eleven

Equity Financing and Shareholders' Equity

TAKEAWAYS

When you complete this chapter you should be able to:

1. Explain the accounting for share issuances and repurchases.
2. Describe why companies issue stock dividends and how they account for them.
3. Explain the motivation behind forward and reverse stock splits.
4. Describe the components of other comprehensive income as reported on the balance sheet.

Where have we been?	Where are we?	Where are we going?
Chapter 10 described the liabilities' section of the balance sheet. The difference between commitments and contingent liabilities was investigated, along with the deferred income tax liability and how a company's deferred income tax obligation increased or decreased. Finally, the topic of retirement obligations was considered, along with how these liabilities are measured and disclosed.	In this chapter, we complete our investigation of corporate financing decisions by examining how companies raise equity capital. Share issuances and repurchases, as well as such free-share distributions as stock dividends and stock splits are investigated. Finally, the components of other comprehensive income and the controversial topic of employee stock options are examined.	In Chapter 12, we consider how investment professionals value the equity of a firm. We show how to develop pro forma financial statements that provide the basic data for a valuation model. The discounted cash flow approach to firm valuation and the earnings-based residual income approach are then illustrated. We examine how to calculate firm operating value, terminal value, and ultimately, the equity value of a business by discounting a business' future free cash flows and residual income using a firm's cost of equity capital. Comparable-firm valuation using price-earnings multiples is also illustrated.

MICROSOFT CORPORATION   Symbol: MSFT

Microsoft Corporation was founded to develop and sell BASIC interpreters for the Altair 8800 computer. Under the guidance of its former CEO and current Chairman Bill Gates, the company eventually grew to a position of dominance in the computer software industry. Microsoft is now a multinational company with global revenue in excess of $40 billion and over 76,000 employees in 102 countries. Although best known for its Windows operating system and Office productivity suite, Microsoft also sells a wide range of other software. In addition to software, the company markets such home entertainment products as the Xbox, music devices such as Zune, and computer accessories like the Microsoft Mouse. Microsoft is also involved in other endeavors, to include MSNBC cable television.

Microsoft went public in 1986 at a price of $21 per share. Since then, the stock has split nine times such that if you held one of the original IPO shares, you would now own 288 shares of the company. As of early 2007, Microsoft stock was trading at $27 per share, making an original $21 investment worth nearly $8,000 and representing an annual share price appreciation rate in excess of 32 percent.

While Microsoft's share price has performed beyond the expectations of even the most optimistic investor, the company's recent share price performance has lagged since its peak in 1999. Despite the mediocre share price performance in recent years, the same cannot be said of Microsoft's financial performance. Microsoft reported record net income of nearly $12.6 billion and cash flow from operations in excess of $14.4 billion for fiscal year 2006. The following news release on Cnet News.com accompanied Microsoft's 2006 annual report release:

> **Microsoft on Thursday reported earnings that were just ahead of analysts' expectations, as the company announced a plan to buy back as much as an extra $40 billion worth of its stock.** *The software maker said it would buy back $20 billion through a tender offer set to be completed on August 17. The company disclosed that its board of directors had also authorized the company to buy back up to $20 billion worth of stock through June 2011. The company said it has completed the $30 billion stock buyback announced two years ago. "With our share repurchase programs announcement today, we reaffirm our confidence and optimism in the long-term future of the company and continue to execute on our strategy of returning capital to shareholders," Microsoft Chief Financial Officer Chris Liddell said in a statement.*

Why is Microsoft buying back its shares? The following explanation appeared on Fool.com: "When a profitable company generates excess cash flow, one of the best ways to return that cash to shareholders is through a share buyback. If a company knows its shares are undervalued, and who else is in a better position to know whether a company's shares are undervalued, repurchasing shares is a surefire way for the company to create value. And even if a company thinks its shares are overvalued, a share buyback is almost always preferable to a cash dividend considering that dividends are taxed at the marginal individual income tax rate, which can be 30 percent or higher."

Many possible reasons exist for a company's share repurchases in addition to sending a signal to the market that management believes that the company's shares are undervalued. One reason, for example, is to acquire shares to be distributed to employees when they exercise their employee stock options. Buying back shares on the open market rather than issuing new shares to these employees prevents existing outstanding shares from being diluted in value.

In this chapter, we discuss the various types of corporate equity transactions, including share issuances and repurchases, dividends, stock splits and employee stock options.

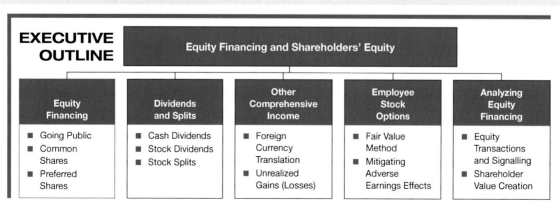

EQUITY FINANCING

Going Public

Small businesses start and grow for many years utilizing financing provided by the business' owners, their family and friends, and occasionally from such external sources as the Small Business Administration, a business development company, a regional bank, or a local "incubator." After a history of operating performance has been established, a small business might find equity funding available through an "angel" investor or possibly a venture capital firm. Only after a firm's business model has been vetted and refined, and a history of operating earnings and cash flow established, will the firm be ready to "go public" through an **initial public offering** (IPO) of its shares. Taking a company public provides the original founders and investors, angel investors, and venture capital investors with an "exit strategy"—that is, a means to gain liquidity by selling some or all of their shareholdings in the business.

Because most businesses do not have direct access to the many individual investors and mutual funds that comprise the capital market (see Chapter 1), companies desiring to go public typically hire an investment advisor or investment banker to assist with the public offering of their shares. Investment advisors and investment bankers have direct access to many potential investors who are their clients. Prior to an IPO, the CEO and CFO of a firm, along with the lead investment advisor for the IPO, will typically go on a "road show" visiting investment professionals, portfolio managers, and other investment bankers in key financial centers around the country. The purpose of the road show is to provide an opportunity for a company to explain and market the firm's business plan and future prospects to financial advisors and investment professionals in hopes that they, in turn, will recommend adding the firm's shares to their clients' investment portfolios.

For a fee, investment bankers advise managers about the appropriate IPO share price, the number of shares to offer for sale, and ultimately, help execute the sale of the firm's shares. Most commonly, IPOs are executed on a **best efforts basis** in which the investment bank attempts to place (sell) all of the shares available for sale but does not guarantee the sale of all available shares. On some occasions, an IPO may be handled on a **firm commitment basis** in which the investment bank agrees to purchase any IPO shares that remain unsold following an IPO. The investment banker's fees for a firm commitment IPO are considerably higher than the fees for a best efforts IPO because of the investment banker bears the risk associated with any unsold shares.

Issuances and Repurchases of Equity

There are two basic forms of equity capital—common (or ordinary) shares and preferred (or preference) shares.

Common Shares

Common shares are the purest form of equity capital and all corporations must have at least one common shareholder. But common shares are also the riskiest form of capital because, in the event the firm liquidates, common shareholders are only paid if there is anything left after paying off all of the other investors in the firm. Thus common shareholders have what is referred to as a **residual interest** in the firm's net assets. With this high risk, however, comes the right to vote for the firm's board of directors and on key corporate governance issues. In most companies, for instance, only common shareholders may vote on such corporate governance matters as the selection of a firm's independent auditors, increasing or decreasing the firm's outstanding equity, whether to offer or amend an executive stock bonus scheme, and whether to approve a

BUSINESS PERSPECTIVE: IPOS AROUND THE WORLD

Historically, the U.S. stock exchanges have attracted the vast majority of the world's initial public offerings (IPOs). Recently, however, as shown in the accompanying graph, IPOs in the U.S. have dropped precipitously. One reason asserted to explain the declining popularity of the U.S. markets is the high regulatory costs imposed by the recently enacted Sarbanes-Oxley Act of 2002 (SOX). For example, in 2006 the largest IPO in history by the Commercial and Industrial Bank of China, scrapped plans to go public in New York citing the high costs of SOX, and instead raised $18.4 billion in Hong Kong. But researchers studying the systematic evidence more carefully, generally conclude that SOX is not the only explanation. Other factors include the increasing quality of foreign stock exchanges as well as changes in the profiles of firms raising capital.* Somewhat related to the decline in IPOs, researchers have also noted a sharp increase in the number of U.S. listed companies fleeing U.S. capital markets by de-listing, or "going dark," since the passage of SOX.**

Percentage of IPOs in the US, Hong Kong, and London

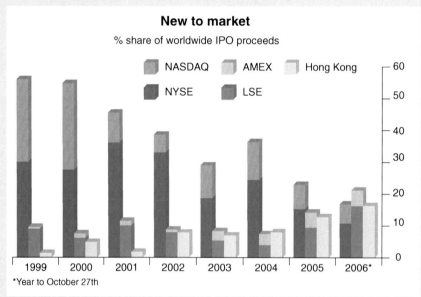

New to market

% share of worldwide IPO proceeds

*Year to October 27th

---

* For example, see Hostak, P., Karaoglu, E,, Lys, T. and Yang, Y,, G., 2007, "An Examination of the Impact of the Sarbanes-Oxley Act on the Attractiveness of US Capital Markets for Foreign Firms", Working paper, Northwestern University, and Piotroski, P., and Srinivasan, S., 2007, "The Sarbanes-Oxley Act and the Flow of International Listings." Working paper, University of Chicago.

** For example, see Engel, E., and Hayes, R., 2007, "The Sarbanes-Oxley Act and Firms' Going Private Decisions." Journal of Accounting and Economics; and Leuz, C., Triantus, A. J., and Wong, T. Y., 2007, "Why do Firms Go Dark? Causes and Economic Consequences of Voluntary SEC Deregistration." Journal of Accounting and Economics.

---

proposed merger or acquisition. The total number of common shares that may be sold by a company is specified in the firm's **charter of incorporation** and is referred to as the **authorized** shares of a firm. When shares are sold, they are said to be **issued**; and, when shares are held by investors they are said to be **outstanding**.

When shares are repurchased by a company with the intent of reissuing them for some future corporate purpose, they are called **treasury shares** and while these shares are no longer outstanding, they are still considered to be issued. Hence, the total number of shares issued is equal to the number of shares outstanding plus any shares held in treasury. Under International Financial Reporting Standards (IFRS) and U.S. GAAP, treasury shares are reported on the balance sheet as a contra-shareholders' equity account; that is, the repurchase cost of any treasury shares is subtracted from total shareholders' equity. In addition, IFRS and U.S. GAAP precludes the recognition of any gain or loss by a company from share transactions involving its own equity. In contrast, some countries such as France and Japan allow treasury shares to be reported on the asset side of the balance sheet as an investment in marketable securities. Under IFRS and U.S. GAAP, treasury shares do not satisfy the definition of an asset, and therefore, cannot be reported as marketable securities. Instead, treasury shares are considered to be equivalent to authorized-but-unissued common shares, which have no value until sold to the investing public.

> Shares which are repurchased without the intent to reissue them are canceled, reducing both the number of shares issued and shares outstanding.

There are several reasons why firms buy back their own shares. Companies that repurchase their own outstanding shares often do so as a means to increase their share price. (In some countries, share buybacks are illegal because they are viewed as a form of price manipulation.) This benefits both the shareholders who retain their shares and former shareholders who sell their shares. The profits on shares sold by investors are often taxed at lower capital gains rates than the rate of taxation on ordinary income. Some companies repurchase their shares to have a sufficient number of shares available to execute an acquisition through a share exchange or to meet the demand for new shares when employees exercise their stock options. Alternatively, some companies repurchase their own shares as a takeover defense, for example, when the company's share price is below its intrinsic value per share. Finally, some companies repurchase their own shares as a means to build shareholder value (the firm has excess cash and a share repurchase is judged to create greater shareholder value than alternative discretionary managerial actions).

Depending upon the securities laws of the state or province of incorporation, a firm will issue either **no-par value** shares or **par value** shares. Par value, sometimes referred to as **stated value**, is a somewhat outdated legal concept that was developed when security markets were largely unregulated, and represents the legal value of a firm's common or preferred shares. It represents the amount of equity capital that cannot be impaired by management (such as paid out in the form of dividends to shareholders) unless a firm is legally restructuring or liquidating itself. In the United States, most shares are now issued without par and because there are no statutes specifying the specific dollar amount of a firm's par value, it is not uncommon to see par values associated with NYSE or NASDAQ-listed shares as low as $0.01 or $.001 per share. In Japan, however, all common shares carry a statutory par value of 50 yen.

When common shares are issued, they are rarely sold at their par value, but instead for some greater amount reflecting the intrinsic value of the firm. **Intrinsic value** refers to the underlying economic value of a business as a going-concern—that is, the value that a business could be sold for in an efficient market. Because intrinsic value is a market-based value, it almost always differs from a firm's **book value**, which is based on the balance sheet value of shareholders' equity.

When shares are sold for an amount greater than their par value, any payment in excess of the par value is placed in a shareholders' equity account called **additional paid-in-capital**, **capital in excess of par value**, **capital surplus**, or the **share premium** account. The total **contributed capital** of a firm is the sum of the par value account and the additional paid-in-capital account. When common shares are issued without a par value, there is no additional paid-in-capital account, and hence, all proceeds from the sale of stock are placed in the common or capital stock account.

In some companies, there may be multiple classes of common shares, often labeled Class A, Class B, Class C, etc. These categories refer either to the **voting rights** of the shares or to the fact that one or

BUSINESS PERSPECTIVE: THE GROWTH IN STOCK REPURCHASES

Stock repurchases were relatively rare in the U.S. until the 1980s, but have mushroomed in recent years, from about $5 billion in 1980 to about $349 billion in 2005. In fact, share repurchases have become so popular that they now account for about half of all cash distributions to shareholders. This means that on an annual basis, companies pay as much to shareholders for stock repurchases as they do as dividends. The accompanying graph shows that combined dividends and stock repurchases more than doubled from 2003 through 2005. One reason for this jump is a 2003 law that reduces the income taxes on payouts to investors.

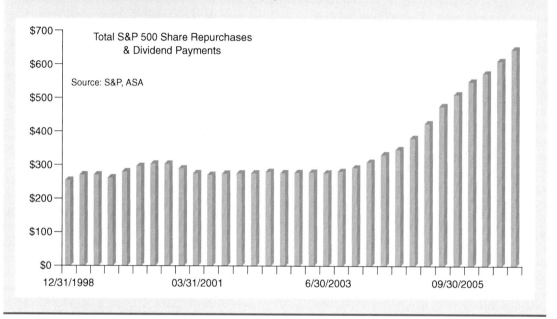

more classes of shares represent **tracking shares**. Class A shares are often the shares issued to the original capital providers of a company (such as the founders of the business, angel investors, and venture capital investors) and may carry voting rights as much as ten to one hundred times greater than the voting rights of Class B shares (one Class A share equals the voting rights of ten Class B shares). In the case of tracking shares, any dividend paid on these shares and their market value are linked to the earnings of a particular operating division of a company—that is, the value of the shares is said to "track" the performance of a specific business unit or division. For example, during the 1990s, **General Motors** had three classes of common shares outstanding—GM, GM-E, and GM-H. The value of the GM common shares was linked to the overall performance of the consolidated company, whereas GM-E and GM-H were tracking shares whose market values were tied to the earnings performance of the EDS and Hughes Aircraft divisions, respectively, of General Motors.

An extreme example of Class A voting power is the **Adolph Coors Company**. The founding Coors' family (and trusts) own 100 percent of the Class A shares of the Adolph Coors Company, whose value is just 3.5 percent of the firm's total market capitalization. Coors Company Class B shares, owned by the public and representing 96.5 percent of firm value, have no voting rights except in the case of a merger; all other issues are decided by the Class A shareholders.

GLOBAL PERSPECTIVE

In some countries, when common shares carry a letter class designation, it is in reference to who may purchase the shares (a citizen of the country or a non-citizen). For instance, in China for many years, Class A shares could only be purchased by Chinese citizens whereas (until 2001) only non-citizens could purchase Class B shares. In 2003, as China began liberalizing its capital markets to facilitate increased foreign investment, its securities laws were relaxed to permit the sale of H shares in Hong Kong, L shares in London, N shares in New York, and S shares in Singapore, available to all foreign investors.

To illustrate the accounting for share issuances and repurchases, consider the following equity transactions for the Ito Company. The Ito Company share transactions are displayed in the spreadsheet below.

1. Ito Company issues 100 shares of $1 par value common stock at an initial market price of $10 per share.
2. Ito Company issues 50 shares of no-par value Class A stock at an initial market price of $6 per share.
3. The market value of the Ito common shares increases to $12 per share.
4. Ito repurchases 30 shares of its common stock at $12 per share.
5. The market value of the Ito common shares increases to $13 per share.
6. Ito reissues 10 shares of its treasury common shares at $13 per share.

The Ito Company Spreadsheet

Transaction	Assets = Cash	Common Stock	Class A Stock	Additional Paid-In-Capital on Common Stock	Treasury Stock
1.	1,000	100		900	
2.	300		300		
3.			No entry		
4.	−360				−360
5.			No entry		
6.	130			10	120

Several items should be noted regarding the accounting for these equity transactions. As illustrated in the first transaction, the recognition of the initial issuance of the $1 par value common stock increases cash by the total proceeds of $1,000 ($10 times 100 shares), increases the common stock account by $100 ($1 par value times 100 shares), and increases the additional paid-in-capital on common stock account by $900, which equals the issuance price per share minus the par value per share times the number of shares issued ([$10 minus $1] times 100 shares). Transaction two reports that the issuance of the no-par class A stock increases cash by the total proceeds of $300 ($6 times 50 shares) and increases the class A stock account by the same amount. Transactions three and five indicate that The Ito Company does not record the changes in the market value of its stock because these changes do not directly impact the firm (although they do impact the firm's shareholders). Transaction four illustrates that treasury stock is recorded in a contra-shareholders' equity account that reduces shareholders' equity by $360 ($12 times 30 shares) and reduces cash by $360. (GAAP allows two different methods to record treasury stock. The method presented here is called the "cost method," and its use is far more widespread than the alternate "stated value method." The stated value method, also known as the "par value method," is described in advanced courses.)

Finally, transaction six reports that the re-issuance of the treasury stock increases cash by the proceeds of $130, removes the 10 treasury shares from the treasury stock account at the price that they were initially purchased at of $120 ($12 times 10 shares), and increases additional paid-in-capital by $10, which equals the difference between the re-issuance price per share minus the original purchase price per share times the number of shares reissued ([$13 minus $12] times 10 shares). If The Ito Company eventually reissues the rest of its treasury stock and the re-issuance price is below its cost of $12 per share, the company first reduces the additional paid-in-capital account for the difference between the re-issuance price and the cost per share, and if the balance in the additional paid-in-capital account is insufficient to absorb the difference, Ito then reduces retained earnings for the remaining amount. For example, if Ito reissues the remaining 20 treasury shares for $9 per share, the transaction increases cash by $180 ($9 times 20 shares), eliminates the remaining balance of $240 ($12 times 20 shares) in the treasury stock account, and reduces additional paid-in-capital by the remaining $$60 ($240 minus $180). If the additional-paid-in-capital account were less than $60, the difference would reduce retained earnings.

Preferred shares

Preferred shares, or preference shares, take their name from the fact that this form of equity is legally entitled to receive dividends before any dividends are paid on the common stock. Unlike common stock, preferred stock receives a periodic fixed dividend, and in the event that the firm liquidates, is paid before the common shareholders. These "preferences" come at a cost, however, in that preferred shares rarely carry the right to vote at shareholder meetings. Further, since the market value of preferred shares is more closely linked to the amount of their fixed dividend payments than to the financial performance of the issuing company, preferred shares rarely experience the share price appreciation that characterize common shares. For these reasons, investment professionals frequently treat preferred shares as a quasi-form of debt, often as part of a firm's **mezzanine financing**. Preferred or preference shares may also have a number of economically important investment features. For example, some preferred shares are **convertible** into common shares at a predetermined share conversion ratio. Preferred shares may also be **participating**, in which case if a company declares a special dividend for the common shareholders, the participating preferred shareholder will share in the special dividend. Some preferred shares are **cumulative**, in which case if a regular dividend is not paid, the company will maintain a record of any unpaid dividends and the cumulative preferred shareholder must be paid the previously unpaid dividends before any new regular dividends can be distributed. An unpaid cumulative dividend is called a **dividend-in-arrears** and represents a contingent liability to the firm that is disclosed in the footnotes to the financial statements. Finally, some preferred shares are **callable**. A callable preferred share is one that can be mandatorily redeemed, or "called," by the issuing

> Preferred shares are frequently referred to as **mezzanine financing** along with the subordinated debt of a business. The concept of mezzanine financing takes its name from the fact that this type of financing is less risky than pure equity financing but is more risky than secured debt financing (bank debt)—that is, mezzanine financing falls somewhere in the middle of the risk continuum. Although accounted for as shareholders' equity on the balance sheet, many investment professionals consider preferred stock to be equivalent to debt for financial analysis purposes.

> The share **conversion ratio** of convertible preferred shares (or convertible bonds and notes) into common shares is established at the time the securities are originally issued. The ratio, however, may be subsequently changed in the event that a firm undergoes a stock split. Changing the share conversion ratio following a forward stock split, for instance, protects the convertible preferred shareholder against the dilutive effect of the split.

company. Companies which issue callable preferred shares often attach a conversion feature to the shares, creating callable convertible preferred stock, to enable preferred shareholders to convert their shares into a company's common shares in the event that the preferred shares are called by the issuing company.

BUSINESS PERSPECTIVE: SHAREHOLDERS' EQUITY DISCLOSURES

The shareholders' equity section of the balance sheet for the General Motors Corporation is below:

December 31 ($ millions)	2005	2004
Shareholders' Equity		
$1 2/3 par value common stock (outstanding 565.5 million and 565.1 million shares)	$ 943	$ 942
Capital surplus (principally additional paid-in-capital)	15,285	15,241
Retained earnings	2,361	14,062
Subtotal	18,589	30,245
Accumulated other comprehensive loss	(3,992)	(2,885)
Total shareholders' equity	$14,597	$27,360

GM's shareholders' equity section reveals that the company had 565.5 million shares of $1 2/3 par value common stock outstanding at year-end 2005. GM's total contributed capital at year-end 2005 amounted to over $16.2 billion ($0.943 + $15.285), whereas its earned capital (or retained earnings) amounted to $2.361 billion. Although the company's book value, or shareholders' equity, totaled $14.597 billion in 2005, its market value, or market capitalization, exceeded $15 billion (565.5 million shares outstanding times $26.57 per share). The difference between these two amounts emphasizes the distinction between a company's book value and its market capitalization—the former reflects the company's past performance whereas the latter reflects the market's expectations regarding the firm's future performance. The final component of GM's shareholders' equity is the Accumulated Other Comprehensive Loss, a subsection of shareholders' equity, which is discussed later in this chapter.

DIVIDENDS

Cash Dividends

As a means to attract investor interest in a company, some companies pay a **regular dividend** on their equity shares. In the case of preferred shares, regular dividends are paid at a fixed rate, much like interest on a bond. In the case of common shares, however, the dividend rate may change over time as a company's performance and operating cash flows increase or decrease. Dividend-paying companies are frequently evaluated by investors on the basis of their **dividend yield**—that is, the dividend paid per share divided by the market price per share. It is noteworthy that dividends on equity shares are never guaranteed; they must be formally approved and declared each fiscal

As a general rule, companies that are considered to be "growth companies" rarely pay dividends on their common shares. Instead, these companies use their available operating cash flow to fund their growth. As the rate of revenue growth declines, companies will often begin to pay dividends as a means to retain their shareholders. Companies which pay large amounts of their earnings out as dividends are often referred to as "mature companies," having little or no revenue growth opportunities other than that caused by inflation or normal market expansion.

period by a company's board of directors. In addition, dividends are never a liability of the firm until such time as they are declared.

Once a dividend has been declared by the board of directors, a **record date** and a **distribution date** are established. To receive a dividend, a shareholder must own the shares on the record date, which is typically four to six weeks after a dividend has been declared by the board of directors. Subsequent to the record date, a stock is said to be "ex-dividend;" that is, the stock is sold without the right to receive the latest declared dividend. The distribution date—that is, the date on which any dividend is actually paid—is approximately two weeks following the record date.

Since the payment of a cash dividend can affect the market price of a stock, dividend changes are approached cautiously by the board of directors. Dividend increases, for example, are rarely instituted unless a firm's projected discretionary cash flows are sufficient to sustain the dividend increase for the foreseeable future. Dividend decreases, on the other hand, are received poorly by equity investors, often interpreted as a negative "signal" about a firm's future prospects. An announced reduction in a firm's dividend is typically accompanied by a dramatic drop in share price, and thus, dividend reductions are avoided at all costs by most firms.

> The **dividend payout ratio** is a measure of the amount of dividends paid by a firm relative to its current net income (dividend-per-share divided by earnings-per-share). A related ratio is the **Dividend yield**, calculated as follows: Dividend paid per share/Market price per share. A common misperception is that dividend-paying companies attempt to maintain a stable payout ratio. In reality, dividend-paying companies determine the dividend to be paid on the basis of their sustainable discretionary cash flow, and not net income.

Dividend increases, on the other hand, are typically accompanied by only modest increases in share price. Since growth companies rarely pay dividends—that is, growth companies reinvest all available cash to fuel continued growth—an increase in a firm's dividend could be interpreted by the equity market as a negative signal about a firm's future prospects. For example, an increase in a firm's dividend may signal that a firm is no longer a growth company or that its industry is no longer a growth industry. To many investors, a dividend increase is a signal from management that they believe that shareholders have investment opportunities superior to those of the company (such as because of slowing industry or firm growth). Hence, under this scenario, a dividend increase is intended to maximize shareholder wealth by distributing cash directly to investors and enabling them to invest in their superior return-generating opportunities.

Occasionally, a firm facing a limited investment opportunity set, but with large amounts of available cash on hand, will pay its shareholders a **special dividend**. A special dividend is a one-time distribution of cash unrelated to a stock's regular dividend. A special dividend may be distributed to avoid an unwanted takeover bid or to maximize shareholder value when management believes that shareholders have superior investment opportunities. For example, by 1998 the **Ford Motor Company** had accumulated over $22 billion in cash on its balance sheet. With few acquisition opportunities available—Ford had already acquired Jaguar, Volvo, and, Land Rover—and since any further automotive acquisitions would likely have encountered antitrust opposition from the both the U.S. Federal Trade Commission and the EU Competition Commission, Ford distributed its excess cash to shareholders as a special dividend of $21.09 per share.

When a company pays a dividend, the share price of the dividend-paying company typically falls by an amount approximately equal to the value of the dividend. For example, in 2004 the **MGM Company** paid its shareholders a special dividend of $8.00 per share. On the day prior to the ex-dividend date, the shares of MGM traded at $20.12 per share. On the ex-dividend date, the price of the shares dropped to $12.18, a decline equal to 99 percent of the special dividend. The share price decline following a special dividend payout may actually exceed the value of the dividend if the market perceives the payout as being

BUSINESS PERSPECTIVE: ALL IN THE FAMILY

The equity ownership structure of U.S. and U.K. public companies is characterized by small diffuse investors, each of whom owns only a small fraction of the firm. But the ownership structure of public companies in most of the rest of the world is strikingly different, and is characterized by the presence of a large investor who holds a controlling interest in the company's stock. These large owners usually consist of families and are typically directly involved in managing the company's operations. The accompanying graph reports the percentage of public companies in seven East Asian countries that are controlled by families. It indicates that more than fifty percent of the public companies in each country are controlled by families and that South Korea has the highest with nearly 80 percent.

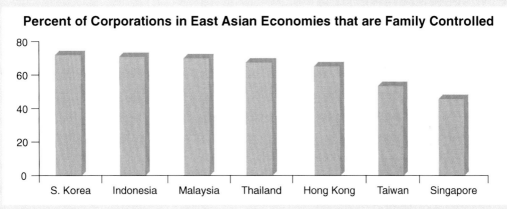

This difference in ownership structure mean that public companies in the U.S. and U.K. have a somewhat different "agency" problems than companies in the rest of the world. While the agency problem for U.S. and U.K. firms involves conflicts of interest between the managers and outside owners, the agency problem in the rest of the world involves conflicts between the large insider-owners and the small minority shareholders.*

Source: Fan, J., and Wong, T. J., 2002. Corporate ownership structure and the informativeness of accounting earnings in East Asia. *Journal of Accounting and Economics.*

so large as to impede the firm's future performance. Similarly, the share price decline following a dividend payout may be less than the value of the dividend if the market perceives the cash outflow as unlikely to adversely impact the firm's future operating performance.

Regular or special cash dividends are a distribution of earned income that is accounted for by reducing both the cash account and retained earnings on the balance sheet. Although interest, the cost of debt financing, is considered to be an expense, dividends, or the cost of equity financing, are not. This differential treatment of the cost of debt and the cost of equity financing reflects the fact that the income statement is prepared from the perspective of a company's shareholders, before any distributions of earnings are made to shareholders.

Free Share Distributions

Investors in publicly-held corporations may obtain their ownership interest by purchasing shares of stock through a firm's initial public offering, a secondary public offering, or by buying the shares from another investor on the open market. Sometimes a company will distribute additional shares of stock to its existing shareholders via a **free share distribution**. Free share distributions occur in two forms—a stock dividend and a stock split. Free share distributions take their name from the fact that investors receive the additional shares without having to pay for them.

Stock Dividends

Cash dividends—that is, a distribution of a firm's earned income—commonly occur as a regular or special dividend to shareholders. Occasionally, a business may distribute a **property dividend** to its share-holders by giving them the product (or a coupon for the product) that the firm produces. For example, **McDonald's Holdings Company (Japan) Ltd.** gives its shareholders a coupon book good for several free "Big Macs." Since customers at a McDonald's restaurant rarely eat just a sandwich, often also ordering French fries and a drink, it may be surmised that McDonald's property dividend is also intended to generate incremental food sales.

> Beverage maker **DyDo Drinco Inc.** mails to its shareholders an annual property dividend of its coffee and other beverages. Companies which distribute property dividends generally believe that this encourages their shareholders to retain their shares by becoming more informed about the company's products.

When a firm desires to reward its shareholders with a dividend but also desires to preserve its operating cash, it may resort to the distribution of a **stock dividend**—that is, the distribution of additional shares of common stock in proportion to the shares already owned by shareholders. For instance, if a firm declares a ten percent stock dividend, the number of new shares to be distributed to shareholders is equal to ten percent of the shares outstanding prior to the free share distribution.

It is important to observe that a firm is not transferring anything of value to the shareholders in a "free" share distribution. While the shareholders hold a larger number of shares after receiving a stock dividend, the value of the shareholders' investment is unchanged. While there is some variation in the way managers account for stock dividends, the most common treatment is to reduce retained earnings by the market value of the distributed shares, increase the common stock account by the par value of the distributed shares, and increase the additional paid-in-capital account by the excess of market value above par value.

For example, consider the case of the Julius Company, with ten million shares outstanding, a par value of $1 per share and a market value of $12 per share. If Julius declares a ten percent stock dividend it will issue an additional 1 million shares to its shareholders (10% times 10 million shares). To account for this stock dividend Julius decreases the retained earnings account by $12 million (1 million shares times $12 market value per share), increases the common stock account by $1 million (1 million shares times $1 par value), and increases the additional paid-in-capital account by $11 million, which equals the difference between the decrease in the retained earnings account and the increase in the additional paid-in-capital account ($12 million minus $1 million). Thus, following a stock dividend, Julius's total shareholders' equity balance remains unchanged, while its retained earnings account declines by the fair value of the distributed shares and the paid-in-capital accounts (common stock at par value plus additional paid-in-capital) increase by the same amount. By transferring the market value of the distributed shares from retained earnings to paid-in capital, the accounting treatment for stock dividends permanently capitalizes a portion of Julius' retained earnings.

Because nothing of value is transferred to the shareholders, the stock's price per share following a stock dividend should fall exactly proportionately to the size of the stock dividend. Empirical evidence indicates, however, that the announcement of a stock dividend results in an increase in share price. One explanation for this increase in shareholder value is that by permanently capitalizing a portion of retained earnings, stock dividends signal to the market that managers expect greater future growth than previously reported.[1]

When stock dividends are proportionally quite large—that is, when the quantity of the distributed shares is 25 percent or more of the existing number of outstanding shares—it is the standing policy of the New York Stock Exchange (and other stock exchanges) that the stock dividend be accounted for in the same way as a stock split, to which we now turn.

Stock Splits

Stock splits are used to both increase and decrease the number of outstanding shares, and hence, the market price per share. A **forward stock split**, for example, increases the number of outstanding shares, whereas a **reverse stock split** reduces the number of outstanding shares.

A forward stock split is used principally to lower the market value of a stock. For example, in January 2003, **Microsoft Corporation** announced a two-for-one split of its common stock. Prior to the split, the firm's shares traded at $48.30 per share. Immediately following the split, the stock traded at $24.96 per share, almost exactly one-half of its prior market value (see bolded area in Exhibit 11.1). Previously, Microsoft had split its stock on eight other occasions. Thus, an original IPO investor in Microsoft with one share of common stock would now own the equivalent of 288 post-split shares, having an aggregate market value in excess of $7,000. (Microsoft originally went public in 1986 at $21.00 per share, with a par value of $.01).

At $7,000 per share (Microsoft's pre-split value per share), only institutional and wealthy investors could afford to buy Microsoft's stock. Thus, the purpose of a forward split is to lower a firm's share price to a price range affordable by most investors. Most stock exchanges charge the lowest transaction fees when shares are purchased or sold in "round lots"—that is, in lots of 100 shares. Thus, to receive the lowest transaction cost per share, a Microsoft investor would need to be able to invest $700,000 in the company's shares if they were trading at $7,000 per share, an amount beyond the means of most individual investors.

EXHIBIT 11.1	**Microsoft's History of Forward Stock Splits**				
				Share Price	
Date of Forward Stock Split		**Stock Split Ratio**	**Par Value After Split**	**Before Split**	**After Split**
September, 1987		2:1	$.005	$114.50	$53.50
April, 1990		2:1	.00025	120.75	60.75
June, 1991		3:2	.00016667	100.75	68.00
June, 1992		3:2	.000111111	112.50	75.75
May, 1994.		2:1	.00005556	97.75	50.63
December, 1996		2:1	.000025[1]	152.88	81.75
February, 1998		2:1	.000025[2]	155.13	81.63
March, 1999		2:1	.0000125	178.13	92.38
February, 2003		2:1	.00000625	48.30	24.96

[1] Rounded from 0.0000277
[2] Stock split effected as a stock dividend

---

[1] G. Rankine and K. Stice, "Accounting Rules and the Signaling Properties of 20% Stock Dividends," *The Accounting Review*, (1997).

BUSINESS PERSPECTIVE: BERKSHIRE HATHAWAY

A contrary example to those firms which use forward stock splits as a means to lower a firm's share price to a trading range affordable by most investors is Berkshire Hathaway. The company's Class A common stock trades on the NYSE at approximately $108,000 per share and may be the most expensive price for a single share of stock worldwide. The company's CEO, Warren Buffett, does not believe in the notion of stock splits or stock dividends; however, to make the Berkshire Hathaway shares affordable by small investors, the company issued a Class B share, with voting rights equal to 1/100 of the company's Class A common shares. The Class B shares trade at approximately $3,800 per share, still expensive for most individual investors.

The traditional accounting for a forward stock split is to proportionally lower the par value of the stock to compensate for the increase in the quantity of shares outstanding. Hence, if a company executes a two-for-one stock split when its par value is $.01, the number of shares outstanding will double and its par value will halve to $.005 per share. Following a stock split, the total par value of the firm is unchanged although the market value of the firm, and of a share of stock, may actually increase. Forward stock splits, like stock dividends, are frequently viewed by the market as a favorable signal about a firm's future operating prospects, and thus, the post-split share price tends to drift upward in anticipation of subsequent favorable corporate news.[2]

A reverse stock split, on the other hand, is used principally to raise the market value of a company's common stock. Consider, for example, the case of Titanium Metals Corporation. Titanium Metals Corporation is an integrated manufacturer of titanium sponge, the basic form of titanium metal used in processed titanium products. A major use of titanium metal is in the construction of aircraft. Prior to the terrorist attack on the New York City World Trade Center in September 2001, Titanium Metals' shares traded at approximately $15 per share. In the days following September 11, 2001, Titanium Metals' share price fell to less than $3 per share, eventually falling to less than $1, as the demand for commercial aircraft, and hence titanium, declined. In early 2003, Titanium Metals announced a one-for-ten reverse split. Earlier the company had been informed by the New York Stock Exchange that since its share price had traded below $1 per share for more than 30 consecutive days, its shares were in danger of being de-listed. Hence, one reason why some firms attempt to raise their share price is to avoid stock exchange de-listing. When a company's shares are de-listed, shareholders face a liquidity crisis in that it is extremely difficult to find buyers for unlisted shares.

> Most stock exchanges maintain a minimum listing price. In the event that a firm's share price falls below the minimum listing price for a consecutive period of time, usually 30 days or more, the shares may be de-listed. Exchange de-listed shares may, and usually do, trade in the over-the-counter market.

Another reason that some firms attempt to raise their share price through a reverse stock split involves the stock "screens" used by many institutional investors and mutual fund managers. There are over 20,000 publicly-traded companies in the U.S., and thus, portfolio managers need an approach to narrow the universe of companies that they consider for their portfolio selections. One way that mutual fund managers constrain the set of firms they evaluate is by the use of "screens," and one such screen is a minimum share price. Many institutional investors and mutual fund managers do not consider companies as potential investments whose share price is consistently below $5 per share (unless, of course, the mutual fund specializes in "low price" stocks). To be sure that mutual fund managers consider a firm's shares for possible purchase and inclusion in their portfolio, some companies execute a reverse split to get their share price

---

[2] R.M. Conroy and R.S. Harris, "Stock Splits and Information: The Role of Share Price," *Financial Management*, 1999.

In Practice 11.1 *Stock Splits: A Glimpse of a Sample of Fortune 1000 Companies* The following chart identifies the stock split ratios disclosed by a sample of 600 *Fortune 1000* companies. The most commonly executed split is a 2-for-1 split:

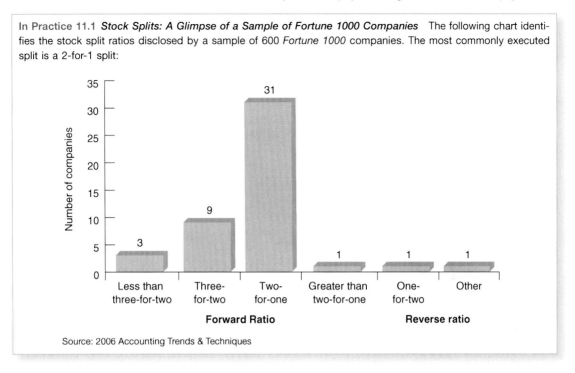

Source: 2006 Accounting Trends & Techniques

above the $5 screen threshold. Stocks whose share price is below the price threshold don't attract institutional investors whose buying in large blocks often drives up share prices.

OTHER COMPREHENSIVE INCOME

Under U.S. GAAP, companies are required to report various increases and decreases in shareholder wealth that have not yet been realized, and thus, not yet reported on the income statement, as a component of shareholders' equity on the balance sheet called other comprehensive income. Examples of such wealth changes which are not reportable as income include:

- Foreign currency translation adjustments
- Minimum pension liability adjustments
- Unrealized gains (losses) on available-for-sale marketable securities
- Unrealized gain (losses) on financial derivatives

As discussed in Chapter 8, when a firm maintains operations in a foreign country, the translated value of those foreign operations will fluctuate as the exchange rate between the currencies of the two countries fluctuates. These unrealized changes in value of the foreign operations are accumulated in a shareholders' equity account on the consolidated balance sheet called the cumulative foreign currency translation adjustment account, or more commonly, the CTA. To illustrate, consider the case of General Motors Corporation, a U.S.-based automotive company with global operations. As of year-end 2004, the value of General Motors' overseas operations had decreased by $1.194 billion as compared to the cost basis of its original investment due to currency fluctuations (see bolded area in Exhibit 11.2). By year-end 2005, the unrealized loss in value was $1.722 billion. Thus, from 2004 to 2005, as a consequence of the increase in the U.S. dollar relative to the foreign currencies of the countries in which GM maintained overseas operations, the value of General Motors' foreign operations declined by $528 million. If General Motors were to liquidate those foreign investments at exchange rates characteristic of year-end 2005 and repatriate those monies back to the U.S., the firm could expect to realize a loss of as much as $1.722 billion. Until that unlikely event (until the loss is actually realized), GM is required to disclose the magnitude of the potential wealth decline on its balance sheet as part of its Other Comprehensive Income.

In Chapter 10, the accounting for retirement obligations was discussed. It was noted that, under U.S. GAAP, companies with under-funded pension plans—that is, a retirement plan in which the present value of the future employee retirement benefits exceeds the value of the pension plan assets—are required to record a liability, called the **minimum pension liability**, for the amount of the under-funding. In some instances, the offsetting balance sheet effect to the minimum liability is the creation of a contra-shareholders' equity account called the **minimum pension liability adjustment**. In the case of General Motors, Exhibit 11.2 reveals that the company's minimum pension liability adjustment amounted to $3,789 million as of year-end 2005, having increased by $758 million from 2004 to 2005. These amounts represent unrealized wealth declines for GM because the disclosed amount has not yet been paid into the GM pension fund nor expensed against the firm's earnings. In essence, the wealth decline remains unrealized until GM satisfies its pension obligation by actually contributing the cash to its pension fund.

In Chapter 8, the accounting for marketable securities was discussed. At that time it was noted that under U.S. GAAP, equity investments classified as "available-for-sale" are valued at their fair market value, with any increase (decrease) in value reflected as part of Other Comprehensive Income as long as the securities remain unsold, and hence, the wealth gain (loss) unrealized. Exhibit 11.2 reveals that General Motors had an unrealized gain on its available-for-sale marketable securities of $786 million as of year-end 2005 and that the unrealized gain increased by $35 million from 2004 to 2005.

EXHIBIT 11.2	Other Comprehensive Income Disclosures		
General Motors Corporation			
December 31 ($ millions)	**2005**	**2004**	**Change**
Accumulated foreign currency translation adjustment	$(1,722)	$(1,194)	$ (528)
Net unrealized losses on derivatives	733	589	144
Net unrealized gains on securities	786	751	35
Minimum pension liability adjustment	(3,789)	(3,031)	(758)
Accumulated other comprehensive income (loss)	$(3,992)	$(2,885)	$(1,107)

Finally, in Appendix 10B, the accounting for financial instruments and derivatives was discussed. It was noted that such instruments should be valued at their fair market value and that any increase (decrease) in their market value above their original cost should be reported on the balance sheet as part of other comprehensive income. As long as the financial instruments remain outstanding, no gain or loss need be reported on the income statement until such time as the instrument expires or is eliminated. Exhibit 11.2 reveals that GM had $733 million in unrealized gains on derivative securities at year-end 2005 and that the unrealized gain increased by $144 million since 2004.

In Practice 11.2 *Other Comprehensive Income Components: A Glimpse of a Sample of Fortune 1000 Companies* The following graph identifies the components of Other Comprehensive Income disclosed by a sample of 600 *Fortune 1000* companies. The most commonly disclosed component was the cumulative translation adjustment:

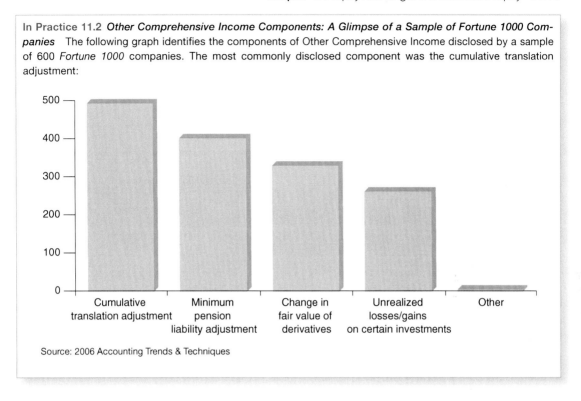

Source: 2006 Accounting Trends & Techniques

In aggregate, Exhibit 11.2 reveals that GM's unrealized losses exceeded its unrealized gains by $3,992 million as of year-end 2005. If all of the unrealized gains and losses disclosed as other comprehensive income in Exhibit 11.2 were realized, GM's pretax net income would decline by $3.992 billion, a massive business loss even by GM's standard.

EMPLOYEE STOCK OPTIONS

An important component of the compensation of many corporate employees is the annual stock option grant. In 2005, for example, **Apple Computer** CEO Steven Jobs received a salary of only $1 and no bonus, although he also received stock options valued at nearly $6 million.

Stock options grant employees the right to buy a company's common shares at a fixed price (the strike price or exercise price) within a specified period of time. A typical employee stock option does not vest—that is, it is not exercisable by the employee—for a number of years, often as long as five to ten years, cannot be sold or transferred, and is ultimately valuable only if the firm's common share price rises above the option strike price.

During the 1990s, stock options became an integral part of employee compensation packages in the U.S. as companies tried to more closely align the shareholder goal of wealth maximization with the employee goal of increased compensation. And, since option exercise prices are typically set at the share's market price at the time of granting, an option is worthless to an employee unless their efforts are successful in raising the company's share price above its strike price. Because employee stock options have no immediate or **intrinsic value** (they are issued "at the money"), and in any case, can't be exercised for

BUSINESS PERSPECTIVE: STATEMENT OF SHAREHOLDERS' EQUITY

The fourth basic financial statement is the statement of shareholders' equity. This statement summarizes the changes during the year of each component of the shareholders' equity section of the balance sheet. Presented below is General Motor's 2005 statement of shareholders' equity and reveals the 2004 and 2005 ending balances of each of GM's shareholders' equity components—common stock, capital surplus, retained earnings, and accumulated other comprehensive income. GM's total shareholders' equity decreased by $12.763 billion from $27.360 billion in 2004 to $14.597 billion in 2005. This $12.763 billion decrease is shown in the statement of shareholders' equity to be made up of (a) a $1 million increase in total capital stock from shares issued, (b) a $44 million increase in capital surplus from shares issued ($102 million) less stock options ($58 million), (c) a $11.701 billion decrease in retained earnings attributable to a $10.567 billion operating loss and a $1.134 billion cash dividend, and (d) a $1.107 billion decrease in accumulated other comprehensive income discussed earlier in the chapter.

General Motors Corporation and Subsidiaries
Consolidated Statements of Shareholders' Equity
For Years Ended December 31, 2005, 2004, and 2003

(Dollars in millions)	Total Capital Stock	Capital Surplus	Comprehensive Income (Loss)	Retained Earnings	Accumulated Other Comprehensive Income (Loss)	Total Stockholders' Equity
Balance at January 1, 2003	$1,032	$21,583		$ 9,629	$(25,832)	$ 6,412
Shares issued	16	1,324	—	—	—	1,340
Net income	—	—	$ 3,859	3,859	—	3,859
Other comprehensive income						
Foreign currency translation	—	—	969	—	—	—
Unrealized gains on derivatives	—	—	256	—	—	—
Unrealized gains on securities	—	—	246	—	—	—
Minimum pension liability adjustment	—	—	20,755	—	—	—
Other comprehensive income	—	—	22,226	—	22,226	22,226
Comprehensive income	—	—	26,085	—	—	—
Effect of Hughes transactions	(111)	(8,056)				(8,167)
Stock Options		334				334
Delphi spin-off adjustment (a)	—	—		20	—	20
Cash dividends	—	—		(1,121)	—	(1,121)
Balance at December 31, 2003	937	15,185		12,387	(3,606)	24,903
Shares issued	5	138		—	—	143
Net income	—	—	2,804	2,804	—	2,804
Other comprehensive income						
Foreign currency translation	—	—	621	—	—	—
Unrealized gains on derivatives	—	—	538	—	—	—
Unrealized gains on securities	—	—	133	—	—	—
Minimum pension liability adjustment	—	—	(571)	—	—	—
Other comprehensive income	—	—	721	—	721	721
Comprehensive income	—	—	3,525	—	—	—
Stock Options		(82)				(82)
Cash dividends	—	—		(1,129)	—	(1,129)
Balance at December 31, 2004	942	15,241		14,062	(2,885)	27,360
Shares issued	1	102		—	—	103
Net (loss) income	—	—	(10,567)	(10,567)	—	(10,567)
Other comprehensive income						
Foreign currency translation	—	—	(528)	—	—	—
Unrealized gains on derivatives	—	—	144	—	—	—
Unrealized gains on securities	—	—	35	—	—	—
Minimum pension liability adjustment	—	—	(758)	—	—	—
Other comprehensive income	—	—	(1,107)	—	(1,107)	(1,107)
Comprehensive income	—	—	$(11,674)	—	—	—
Stock Options		(58)				(58)
Cash dividends	—	—		(1,134)	—	(1,134)
Balance at December 31, 2005	$ 943	$15,285		$ 2,361	$(3,992)	$ 14,597

years, the traditional accounting treatment was to ignore the options for financial statement purposes—that is, the options were described in the footnotes to the financial statements but were not actually reflected in the financial statements. This accounting approach, called the intrinsic value method, was quite controversial since it was believed by many investment professionals that stock options have a fair value at the time of granting since there is an expected value associated with the possibility that the options will be exerciseable at a profit in the future when, and if, the share price increases. The FASB concluded that stock options represented a real employee compensation cost to the firm and proposed that the options be expensed in the period in which they were granted. This proposal met with stiff opposition from the business community, and consequently, the proposal was defeated (recall the discussion from Chapter 1). The topic of expensing employee stock options resurfaced, however, following the accounting scandals at Enron and WorldCom, where some attributed the fraudulent activity of management at least in part to the earnings' management incentives provided by their stock options.

The FASB's proposal to expense stock options met with particularly strong opposition from companies in the high tech industry. High tech companies are some of the biggest stock option users and executives in this industry argued that expensing stock options would dramatically reduce their profitability. For example, if Apple computer had been forced to expense stock options in 2003, instead of reporting earnings of $0.19 per share, they would have reported a loss of $0.27 per share! In response to claims that lower reported profits would hurt the competitiveness of U.S. businesses and cost jobs, the House of Representatives passed HR 3574 in 2004, a bill that outlawed the FASB from requiring companies to expense stock options. While the bill ultimately failed to become law, its existence demonstrates the political nature of accounting standard setting.

Internationally, the prevailing view has been that despite the fact that employee stock options are rarely granted "in the money," the options are valuable because they may assume significant future value for an employee if, and when, the share price rises. As a consequence, both the IASB and the FASB mandated that, effective 2005, companies granting employee stock options must estimate the fair market value of the options at the time of granting and deduct that value as employee compensation expense on a

BUSINESS PERSPECTIVE: CISCO SYSTEMS, INC.

The impact on the income statement of expensing stock options using the fair value method required under FAS 123R can be quite significant. To illustrate, consider the case of Cisco Systems, Inc., a worldwide leader in networking hardware and software for the internet. The following table presents Cisco's earnings per share both with and without the cost associated with issuing employee stock options. The cost of employee stock options represents as much as $0.15 to $0.24 per share of the firm's total EPS from 2000 to 2003, or approximately 42 to 65 percent of Cisco's net earnings. Thus, it is clear that Cisco's employee stock options had a material impact on the firm's reported performance. For the period 2000 to 2003, Cisco reported the financial impact of its employee stock options in its footnotes but not as an expense on its income statement.

| | Net Income Per Share | | |
Effect of Stock Options on Reported Net Income (Fiscal Year)	As Reported	After Stock Option Expense	Difference
2000	$ 0.36	$ 0.21	(0.15)
2001	(0.14)	(0.38)	(0.24)
2002	0.25	0.05	(0.20)
2003	0.50	0.32	(0.18)

Source: U.S. Securities and Exchange filings

straight-line basis over the vesting period. This accounting method is known as the fair value method and became U.S. GAAP with the adoption of FAS 123R in 2005.

Although stock options must now be expensed, controversy remains over how to measure an option's fair value. Two widely used approaches to estimate the value of employee stock options are the **Black-Sholes model** and the **binomial model**.[3] Although easier to apply, the Black-Sholes model does not consider the likelihood that changes in a stock's market price will influence the timing of when employees exercise their options. As a consequence, the binomial model is becoming more widely used. Consider, for example, the **American International Group, Inc.** (AIG). AIG disclosed that in 2002, it changed the method it used to value its employee stock options from the Black-Sholes approach to the binomial approach. By switching methods, AIG was able to lower its option expense by $30 million in 2000 and by $18 million in 2001. In 2002, the company deducted $140 million as its cost of granting options under the binomial method, a savings of $30 million as compared to the Black-Sholes method. In 2007, the U.S. Securities and Exchange Commission approved a new approach to value employee stock options called ESOARS, or employee stock option appreciation rights securities. ESOARS use an auction process to assign value to employee stock options. Recently, **Google Inc.** announced that it would use an online auction process to enable its employees to trade, and hence value, their stock options granted by the company.

In the response to the requirement that the cost of employee stock options be immediately expensed, a study by **New Constructs** research firm found that many firms affected by the new accounting requirement attempted to mitigate the adverse earnings effect of the new accounting by altering the projected volatility assumptions used in their option pricing models.[4] The research study found that over 20 percent of the Russell 1,000 companies changed their model volatility assumptions in 2004 to reduce the adverse earnings effect associated with recognizing the cost of employee stock options. The volatility assumption change refers to the degree to which the price of a company's shares fluctuate in the capital market. For some companies, the effect of the volatility assumption change reduced the negative earnings effect of expensing employee stock options by 50 percent (such as see **Echostar Communications** in In Practice 11.3).

In Practice 11.3 *Reducing the Adverse Earnings Effect of Employee Stock Option Expensing*

Company	EPS 2004	Adverse Earnings Affect		Percentage Change
		Before Assumption Change	After Assumption Change	
Echostar Communications.............	$0.46	$0.08	$0.04	50%
Edison International	2.81	0.17	0.07	47
Lexmark International.................	4.38	0.41	0.25	39
XTO Energy	2.03	0.29	0.20	31

Source: New Constructs

---

[3] F. Black and M. Scholes, "The Pricing of Options and Corporate Liabilities," *Journal of Political Economy*, 1973.
[4] E. MacDonald, "A Volatile Brew," *Forbes*, August 1, 2005.

BUSINESS PERSPECTIVE: THE BACKDATING SCANDAL

In 2004, finance Professor David Lie at the University of Iowa published research reporting that the option grant dates of many U.S. corporations happened to coincide with the day of the year in which the stock was at its annual low. This research was followed by a series of investigative articles in the Wall Street Journal in 2006 that alleged large numbers of U.S. companies were deceptively "backdating" their option grant dates. An example is United Health, a large managed health care company. United Health reported that it granted 250,000 options to its CEO in October 1999 when the stock was selling at $35 per share, and hence assigned a $35 exercise price to the options (see the accompanying graph). With a grant date and exercise price both equaling $35 per share, the options have an intrinsic value of zero, and the proper accounting is to make no adjustments to the books. In 2006, however, the SEC and the Internal Revenue Service launched investigations into allegations that the options were actually granted in December 1999, when the stock was trading at $85 per share. If true, the stock options actually had an intrinsic value of $30 million ($85 minus $30, times 250,000 options) and the proper accounting is to increase compensation expenses by $30 million, an event that also has tax consequences. As of this writing, the SEC has opened investigations of more than 130 companies suspected of backdating their executive stock options.

United Healthcare's 1999 Share Price Performance

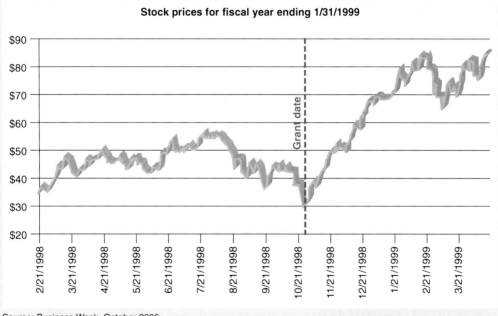

Stock prices for fiscal year ending 1/31/1999

Source: Business Week, October 2006

ANALYZING EQUITY FINANCING AND SHAREHOLDERS' EQUITY

The analysis of equity transactions requires a substantial amount of judgment on the part of financial statement users. As discussed in this chapter, there are multiple reasons why a firm may elect to engage in transactions like share buybacks or dividend payments. Both share repurchases and dividend

In Practice 11.4 *Title of the Shareholders' Equity Section on the Balance Sheet: A Glimpse of a Sample of Fortune 1000 Companies*   The following chart identifies the title used on the balance sheet for the shareholders' equity section by a sample of 600 *Fortune 1000* companies. Over 50 percent of the surveyed firms used the label "stockholders' equity:"

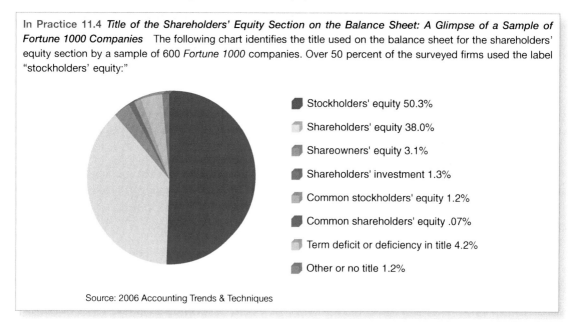

Stockholders' equity 50.3%

Shareholders' equity 38.0%

Shareowners' equity 3.1%

Shareholders' investment 1.3%

Common stockholders' equity 1.2%

Common shareholders' equity .07%

Term deficit or deficiency in title 4.2%

Other or no title 1.2%

Source: 2006 Accounting Trends & Techniques

increases are often considered to be shareholder-value increasing events because they signal the market about management's optimistic beliefs regarding a firm's future prospects. For example, share repurchases often signal that management feels that the current share price under values a firm's intrinsic value, while increases in a firm's dividend payout signals that management believes that future operating cash flow will be more than adequate to support the larger dividend payments. Unfortunately, negative signals can also be associated with each of these events. Both share repurchases and dividend increases can be interpreted by the capital market as indicating that a firm no longer has good revenue growth prospects.

Shareholder value creation can arise in two ways—share price appreciation and dividend payments. Two measures of the latter include the dividend payout ratio and the dividend yield. The dividend payout ratio compares the amount of dividends paid to shareholders relative to a firm's net income, while the dividend yield computes dividends paid relative to a firm's share price. According to modern financial theory, in the absence of income taxes, it should not matter to shareholders whether or not a firm chooses to pay dividends since any dividend paid would cause an equivalent decrease in share price. Still, many investment professionals pay close attention to the dividend policy adopted by a firm because many shareholders prefer a steady, dependable dividend to the uncertainty of share price appreciation.

As noted in prior chapters, it is the responsibility of the financial statement user to not only analyze the numbers that appear in a company's financial statements, but also to adjust the financial statements for any business risks (such as operating leases and pending lawsuits) that they feel are not adequately reflected in the financial data. Examples of the latter that are discussed in this chapter include dividends-in-arrears and employee stock option expense. Dividends-in-arrears result from the failure of a firm to pay dividends on its cumulative preferred stock. Since dividends are not recorded as liabilities until they are actually declared by the board of directors, dividends-in-arrears represent a contingent liability and thus require only footnote disclosure. The presence of dividends-in-arrears, however, serves as a red flag to financial statement users that a firm is (or at least, was) in financial distress, and consequently, has been forced to conserve its operating cash flow by not paying its preferred stock dividends.

Prior to 2007 managers had considerable discretion as to how they reported the cost of employee stock options in corporate financial statements. Most managers elected to simply disclose this cost in the financial statement footnotes rather than reporting the expense as a deduction against earnings on the income statement. With the passage of SFAS 123R, firms are now required to expense employee stock option costs as an operating expense on the income statement. Nonetheless, if an analysis of a firm includes prior years (2006 and before), it is important to consider the earnings impact of the employee stock option expense that can be found in a firm's footnotes.

Finally, the financial statement user should pay careful attention to items that appear in the Accumulated Other Comprehensive Income section of shareholders' equity. The items reported in this section of the balance sheet represent unrealized wealth changes to a firm that bypass the income statement, at least temporarily. The financial statement user should, at a minimum, consider whether their inclusion is warranted in any analysis of a firm's future cash flow and sustainable earnings.

ETHICS PERSPECTIVE

One of the basic tenets of modern financial theory is that the primary goal of a public corporation is to maximize shareholder value. The rationale underlying this argument is that the shareholders are the owners of the corporation, and as the residual claimants, they bear all of the risks and rewards of ownership. Further, economic theory dating from the teachings of Adam Smith argues that capital will flow to those firms that provide the best returns and that this flow of capital will benefit society as a whole. The construct of shareholder value maximization, however, is not universally embraced. Some would call "stakeholder theory" a competing theory of the firm. Under stakeholder theory, shareholders are but one of the many stakeholders of the corporation, with other stakeholders being a company's employees, customers, suppliers, the government, the surrounding community, and the environment. Stakeholder theory proponents believe that it is the obligation of the corporation to balance the needs of each of its stakeholder groups, rather than to focus solely on shareholder maximization. Some have gone so far as to equate the doctrine of shareholder maximization with corporate greed.

REVIEW PROBLEM

The Arcadia Company began operations on January 1, 2006, by issuing 500,000 shares of $1 par value common stock at a price of $10.00 per share. During the first year of operations, the company generated revenue of $2 million and incurred expenses totaling $800,000. (Assume all transactions are in cash.) During its second year of operations, the company executed the following events in the sequence listed:

  a. Declared a 2-for-1 forward stock split.
  b. Repurchased 10,000 shares of its common stock for cash at a price of $15 per share.
  c. Declared and distributed a ten percent stock dividend on the outstanding shares at a time when the market price per common share was $18 per share.
  d. Paid a cash dividend of $.10 per share on all outstanding common shares.
  e. Generated revenue of $3 million and incurred expenses of $1.2 million.

Required

Using a spreadsheet approach, record the transactions for Years 1 and 2 for The Arcadia Company. Using the account balances at the end of Year 2, prepare the shareholders' equity section of the balance sheet for The Arcadia Company.

	Assets	=	Equity			
	Cash		Common Stock ($1 par)	Additional Paid-in-Capital	Retained Earnings	Treasury Stock
2006						
Jan 1....	5,000,000		500,000	4,500,000		
Dec 31 ..	2,000,000				2,000,000 (R)	
	−800,000				−800,000 (E)	
EOY	6,200,000		500,000	4,500,000	1,200,000	0
2007						
a.......			Reduce par value to $0.50 per share; increase shares			
b.......	−150,000					−150,000
c.......			49,500[1]	1,732,500	−1,782,000[1]	
d.......	−108,900				−108,900[2]	
e.......	3,000,000				3,000,000 (R)	
	−1,200,000				−1,200,000 (E)	
EOY	7,741,100		549,500	6,232,500	1,109,100	(150,000)

1. 990,000 outstanding shares × $18 per share = $1,782,000.
   990,000 outstanding shares × $0.50 par value = $49,500.
2. 1,089,000 outstanding shares × $0.10 = $108,900.

The Arcadia Company Partial Balance Sheet	
Shareholders' Equity	
Common stock, $0.50 par value 1,099,000 shares issued; 1,089,000 shares outstanding	$ 549,500
Additional paid-in-capital	6,232,500
Retained earnings	1,109,100
Treasury stock	(150,000)
Total shareholders' equity	$7,741,100

EXECUTIVE SUMMARY

This chapter investigated the shareholders' equity section of the balance sheet. Specifically, we considered how companies raise equity capital through the sale of common and preferred shares, and how and why they sometimes execute free share distributions through stock dividends and stock splits. Finally, we examined the Other Comprehensive

Income section of the shareholders' equity section of the balance sheet, and the accounting for, and disclosure of, employee stock options.

As a validation of your understanding of the content of this chapter, you should now be able to:

- Explain the accounting for share issuances and repurchases.
- Explain why companies issue stock dividends and how they account for them.
- Explain the motivation behind forward and reverse stock splits.
- Explain the various components of the Other Comprehensive Income section of shareholders' equity on the balance sheet.

In the next and final chapter, we illustrate the discounted cash flow approach and the residual income approach to firm valuation.

KEY CONCEPTS AND TERMS

Additional paid-in capital, 11.5
Authorized shares, 11.4
Best efforts basis, 11.3
Binomial model, 11.20
Black-Scholes model, 11.20
Book value, 11.5
Callable preferred stock, 11.8
Capital-in-excess of par value, 11.5
Capital surplus, 11.5
Charter of incorporation, 11.4
Common shares, 11.3
Conversion ratio, 11.8
Convertible preferred stock, 11.8
Cumulative foreign currency
   translation adjustment, 11.15
Cumulative preferred stock, 11.8
Distribution date, 11.10

Dividend payout ratio, 11.10
Dividend yield, 11.10
Dividends-in-arrears, 11.8
Exercise price, 11.17
Fair value method, 11.20
Firm commitment basis, 11.3
Forward split, 11.13
Free share distribution, 11.12
Initial public offering, 11.3
Intrinsic value method, 11.5
Issued shares, 11.4
Market capitalization, 11.9
Mezzanine financing, 11.8
No-par value, 11.5
Other comprehensive income, 11.15
Outstanding shares, 11.4
Par value, 11.5

Participating preferred stock, 11.8
Preferred shares, 11.8
Property dividend, 11.12
Record date, 11.10
Regular dividend, 11.9
Residual interest 11.3
Reverse split, 11.14
Share premium, 11.5
Special dividend, 11.10
Stated value, 11.5
Stock dividend, 11.12
Stock option, 11.17
Stock split, 11.13
Strike price, 11.17
Tracking shares, 11.6
Treasury shares, 11.7

APPENDIX 11A: Recording Equity Financing Transactions using the Debit and Credit Paradigm

In this appendix, the traditional approach to recording accounting transactions—that is, the debit and credit paradigm—is used to illustrate the journal entries for various equity financing transactions. For purposes of this appendix, the following illustrative transactions are assumed to have occurred during 2005:

- Claremont Company incorporated on January 1, 2005, and authorized the issuance of 100,000 shares of $1 par value common stock and 50,000 shares of no-par value preferred stock. The preferred stock had a stated dividend of $5 per share.
- On January 10, 2005, Claremont Company sold 25,000 shares of common stock for $500,000 cash and 10,000 shares of preferred stock for $100,000 cash.
- On June 30, 2005, the Board of Directors of Claremont Company declared and paid a cash dividend of $0.10 per share on each outstanding common share and $2.50 per share on each outstanding preferred share, or a total of $27,500 in cash dividends ($2,500 + $25,000).

- On September 1, 2005, Claremont Company repurchased 5,000 shares of common stock at a cost of $15 per share, or a total outlay of $75,000,
- On December 31, 2005, the Board of Directors of Claremont Company declared a 2:1 forward stock split on the issued and outstanding common shares.
- On December 1, 2005, the Board of Directors of Claremont Company issued 1,000 treasury shares to company executives who exercised stock options at an exercise price of $10 per share.

The following journal entries would be recorded to reflect the above equity transactions.

Date	Accounts	Debit	Credit
Jan 1, 2005	No entry is recorded to reflect the authorization to sell equity shares		
Jan 10, 2005	Cash (A)	500,000	
	Common stock, $1 par (SE).		25,000
	Additional paid-in-capital (SE)		475,000
	To record the sale of 25,000 shares of $1 par value common stock.		
	Cash (A)	100,000	
	Preferred stock (SE)		100,000
	To record the sale of 10,000 shares of no-par value preferred stock.		
Jun 30, 2005	Retained Earnings (D)	27,500	
	Cash (A)		27,500
	To record the declaration and payment of a cash dividend on the outstanding common and preferred shares.		
Sep 1, 2005	Treasury Stock (SE)	75,000	
	Cash (A)		75,000
	To record the repurchase of 5,000 common shares at $15 per share.		
Dec 31, 2005	Common Stock, $1 par value.	25,000	
	Common Stock, $0.50 par value		25,000
	To record a reduction in the par value on the common shares from $1.00 to $0.50 per share, and to increase the shares issued and outstanding from 25,000 to 50,000 shares.		
	Retained Earnings (E)	5,000	
	Cash (A)	10,000	
	Treasury Shares (SE)		15,000
	To record the exercise of stock options on 1,000 shares of common stock valued at $15 per share		

To validate your understanding of the above journal entries, create a set of T-accounts and calculate the value of shareholders' equity for Claremont Company at year-end 2005. Your answer should appear as follows:

Shareholders' Equity	
Common stock, $0.50 par value	$ 25,000
Additional paid-in-capital	475,000
Preferred stock, no par value	100,000
Retained earnings	(32,500)
Treasury stock	(60,000)
	$507,500

DISCUSSION QUESTIONS

Q11.1   **Book Value versus Market Capitalization.**   **Home Depot Inc.** has a book value of $23 billion but a market capitalization of over $88 billion (almost four times its book value). Discuss why Home Depot's book value is so much less than its market capitalization. Describe the circumstances in which a company's book value might exceed its market capitalization.

Q11.2   **Free Share Distributions.**   Stock dividends and stock splits are often referred to as "free share distributions." Discuss why the use of the label "free share distribution" is an appropriate description of these shareholders' equity transactions.

Q11.3   **Dividend-in-Arrears.**   When dividends are unpaid on a cumulative preferred stock, they are referred to as a dividend-in-arrears. Discuss why dividends-in-arrears are disclosed as a contingent liability in the footnotes to the financial statements and not as a liability on the balance sheet. What message do dividends-in-arrears convey about the financial health of a business?

Q11.4   **Multiple Classes of Voting Rights.**   The April 19, 2006 edition of *The Wall Street Journal* carried the following headline and lead paragraph:

> **New York Times Faces Share Class Challenge**   The *New York Times Co.* became the latest newspaper company to come under fire from some of its restive investors, this time for its use of two classes of shares with unequal voting power. Morgan Stanley's money-management division, which holds more than 5% of the New York time's Class A shares, pressed the company to eliminate its Class B stock.

The Times' Class B shares, which are primarily owned by the family of Chairman Arthur Sulzberger, carry significantly more voting power than the newspaper company's Class A shares. Discuss why Morgan Stanley would want to see the two class share structure eliminated. Why would the family of Chairman Sulzberger prefer to maintain a two class share structure?

Q11.5   **Oversubscribed Initial Public Offering.**   In early 2006, **India's Reliance Petroleum** announced that it would hold an initial public offering (IPO) of its common shares. The announced IPO was for 1.8 million shares at an estimated price range of 57 to 62 rupees per share, or approximately $2.5 billion to $2.7 billion. Because of exceptionally strong investor interest worldwide for Indian company shares, and especially for oil and gas company shares, the Reliance Petroleum IPO was over subscribed by 7.5 times (the total number of shares sought by investors was 13.5 million). Discuss what strategies Reliance Petroleum might adopt in response to this dramatic over-subscription of its initial public offering. If Reliance's outstanding shares total 7.2 million shares following the IPO, what is the implicit value of the entire company? (Reliance Petroleum's remaining outstanding shares were held by its parent company Reliance Industries.)

Q11.6   **Stock Splits and Share Prices.**   In early 2006, the **Loews Corporation**, a property and casualty insurance company, announced that its board of directors had approved a 3-for-1 forward stock split. At the time of the stock split announcement, Loews' common shares were trading at $99 per share but gained nearly $2 per share in after-hours trading following the announcement. In the year prior to the split announcement, the Loews shares had steadily increased in price from $70 per share to its current price of $99 per share, an increase of nearly 42 percent in just one year. Discuss why the board of directors might have approved the stock split. Is the announcement of a stock split "positive news" to the market? If so, why?

Q11.7 **Dividend Reduction.** In early 2006, the Mills Corporation announced that it would cut its dividend payment to shareholders from $0.63 per share to just $0.25 per share. In response to the announcement, Mills share price rose about $4 per share, or approximately 13 percent. Over the past year, Mills' share price had fallen about 53 percent, from $64 per share to $30 per share, after the real estate investment trust (REIT) company had revealed to its shareholders that it was incurring significant operating losses on a number of its real estate projects. Analysts had been predicting a dividend cut since Mills had been unable to cover its dividend payout through its ongoing operating cash flow. REITs are usually reluctant to cut their dividend because the dividend yield on such investments is one of the principal attractions for investors. Discuss how the equity market is likely to react to news of a dividend cut. Discuss how companies set their dividend policy and under what conditions they are likely to increase or decrease a dividend.

Q11.8 **Dividend Payout Ratio.** The dividend payout ratio, or the percentage of net income paid out to shareholders in the form of a dividend (Dividends paid/Net income), is used by some investors to identify securities to add to their portfolio of investments. For example, in 2005, the dividend payout ratio for The Proctor & Gamble Company was 37.6 percent, The Johnson and Johnson Company was 36.4 percent, and for Pfizer, Inc. was 68.7 percent. Discuss whether having a high payout ratio (such as Pfizer, Inc.) is a good strategy for a company. What type of investor would prefer a high payout ratio versus a low (or zero) payout ratio? What does a high payout ratio suggest about a company's future growth prospects?

Q11.9 **Cost of Employee Stock Options.** The April 19, 2006 edition of *The Wall Street Journal* carried the following headline: "Yahoo's Net Declines 22% After Accounting Change." The article explained that while the internet company's revenue had increased by 30 percent over the same period one year earlier, its profit had fallen 22 percent as a consequence of the mandatory adoption of a new accounting standard regarding the accounting for employee stock options. Without the adoption of the accounting change, Yahoo's first quarter earnings would have been $231 million, or $0.15 per share. Including the cost of employee stock options issued to Yahoo employees during the first quarter caused Yahoo's earnings to fall $71 million, a $0.04 per share, to just $160 million, or $0.11 per share. Yahoo's share price rose six percent in response to the news announcement while the S&P 500 index closed slightly down for the day. Discuss why the capital market may have responded positively to Yahoo's earnings announcement. Do you agree that the cost of employee stock options should be expensed in the period in which they are granted?

Q11.10 **Directors' Compensation.** In 2006, the Coca-Cola Company announced a major change in company policy regarding the compensation of its board of directors. Under the new director compensation plan, non-executive directors would be paid an annual director's fee of $175,000 only if the soft drink company met its target of eight percent compounded annual earnings growth over a three-year period. If the target was missed, directors would receive nothing. Coca-Cola director Warren Buffett hailed the program as "pioneering," noting that the new policy would align the interests of the board of directors and Coke's shareholders more closely than in any other large company. Discuss whether you think Coke's new director compensation scheme will achieve its intended goal.

Q11.11 **Special Dividends: Return on Capital or Return of Capital.** On April 24, 2006, Cablevision Systems Corporation paid its shareholders a special dividend of $10 per share. At the time that the special dividend was announced, the company's share price was trading at $27 per share. Following the dividend distribution, the company's share price dropped to $18 per share. Special dividends that represent a return *on* capital are taxed at regular dividend tax rates (currently 15 percent), whereas special dividends that represent a return *of* capital are not subject to any income tax. Discuss under what circumstances a special dividend would be considered a return of capital versus a return on capital. Describe the financial performance of a company that might justify classification of a special dividend as a return of capital.

Q11.12 **(Ethics Perspective) Stakeholder Theory and Shareholder Wealth Maximization.** To whom do you feel corporate manager's owe their responsibility? Do you feel that shareholder wealth maximization and stakeholder theory are necessarily competing theories? If you feel that managers owe a responsibility to more than just shareholders, how should they resolve the ethical dilemma of the competing needs of each group (such as profits for shareholders, quality and fair prices for customers, good wages for employees, etc.)?

⊘ **indicates that check figures are available on the book's Website.**

EXERCISES

E11.13 **Shareholders' Equity Transactions.** The following transactions occurred during 2006 for The Niagara Company:

1. Generated net income of $2.5 million.
2. Sold common stock having a par value of $0.01 for $22 per share.
3. Paid a cash dividend of $2 per share to its preferred shareholders.
4. Issued a ten percent stock dividend on its outstanding common stock.
5. Repurchased 10,000 shares of common stock at $18 per share.
6. Declared a 2-for-1 forward stock split on its common stock.

Identify whether the above transactions increased, decreased, or had no effect on total shareholders' equity. Identify the specific shareholders' equity accounts affected by each transaction and indicate whether the accounts increased, decreased, or remained unchanged.

⊘ E11.14 **Accounting for Shareholders' Equity Transactions.** The shareholders' equity section of the balance sheet of The Claremont Company appeared as follows on December 31, 2005.

Common stock, $0.10 par value	$ 600,000
Additional paid-in-capital	89,400,000
Retained earnings	32,000,000
Treasury stock	(7,500,000)
Shareholders' equity	$114,500,000

During 2006, the following transactions occurred:

1. Generated net income of $6 million.
2. Paid a cash dividend of $1.5 million.
3. Purchased 100,000 shares of common stock at $9.50 per share.
4. Executed a 1-for-2 reverse stock split.

Prepare the shareholders' equity section of the balance sheet of Claremont Company at December 31, 2006.

E11.15 **Shareholders' Equity Transactions.** The following transactions occurred during 2006 for The Manhattan Company:

1. Incurred an operating loss of $12 million.
2. Paid the regular dividend to its common shareholders.
3. Repurchased 100,000 shares of common stock.
4. Executed a 1-for-3 reverse stock split to raise its common share price.
5. Issued treasury shares to executives who exercised their stock options.

Identify whether the above transactions increased, decreased, or had no effect on total shareholders' equity. Identify which shareholders' equity accounts were affected by each transaction and indicate whether the accounts increased, decreased, or remained unchanged.

E11.16 **Accounting for Shareholders' Equity Transactions.** The shareholders' equity section of the consolidated balance sheet of **The Tortuga Rum Cake Company** appeared as follows on December 31, 2005.

Common stock, $1.00 par value	$ 100,000
Additional paid-in-capital...	1,200,000
Convertible preferred stock, no par value	800,000
Retained deficit	(600,000)
Treasury stock	(250,000)
Shareholders' equity	$1,250,000

During 2006, the following transactions occurred:

1. Generated net income of $80,000.
2. Paid cash dividends of $220,000.
3. Issued a ten percent common stock dividend; the fair value of the stock was $10 per share at this time.
4. Declared and issued a 2-for-1 forward stock split.
5. Converted 10,000 shares of convertible preferred stock with a book value of $300,000 into 30,000 shares of common stock.

Prepare the shareholders' equity section of the balance sheet of Tortuga Rum Cake Company at December 31, 2006.

E11.17 **Dividend Yield and Dividend Payout.** The following information is available for West Texas Waste Management Inc. (WTWM).

	2004	**2005**	**2006**
Dividends per share	$ 0.04	$ 0.08	$ 0.16
Earnings per share............................	1.07	1.28	1.41
Market price per share........................	16.00	19.00	21.00

Calculate WTWM's dividend payout ratio and dividend yield for 2004, 2005, and 2006. Describe the trend in WTWM's dividend payout and dividend yield. Which factor—dividends or earnings—seem to be driving WTWM's share price movement.

⊘ E11.18 **Accounting for Stock Dividends and Stock Splits.** The Irvine Corporation reported the following data at year-end 2005:

Common stock, par value $1.......................................	$ 100,000
Additional paid-in-capital...	300,000
Retained earnings	1,400,000
Treasury shares	(600,000)
Other comprehensive income	200,000
Total shareholders' equity	$1,400,000

The following transactions occurred during 2006 in the following sequence:

1. Declared and distributed a ten percent stock dividend on the outstanding common shares at a time when the common shares were selling for $15 per share.
2. Declared a 3-for-2 forward stock split on the outstanding common shares.

3. Declared and issued a 20 percent stock dividend on the outstanding common shares at a time when the shares were selling for $30 per share.
4. Declared a 2-for-1 forward stock split on the outstanding common shares.

Calculate the par value per share and number of shares outstanding at year-end 2006. Prepare the shareholders' equity section of the balance sheet for the Irvine Corporation at year-end 2006.

E11.19 **Interpreting the Foreign Currency Translation Adjustment Account.** The following information is taken from the 2004 annual report of **Home Depot Inc.**:

Other Comprehensive Income (in millions)	2002	2003	2004
Foreign currency translation adjustment account	$(124)	$109	$172

Discuss why the Foreign Currency Translation Adjustment account was negative for Home Depot in 2002. Explain why the account balance became positive in 2003 and grew larger in amount in 2004. Are the changes in this account reported on the income statement or in the statement of cash flow for Home Depot? Why or why not?

E11.20 **Analyzing the Net Unrealized Gain on Available-for-Sale Securities.** The following information is taken from the 2005 annual report of Smith & Sons Inc. :

Other Comprehensive Income (in millions)	2002	2003	2004
Net unrealized gain (loss) on available-for-sale securities	$(9,324)	$47,230	$19,238

Explain why the net unrealized gain on available-for-sale securities was negative in 2003. Explain why the account balance became positive in 2004 but then declined in 2005. Are the changes in this account reported on the company's income statement? Would this account appear on Smith & Sons' statement of cash flow? Why or why not?

⊘ E11.21 **Adjusting Conversion Ratios for Stock Splits and Stock Dividends.** R.J. Miller & Company has the following securities outstanding:

- Common stock, $0.10 par value
- Convertible preferred stock
- Convertible debentures

The convertible preferred stock carried a conversion ratio of 3-to-1 (each share of preferred stock may be converted into three shares of common stock), whereas the convertible debentures carried a conversion ratio of 46-to-1 (each debenture may be converted into 46 shares of common stock). During the year, R.J. Miller & Company declared and issued a ten percent common stock dividend, followed by a 2-for-1 forward common stock split. Calculate the new conversion ratios for the convertible preferred stock and convertible debentures following the common stock dividend and common stock split. Why is it appropriate to adjust the conversation ratios of the convertible preferred stock and the convertible debentures following the stock dividend and stock split?

E11.22 **Contrasting the Contributed Capital of a Firm with Treasury Stock.** The following information is taken from the 2005 annual reports of **Cisco Systems Inc., Intel Inc.,** and **Microsoft Inc.**:

Shareholders' Equity (amounts in millions)	Cisco Systems	Intel	Microsoft
Contributed capital.	$27,096	$ 7,698	$62,150
Retained earnings	22,957	38,994	(5,978)
Treasury stock	(27,153)	(10,637)	(8,057)
Other comprehensive income	274	127	0
	$23,174	$36,182	$48,115

For each company, calculate the ratio of treasury stock divided by contributed capital. What does this ratio tell you about each of the three companies?

E11.23 **Analyzing Shareholders' Equity.** Presented below is the consolidated statement of shareholders' equity for **The Johnson and Johnson Company** (J&J) at year-end 2005:

(in millions)	Total	Compre-hensive Income	Retained Earnings	Notes Receivable From ESOP	Accumulated Other Comprehensive Income	Common Stock	Treasury Stock
Balance, January 2, 2005. . .	$31,813		$35,223	$(11)	$(515)	$3,120	$(6,004)
Net earnings.	10,411	$10,411	10,411				
Cash dividends paid.	(3,793)		(3,793)				
Employee stock compensation and stock option plans.	1,017		(441)				1,458
Conversion of subordinated debentures	369		(132)				501
Repurchase of common stock	(1,717)		203				(1,920)
Other comprehensive income, net of tax Currency translation adjustment	(415)	(415)			(415)		
Unrealized losses on securities	(16)	(16)			(16)		
Pension liability adjustment	26	26			26		
Gains on derivatives & hedges	165	165			165		
Reclassification adjustment		(15)					
Total comprehensive income.		$10,156					
Note receivable from ESOP.	11			11			
Balance, January 1, 2006. . .	$37,871		$41,471	—	$(755)	$3,120	$(5,965)

Based on your review of this data, consider the following questions:

1. How much cash dividends did J&J pay in 2005?
2. What was the value of the common stock distributed to employees in 2005 under J&J's stock compensation plan and stock option plan? Where did J&J get the shares to distribute to its employees?

3. What was the value of the convertible subordinated debentures converted into common stock in 2005? Where did J&J get the shares to give to the debentureholders?
4. What was the value of the treasury stock repurchase in 2005?
5. What happened to J&J's currency translation adjustment account? Did the U.S. dollar appreciate, depreciate, or remain unchanged during 2005?

E11.24 **Analyzing Shareholders' Equity.**   Presented below is the Shareholders' Equity section of the consolidated balance sheet of **Pfizer Inc.** The data is taken from the company's 2005 annual report:

(in millions)	2005	2004
Convertible preferred stock (no par).	$ 169	$ 193
Common stock, $0.05 par value	439	438
Additional paid-in-capital.	67,622	67,098
Employee benefit trust	(923)	(1,229)
Treasury stock, at cost.	(39,767)	(35,992)
Retained earnings	37,608	35,492
Other comprehensive income	479	2,278
Total shareholders' equity	$65,627	$68,278

Based on your review of this data, develop an explanation as to why each of the account balances changed from 2004 to 2005?

PROBLEMS

P11.25 **Accounting for Share Transactions.**   During 2005, The Mann Corporation, a private entity, decided to go public. A charter of incorporation was constructed which authorized the sale of ten million shares of $1 par value common stock, 100,000 shares of $100 par value, eight percent preferred stock, and 200,000 shares of $5 no-par value convertible preferred stock. The following shares were sold as part of the firm's initial public offering:

-   1,000,000 shares of common stock at $10 per share.
-   100,000 shares of $100 par value, eight percent preferred stock at $105 per share.
-   100,000 shares of $5 convertible, no-par preferred stock at $55 per share.

At the end of 2005, the full dividend was declared and paid on both preferred stock offerings.

Required
Using a spreadsheet, record the financial effects of the shareholders' equity transactions for The Mann Corporation for 2005.

⊘ P11.26 **Accounting for Share Transactions.**   The Mayfair Corporation went public on January 1, 2002 with an initial public offering of 10,000,000 common shares, $1 par value, at a market price of $3 per share. Since then, the following equity transactions had occurred:

1. In 2003, a ten percent stock dividend was issued. At the time, the Mayfair common shares were trading at $6 per share.
2. In 2004, a three-for-one forward stock split was executed. At the time, the Mayfair common shares were trading at $12 per share.
3. In 2005, 500,000 common shares were repurchased on the open market at a price of $15 per share.

4. On December 31, 2005, the company declared and paid its first cash dividend of $0.10 per share on all outstanding common shares.

Required

1. Calculate the par value per share and the number of shares outstanding for the Mayfair Corporation on December 31, 2005.
2. Prepare a spreadsheet to illustrate the financial effects of each of the above share transactions.

P11.27   **Accounting for Share Transactions.**   The shareholders' equity section of the consolidated balance sheet of **CompX International** appeared as follows at the beginning of the year:

Shareholders' Equity	
Class A common stock, $.01 par value; 20,000,000 shares authorized;	$ 61,000
6,100,000 shares issued	
Additional paid-in-capital	118,127,000
Retained earnings	14,270,000
Currency translation adjustment	(2,412,000)
Total equity	$130,046,000

The following events occurred sequentially during the year:

1. A 2-for-1 forward stock split was executed.
2. A ten percent stock dividend was distributed when the CompX share price was $20 per share.
3. Treasury stock valued at $3,000,000 was repurchased when the CompX share price was $15 per share.

Required

1. How many Class A common shares are outstanding following the above events?
2. What is the par value per share of the Class A common stock following the above events?
3. Identify the financial effects associated with the above three share transactions.
4. Calculate the total value of shareholders' equity following the above events.

P11.28   **Stock Dividends.**   Mic Dundee, President of Aussie Steaks Inc., is contemplating issuing a stock dividend that would lower the company's share price to the $24 to $25 per share range. Aussie Steaks' share price is currently trading at $30 per share. The shareholders' equity section of Aussie Steaks' balance sheet at December 31, 2005 is as follows:

Common stock ($1 par)	$ 500,000
Additional paid-in-capital	2,000,000
Retained earnings	3,100,000
Total shareholders' equity	$5,600,000

For the past several years, Aussie Steaks has paid annual cash dividends of $0.80 per share. Mic would like to maintain this level of cash dividends after the stock dividend is issued. Mic expects net income for the next few years to average $300,000 per year. Some members of Aussie Steaks' board of directors want a 20 percent stock dividend; others want a 25 percent stock dividend.

Required

1. Identify the financial effects associated with a 25 percent stock dividend.
2. Identify the financial effects associated with a 20 percent stock dividend.
3. Is there any reason why the Aussie Steaks' shareholders would prefer a small stock dividend to a large stock dividend?

4. Should Aussie Steaks declare a 20 percent stock dividend or a 25 percent stock dividend? Why?
5. What event must have occurred if the shareholders' equity section of Aussie Steaks' balance sheet at January 1, 2006 was reported as follows:

Common stock ($1 par)	$1,000,000
Additional paid-in-capital	1,500,000
Retained earnings	3,100,000
Total shareholders' equity	$5,600,000

P11.29 **Convertible Preferred Stock: A Redemption.** The *Financial Times* and the *Wall Street Journal* carried a legal notice entitled "**The Thomas Regout Company** has called for the redemption of all of its €3.50 Convertible Preferred Stock." According to the notice Thomas Regout, a Dutch company, had decided to exercise the redemption feature on its outstanding preferred stock and to redeem all of the outstanding shares at a price of €52.45 per share plus accrued dividends of €0.16 per share, for a total of €52.61, on August 31. The Thomas Regout preferred stock also carried a conversion feature that would permit the owner to convert the preferred stock into 1.9608 shares of common stock (par value of €1). The market price of the common stock on August 13 was €32.625 per share. The legal notice of redemption emphasized that the conversion feature of the preferred stock expired on August 27.

Required
1. Assume that Thomas Regout has 1 million shares of preferred stock outstanding and that its par value is €5. How would the company account for (1) the redemption of all of the preferred shares and (2) the conversion of all of the preferred shares?
2. If you held 100 shares of Thomas Regout preferred stock, which alternative (conversion or redemption) would you choose, and why?
3. If you were the CEO of Thomas Regout, which alternative (conversion or redemption) would you prefer, and why?

P11.30 **Common Shares for Convertible Debt Exchange.** In 1999, the **M. Edgar Barrett Company** was taken private by Kohlberg Kravis Roberts & Co. (KKR) in a leveraged buyout. A central feature of the buyout was that the Barrett Company would issue large amounts of high yield "junk" bonds (a bond having a high risk rating and consequently, yielding a high return). For example, one phase of the leveraged buyout involved the issuance of $2.86 billion of twelve percent bonds due in 2009. Beginning in 2004, KKR began efforts to reduce the level of debt carried on the books of the Barrett Company in anticipation of taking the Barrett Company public again. One aspect of the debt reduction program called for the issuance of 82.8 million shares of Barrett Company common stock in exchange for $753 million (face value) of the twelve percent bonds.

Required
1. Assume that the Barrett Company common stock has a par value of $1 and that the $753 million of twelve percent bonds are trading at an aggregate market value of $850 million (or approximately $1,129 per $1,000 bond). Why would KKR want to undertake the stock-for-debt exchange in 2004?
2. Describe the financial effects of the stock-for-debt exchange assuming it occurs as planned.
3. How are the financial effects of the stock-for-debt exchange altered if the bonds are trading at $800 per bond rather than $1,129 per bond?

P11.31 **Analyzing Shareholders' Equity.** **Microsoft Corporation** is one of the world's leading developers and retailers of PC software. Presented below are excerpts from Microsoft's 2004 annual report regarding its shareholders' equity:

Shareholders' Equity Statements		
Year Ended June 30 ($ millions)	**2003**	**2004**
Common stock and paid-in-capital		
Balance, beginning of period	$41,845	$49,234
Common stock issued	2,966	2,815
Common stock repurchased	(691)	(416)
Stock-based compensation expense	3,749	5,734
Stock option income benefits/(deficiencies)	1,365	(989)
Other, net	—	18
Balance, end of period	$49,234	$56,396
Retained earnings		
Balance, beginning of period	$12,997	$15,678
Net income	7,531	8,168
Other comprehensive income		
Net gains/(losses) on derivative instruments	(102)	101
Net unrealized investments gain/(losses).	1,243	(873)
Translation adjustments and other.	116	51
Comprehensive income	8,788	7,447
Common stock dividend	(857)	(1,729)
Common stock repurchased	(5,250)	(2,967)
Balance, end of period	$15,678	$18,429
Total stockholders' equity	$64,912	$74,825

Required

Prepare a list of the key events and their financial effects that impacted Microsoft's shareholders' equity in 2004. Where possible, explain why these transactions occurred. You may wish to access Microsoft's 2004 annual report at www.microsoft.com to assist you with your answer.

P11.32 **Analyzing Shareholders' Equity.** **Entrust, Inc.** designs, produces, and sells software products and services for securing digital information and identities. Presented below is the company's statement of shareholders' equity from its 2004 annual report:

	Common Stock		Additional Paid-In Capital	Unearned Compensation	Accumulated Deficit	Accumulated Other Comprehensive Income (Loss)	Comprehensive Income (Loss)	Total Shareholder's Equity
($ thousands, except share data)	**Shares**	**Amount**						
Balances at December 31, 2002 . .	64,491,634	$645	$781,842	$ (39)	$(663,502)	$(1,081)		$117,865
Unearned compensation related to non-employee								
Stock options granted	—	—	(25)	25	—	—	—	—

Entrust, Inc.
Consolidated Statements of Shareholders' Equity and Comprehensive Income
For years ended December 31, 2004 and 2003

continued

continued from previous page

Entrust, Inc.
Consolidated Statements of Shareholders' Equity and Comprehensive Income
For years ended December 31, 2004 and 2003

($ thousands, except share data)	Common Stock		Additional Paid-In Capital	Unearned Compen-sation	Accu-mulated Deficit	Accumu-lated Other Compre-hensive Income (Loss)	Compre-hensive Income (Loss)	Total Sharehold-er's Equity
	Shares	Amount						
Unearned compensation amortized	—	—	—	88	—	—		88
Common shares issued								
Stock option exercises	331,063	3	688	—	—	—		691
Employee stock purchase plan. . . .	173,891	2	386	—	—	—		388
Stock awards and restricted stock.	40,800	—	125	(125)	—	—		—
Common shares repurchased and retired	(1,444,200)	(14)	(3,677)	—	—	—		(3,961)
Comprehensive income (loss)								
Net loss	—	—	—	—	(35,866)	—	$(35,866)	(35,866)
Translation adjustment	—	—	—	—	—	1,197	1,197	1,197
Total comprehensive loss							$(34,669)	
Balances at December 31, 2003 . .	65,593,188	636	779,339	(51)	(699,368)	116		80,672
Unearned compensation amortized	—	—	—	64	—	—		64
Common share issued								
Stock option exercises	379,831	4	828	—	—	—		832
Stock awards and restricted stock. . .	28,250	—	97	(97)	—	—		—
Common shares repurchased and retired	(1,661,440)	(17)	(7,237)	—	—	—		(7,254)
Comprehensive income								
Net income	—	—	—	—	1,078	—	$1,078	1,078
Translation adjustment	—	—	—	—	—	602	602	602
Total comprehen-sive income							$ 1,680	
Balances at December 31, 2004 . .	62,339,829	$ 623	$ 773,027	$ (84)	$(698,290)	$ 718		$ 75,994

Required
Prepare a list of the key events that impacted Entrust's shareholders' equity in 2004. Where possible, explain why the transaction occurred. You may wish to access Entrust's 2004 annual report at www.entrust.com to assist you with your answer.

P11.33 **Other Comprehensive Income: Calculating the Cumulative Foreign Currency Translation Adjustment.** Graham International Ltd., an Australian Company, is a wholly-owned but financially-independent operating subsidiary of its U.S.-parent company and reports its financial results in Australian dollars. As of January 1, 2005, Graham International had a balance of $(10,780) U.S. in its cumulative foreign currency translation adjustment account (see translated balance sheet). During 2005, the exchange rates between the Australian and U.S. dollars were as follows:

January 1, 2005:	0.75	($1A = $0.75 U.S.)
December 31, 2005:	0.78	($1A = $078 U.S.)
Average for 2005:	0.76	

Graham International Ltd.'s balance sheet as of January 1, 2005, was as follows:

January 1, 2005	$A	Exchange Rate	$US
Assets			
Cash	$ 28,000	0.75	$ 21,000
Accounts receivable.	84,000	0.75	63,000
Inventory.	98,000	0.75	73,500
Property and equipment, net	476,700	0.75	357,525
Total	$686,700		$515,025
Liabilities.	$434,700	0.75	$326,025
Common stock.	42,000	H *	25,830
Retained earnings	210,000	H *	173,950
Translation adjustment	—		(10,780)
Total	$686,700		$515,025

*H = the historical exchange rate in effect at the time the account balance was created.

At the end of 2005, Graham International's income statement and balance sheet appeared as follows:

2005 Income Statement (Australian Dollars)	
Sales.	$1,148,000
Less: Operating expenses	(781,200)
Net income before taxes	366,800
Income tax expense.	(186,200)
Net income.	$ 180,600

Balance Sheet: Year-End 2005	
(Australian Dollars)	
Assets	
Cash..	$ 63,000
Accounts receivable.....................................	103,600
Inventory..	140,000
Property and equipment, net.............................	462,000
Total	$768,600
Liabilities..	$336,000
Common stock..	42,000
Retained earnings	390,600
Total	$768,600

Required
1. Translate Graham International's 2005 income statement using the average exchange rate for the year.
2. Translate Graham International's year-end 2005 balance sheet using the current rate method (all assets and liabilities are translated at the end-of-year exchange rate).
3. Explain the change in Graham's cumulative foreign currency translation adjustment from $(10,780) at the beginning of 2005 to $392 at year-end 2005. Why did the currency translation adjustment increase from an unrealized loss to an unrealized gain? When will this unrealized gain be realized?

P11.34 **Analyzing Shareholders' Equity.** **Wal-Mart Stores Inc.** is the world's largest retailer as measured by total revenues. Domestically, at year-end 2001, the Company operated 1,736 discount stores, 888 Super-Centers, 475 SAM'S Clubs, and 19 Neighborhood Markets. Internationally, at January 31, 2001, the Company operated units in Argentina (11), Brazil (20), Canada (174), Germany (94), Korea (6) Mexico (499), Puerto Rico (15), and the United Kingdom (241), and, under joint venture agreements, in China (11). Presented below are selected parts of Wal-Mart's 2000 10-K report:

Required
- During fiscal year 2001, Wal-Mart repurchased some of its outstanding shares. What was the average price paid for the repurchased treasury shares?
- Wal-Mart reports a minority interest account on its consolidated balance sheet. What does the existence of this account reveal about Wal-Mart's investments in its subsidiaries?
- Wal-Mart uses the current rate method to account for its foreign subsidiaries. During fiscal year 2001, did the U.S. dollar appreciate, remain unchanged or depreciate relative to the currencies of the countries in which these subsidiaries operate?
- On March 4, 1999, the Company announced a two-for-one forward stock split in the form of a 100 percent stock dividend. Prior to the announcement, the company's stock price was $89 3/8 per share. What was the target share price that the company achieved with the March 1999 forward stock split?
- On March 4, 1998, Wal-Mart's share price was $48 per share. Why did Wal-Mart split its stock in 1999?
- How much would retained earnings change if Wal-Mart had declared a 20 percent stock dividend instead of a 100 percent stock dividend?

Wal-Mart Stores Inc. Consolidated Balance Sheet (selected)		
(In millions for period ended)	01/31/01	01/31/00
Commercial paper	$ 2,286	$ 3,323
Accounts payable.	15,092	13,105
Accrued liabilities	6,355	6,161
Accrued income taxes	841	1,129
Long-term debt due within one year	4,234	1,964
Obligations under capital leases due within one year	141	121
Total current liabilities.	$28,949	$25,803
Long-term debt	$12,501	$13,672
Long-term obligations under capital leases.	3,154	3,002
Deferred income taxes and other.	1,043	759
Minority interest	1,140	1,279
Shareholders' equity		
Preferred stock ($0.10 par value; 100 shares authorized, none issued)	—	—
Common stock ($0.10 par value; 11,000 shares authorized, 4,470 and 4,457 issued and outstanding in 2001 and 2000, respectively).	447	446
Capital in excess of par value	1,411	714
Retained earnings	30,169	25,129
Other accumulated comprehensive income	(684)	(455)
Total shareholders' equity	$31,343	$25,834
Total liabilities and shareholders' equity.	$78,130	$70,349

Wal-Mart Stores Inc. Consolidated Statements of Stockholders' Equity						
In millions except per share data	Number of shares	Common stock	Capital in excess of par	Retained earnings	Other accumulated comprehensive income	Total
Balance–January 31, 1998. . . .	2,241	$224	$ 585	$18,167	($473)	$18,503
Comprehensive income						
Net income.				4,430		4,430
Other accumulated comprehensive income. . . .						
Foreign currency translation adjustment					(36)	(36)
Total comprehensive income.						4,394
Cash dividends ($.16 per share)				(693)		(693)
Purchase of Company stock	(21)	(2)	(37)	(1,163)		(1,202)

continued

continued from previous page

Wal-Mart Stores Inc.
Consolidated Statements of Stockholders' Equity

In millions except per share data	Number of shares	Common stock	Capital in excess of par	Retained earnings	Other accumulated comprehensive income	Total
Two-for-one stock split.......	2,224	223	(223)			—
Stock options exercised and other	4		110			110
Balance–January 31, 1999....	4,448	$445	$ 435	$20,741	$(509)	$21,112
Comprehensive income						
Net income...............				5,377		5,377
Other accumulated comprehensive income .						
Foreign currency translation adjustment...........					54	54
Total comprehensive income................						5,431
Cash dividends ($.20 per share)..........				(890)		(890)
Purchase of Company stock	(2)		(2)	(99)		(101)
Stock options exercised and other..............	11	1	281			282
Balance–January 31, 2000....	4,457	$446	$ 714	$25,129	$(455)	$25,834
Comprehensive income						
Net income...............				6,295		6,295
Other accumulated comprehensive income						
Foreign currency translation adjustment					(229)	(229)
Total Comprehensive Income..						6,066
Cash dividends ($.24 per share)				(1,070)		(1,070)
Purchase of Company stock	(4)		(8)	(185)		(193)
Issuance of Company stock	11	1	580			581
Stock options exercised and other..............	6		125			125
Balance—January 31, 2001...	4,470	$447	$1,411	$30,169	($684)	$31,343

P11.35 **(Appendix 11A) Recording Shareholders' Equity Transactions using the Debit/Credit Paradigm.** The following transactions occurred during 2006 for The Niagara Company:

1. Sold 10,000 shares of common stock having a par value of $0.01 for $22 per share.
2. Paid a cash dividend of $2 per share to its preferred shareholders when 5,000 shares were outstanding.

3. Issued a ten percent stock dividend on its outstanding common stock.
4. Repurchased 10,000 shares of common stock at $18 per share.
5. Declared a 2-for-1 forward stock split on its common stock.

Required

Using journal entries, record the shareholders' equity transactions for 2006 for The Niagara Company.

P11.36 (Appendix 11A) Recording Shareholders' Equity Transactions using the Debit/Credit Paradigm. During 2006, The Mann Corporation, a private entity, decided to go public. A charter of incorporation was constructed which authorized the sale of ten million shares of $1 par value common stock, 100,000 shares of $100 par value eight percent preferred stock, and 200,000 shares of $5 no-par value convertible preferred stock. The following shares were sold as part of the firm's initial public offering:

- 1,000,000 shares of common stock at $10 per share.
- 100,000 shares of $100 par value, eight percent preferred stock at $105 per share.
- 100,000 shares of $5 convertible, no-par preferred stock at $55 per share.

At the end of 2006, the full dividend was declared and paid on both preferred stock offerings.

Required

Using journal entries, record the financial effects of the shareholders' equity transactions for The Mann Corporation for 2006.

CORPORATE ANALYSIS

CA11.37 **The Procter and Gamble Company.** The 2005 annual report of **The Procter and Gamble Company** (**P & G**) is available at www.pg.com/annualreports/2005/pdf/pg2005annualreport.pdf. After reviewing P & G's annual report, respond to the following questions.

a. What types of equity securities does P & G have outstanding? What is their par or stated value, how many shares are authorized, and how many shares are outstanding at year-end 2005?

b. What percentage of P & G's assets are debt-financed versus equity-financed in 2004 and 2005? Why do you think the company has followed this strategic financing policy? What is P & G's cost of debt in 2005?

c. How many common shares did P & G repurchase in 2005 and at what aggregate price? How much did P & G expect to spend in 2006 to repurchase its common shares?

d. How many common shares were issued in 2005 to employees under P & G's employee stock option plan? If P & G had implemented SFAS No. 123R, "Accounting for Stock-Based Compensation," what would have been the effect on P & G's basic and diluted EPS for 2005?

CA11.38 **Internet-based Analysis.** Consider a publicly-held company whose products you are familiar with. Some examples might include:

Company	Product	Corporate Website
• **Johnson & Johnson Company**	• Band-Aids	• www.jnj.com
• **Microsoft Corporation**	• Windows XP software	• www.microsoft.com
• **Nokia Corporation**	• Cellular phones	• www.nokia.com
• **Intel Corporation**	• Pentium processors	• www.intel.com
• **Kimberly-Clark Corporation**	• Kleenex	• www.kimberly-clark.com

Access the company's public website and search for its most recent annual report. (Some companies provide access to their financial data through an "investor relations" link, while others provide a direct link to their "annual reports.") After locating your company's most recent annual report, open the file and review its contents. After reviewing the annual report for your selected company, prepare answers to the following questions:

1. How many common shares are authorized, issued, and outstanding? What is the par (or stated) value of the common stock? What is the company's market capitalization?

2. Does the company have any preferred stock issued and outstanding? If so, what is its par (or stated) value and what is the amount of the annual dividend? Is the preferred stock callable, convertible, or participating?

3. Has the company repurchased any of its common shares in the last two years? If so, how much was spent on treasury stock in each of the last two years?

4. Does the company give stock options to its management team? If so, how many shares might be issued if all of the outstanding stock options are exercised? What would happen to the company's earnings per share if the options are exercised?

5. Does the company pay dividends on its common stock? If so, what is the company's dividend payout ratio? What is the company's dividend yield? Is the company a "growth" company?

Chapter Twelve

Using Accounting Information in Equity Valuation

TAKEAWAYS

When you complete this chapter you should be able to:

1. Construct pro forma financial statements.

2. Estimate the value of a company using the discounted cash flow approach.

3. Estimate the value of a company using the residual income approach.

4. Estimate the value of a company using price-earnings multiples.

Where have we been?	Where are we?
Chapter 11 examined the shareholders' equity section of the balance sheet and investigated how firms account for share issuances and repurchases, as well as how and why stock dividends and stock splits are executed. In addition, the other comprehensive income section of shareholders' equity that characterizes U.S. corporate balance sheets was considered. Finally, the chapter investigated the controversial topic of accounting for stock options.	In this final chapter, we investigate how investment professionals, equity investors, and managers use financial statement information to value a company. We first illustrate how to develop the pro forma financial statements needed to value a company. We then examine how a business' free cash flow can be used to estimate the firm's operating value, and when combined with the firm's terminal value, can be used to estimate its equity value by discounting the various cash flows using the firm's cost of equity capital. We also illustrate the residual income approach to firm valuation and observe that both valuation approaches yield exactly the same estimate of firm value so long as equivalent forecasting assumptions are used. Finally, the comparable-firms approach to firm valuation is illustrated using price-earnings multiples.

WHOLE FOODS MARKET   Symbol: WFMI

CEO John Mackey, along with two other Austin, Texas investors, decided that the natural foods industry was ready for a supermarket format and founded Whole Foods Market. The first Whole Foods Market opened in 1980 with a staff of only 19 people. The Company is now the world's leading retailer of natural and organic foods, with 194 stores in North America and the United Kingdom.

Whole Foods Market is a mission driven company with a strong belief in a "virtuous circle," including the food chain, people, and the planet. The company motto is "Whole Foods, Whole People, Whole Planet." The company is consistently honored for its commitment to corporate social responsibility, ranking among "The Top 50 Best Corporate Citizens" by *Business Ethics* Magazine and among "The Top 10 Companies To Work For" by *Fortune* Magazine.

Whole Foods Market is also customer driven. The company strives to provide a high level of customer satisfaction and believes that by "offering the highest quality food available, we are helping to transform the diet of America, helping people live longer, healthier, more pleasurable lives while responding positively to the challenge of environmental sustainability."

Whole Foods Market understands that profits are an essential ingredient if they wish to be a responsible corporate citizen and provide benefits to their many stakeholders. As the company states, profits are "the 'seed corn' for next year's crop. We are the stewards of our shareholders' investments and we are committed to increasing long-term shareholder value." The company utilizes Economic Value Added (EVA), a variation of the residual income method discussed in this chapter, to help evaluate the firm's progress in reaching this goal.

What does it mean to increase long-term shareholder value? Shareholder value is increased when the return on the shareholders' investment in a business enterprise is increased through a combination of dividend distributions and share price appreciation. To determine whether this goal is attained requires that a value be calculated as to what an enterprise is worth. In this chapter, we examine various methodologies that allow a financial statement user to estimate the value of a company like Whole Foods Market.

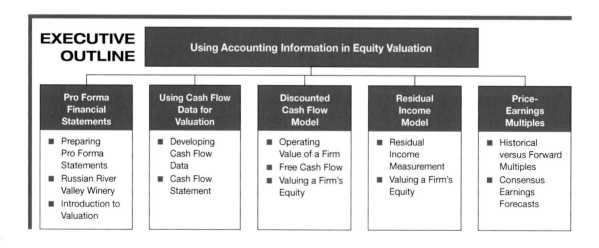

EXECUTIVE OUTLINE

Using Accounting Information in Equity Valuation

Pro Forma Financial Statements	Using Cash Flow Data for Valuation	Discounted Cash Flow Model	Residual Income Model	Price-Earnings Multiples
■ Preparing Pro Forma Statements ■ Russian River Valley Winery ■ Introduction to Valuation	■ Developing Cash Flow Data ■ Cash Flow Statement	■ Operating Value of a Firm ■ Free Cash Flow ■ Valuing a Firm's Equity	■ Residual Income Measurement ■ Valuing a Firm's Equity	■ Historical versus Forward Multiples ■ Consensus Earnings Forecasts

PRO FORMA FINANCIAL STATEMENTS

We first considered pro forma financial statements in Appendix 4B. At that time, we observed that investment professionals, managers, and shareholders are often interested in knowing how a firm might perform in the future under various economic scenarios. Pro forma financial statements are a good source of information to address these kinds of questions. In this chapter, we continue our exploration of pro forma financial statements to value the shareholders' equity of a business. As we will soon see, pro forma statements provide the raw data to develop an assessment of the fair value of a business.

To facilitate the calculations necessary to develop pro forma financial statements, we utilize an electronic spreadsheet. To illustrate the process of setting up a spreadsheet, we again turn to the financial data of the Russian River Valley Winery, Inc. that were developed in Chapter 2. In Chapter 2, we prepared a forecast of the firm's first year of operations in conjunction with the winery's request for bank financing. The winery's actual first-year results were stronger than predicted as the firm was able to sell more wine than its owners initially forecasted (sales of $1.9 million were forecasted while actual sales of $2.2 million were achieved). This positive turn-of-events lead to a higher-than-expected net income for the first year ($317,000 forecasted net income versus $521,000 actual net income). The second year of operations proved to be even better than the first, with an additional ten percent increase in sales (actual sales of $2.42 million). We now turn our attention to forecasting the next five years of performance for the winery to estimate the value of Matt's and Kate's investment in the business.

Exhibit 12.1 presents a spreadsheet for the winery, reflecting both its historical and forecasted financial performance. Columns Two and Three, for example, display the two years of actual performance data for the winery (2004 and 2005). This historical performance data, along with our knowledge of the operating environment of the winery, provides the necessary data for forecasting the winery's future financial performance. Our goal is to develop pro forma financial statements for the period 2006 through 2010.

EXHIBIT 12.1	Pro Forma Financial Statements: Russian River Valley Winery, Inc							

Panel A Income Statement

	Actual		Forecast					
($ thousands)	2004	2005	2006	2007	2008	2009	2010	Terminal
Sales (net)...............	$2,200	$2,420	$2,662	$2,928	$3,221	$3,543	$3,897	$4,092
Cost of goods sold..........	(330)	(363)	(399)	(439)	(483)	(531)	(585)	(614)
Gross profit...............	1,870	2,057	2,263	2,489	2,738	3,012	3,313	3,478
SG&A expense.............	(506)	(557)	(612)	(673)	(741)	(815)	(896)	(941)
Depreciation and amortization .	(275)	(275)	(275)	(275)	(275)	(275)	(275)	(289)
Interest expense............	(288)	(230)	(202)	(173)	(144)	(115)	(86)	(91)
EBT......................	801	995	1,174	1,368	1,578	1,807	2,055	2,158
Income taxes	(280)	(348)	(411)	(479)	(552)	(632)	(719)	(755)
Net income...............	$ 521	$ 647	$ 763	$ 889	$1,026	$1,174	$1,336	$1,403

continued

continued from previous page

EXHIBIT 12.1	Pro Forma Financial Statements: Russian River Valley Winery, Inc

Panel B Balance Sheet

	Actual		Forecast					
($ thousands)	2004	2005	2006	2007	2008	2009	2010	Terminal
Cash.	$ 860	$ 726	$ 799	$ 878	$ 966	$ 1,063	$ 1,169	$ 1,228
Other current assets.	1,180	968	1,065	1,171	1,288	1,417	1,559	1,637
Total current assets	2,040	1,694	1,863	2,050	2,255	2,480	2,728	2,865
PP&E (net)	9,275	9,275	9,275	9,275	9,275	9,275	9,275	9,739
Intangibles	50	0	0	0	0	0	0	0
Total assets.	$11,365	$10,969	$11,138	$11,325	$11,530	$11,755	$12,003	$12,603
Current debt.	$ 480	$ 480	$ 480	$ 480	$ 480	$ 480	$ 480	$ 504
Other current liabilities	384	605	666	732	805	886	974	1,023
Total current liabilities.	864	1,085	1,146	1,212	1,285	1,366	1,454	1,527
Long-term debt	3,840	3,360	2,880	2,400	1,920	1,440	960	1,008
Total liabilities	4,704	4,445	4,026	3,612	3,205	2,806	2,414	2,535
Paid-in-capital	6,400	6,400	6,400	6,400	6,400	6,400	6,400	6,720
Retained earnings	261	124	713	1,313	1,924	2,549	3,189	3,348
Total equity.	6,661	6,524	7,113	7,713	8,324	8,949	9,589	10,068
Total liabilities and equity	$11,365	$10,969	$11,138	$11,325	$11,530	$11,755	$12,003	$12,603

Panel C Statement of Retained Earnings

	Actual		Forecast					
($ thousands)	2004	2005	2006	2007	2008	2009	2010	Terminal
Beg. retained earnings	$ 0	$261	$124	$ 713	$1,313	$1,924	$2,549	$3,189
+ Net income.	521	647	763	889	1,026	1,174	1,336	1,403
− Dividends	(260)	(784)	(174)	(289)	(414)	(549)	(696)	(1,243)
= End. retained earnings	$261	$124	$713	$1,313	$1,924	$2,549	$3,189	$3,348

continued

To begin, the single most important assumption when developing pro forma financial statements is the forecast of future revenue. Many of the other income statement and balance sheet accounts will be forecasted as a function of a firm's future sales. Thus, a poor forecast of future sales revenue is very likely to result in a poorly constructed set of pro forma financial statements, and hence, an incorrect estimate of firm value. Consequently, it is essential to utilize whatever data may be available, such as a firm's prior operating history, the expected demand for new products, and demographic trends, to make the sales forecast as realistic as possible.

The process of preparing pro forma financial statements typically progresses with the following set of steps:

1. Forecast sales revenue.
2. Forecast the cost of goods sold, gross profit, and other operating expenses on the income statement as a function of forecasted sales (such as using the historical common-size percentages for those accounts where a linear relationship with sales is evident).

continued from previous page

EXHIBIT 12.1	Pro Forma Financial Statements: Russian River Valley Winery, Inc

Panel D Statement of Cash Flow

($ thousands)	Actual		Forecast					
	2004	2005	2006	2007	2008	2009	2010	Terminal
Operating activities								
Net income.	$ 521	$ 647	$ 763	$ 889	$1,026	$1,174	$1,336	$1,403
+ Depreciation and amortization.	275	275	275	275	275	275	275	289
− Increase in other current assets	(1,180)	212	(97)	(106)	(117)	(129)	(142)	(78)
+ Increase in other current liabilities.	384	221	61	67	73	81	89	49
= Cash from operations	(0)	1,355	1,002	1,124	1,257	1,401	1,558	1,662
Investing activities								
− Capital expenditures	(9,550)	(275)	(275)	(275)	(275)	(275)	(275)	(753)
− Purchases of intangibles . . .	(50)	50	0	0	0	0	0	0
= Cash from investing	(9,600)	(225)	(275)	(275)	(275)	(275)	(275)	(753)
Financing activities								
+ Increase in Debt	4,320	(480)	(480)	(480)	(480)	(480)	(480)	72
− Dividends	(260)	(784)	(174)	(289)	(414)	(549)	(696)	(1,243)
Issuance of common stock . . .	6,400	0	0	0	0	0	0	320
= Cash from financing	10,460	1,264)	(654)	(769)	(894)	(1,029)	(1,176)	(851)
Change in cash.	$ 860	$ (134)	$ 73	$ 80	$ 88	$ 97	$ 106	$ 58
+ Beg. cash	0	860	726	799	878	966	1,063	1,169
Ending cash balance	$ 860	$ 726	$ 799	$ 878	$ 966	$1,063	$1,169	$1,228

3. Forecast the balance sheet working capital accounts such as cash, accounts receivable, inventory, and accounts payable needed to support the forecasted sales (such as using such historical relationships as revealed by the receivable, inventory, and payable turnover ratios).

4. Forecast the property, plant and equipment and intangible assets needed to support the forecasted level of sales (such as using such historical relationships as revealed by the fixed asset turnover and intangible asset turnover ratios).

5. Forecast depreciation and amortization expense as a function of forecasted property, plant, and equipment and intangible assets. (Investment professionals frequently adopt a half-year convention when forecasting the depreciation and amortization expense associated with these capital investments to compensate for the uncertainty regarding the timing of such investments.)

6. Forecast the level of debt financing based on such strategic factors as the desired capital structure and the forecasted growth in sales.

7. Forecast interest expense based on the level of forecasted debt.

8. Forecast any remaining items on the income statement and then forecast the income tax expense based on forecasted earnings before tax and the firm's effective tax rate.

9. Forecast the statement of retained earnings based on the forecasted income statement and any expected dividend payments.

10. Prepare the pro forma statement of cash flow from the forecasted income statement and forecasted balance sheets using the indirect method (see Chapter 3).

11. Determine a **terminal year growth rate** for the pro forma terminal year. The terminal year is the year following the final forecast period (2011 for the Russian River Valley Winery). It is assumed that this growth rate will persist into perpetuity.

The above steps illustrate one approach to preparing pro forma financial statements. Other approaches also exist. For example, while accounts receivable, inventory, and accounts payable may be forecasted based on their respective turnover ratios, some investment professionals instead use the historical common-size balance sheet percentages to forecast these operating assets. And, some investment professionals will use a combination of ratios and common-size percentages to develop their pro forma estimates. As a consequence of the alternative approaches that may be used to forecast the individual balance sheet accounts, it is not unusual for a pro forma balance sheet to be out-of-balance. When this occurs, it is common to create a plug figure to achieve the necessary equality demanded by the balance sheet equation. Possible plug figures include cash and marketable securities when a plug figure is needed to balance the asset side of the balance sheet, and short-term debt or a line-of-credit when a plug figure is needed to balance the liability side of the balance sheet.[1]

Exhibit 12.2 presents the various assumptions that were used to construct the pro forma financial statements for the Russian River Valley Winery that appear in the forecast columns (2006 through the Terminal Year) of Exhibit 12.1. As detailed in Exhibit 12.2, the following assumptions were utilized:

- Sales are expected to grow by ten percent per year for five years and by five percent annually thereafter.
- Cost of goods sold will remain a constant fifteen percent of sales.
- Selling, general, and administrative (SG&A) expenses will remain a constant 23 percent of sales.
- The Russian River Valley Winery has sufficient capacity to produce enough wine to satisfy projected sales for the next five years without any new capital investment. As a consequence, depreciation will remain constant at the 2005 level.
- Interest expense will be six percent of the outstanding beginning-of-year balance of bank debt.
- Income taxes will be 35 percent of earnings before income taxes.
- Cash will be maintained at thirty percent of sales.
- Other current assets will be maintained at forty percent of sales.
- The only capital outlay will be an amount equal to the annual depreciation expense. As a consequence, net PP&E will remain constant for five years. After 2010, PP&E will grow at a rate equal to the rate of growth of sales.
- The current debt will continue to be paid down at a constant rate ($480,000 per year) for five years. After 2010, debt will grow at a rate equal to sales growth.
- Other current liabilities will remain a constant 25 percent of sales.
- Dividend payments are forecasted as a plug figure to balance retained earnings on the balance sheet.

---

[1] Care must be taken, however, when choosing a plug figure account as there are many inter-dependencies in the financial statements. For example, if debt is used as a plug figure to balance the liability side of the balance sheet, then interest expense on the income statement will need to be recomputed each time that the level of debt changes. This will alter net income, and therefore retained earnings, forcing another change to debt. While such situations can be resolved with more advanced mathematical techniques, it is often easier to use an account that has fewer dependencies (such as cash). It is also possible to solve these "circular reference" situations with the iteration function within Excel.

EXHIBIT 12.2	Pro Forma Assumptions
Item	Assumption
Sales	Grows annually at 10% until terminal year
Cost of goods sold	15% of sales
SG&A expense	23% of sales
Depreciation	Constant until terminal year
Interest expense	6% of outstanding debt
Income taxes	35% of earnings before taxes
Cash	30% of sales
Other current assets	40% of sales
PP&E	Constant net PP&E until terminal year
Debt	Constant payments of $480 until terminal year
Other current liabilities	25% of sales
Dividends	Plug figure to balance the balance sheet
All items	Terminal 5% annual growth

The spreadsheet in Exhibit 12.1 reveals that based upon the above set of assumptions, the Russian River Valley Winery will likely have both increasing profits and increasing cash flow from operations throughout the forecast period and beyond. Therefore, our assumptions regarding the need for debt and continuing dividend payments appear reasonable. One advantage of the electronic spreadsheet approach is that it is possible to conduct "what if" analyses—that is, to evaluate how the winery's financial performance would be affected if, for instance, sales growth is reduced to, say, five percent or if gross profit percentages are increased to reflect the realization of economies of scale that come with greater levels of output. In the next section, we will see how the pro forma financial statements can be used to help assess the equity value of a firm.

Introduction to Equity Valuation

How much is the Russian River Valley Winery worth? Recall from Chapter 2 that Matt and Kate sold 200,000 shares of the winery's common stock to an outside investor for $2 per share. How can we determine if this was a reasonable price to pay for the Russian River Valley Winery shares? An important role for accounting information is its use in valuing a business. To answer the question of what a share of stock in the Russian River Valley Winery is worth, it is first necessary to select a valuation framework to estimate the company's value. There are several valuation models that are widely used. If done correctly, each model will yield an identical estimate of firm value since they are based on the same fundamental theory of economic risk and reward. Which model is used is usually determined by individual investor preference or practical considerations such as data availability.

The two models that we illustrate are the discounted cash flow model, which is based on a firm's free cash flow, and the residual income model, which is based on a firm's accrual earnings. We also explore the popular price-earnings multiple model—a model that is not based on theory but whose popularity can be traced to its ease of use and ease in understanding.

USING CASH FLOW DATA TO VALUE A COMPANY

A fundamental tenet of modern financial theory is that the value of an asset or a bundle of assets (such as an entire company), is equal to the present value of the future cash flows that accrue from ownership of the asset (or company). Thus, this tenet suggests that the primary source of firm value is a firm's operating cash flows. Hence, the task that investment professionals, equity investors, and managers face when trying to value a company is to forecast a firm's future cash flows using pro forma financial statements and to then discount the projected cash flows using an appropriate discount rate. This valuation framework is called the **discounted cash flow approach**.

Developing Cash Flow Data

Use of the discounted cash flow approach to firm valuation assumes an understanding of, and capability of, developing cash flow data. As indicated above, pro forma cash flow data is extracted from the pro forma income statements and balance sheets using the indirect method format. In Chapter 3, we illustrated a five-step process for preparing a statement of cash flow using the indirect method. That illustration was, of necessity, highly simplistic. We now return to that five-step process and consider a more sophisticated cash flow example which integrates some of the accounting measurement concepts and approaches discussed in Chapters 5 through 11. Specifically, we now consider how the accounting for zero-coupon bonds (Chapter 10), the use of the equity method to account for unconsolidated affiliates, joint ventures or special purpose entities (Chapter 8), and the accounting for a gain or loss on the sale or retirement of a long-lived asset (Chapter 7) affects the cash flow of a business.

   Our current illustration involves the **Arctic Sea Oil & Gas Company Ltd.**, a Canadian energy company. Financial information for the company for 2004 and 2005 is presented in Panels A and B of Exhibit 12.3. As discussed in Chapter 3, the five-step process to prepare a statement of cash flow using the indirect method format is as follows:

1. Measure the change in all balance sheet accounts by subtracting the beginning balance from the ending balance. Recall that the increase or decrease in the cash and cash equivalents account is the check figure for the cash flow statement.

2. Classify each of the balance sheet accounts into one of the three cash flow activity categories: Operating, Investing, and Financing.

3. Prepare a preliminary statement of cash flow using the values from Step One and the activity classifications from Step Two. Remember that the sign of the change of the asset accounts are reversed, but the sign of the change of the liability and shareholders' equity accounts are not.

4. Integrate the income statement data (such as depreciation and amortization expense) into the preliminary statement of cash flow, remembering that it is necessary to always balance to the change in cash.

5. Make any necessary refinements to the cash flow from operations (CFFO) to identify the sustainable operating cash flow of the business by removing any non-recurring, non-operating gains or losses.

   Panel A of Exhibit 12.3 presents the results of Steps 1 and 2 of our five-step process; and, Panel C presents the results of Step 3—Arctic's preliminary statement of cash flow using only the company's balance sheet data. As required, Arctic's preliminary statement of cash flow balances to the change in cash on Arctic's balance sheet of negative $10.183 million. Can you replicate Arctic's preliminary statement of cash flow in Panel C using the data from Panel A of Exhibit 12.3?

Step 4 involves the introduction of Arctic's income statement data presented in Panel B of Exhibit 12.3. The adjustments (in thousands) to the preliminary statement of cash flow required at this step include the following:

1. Replace Arctic's change in retained earnings of $22,668 with net income of $46,168 under the operating activities section. The difference of $23,500 ($46,168 – $22,668) is also shown as a cash outflow for dividends paid to shareholders under the financing activities section.

2. Depreciation and depletion expense of $24,800, a non-cash expense, is added back to accrual net income under the operating activities section and also subtracted from the change in the oil and gas properties (net) under the investing activities section.

3. Amortization expense of $750, a non-cash expense, is added back to accrual net income under the operating activities section and subtracted from the change in intangible assets under the investing activities section.

4. Zero-coupon interest expense of $4,757, a non-cash expense, is added back to accrual net income under the operating activities section and subtracted from the change in zero-coupon debenture issuance under the financing activities section.

5. The equity in the earnings of unconsolidated affiliates of $36,650, representing Arctic's ownership interest in the earnings of its affiliates that it does not control (and thus which remain unconsolidated), is subtracted from accrual net income under the operating activities section and added to the change in the Investment in Affiliated Companies under the investing activities section.

6. The gain on the sale of property and equipment of $1,000, a non-recurring and non-operating event, is subtracted from net income under the operating activities section and added to the change in oil and gas properties (net) under the investing activities section.

EXHIBIT 12.3	Financial Data: Arctic Sea Oil & Gas Company Ltd.				
Panel A Consolidated Balance Sheet					
(in thousands)		**2005**	**2004**	**Δ**	**Category**
Assets					
Current assets					
Cash.		$100,067	$110,250	$ (10,183)	Ck Figure
Accounts receivable.		69,100	53,200	15,900	O
Inventory		58,950	46,800	12,150	O
Prepaid expenses		11,108	13,850	(2,742)	O
		239,225	224,100		
Investments					
In affiliated companies.		159,000	151,000	800,000	I
Marketable equity securities		2,500	0	2,500	I
Long-term assets					
Oil & Gas properties, equipment (net)		237,850	246,900	(9,050)	I/O
Intangible assets		3,000	3,750	(750)	I/O
Total assets.		$641,575	$625,750	$ 15,825	
Liabilities and Shareholders' Equity					
Current liabilities					
Accounts payable		$ 1,650	$ 8,000	$ (6,350)	O
Income taxes payable		4,750	3,250	1,500	O

continued

continued from previous page

EXHIBIT 12.3	Financial Data: Arctic Sea Oil & Gas Company Ltd.

Panel A Consolidated Balance Sheet

(in thousands)	2005	2004	Δ	Category
Long-term liabilities				
Zero-coupon debentures...............	53,507	0	53,507	F
Deferred income taxes.................	46,000	40,000	6,000	O
Employee retirement benefits	62,500	60,000	2,500	O
Total liabilities.........................	$168,407	$111,250		
Shareholders' Equity				
Common shares at par	$103,000	$ 75,000	28,000	F
Capital in excess of par...............	157,500	150,000	7,500	F
Preferred shares, no par	0	100,000	(100,000)	F
Retained earnings	212,168	189,500	22,668	O/F
Other Comprehensive Income				
Unrealized gain on available-for-sale				I
securities........................	500	0	500	
Total liabilities and shareholders' equity.......	$641,575	$625,750	$ 15,825	

Panel B Consolidated Income Statements

(in thousands)	2005
Revenue..	$483,135
Costs and expenses	
Cost of goods sold	345,920
Depreciation and depletion expense............................	24,800
Selling and general expenses	54,215
Amortization expense	750
Operating income......................................	$ 57,450
Other (expense) income	
Interest expense	(4,757)
Equity in earnings of unconsolidated affiliates	36,650
Gain on sale of property and equipment.......................	1,000
Income before income taxes	$ 90,343
Less: Income tax provision......................................	(44,175)
Net income...	$ 46,168

continued

    Following the set of six adjustments, it is now possible to develop Arctic's final statement of cash flow using the indirect method format, and this final statement is presented in Exhibit 12.4. Arctic's statement of cash flow in Exhibit 12.4 reveals that the company's sustainable CFFO is $17.167 million, its CFFI is $11.9 million, and its CFFF is negative $39.25 million, aggregating to a decrease in cash of $10.183 million. Now that you have a more complete understanding of how to construct a complex statement of cash flow, let's consider how this data can be used to value a company using the discounted cash flow approach.

continued from previous page

EXHIBIT 12.3	Financial Data: Arctic Sea Oil & Gas Company Ltd.

Panel C Preliminary Statement of Cash Flow

(in thousands)	2005
Operating activities	
Retained earnings	$ 22,668
Accounts receivable.	(15,900)
Inventory	(12,150)
Prepaid expenses	2,742
Accounts payable	(6,350)
Income tax payable	1,500
Deferred income taxes.	6,000
Employee retirement benefits	2,500
Cash flow from operations	1,010
Investing activities	
Investment in affiliated companies	(8,000)
Marketable equity securities	(2,500)
Unrealized gain on long-term marketable securities	500
Oil and gas properties, equipment (net).	9,050
Intangible assets	750
Cash flow for investing.	$(200)
Financing activities	
Zero-coupon debenture issuance	53,507
Common stock issuance	35,500
Preferred share retirement	(100,000)
Cash flow for financing.	(10,993)
Change in cash.	$ (10,183)

VALUATION USING THE DISCOUNTED CASH FLOW MODEL

Operating Value of a Firm

One of the well-documented limitations of humans is an inability to forecast the future. Weatherman routinely forecast the temperature and weather conditions for days, and sometimes even weeks in advance with considerable accuracy; but, they never attempt to forecast weather conditions years in advance because they lack the skill to do so. This same situation confronts financial analysts, investment professionals, and managers as they try to estimate the value of a business. Since firm value depends on what will happen in the future, it is necessary to forecast the future, or at least some part of the future.

In general, most investment professionals and managers feel comfortable forecasting a firm's performance for the coming year, at least for most industries. But, that confidence quickly erodes as they attempt to forecast beyond one or two years. Fortunately, as a consequence of the discounting process, the value of near-term forecasts is far more important when assessing firm value than are longer-term forecasts (since the value of $1 in one year is considerably greater than the value of $1 in ten years).

Because of our inability to accurately forecast far into the future, we dichotomize a company's future into two time periods—a specific forecast period (the pro forma statement preparation period) and the

EXHIBIT 12.4	Statement of Cash Flow: Arctic Sea Oil & Gas Company Ltd	
(in thousands)	**Consolidated Statement of Cash Flow**	**2005**
Operating activities		
Net income.		$ 46,168
Accounts receivable.		(15,900)
Inventory		(12,150)
Prepaid expenses		2,742
Accounts payable		(6,350)
Income tax payable		1,500
Deferred income taxes.		6,000
Employee retirement benefits		2,500
Depreciation and depletion expense.		24,800
Amortization expense		750
Zero-coupon interest expense.		4,757
Equity in earnings of unconsolidated affiliates		(36,650)
Gain on sale of property and equipment.		(1,000)
Cash flow from operations.		17,167
Investing activities		
Investment in affiliated companies		28,650
Marketable equity securities		(2,000)
Oil and gas properties, equipment (net).		(14,750)
Cash flow for investing.		11,900
Financing activities		
Zero-coupon debenture issuance		48,750
Common stock issuance.		35,500
Preferred share retirement.		(100,000)
Dividend paid.		(23,500)
Cash flow for financing.		(39,250)
Change in cash.		$(10,183)

period thereafter. The pro forma forecast period is that period of time for which investment professionals, managers and shareholders feel confident in their ability to prepare specific pro forma financial statements, and thereafter is all periods in which they feel unable to do so. Using this simple dichotomy, we define the **operating value** of a business as follows:

$$\text{Operating Value of a Business} = \text{Present Value of Operating Cash Flows During the Specific Forecast Period} + \text{Present Value of Operating Cash Flows Thereafter}$$

The second component of operating value is commonly referred to as the **continuing value** of a business, or alternatively, as its **terminal value** (TV). It is the value of a business from the end of the specific forecast period (the pro forma statement preparation period) until the business is sold or otherwise terminated. Thus, we can refine the definition of firm operating value as follows:

$$\text{Operating Value of a Business} = \text{Present Value of Operating Cash Flows During the Specific Forecast Period} + \text{Present Value of a Firm's TV}$$

We will have more to say about computing terminal values shortly.

Free Cash Flow

As noted earlier, the primary source of a firm's value is its operating cash flows—that is, the cash generated from its sustainable, recurring operations. There are two approaches to discounting the operating cash flow to value a company. One approach is to utilize a measure of the cash flow to all capital providers, both creditors and equity investors. This approach leads to a value for the entire enterprise. To obtain a value for just the equity of a business—that is, the value of a business' common shares—it is necessary to obtain a separate value for the firm's debt (as discussed in Chapter 9). The value of a firm's debt is then subtracted from the enterprise's total value to yield its equity value. In this chapter, we illustrate a second discounted cash flow approach that is used to directly value the equity of a firm.

To be a going concern, a business must constantly re-invest in itself, replacing those assets consumed by its operations each period. As discussed in Chapter 3, a firm's **free cash flow** (FCF) is defined as the cash flow from operations (CFFO) available to capital contributors (debtholders and shareholders) less the capital expenditures necessary to enable a firm to maintain itself as a going concern (to replace or replenish any assets consumed).[2] A variant of a firm's FCF is its **free cash flow to common equity**, which is nothing more than the net cash distributions to common shareholders.[3] Free cash flow to equity can be measured in multiple ways; however, all definitions are equivalent and must yield the same result. Exhibit 12.5 illustrates the computation of free cash flow to equity for the Russian River Valley Winery utilizing the financial statement data from Exhibit 12.1.[4]

EXHIBIT 12.5	Free Cash Flow to Equity Computation					
Panel A						
Year of Forecast (in 000's)	**2006**	**2007**	**2008**	**2009**	**2010**	**Terminal**
Financing flows						
Dividends paid	$ 174	$ 289	$ 414	$ 549	$ 696	$1,243
− Net issuance of common stock	0	0	0	0	0	(320)
Free cash flow to equity	174	289	414	549	696	923
Panel B						
Cash flow from operations	$1,002	$1,124	$1,257	$1,401	$1,558	$1,662
− Increase in operating cash	(73)	(80)	(88)	(97)	(106)	(58)
+ Cash from investing	(275)	(275)	(275)	(275)	(275)	(753)
+ Increase in debt	(480)	(480)	(480)	(480)	(480)	72
Free cash flow to equity	174	289	414	549	696	923

continued

---

[2] Recall from Chapter 3 that we defined a firm's free cash flows (FCF) as: FCF = CFFO − Capital expenditures.

[3] We will refer to free cash flow to common equity as simply "free cash flow to equity" under the assumption that a firm does not have any preferred shareholders.

[4] Valuation computations for the Russian River Valley Winery were done with the aid of the spreadsheet program eVal. Russel Lundholm and Richard Sloan, Equity Valuation and Analysis with eVal. McGraw Hill, 2004.

continued from previous page

EXHIBIT 12.5	Free Cash Flow to Equity Computation					
Panel C						
Year of Forecast (in 000's)	**2006**	**2007**	**2008**	**2009**	**2010**	**Terminal**
Net income.	$ 763	$ 889	$1,026	$1,174	$1,336	$1,403
− Increase in common equity	(589)	(600)	(612)	(625)	(639)	(479)
Free cash flow to equity.	174	289	414	549	696	923

The first definition of free cash flow to equity in Panel A is perhaps the simplest and most straightforward. It merely looks to the financing section of the statement of cash flow and identifies the two items that are cash flow transactions involving the common shareholders. For the Russian River Valley Winery in 2006, projected dividend payments are $174,000, but there are no other forecasted cash flows to or from shareholders (such as no sales or repurchases of common shares). Therefore, the free cash flow to equity is $174,000.

The second definition of free cash flow to equity, illustrated in Panel B of Exhibit 12.5, uses the statement of cash flow and backs into the amount of cash flow to equity by removing all other cash flows. This definition starts with the CFFO and subtracts any increase in the cash account (if the cash account increased, this would suggest that the cash was not paid to shareholders). Next, any cash from investing is added if it is positive and subtracted if it is negative. Finally, any cash received from borrowings is added and any cash paid to a firm's creditors is subtracted. What remains is the free cash flow to equity since the cash retained by the firm, used to purchase assets, or used to retire debt has been removed. For the Russian River Valley Winery in 2006, projected cash flow from operations is $1,002,000; however, the company retained $73,000 of this amount. From this net cash of $929,000 ($1,002,000 − $73,000), $275,000 was invested in long-term assets and $480,000 was used to retire debt, yielding a cash flow to equity of $174,000 ($929,000 − $480,000 − $275,000).

The final definition of free cash flow to equity uses only the income statement and the balance sheet. As noted in Panel C, the free cash flow to equity is simply net income less any increase in common shareholders' equity. For the Russian River Valley Winery in 2006, projected net income is $763,000 and the only change in common equity is an increase of $589,000 in retained earnings. Therefore, the free cash flow to equity is again computed to be $174,000 ($763,000 − $589,000).

Russian River Valley's free cash flows for years 2007 through 2010, along with the terminal year forecast, are calculated in a similar fashion and are presented in Exhibit 12.5. Having determined the free cash flow to equity for the winery, we now turn to the valuation of the firm's equity.

Valuing a Firm's Equity

The first step in valuing any asset, such as a piece of equipment or a whole company, is to realize that the payoffs received from ownership of the asset are worth less the longer it takes to receive the payoffs. This economic fact is referred to as the time value of money. (See the appendix at the end of this book for a discussion of the time value of money.) In essence, $1 received in ten years is worth much less than $1 received immediately. In fact, $1 received in ten years would be worth only $0.39 if you could earn ten percent per year by putting your money in an investment elsewhere. Thus, if you were offered a deal in which you had to pay a sum of money today to receive $1 in ten years, the most you should be willing to pay is $0.39. The value today—$0.39—is called the present value of $1 to be received in ten years with a rate of return of ten percent per year. The ten percent per year is the opportunity cost or required rate of return on your investment. The opportunity cost is also known as the discount rate for the investment.

Financial theory postulates that the value of any financial asset is simply the sum of the future cash flows to be received from the asset, discounted at an appropriate risk-adjusted rate. In Chapter 9, we saw that the value of a bond could be calculated by discounting each of the future interest payments along with the final principal payment. While the same definition applies to the valuation of a firm's equity, several factors make the calculation more complex. The first complexity involves the degree of uncertainty associated with the future cash flows. We incorporate this uncertainty into our valuation analysis through the use of a discount rate based on the firm's cost of equity capital, an amount that is commonly several percentage points greater than a firm's cost of debt.

A widely-accepted tenet of modern financial theory is that the appropriate rate to discount a stream of cash is that rate which best reflects the riskiness of the flows. In the case of a business' free cash flow to equity, since the cash flows are net of the interest expense paid to debtholders, the valuation model discounts these payoffs—that is, finds their present value—at the rate of return required by the firm's shareholders, or what is commonly referred to as the firm's **cost of common equity** (r_e). This topic is covered extensively in basic finance courses but the idea is simple. Finance professionals use the **capital asset pricing model** (CAPM) to establish the point that there is a linear relationship between a company's risk (β) and the expected return required by equity investors (r_e). The model says that if investors can earn the risk-free rate of return (r_f) by investing in government securities, the expected return on a risky investment should be the risk-free (r_f) rate *plus* a risk premium that is proportional to the company's risk. That is, $r_e = r_f + \beta \times$ risk premium, where β is the company's **beta**. (See Appendix C to Chapter 4 for additional information on CAPM.)

> Beta is a measure of the historical volatility of a company's share price relative to the capital market as a whole. Betas can be found in Standard and Poor's publications, Yahoo!Finance on the Worldwide Web, or in ValueLine publications, among others.

To facilitate our illustration, assume that: (1) the beta for the Russian River Valley Winery is 0.70, compared to 1.0 for the U.S. stock market as a whole (such as the Standard & Poor's 500 index); (2) the yield rate on ten-year U.S. Treasury Bonds, a long-term risk-free rate of interest, is 4.75 percent; and (3) the historical risk premium of 7.5 percent is estimated as the average difference between the annual returns on U.S. Treasury Bonds and an index of common stocks over a long period of time. (The calculation of an appropriate risk premium is a hotly debated topic in financial circles; a full discussion of this issue is beyond the scope of this book.) Under these assumptions, the cost of equity (r_e) for the Russian River Valley Winery is ten percent (4.75% + 0.7*7.5%).

The second complexity involves the timing and duration of the future cash flows associated with a business. When finding the value of a bond in Chapter 9, we knew when and for how long the various cash flows associated with the bond would be received. The same cannot be said for a firm's equity. In fact, we assume in most cases that a firm will continue indefinitely. Since the value of the equity requires us to discount to the present all future cash flows, we are presented with a dilemma. Fortunately, there is an accepted shortcut that allows us to forecast a relatively small number of years (such as five years for Russian River Valley Winery) and then create a terminal year forecast to reflect the cash flows for all years thereafter.

Because we assume that a business is a going-concern, the terminal value is an aggregate measure of a business' free cash flows for all periods beyond the specific forecast period; it is a proxy measure for the future free cash flow of a business that an analyst is unable to forecast on a period-by-period basis using pro forma financial statements. As a practical matter, the longer the forecast period, the smaller will be the terminal value (TV). For short forecast periods (such as five years for the Russian River Valley Winery), the TV may constitute the majority of a business' total operating value.

A widely used approach to estimate a firm's TV is the perpetuity growth formula. Under the perpetuity growth formula, a business is assumed to grow at some constant annual rate, g, in perpetuity. Since g is likely to be unknown, it is common practice to set g equal to the expected rate of inflation. Under this formula, a firm's TV is estimated as follows:

$$TV = FCF/(r_e - g)$$

where FCF is the firm's free cash flow to equity in the terminal year and r_e is the firm's cost of equity capital, which can be calculated using the CAPM.

Valuing the Russian River Valley Winery Shares

Exhibit 12.6 presents a discounted cash flow analysis of the Russian River Valley Winery's operating cash flow assuming a five-year forecast horizon. The free cash flow to equity values were obtained from Exhibit 12.5. Each of these cash flows for the five year forecast horizon is discounted to the present using the firm's ten percent cost of equity. The sum of these present values is shown to be $1.516 million.

The terminal year FCF of $923,000 produces a terminal value of $18.460 million ($923,000/0.05) using the perpetuity growth formula and assuming a growth rate of five percent and a cost of equity of ten percent. This value, discounted back to the present, equals $11.463 million.

$$TV = \frac{FCF}{(r_e - g)}$$
$$= \frac{\$923}{(1 + .10)^5}$$
$$= \$18,460$$
$$= \frac{\$18,460}{(1 + .10)^5}$$
$$= \$11,463$$

The $12.979 million value of Russian River Valley equity is the sum of these two amounts ($1.516 million + $11.463 million), or $2.09 per share when divided by the 6.2 million shares outstanding. Obviously, this value is highly dependent on the reasonableness of the assumptions that were used to build the winery's pro forma financial statements in Exhibit 12.3. An error in any of the key assumptions, such as the growth rate of revenue, could result in a material error in the discounted cash flow estimate of firm value. Thus, considerable effort should be expended developing reasonable assumptions, and hence, generating reliable pro forma data.

In the next section, an accounting-based valuation model, the residual income (RI) model, is illustrated. This model uses accounting variables that are found in a company's basic financial statements to assess firm value. Following a discussion of RI valuation, valuation using price-earnings multiples is considered.

EXHIBIT 12.6	Discounted Cash Flow						
Year of forecast (in 000's)		**2006**	**2007**	**2008**	**2009**	**2010**	**Terminal**
Free cash flow to common equity		$ 174	$289	$414	$549	$696	$923
Present value of FCF		$ 158	$239	$311	$375	$432	
Present value of first 5 years		$ 1,516					
Present value beyond 5 years		$11,463					
Value attributable to common equity		$12,979					
Common shares outstanding		6,200					
Forecast price per share.		$ 2.09					

VALUATION USING THE RESIDUAL INCOME MODEL

Unlike the free cash flow model, the **residual income** model (RI) focuses on accounting variables rather than cash flows.[5] Residual income is derived from the basic financial tenet that a firm only adds value to its shareholders if it is able to earn a return greater than its cost of capital. As with the free cash flow to equity valuation model just discussed, the cost of capital is simply the firm's cost of equity (r_e). More formally, residual income, also known as **excess earnings**, is defined as the firm's net income, or **normal earnings**, less the opportunity cost associated with common shareholders' equity:

$$RI_t = NI_t - r_e CE_{t-1}$$

The opportunity cost associated with shareholders' equity, $r_e CE_{t-1}$, is defined as the firm's cost of equity times its beginning-of-period common shareholders' equity. In other words, residual income is the amount of net income the firm earns above the amount that could have been earned by the shareholders if they had invested their money elsewhere at their required rate of return. This is best illustrated by thinking of a savings account that pays five percent interest in which you deposit $1,000 at the beginning of the year. Your opportunity cost of withdrawing your savings and investing elsewhere is the foregone interest you would no longer earn—$50 in this case. If you took your savings and invested in a project that earned eight percent, the residual income would be the excess earning of three percent (eight percent less five percent) times your investment of $1,000—$30 in this example ($80 − $50). Further, since this project can earn a rate of return in excess of the cost of capital, it will be popular with other investors. These other investors, in an effort to also earn the higher rate of return, will try to acquire ownership shares in the project, and in so doing, will bid up the price of the project so that your investment will be worth more than its original $1,000. In other words, by earning residual income, the project will be able to add value and this additional value is equal to the present value of all expected future residual income.

Under the RI approach, the value of a firm's equity (E_t)—that is, the value of its outstanding common shares—is equal to the book value of shareholders' equity (CE_{t-1}) from the balance sheet plus the firm's future residual income (RI_t) discounted at the cost of equity (r_e) over the life of the firm (t):

$$E_0 = CE_{t-1} + \Sigma\, RI_t/(1 + r_e)^t$$

---

[5] For a complete discourse on the residual income valuation model, see S. Penman, *Financial Statement Analysis and Security Valuation,* 2nd edition, McGraw-Hill International (2004).

Stated alternatively, the residual income model assumes that a firm's equity value (E_0) is equal to the current book value of shareholders' equity (CE_{t-1}) plus the present value of the firm's expected future residual income (future earnings less normal earnings).

A natural question to ask is how a firm's equity can be valued as the present value of its future free cash flow to equity, a measure based on cash flows, and also as the present value of its future residual income, a measure based on earnings, and come to the same valuation result. You may even be wondering how it is even possible to perform a valuation using earnings given all the myriad of accounting policy choices and estimates present under the GAAP framework. How can a consistent valuation be achieved when so many different earnings numbers are possible depending upon which accounting policy choices and estimates are made? These are good questions and luckily there is a good answer for each.

First, it can be demonstrated mathematically that the present value of free cash flow and of residual income over the life of a firm are identical. With some simple algebra, it can be demonstrated that operating cash flow and residual income valuation will lead to the exact same valuation result. Therefore, which method is used comes down to practical issues such as data availability and one's ability to forecast earnings versus cash flows.[6]

It can also be shown with some simple algebra that the types of accounting policy choices and estimates made by managers will not effect the ultimate equity valuation.[7] The reason behind this resides in the way that the balance sheet and the income statement work together, along with the way that the residual income computation is discounted. For example, if a firm's assets are depreciated using the double-declining balance method, then net income will be lower in the early years. At the same time, the common equity account (through retained earnings) will also be lower, leading to a lower charge against net income to compute residual income. These offsetting amounts, when discounted at the cost of equity, exactly cancel each other out and lead to the same valuation result regardless of the accounting policy choices and estimates.

Valuing the Russian River Valley Winery Shares

Exhibit 12.7 illustrates the valuation of the Russian River Valley common equity using the residual income method. We first compute the residual income for the five-year forecast period, along with the terminal year. The computation begins with net income, which we obtain from Panel A of Exhibit 12.1. We then subtract the opportunity cost of the shareholders' investment, defined as beginning-of-year common equity (obtained from Panel B of Exhibit 12.1) multiplied by the firm's ten percent cost of equity capital (such as in 2006, 10 percent × $6.524 million = $652,000). For 2006, this yields residual income of $111,000 ($763,000 − $652,000). We next discount the future residual incomes back to the present using the firm's ten percent cost of equity capital. The present values of the five years of forecasted residual income are then aggregated to $946,000. As we did with the free cash flow valuation, the terminal year residual income is first divided by the difference between the cost of equity capital (ten percent) and the assumed growth rate (five percent), and this amount is then discounted to the present at the cost of equity, yielding $5.510 million. These two amounts are combined with the initial common equity of $6.524 million to yield a $12.979 million valuation of common equity. When divided by the outstanding shares of 6.2 million, we get a value of $2.09 per share, exactly as we did with the free cash flow to equity valuation.

It is instructive to compare the results of the two valuations methods. While each yields the same $12.979 million valuation estimate for equity, the component parts of the valuation analysis are much different. The discounted cash flow approach attributes far more of the firm's value to the firm's terminal value—$11.463 million compared to $5.509 million—than does the residual income approach. In con-

---

[6] Ohlson, James A.,"Earnings, book value, and dividends in equity valuations," Contemporary Accounting Research 11, pp. 661–687
[7] R. Lundholm and R. Sloan, *Equity Valuation and Analysis with eVal*. McGraw Hill, 2004.

EXHIBIT 12.7	Residual Income Valuation					
Year of Forecast (in 000's)	2006	2007	2008	2009	2010	Terminal
Net income.	$ 763	$ 889	$1,026	$1,174	$1,336	$1,403
Common equity at beginning of year.	6,524	7,113	7,713	8,324	8,949	9,589
Residual income.	111	178	254	342	441	444
Present value of residual income	101	147	191	233	274	
Present value of first 5 years	946					
Present value beyond 5 years	5,509					
Common equity as of 2005	6,524					
Value attributable to common equity	12,979					
Common shares outstanding.	6,200					
Forecast price per share.	2.09					

trast, the residual income approach attributes far more of the firm's value to the first five years of forecasted operations—$7.470 million compared to $1.516 million. Why is this?

These differences are a consequence of how each approach considers value creation. The residual income approach considers the existing investment to have value—$6.524 million in this case—and then considers future excess earnings above the firm's cost of capital as incremental value. The discounted cash flow approach, in contrast, only considers future cash flows as value-relevant, and therefore, places a greater percentage of the equity's value on the firm's future cash flows.

VALUATION USING PRICE-EARNINGS MULTIPLES

Both the free cash flow to equity and the residual income valuation approaches are premised on the basic financial concept that the value of any asset is simply the present value of the future cash flows generated by the asset. Unfortunately, while these valuation methods are widely accepted as theoretically sound, they are not easy to apply. Each requires forecasted pro forma financial statements and each is subject to the various uncertainties inherent in forecasting the future. Recent academic research indicates that investment professionals often use a much simpler approach based on comparable firms to value a company, although they often later supplement this simple approach with one of the two approaches discussed.[8]

This simplified approach is based on the concept that equally risky financial assets that provide similar payouts should sell for prices that are similar. One of the most common forms of the comparable firms approach is price-earnings (P/E) multiples valuation. The P/E multiple—or the market price per share divided by the earnings per share—indicates the relative amount that investors are willing to pay for $1 of sustainable corporate earnings. Thus, a P/E multiple of 20 indicates that investors are willing to pay $20 for each dollar of future recurring income earned by a company.

Earnings multiples can be calculated for a variety of earnings-based metrics but are most often calculated for earnings after taxes (P/E), earnings before interest and taxes (P/EBIT), and earnings before interest, taxes, depreciation, and amortization (P/EBITDA). The two most popular earnings multiples are P/E and P/EBITDA, the latter largely because of its close proximity to a firm's CFFO.

Earnings multiples can also be calculated for a variety of time periods. A **trailing multiple**, for example, is obtained by dividing a company's recent closing share price by its *historical* earnings per share

---

[8] Demirakos, N. Strong, and M Waller, "What Valuation Models Do Analysts Use," *Accounting Horizons*, December, 2004.

(EPS) for the most recently completed fiscal period (quarter or year). (Most analysts use basic EPS but some use diluted EPS.) A *forward multiple*, on the other hand, is a company's current closing share price divided by *forecasted* earnings per share. Since a firm's share price is thought to be a function of future earnings, forward multiples are conceptually superior to historical multiples.

Most businesses routinely develop budgeted (or pro forma) financial statements for internal planning purposes; hence, forecasted EPS values are readily available to managers to assess a firm's value. These internal forecasts of profitability are rarely externally publicized, however; and thus, investment professionals and shareholders must develop their own forecasts of EPS, or alternatively subscribe to such data services as *Zacks Investment Research*, *Institutional Brokers' Estimate System*, or *First Call/Thompson Financial* which provide consensus earnings forecasts for most publicly-held companies. *Consensus earnings forecasts* are the average forecast of future earnings from a group of professional analysts that routinely follow a particular company's performance.

Perhaps the most difficult aspect of the comparable companies approach is to find comparable companies. While most professionals simply look at similar size firms in the same industry, care must be taken to consider such factors as firm risk, accounting policy differences and growth options. Each of these factors should be value relevant and result in different P/E multiples. Once a group of comparable firms is determined, the P/E multiples approach is quite easy to implement. This process is best illustrated by way of an example.

To value the common equity of the Russian River Valley Winery, Kate and Matt found four wineries that appeared to be comparable. The earnings per share and share price, along with the computed P/E ratio of each winery, are presented in Exhibit 12.8.

EXHIBIT 12.8	Comparable Price-Earnings Ratios		
Winery	**EPS**	**Share Price**	**P/E ratio**
A.	$0.50	$ 9.00	18
B.	$0.06	$ 1.32	22
C.	$1.25	$20.00	16
D.	$0.60	$14.40	24
Average			20

Russian River Valley's 2005 net income was $647,000. Since the outstanding number of shares was 6.2 million, the winery's EPS for 2005 is $0.104. Using an average P/E multiple of 20, based on the identified comparable firms (see Exhibit 12.8), yields a share price of $2.09 ($0.104 × 20) for the Russian River Valley Winery.

ETHICS PERSPECTIVE

Historically, there have been three approaches to developing and teaching ethics. Utilitarianism, which is closely associated with John Stuart Mill, teaches that ethical behavior leads to the best consequences. Deontology, associated with Immanuel Kant, teaches that ethics is a matter of finding the right rule. Finally, a virtue-based approach to ethics states that ethics is a matter of acquiring and putting into practice the relevant "virtue." Which of the three approaches do you feel most accurately describes your personal philosophy of ethics?

BUSINESS PERSPECTIVE: JOHNSON & JOHNSON INC.

To illustrate the use of P/E multiple valuation, consider the case of Johnson & Johnson Inc. (J&J), a leading pharmaceutical and consumer products' company. J&J reported EPS for the year ending December 31 of $3.05 per share and had a closing share price of $63.20 per share. Hence, the company's trailing P/E multiple was 20.7 times earnings:

$$\text{Trailing P/E Multiple} = \$63.20/\$3.05 = 20.7$$

The consensus EPS forecast of a survey of 18 professional analysts that tracked the company was $3.35 for the following fiscal year , yielding a forward P/E multiple of:

$$\text{Forward P/E Multiple} = \$63.20/\$3.35 = 18.7$$

Presumably, J&J's year-end price of $63.20 reflects the consensus earnings estimate, and thus, conceptually, the forward multiple of 18.7 would more accurately reflect the market's consensus of the value of the firm.

How can the forward multiple be used to value J&J? As new information is obtained, such as actual first quarter earnings for the following year, the multiple can be used to calculate whether the firm's current share price is undervalued (a buy), overvalued (a sell), or fairly valued (a hold). For instance, if J&J reports first quarter earnings of $0.80 per share, the annualized earnings would equal $3.20 per share (4 × $0.80). On the basis of its annualized earnings and a forward P/E multiple of 18.7, J&J's shares would be fairly priced at $59.84 per share. If J&J's share price is below (above) $59.84, it would be considered undervalued (overvalued) using the P/E multiple framework.

EXECUTIVE SUMMARY

Accounting information can be used to benchmark a firm's performance, to help managers make important operating decisions, and to help assess the value of a firm. The focus of this final chapter was firm valuation. Using the discounted cash flow framework, we saw that it was possible to value a firm by discounting the various operating cash flows expected to be generated by the firm. We also saw that it was possible to value a firm using its book value and its residual income. Finally, we saw that some professionals value a firm by reference to earnings multiples.

As a validation of your understanding of the content of this chapter, you should not be able to:

- Develop pro forma financial statements.
- Estimate the value of a company using the discounted cash flow approach.
- Estimate the value of a company using the residual income approach.
- Estimate the value of a company using price-earnings multiples.

KEY CONCEPTS AND TERMS

Beta, 12.15
Capital asset pricing model
   (CAPM), 12.15
Continuing value, 12.12
Cost of common equity, 12.15
Discount rate, 12.15
Discounted cash flow
   approach, 12.8

Excess earnings, 12.17
Forward P/E multiple, 12.20
Free cash flow, 12.13
Free cash flow to common
   equity, 12.13
Operating cash flow, 12.13
Operating value, 12.12

Normal earnings, 12.17
Perpetuity growth formula, 12.16
Residual income, 12.17
Terminal value, 12.12
Terminal year growth rate, 12.6
Trailing P/E multiple, 12.21

DISCUSSION QUESTIONS

Q12.1 **Discounted Cash Flow versus Residual Income Valuation.** Describe the general steps followed to value the common equity of a business using (a) the discounted cash flow method and (b) the residual income method. Discuss what circumstances will yield equivalent valuation results under the two approaches.

Q12.2 **Pro Forma Financial Statements.** Describe the basic steps to be followed in developing pro forma financial statements. Discuss why it is unnecessary to make a separate set of pro forma assumptions for the statement of cash flow. Discuss why it is necessary to develop a terminal year projection.

Q12.3 **Free Cash Flow versus Residual Income.** Discuss how (a) the free cash flow and (b) the residual income of a business are calculated. Describe how these two measures are related.

Q12.4 **Capital Asset Pricing Model and Beta.** Explain the Capital Asset Pricing Model. What does it mean if a company has a beta of 1.3? What does it mean if a company has a beta of 1.0?

Q12.5 **Analyzing and Reporting Operating-loss Carryforwards.** The following information is taken from the 2005 annual report of **Coca-Cola Enterprises**:

> At December 31, 2005, we had U.S. federal tax operating loss carryforwards totaling $646 million. These carryforwards are available to offset future taxable income until they expire at varying dates through 2024. We also had U.S. state operating loss carryforwards totaling $2 billion, which expire at various dates through 2005 . . . .

Discuss how the existence of operating-loss carryforwards affects firm value. Discuss how the financial effects of operating-loss carryforwards are reflected in the calculation of firm value using (a) the discounted cash flow model and (b) the residual income model.

Q12.6 **Forecasting the Cost of Goods Sales: Economies and Dis-Economies of Scale.** Many investment professionals forecast the cost of goods sales on the pro forma income statement using recent historical common-size percentages. Common-size percentages, however, may be significantly impacted by economies of scale or dis-economies of scale. Discuss what an economy of scale is and how it can impact the historical relation of the cost of goods sales divided by sales. Discuss what a dis-economy of scale is; under what circumstances can dis-economies of scale arise?

Q12.7 **Unlevering Cash Flow from Operations.** Some investment professionals "unlever" the cash flow from operations by adding the following term $i(1-t_x)$ to the cash flow from operations (CFFO). Discuss why these professionals might modify the CFFO in this fashion. How does unlevering change the CFFO?

Q12.8 **Discounting Cash Flows and Earnings.** Under the residual income approach and the discounted cash flow approach to firm valuation, earnings and cash flows, respectively, are discounted using a firm's cost of equity. Discuss why the cost of equity is the appropriate discount rate to use to discount a firm's earnings and cash flows. Why is the cost of debt inappropriate to use to discount a firm's earnings or cash flows?

Q12.9 **(Ethics Perspective) Virtue-based approach to Ethics.** The virtue-based approach to ethics asks the following questions—What role should an individual occupy in an organization? What good traits (or virtues) are needed to succeed at that role? And, how should someone with those virtues act when confronted with ethical dilemmas? Discuss the role that accountants are meant to occupy. Discuss the traits or virtues that an accountant should have to succeed in that role. Discuss how an accountant should act when faced with an ethical dilemma.

✅ indicates that check figures are available on the book's Website.

EXERCISES

E12.10 **Calculating the Cost of Equity.** Assume that the Coffman Company has a beta of 1.2 and that the risk-free rate of return is five percent. If the equity-risk premium is six percent, calculate the cost of equity for the Coffman Company using the capital asset pricing model.

⊘ E12.11 **Calculating the Cost of Equity.** Assume that The Jackson Company has a beta of 0.8 and the risk-free rate of return is 4.5 percent. If the equity-risk premium is seven percent, calculate the cost of equity for The Jackson Company using the capital asset pricing model.

E12.12 **Valuation using Price-Earnings Multiples.** The Claremont Company is planning an initial public offering (IPO) and management would like to have an idea of an appropriate price to charge for a share of its stock. The company plans to issue 100,000 shares. The Claremont Company's most recent earnings per share (EPS) are $1.25; however, the consensus forecast among analysts who follow the company is for EPS to be $1.50. The EPS and share price of four comparable firms are shown below:

Firm	EPS	Share Price	P/E ratio
A.	$ 1.00	$ 18.00	18
B.	0.60	13.20	22
C.	10.00	140.00	14
D.	2.20	57.20	26

Compute the value of a share of Claremont Company stock using the price-earnings multiples method.

E12.13 **Valuation using Price-Earnings Multiples.** The Pomona Company is planning an initial public offering (IPO) and management would like to have an idea of an appropriate price to charge for a share of its stock. The company plans to issue 200,000 shares. The Pomona Company's most recent earnings per share (EPS) are $2.50, however, the consensus forecast among analysts who follow the company is for EPS to be $2.75. The EPS and share price of four comparable firms are shown below:

Firm	EPS	Share Price
A.	$ 2.00	$ 18.00
B.	1.20	13.20
C.	20.00	140.00
D.	4.40	57.20

Compute the value of a share of Pomona Company stock using the price-earnings multiples method.

E12.14 **Calculating Terminal Values.** Scripps Inc. is projected to generate free cash flow (FCF) of $950,000 in its terminal year, at which point it is forecasted to have a four percent growth rate. The firm's cost of equity is estimated to be twelve percent. Calculate the terminal value of Scripps Inc.

E12.15 **Calculating Terminal Values.** Pitzer Inc. is projected to generate residual income (RI) of $875,000 in its terminal year, at which point it is forecasted to have a five percent growth rate. The firm's cost of equity is estimated to be nine percent. Calculate the terminal value of Pitzer Inc.

E12.16 **Calculating Free Cash Flow.** Below are data from the financial statements of Sand and Glass Audio:

Net income.	$ 900
Common stock issued (net)	200
Cash from operations (net).	1,150
Cash from investing (net)	(400)
Change in debt (net).	(475)
Dividends paid	300
Change in operating cash (net)	175
Change in common equity (net).	800

Compute the company's free cash flow to equity using three different methods. (Each method should yield the same answer.)

⊘ E12.17 **Calculating Free Cash Flow.** Below are data from the financial statements of Ann A. Logg Audio.

Net income.	$1,800
Common stock issued (net)	400
Cash from operations (net).	2,300
Cash from investing (net)	(800)
Change in debt (net).	(950)
Dividends paid	600
Change in operating cash (net)	350
Change in common equity (net).	1,600

Compute the company's free cash flow to equity using three different methods. (Each method should yield the same answer.)

E12.18 **Discounted Cash Flow Valuation.** Presented below are data for Boso Audio:

	Forecast Year					
	1	2	3	4	5	Terminal
No. of outstanding shares	500	500	500	500	500	500
Terminal year growth rate.						5%
Cost of common equity	10%	10%	10%	10%	10%	10%
Net income.	$ 79	$ 94	$111	$130	$150	$157
Beginning of year common equity	$649	$683	$720	$758	$797	$839
Free cash flow to common equity	$ 44	$ 58	$ 73	$ 90	$108	$115

Compute the value of a share of Boso common stock using the discounted cash flow method.

E12.19 **Residual Income Valuation.** Presented below are data for Boso Audio:

	Forecast Year					
	1	2	3	4	5	Terminal
No. of outstanding shares	500	500	500	500	500	500
Terminal year growth rate.						5%
Cost of common equity	10%	10%	10%	10%	10%	10%
Net income.	$ 79	$ 94	$111	$130	$150	$157
Beginning of year common equity	$649	$683	$720	$758	$797	$839
Free cash flow to common equity	$ 44	$ 58	$ 73	$ 90	$108	$115

Compute the value of a share of Boso common stock using the residual income method.

E12.20 **Discounted Cash Flow Valuation.** Presented below are data for Hero Cable:

	Forecast Year					
	1	2	3	4	5	Terminal
No. of outstanding shares	1000	1000	1000	1000	1000	1000
Terminal year growth rate.						4%
Cost of common equity	12%	12%	12%	12%	12%	12%
Net income.	$128	$148	$170	$194	$221	$230
Beginning of year common equity	$698	$738	$780	$824	$870	$919
Free cash flow to common equity	$ 88	$106	$126	$148	$172	$193

Compute the value of a share of Hero common stock using the discounted cash flow method.

⊘ E12.21 Residual Income Valuation. Presented below are data for Hero Cable:

	Forecast Year					
	1	**2**	**3**	**4**	**5**	**Terminal**
No. of outstanding shares	1000	1000	1000	1000	1000	1000
Terminal year growth rate.						4%
Cost of common equity	12%	12%	12%	12%	12%	12%
Net income.	$128	$148	$170	$194	$221	$230
Beginning of year common equity	$698	$738	$780	$824	$870	$919
Free cash flow to common equity	$ 88	$106	$126	$148	$172	$193

Compute the value of a share of Hero common stock using the residual income method method.

⊘ E12.22 Price-Earnings Multiple Valuation. **Titanium Metals Corporation (TIMET)** is one of the world's leading producers of titanium melted and mill products, used principally in the manufacture of commercial and military aircraft and aerospace products. On August 1, 2005, the company's trailing (twelve months) earnings-per-share was $4.17, and with a market price-per-share of $64.00, indicated a trailing price-earnings multiple of 15.35.

Required:

1. According to Thomson Financial, the consensus forward price-earnings multiple is 10.33. What is the consensus forecasted earnings-per-share?

2. Using your consensus forecast of future earnings-per-share from question one, and the current trailing price-earnings multiple of 15.35, what should TIMET's target share price be? According to Thomson Financial, TIMET's one-year target price was $70 per share. How does the Thomson Financial one-year target price compare to your target price?

E12.23 Pro Forma Income Statements. Using the Mann & Miller Inc. (M&M) consolidated statement of earnings in Problem 4.32 (see Chapter 4) as your base year, prepare pro forma income statements for M&M for 2006 and 2007 using an EXCEL spreadsheet. Relevant assumptions that you should use include:

- Sales growth is twelve percent per year.
- Gross profit margin is 70 percent.
- Effective income tax rate is 29 percent.
- All expenses, except interest expense, vary as a function of sales.
- Interest expense is eight percent of the beginning balance of long-term debt.

PROBLEMS

P12.24 Generating Cash Flow Information. Presented below are recent financial statements for The Gamble Company.

The Gamble Company Consolidated Balance Sheet		
	2006	**2005**
Assets		
Cash & cash equivalents	$ 1,549	$ 2,350
Marketable securities.	857	760
Trade receivables.	2,781	2,738
Inventories	3,284	3,087
Prepaid expenses	1,511	1,190
Total current assets	9,982	10,125

continued

continued from previous page

The Gamble Company Consolidated Balance Sheet	2006	2005
Property, plant & equipment (net)	12,180	11,376
Intangible assets (net)	7,011	3,949
Other noncurrent assets	1,198	1,433
Total assets	$30,371	$26,883
Liabilities & Shareholders' Equity		
Accounts payable	$ 2,051	$ 2,203
Accrued expenses & other liabilities	3,942	3,802
Taxes payable	976	944
Debt due within one year	2,281	849
Current liabilities	9,250	7,798
Long-term debt	5,765	4,143
Deferred income taxes	(167)	(102)
Other noncurrent liabilities	3,287	2,998
Shareholders' equity		
Capital stock (at par)	3,158	3,210
Additional paid-in-capital	907	559
Retained earnings	11,144	10,730
Cumulative translation adjustment account	(2,973)	(2,453)
Total liabilities & shareholders' equity	$30,371	$26,883

The Gamble Company Consolidated Statement of Earnings	2006	2005
Net sales	$37,154	$35,764
Cost of goods sold*	(21,064)	(20,510)
Marketing research & administrative expenses**	(10,035)	(9,766)
Operating income	6,055	5,488
Interest expense	(548)	(457)
Other income (net)†	201	218
Earnings before income taxes	5,708	5,249
Income taxes	(1,928)	(1,834)
Net earnings	$ 3,780	$ 3,415

* Includes depreciation on plant & equipment of 1,480 in 2006 and 1,387 in 2005.
** includes amortization of intangible assets of 118 in 2006 and 1000 in 2005.
† includes one-time gains of 150 in 2006 and 125 in 2005 from the sale of equipment.

Required

Prepare a statement of cash flow using the indirect method.

P12.25 **Generating Cash Flow Information.** Presented below are recent financial data for the Coca-Cola Company.

The Coca-Cola Company
Consolidated Balance Sheet

	Year 9	Year 8
Assets		
Cash & cash equivalents	$ 1,611	$ 1,648
Marketable securities	201	159
Trade accounts receivable (net)	1,798	1,666
Inventories	1,076	890
Prepaid expenses & other current	1,794	2,017
Total current assets	6,480	6,380
Equity investment in affiliated companies	6,792	6,686
Marketable securities	2,124	1,863
Property, plant & equipment (net)	4,267	3,669
Goodwill & other intangibles (net)	1,960	547
Total assets	$21,623	$19,145
Liabilities & Shareholders' Equity		
Accounts payable & accrued expenses	$ 3,714	$ 3,141
Loans & notes payable	5,112	4,459
Current maturities of long-term debt	261	3
Accrued income taxes	769	1,037
Total current liabilities	9,856	8,640
Long-term debt	854	687
Long-term pension liabilities	902	991
Deferred income taxes	498	424
Shareholders' equity		
Common stock @ par	867	865
Additional paid-in-capital	2,584	2,195
Reinvested earnings	20,773	19,922
Cumulated currency translation adjustment	(1,551)	(1,434)
Treasury stock	(13,160)	(13,145)
Total Liabilities & Shareholders' Equity	$21,623	$19,145

The Coca-Cola Company
Consolidated Statement of Income

	Year 9
Net operating revenues	$19,805
Less: Cost of goods sold [1]	6,009
Gross profit	13,796
Less: Selling and administrative expenses [2]	9,001
Other operating charges	813
Operating income	3,982
Interest expense (net of income)	(77)
Equity income (loss)	(184)
Other income (net)	68
Gains on issues of stock by equity investors	30
Income before income taxes	3,819
Income taxes	1,388
Net income	$ 2,431

[1] Includes depreciation on property & equipment of $528.
[2] Includes amortization of intangible assets of $264.

Required

Prepare a statement of cash flow for Year 9 using the indirect method format.

P12.26 **Generating Cash Flow Information: International.** China Yuchai International Ltd. is a Bermuda holding company that owns 76.4 percent of the outstanding common shares of Guangxi Yuchai Machinery Company Ltd. Guangxi Yuchai is one of the leading manufacturers of diesel engines in China. Presented below are recent financial statements for China Yuchai International:

China Yuchai International Ltd. Consolidated Statement of Income		
	Year 3	Year 4
Assets		
Current assets		
Cash.	173,038	285,831
Inventories	301,366	292,192
Receivable from related company	98,270	60,263
Trade receivables (net).	548,128	475,254
Prepaid expenses	69,343	84,252
Investments	—	800
Total current assets	1,190,145	1,198,592
Noncurrent assets		
Property, plant, & equipment (net)	1,136,242	1,082,976
Investments	99,446	50,063
Goodwill (net).	263,211	246,353
Deferred income tax	21,703	22,322
Total assets	2,710,747	2,600,306
Liabilities & Shareholders' Equity		
Current liabilities		
Short-term bank loans	128,016	90,000
Current maturities of long-term loans	183,800	294,800
Trade accounts payable.	209,954	134,696
Income taxes payable	559	1,057
Accrued expenses payable	138,374	138,472
Total current liabilities	660,703	659,025
Long-term bank loans	208,800	60,000
Total liabilities.	869,503	719,025
Minority interest	358,589	354,926
Shareholders' equity		
Common stock	30,349	30,349
Contributed surplus	1,486,934	1,486,934
Statutory reserves	98,868	108,095
Accumulated deficit.	(133,496)	(99,023)
Total Liabilities & Shareholders' Equity	2,710,747	2,600,306

China Yuchai International Ltd. Consolidated Statement of Operations	Year 4
Net sales.	1,270,337
Cost of goods sold.	828,865[1]
Gross profit.	441,472
Selling, general & administrative expenses	309,995
Amortization of goodwill.	16,859
Impairment of plant & equipment.	4,449
Operating income.	110,169
Interest expense.	36,602
Income before income taxes & minority interest	73,567
Income tax expense.	11,217
Income before minority interest	62,350
Minority interest in income of consolidated subsidiaries.	(18,650)
Net income.	43,700

[1] Includes depreciation expense of 127,892

Required
Prepare a statement of cash flow using the indirect method.

P12.27 **Generating Cash Flow Information: International.** Minebea Co., Ltd was established in 1951 as Japan's first specialized manufacturer of high-precision miniature ball-bearings. Today, the company is the world's leading manufacturer of miniature ball-bearings and high-pressure components supplying customers worldwide. Presented below are excerpts from Minebea's annual report.

Minebea Co., Ltd. Consolidated Balance Sheet		
(in millions of yen)	Year 5	Year 4
Current assets		
Cash & cash equivalents	13,952	11,930
Accounts & notes receivable (net)	53,416	57,773
Inventories	49,887	52,764
Prepaid expenses & other current assets	14,293	14,639
	131,548	137,106
Noncurrent assets		
Property, plant, & equipment.	361,348	331,481
Less: Accumulated depreciation	(195,321)	(179,299)
	166,027	152,182
Land.	17,411	16,551
	183,438	168,733

continued

continued from previous page

Minebea Co., Ltd. Consolidated Balance Sheet		
(in millions of yen)	**Year 5**	**Year 4**
Investments & other assets		
Excess of cost over net assets acquired (net)	14,595	15,344
Investments in affiliates	206	303
Investments in securities	5,524	8,574
Long-term loans receivable	11,189	13,320
Other	3,537	3,585
	35,051	41,126
Total assets.	350,037	346,965
Current liabilities		
Short-term loans payable	61,618	62,724
Current portion of long-term debt	41,843	3,807
Trade accounts & notes payable	30,787	37,315
Income taxes payable	4,162	3,985
Accrued expenses payable	18,498	19,459
	156,908	127,290
Long-term liabilities		
Long-term debt	79,212	118,629
Pension liability	1,089	350
	80,301	118,979
Minority interest in consolidated subsidiaries	96	122
Shareholders' equity		
Common stock, ¥50 par value.	68,259	68,259
Capital reserve.	94,757	94,757
Retained earnings	4,774	3,303
Difference on revaluation of marketable securities	(1,719)	(953)
Foreign currency translation adjustment	(53,333)	(64,791)
Treasury stock	(6)	(1)
	112,732	100,574
Total liabilities & shareholders' equity	350,037	346,965

[1] Depreciation expense for Year 5 totaled 23,656.
[2] Amortization expense for Year 5 totaled 749.

Minebea Co., Ltd. Consolidated Statements of Income	
(in millions of yen)	**Year 5**
Net sales.	279,344
Cost of sales.	(206,061)
Gross profit.	73,283
Selling, general & administrative expenses	(51,311)
Operating income.	21,972

continued

continued from previous page

Minebea Co., Ltd. Consolidated Statements of Income	
(in millions of yen)	Year 5
Other income (expenses)	
Interest income	586
Equity in loss of non-consolidated subsidiaries & affiliates.	(21)
Interest expense	(5,673)
Gains (losses) on sales of marketable securities, investment securities & investment securities in affiliates	(6)
Gains (losses) on revaluation of marketable & investment securities	(1,466)
Foreign currency exchanges losses	(827)
Losses on disposals of inventories	(1,125)
Losses on sales & disposals of property, plant, & equip.	(612)
Losses on liquidation of subsidiaries & affiliates	(937)
Other, net	(1,058)
	(9,023)
Income before income taxes	12,949
Income taxes	
Current.	4,919
Deferred.	2,717
	7,630
Minority interests in earnings of consolidated subsidiaries	21
Net income.	5,298

Required

Prepare a statement of cash flow for Year 5 using the indirect method format.

P12.28 Generating Cash Flow Information: International. Presented below are recent financial statements of **Kubota Corporation**, a leading Japanese manufacturer of machinery and equipment:

Kubota Corporation Consolidated Balance Sheet		
(in millions of yen)	Year 2	Year 1
Assets		
Cash and cash equivalents	80,215	91,774
Short-term investments	25,516	36,925
Trade notes and accounts receivable (net).	361,812	393,852
Other receivables (net)	109,310	88,286
Inventories	185,683	181,537
Prepaid expenses.	23,322	23,687
Total current assets	785,858	816,061
Investments in affiliate companies	145,195	158,824
Property, plant and equipment (net).	296,317	296,828
Other noncurrent assets.	83,996	65,034
Total assets.	1,311,366	1,336,747

continued

continued from previous page

Kubota Corporation
Consolidated Balance Sheet

(in millions of yen)	Year 2	Year 1
Liabilities & Shareholders' Equity		
Short-term borrowings......................................	150,342	167,611
Trade notes and accounts payable	217,305	242,543
Advances from customers......................................	8,483	12,801
Notes and accounts payable for capital expenditures..............	22,323	20,991
Accrued expenses payable	26,439	27,763
Income taxes payable	5,792	23,471
Current portion of long-term debt	136,732	100,847
Total current liabilities.......................................	567,416	596,027
Long-term liabilities		
Long-term debt...	254,354	291,657
Accrued retirement and pension costs	119,823	76,197
Other long-term liabilities................................	19,087	18,126
Total long-term liabilities	393,264	385,980
Shareholders' equity		
Common stock	78,107	78,107
Additional paid-in-capital................................	87,213	87,213
Retained earnings	213,418	200,098
Cumulative foreign currency translation account	(28,052)	(10,678)
Total shareholders' equity	350,686	354,740
Total liabilities & shareholders' equity	1,311,366	1,336,747

Kubota Corporation
Consolidated Income Statement

(in millions of yen)	Year 2
Net sales..	1,029,437
Cost of sales*...	767,588
Selling, general, & administrative expenses................	214,345
Operating income	47,504
Other income (expenses)	
Interest & dividend income	10,969
Interest expense	(12,687)
Other (net)	(15,653)
Other income (expenses), net	(17,371)
Income before income taxes & gain on sales of affiliated companies...............	30,133
Income taxes	
Current..	9,694
Deferred...	(204)
Total income taxes..................................	9,490
Gain (loss) on sale of affiliated companies................	1,135
Net income...	21,778

* Includes depreciation of $37,000.

Required

Prepare a statement of cash flow for Year 2 using the indirect method format.

P12.29 **Statement of Cash Flow: International.** Presented below are the financial statements of the **Wacoal Corporation**, a leading manufacturer of women's apparel in Japan. Wacoal's footnotes and other supplementary data revealed the following additional information:

1. Depreciation and amortization on property, plant, and equipment taken in 2001 amounted to ¥3,265 million.
2. Effective April 1, 2001, Wacoal changed its method of accounting for employee retirement benefits. As a result of this change in accounting principle, net income for 2001 decreased by ¥1,429 million, **including** the cumulative effect of the change as of the beginning of the year of ¥1,286 million.
3. The consolidated statement of shareholders' equity revealed that cash dividends paid in 2001 were ¥2,544 million, and that treasury stock in the amount of ¥2,803 million had been repurchased and had been deducted against retained earnings.

Wacoal Corporation Consolidated Balance Sheet		
(in millions of Yen)	2001	2000
Assets		
Cash.	¥ 7,634	¥ 9,403
Time deposits & certificates of deposit	33,562	40,486
Total cash & cash equivalents	41,196	49,889
Marketable securities.	34,499	24,178
Notes & accounts receivable		
Trade notes	2,651	2,902
Trade accounts	22,049	21,851
Allowance for returns & doubtful receivables	(2,869)	(2,633)
Inventories	25,601	25,515
Deferred income taxes.	4,647	4,142
Other current assets	1,734	1,890
Total current assets	129,508	127,734
Property, plant & equipment		
Land.	25,284	25,247
Buildings	55,197	54,784
Machinery & equipment.	11,530	11,148
Total	92,011	91,179
Accumulated depreciation.	(33,367)	(31,189)
Net property, plant, & equipment.	58,644	59,990
Other assets		
Investments in affiliates	8,670	7,305
Investments	28,877	37,327
Lease deposits & other	6,563	5,365
Total other assets.	44,110	49,997
Total	¥232,262	¥237,721

continued

continued from previous page

Wacoal Corporation Consolidated Balance Sheet		
(in millions of Yen)	**2001**	**2000**
Liabilities and Shareholders' Equity		
Short-term bank loan....................................	¥ 8,088	¥ 8,125
Trade notes	8,513	7,391
Trade accounts	7,214	6,769
Accrued payroll & bonuses	7,743	8,053
Income taxes payable	3,093	3,033
Other current liabilities...............................	6,281	4,340
Current portion of long-term debt	517	779
Total current liabilities	41,449	38,490
Long-term liabilities		
Long-term debt	892	1,369
Liability for termination & retirement benefits	6,709	11,734
Deferred income taxes...............................	8,957	10,675
Total long-term liabilities	16,558	23,778
Minority interests	1,697	1,84134
Shareholders' equity		
Common stock par value of ¥50 per share-authorized, 237 million & 240 million shares in 2001 & 2000; issued & outstanding 151,116,685 and 154,116,685 shares in 2001 & 2000	13,260	13,260
Additional paid-in-capital.............................	25,242	25,242
Retained earnings	132,322	126,780
Accumulated other comprehensive income (loss)		
Foreign currency translation adjustments	(2,418)	(3,231)
Unrealized gain on securities.........................	4,152	11,561
Total	1,734	8,330
Total shareholders' equity	172,558	173,612
Total	¥232,262	¥237,721

Wacoal Corporation Consolidated Statement of Income	
(in millions of Yen)	**2001**
Net sales...	¥162,023
Operating costs and expenses	
Cost of sales	87,493
Selling, general & administrative expense...............	64,906
Total operating costs and expenses	152,399
Operating income....................................	9,624

continued

continued from previous page

Wacoal Corporation Consolidated Statement of Income	
(in millions of Yen)	**2001**
Other income and expenses	
Interest income	395
Interest expense	(333)
Dividend income	268
Equity in net income of affiliated companies.	1,271
Gain (loss) on sale, transfer or exchange of investments	11,025
Other (net)	(850)
Total other income and expenses	11,776
Income before income taxes, minority interests and cumulative	
effect of accounting change	21,400
Income taxes	
Current.	5,181
Deferred.	3,877
Total income taxes.	9,058
Income before minority interests and cumulative effect of accounting change.	12,342
Minority interests	(167)
Income before cumulative effect of accounting change	12,175
Cumulative effect of accounting change	(1,286)
Net income.	¥ 10,889

Required

Prepare a statement of cash flow for 2001 using the indirect method format.

P12.30 **Firm Valuation: Discounted Cash Flow.** The Mann Corporation is a small manufacturer of office products. Until recently, the company was all equity-financed (shareholders' equity totaled $20 million), having
a cost of equity of twelve percent. The company decided to expand its productive capacity by investing in
new plant and equipment at a cost of $12 million. Executives at Mann decided to finance the capital invest-
ment with lower costing debt financing which carried an interest rate of only eight percent. The CEO of
The Mann Corporation wondered what the company was now worth following the plant expansion; consequently, the CEO instructed the company's CFO to prepare a forecast of the firm's free cash flows. The
CFO's forecast was as follows:

(in thousands)	**Year 1**	**Year 2**	**Year 3**	**Year 4**
Free cash flow	$2,500	$4,675	$5,573	$ 5,930
Terminal value.				30,000

Required

1. Calculate the value of The Mann Corporation.
2. Is the company's decision to invest in new plant and equipment a good operating decision? Why?

P12.31 **Pro Forma Financial Statements.** The venture capital division of a major U.S. financial institution has elected to fund an investment in an oil and gas exploration and production company that will operate both onshore and offshore in Texas and Louisiana in the United States. The initial financing commitment from the bank is for $40 million.

The company's strategic plan calls for an aggressive drilling program to be carried out during 2004. Hofstedt Oil & Gas estimates that it will drill 50 wells at an average cost of $800,000 per well and that 30 of those wells will yield aggregate crude oil reserves of approximately 10 million barrels. The remaining 20 wells are expected to be dry or commercially unproductive. These forecasts were based on the expert opinion of geologists familiar with the properties and were confirmed by petroleum engineers employed directly by the bank.

The company's production plan calls for a maximum exploitation effort to earn the highest financial return. Tom Hofstedt, president of the company, developed the following production scenario:

Year	Number of Barrels To Be Produced	Estimated Selling Price Per Barrel	Estimated Lifting Cost Per Barrel
2004	1,000,000	$30	$5
2005	1,500,000	30	5
2006	1,500,000	35	6
2007	2,500,000	40	7
2008	3,500,000	45	8

Hofstedt Oil & Gas is concerned about the impact of this operation on its financial statements and on the company's stock price. Consequently, any available accounting policy choices loom as very important in the overall evaluation of the investment. As a result, Hofstedt sent a terse memo to the company's controller, the closing line of which stated, "Prepare pro forma statements showing the alternative accounting effects on cash flow, income before tax, and financial position if we elect to use the successful efforts method or the full-cost method." Under the full-cost method, the cost of all wells—successful and unsuccessful—are capitalized to the balance sheet and then depleted over the expected productive life of the successful wells. Under the successful efforts method, only the cost of the successful wells are capitalized (the cost of any unsuccessful wells are immediately expensed) to be depleted over their expected productive life.

Required

For purposes of pro forma statement preparation, assume that the $40 million loan agreement will be repaid as follows: (1) $10 million principal repayment per year to be paid on December 31 beginning on December 31, 2005; and (2) interest payments of 10 percent per year on the balance of the loan outstanding as of the beginning of the year. Ignore income taxes and all other operations. Based on your pro forma cash flows, income statements, and balance sheets for the period 2004 through 2008, what accounting method (successful efforts or full cost) recommendation would you make to Hofstedt, and why?

P12.32 **Pro Forma Financial Statements.** Handy Dan, Inc. operates warehouse-style stores, selling a variety of home building products and lawn and garden supplies. Presented below are Handy Dan's historical financial statements for Year 1 and Year 2:

Handy Dan, Inc.
Statement of Income

(amounts in millions)	Year 2
Sales.	$980
Cost of goods sold.	(727)
Gross profit.	253
Depreciation expense.	(8)
Other operating expenses	(217)
Operating income.	28
Interest expense.	(21)
Income before taxes.	7
Income tax expense.	(2)
Net income.	$ 5

Handy Dan, Inc.
Balance Sheets

	Year 1	Year 2		Year 1	Year 2
Assets			**Equities**		
Cash	$ 10	$ 14	Accounts payable.	$ 74	$104
Accounts receivable (net)	27	38	Short-term loans payable.	10	29
Inventory.	153	214	Long-term debt	207	289
Total current assets	190	266	Total liabilities	291	422
Property & equipment (cost).	199	279	Contributed capital.	50	62
Accumulated depreciation	(9)	(17)	Retained earnings	39	44
Net property & equipment	190	262	Total shareholders' equity	89	106
Total assets.	$380	$528	Total equities	$380	$528

Handy Dan, Inc.
Statement of Retained Earnings

	Year 2
Retained earnings (Year 1)	$29
Add: Net income	5
Less: Dividends	0
Retained earnings (Year 2)	$44

Handy Dan, Inc.	
Statement of Cash Flow	
Operations	
Net income.	$ 5
Depreciation expense	8
Accounts receivable (net).	(11)
Inventory	(61)
Accounts payable	30
Cash flow from operations.	(29)
Investing	
Purchase of property & equipment	(80)
Cash flow from investing	(80)
Financing	
Short-term borrowing	19
Long-term borrowing.	82
Stock sales	12
Dividend payment	0
Cash flow from financing.	113
Change in cash.	$ 4

Required

Using the following set of assumptions, prepare pro forma financial statements for Handy Dan, Inc. for Year 3:

- Sales are projected to grow by 40 percent.
- Cash is expected to increase at the same rate as sales.
- Assume the following ratios to forecast the identified accounts:

Account	Financial Ratio		
Accounts receivable.	Receivable turnover	=	25.9
Inventory.	Inventory turnover	=	3.39
Property & equipment	Fixed asset turnover	=	3.52
Cost of goods sold.	Gross profit margin %	=	25.9%
Operating expenses	Operating expenses/sales	=	22.1%
Accounts payable.	Payable turnover	=	7.55

- Depreciation expense is based on a 30 year expected life with no salvage value; any property and equipment acquired during the year is depreciated for only one-half year.
- Interest expense is based on a six percent short-term cost of debt and eight percent long-term cost of debt; only one-half year of interest is charged on loans taken out during the year.
- Effective income tax rate is 33.33 percent.
- The mix of short-term loans payable, long-term debt and contributed is set to satisfy an existing debt covenant that requires the company to maintain a current ratio of 2.0 (or greater) and a total debt-to-total assets ratio of 80 percent (or less).

P12.33 Residual Income Valuation. Lowe's Companies Inc. is the second largest retailer of home improvement products in the world, with a specific emphasis on retail do-it-yourself (DIY) and commercial business customers. Lowe's specializes in offering products and services for home improvement, home decor, home maintenance, home repair and remodeling and maintenance of commercial buildings.

Required

On July 8, 2003, Lowe's stock price closed at $45.30 per share. Lehman Brothers set a price target of $52 per share based on an EPS forecast of $2.22 per share for fiscal 2003. Assume that the company's cost of equity is 14 percent. Using the Residual Income valuation model calculate the equity value of the Lowe's Companies. [As a base case, a company whose expected ROE is 25 percent per year, whose cost of equity is 14 percent, and whose growth in book value is expected to be 20 percent per year for the first ten years and five percent per year thereafter, would have an intrinsic value of 4.015 times current book value.] Do you think Lowe's is worth $52 per share? Why?

Lowe's Cos. Inc. Consolidated Balance Sheet		
($ millions)	01/31/03	02/01/02
Cash and cash equivalents	$ 853	$ 799
Short-term investments	273	54
Accounts receivable—net	172	166
Merchandise inventory.	3,968	3,611
Deferred income taxes	58	93
Other current assets.	244	197
Total current assets	5,568	4,920
Property, less accumulated depreciation.	10,352	8,653
Long-term investments	29	22
Other assets.	160	141
Total assets.	$16,109	$13,736
Short-term borrowings.	$ 50	$ 100
Current maturities of long-term debt	29	59
Accounts payable.	1,943	1,715
Employee retirement plans.	88	126
Accrued salaries and wages	306	221
Other current liabilities	1,162	796
Total current liabilities.	3,578	3,017
Long-term debt, excluding current maturities	3,736	3,734
Deferred income taxes	478	305
Other long-term liabilities	15	6
Total liabilities	7,807	7,062
Shareholders' Equity		
Preferred stock - $5 par value, none issued	—	—
Common stock - $.50 par value; shares issued and outstanding January 31, 2003, 782; February 1, 2002 776.	391	388
Capital in excess of par value	2,023	1,803
Retained earnings	5,887	4,482
Accumulated other comprehensive income.	1	1
Total shareholders' equity	8,302	6,674
Total liabilities and shareholders' equity.	$16,109	$13,736

Lowe's Cos. Inc. Consolidated Statements of Income			
($ millions except per share amounts for period ended)	1/31/03	2/1/02	2/2/01
Net sales.	$26,491	$22,111	$18,779
Cost of sales.	18,465	15,743	13,488
Gross margin	8,026	6,368	5,291
Expenses			
Selling, general and administrative	4,730	3,913	3,348
Store opening costs	129	140	132
Depreciation	626	517	409
Interest	182	174	121
Total expenses	5,667	4,744	4,010
Pretax earnings	2,359	1,624	1,281
Income tax provision	888	601	471
Net earnings.	$ 1,471	$ 1,023	$ 810
Basic earnings per share	$ 1.89	$ 1.33	$ 1.06
Diluted earnings per share	1.85	1.30	1.05
Cash dividends per share.	0.09	0.08	0.07

Selected Financial Data for Lowe's					
Lowe's Companies	2002	2001	2000	1999	1998
Net sales.	$26,491	$22,111	$18,779	$15,906	$13,331
Growth in net sales (%)	19.8%	17.7%	18.1%	19.3%	—
Net earnings	1,471	1,023	810	673	500
Total assets.	16,109	13,736	11,358	9,007	7,087
Shareholders' equity	8,302	6,674	5,494	4,695	3,620
Growth in shareholders' equity (%)	24.4%	21.5%	17.0%	29.7%	—
ROE Analysis					
ROE (net earnings/beginning shareholder's equity)	22.04%	18.62%	17.25%	18.59%	—
Return on sales (net earnings/net sales)	5.55%	4.63%	4.31%	4.23%	3.75%
Asset turnover (net sales/total assets)	1.64	1.61	1.65	1.77	1.88
Leverage (total assets/beginning shareholders' equity)	2.41	2.50	2.42	2.49	—

P12.34 **Integrative Case Analysis.** CSK Auto Corp. is the largest retailer of automotive parts and accessories in the Western United States and one of the largest retailers of such products in the United States based on the number of stores. As of February 4, 2001, the company operated 1,152 stores as one fully integrated company under three brand names: Checker Auto Parts, Schuck's Auto Supply, and Kragen Auto Parts. Presented below is selected information from CSK Auto Corp.'s 2000 10-K report. Assume an effective tax rate of 40 percent.

Required
1. On March 17, 1998, the Company completed an initial public offering (IPO). What was the average price (net of underwriting fees) that CSK sold its shares for?

2. In 1999, CSK Auto spent $260.221 million on investing activities. How did the company finance this investment?

3. On February 4, 2001, the company's share price was $6.10 per share. The Board of Directors believes that the company's share price is too low and has recommended a share buyback program. What would be the financial effect of a share buyback, and what accounts would be affected if the company repurchased ten percent of its outstanding shares?

4. On March 1, 2000, the company participated in the formation of a new joint venture, PartsAmerica. com (PA) by acquiring 37 percent of the outstanding equity of PA. The company accounted for its investment in PA under the equity method.

    a. What financial effects did the company record to reflect its investment in PartsAmerica on its financial statements?

    b. During fiscal 2000, the company recognized its proportionate share of PA's net loss and wrote off the remaining investment in the joint venture. What did the company record to reflect these events in its financial statements?

5. CSK Auto reports that included in property and equipment (net) are assets under capital leases (net of accumulated amortization) of $38.067 million and $35.676 million on February 4, 2001 and January 30, 2000, respectively. Consider the information on leases provided in the financial statements and footnotes.

    a. What cash payment is CSK Auto expecting to make for operating leases for the year ending February 4, 2002?

    b. What financial effects will CSK Auto record for its capital leases for the year ending February 4, 2002?

6. CSK Auto recognizes income taxes based on pretax income.

    a. What financial effects did CSK record to recognize income taxes in 2000?

    b. Has CSK Auto reported more or less income to its shareholders cumulatively through February 4, 2001 than to the tax authorities? How much more or less?

7. On February 4, 2001, CSK Auto's share price closed at $6.10 per share. Using the Residual Income valuation model, calculate the equity value of the company? Assume that the company's cost of equity is approximately 10.4 percent. Top management thinks the share price should be considerably higher. How would you explain the situation to management?

CSK Auto Corp. Consolidated Balance Sheet		
($ thousands)	02/04/01	01/30/00
Cash and cash equivalents	$ 11,131	$ 11,762
Receivables, net of allowances of $4,236 and $3,294, respectively	79,901	69,129
Inventories	621,814	625,480
Deferred income taxes	3,133	—
Assets held for sale	1,497	4,745
Prepaid expenses and other current assets	19,169	18,471
Total current assets	736,645	729,587
Property and equipment, net	175,358	160,561
Leasehold interests, net	20,244	8,341
Goodwill, net	130,544	124,750
Other assets, net	14,190	12,413
Total assets	$1,076,981	$1,035,652

continued

continued from previous page

CSK Auto Corp. Consolidated Balance Sheet		
($ thousands)	02/04/01	01/30/00
Liabilities and Stockholders' Equity		
Accounts payable..	$ 199,483	$ 168,770
Accrued payroll and related expenses............................	27,673	38,910
Accrued expenses and other current liabilities	42,448	50,663
Current maturities of amounts due under Senior Credit Facility	54,640	3,340
Current maturities of capital lease obligations.......................	10,878	9,893
Deferred income taxes......................................	—	1,417
Total current liabilities......................................	335,122	272,993
Facility	471,840	505,480
Subordinated Notes......................................	81,250	81,250
Obligations under capital leases	29,273	27,170
Deferred income taxes......................................	10,544	5,801
Other..	9,339	8,411
Total non-current liabilities	602,246	628,112
Stockholders' Equity		

Common stock, $0.01 par value, 50,000,000 shares authorized,
  27,841,178 and 27,834,574 shares issued and outstanding at
  February 4, 2001 and January 30, 2000, respectively................
	278	278

Additional paid-in-capital....................................	291,063	291,004
Stockholder receivable.....................................	(745)	(584)
Deferred compensation	(156)	(324)
Accumulated deficit.......................................	(150,827)	(155,827)
Total stockholders' equity	139,613	134,547
Total liabilities and stockholders' equity.........................	$1,076,981	$1,035,652

CSK Auto Corp. Consolidated Statements of Income			
($ thousands)	2/4/01	1/30/00	1/31/99
Net sales......................................	$1,452,109	$1,231,455	$1,004,385
Cost of sales...................................	769,043	636,239	531,073
Gross profit....................................	683,066	595,216	473,312
Other costs and expenses.......................	—	—	—
Operating and administrative....................	568,873	471,340	391,528
Store closing costs	6,060	4,900	335
Legal settlement	8,800	—	—
Transition and integration expenses	23,818	30,187	3,075
Equity in loss of joint venture....................	3,168	—	—
Goodwill amortization	4,799	1,941	—
Write-off of unamortized management fee	—	—	3,643

continued

continued from previous page

CSK Auto Corp. Consolidated Statements of Income			
($ thousands)	2/4/01	1/30/00	1/31/99
Secondary stock offering costs.	—	—	770
Operating profit	67,548	86,848	73,961
Interest expense, net	62,355	41,300	30,730
Income before income taxes, extraordinary loss and cumulative effect of change in accounting principle	5,193	45,548	43,231
Income tax expense.	193	17,436	15,746
Income before extraordinary loss and cumulative effect of change in accounting principle	5,000	28,112	27,485
Extraordinary loss, net of $4,236 of income taxes.	—	—	(6,767)
Income before cumulative effect of change in accounting principle.	5,000	28,112	20,718
Cumulative effect of change in accounting principle, net of $468 of income taxes	—	(741)	—
Net income.	$ 5,000	$ 27,371	$ 20,718

CSK Auto Corp. Consolidated Statements of Cash Flow			
($ thousands)	02/04/01	01/30/00	01/31/99
Cash flows provided by (used in) operating activities			
Net income.	$ 5,000	$ 27,371	$ 20,718
Adjustments to reconcile net income to net cash provided by (used in) operating activities	—	—	—
Depreciation and amortization of property and equipment	33,120	26,066	20,930
Amortization of goodwill.	4,799	1,941	—
Amortization of leasehold interests	1,841	761	919
Amortization of other deferred charges	1,067	607	563
Amortization of deferred financing costs	2,224	1,406	1,016
Tax benefit relating to stock option exercises	—	393	184
Equity in loss of joint venture	3,168	—	—
Extraordinary loss on early retirement of debt, net of income taxes	—	—	6,767
Cumulative effect of change in accounting principle, net of income taxes . .	—	741	—
Write-off of unamortized deferred charge	—	—	3,643
Deferred income taxes.	193	15,637	15,542
Change in operating assets and liabilities, net of effects of acquisitions . . .	—	—	—
Receivables	(11,915)	(5,812)	(21,056)
Inventories	(7,577)	(93,567)	(45,848)
Prepaid expenses and other current assets	(208)	7,240	(200)
Accounts payable	25,172	11,203	7,925

continued

continued from previous page

CSK Auto Corp. Consolidated Statements of Cash Flow			
($ thousands)	02/04/01	01/30/00	01/31/99
Accrued payroll, accrued expenses and other current liabilities	(23,332)	2,793	(947)
Other operating activities.	(1,083)	(811)	(6,753)
Net cash provided by (used in) operating activities	32,469	(4,031)	3,403
Cash flows provided by (used in) investing activities			
Business acquisitions, net of cash acquired	(1,182)	(218,201)	(892)
Capital expenditures	(32,080)	(41,358)	(37,846)
Expenditures for assets held for sale	(5)	(7,400)	(19,144)
Proceeds from sale of property and equipment and assets held for sale . . .	5,029	8,760	21,650
Investment in joint venture	(3,168)	—	—
Due to affiliate	—	—	(1,000)
Other investing activities	(3,136)	(2,022)	(292)
Net cash used in investing activities	(34,542)	(260,221)	(37,524)
Cash flows provided by (used in) financing activities			
Borrowings under Senior Credit Facility.	309,500	502,000	126,000
Payments under Senior Credit Facility	(291,840)	(218,340)	(87,065)
Issuance of common stock in initial public offering	—	—	172,482
Underwriter's discount and other IPO costs	—	—	(13,859)
Premiums paid upon early retirement of debt	—	—	(4,875)
Retirement of 11% Senior Subordinated Notes.	—	—	(43,750)
Retirement of 12% Subordinated Notes	—	—	(50,000)
Payment of Senior Credit Facility with public offering proceeds	—	—	(53,825)
Payment of debt issuance costs	(1,815)	(4,730)	—
Payments on capital lease obligations.	(10,934)	(10,905)	(8,634)
Advances to stockholders	(189)	—	—
Recovery of stockholder receivable	28	434	150
Exercise of options.	59	791	367
Other financing activities	(3,367)	(726)	(232)
Net cash provided by financing activities.	$ 1,442	$268,524	$ 36,759
Net increase (decrease) in cash and cash equivalents	(631)	4,272	2,638
Cash and cash equivalents, beginning of period	11,762	7,490	4,852
Cash and cash equivalents, end of period.	$ 11,131	$ 11,762	$ 7,490

CSK Auto Corp.
Consolidated Statements of Stockholders' Equity (Deficit)

($ thousands)	Common Stock Shares	Common Stock Amount	Additional Paid-in Capital	Shareholder Receivable	Deferred Compensation	Accumulated Deficit	Total Equity (Deficit)
Balances at February 1, 1998	19,113,399	$191	$130,513	−$1,168	−$675	−$203,916	−$ 75,055
Amortization of deferred compensation					182		182
Recovery of stockholder receivable				150			150
Issuance of common stock in initial public offering, net of transactions costs	8,625,000	86	158,537				158,623
Stock compensation			220				220
Exercise of options..................	30,444	1	366				367
Tax benefit of options................			184				184
Net income........................						20,718	20,718
Balances at January 31, 1999	27,768,843	278	289,820	−1,018	−493	−183,198	105,389
Amortization of deferred compensation					169		169
Recovery of stockholder receivable				434			434
Exercise of options..................	65,742		791				791
Tax benefit of options................			393				393
Net income........................						27,371	27,371
Balances at January 30, 2000	27,834,574	278	291,004	−584	−324	−155,827	134,547
Amortization of deferred compensation					168		168
Recovery of stockholder receivable				28			28
Advances to stockholders				−189			189
Exercise of options..................	6,604		59				59
Net income........................						5,000	5,000
Balances at February 4, 2001	$27,841,178	$278	$291,063	−$745	−$156	−$150,827	$139,613

8. The Company leases its office and warehouse facilities, all but three of its retail stores, and a majority of its equipment. Generally, store leases provide for minimum rentals and the payment of utilities, maintenance, insurance and taxes. Certain store leases also provide for contingent rentals based upon a percentage of sales in excess of a stipulated minimum. The majority of lease agreements are for base lease periods ranging from 15 to 20 years, with three to five renewal options of five years each.

Operating lease rental expense is as follows (in thousands):

Fiscal Year	2000	1999	1998
Minimum rentals.	$123,298	$97,748	$75,689
Contingent rentals	945	976	1,088
Sublease rentals.	−6,970	−5,395	−5,089
	$117,273	$93,329	$71,688

Future minimum lease obligations under non-cancelable leases at February 4, 2001, follows:

For Fiscal Years (in thousands)	Operating Leases	Capital Leases
2001	$122,985	$14,800
2002	115,549	13,387
2003	103,244	10,002
2004	87,459	6,496
2005	77,683	1,456
Thereafter	387,218	3,410
	$894,138	49,551
Less amounts representing interest		9,400
Present value of obligations		40,151
Less: current portion		(10,878)
Long-term obligation		$29,273

P12.35 **Integrative Case Analysis.** **Wal-Mart Stores, Inc.** is the world's largest retailer as measured by total revenues. During the fiscal year ended January 31, 2003, Wal-Mart had net sales of $244.5 billion. Presented below is information from Wal-Mart Stores, Inc.'s 2002 10-K report. (Wal-Mart refers to the ending January 31, 2003 as the year 2003. Assume that Wal-Mart's effective tax rate is 40 percent.)

Required
1. Was 2003 a good or bad year for Wal-Mart?
2. Wal-Mart uses the current rate method to account for the currency translation effects associated with its foreign subsidiaries. In 2003, relative to the currencies of the countries in which these subsidiaries operate, did the U.S. dollar appreciate, remain unchanged, or depreciate?
3. How has Wal-Mart generally financed its investment in new domestic and international stores?
4. What financial effects will Wal-Mart record with regard to its capital leases in 2004?
5. On January 31, 2003, Wal-Mart's share price was $47.56 per share. The Board of Directors has recommended declaring a 20 percent stock dividend.
   a. What is the target share price the Director's have in mind?
   b. What financial effects would the company record to give effect to the stock dividend?
   c. Why might the company consider undertaking a stock dividend?

6. Wal-Mart recognizes income taxes based on pretax income.
   a. What financial effects would the company record to recognize income taxes in 2003?
   b. Wal-Mart reported that its net deferred tax liability (deferred tax assets less deferred tax liabilities) was $759 million at January 31, 2003. What is the difference in the income Wal-Mart reported to its shareholders and to the tax authorities cumulatively through January 31, 2003? Is it more or less?

7. On January 31, 2004, Wal-Mart issued $200 million in zero-coupon notes due January 31, 2008. The proceeds from the sale of the Notes were $177.60 million. What was the yield, or market rate of interest, on the Notes?

8. On May 1, 2003, Wal-Mart's share price closed at $55.76 per share. Value Line forecasted sales of $259,800 million and $291,600 million and EPS of $2.05 and $2.35 per share for fiscal 2004 and 2005, respectively. The company's cost of equity is approximately thirteen percent. Using the Residual Income valuation model, calculate the equity value of the firm. [As a base case, a company whose expected ROE is 20 percent (25 percent) per year, whose cost of equity is thirteen percent, and whose growth in book value is expected to be twelve percent per year for the first ten years and three percent per year thereafter, would have an intrinsic value of 2.18 (3.03) times current book value.] Do you think Wal-Mart is worth $55.76 per share?

Wal-Mart Stores Inc. **Consolidated Balance Sheet**		
($ millions)	**01/31/03**	**01/31/02**
Cash and cash equivalents	$ 2,758	$ 2,161
Receivables	2,108	2,000
Inventories	—	—
At replacement cost	25,056	22,749
Less LIFO reserve.	165	135
Inventories at LIFO cost	24,891	22,614
Prepaid expenses and other	726	1,103
Total current assets	30,483	27,878
Property, plant and equipment, at cost		
Land	11,228	10,241
Building and improvements	33,750	28,527
Fixtures and equipment	15,946	14,135
Transportation equipment	1,313	1,089
	62,237	53,992
Less accumulated depreciation	13,537	11,436
Net property, plant and equipment	48,700	42,556
Property under capital lease.	4,814	4,626
Less accumulated amortization	1,610	1,432
Net property under capital leases	3,204	,194
Other assets and deferred charges		
Goodwill	9,521	8,566
Other assets and deferred charges	2,777	1,333
Total assets.	$94,685	$83,527

continued

continued from previous page

Wal-Mart Stores Inc.
Consolidated Balance Sheet

($ millions)	01/31/03	01/31/02
Commercial paper	$ 1,079	$ 743
Accounts payable.	17,140	15,617
Accrued liabilities	8,945	7,174
Accrued income taxes	739	1,343
Long-term debt due within one year	4,538	2,257
Obligations under capital leases due within one year	176	148
Total current liabilities.	32,617	27,282
Long-term debt	16,607	15,687
Long-term obligations under capital leases.	3,001	3,045
Deferred income taxes and other.	1,761	1,204
Minority Interests	1,362	1,207
Shareholders' Equity		
Preferred stock ($0.10 par value; 100 shares authorized, none issued)		
Common stock ($0.10 par value; 11,000 shares authorized, 4,395 and		
4,453 issued and outstanding in 2003 and 2002, respectively).	440	445
Capital in excess of par value	1,482	1,484
Retained earnings	37,924	34,441
Other accumulated comprehensive income	(509)	(1,268)
Total shareholders' equity	39,337	35,102
Total liabilities and shareholders' equity.	$94,685	$83,527

Wal-Mart Stores Inc.
Consolidated Statements of Income

($ millions)	1/31/03	1/31/02	1/31/01
Revenues			
Net sales.	$244,524	$217,799	$191,329
Other income	2,001	1,873	1,787
	246,525	219,672	193,116
Costs and expenses			
Cost of sales.	191,838	171,562	150,255
Operating, selling and general and			
administrative expenses	41,043	36,173	31,550
Operating income.	13,644	11,937	11,311
Interest			
Debt	803	1,083	1,104
Capital leases.	260	274	279
Interest income.	(138)	(171)	(188)
	925	1,186	1,195
Income before income taxes and minority interest	12,719	10,751	10,116
Provision for income taxes.	4,487	3,897	,692
Income before minority interest	8,232	6,854	6,424
Minority interests	(193)	(183)	(129)
Net income.	$ 8,039	$ 6,671	$ 6,295

Wal-Mart Stores Inc. Consolidated Statements of Cash Flow			
($ millions)	01/31/03	01/31/02	01/31/01
Cash flows from operating activities			
Net Income..	$ 8,039	$ 6,671	$ 6,295
Adjustments to reconcile net income to net cash provided by operating activities			
Depreciation and amortization..........................	3,432	3,290	2,868
Increase in accounts receivable........................	(101)	(210)	(422)
Increase in inventories................................	(2,236)	(1,235)	(1,795)
Increase in accounts payable..........................	1,447	368	2,061
Increase in accrued liabilities.........................	1,106	1,125	11
Deferred income taxes................................	520	185	342
Other..	325	66	244
Net cash provided by operating activities	12,532	10,260	9,604
Cash flows from investing activities......................	—	—	—
Payments for property, plant and equipment...............	(9,355)	(8,383)	(8,042)
Investment in international operations.....................	(749)	—	(627)
Proceeds from the disposal of fixed assets................	455	331	284
Proceeds from termination or sale of net investment hedges	—	1,134	—
Other investing activities	(60)	(228)	(329)
Net cash used in investing activities.....................	(9,709)	(7,146)	(8,714)
Cash flows from financing activities......................	—	—	—
Increase/(decrease) in commercial paper	1,836	(1,533)	(2,022)
Proceeds from issuance of long-term debt	2,044	4,591	3,778
Purchase of Company stock	(3,232)	(1,214)	(193)
Dividends paid.......................................	(1,328)	(1,249)	(1,070)
Payment of long-term debt	(1,263)	(3,519)	(1,519)
Payment of capital lease obligations	(216)	(167)	(173)
Proceeds from issuance of Company stock	—	—	581
Other financing activities	(63)	113	176
Net cash used in financing activities	(2,222)	(2,978)	(442)
Effect of exchange rate changes on cash	(4)	(29)	(250)
Net increase in cash and cash equivalents	597	107	198
Cash and cash equivalents at beginning of year.............	2,161	2,054	1,856
Cash and cash equivalents at end of year.................	$ 2,758	$ 2,161	$ 2,054

Wal-Mart Stores Inc.
Consolidated Statements of Shareholders' Equity

($ millions)	Number of shares	Common Stock	Capital in Excess of Par Value	Retained Earnings	Other Accumulated Comprehensive Income	Total
Balance, January 31, 2002.........	$4,453	$445	$1,484	$34,44	$(1,268)	$35,102
Comprehensive income						
Net income....................				8,039		8,039
Other comprehensive income						
Foreign currency translation adjustment..................					1,113	1,113
Hedge accounting adjustment.....					(148)	(148)
Minimum pension liability adjustment..................					(206)	(206)
Total comprehensive income						
Cash dividends ($.30 per share) ...				(1,328)		(1,328)
Purchase of Company stock	(63)	(5)	(150)	(3,228)		(3,383)
Stock options exercised and other .	5		148			148
Balance, January 31, 2003.........	$4,395	$440	$1,482	$37,924	$(509)	$39,337

9.   The Company and certain of its subsidiaries have long-term leases for stores and equipment. Rentals (including, for certain leases, amounts applicable to taxes, insurance, maintenance, other operating expenses and contingent rentals) under all operating leases were $1,091 million, $1,043 million, and $893 million in 2003, 2002, and 2001, respectively. Aggregate minimum annual rentals at January 31, 2003, under non-cancelable leases are as follows:

Fiscal year (in millions)	Operating Leases	Capital Leases
2004	$ 589	$ 440
2005	576	431
2006	560	428
2007	546	419
2008	515	412
Thereafter......................................	5,202	3,095
Net minimum rentals	$7,988	5,225
Less imputed interest at rates ranging from 6.1% to 14.0%......		2,048
Present value of minimum lease payments		$3,177

(in millions (except %))	Wal-Mart Stores Inc. Fiscal Year Ending				
	1/31/03	1/31/02	1/31/01	1/31/00	1/31/99
Net income.	$8,039	$6,671	$6,295	$5,377	$4,430
Growth (%).	21%	6%	17%	21%	26%
Net sales.	$244,524	$217,799	$191,329	$165,013	$137,634
Growth (%).	12%	14%	16%	20%	17%
Shareholders' equity	$39,337	$35,102	$31,343	$25,834	$21,112
Growth (%).	12%	12%	21%	22%	14%
Total assets.	$94,685	$83,527	$78,130	$70,349	$49,996
Growth (%).	13%	7%	11%	41%	10%

P12.36 **Financial Statement Analysis and Firm Value.** **Weis Markets, Inc.** is a Pennsylvania business founded by Harry and Sigmund Weis in 1912. The company is engaged principally in the retail sale of food and pet supplies in Pennsylvania and surrounding states. The Weis family currently owns approximately 62 percent of the outstanding shares. The company's retail food stores sell groceries, dairy products, frozen foods, meats, seafood, fresh produce, floral, prescriptions, deli/bakery products, prepared foods, fuel and general merchandise items, such as health and beauty care and household products.

Required
1. Was 2004 a good year or a bad year for Weis? Why?
2. What was the company's interest coverage ratio in 2004 and 2003? On July 1, 2004, Weis considered borrowing $100 million of long-term debt at an interest rate of ten percent per year to finance a $100 million investment in additional stores. The new properties would not generate earnings until 2005. What would the company's interest coverage ratio have been for 2004 if it had completed the borrowing?
3. Evaluate Weis' profitability in 2003 and 2004 using the ROE Model discussed in Chapter 4. On March 31, 2005, Weis's share price closed at $29.85 per share. Value Line forecasted sales of $2,050 million and $2,125 million and EPS of $2.00 and $2.10 per share for fiscal 2005 and 2006, respectively. The company's cost of equity is approximately nine percent. Using the Residual Income valuation model, calculate the equity value of the company. [As a base case, a company whose expected ROE is twelve percent (14 percent) per year, whose cost of equity is nine percent, and whose growth in book value is expected to be four percent per year for the first ten years and three percent per year thereafter, would have an intrinsic value of 1.54 (1.90) times current book value.] Do you think Weis is worth $29.85 per share? Why?

Weis Markets Inc.
Consolidated Balance Sheet

($ thousands, for period ended)	12/29/04	12/29/03
Assets		
Cash.	$ 3,929	$ 3,255
Marketable securities	43,510	28,675
Accounts receivable, net	30,188	26,530
Inventories	182,832	169,952
Prepaid expenses.	3,980	8,294
Income taxes recoverable	—	3,395
Total current assets	264,439	240,101
Property and equipment, net	428,153	439,977
Intangible and other assets	24,107	24,107
	$716,699	$704,185
Liabilities		
Accounts payable.	$101,917	$ 98,382
Accrued expenses	15,704	11,043
Accrued self-insurance.	16,117	15,040
Payable to employee benefit plans	8,950	8,672
Income taxes payable	6,112	—
Deferred income taxes	702	4,633
Total current liabilities.	149,502	137,770
Deferred income taxes	14,765	16,051
Long-term debt	—	25,000
Shareholders' Equity		
Common stock, no par value, 100,800,000 shares authorized,		
32,986,337 and 32,978,037 shares issued, respectively.	7,882	7,630
Retained earnings	678,294	648,522
Accumulated other comprehensive income.	4,145	6,479
	690,321	662,631
Treasury stock at cost, 5,792,800 and 5,774,830 shares, respectively . . .	(137,889)	(137,267)
Total shareholders' equity	552,432	525,364
	$716,699	$704,185

Weis Markets Inc.
Consolidated Statements of Income

($ thousands except per share amounts, for period ended)	12/30/04	12/30/03	12/30/02
Net sales.	$1,999,364	$1,971,665	$2,042,329
Cost of sales, including warehousing and distribution expenses.	1,471,479	1,457,002	1,518,136
Gross profit on sales	527,885	514,663	524,193
Operating, general and administrative expenses.	448,478	451,723	444,110
Income from operations	79,407	62,940	80,083
Investment income.	879	9,860	18,557
Interest expense.	(394)	(1,400)	—

continued

continued from previous page

Weis Markets Inc.
Consolidated Statements of Income

($ thousands except per share amounts, for period ended)	12/30/04	12/30/03	12/30/02
Other income	14,794	10,447	18,172
Income before provision for income taxes	94,686	81,847	116,812
Provision for income taxes	35,537	31,792	42,989
Net income	$ 59,149	$ 50,055	$ 73,823
Cash dividends per share	$1.08	$1.08	$1.06
Basic and diluted earnings per share	2.17	1.55	1.77

Weis Markets Inc.
Consolidated Statements of Cash Flow

($ thousands, for period ended)	12/30/04	12/30/03	12/30/02
Cash flows from operating activities			
Net income	$ 59,149	$ 50,055	$ 73,823
Adjustments to reconcile net income to net cash provided by operating activities			
Depreciation	41,885	43,755	44,169
Amortization	5,797	7,222	6,682
(Gain) loss on sale of fixed assets	(3,620)	1,629	(5,913)
Gain on sale of marketable securities	—	(570)	(1,279)
Changes in operating assets and liabilities			
Inventories	(12,880)	(1,411)	(1,395)
Accounts receivable and prepaid expenses	656	(2,923)	8,508
Income taxes recoverable	3,395	(251)	1,194
Accounts payable and other liabilities	9,551	14,993	(2,696)
Income taxes payable	6,112	—	—
Deferred income taxes	(3,561)	1,381	2,472
Net cash provided by operating activities	106,484	113,880	125,565
Cash flows from investing activities			
Purchase of property and equipment	(46,056)	(48,046)	(56,331)
Proceeds from the sale of property and equipment	14,520	86	11,714
Purchase of marketable securities	(21,754)	(299,064)	(259,574)
Proceeds from maturities of marketable securities	2,929	556,141	108,154
Proceeds from sale of marketable securities	—	123,660	127,043
Increase in intangible and other assets	(702)	(19)	(13,379)
Net cash provided by (used in) investing activities	(51,063)	332,758	(82,373)
Cash flows from financing activities			
Proceeds (payments) of long-term debt, net	(25,000)	25,000	–0–
Proceeds from issuance of common stock	252	36	35
Dividends paid	(29,377)	(37,202)	(44,191)
Purchase and cancellation of stock	—	(434,317)	—
Purchase of treasury stock	(622)	(289)	(199)
Net cash used in financing activities	(54,747)	(446,772)	(44,355)
Net increase (decrease) in cash	$ 674	$ (134)	$ (1,163)

CORPORATE ANALYSIS

CA12.37 The Procter and Gamble Company. The 2005 annual report of **The Procter and Gamble Company** (**P & G**) is available at www.pg.com/annualreports/2005/pdf/pg2005annualreport.pdf. After reviewing P & G's annual report, respond to the following questions:

a. Prepare pro forma income statements for 2006, 2007, and 2008, using the following assumptions.
   - Sales will grow by five percent annually.
   - Cost of goods sold will remain 49 percent of sales.
   - Selling, general and administrative expense will amount to 31 percent of sales.
   - Interest expense will be 3.5 percent times the beginning-of-year "debt due in one year" plus 4.0 percent times the beginning-of-year "long-term debt."
   - Other non-operating income will amount to 0.5 percent of sales.
   - The effective tax rate will remain 30.5 percent.
   - Round all amounts to the nearest million.

b. Prepare pro forma balance sheets for 2006, 2007, and 2008, using the following assumptions:

Assets:
   - Total assets will maintain a turnover rate of 0.92 times.
   - Cash and cash equivalents will grow at the same rate as sales.
   - Investment securities will be a plug figure to balance the asset side of the balance sheet.
   - Accounts receivable will maintain a turnover rate of 14 times.
   - Inventories (total) will maintain a turnover rate of 5.6 times.
   - Deferred income taxes will grow at ten percent per year.
   - Prepaid expenses and other current assets will grow at six percent per year.
   - Net property, plant and equipment will maintain a fixed asset turnover of four times.
   - Net goodwill and other intangible assets will maintain an intangible assets turnover of 2.4 times.
   - Other current assets will remain constant at $2,703.

Liabilities:
   - Total liabilities and shareholders' equity will equal forecasted total assets.
   - Accounts payable will maintain a turnover rate of 7.3 times.
   - Accrued and other liabilities will remain constant at $7,531.
   - Taxes payable will remain a constant 70 percent of the income tax expenses (from the income statement).
   - Debt due within one year is a plug figure to balance the total liabilities and total shareholders' equity.
   - Long-term debt will grow to $13,000 in 2006 and remain constant thereafter.
   - Deferred income taxes will grow by 20 percent of the change in net property, plant and equipment.

Shareholders' equity:
   - Convertible preferred stock, common stock (at par), and Additional paid-in-capital will remain constant as the company will finance all growth and operating needs using short-term debt.
   - The Reserve for ESOP debt retirement and other comprehensive income will remain constant.
   - Ending retained earnings equals beginning retained earnings plus net income less dividends paid. Consistent with its past behavior, P & G is assumed to grow its dividend eleven percent annually as follows:

2006	$3,035
2007	3,369
2008	3,740

c. Using the pro forma income statements from part (a) and pro forma balance sheets from part (b), prepare pro forma statements of cash flow for 2006, 2007, and 2008. Assume that the depreciation and amortization expense equals five percent of the beginning-of-year balance of net property, plant and equipment plus net goodwill and other intangible assets.

d. Calculate the equity value of Procter and Gamble using the discounted cash flow approach and the following assumptions:
   - P & G's cost of equity is ten percent.
   - Assume that the growth rate (g) of free cash flow is three percent after 2008.

How does your estimate of firm value compare to P & G's current market capitalization?

CA12.38 Internet-based Analysis. Consider a publicly-held company whose products you are familiar with. Some examples might include:

Company	Product	Corporate Website
• Johnson & Johnson Company	• Band-Aids	• www.jnj.com
• Microsoft Corporation	• Windows XP software	• www.microsoft.com
• Nokia Corporation	• Cellular phones	• www.nokia.com
• Intel Corporation	• Pentium processors	• www.intel.com
• Kimberly-Clark Corporation	• Kleenex	• www.kimberly-clark.com

Access the company's public website and search for its most recent annual report. (Some companies provide access to their financial data through an "investor relations" link, while others provide a direct link to their "annual reports.") After locating your company's most recent annual report, open the file and review its contents. After reviewing the annual report for your selected company, prepare answers to the following questions:

1. What is the book value of the company? What is the market capitalization of the company? Why are they different?

2. What is the company's current price-to-book value multiple, price-to-sales multiple, and price-to-earnings multiple?

3. Calculate the company's cost of equity, assuming a risk-free rate of 4.5 percent and an equity-risk premium of 7.0 percent. How does the company's cost of equity compare to its ROE? What does the comparison tell you about the company?

4. Calculate the equity value of the company using the residual income model.

The Time Value of Money

In this appendix, the concepts of compounding and the time value of money—important concepts that affect your everyday life—are illustrated. To set the stage, consider the following information regarding a loan made by Mr. Jacob DeHaven to General George Washington in 1777:

> The U.S. Supreme Court has upheld a refusal to repay a loan that helped save the American Revolution as George Washington's beleaguered army camped in the snow at Valley Forge. Jacob DeHaven of Philadelphia made the loan of gold, food and other supplies with an estimated value of $450,000 in February 1777. The failure of the United States ever to repay the loan obsesses Hershel Weasenforth, one of DeHaven's descendants. Before he died in 1984 at age 79, his daughter, Thelma Lunaas, promised him she would strive to get the U.S. government to settle the debt...Jacob DeHaven, a wealthy merchant and wine importer, was one of the patriots who responded to a desperate plea for aid for Washington's army at Valley Forge. . . . His descendants have made periodic efforts to get repayment over the past 215 years. (*Houston Chronicle*, January 29, 1992, p. 13A).

The information is not explicit as to whether Mr. DeHaven and General Washington discussed the interest rate on the loan, and if they did, whether they agreed on a specific interest rate. However, if Mr. DeHaven had written a loan agreement with a five percent annual rate of interest and the U.S. Supreme Court had upheld the claim, Mr. DeHaven's heirs would be owed an astounding $32 billion some 229 years later in 2006. This case illustrates that even a modest sum of money invested at a low rate of interest for a long period of time can accumulate to a substantial sum as a consequence of the phenomenon of compounding. Compounding is a process in which interest is earned not only on an outstanding loan amount but also on any prior unpaid interest.

The key to understanding the concept of compounding is that the value of invested funds grows over time. Another way to think of this is that having $1 now is not the same as having $1 one year from now. If you have $1 now, you can invest it and have more than $1 in a year because your investment can earn interest. This notion—the time value of money—is important when evaluating the attractiveness of any investment.

How did we arrive at the $32 billion figure owed to Mr. DeHaven by the U.S. government? If Mr. DeHaven had written a loan for one year at five percent interest, he would expect to receive his original investment of $450,000 plus interest of $22,500 (5 percent of $450,000), or a total of $472,500 at the end of year one. If General Washington had wanted to roll the loan over for a second year, Mr. DeHaven could expect to receive $496,125 ($472,500 plus interest of $23,625 (5 percent of $472,500)) at the end of year two. If we repeated the exercise 227 more times (i.e., until 2006), you arrive at $32 billion.

Time	0		1		2			229
	1777	1778		1779			2006	
Principle $450,000.....		$450,000		$472,500				
Interest		22,500		23,625				
Amount owed..........		$472,500		$496,125				$32 billion

An interesting twist to the story is that Jacob DeHaven's relatives actually sued the U.S. government for $100 billion! What rate of interest would yield that amount? You may be surprised to learn that it would only take an interest rate of 5.52 percent compounded annually over 229 years to grow to $100 billion. In fact, at six percent interest, the amount owed would be over $280 billion! A one percent increase in the rate of interest results in almost a ten-fold increase in the future amount, reflecting the power of compounding.

FUTURE VALUE OF A SINGLE AMOUNT

The DeHaven loan example illustrates the concept of **future value**. The future value of an investment is the amount that an initial investment, or a series of payments, will be worth at some point in the future. In the above example, $32 billion is the future value of an initial investment of $450,000 earning five percent interest per year for 229 years. The following formula can be used to compute future values:

$$\text{Future Value} = \text{Present Value} \times (1 + r)^n$$

where the present value is the amount currently invested, r is the prevailing rate of interest, and n is the number of periods (e.g., months, quarters, or years) until the cash inflow occurs. For example, if you can earn eight percent on your investment, how much would an investment of $2,000 today be worth in five years? Using the formula above, we see that the future value of your investment is $2,938, calculated as follows:

$$\text{Future Value} = \$2,000(1+.08)^5 = \$2,938.$$

Alternatively, you can use a future value table (see Table 3 at the end of this appendix), which shows that the future value of $1 to be received in 5 years at an interest rate of 8 percent, PV(5, 8%), is equal to 1.469.[1] Hence,

$$FV = \$2,000 \times PV(5,8\%) = \$2,000 \times 1.469 = \$2,938.$$

What if you want to find the future value of more than one deposit? This is not a problem as you simply add the individual future value computations together using the following formula:

$$FV = \sum_{t=1}^{n} CF_i(1 + r)^{n-t}$$

where CF represents the individual deposits.

To illustrate, suppose you deposit $200 today into a savings account, $150 one year from today, and $300 in three years from today. What will all of this be worth in five years, assuming a six percent rate of interest? Your first deposit will earn interest for five years and therefore will have a future value of $267.60. The future value of our second and third deposit are $189.30 and $337.20, respectively, for a total future value of $794.10. (You should be certain that you can compute these amounts on your own.)

---

[1] In order to use Tables 1 through 4 at the end of this appendix, you simply find the number, called an interest factor, which is at the intersection of the appropriate interest rate column and the period row. Can you find the interest factor of 1.469 in Table 3, at the intersection of row n = 5 and the column i = 8%?

FUTURE VALUE OF AN ANNUITY

Rather than investing a single lump sum, or several deposits of differing value, you might invest a fixed amount on a regular basis. To illustrate this, assume that you plan to deposit $100 in a savings account on January 1st of each year for ten years and that you can earn seven percent interest on your deposits. How much would you have at the end of the tenth year? One way to solve this problem would be to use the future value (FV) formula (or Table 3) and compute the sum of the future value of each of the ten deposits. The first $100 deposit will be able to earn interest for ten years so it will be worth $196.70 at the end of ten years. Similarly, the second $100 deposit will earn interest for nine years and be worth $183.80. If we were to do the same calculations for each of the ten deposits and then sum the results, we would have our answer, $1,381.60. Luckily, there is an easier way to solve this type of problem.

An **annuity** is defined as a stream of equal size payments occurring at equal intervals.[2] Fortunately, a formula has been derived that can shorten the computation of the present value of an annuity:

$$\text{Future Value of an Annuity} = \text{Payment} \times FV_a(n, r\%) = \text{Payment} \times ((1+r)^n - 1)/r$$

Using the above formula, we see that $1,381.60 = $100 \times ((1.07^{10} - 1) / .07)$. To facilitate this calculation, we can use Table 4 and find the interest factor of 13.816, which when multiplied by the recurring deposit of $100 yields our future value of $1,381.60.

To this point, all of our examples have assumed that the payments and the compounding of interest occur just once per year. This, however, may not be the case in all situations. The only adjustment needed to compute a non-annual compounding is to convert the annual interest rate into a per-period rate of interest and to work with the number of periods rather than the number of years. The per-period interest rate is calculated by dividing the annual interest rate by the number of periods per year (e.g., a twelve percent annual rate would be a one percent monthly rate.) In the above example, rather than making one payment per year for ten years, let's compute the future value for ten semiannual payments of $100 with annual interest at eight percent.

We first need to convert the eight percent annual interest rate to a four percent per-period rate. Our formula then becomes $100 \times ((1.04^{10} - 1) / .04 = $1,200.60$. Note that we could also use the interest factor from Table 4 and compute the future value as $100 \times 12.006 = $1,200.60$.

PRESENT VALUE OF A SINGLE AMOUNT

Thus far, we have been focusing on what an amount will be worth in the future. So, let's reverse our thinking and now consider what an amount to be received in the future is worth today. For example, consider a $100 investment today that will pay back $121.90 in ten years. Intuitively, this doesn't seem like a very good investment. It seems like you could do better just putting your money in a money market account at a bank. A common way to evaluate an investment opportunity like this is to compute the **present value** of the $121.90—that is, the amount that you would have to invest now, at a specified rate of interest, that would grow to $121.90 in ten years. In this case, if we assume that the prevailing interest rate is twelve percent, the present value of $121.90 to be received in ten years is $39.25—that is, if you invested $39.25 now at twelve percent annual interest, in ten years your investment would grow to a future value of $121.90.

The present value (PV) of a single amount is computed like this:

$$\text{Present Value} = \text{Future Amount} \times (1/(1+r)^n)$$

---

[2] In this appendix we assume that the deposits (often referred to as payments) occur at the end of each period. This type of annuity is called an ordinary annuity or an annuity-in-arrears. An annuity-in-advance is an annuity in which the payments occur at the beginning of each period.

where r is the prevailing rate of interest and n is the number of periods (e.g., months, quarters, or years) until the cash inflow occurs. In the example just shown, the present value of the $121.90 would be computed as follows:

$$\text{Present Value} = \$121.90 \times (1/(1 + 0.12)^{10}) = \$39.25$$

Alternatively, you can use a present value table (see Table 1), which shows that the present value of $1 to be received in 10 years at an interest rate of twelve percent, PV(10, 12%), is equal to 0.322. Hence,

$$\text{PV} = \$120 \times \text{PV}(10,12\%) = \$121.90 \times 0.322 = \$39.25$$

To help us decide whether to undertake an investment, we can compute the **net present value (NPV)** of the investment as follows:

> **NPV = Present value of cash flows − cost of investment**

An investment is considered to be a good one if the NPV $\geq$ 0—that is, if the present value of the expected cash inflow is greater than the cost of the investment. Conversely, if the NPV $<$ 0, it is considered to be a bad investment. In our case, the NPV of the $100 investment is equal to negative $61.36 ($38.64 − $100) assuming a prevailing interest rate of twelve percent, and, since the NPV of the investment is less than zero, it would be considered a bad investment.[3]

Let's consider another present value example. Anna Amphlett recently learned that in ten years she would receive $1 million from a trust fund established by her uncle when Anna was born. Given that she could earn about eight percent per year, Anna wondered how much her trust fund was currently worth. Using the present value approach, Anna's trust fund would be currently worth $463,000, calculated as follows:

$$\text{PV} = \$1,000,000 \times \text{PV}(10, 8\%) \text{ [from Table 1, PV}(10,8\%) \text{ is equal to 0.463]}$$
$$= \$1,000,000 \times 0.463$$
$$= \mathbf{\$463,000}$$

In ten years, with an interest rate of eight percent per year, Anna's trust fund will grow to be worth $1 million, its future value.

PRESENT VALUE OF AN ANNUITY

Investments often involve a series of cash flows rather than a single lump sum cash payment at the end of the investment. For example, consider a $60,000 investment in an MBA degree that is expected to yield an increment to your salary of $5,000 a year for the next 25 years. Is this a good investment? Unlike the previous example, this education investment pays off each year. One way to compute the present value of the incremental cash flows would be to compute the present value of each of the $5,000 annual salary flows and then add the 25 amounts up as follows:

---

[3] You may wonder what interest rate resulted in the deposit of $100.00 growing to $121.90 in ten years. This can be found with the use of Table 1 and the present value formula. Simply rearrange the present value (PV) formula as follows:

$$\text{PV} = \text{FV} \times \text{PV factor}$$
$$\text{PV} / \text{FV} = \text{PV factor}$$

We can then compute the PV factor as $100.00 / $121.90 = .820. We then search for this PV factor in Table 1 by scanning across the ten period row until we find this a factor of 0.82 in the two percent column.

$$5,000 \times PV(1, 10\%)$$
$$5,000 \times PV(2, 10\%)$$
$$\cdot$$
$$\underline{5,000 \times PV(25, 10\%)}$$
$$\underline{\$45,385}$$

Fortunately, a formula similar to the future value of an annuity has been derived that can shorten the computation of the present value of an annuity:

Present Value of an Annuity $= $ Payment $\times PV_a(n, r\%) = $ Payment $\times (1-(1/(1+r)^n))/r$

The present value of the 25 years of extra salary, assuming an interest rate of ten percent, is computed as follows:

Present Value of an Annuity $= \$5,000 \times (1-(1/(1+.10)^{25}))/.10 = \$45,385$

Alternatively, you can use a present value table (see Table 2), which shows that the present value of $1 to be received every year for 25 years at an interest rate of ten percent, $PV_a(25, 10\%)$, is equal to 9.077. Hence,

Present Value of an Annuity $= \$5,000 \times 9.077 = \$45,385$

But is this a good investment? Using the formula to calculate the net present value of an investment reveals that the NPV of receiving $5,000 per year for 25 years, with a prevailing interest rate of ten percent, is negative $14,615, calculated as follows:

$$NPV = \$5,000 \times PV_a(12,10\%) - \$60,000$$
$$= \$5,000 \times 9.077 - \$60,000$$
$$= \$45,385 - \$60,000$$
$$= -\$14,615 < 0$$

In this case, since the NPV of the investment is less than zero, the investment in the MBA degree is a bad one from a financial standpoint.

Consider a final example of an annuity. Josie Walsh recently won the lottery which will pay her $500,000 every year for the next 20 years. Josie's friend, Paul, offered her $3.5 million now if she will give him the winning ticket. Josie figures that she could always put the money in a 20-year U.S. government bond earning twelve percent. Should Josie sell her winning ticket for $3.5 million? Calculating the net present value of 20 payments of $500,000 reveals that the NPV is $234,500, calculated as follows:

$$NPV = \$500,000 \times PV_a(20, 12\%) - \$3,500,000 \text{ [from Table 2, } PV_a(20,12\%) \text{ is equal to 7.469]}$$
$$= \$500,000 \times 7.469 - \$3,500,000$$
$$= \$3,734,500 - \$3,500,000$$
$$= \$234,500 > 0,$$

Since the NPV of the offer is $234,500, which is greater than zero, Josie should not accept Paul's offer to buy her winning lottery ticket.

TABLE 1	Present Value of $1										
Period	**1%**	**2%**	**3%**	**4%**	**5%**	**6%**	**7%**	**8%**	**9%**	**10%**	**11%**	**12%**
1	0.990	0.980	0.971	0.962	0.952	0.943	0.935	0.926	0.917	0.909	0.901	0.893
2	0.980	0.961	0.943	0.925	0.907	0.890	0.873	0.857	0.842	0.826	0.812	0.797
3	0.971	0.942	0.915	0.889	0.864	0.840	0.816	0.794	0.772	0.751	0.731	0.712
4	0.961	0.924	0.888	0.855	0.823	0.792	0.763	0.735	0.708	0.683	0.659	0.636
5	0.951	0.906	0.863	0.822	0.784	0.747	0.713	0.681	0.650	0.621	0.593	0.567
6	0.942	0.888	0.837	0.790	0.746	0.705	0.666	0.630	0.596	0.564	0.535	0.507
7	0.933	0.871	0.813	0.760	0.711	0.665	0.623	0.583	0.547	0.513	0.482	0.452
8	0.923	0.853	0.789	0.731	0.677	0.627	0.582	0.540	0.502	0.467	0.434	0.404
9	0.914	0.837	0.766	0.703	0.645	0.592	0.544	0.500	0.460	0.424	0.391	0.361
10	0.905	0.820	0.744	0.676	0.614	0.558	0.508	0.463	0.422	0.386	0.352	0.322
11	0.896	0.804	0.722	0.650	0.585	0.527	0.475	0.429	0.388	0.350	0.317	0.287
12	0.887	0.788	0.701	0.625	0.557	0.497	0.444	0.397	0.356	0.319	0.286	0.257
13	0.879	0.773	0.681	0.601	0.530	0.469	0.415	0.368	0.326	0.290	0.258	0.229
14	0.870	0.758	0.661	0.577	0.505	0.442	0.388	0.340	0.299	0.263	0.232	0.205
15	0.861	0.743	0.642	0.555	0.481	0.417	0.362	0.315	0.275	0.239	0.209	0.183
16	0.853	0.728	0.623	0.534	0.458	0.394	0.339	0.292	0.252	0.218	0.188	0.163
17	0.844	0.714	0.605	0.513	0.436	0.371	0.317	0.270	0.231	0.198	0.170	0.146
18	0.836	0.700	0.587	0.494	0.416	0.350	0.296	0.250	0.212	0.180	0.153	0.130
19	0.828	0.686	0.570	0.475	0.396	0.331	0.277	0.232	0.194	0.164	0.138	0.116
20	0.820	0.673	0.554	0.456	0.377	0.312	0.258	0.215	0.178	0.149	0.124	0.104
25	0.780	0.610	0.478	0.375	0.295	0.233	0.184	0.146	0.116	0.092	0.074	0.059
30	0.742	0.552	0.412	0.308	0.231	0.174	0.131	0.099	0.075	0.057	0.044	0.033
35	0.706	0.500	0.355	0.253	0.181	0.130	0.094	0.068	0.049	0.036	0.026	0.019
40	0.672	0.453	0.307	0.208	0.142	0.097	0.067	0.046	0.032	0.022	0.015	0.011
50	0.608	0.372	0.228	0.141	0.087	0.054	0.034	0.021	0.013	0.009	0.005	0.003

TABLE 2	Present Value of an Ordinary Annuity of $1 per period										
Period	**1%**	**2%**	**3%**	**4%**	**5%**	**6%**	**7%**	**8%**	**9%**	**10%**	**11%**	**12%**
1	0.990	0.980	0.971	0.962	0.952	0.943	0.935	0.926	0.917	0.909	0.901	0.893
2	1.970	1.942	1.913	1.886	1.859	1.833	1.808	1.783	1.759	1.736	1.713	1.690
3	2.941	2.884	2.829	2.775	2.723	2.673	2.624	2.577	2.531	2.487	2.444	2.402
4	3.902	3.808	3.717	3.630	3.546	3.465	3.387	3.312	3.240	3.170	3.102	3.037
5	4.853	4.713	4.580	4.452	4.329	4.212	4.100	3.993	3.890	3.791	3.696	3.605
6	5.795	5.601	5.417	5.242	5.076	4.917	4.767	4.623	4.486	4.355	4.231	4.111
7	6.728	6.472	6.230	6.002	5.786	5.582	5.389	5.206	5.033	4.868	4.712	4.564
8	7.652	7.325	7.020	6.733	6.463	6.210	5.971	5.747	5.535	5.335	5.146	4.968
9	8.566	8.162	7.786	7.435	7.108	6.802	6.515	6.247	5.995	5.759	5.537	5.328
10	9.471	8.983	8.530	8.111	7.722	7.360	7.024	6.710	6.418	6.145	5.889	5.650
11	10.368	9.787	9.253	8.760	8.306	7.887	7.499	7.139	6.805	6.495	6.207	5.938
12	11.255	10.575	9.954	9.385	8.863	8.384	7.943	7.536	7.161	6.814	6.492	6.194
13	12.134	11.348	10.635	9.986	9.394	8.853	8.358	7.904	7.487	7.103	6.750	6.424

continued

continued from previous page

TABLE 2	Present Value of an Ordinary Annuity of $1 per period										
Period	1%	2%	3%	4%	5%	6%	7%	8%	9%	10%	11%	12%
14	13.004	12.106	11.296	10.563	9.899	9.295	8.745	8.244	7.786	7.367	6.982	6.628
15	13.865	12.849	11.938	11.118	10.380	9.712	9.108	8.559	8.061	7.606	7.191	6.811
16	14.718	13.578	12.561	11.652	10.838	10.106	9.447	8.851	8.313	7.824	7.379	6.974
17	15.562	14.292	13.166	12.166	11.274	10.477	9.763	9.122	8.544	8.022	7.549	7.120
18	16.398	14.992	13.754	12.659	11.690	10.828	10.059	9.372	8.756	8.201	7.702	7.250
19	17.226	15.678	14.324	13.134	12.085	11.158	10.336	9.604	8.950	8.365	7.839	7.366
20	18.046	16.351	14.877	13.590	12.462	11.470	10.594	9.818	9.129	8.514	7.963	7.469
25	22.023	19.523	17.413	15.622	14.094	12.783	11.654	10.675	9.823	9.077	8.422	7.843
30	25.808	22.396	19.600	17.292	15.372	13.765	12.409	11.258	10.274	9.427	8.694	8.055
35	29.409	24.999	21.487	18.665	16.374	14.498	12.948	11.655	10.567	9.644	8.855	8.176
40	32.835	27.355	23.115	19.793	17.159	15.046	13.332	11.925	10.757	9.779	8.951	8.244
50	39.196	31.424	25.730	21.482	18.256	15.762	13.801	12.233	10.962	9.915	9.042	8.304

TABLE 3	Future Value of $1										
Period	1%	2%	3%	4%	5%	6%	7%	8%	9%	10%	11%	12%
1	1.010	1.020	1.030	1.040	1.050	1.060	1.070	1.080	1.090	1.100	1.110	1.120
2	1.020	1.040	1.061	1.082	1.103	1.124	1.145	1.166	1.188	1.210	1.232	1.254
3	1.030	1.061	1.093	1.125	1.158	1.191	1.225	1.260	1.295	1.331	1.368	1.405
4	1.041	1.082	1.126	1.170	1.216	1.262	1.311	1.360	1.412	1.464	1.518	1.574
5	1.051	1.104	1.159	1.217	1.276	1.338	1.403	1.469	1.539	1.611	1.685	1.762
6	1.062	1.126	1.194	1.265	1.340	1.419	1.501	1.587	1.677	1.772	1.870	1.974
7	1.072	1.149	1.230	1.316	1.407	1.504	1.606	1.714	1.828	1.949	2.076	2.211
8	1.083	1.172	1.267	1.369	1.477	1.594	1.718	1.851	1.993	2.144	2.305	2.476
9	1.094	1.195	1.305	1.423	1.551	1.689	1.838	1.999	2.172	2.358	2.558	2.773
10	1.105	1.219	1.344	1.480	1.629	1.791	1.967	2.159	2.367	2.594	2.839	3.106
11	1.116	1.243	1.384	1.539	1.710	1.898	2.105	2.332	2.580	2.853	3.152	3.479
12	1.127	1.268	1.426	1.601	1.796	2.012	2.252	2.518	2.813	3.138	3.498	3.896
13	1.138	1.294	1.469	1.665	1.886	2.133	2.410	2.720	3.066	3.452	3.883	4.363
14	1.149	1.319	1.513	1.732	1.980	2.261	2.579	2.937	3.342	3.797	4.310	4.887
15	1.161	1.346	1.558	1.801	2.079	2.397	2.759	3.172	3.642	4.177	4.785	5.474
16	1.173	1.373	1.605	1.873	2.183	2.540	2.952	3.426	3.970	4.595	5.311	6.130
17	1.184	1.400	1.653	1.948	2.292	2.693	3.159	3.700	4.328	5.054	5.895	6.866
18	1.196	1.428	1.702	2.026	2.407	2.854	3.380	3.996	4.717	5.560	6.544	7.690
19	1.208	1.457	1.754	2.107	2.527	3.026	3.617	4.316	5.142	6.116	7.263	8.613
20	1.220	1.486	1.806	2.191	2.653	3.207	3.870	4.661	5.604	6.727	8.062	9.646
25	1.282	1.641	2.094	2.666	3.386	4.292	5.427	6.848	8.623	10.835	13.585	17.000
30	1.348	1.811	2.427	3.243	4.322	5.743	7.612	10.063	13.268	17.449	22.892	29.960
35	1.417	2.000	2.814	3.946	5.516	7.686	10.677	14.785	20.414	28.102	38.575	52.800
40	1.489	2.208	3.262	4.801	7.040	10.286	14.974	21.725	31.409	45.259	65.001	93.051
50	1.645	2.692	4.384	7.107	11.467	18.420	29.457	46.902	74.358	117.391	184.565	289.002

continued from previous page

TABLE 4	Future Value of an Ordinary Annuity of $1 per period											
Period	1%	2%	3%	4%	5%	6%	7%	8%	9%	10%	11%	12%
1	1.000	1.000	1.000	1.000	1.000	1.000	1.000	1.000	1.000	1.000	1.000	1.000
2	2.010	2.020	2.030	2.040	2.050	2.060	2.070	2.080	2.090	2.100	2.110	2.120
3	3.030	3.060	3.091	3.122	3.153	3.184	3.215	3.246	3.278	3.310	3.342	3.374
4	4.060	4.122	4.184	4.246	4.310	4.375	4.440	4.506	4.573	4.641	4.710	4.779
5	5.101	5.204	5.309	5.416	5.526	5.637	5.751	5.867	5.985	6.105	6.228	6.353
6	6.152	6.308	6.468	6.633	6.802	6.975	7.153	7.336	7.523	7.716	7.913	8.115
7	7.214	7.434	7.662	7.898	8.142	8.394	8.654	8.923	9.200	9.487	9.783	10.089
8	8.286	8.583	8.892	9.214	9.549	9.897	10.260	10.637	11.028	11.436	11.859	12.300
9	9.369	9.755	10.159	10.583	11.027	11.491	11.978	12.488	13.021	13.579	14.164	14.776
10	10.462	10.950	11.464	12.006	12.578	13.181	13.816	14.487	15.193	15.937	16.722	17.549
11	11.567	12.169	12.808	13.486	14.207	14.972	15.784	16.645	17.560	18.531	19.561	20.655
12	12.683	13.412	14.192	15.026	15.917	16.870	17.888	18.977	20.141	21.384	22.713	24.133
13	13.809	14.680	15.618	16.627	17.713	18.882	20.141	21.495	22.953	24.523	26.212	28.029
14	14.947	15.974	17.086	18.292	19.599	21.015	22.550	24.215	26.019	27.975	30.095	32.393
15	16.097	17.293	18.599	20.024	21.579	23.276	25.129	27.152	29.361	31.772	34.405	37.280
16	17.258	18.639	20.157	21.825	23.657	25.673	27.888	30.324	33.003	35.950	39.190	42.753
17	18.430	20.012	21.762	23.698	25.840	28.213	30.840	33.750	36.974	40.545	44.501	48.884
18	19.615	21.412	23.414	25.645	28.132	30.906	33.999	37.450	41.301	45.599	50.396	55.750
19	20.811	22.841	25.117	27.671	30.539	33.760	37.379	41.446	46.018	51.159	56.939	63.440
20	22.019	24.297	26.870	29.778	33.066	36.786	40.995	45.762	51.160	57.275	64.203	72.052
25	28.243	32.030	36.459	41.646	47.727	54.865	63.249	73.106	84.701	98.347	114.41	133.33
30	34.785	40.568	47.575	56.085	66.439	79.058	94.461	113.28	136.31	164.49	199.02	241.33
35	41.660	49.994	60.462	73.652	90.320	111.43	138.24	172.32	215.71	271.02	341.59	431.66
40	48.886	60.402	75.401	95.026	120.80	154.76	199.64	259.06	337.88	442.59	581.83	767.09
50	64.463	84.579	112.80	152.67	209.35	290.34	406.53	573.77	815.08	1,163.9	1,668.8	2,400.0

EXERCISES

A-1 Margaret Diver invests $7,000 into her bank account that pays 12 percent, compounded annually. How much will she have if:

a) She leaves the money in her account for two years?
b) She leaves the money in her account for three years?
c) She leaves the money for two years but the bank's 12 percent annual rate is compounded quarterly?

A-2 Christina Smiley invests $10,000 into her bank account that pays 8 percent, compounded annually. How much will she have if:

a) She leaves the money in her account for four years?
b) She leaves the money in her account for six years?
c) She leaves the money for two years but the bank's 8 percent annual rate is compounded semi-annually?
d) She leaves the money for two years but the bank's 8 percent annual rate is compounded quarterly?

A-3 Jay Stone invested $3,000 he won in a poker match at 8 percent annual interest for 10 years. At the end of the 10 years he took all the money out and went on a spending spree. How much can he spend if:

    a)   The interest is compounded annually?

    b)   The interest is compounded semi-annually?

    c)   The interest is compounded quarterly?

A-4 Ira Jackman invested $6,000 he won at the track at 4 percent annual interest for 5 years. At the end of the 5 years he took all the money out and went on a spending spree. How much can he spend if:

    a)   The interest is compounded annually?

    b)   The interest is compounded semi-annually?

    c)   The interest is compounded quarterly?

A-5 Julie Lynch invests $1,000 annually into her bank at the end of each year for five years. Her bank pays interest at the annual rate of 6 percent. How much will she have at the end of the four years?

A-6 Scott Drucker invests $1,500 semi-annually into his bank for ten years. He hopes to have $40,000 at the end of the ten years. Will Scott have the required $40,000 is he is able to earn a 6 percent annual rate compounded semi-annually?

A-7 Murat Borat just opened an Individual Retirement Account (IRA) and plans to contribute $4,000 per year for 30 years and which time he will retire. Assume he funds his IRA at the end of each of the 30 years and he can earn 12 percent compounded annually, how much will he have at retirement?

A-8 Murat Borat just opened an Individual Retirement Account (IRA) and plans to contribute $4,000 per year for 35 years and which time he will retire. Assume he funds his IRA at the end of each of the 35 years and he can earn 12 percent compounded annually, how much will he have at retirement?

A-9 Debra Moore needs $20,000 3 years from now. How much should she invest today in order to reach her goal if

    a)   She can earn 6 percent compounded annually?

    b)   She can earn an annual rate of 6 percent compounded semi-annually?

A-10 Steve Lesley needs $15,000 4 years from now. How much should he invest today in order to reach his goal if

    a)   He can earn 8 percent compounded annually?

    b)   He can earn an annual rate of 8 percent compounded quarterly?

A-11 Abe Washington sold some property in Oregon and will receive $40,000 in 5 equal payments of $8,000 at the end of each year from today. What is the present value of these future payments at an interest rate of 9 percent compounded annually?

A-12 Kate Eckstein sold some property in Nevada and will receive $60,000 in 10 equal payments of $6,000 at the end of each year from today. What is the present value of these future payments at an interest rate of 7 percent compounded annually?

A-13 Lucky Lewis won a jackpot that offered him the option of receiving $15,000 immediately or $30,000 20 years from now. Assuming Lucky can earn a rate of 8 percent compounded annually, which option should he select?

A-14 Happy Johnson won a jackpot that offered her the option of receiving $20,000 immediately or $35,000 10 years from now. Assuming Lucky can earn a rate of 6 percent compounded annually, which option should she select?

A-15 You have been offered an investment that will pay you a lump sum of $30,000 25 years from today, along with a payment of $1,000 per year for 25 years starting one year from today. How much are you willing to invest today to have this investment in your portfolio assuming you wish to earn a rate of 6 percent compounded annually?

A-16 You have been offered an investment that will pay you a lump sum of $20,000 20 years from today, along with a payment of $1,500 per year for 20 years starting one year from today. How much are you willing to invest today to have this investment in your portfolio assuming you wish to earn a rate of 8 percent compounded annually?

A-17 Jesse would like to have $1 million dollars in 10 years. Jesse will invest $75,000 in a money market account at the end of each year for the next 10 years. His account will earn an annual rate of 6 percent compounded annually. Will Jesse reach his goal of becoming a millionaire? If not, how much will his mother have to gift him at the end of 10 years?

A-18 Muir would like to have $6 million dollars in 20 years. Muir will invest $150,000 in a money market account at the end of each year for the next 20 years. His account will earn an annual rate of 7 percent compounded annually. Will Muir reach his goal of becoming a millionaire? He told his business partner that if he exceeds his goal he will contribute the excess to charity. How large of a contribution, if any, will he make?

Financial Statement Ratios and Metrics

Asset Management

Accounts receivable turnover
Receivable collection period
Intangible asset turnover
Inventory turnover
Inventory-on-hand period
Fixed asset turnover
Total asset turnover

Cash flow

Cash conversion ratio
Discretionary cash flow
Free cash flow
Free cash flow yield
Operating funds ratio

Profitability

Common equity share of operating earnings
Earnings per share (basic, diluted)
Earnings before interest, income taxes,
    depreciation and amortization (EBITDA)
Gross profit margin
Pro forma earnings
Return on assets
Return on equity
Return on sales

Liquidity

Accounts payable turnover
Days' payable period
Cash collection period
Cash and marketable securities-to-total assets
Current ratio
Operating cash flow-to-current liabilities
Quick ratio

Solvency

Financial leverage
Interest coverage
Long-term debt-to-equity
Long-term debt-to-total assets
Total debt-to-total assets

Miscellaneous

Accumulated depreciation-to-gross property,
    plant and equipment
Allowance for uncollectible accounts-to-gross
    accounts receivable
Capital intensity
Conservatism ratio
Cost of debt
Cost of equity
Dividend payout
Dividend retention rate
Dividend yield
Inventory reserve
Sustainable growth rate

Accelerated depreciation A cost allocation method in which depreciation deductions are largest in an asset's earlier years but decrease over time.

Account (T account) An accounting information file usually associated with the general ledger, which appears as follows:

Account	
Debit side	Credit side

Accounting A language used by businesspeople to communicate the financial status of their enterprise to interested parties.

Accounting cycle The process of analyzing a transaction and then journalizing it, followed by posting it to the ledger accounts, and then preparing a trial balance, any necessary adjusting entries, financial statements, and closing entries.

Accounting equation Assets = Equities; Assets = Liabilities + Shareholders' equity. An equation depicting the balance sheet or statement of financial position.

Accounting exposure (risk) The hazard of recognizing and reporting foreign exchange gains (losses) in the income statement for a given period.

Accounting period The time period, usually a quarter or one year, to which accounting reports are related.

Accounting policies The specific accounting principles and practices adopted by a company to report its financial results.

Accounting Principles Board (APB) An organization of the AICPA that established GAAP during the 1957-1973 period; some of the APB's opinions remain in force today.

Accounts payable (trade payable) Amounts owed to suppliers for merchandise purchased on credit but not yet paid for; normally classified as a current liability.

Accounts receivable (trade receivable) Amounts due to a company from customers who purchased goods or services on credit; payment is normally expected in 30, 60, or 90 days.

Accounts receivable turnover ratio A measure of the effectiveness of receivable management calculated as net credit sales for the period divided by the average balance in accounts receivable.

Accrual method (accrual basis of accounting) An accounting measurement system that records the financial effects of transactions when a business transaction occurs without regard to the timing of the cash effects of the transaction.

Accumulated depreciation (allowance for depreciation) A contra asset account deducted from the acquisition cost of property, plant, and equipment that represents the portion of the original cost of an asset that has been allocated to prior accounting periods.

Active investment An intercorporate investment by an investor-company that allows the investor to exercise influence or control over the operations of the investee-company.

Additional paid-in-capital Amounts paid by shareholders in excess of the minimum amount required for the shares to be fully paid (that is, par or stated value); also known as paid-in capital in excess of par value and share premium reserve.

Adjusting entries Journal entries recorded to update or correct the accounts in the general ledger.

Administrative expense A general operating expense, such as depreciation on a company's headquarters building, associated with the overall management of a company; a period expense.

Affiliated company A company in which an investor-company holds an equity investment in excess of 20 percent of the voting capital stock.

Aging of accounts receivables A method of accounting for uncollectible trade receivables in which an estimate of the bad debts expense is determined by classifying the specific receivable balances into age categories and then applying probability estimates of noncollection.

Allocation principle An accounting principle that permits the financial effects of business transactions to be assigned to or spread over multiple accounting periods.

Allowance for Decline in Value of Inventory A contra asset account deducted from the cost basis of ending inventory to reflect the write-down of inventory to its replacement value under the lower-of-cost-or-market method.

Allowance for Change in Value of Marketable Securities A contra asset (addendum) account deducted from (added to) the cost basis of marketable securities; represents the unrealized change in a portfolio of securities resulting from the application of the mark-to-market method.

Allowance for Uncollectible Accounts (allowance for bad debts) A contra asset account deducted from accounts or notes receivable; represents the portion of the outstanding receivable balance whose collection is doubtful.

American depositary receipt (ADR) A security issued by a bank or other recognized trustee representing an actual shareholding in a foreign company; these beneficial ownership shares are issued to avoid problems relating to the collection of dividends denominated in a foreign currency and to facilitate rapid ownership transfer; also referred to as stock depositary receipts.

American Institute of Certified Public Accountants (AICPA) The national professional association of certified public accountants (CPAs) in the United States.

Amortization A cost allocation process that spreads the cost of an intangible asset over the asset's expected useful life.

Annual report The report prepared by a company at year end for its stockholders and other interested parties. It frequently includes a letter to the shareholders from the chairperson of the board of directors, a management discussion and analysis of financial performance, and a variety of financial highlights in addition to the basic financial statements. It also includes the auditor's report in which the independent accountants express an opinion as to the fairness of the financial data presented in the financial statements.

Annuity A payment, or a receipt, occurring every period for a set number of periods (for example, interest expense or interest income on a debt instrument).

Antidilutive security A security that, if converted or assumed to be converted into common stock, causes the level of earnings per share to increase.

Asset management The effective utilization of a company's revenue-producing assets; a measure of management's ability to effectively utilize a company's assets to produce revenue.

Asset turnover The rate at which sales (or revenues) are generated from a given level of assets; a measure of a company's effectiveness in generating revenues from the assets at its disposal, calculated as net sales divided by average total assets.

Assets Tangible and intangible resources of an enterprise that are expected to provide the enterprise with future economic benefits.

Associated company One that is not a legal subsidiary of another company (control is less than 50+ percent) but in which the other company exercises significant influence (presumably at least a 20 percent shareholding).

Audit A process of investigating the adequacy of a company's system of internal controls, the company's consistent use of generally accepted accounting principles, and the presence of material errors or mistakes in the company's accounting data.

Auditor's opinion A report to a company's shareholders and the board of directors issued by an independent auditor summarizing his or her findings with regard to the company's financial statements. The four types of opinions that may be issued are clean or unqualified, qualified, adverse, and disclaimer.

Authorized shares The total number of shares of capital stock that are authorized to be sold under a company's charter of incorporation.

Available-for-sale investments Securities owned by a company where management's intent is not to trade them on a frequent basis but to sell if and when they deem best.

Average cost method An inventory cost-flow method that assigns the average cost of available finished goods to units sold and, thus, to cost of goods sold.

Bad debt An account receivable considered to be uncollectible.

Bad debt expense An estimate of the dollar amount of accounts receivable that will eventually prove to be uncollectible; the actual bad debts that are written off if the direct write-off method is used.

Balance The difference between the total left-side (debit) entries and the total right-side (credit) entries made in an account.

Balance sheet (statement of financial position) An accounting statement describing, as of a specific date, the assets, liabilities, and shareholders' equity of an enterprise.

Basic earnings per share (EPS) A measure of EPS, calculated as net income after taxes minus preferred dividends, divided by the weighted average number of common (or ordinary) shares outstanding.

Betterment An expenditure that extends the useful life or productive capability of an asset and that is capitalized to the balance sheet as an asset.

Blocked funds risk The hazard that a government will restrict the flow of funds either into or out of a given locale.

Board of directors A group of individuals elected by a company's shareholders to oversee the overall management of the company (that is, a board of advisers for the company's managers).

Bond (debenture) An interest-bearing obligation issued by a company to various creditors, usually in amounts of $1,000 or $5,000 and payable at some future maturity date.

Bond discount The amount by which the net proceeds of a bond issue are less than the amount of the principal that must be repaid at maturity date. The amount of the bond discount must be amortized over the life of the bond, thereby making the bond's effective rate of interest greater than its coupon rate of interest.

Bond indenture The document in which the details associated with a bond issue are specified.

Bond payable A financial instrument sold in the capital markets, carrying a specified rate of interest (coupon rate) and a specified repayment date (maturity date); usually classified as a long-term liability.

Bond premium The amount by which the net proceeds of a bond issue exceed the amount of the bond principal that must be repaid at maturity date. The amount of the bond premium that must be amortized over the life of the bond, thereby making its effective rate of interest less than its coupon rate of interest.

Book value (per share) The dollar amount of the net assets of a company on a per share of common stock basis; calculated as (total assets minus total liabilities) divided by the number of outstanding shares of class A common stock.

Book value (of an asset) The original cost of an asset less any accumulated depreciation (depletion or amortization) taken to date; also known as carrying value.

Business combination When one or more businesses are brought together into one accounting entity but not necessarily into one legal entity.

C

Callable debt Bonds or other obligations that may be legally retired before maturity at the discretion of the debtor-company.

Capital Another term for shareholders' equity; also used to mean the total assets of an organization.

Capital budgeting The process of proposing and selecting from among a variety of investment proposals or certain long-lived assets to be acquired. This process frequently considers the net present value of projected cash flows for proposed investments.

Capital expenditure An expenditure for the purchase of a noncurrent asset, usually property, plant, or equipment.

Capital intensity ratio A measure of a company's investment in long-lived assets, calculated as fixed assets plus intangible assets divided by total assets.

Capitalization (of an expenditure) The process of assigning value to a balance sheet account—for example, a capitalized asset (that is, a leased asset) or a capitalized liability (such as a lease liability).

Capitalization (of a company) The composition of a company's long-term financing, specifically, shareholders' equity and long-term debt.

Capital lease A noncancelable lease obligation accounted for as a liability on the balance sheet; a lease agreement in which the risks and rewards of asset ownership are passed (either formally or informally) to the lessee.

Capital stock A certificate representing an ownership interest in an enterprise. See also common stock and preferred stock.

Cash A current asset account representing the amount of money on hand or in the bank.

Cash basis of accounting An accounting measurement system that records the financial effects of business transactions when the underlying event has a cash effect.

Cash discount An amount, usually 2 percent of the gross purchase price, that a buyer may deduct from the final price of an asset if cash is remitted within the discount period, usually 10 days of purchase.

Cash dividend payout A measure of the cash return to common shareholders, calculated as the cash dividend per common share divided by the basic earnings per share.

Cash dividend yield A measure of the cash return to common shareholders, calculated as the cash dividend per common share divided by the average market price per common share.

Cash equivalents Bank deposits, usually in the form of certificates of deposit, whose withdrawal may be restricted but whose maturity is expected in the current accounting period.

Cash flow adequacy ratio A cash flow ratio calculated as the cash flow from operations divided by the sum of capital expenditures, dividends paid, and long-term debt repayment; indicates the extent to which cash flows from operations are sufficient to cover asset replacement and capital carrying costs.

Cash flow from operations (CFFO) A measure of the net cash flows from transactions involving sales of goods or services and the acquisition of inputs used to provide the goods or services sold; the excess of cash receipts over cash disbursements relating to the operations of a company for a given period; net income calculated on a cash basis.

CFFO to current liabilities ratio A measure of firm liquidity, calculated as the cash flow from operations (CFFO) divided by average current liabilities; reflects the short-term debt coverage provided by current cash flows from operations.

CFFO to interest charges ratio A measure of solvency, calculated as the cash flow from operations divided by interest charges; reflects the extent to which interest charges are covered by current cash flows from operations.

CFFO to total liabilities ratio A measure of solvency, calculated as the cash flow from operations divided by average total liabilities; reflects the extent to which current cash flow from operations is sufficient to satisfy both long-term and short-term obligations.

Certified public accountant (CPA) An accountant who has passed the Uniform CPA Examination prepared by the American Institute of CPAs and who has met prescribed requirements of the state issuing the CPA certificate.

Chartered accountant (CA) A certified public accountant in the U.K.

Charter of incorporation A legal document creating a corporate entity; specifies (among other things) the number and type of shares of capital stock that the corporate entity can sell.

Chart of accounts A list of the general ledger accounts used by an enterprise in its accounting system.

Class B common stock A form of common stock that usually carries a lower voting power and lower dividend return than Class A common stock.

Classified balance sheet A balance sheet that delineates the assets and liabilities as current and noncurrent.

Closing entries Accounting data entries prepared at the end of an accounting period; designed to close or set equal to zero the temporary accounts.

Collateral The value of various assets used as security for various debts, usually bank borrowings, that will be transferred to a creditor if the obligation is not fully paid.

Commitment A type of contingent liability in which the value of the future obligation is known but that is not currently an obligation because various future events or conditions have not transpired or are currently satisfied.

Common equity share of operating earnings (CSOE) A measure of the proportion of a company's operating earnings allocable to common shareholders.

Common shareholders' capital structure leverage ratio (CSL) A measure of a company's financial leverage, calculated as average total assets divided by average common equity.

Common-size balance sheet A balance sheet in which all account balances are expressed as a percentage of total assets or total equities.

Common-size financial statement Financial statements in which the dollar amounts are expressed as a percentage of some common statement item (for example, a common-size income statement might express all items as a percentage of sales).

Common-size income statements An income statement in which all revenue and expense items are expressed as a percentage of net sales.

Common stock A form of capital stock that usually carries the right to vote on corporate issues; a senior equity security.

Common stock equivalent A security that is not a common stock but that contains provisions to enable its holder to become a common stockholder.

Compensating balances The percentage of a line of credit or of a loan that a bank requires a borrower to keep on deposit at the bank. Its amount has the effect of increasing the effective interest rate of any amount borrowed.

Completed contract A revenue recognition method in which project or contract revenues are unrecognized until the project or contract is substantially completed.

Compound interest A method of calculating interest by which interest is figured on both the principal of a loan and any interest previously earned but not distributed.

Conservatism principle An accounting principle that stipulates that when there is a choice between two approaches to record an economic event, the one that produces the least favorable yet realistic effect on net income or assets should be adopted.

Consignment Inventory placed with a retailer for sale to a final consumer but not sold to the retailer; title to the inventory is retained by the manufacturer until a final sale occurs.

Consistency principle An accounting principle underlying the preparation of financial statements that stipulates that an enterprise should, when possible, use the same set of GAAP from one accounting period to the next.

Consolidated financial statements Financial statements prepared to reflect the operations and financial condition of a parent company and its wholly or majority-owned subsidiaries.

Consolidated reporting A reporting approach in which the financial statements of the parent and subsidiary companies are combined to form one set of financial statements.

Contingent asset An asset that may arise in the future if certain events occur.

Contingent liability A liability that may arise in the future if certain events occur.

Contra account (contra asset, contra liability, contra shareholders' equity) An account that is subtracted from a related account; for example, accumulated depreciation is subtracted from the Building or Equipment account; other examples include the Allowance for Uncollectible accounts, the Bond Discount account, and the Treasury Stock account.

Contributed capital The sum of the capital stock accounts and the capital in excess of par (or stated) value accounts. Also called paid-in capital.

Convenience statement A set of foreign financial statements translated into the language and the currency of another country.

Convenience translation A set of foreign financial statements translated into the language (not currency) of another country.

Conversion The exchange of convertible bonds or convertible preferred stock for a predetermined quantity of common stock.

Conversion ratio The exchange ratio used to determine the number of common shares that will be issued on conversion of a convertible bond or a convertible preferred stock.

Convertible debt (bond) An obligation or debt security exchangeable, or convertible, into the common stock of a company at a prespecified conversion (or exchange) rate.

Convertible preferred stock A preferred stock that is exchangeable or convertible into the common stock of a company at a prespecified conversion (or exchange) rate.

Corporation A business enterprise owned by one or more owners, called shareholders, that has a legal identity separate and distinct from that of its owners.

Cost The total acquisition value of an asset; the value of resources given up to acquire an asset.

Cost of goods manufactured The total cost of goods manufactured in an accounting period; the sum of all product costs (such as direct materials, direct labor, and manufacturing overhead).

Cost of goods sold The value assigned to inventory units actually sold in a given accounting period.

Coupon interest rate (face rate) The rate of interest stated on the face of a debt instrument.

Countertrade A trade practice equivalent to barter or the exchange of goods and/or services for other goods and services (that is, no currency is exchanged); typically occurs as a consequence of restrictive currency laws.

Country risk analysis A process of identifying the various types of risks associated with investing or doing business in a given country.

Credit An entry on the right side of an account; credits increase liability, shareholders' equity, and revenue accounts but decrease asset and expense accounts.

Creditor An individual or company that loans cash or other assets to another person or company.

Cross-sectional analysis A process of analyzing financial data between or among firms in the same industry, or between a firm and industry averages, to identify comparative financial strengths and weaknesses.

Cumulative preferred stock A preferred stock in which any unpaid prior dividends accumulate year to year (called dividends in arrears) and must be paid in full before any current period dividends may be paid to either preferred or common shareholders.

Currency risk See foreign exchange risk.

Current asset Those resources of an enterprise, such as cash, inventory, or prepaid expenses, whose consumption or use is expected to occur within the current operating cycle.

Current cost accounting A method of accounting in which financial data are expressed in terms of current rather than historical cost.

Current liability An obligation of an enterprise whose settlement requires the use of current assets or the creation of other current liabilities and occurs within one year.

Current maturity of long-term debt That portion of a long-term obligation that is payable within the next operating cycle or one year.

Current rate method A method of restating foreign financial statements using the current exchange rate.

Current ratio A measure of liquidity and short-term solvency calculated as current assets divided by current liabilities.

Date of declaration The calendar date on which the payment of a cash or stock dividend is officially declared by a company's board of directors.

Date of payment The calendar date on which a cash or stock dividend is actually paid or distributed.

Date of record The calendar date on which a shareholder must own a company's stock to be entitled to receive a declared dividend.

Debenture A general obligation bond of a company.

Debit An entry on the left side of an account; debits increase asset and expense accounts but decrease liability, shareholders' equity, and revenue accounts.

Debt-to-equity ratio A measure of solvency, calculated as long-term debt divided by total shareholders' equity.

Debt-to-total assets ratio A measure of solvency or long-term liquidity calculated as total debt divided by total assets.

Debt-to-total capitalization ratio A measure of solvency, calculated as long-term debt divided by the sum of total shareholders' equity and long-term debt.

Debtors An alternative designation for accounts and notes receivables, principally used in the financial statements of Great Britain and other Commonwealth companies.

Declining balance method A method to depreciate the cost of a tangible asset in which the allocated cost is greater in the early periods of the asset's life (that is, an accelerated method).

Default risk The probability (or risk) that a company will be unable to meet its short-term or long-term obligations.

Defeasance A method of early retirement of debt in which risk-free securities are purchased and then placed in a trust account to be used to retire the outstanding debt at its maturity.

Deferral A postponement in the recognition of an expense (such as Prepaid Insurance) or a revenue (such as Unearned Rent) account.

Deferred charge An asset that represents an expenditure whose related expense will not be recognized in the income statement until a future period. Prepaid rent is an example.

Deferred income taxes The portion of a company's income tax expense not currently payable that is postponed because of differences in the accounting policies adopted for financial statement purposes versus those policies used for tax reporting purposes.

Deferred revenue Revenue received as cash but not yet earned.

Deficit An accumulated loss in the retained earnings account; a debit balance in retained earnings.

Defined benefit plan A pension plan in which an employer promises to pay certain levels of future benefits to employees on their retirement from the company.

Defined contribution plan A pension plan in which an employer promises to make periodic payments to the plan on behalf of its employees.

Demand deposit A bank account that may be drawn against on demand.

Depletion A cost allocation method for natural resources.

Depreciation A systematic allocation process that allocates the acquisition cost of a long-lived asset over the expected productive life of the asset.

Devaluation A material downward adjustment of the exchange rate between two currencies.

Diluted earnings per share A standardized measure of performance calculated as net income applicable to common stock divided by the weighted-average number of common shares outstanding plus common stock equivalents and any other potentially dilutive securities.

Direct-financing-type lease A capital lease in which the lessor receives income only from financing the "purchase" of the leased asset.

Direct write-off method A method of accounting for uncollectible trade receivables in which no bad debt expense is recorded until specific receivables prove to be uncollectible.

Discount A reduction in the price paid for a security or a debt instrument below the security's face value.

Discount rate The rate of interest used to discount a future cash flow stream when calculating its present value.

Discounted cash flows The present value of a future stream of cash flows.

Discounting receivables The process of selling accounts or notes receivables to a bank or other financial company at a discount from the maturity value of the account or note.

Discretionary cash flows A measure of a company's cash flows from operations that are available to finance such discretionary corporate activities as the acquisition of another company, the early retirement of debt or equity, or some form of capital asset expansion.

Dividend A distribution of the earned income of an enterprise to its owners.

Dividend payout ratio A measure of the percentage of net income (or cash flows from operations) paid out to shareholders as dividends; calculated as cash dividends divided by net income (or cash dividends divided by the cash flow from operations).

Dividends in arrears The dividends on a cumulative preferred stock that have been neither declared nor paid; not a legal liability of a company until declared.

Dividend yield A measure of the level of cash actually distributed to common shareholders, calculated as the cash divided per common share divided by the market price per common share.

Donated capital The increase in shareholders' equity resulting from a donation of an asset to a company.

Double-declining-balance depreciation A method of calculating depreciation by which a percentage equal to twice the straight-line percentage is multiplied by the declining book value to determine the depreciation expense for the period. Salvage value is ignored when calculating it.

Double-entry system An accounting recordkeeping system that records all financial transactions in the accounting system using (at least) two data entries.

Double taxation The taxation of income at the company level plus the taxation of dividends declared and paid to investors from the company earnings.

Doubtful account An account receivable thought to be uncollectible.

Du Pont formula An overall indicator of corporate performance obtained by multiplying a company's asset turnover by its profit margin; equivalent to ROA or ROI.

E

Early retirement The process of prepaying, or retiring, outstanding debt before its stated maturity.

Earned surplus A term synonymous with retained earnings.

Earnings Income or profit.

Earnings per share A standardized measure of performance calculated as net income divided by the weighted-average number of common shares outstanding during an accounting period. Also known as basic earnings per share.

Economic exposure (risk) The risk of experiencing a real gain (loss) in purchasing power as a consequence of foreign exchange rate fluctuations.

Economic income The excess or additional resources of an enterprise resulting from its primary business activity and measured relative to the beginning level of resources.

Effective interest method A method to amortize a discount or a premium on a debt instrument based on the time value of money.

Effective interest rate The real rate of interest paid (or earned) on a debt instrument.

Efficient market hypothesis A theory to explain the functioning of capital markets in which stock and bond prices always reflect all publicly available information, and any new information is quickly impounded in security prices.

Emerging Issues Task Force (EITF) An affiliate organization of the FASB whose purpose is to address new accounting and reporting issues before divergent practice can become widely adopted.

Employee Retirement Income and Security Act (ERISA) Legislation passed by the U.S. Congress in 1974 to govern the funding of private pension plans.

Entity principle An accounting convention that views a corporate enterprise as separate and distinct from its owners; thus, the financial statements of the corporation describe only the financial condition of the enterprise itself, not that of its shareholders.

Equity A claim against the assets of a company by creditors or the shareholders.

Equity in earnings of affiliate An income statement account representing an investor-company's percentage ownership of an investee's (or affiliate's) net earnings.

Equity method A method to value intercorporate equity investments by adjusting the investor's cost basis for the percentage ownership in the investee's earnings (or losses) and for any dividends paid by the investee.

European currency unit (ECU) A currency intended to be used by all European Union members in conducting trade, called the euro.

European exchange rate mechanism (ERM) A system created by the EU to stabilize the rate of exchange of currency between EU member nations.

European Union (EU) An organization of politically independent European nations (currently numbering 21), united to act as a single economic (trading) entity (or bloc); includes three cooperative alliances intended to improve the efficiency and competitive ability of its member nations: the European Coal and Steel Community, the European Atomic Energy Commission, and the European Economic Community.

Exchange Currency or legal tender used to facilitate trade between parties.

Exchange rate The rate at which one unit of currency may be purchased by another unit of currency.

Ex-dividend A condition of capital stock if sold (or purchased) after the date of record; that is, the purchaser of an ex-dividend stock is not entitled to receive the most recently declared dividend.

Executory contracts A category of legal agreements requiring some type of future performance.

Expenditure An outflow of cash, usually representing the acquisition of an asset or the incurring of an expense.

Expense An outflow of assets, an increase in liabilities, or both, from transactions involving an enterprise's principal business activity (such as sales of products or services).

Expropriation exposure (risk) The likelihood that a company's assets located in a foreign domain will be involuntarily appropriated by the local government, with or without compensation.

External reporting Financial reporting to shareholders and others outside an enterprise.

Extraordinary item A loss or gain that is both unusual in nature and infrequent in occurrence.

F

Face amount (maturity value) The value of a security as stated on the instrument itself.

Factor A financial corporation, bank, or other financial institution that buys accounts and notes receivables from companies; receivables may be purchased with or without recourse.

Factory overhead Another name for manufacturing overhead. For inventory valuation purposes, it is allocated to units of production by some type of rational systematic method.

Federal income tax The tax levied by the federal government on corporate and individual earnings.

Financial accounting The accounting rules and conventions used in preparing external accounting reports.

Financial Accounting Standards Board (FASB) An independent, private sector organization responsible for establishing generally accepted accounting principles.

Financial Reporting Council (FRC) An accounting standard-setting organization in the United Kingdom founded in 1990 that succeeded the Accounting Standards Committee; issues financial reporting standards.

Financial reporting standard (FRS) An official accounting pronouncement issued by the Financial Reporting Council of the United Kingdom.

Financial statements The basic accounting reports issued by a company, including the balance sheet, the income statement, the statement of shareholders' equity, and the statement of cash flows.

Financial statement analysis The process of reviewing, analyzing, and interpreting the basic financial statements to assess a company's operating performance and/or financial health.

Finished goods Inventory having completed the manufacturing process and ready for sale.

Finished goods inventory Fully assembled or manufactured goods available for sale and classified as a current asset on the balance sheet.

First-in, first-out (FIFO) An inventory cost-flow method that assigns the first cost value in finished goods inventory to the first unit sold and thus to cost of goods sold.

Fiscal year Any continuous 12-month period, usually beginning after a natural business peak.

Fixed assets A subcategory of noncurrent assets; usually represented by property, plant, and equipment.

FOB Free-on-board, some location. Examples are FOB shipping point and FOB destination. The location denotes the point at which title passes from the seller to the buyer.

Footnotes Written information by management designed to supplement the numerical data presented in a company's financial statement.

Foreign currency option contract A contract providing the right to buy or sell a set quantity of foreign currency at a present exchange rate within a specified future time frame; typically used to hedge foreign exchange risk exposure, and often thought of as currency insurance.

Foreign currency translation adjustment An shareholders' equity account measuring the change in value of a company's net assets held in a foreign country, attributable to changes in the exchange rate of a foreign currency as compared to the U.S. dollar (or some other base currency).

Foreign exchange Any currency other than the one in which a company prepares its basic financial statements.

Foreign exchange risk The risk associated with changes in exchange rates between the U.S. dollar (or some other base currency) and foreign currencies when a company maintains operations in a foreign country.

Form 8-K A special U.S. SEC filing required when a material event or transaction occurs between Form 10-Q filing dates. Events that usually necessitate the filing of Form 8-K include a change in control or ownership of an enterprise, the acquisition or disposition of a significant amount of assets, a bankruptcy declaration, the resignation of an executive or director of an enterprise, or a change in the independent external auditor.

Form 10-K The annual financial report filing with the U.S. SEC required of all publicly held enterprises.

Form 10-Q The quarterly financial report filing with the U.S. SEC required of all publicly held enterprises; it is filed only for the first three quarters of a fiscal year.

Form 20-F The annual financial report filing with the U.S. SEC required of all foreign companies whose debt or equity capital is available for purchase/sale on a U.S. exchange.

Forward exchange contract A contract providing for the payment (receipt) of a foreign currency at a future date at a specified exchange rate; typically used to hedge foreign exchange risk exposure.

Forward exchange rate An exchange rate between two currencies quoted for 30, 60, 90, or 180 days in the future; a rate quoted currently for the exchange of currency at some future specified date.

Free cash flows A measure of a company's internally generated operating cash flows available for distribution to investors.

Freight-in Freight costs associated with the purchase and receipt of inventory.

Freight-out Freight costs associated with the sale and delivery of inventory.

Front-end loading An accounting process by which revenues (expenses) are recognized for income statement purposes before they have been earned (incurred).

Functional currency The currency of the primary business environment (country) of a company's operations.

G

Gain An increase in asset values, usually involving a sale (realized) or revaluation (unrealized), unrelated to the principal revenue-producing activity of a business.

General journal An accounting data file containing a chronological listing of financial transactions affecting an enterprise.

General ledger An accounting data file containing aggregate account information for all accounts listed in an enterprise's chart of accounts.

Generally accepted accounting principles (GAAP) Those methods identified by authoritative bodies (APB, FASB, SEC) as being acceptable for use in the preparation of external accounting reports.

Generally accepted auditing standards (GAAS) Those auditing practices and procedures established by the AICPA that are used by CPAs to evaluate a company's accounting system and financial results.

Going-concern concept An accounting concept underlying the preparation of financial statements that assumes that the enterprise will continue its operations for the foreseeable future.

Goodwill An intangible asset representing the excess of the purchase price of acquired net assets over their fair market value.

Gross profit (gross margin) A measure of a company's profit on sales calculated as net sales minus the cost of goods or services sold.

Gross profit margin ratio A measure of profitability that assesses the percentage of each sales dollar that is recognized as gross profit (after deducting the cost of goods sold) and that is available to cover other operating expenses (such as selling, administrative, interest, and taxes).

H

Harmonization The attempt by various organizations (such as the IASC, the EU, and TOSCO) to establish a common set of international accounting and reporting standards.

Hedge A process of buying or selling commodities, forward contracts, or options for the explicit purpose of reducing or eliminating foreign exchange risk.

Hedged items Those accounts (assets, liabilities, revenues) or contracts for which an artificial or natural hedge exists.

Hedging instrument A forward exchange contract or option contract acquired to hedge some type of exposure (such as currency risk, expropriation risk, political risk).

Highest-in, first-out (HIFO) An inventory cost-flow method that assigns the highest cost value available in finished goods inventory to the first unit sold and thus cost of goods sold.

Historical cost principle An accounting principle that stipulates that all economic transactions should be recorded using the dollar value incurred at the time of the transaction.

Hold-to-maturity investments Securities, usually debt securities, owned by a company where management's intent is to hold them until the securities' stipulated maturity date.

Holding company (parent company) A company that owns a majority of the voting capital shares of another company.

I

Impairment A temporary or permanent reduction in asset value; usually necessitates a write-down in the asset's balance sheet value.

Income A generic term that may be used to indicate revenue from miscellaneous sources (such as interest income or rent income) or the excess of revenue over expenses for product sales or services.

Income and Loss Summary A temporary account used to transfer the net income or loss of an enterprise from the income statement to the retained earnings account on the balance sheet.

Income smoothing An accounting practice that implicitly or explicitly attempts to present a stable (but growing) measure of net income.

Income statement (statement of earnings) An accounting statement describing the revenues earned and expenses incurred by an enterprise for a given period.

Independent auditor A professionally trained individual whose responsibilities include the objective review of a company's financial statements prepared for external distribution.

Inflation A phenomenon of generally rising prices.

Initial public offering (IPO) The first or initial sale of voting shares to the general market by a previously privately held concern.

Insolvent (bankrupt) A condition in which a company is unable to pay its current obligations as they come due.

Installment basis A method of recognizing revenue that parallels the receipt of cash.

Installment sale A credit sale in which the buyer agrees to make periodic payments, or installments, on the amount owed.

Intangible assets Those resources of an enterprise, such as goodwill, trademarks, or tradenames, that lack an identifiable physical presence.

Intercompany profit The profit resulting when one related company sells to another related company; intercompany profits are removed from the financial statements when consolidated financial statements are prepared.

Intercorporate investments Investments in the stocks and bonds of one company by another.

Interest coverage ratio See times-interest-earned ratio.

Interest expense The cost of borrowing funds.

Interim financial statements Financial statements prepared on a monthly or quarterly basis; usually unaudited.

Internal control structure The policies and procedures implemented by management to safeguard a company's assets and its accounting system against misapplication or misuse.

International accounting standards (IAS) The accounting and reporting standards adopted and promulgated by the IASB.

International Accounting Standards Board (IASB) An association of professional accounting bodies formed in 1973 to develop and issue international accounting and reporting standards.

International Federation of Accountants (IFAC) An association of professional accounting organizations from more than 70 nations founded in 1977; largely concerned with developing international guidelines for the accounting profession in the areas of auditing, ethics, and education.

International Organization of Securities Commissions and Similar Organizations (IOSCO) An organization of securities regulatory agencies representing various member countries, whose goal is to assist in the creation and regulation of orderly international capital markets.

International Stock Exchange (ISE) The largest securities exchange in the United Kingdom.

Interperiod tax allocation The process of allocating the actual taxes paid by a company over the periods in which the taxes are recognized for accounting purposes.

Inventory The aggregate cost of salable goods and merchandise available to meet customer sales.

Inventory-on-hand ratio A measure of the effectiveness of inventory management calculated as 365 days divided by the inventory turnover ratio; a measure of the appropriateness of current inventory levels given current sales volume.

Inventory turnover A measure of the rate of inventory sales.

Inventory turnover ratio A measure of the effectiveness of inventory management calculated as the cost of goods sold for a period divided by the average inventory held during that period.

Investment ratio A cash flow ratio calculated as capital expenditures divided by the sum of depreciation and proceeds from the sale of assets; indicates the relative change in a company's investment in productive assets.

Investment tax credit A reduction in the current income taxes payable earned through the purchase of various applicable assets.

Investor company A company that holds an equity investment in another company (the investee company).

Issued shares The number of authorized shares of capital stock sold to shareholders less any shares repurchased and retired.

J

Journal A chronological record of events and transactions affecting the accounts of a company recorded by means of debits and credits; a financial diary of a company.

Journal entry A data entry into a company's journal system.

Journalize The process of recording data in the journal system of a company by means of debits and credits.

L

Last-in, first-out (LIFO) An inventory cost-flow method that assigns the last cost value in finished goods inventory to the first unit sold and thus to cost of goods sold.

Lease An agreement to buy or rent an asset.

Leasehold improvement Expenditures made by a lessee to improve or change a leased asset.

Lessee An individual or company who leases an asset.

Lessor The maker of a lease agreement; an individual or company who leases an asset to another individual or company.

Leverage The extent to which a company's long-term capital structure includes debt financing; a measure of a company's dependency on debt. A company with large quantities of debt is said to be highly leveraged.

Liabilities The dollar value of an enterprise's obligations to repay monies loaned to it, to pay for goods or services received by it, or to fulfill commitments made by it.

LIFO liquidation The sale of inventory units acquired or manufactured in a prior period at a lower cost; results when the level of LIFO inventory is reduced below its beginning-of-period level.

LIFO reserve An amount presented in the footnotes to the financial statements of companies employing the LIFO method of inventory valuation; calculated as the current cost of ending inventory minus the LIFO cost of ending inventory.

Limited company (Ltd) A limited liability but privately held company in the United Kingdom having no minimum capital requirement.

Limited liability The concept that shareholders in a corporation are not held personally liable for its losses and debts.

Limited partnership A partnership composed of at least one general partner and at least one limited partner, in which the general partner(s) assumes responsibility for all debts and losses of the partnership.

Line of credit An agreement with a bank by which an organization obtains authorization for short-term borrowings up to a specified amount.

Liquid assets Those current assets, such as cash, cash equivalents, or short-term investments, that either are in cash form or can be readily converted to cash.

Liquidating dividend A cash dividend representing a return of invested capital and, hence, a liquidation of a previous investment.

Liquidation The process of selling off the assets of a business, paying any outstanding debts, and then distributing any remaining cash to the owners.

Liquidity The short-term debt repayment ability of a company; a measure of a company's cash position relative to currently maturing obligations.

Listed company A company whose shares or bonds have been accepted for trading on a recognized securities exchange (such as the NYSE).

Long-term liabilities (noncurrent liabilities) The obligations of a company payable after more than one year.

Loss The excess of expenses over revenues for a single transaction.

Lower of cost or market A method to value inventories; the lower of an asset's cost basis or current market value is used to value the asset account for balance sheet purposes.

M

Machine-hour method A method to depreciate the cost of a machine or other equipment based on its actual usage.

Maintenance expenditure An expenditure to maintain the original productive capacity of an asset; deducted as an expense.

Managerial accounting The accounting rules and conventions used in the preparation of internal accounting reports.

Manufacturing overhead The factory-related costs indirectly associated with the manufacture or production of a good; for example, the costs of production-line supervision, maintenance of the production equipment, and depreciation of the factory building.

Market price The current fair value of an asset as established by an arm's length transaction between a buyer and a seller.

Marketable securities Short- or long-term investments in the shares or bonds of other corporations.

Mark-to-market A method to value investments in trading or available-for-sale securities wherein they are reported on corporate balance sheets at their fair market value, not at cost.

Matching principle An accounting principle that stipulates that when revenues are reported, the expenses incurred to generate those revenues should be reported in the same accounting period.

Materiality principle An accounting principle underlying the preparation of financial statements; stipulates that only those transactions that might influence the decisions of a reasonable person should be disclosed in detail in the financial statements; all other information may be presented in summary format.

Maturity date The principal repayment date for a bond or debenture, specified as part of the indenture agreement.

Maturity value (face amount) The amount of cash required to satisfy an obligation at the date of its maturity.

Merger A combination of one or more companies into a single corporate entity.

Minority interest The percentage ownership in the net assets of a subsidiary held by investors other than the parent company.

Modified Accelerated Cost Recovery System (MACRS) A method to depreciate tangible assets placed in service after 1986 for U.S. income tax purposes.

Monetary assets Resources of an enterprise, such as cash and marketable securities, whose principal characteristic is monetary denomination.

Mortgage An agreement in which a lender (the mortgagee) agrees to loan money to a borrower (the mortgagor) to be repaid over a specified period of time and at a specified rate of interest.

Mortgage bond A bond secured or collateralized by a company's noncurrent assets, usually its property, plant, and equipment.

Multinational corporation (MNC) A for-profit organization with operations in two or more countries.

Multinational enterprise (MNE) A for-profit or not-for-profit organization with operations in two or more countries (such as a multinational corporation).

Multiple reporting Reporting by a company that requires the preparation of multiple sets of financial statements in the language and currency of another country.

N

Natural hedge A hedging instrument that exists as a consequence of the normal course of business.

Natural resources Noncurrent, nonrenewable resources such as oil and gas, coal, ore, and uranium.

Negative goodwill The excess of the net book value of an acquired company over the consideration paid for it.

Negotiable instruments Receivables, payables, or securities that can be bought and sold (that is, negotiated) between companies.

Net assets Total assets minus total liabilities; equal to total shareholders' equity.

Net current assets Current assets minus current liabilities; working capital.

Net income (net earnings) The difference between the aggregate revenues and aggregate expenses of an enterprise for a given accounting period; when aggregate expenses exceed aggregate revenues, the term net loss is used.

Net realizable value The amount of funds expected to be received upon the sale or liquidation of an asset.

Net sales Total sales less sales returns and allowances and sales discounts.

Net worth (of an enterprise) Total assets minus total liabilities, or the value of shareholders' equity; also known as the book value of an enterprise.

Nonclassified balance sheet A balance sheet in which the assets and liabilities are not classified as current or noncurrent;

in nonclassified balance sheets, assets and liabilities are considered to be noncurrent.

Noncurrent assets The long-lived resources of an enterprise, such as property, plant, and equipment, whose consumption or use is not expected to be completed within the current operating cycle.

Noncurrent asset turnover ratio A measure of the effectiveness of noncurrent asset management calculated as net sales for the period divided by the average balance of noncurrent assets.

Noncurrent liability An obligation of an enterprise whose settlement is not expected within one year.

Nondiversifiable risk Unique, nonsystematic risk associated with an investment that cannot be effectively hedged (through, for example, portfolio diversification).

Nonmonetary assets Those resources of an enterprise, such as inventory or equipment, whose principal characteristic is other than its monetary denomination or value.

Notes payable An obligation to repay money or other assets in the future evidenced by a signed contractual agreement or note.

Notes receivable Amounts due a company from customers who purchased goods or services on credit; the obligation is evidenced by a legal document called a note.

Off-balance-sheet debt Economic obligations that are not reported on the face of the balance sheet (such as operating leases).

Operating cycle The average length of time between the investment in inventory and the subsequent collection of cash from the sale of that inventory.

Operating expenses Expenses incurred in carrying out the operations of a business, for example, selling expenses.

Operating funds index A cash flow ratio calculated as net income divided by cash flow from operations that indicates the portion of operating cash flow provided by net income.

Operating lease A lease agreement in which the risks and rewards of asset ownership are retained by the lessor.

Operating leverage The extent to which a company operates with a high proportion of fixed costs.

Operational risk The probability that unforeseen or unexpected events will occur and consequently reduce or impair the revenue, earnings, and cash flow streams of a company.

Option A contract in which a buyer receives the right to buy inventory or shares in the future at a prespecified price.

Option contract Usually used for hedging purposes to grant one party the right to choose whether (and sometimes when) a currency exchange will actually take place.

Organization costs The expenditures associated with starting a new business venture, including legal fees and incorporation

fees; frequently accounted for as an intangible asset of a company.

Outstanding shares The number of authorized shares of capital stock that have been sold to shareholders and are currently in the possession of shareholders; the number of issued shares less the shares held in treasury.

Owners' equity (shareholders' equity) The dollar value of the owners' (or shareholders') investment in an enterprise; may take two forms-the purchase of shares of stock or the retention of earnings in the enterprise for future use.

Paid-in-Capital in Excess of Par Value (Contributed Capital in Excess of Par Value) An shareholders' equity account reflecting the proceeds from the sale of capital stock in excess of the par value (or stated value) of the capital stock.

Participating preferred stock A preferred stock that entitles shareholders to share in any "excess dividend payments" (that is, after the common shareholders have received a fair dividend return).

Partnership A business enterprise jointly owned by two or more persons.

Par value A legal value assigned to a share of capital stock that must be considered in recording the proceeds received from the sale of the stock. See also stated value.

Passive investment An intercorporate investment in which the investor cannot (or does not) attempt to influence the operations of the investee-company.

Past service cost The cost of committed pension benefits earned by employees for periods of work prior to the adoption of a formal pension plan.

Payback period The period of time required to recover the cash outlay for an asset or other investment.

Pension A retirement plan for employees that will provide income to the employee upon retirement.

Percentage of completion A revenue recognition method in which total project or contract revenues are allocated between several accounting periods on the basis of the actual work completed in those periods.

Percentage of credit sales method A method of accounting for uncollectible trade receivables in which an estimate of the bad debts expense is recorded each period on the basis of the credit sales for the period.

Period costs Costs, such as administrative and selling expenses, associated with the accounting period in which they were incurred.

Periodic inventory system An inventory recordkeeping system that determines the quantity of inventory on hand by a physical count.

Permanent accounts Those accounts, principally the balance sheet accounts, that are not closed at the end of an accounting period and that carry accounting information forward from one period to the next.

Permanent difference A difference in reported income or expenses between a company's tax return and its financial statements that will never reverse (that is, the difference is permanent).

Permanent earnings (cash flows) The recurring earnings (cash flows) of a company; earnings (cash flows) expected to recur in future periods.

Perpetual inventory system An inventory recordkeeping system that continuously (or perpetually) updates the quantity of inventory on hand on the basis of units purchased, manufactured, and sold.

Pledging When assets are used as collateral for a bank loan, the assets are said to have been pledged.

Political exposure (risk) The degree of stability (or lack thereof) among political groups and the established government in a given country.

Pooling-of-interests A consolidation method that combines the financial results of a parent company and its subsidiary on the basis of existing book values.

Posting An accounting process involving the transfer of financial data from the general journal to the general ledger.

Preemptive right The privilege of a shareholder to maintain his or her proportionate ownership in a corporation by being able to purchase an equivalent percentage of all new capital stock offered for sale.

Preferred stock A (usually) nonvoting form of capital stock whose claims to the dividends and assets of a company precede those of common shareholders.

Premium An amount paid in excess of the face value of a security or debt instrument.

Prepaid expenses A current asset that represents prior expenditures and whose consumption is expected to occur in the next accounting period.

Present value The value today of a future stream of cash flows calculated by discounting the cash flows at a given rate of interest.

Price-earnings (P/E) ratio A market-based measure of the investment potential of a security, calculated as the market price per share divided by the earnings per share; also known as P/E multiple.

Price-level-adjusted financial statements Financial statements in which the account balances have been restated to reflect changes in price levels due to inflation.

Prime rate The interest rate charged by banks on borrowings by preferred customers.

Principal The remaining balance of an outstanding obligation to be paid in the future.

Prior period adjustment An accounting event or transaction that does not affect the current period's earnings but instead is reflected as an adjustment to retained earnings.

Private placement The sale, or "placement," of a significant number of shares of stocks or bonds to a limited group of buyers; the securities are not offered for sale to the general marketplace.

Privatization The sale of all or part of a previously state-controlled entity to the general public.

Product cost A cost directly related to the production of a good or service-for example, the cost of goods sold.

Productivity index A cash flow ratio calculated as the cash flow from operations divided by the capital investment; indicates the relative cash productivity of a company's capital investments.

Profit The excess of revenues over expenses for a single transaction.

Profit and loss reserve The amount of retained earnings of a company; see retained earnings.

Profit margin The excess (or insufficiency) of operating revenues over operating expenses; a measure of a company's ability to generate profits from a given level of revenues; calculated as net income after tax divided by net sales; also known as the return on sales ratio.

Profitability The relative success of a company's operations; a measure of the extent to which accomplishment exceeded effort.

Pro forma (financial statement) A forecast or projected financial statement for a future accounting period.

Promissory note A written promise to pay a specific sum of money at a specific date; a liability.

Property, plant, and equipment The noncurrent assets of a company, principally used in the revenue-producing operations of the enterprise.

Proportionate consolidation A method of consolidating the financial results of a parent company and its subsidiary, in which only the proportion of net assets owned by the parent are consolidated; as a consequence there is no need for a minority interest account.

Proprietary company A label used in some countries to describe a privately held (or nonpublic) company.

Prospectus A document describing the nature of a business and its recent financial history, usually prepared in conjunction with an offer to sell capital stock or bonds by a company.

Proxy A legal document granting another person or company the right to vote for a shareholder on matters involving a shareholder vote.

Public company One whose voting shares are listed for trading on a recognized securities exchange or are otherwise available for purchase (sale) by public investors.

Public limited company (Plc) A limited liability publicly held company in the United Kingdom; must have share capital of at least £50,000.

Purchase accounting A consolidation method in which the financial results of a parent-company and its subsidiary are combined using the fair market value of the subsidiary's net worth.

Purchase discount A cash discount (usually 2 percent) given to a buyer if the buyer pays for the purchases within the discount period (usually 10 days after purchase).

Purchase Discounts Lost An expense account representing the finance or interest costs incurred as a consequence of not paying for goods purchased on credit on a timely basis (such as 2/10, net 30).

Purchases Goods or inventory acquired for sale or manufacture.

Q

Qualified opinion An opinion issued by an independent auditor indicating that the financial statements of a company are fairly presented on a consistent basis and use generally accepted accounting principles, but for which some concern or exception has been noted.

Quick assets Highly liquid, short-term assets such as cash, cash equivalents, short-term investments, and receivables.

Quick ratio (acid test ratio) A measure of liquidity and short-term solvency calculated as quick assets divided by current liabilities.

R

Ratio A financial indicator (such as the current ratio) formed by comparing two account balances (such as current assets and current liabilities).

Ratio analysis The process of analyzing and interpreting the ratios formed from two or more financial statement numbers.

Raw material inventory Materials and purchased parts awaiting assembly or manufacture; classified as a current asset on the balance sheet.

Realized loss (gain) A loss (gain) that is recognized in the financial statements, usually due to the sale of an asset.

Rear-end loading An accounting process by which expenses (revenues) are deferred for income statement purposes despite being incurred (earned).

Receivable collection period A measure of the effectiveness of accounts receivable management calculated by dividing the receivable turnover ratio into 365 days.

Receivable turnover A measure of the rate of collections on sales.

Receivable turnover ratio A measure of the rate of collections on sales, calculated as net sales divided by the average receivable balance: the rate at which a company's receivables are converted to cash.

Recognition principle An accounting principle that stipulates that revenues should not be recorded in the accounting records until earned and that expenses should not be recorded until incurred.

Reconciliation report A statement or report reconciling the financial statements of a foreign entity to the accepted or prevailing accounting practice of another country.

Redeemable (callable) preferred stock A preferred stock that may be retired (redeemed or called) at the discretion of the issuing company, usually after a specified date and usually at a premium above the stated (or par) value of the preferred stock.

Redemption The retirement of preferred stock or bonds before a specified maturity date.

Registrar An independent agent, normally a bank or a trust company, that maintains a record of the number of shares of capital stock of a company that have been issued and to whom.

Relevance principle An accounting principle used to select which accounting information should be presented in a company's financial statements.

Reliability principle An accounting principle that stipulates that accounting information, and hence accounting reports, must be reliable to be useful to financial statement users.

Reorganization (quasi-reorganization) A process of changing the ownership structure of a company, usually as a direct result of a deficit in retained earnings.

Replacement cost The cost to reproduce or repurchase a given asset (such as a unit of inventory).

Reporting currency The currency used to measure and report a company's net assets (that is, the "local" currency).

Reserve An shareholders' equity account including the profit and loss reserve (retained earnings), revaluation reserve, capital reserve or share premium reserve (paid-in-capital in excess of par value), and legal reserves (those mandated by a given country's laws of incorporation).

Retained earnings Those earnings of an enterprise that have been retained in the enterprise (have not been paid out as dividends) for future corporate use.

Retained earnings—appropriated The amount of total retained earnings that has been allocated for specific corporate objectives, such as the redemption of debt or capital stock.

Retained earnings—restricted The amount of total retained earnings that is legally restricted from being paid out as dividends to shareholders; the restriction usually results from a borrowing agreement with a bank or other financial institution.

Return on common equity (ROCE) ratio A measure of profitability, calculated as the net income available to common shareholders divided by the average total common equity for the period.

Return on shareholders' equity (ROE) A measure of profitability; a measure of the relative effectiveness of a company in using the assets provided by the owners to generate net income; calculated as net income divided by average shareholders' equity.

Return on sales ratio (net profit margin ratio) A measure of profitability, calculated as the percentage of each sales dollar that is earned as net income; may be either retained in the company or paid out as a dividend.

Return on total assets (ROA) A measure of profitability that assesses the relative effectiveness of a company in using available resources to generate net income; also called the return on investment, or ROI; calculated as net income divided by average total assets.

Revaluation A material upward adjustment of the exchange rate between two currencies; an upward adjustment in asset value, usually undertaken to reflect the economic effects of inflation.

Revenue bond A bond secured or collateralized by a revenue stream from a particular group of assets.

Revenues The inflow of assets, the reduction in liabilities, or both, from transactions involving an enterprise's principal business activity (for example, sales of products or services).

Sale A legal term suggesting that the title to an asset has passed from a seller to a buyer.

Sale/Leaseback An accounting transaction in which an asset is first sold and then immediately leased back by the selling entity; a financing transaction.

Sales-type lease A capital lease that generates two income streams: (1) from the "sale" of the asset and (2) from financing the "purchase" of the asset.

Salvage value (residual value) The amount that is expected to be recovered when an asset is retired, removed from active use, and sold.

Securities Act of 1933 A 1933 legislative act of the U.S. Congress that requires certain disclosures by enterprises issuing (or desiring to issue) shares of capital stock.

Securities and Exchange Commission (SEC) A government agency responsible for the oversight of U.S. securities markets; this agency also specifies the form and content of all financial reports by companies issuing securities to the public.

Securities Exchange Act of 1934 A 1934 legislative act of the U.S. Congress that created the Securities and Exchange Commission.

Self-sustaining foreign operation A foreign entity financially and operationally independent of its parent company.

Selling expense Expenses incurred directly as a consequence of selling and delivering a product to customers.

Sensitivity analysis A process by which the effect of a change in a given assumption is assessed (as in a pro forma analysis).

Sinking fund A trust account established in conjunction with the issuance of bonds into which funds are paid periodically to be used to retire the debt at maturity; an asset account.

Sole proprietorship A business enterprise owned by one person.

Solvency The long-term debt repayment ability of a company; a measure of a company's long-term liquidity.

Special journal An accounting data file containing a chronological listing of special financial transactions (for example, cash purchases or cash receipts) affecting an enterprise.

Specific identification An inventory cost-flow method that assigns the actual cost of producing a specific unit to that unit;

the only inventory method that matches exactly the cost flow and physical flow.

Spot rate The prevailing exchange rate between two currencies on a given date.

Standard product cost An inventory valuation method that uses estimated or projected costs of producing a product rather than actual costs.

Stated value The recorded accounting value of capital stock. See also par value.

Statement of cash flows An accounting statement describing the sources and uses of cash flows for an enterprise for a given period.

Statement of fund flows An accounting statement describing a company's inflows and outflows of funds over a given period; funds defined with reference to a company's cash, liquid assets, or working capital.

Statement of shareholders' equity (statement of owners' equity) An accounting statement describing the principal transactions affecting the shareholders' interests in an enterprise for a given period.

Statement of retained earnings An accounting statement describing the beginning and ending balances in retained earnings and the major changes to the retained earnings account (for example, dividends and net income).

Statements of financial accounting standards (SFAS) The official pronouncements of the FASB.

Stewardship The management and supervision of enterprise resources.

Stock certificate A legal document evidencing the purchase of capital stock in a company.

Stock depositary receipt (SDR) A beneficial ownership share in a foreign entity held by a trustee (such as a bank or brokerage firm) on behalf of the investor; see American depositary receipt.

Stock dividend A distribution of additional shares of capital stock to a company's shareholders.

Shareholders' equity The owners' equity of a corporation; comprises paid-in capital and retained earnings.

Stock option A right issued by a company to its employees entitling an employee to buy a set quantity of capital stock in the future at a prespecified price.

Stock split An increase (a forward split) or a decrease (a reverse split) in the number of shares issued by a company; equivalent to a large stock dividend.

Stock warrant (stock right) A certificate issued by a company that carries the right or privilege to buy a set quantity of capital stock in the future at a prespecified price.

Straight-line method A method to depreciate the cost of a tangible asset or to amortize the cost of an intangible asset in which the allocated cost is constant over the life of the asset.

Subchapter S corporation A small corporation that pays no corporate taxes; all earnings are divided among the owners and are taxed at the individual level.

Subsidiary A company in which an investor company (the parent) holds an equity investment in excess of 50 percent of the voting shares of the investee company.

Subsidiary ledger An accounting data file containing detailed account information to supplement or explain the aggregate account balance contained in the general ledger.

Sum-of-the-years' digits method A method to depreciate the cost of a tangible asset in which the allocated cost is greater in the early periods of the asset's life (that is, an accelerated method).

T

Take-or-pay contract An executory contract by which one party agrees to pay for certain inventory (or other products) regardless of whether the inventory is physically received or not.

Tangible asset Those resources of an enterprise, such as property, plant, and equipment, that possess physical characteristics or have a physical presence.

Temporal method A method of translating foreign financial statements in which cash, receivables, and payables are translated at the exchange rate in effect at the balance sheet date; other assets and liabilities translated at historical rates; revenues and expenses translated at the weighted-average rate for the period.

Temporary accounts Those accounts that are closed at the end of each accounting period-for example, the income statement accounts, dividends, and the income and loss summary.

Temporary difference A difference in reported income or expenses between a company's tax return and its financial statements that will reverse out in some future period.

Times-interest-earned ratio A measure of solvency and leverage calculated as net income plus interest and income taxes divided by interest charges; a measure of the extent to which current interest payments are covered by current earnings.

Time value of money Because money can always be invested at a bank to earn interest for the period it is on deposit, money is said to have a "time value."

Timing differences Differences in the timing of the reporting of certain revenues and expenses for tax purposes and for external financial reporting purposes.

Total asset turnover ratio A measure of asset management effectiveness reflecting the rate at which sales are generated from a company's investment in assets; calculated as net sales divided by average total assets.

Total debt-to-total assets ratio A measure of solvency or long-term liquidity, calculated as total debt divided by total assets.

Trade payables See accounts payable and notes payable.

Trade receivables See accounts receivable.

Trading security A security owned by a company where management's intent is to sell it in the very near term.

Transaction exposure (risk) A source of foreign exchange risk resulting from exchange rate fluctuations between the date on which a contract is signed or goods delivered and the date of payment.

Transaction principle A concept underlying the preparation of financial statements that requires that the source of all accounting information be economic transactions affecting an enterprise and its resources.

Transfer agent An independent agent, usually a bank or a trust company, that maintains a record of, and executes all, capital stock transfers and sales, as well as the payment of dividends on those shares.

Transitory earnings (cash flows) The nonrecurring earnings (cash flows) of a company; earnings (cash flows) that are not expected to reoccur in future periods.

Translation exposure (risk) A source of foreign exchange risk resulting from the restatement of foreign financial statements denominated in a foreign currency into U.S. dollar-equivalents (or some other base currency); also known as accounting exposure.

Treasury stock Outstanding capital stock that has been repurchased but not retired and is usually held to be reissued at some future date.

Trend analysis The analysis of ratios or absolute account balances over one or more accounting periods to identify the direction or trend of a company's financial health.

Trial balance A listing of the preadjusted, preclosing account balances from the general ledger designed to verify that the sum of the accounts with debit balances equals the sum of the accounts with credit balances.

True and fair view The current standard of precision required of all audited financial data in the EU; analogous to the "fairly presented" standard used in the United States.

Turnover A measure of the rate of sales of goods or services; in the United Kingdom, a measure of net sales or net revenues.

U

Uncollectible account An account receivable that a company expects not to be able to collect.

Underwriter A brokerage house or investment banker hired by a company to help sell a bond or stock offering.

Unearned revenue Revenue that is received as cash but that has not yet been earned.

Unit-of-production method A method to depreciate the cost of a tangible asset or to deplete the cost of a natural resource; the allocated cost is based on the actual production by the asset.

Unleveraged ROA (UROA) A refinement of the return on assets (ROA) ratio, obtained by restating net income to include interest charges on an after-tax basis (that is, net income plus interest expense net of tax benefits).

Unrealized change in value of available-for-sale investment portfolio A contra shareholders' equity account representing a write-down (write-up) in the available-for-sale portfolio for temporary market fluctuations, as a consequence of the mark-to-market method.

Unrealized loss (gain) A loss (gain) that is recognized in the financial statements but is not associated with an asset sale; usually involves a revaluation of an asset value.

Useful life The estimated productive life of a noncurrent asset.

V

Value-added statement A financial statement prepared by some foreign companies reflecting a measure of the wealth created by the operations of the company and the distribution of that wealth among its major constituents (for example, employees, investors, and the government).

Value-added tax A tax levied at each stage in the production and distribution chain on the basis of the value that is added to a product as it passes through a given stage.

Vendor A company selling goods or services.

Vested benefits Pension benefits owed to employees at retirement regardless of whether they continue to be employed by the company until they reach retirement age.

W

Warrant A legal document enabling the holder to buy a set number of shares of capital stock at a prespecified price within a set period of time.

Warranty obligation An obligation for future costs to maintain a product sold in good working condition.

Wasting assets Noncurrent assets, such as natural resources, that decrease in value as a result of depletion or consumption of the asset.

Weighted-average cost method An inventory cost-flow method that assigns the average cost of available finished goods, weighted by the number of units available at each price, to a unit sold and thus cost of goods sold, and to ending inventory.

With (without) recourse Terms of the sale of an account or note receivable. A sale with recourse obligates the selling company to "make good" the receivable in the event that the factor is unable to collect on the receivable; a sale without recourse obligates the factor to assume all liability for noncollectibility.

Work in process inventory Partially completed goods or products; classified as a current asset on the balance sheet.

Working capital A measure of liquidity or short-term solvency, calculated as total current assets minus total current liabilities.

Working capital maintenance agreement An executory contract by which one entity guarantees to maintain the level of working capital of a second entity; usually arises as a consequence of a borrowing agreement by the second entity for which the first party becomes a guarantor.

World standards report A set of financial statements prepared according to IASB accounting standards.